ZWK 320.09 12.99
YOU

Political Lives

Political Lives

Selected by **Hugo Young**

OXFORD
UNIVERSITY PRESS

OXFORD

UNIVERSITY PRESS

Great Clarendon Street, Oxford OX2 6DP

Oxford University Press is a department of the University of Oxford.
It furthers the University's objective of excellence in research, scholarship,
and education by publishing worldwide in

Oxford New York

Auckland Bangkok Buenos Aires Cape Town Chennai
Dar es Salaam Delhi Hong Kong Istanbul Karachi Kolkata
Kuala Lumpur Madrid Melbourne Mexico City Mumbai Nairobi
São Paulo Shanghai Singapore Taipei Tokyo Toronto

Oxford is a registered trade mark of Oxford University Press
in the UK and in certain other countries

Published in the United States
by Oxford University Press Inc., New York

First published 2001
First issued as an Oxford University Press paperback 2002

British Library Cataloguing in Publication Data
Data available

Library of Congress Cataloging in Publication Data
Data available

ISBN 0-19-860643-5

10 9 8 7 6 5 4 3 2 1

Typeset in DanteMT
by Alliance Phototypesetters, Pondicherry, India
Printed in Great Britain
by T. J. International, Padstow, Cornwall

Preface

'The best record of a nation's past that any civilization has produced': G. M. Trevelyan's view in 1944 of the *Dictionary of National Biography* highlights the achievement of its first editor Leslie Stephen. Between 1885 and 1900 quarterly volumes rolled out from the presses in alphabetical order by subject. A national institution had come into existence, making its distinctive contribution to the national aptitude for the art of biography.

In his initial prospectus for the *DNB*, Stephen emphasized the need to express 'the greatest possible amount of information in a thoroughly business-like form'. Dates and facts, he said, 'should be given abundantly and precisely', and he had no patience with the sort of 'style' that meant 'superfluous ornament'. But he knew well enough that for 'lucid and condensed narrative', style in the best sense is essential. Nor did he content himself, in the many longer memoirs he himself contributed to the *DNB*, with mere dates and facts: a pioneer in the sociology of literature, he was not at all prone to exaggerate the individual's impact on events, and skilfully 'placed' people in context.

Stephen's powerful machine was carried on by his work-horse of a successor Sidney Lee, who edited the first of the ten supplements (usually decennial) which added people who died between 1901 and 1990. It was in these supplements that all of the memoirs published in this series first appeared, so they were often written soon after the subject died; their authors were frequently able to cite 'personal knowledge' and 'private information'. In such cases there is always a balance to be struck between waiting for written sources to appear and drawing upon living memory while still abundant and fresh. Stephen had no doubts where he stood: he published book-length biographies of his Cambridge friend Henry Fawcett and of his brother Fitzjames within a year of their deaths, and cited Boswell's *Johnson* and Lockhart's *Scott* as proof that the earliest biographies are often the best. Furthermore, memoirs of the recently dead were included in the *DNB* right up to the last possible moment, the press often being stopped for the purpose. Roundell Palmer, for example, died on 4 May 1895 and got into the 43rd volume published at the end of June.

Preface

So the memoirs published in this series are fully in line with what was *DNB* policy from the outset. Furthermore, all have the virtue of reflecting the attitudes to their subjects that were taken up during their lifetimes. They may not always reflect what is now the latest scholarship, but as G. M. Young insisted, 'the real, central theme of history is not what happened, but what people felt about it when it was happening'. So they will never be superseded, and many are classics of their kind—essential raw material for the most up-to-date of historians. They have been selected by acknowledged experts, some of them prominent in helping to produce the *New Dictionary of National Biography*, which will appear in 2004. All are rightly keen that this ambitious revision will not cause these gems of the *DNB* to be lost. So here they are, still sparkling for posterity.

Brian Harrison
Editor, *New Dictionary of National Biography*

Political Lives—selections from the twentieth-century DNB

Introduction

It seems strange that two of my choices for twentieth-century political lives were born in 1830. Surely they belonged to a different age. But this anthology is of lives across a century, and the century seems a long one, richer at the beginning than the end for the mundane reason that many politicians from the age we think of as ours have yet to have their lives memorialized. Four twentieth-century prime ministers are still living, and the *DNB* will know them only when they are dead. Cohorts of cabinet ministers from the modern era await their place in the annals of immortality. So the third Marquis of Salisbury, prime minister when the century opened, was the necessary life to begin with. He tells us something about political life now as well as then. The Victorians and Edwardians have things to say, comparatively, about their successors. From Lord Salisbury to Tony Blair in the span of a hundred years is a provocative transition.

Most striking about the sift has been the change of political type it revealed, and most compelling among the changes is the decline of hinterland. In the old days politicians had a breadth of character and interest their successors cannot dream of. Arthur Balfour was a serious philosopher, Joseph Chamberlain a risk-taking businessman, Charles Dilke a global traveller of quite startling range. Travel, in fact, is what strikes me as distinguishing the early-century politician most from the modern version. Those old imperialists, without an aircraft in sight, really knew the world. Today, the higher the summit and faster the globe-trotting, the less ministers take in about the place where they chance to land.

Dilke was a cool observer wherever his mission took him. Read the minor lives as well, and you enter a world of far horizons and decidedly unmodern manners. 'He professed in casual conversation a lower standard of conduct than he really acted upon', the biographer writes of the laid-back Sir Henry Wolff, a serpentine operator in Turkey, Persia, and Spain when Great Britain mattered more than any country in the world. John Edward Jenkins, author, satirist, imperialist, radical, is a little cameo of eccentric Victorian breadth. Salisbury's youngest son, Hugh Cecil, was an aviator, orator, and serious Anglican as well as Tory MP and provost of Eton, whose retirement line when he left the place was 'I go to Bournemouth in lieu of Paradise.' Aubrey Herbert, who travelled with seven languages round the Balkans and the Middle East, died, according to Auberon Waugh, of blood poisoning after being told that the best cure for blindness was to have his teeth extracted. Osbert Sitwell writes of Sir Philip Sassoon, a Tory MP for twenty-seven years, that 'his great entertainments were imbued with his personality and with imagination, as if with a kind of magic.' Those were the days.

The century's mainstream characters attracted a less diverting authorial tone. I've taken the irreverent step of excluding Winston Churchill, on the grounds that the piece is very long, the writing undistinguished, and the subject pretty familiar. But consider three other prime ministers: Lloyd George, Bonar Law, and Baldwin. All are handled here by the same writer, Thomas Jones, who was not a professional historian and sets down rather pedestrian narratives. On the other hand, he was an insider. He worked as a top civil servant for all three men. The *DNB* thus had a series of rare scoops, since it was unusual for officials ever to write about their political superiors. But the pattern continued, and it seemed worth retaining a whiff of it in this collection. In the pages of the dictionary, possibly because they were seldom read, the establishment continued to break its codes of silence. Here is Burke Trend, mandarin of mandarins in the 1960s and 1970s, discreetly marking the cards of his predecessors, Lords Bridges and Normanbrook. Reversing the compliment, Edward Heath chronicles his admiration for William Armstrong, the top official at his side during the 1974 miners' strike, and only thinly veils the nervous breakdown that drove Armstrong out of office. John Wyndham, a high-level personal retainer—'very devoted to the interests of what he used to call his "master"'—is affectionately recalled by that master himself, Harold Macmillan. Horace Wilson, head of the Civil Service at the start of the Second World War, acquires extra fascination under the hand of Robert Armstrong, cabinet secretary forty years later, who could be exalting in Wilson the very qualities he himself doubtless wanted to reflect: 'intelligence, clarity of mind and expression, skill in conciliation, impartiality, and integrity.'

It seemed necessary to include these administrators in a collection of political lives. They did, after all, run the country much more fully than the Civil Service which was later put in its subordinate place by Margaret

Thatcher and Tony Blair. Other adjacent categories also suggested themselves, notably top judges and senior spies. Cyril Radcliffe, another Robert Armstrong subject, bridged just about every class of power-handler save elected politician. David Maxwell Fyfe and Reginald Manningham-Buller, in the hands of the discreetly sardonic judicial biographer, R. F. V. Heuston, deserve their place. Donald Somervell was the perfect model of politician-turned-judge, a breed virtually extinct in modern times. With the spies, we get back to the delights of like-on-like, in still more rarefied form. Dick White, former head of MI6, on John Sinclair and Roger Hollis, two tarnished figures from the secret world: who could resist such guileful pieces? Or the entry for Stewart Menzies, plainly from the same authorial quarter, but (uniquely) attributed to 'Anon.'?

There was a problem with the royals. All kings, one might argue, justify inclusion as political lives. But the pieces on Edward VII, George V, and George VI are very long. With a limit of a hundred lives, there had to be a line drawn somewhere. Edward VIII, on the other hand, was at the heart of one of the most resonant political crises of the century, and, besides, was lucky enough to have John Grigg as his biographer. Through Lord Louis Mountbatten, equally, whole political terrains open up: war, the peacetime army, the future of royalty itself. Mountbatten was the most political royal of the century, not least through his supervision of Indian independence. The imperial connection, in any case, had to come full circle. Out of the *DNB*'s copious subsuming of empire within the definition of what is 'national'—itself a distinctly imperialistic mind-set—there needed to be some examples here. I chose Nehru, Kenyatta, Nkrumah, and Frank Longford's graphic piece on Eamon de Valera.

Some lives became most famous for a single happening, and their biographies reflect it, giving climactic weight to what made them matter: Dilke for his shocking divorce, John Seely for the Curragh Mutiny, Samuel Hoare for the Hoare–Laval Plan. Of others it can be said that they are here because they recall a very different calibre of British leftism than is easy to comprehend today: see Rajani Palme Dutt, James Maxton, Shaparji Saklatvala. I preferred such minor exoticism to the dreary recitations of a good many lives from the trade union and Labour tradition. The purpose of the book, after all, is more to give pleasure than construct a thorough account of twentieth-century history.

For the same reason, I think the brightest gems dug out from the *DNB* mine tend to be the work of professional authors, often paired with exceptionally appropriate subjects. Two in that category are Ian Gilmour on Iain Macleod—'Macleod's faith in democracy was unusually strong for a democratic politician'—and Roy Jenkins on Anthony Crosland: 'his personality, if not his fame, was a match for that of his principal confrère,

Introduction

Henry Kissinger.' There are also Kenneth Rose and Robert Blake. William Haley on Violet Bonham Carter brings the editor of *The Times*, virtually anonymous in his day, out into the light, as well as his coruscating subject. Nancy Astor provides John Grigg with another opportunity for a little *tour de force*. John Mackintosh on Herbert Morrison (bracketed with Tam Dalyell on John Mackintosh) reminds us what a sad loss Mackintosh was to letters as well as politics, dying at 49. Most timeless of all are Harold Nicolson's two entries, on Curzon and Duff Cooper. Nicolson, perhaps the most stylish biographer of second-rank politicians in the twentieth century, is a pleasure to unearth, and present to a wider public.

That is the unique merit of an anthology like this one. The *DNB* is a source of hidden treasure, until recently kept that way by the practical difficulty of consulting its cumbrous volumes. It was a mausoleum for its authors as well as its subjects. Much that I have read and excluded strikes the modern reader as, to be frank, too earnest and long-winded. When the *DNB* was started, diligent Victorians liked to set down accounts that were more thorough than they were enlightening, still less entertaining. It is in the more recent pieces that shafts of wit and anecdote are more likely to appear, to excite the browsing as distinct from scholarly reader.

One of my favourite characters is one that hardly any reader will have heard of, Sir Edmund Hall-Patch, civil servant. Raised in France, and gassed in the First World War, he was recruited from a Paris cabaret band into the Reparations Commission. After a spell as finance officer there, he became, under Treasury auspices, financial adviser to the government of Siam, before resigning on some matter of principle and being obliged to return to his saxophone. After a couple of years, though, he was again picked up by the Treasury, prelude to a spell as financial adviser to the embassies in both Peking and Tokyo. He was pressed into big economic jobs during the next war, served Ernest Bevin, and finished with the top Whitehall gong, a GCMG.

Hall-Patch was a genuine British eccentric, gifted with both prescience and independence. At the policy level he was one of the first men in the Foreign Office to understand that Britain could not survive outside the European Economic Community. More personally, his biographer summons up a man about whom 'stories abounded'. These were 'seldom confirmed but few were finally denied; stories of sorrows and romances, of the anonymous authorship of a daring French novel, or of popular music for film or review, of unusual friends—Chou En Lai and Syngman Rhee, Yvonne Printemps and Sacha Guitry.'

This was not a Great Man. He would not merit a biography. But he is the sort of Briton whom the *DNB* exists to memorialize. This highly selective anthology of its political lives from one century will, I hope, revive interest in others from a varied cadre of characters great and smaller.

HUGO YOUNG

December 2000

Contents

xiii

Contents

Contents

Contents

Contents

Contents

AITKEN William Maxwell

(1879–1964)

First Baron Beaverbrook

Newspaper proprietor, was born 25 May 1879 at Vaughan, Maple, Ontario, the third son in the family of ten children of a Presbyterian minister, William Cuthbert Aitken, who had emigrated to Canada from Torpichen, West Lothian. The mother was Jane, daughter of Joseph Noble, storekeeper and farmer in Vaughan. The year after 'Max' Aitken was born, his father received a call from St. James's church at Newcastle, a township on the Miramichi river in New Brunswick where the boy spent a happy and adventurous childhood and attended the local school until he was sixteen, but failed in Latin in the entrance examination to Dalhousie University. Instead, he entered a law firm in Chatham, down river from Newcastle, but soon began to sell insurance, then switched successfully to selling bonds at the right moment in the Canadian boom. He found a patron in John F. Stairs, the leading financier and Conservative in Halifax, Nova Scotia, who helped to set him up in a finance company, Royal Securities Corporation.

One of the talents Max Aitken exhibited throughout his life lay in confecting combines and alliances. He used his knowledge of local banking to negotiate the sale of the Commercial Bank of Windsor to Stairs's Union Bank of Halifax, a merger which brought him a personal profit of 10,000 dollars. He was soon venturing too in the West Indies. On 30 January 1906 he married Gladys Henderson, the beautiful nineteen-year-old daughter of Colonel (later General) Charles William Drury, the first Canadian to command the Halifax garrison, Nova Scotia. They moved to Montreal where Aitken acquired a seat on the Stock Exchange. By 1907 'the little fellow with the big head' was a dollar millionaire. In 1909 he formed the Canada Cement Company, a controversial amalgamation much criticized in some quarters, the echoes of which, much to his righteous indignation, were to reverberate about his ears for years to come.

In the following year the Aitkens came to England. Aided by Andrew Bonar Law, himself the son of a New Brunswick manse, Max Aitken stood as a Conservative in the Liberal-held Lancashire seat of Ashton-under-Lyne and, after a whirlwind campaign, he won by 196 votes, one of the few Unionist gains in the general elections of that December.

He had bounced into the political limelight, but he spoke rarely in the House where he was regarded as a 'Canadian adventurer'; however, he had the friendship of Bonar Law, as well as financial links, and he soon gained

1

the support of F. E. Smith (later the Earl of Birkenhead) through whom he came to know (Sir) Winston Churchill. In 1911 Aitken's name appeared in the coronation honours; his knighthood was not universally well received. When Bonar Law, whose resolution Aitken had helped to stiffen (and this was but the first instance in their close friendship), came to succeed Arthur Balfour as Conservative leader, Aitken's political stock, as his intimate, was correspondingly strengthened. He bought a large Victorian country house in Surrey, Cherkley Court, near Leatherhead, where he would entertain friends and leading politicians whilst he continued to expand his Canadian business interests. He refused to eat in other people's houses: he preferred to be the focus of attention from the middle of his own dinner table. After the war he was to acquire The Vineyard, a tiny Tudor house with a tennis court at Hurlingham Road, Fulham, more intimate than Cherkley.

In July 1914 it was 'Max Aitken, Bonar Law's financier and jackal', as one of Asquith's Cabinet described him, who was the intermediary through whom the abortive Buckingham Palace conference over the Ulster question came to be held: the silhouette of a future political merger.

When war broke out Sir Max Aitken soon became the Canadian Government representative at British GHQ at St. Omer with the rank of lieutenant-colonel in the Canadian Militia—as 'Canadian eyewitness.' He initiated the *Canadian Daily Record*, which lasted until 31 July 1919, for Canadian troops in Europe, and published a historical narrative, *Canada in Flanders*, the first two volumes of which he wrote himself. He created the Canadian War Records Office, set up a war memorial fund, and was the first to commission war artists. Impatient at the muddles of the military men, he soon came to spend much of his time in Whitehall. Living in the Hyde Park Hotel, not far from Bonar Law's house in Edwardes Square, by July 1916 he had acquired a room in the War Office, two doors down the corridor from Lloyd George's.

Aitken was to play a special part in the downfall of Asquith, who disdained him, and in the manœuvring which made Lloyd George war minister and then, in December 1916, prime minister. The details of the struggle to overthrow Asquith and to replace him by Bonar Law or Lloyd George, in which Aitken acted as spur and go-between, he was to record in his incomparable *Politicians and the War* (2 vols. 1928–32) which will remain, despite all carping, the authoritative narrative; nor does the story want in the telling thereof.

Confident, according to his own account, that he would be recompensed with office for the decisive part he believed himself to have played in the new arrangements, Aitken awaited a call from the new prime minister. Instead, since a seat in the Commons was required for Sir Albert Stanley (later Lord Ashfield), the incoming president of the Board of

Trade, the very post which he himself had his eye on, Aitken hesitated before reluctantly accepting Lloyd George's offer of a peerage, vacating his seat at Ashton-under-Lyne (to which Stanley was promptly elected), and becoming—he was already a baronet (January, 1916)—Lord Beaverbrook, an elevation which he claimed to regret to the end of his days.

Whilst the war lasted Beaverbrook gave what help he could to the Government in his own idiosyncratic way on becoming chancellor of the Duchy of Lancaster, despite the King's objection, then, from February to November 1918, minister of information. In March 1918 he was sworn of the Privy Council. He was still entertaining freely: 'It was during Duff's time in France' (from May 1918), Lady Diana Duff Cooper (later Lady Norwich) was to write, 'that the Montagus and I saw almost daily this strange attractive gnome with an odour of genius about him. He was an impact and a great excitement to me, with his humour, his accent, his James the First language, his fantastic stories of his Canadian past, his poetry and his power to excoriate or heal' (*The Rainbow Comes and Goes*, 1958).

Since 1910 Beaverbrook had been a close friend of R. D. Blumenfeld, who had been editor of the *Daily Express* since 1904. Although a lively, well-written, and politically influential newspaper, it was losing money and in danger of closing. In December 1916 Blumenfeld on Bonar Law's advice turned to Aitken (who had been interested in the paper at least as early as May), who bought the paper—and its debts—for £17,500 and so acquired not only a platform for his views and additional political leverage, but what was to prove his dominant interest for the rest of his life.

The partnership with R.D.B., who remained as editor-in-chief until 1929 and paterfamilias until he died in 1948, was faithful, fruitful, and at times explosive. 'Blum', Beaverbrook once remarked, 'taught me the business of journalism.' Beaverbrook for his part taught his editor how to make a newspaper pay. He introduced 'more money, better management', and, above all, he made the paper controversial. Advertisements became a major source of revenue. Beaverbrook personally sold space to Gordon Selfridge. Blumenfeld said that Max was the most gifted natural journalist he had ever met, not excluding Lord Northcliffe. Together, they gathered a remarkable team of writers, cartoonists, and business managers into the building in Shoe Lane and set off after the circulation leadership of the *Daily Mail*. Foremost among them was John Gordon, together with two Canadians, (Sir) Beverley Baxter and, on the management side, E. J. Robertson. After Northcliffe's death in 1922 the struggle for circulation amongst the popular dailies became intense, but eventually by 1936, with Arthur Christiansen as editor (since 1934), the *Daily Express*, with a two and a quarter million sale, achieved the largest circulation in the world and

Beaverbrook by then was the unchallenged leader. By 1954 the circulation was exceeding four million a day. Meanwhile the *Sunday Express* had been launched in December 1918, and in 1923 Beaverbrook acquired from Sir Edward Hulton control of the *Evening Standard*, in which the cartoons of (Sir) David Low achieved their uncensored popularity. Beaverbrook impishly liked to pretend that he left his newspapers to run themselves, but it is evident that the chief shareholder's telephonic interventions were menacingly perpetual and his flair for informed gossip—and malice—unexampled. For good or ill, his newspapers were the extension of Beaverbrook's complex personality and friendships. Amongst those who wrote for them were men as varied as Arnold Bennett, Dean Inge, (Sir) Robert Bruce Lockhart, and Harold Nicolson, Lord Castlerosse, and, later, Michael Foot. 'Vicky' in his day was allowed as much freedom as Low had had when he would portray Beaverbrook's characteristic features with the huge urchin grin lurking in the corner of many of his cartoons. Timothy Healy, the Duff Coopers, H. G. Wells, and subsequently Brendan Bracken, and much later the Aneurin Bevans, Stanley Morison, and A. J. P. Taylor, who was to write his biography (1972), were among Beaverbrook's intimates; but nobody could ever replace Bonar Law in his heart. After the war of 1939–45 he eventually resumed his highly personal account of affairs in *Men and Power 1917–1918* (1956) and *The Decline and Fall of Lloyd George* (1963). It was he, for example, who had seen to it that Bonar Law attended the Carlton Club meeting in October 1922 which brought about the downfall of the very wartime coalition which Beaverbrook himself had helped to initiate, a meeting which enabled Stanley Baldwin to reveal those unexpected qualities which were to deprive Beaverbrook—and Churchill—of the influence each, very independently, sought to exert upon Conservative policy between the wars. Years passed before he and Churchill came to work together again—they had crossed tempers during the general strike—and then once again, those ten years later, it was Baldwin who won the day. In 1936 King Edward VIII sought Beaverbrook's advice on the public handling of his decision to marry Mrs Simpson. Beaverbrook, joined by Churchill, strove mightily to delay the issue, advising the King to wait rather than precipitate a clash with Church and Cabinet with an inevitable outcome. It was in vain. After Beaverbrook's death his version of the struggle behind the scenes, *The Abdication of King Edward VIII*, was published (1966). It is perhaps significant that, whereas both Baldwin and Churchill were most distressed by what took place, Beaverbrook, for his part, had 'never had so much fun in my life'.

Bonar Law's death in 1923 had left Beaverbrook outside the innermost circles of power, and he threw himself into battle after battle with Baldwin over the issue of imperial preferences, which Beaverbrook chose to call

'Empire Free Trade', or, again, his 'Empire Crusade'. He campaigned in by-elections; he wrote at length week after week on a theme which he had made his own, and he used his three papers relentlessly to press his ideas on imperial preferences; the iniquity, in Beaverbrook's view, of Baldwin's settlement of the British war debt to the United States; and the neglect of the Empire, about which Beaverbrook himself knew very little outside Canada. Beaverbrook frankly admitted that 'S. B.' defeated him every time and he was intensely irritated by the public image of Baldwin as 'a quiet, honest country gentleman', to him a successful travesty. Starting as admirers of Bonar Law, they had soon parted company and they were never reconciled. It was probably Beaverbrook whom Baldwin chiefly had in mind rather than Lord Rothermere when, deeply wounded by the press campaigns against him, he spoke (24 June 1930) in the words of his cousin Rudyard Kipling (who had earlier parted from Beaverbrook over the Irish treaty) of newspaper proprietors who exercised 'power without responsibility, the prerogative of the harlot throughout the ages'.

The political merger of 1931 might seem to have been 'made' for Beaverbrook, yet he was not involved in the formation of the 'national' Government: he seemed to have shot his political bolt. It appeared that Churchill was not the only 'busted flush.' It was noteworthy, as his biography was to reveal, that 'no Prime Minister came to Cherkley between 1922 and 1941'.

During the rise of Hitler Beaverbrook used his newspapers to damp down the threat of war. He accompanied Lord Vansittart to Paris in December 1935 and sustained him and Sir Samuel Hoare (later Viscount Templewood) at the time of the Hoare-Laval pact. From 1938 Beaverbrook made Hoare (who had served with him in the Commons before 1914) an allowance of £2,000 a year. He supported Neville Chamberlain over Munich and as late as mid 1939 the *Daily Express* was busily informing its public that 'there will be no war this year'. During the 'phoney war' he visited President Roosevelt, a kindred spirit, a visit which was to bear fruit. When Churchill became prime minister, Beaverbrook re-entered the *arcana imperii* and the old intimacy was renewed. On 14 May 1940 he became minister of aircraft production and later a member of the War Cabinet. He accompanied Churchill to Tours whilst France was collapsing, because the premier knew that 'in trouble' Beaverbrook was 'always buoyant'. Beaverbrook's contribution to victory in the Battle of Britain was immense and unique: Churchill and Dowding paid public tribute to it. The hour and the man proved a fit match. By the most ruthless methods Beaverbrook burst through the entrenched conventions of the Air Ministry and long-term plans of 'the bloody Air Marshals', as he called them, and demanded successfully that every ounce of the war effort be thrown into producing the fighter aircraft which the Royal Air Force (in which his son and heir was gallantly serving) needed to deny the Luftwaffe control of the narrow seas, without which the invasion of Britain was impossible. His torrential, piratical energy was centred in Stornoway House in St. James's which he had acquired in the 1920s. He made plenty of enemies not only in the Air Staff, but also, for example, Lord Nuffield and Ernest Bevin, but he carried the day. The story of his tempestuous handling of the new Ministry remains an epic. He gave a new and primal urgency to the cycle: production, cannibalization, repair, and dispersal. Beaverbrook, said Churchill, was 'at his very best when things are at their worst'. Nothing that he did in his long life was as important as the part Beaverbrook played in winning the Battle of Britain.

Typically, when the battle in the air was won, the man who had done most to make it possible tired of the burden, and in May 1941 he became simple minister of state; in June he succeeded Sir Andrew Duncan as minister of supply—'he believes in orderly advance', he announced, 'I am given to immediate methods.' In August he visited Washington; in September Moscow, with Averell Harriman, to bargain with Stalin over war supplies. He returned to Washington with Churchill after Pearl Harbor to press for more tanks, aircraft, and—his own significant contribution to the debate—landing craft. In February 1942 he became minister of production, again in succession to Duncan, but a couple of weeks later ill health—which was never far away and his asthma may have been partly psychosomatic—gave him the excuse to leave the Government. He loathed committees. His letters of resignation had become as frequent as those of Gladstone or John Morley. In September 1943, however, he agreed to become lord privy seal and so remained until the war ended. Beaverbrook was never a team man but he was a very present help in time of trouble, especially to Churchill. It was Harry Hopkins who spotted that Beaverbrook was a member of that inner cabinet 'of the men who saw Churchill after midnight'. They might not always agree. Beaverbrook pressed for an early Second Front, especially after his return from Moscow, just as from 1940 onwards he continued to stress the strategic ineffectiveness of massive bombing. But the court favourite no longer had quite the same influence. Yet it was he who arrived at Marrakesh in December 1943 when Churchill was taken ill there after the Big Three meeting at Tehran, just as it had been Beaverbrook who had been summoned to Chequers when Germany declared war on Russia in June 1941.

Beaverbrook took a leading—and, in some people's view, a disastrous—part in Churchill's 1945 election campaign. With 393 Labour seats compared with 189 Conservative, the Carlton Club, which Beaverbrook rarely visited, and the Tory backbenchers whom he derided, turned their wrath on him. He bore it as he always did (with irritated interruptions) with buoyancy, and his friendship with Churchill survived undamaged. Indeed, it was the 'best of foul weather friends' who realized that Churchill would feel especially deprived in his moment of defeat and saw to it that a motor car and chauffeur were at his door when the familiar government per-quisites had abruptly disappeared. It was typical—a point which Lord Rosebery was to make at the memorial service at St. Paul's—of Bea-verbrook's many secret acts of kindness when people were down on their luck—to the Asquiths, or the Snowdens, or, until she died in 1952, Lady Brade, the widow of Sir Reginald, who had befriended him in far-off days as secretary to the War Office. More formally, in 1954 he set up the Beaverbrook Foundation.

Two more campaigns remained for the happiest of warriors: he op-posed Maynard Keynes over the American loan in 1947 and Harold Macmillan's attempt in 1961 to put Britain into 'that blasted Common Market'. Much of his old resilient fire returned and, at the age of eighty-two, with most of his friends long since dead, he waged a tremendous fight against what he believed would mark the end of British independence. He had never really liked allies. When the Common Market proposal tem-porarily foundered, his headline was a characteristic 'Hallelujah Halle-lujah.'

In his last years, although Maurice Woods who had furnished the first drafts for his political memoirs had died as long ago as 1929, Beaverbrook resumed his career as political historian, a special talent about which he was curiously modest. He was able to draw upon his extensive collection of political papers (now in the House of Lords Library), from those left to him by Bonar Law, Lord Wargrave's papers which he had acquired, and the Lloyd George papers, which he had purchased from the widow to-gether with her diaries. He had already made use of Asquith's letters to Mrs Edwin Montagu and Mrs Reginald McKenna in his *Politicians and the War*. He had published further books in the series of memoirs, but *The Age of Baldwin*, the final volume, long-plotted, somehow never seemed to get written.

At the end of his long life Canada came to give him full recognition as one of her foremost sons. Since the war of 1939–45 he had endowed the university of New Brunswick, of which he had become chancellor in 1953, with impatient generosity. He founded scholarships there and provided new buildings, notably the library and the Beaverbrook Art Gallery, which he ensured was filled with masterpieces of every age, few of which he himself appreciated.

On 9 June 1964 at the age of eighty-five, he died at Cherkley of cancer. But a fortnight earlier he had attended a mammoth dinner in his honour given in London by his fellow Canadian, Lord Thomson of Fleet. At the end 'the Beaver' rose, old and frail, and held his audience spellbound. He spoke for half an hour, in the inimitable Canadian twang he never lost, of his successes and his failures, what he had hoped for and what he had lived for. 'And now', he said, 'I am to become an apprentice again, somewhere, soon.' As he walked steadfastly out the six hundred guests, men of all ages, stood and cheered him. It was his farewell, wholly typical of the man, full of wisdom, rich in humour, glowing with courage.

Beaverbrook achieved eminence in three worlds—finance, politics, and journalism. (Some, perhaps a minority, might add a fourth, as an annalist, of the school of John Aubrey.) In the first and last of these three he was pre-eminent. He made a vast fortune and he owed no man a penny, making money for others as well as himself. He helped to make and unmake prime ministers, yet never succeeded in winning the trust and confidence of the Conservative Party to which, almost by accident, he belonged. He was a radical by temperament, yet he could never have fitted with any comfort into the ranks of radicals or liberals, and certainly not of socialists: he was a lone fighter, in politics as in everything else.

His influence on popular journalism was great, founded as it was on an inborn sense of news values and an unfailing gift for knowing what would interest ordinary men and women. Moreover, the mass circulations he achieved were built on sheer efficiency in a difficult art, and he accepted nothing less than the best of its kind; smut was anathema to him. His papers sparkled with controversy, and it was his particular genius that made them appeal to all classes of reader, whether or not they agreed with his point of view. The man who read *The Times* was likely to read the *Daily Express* as well. Beaverbrook's tendency at times to indulge in personal vendettas, such as that against Earl Mountbatten whom he blamed for the Canadian losses at Dieppe, or his running feud against the British Council, perhaps contradicted the high standards by which he judged himself and other people. The secrets of his long and at times fantastic career were the brilliance and shrewdness of his intellect, the restless energy which only left him in his last year, and the courage and ruthlessness with which he attacked his every objective. In private life he had friends everywhere who throughout the years remained as devoted to him as he to them. His loves and his hatreds came all alike to him, and once generated they seldom changed. Once dropped, a friend remained unforgiven. Not everybody who came under his patronage was improved by the contact. He had an original and at times hilarious wit, stuffed shirts his instinctive target. The son of a Christian minister, he retained from first to last a vocabulary based on the Bible and a strong religious faith, unorthodox, sporadic, but real, to which his little book *The Divine Propagandist* (1962) bears witness. For his father and mother, for whom from 1902 until their deaths he ensured every comfort, he had a deep love and respect. He himself believed, towards the end of his life, that he had failed in the things he had sought most; if so, it was perhaps because of an impish streak which he enjoyed, and also because, despite his half-century of life in England, he remained at heart a Canadian. Although he loved and admired the British people, he never fully understood their mental processes or the traditions in which their lives were rooted, and in 1956 he wrote: 'My last home will be where my heart has always been.'

His first wife, who bore him two sons and a daughter, died at Cherkley in 1927. Beaverbrook had often been a neglectful husband. For twenty years, until she died in 1945, Mrs Jean Norton was his most intimate woman friend. In 1963 he married Marcia Anastasia, daughter of John Christopher and widow of his friend Sir James Dunn, first baronet. Beaverbrook's elder son, John William Max (born 1910), succeeded to the baronetcy created in 1916 but disclaimed the barony, maintaining that 'there will be only one Lord Beaverbrook'.

There is a portrait by Sickert and another (1950) by Graham Sutherland which Beaverbrook bequeathed to his widow. There are also two busts: one by Oscar Nemon on the plinth in the town square, Newcastle, New Brunswick, above Beaverbrook's ashes; the other by Epstein.

[A. J. P. Taylor, *Beaverbrook*, 1972; Beaverbrook's own writings; private information; personal knowledge.]

JOHN ELLIOT

published 1981

ARMSTRONG William

(1915–1980)

Baron Armstrong of Sanderstead

Civil servant and banker, was born in Clapton, London, 3 March 1915, the elder son (there were no daughters) of William Armstrong, of Stirling, a colonel in the Salvation Army, and his wife, Priscilla Hopkins, also a Salvation Army officer. He was educated at Bec School, Tooting, and at Exeter College, Oxford, to which he won an open scholarship. He obtained first classes in both classical honour moderations (1936) and *literae humaniores* (1938).

Armstrong entered the Civil Service as an assistant principal at the Board of Education in 1938, becoming assistant private secretary to the president of the Board of Education in 1940. From 1943 to 1945 he was private secretary to Sir Edward (later Lord) Bridges, secretary of the War Cabinet, after which he moved to the Treasury. During the period 1949–53 he served as principal private secretary to three successive chancellors of the Exchequer, Sir R. Stafford Cripps, Hugh Gaitskell, and R. A. Butler (later Lord Butler of Saffron Walden), being responsible on five different occasions for the co-ordination of the contributions to the budget speech and to a considerable extent for the writing of it. To work so closely with three such different personalities and in addition to accommodate himself to a change of government in 1951 undoubtedly expedited his development as a civil servant and immeasurably broadened his outlook. At the same time Westminster and Whitehall were endeavouring to adjust themselves to the economic and social changes of the post-war world, to the emergence of the first European community, that for coal and steel, and to the increased tension between the Atlantic alliance and the Soviet bloc. It was a testing but exhilarating time for Armstrong to be so close to the centres of power.

He then became under-secretary to the overseas finance division of the Treasury where for four years, from 1953 to 1957, he had to handle external financial problems, in particular those of the sterling balances, after which he moved over to the home finance division until 1958. From then until 1962 he was third secretary and Treasury officer of accounts. When the Treasury was reorganized at the end of this period, Armstrong became joint permanent secretary in charge of economic and financial policy at the early age of forty-seven. It had always been obvious that he was a high-flyer, but even this was exceptionally rapid promotion. Responsible now for both the home and overseas finance divisions of the Treasury, which had been amalgamated, he had to handle the economic problems of the recession and to implement the policy for expanding the economy pursued by Reginald Maudling when he became chancellor of the Exchequer in mid-1962.

The narrow defeat of the Conservative Party at the general election of 1964 and the formation of a Labour government led to the creation of the Department of Economic Affairs. This was the consequence of a widely felt dissatisfaction with the Treasury's handling of economic policy over a number of years. The tension which existed between the new department and the Treasury lasted until the department's abolition in 1969. Within a few weeks of taking office the government found itself facing a major financial crisis which was very largely a crisis of confidence. The governor of the Bank of England, Lord Cobbold, working closely with Armstrong, managed through the other central banks to mobilize the funds necessary to stabilize the situation.

In 1968 Armstrong was appointed head of the Home Civil Service and when the department at the Treasury responsible for the management of the Service was hived off to become the Civil Service Department he became its first permanent secretary. After more than twenty years' intensive activity at the Treasury during which he suffered not a little stress and strain, he was able to use his immense knowledge of Whitehall and his widespread experience of international affairs for the benefit of the Civil Service as a whole. As head of the Civil Service, the first not to be burdened with the work of secretary to the Cabinet or head of the Treasury, and permanent secretary to the Civil Service Department, he was able to devote all his skill and energies to the management of the Service he loved, and in particular to the implementation of the recommendations of the committee on the Civil Service chaired by Lord Fulton. In this wider field and freer atmosphere he blossomed and flourished.

He created the new Civil Service College, used it as a basis for greatly improved training in the Service, and introduced many innovations into methods of training. He brought about increased mobility of civil servants both between their different classes and between various departments. This was especially the case with those members with professional qualifications. He tried to spread his enthusiasm for modern methods of management and the equipment required for it throughout the Service. All this gave much encouragement to the newer and younger members of the Service as well as to those in the middle ranks. When critics complained that the Fulton committee's recommendations had not been fully carried out it had to be remembered that although he had the support of the ministers concerned he had to work against the inertia of the establishment including at times the Civil Service unions. This did not prevent him from opening up opportunities for civil servants to take part in discussions about current problems on radio and television and from participating in them himself. It was, as he saw it, an important aspect of open government.

In mid-1973 the Conservative government called together representatives of the employers and trade unions for discussions on a prices and incomes policy. Although nominally under the umbrella of the National Economic Development Council, the latter's secretariat took no part. The prime minister asked Armstrong to co-ordinate the work of the director-general of the Confederation of British Industry, the secretary-general of the Trades Union Congress, and the permanent secretary to the Treasury in preparation for such meetings. This task he fulfilled admirably for more than fifty meetings. He was appointed not because of any mistrust of the Treasury, as has been alleged, but so as to allow the Treasury, representing all Whitehall departments, to play an equal part with the representatives of the CBI and TUC under a chairman who could concentrate on reconciling different views. It was moreover uncharacteristically foolish of Victor (later Lord) Feather, the general secretary of the TUC, to remark that Armstrong had become deputy prime minister, presumably because he sat next to the prime minister at conferences, something which is no more than a departmental official does for his minister. At no time did Armstrong exceed his functions as an official. He was trusted and admired by those who were present at that series of meetings. Unfortunately his health suddenly broke down early in 1974 and he was unable to take any further part in them. Later in that year he retired from the Civil Service and became a member of the board of the Midland Bank. In 1975 he was elected its chairman and on becoming chairman also of the Committee of London Clearing Bankers (1978–80) he played a major role in their collective campaign against the Labour Party's proposals for their nationalization. The chairmanship was a position he enjoyed although, or perhaps because, its circumstances were so entirely different from his own background, upbringing, and life's work.

Armstrong was unassuming, friendly, and approachable. Wise in judgement, he never attempted to force his views on those with whom he worked. Indeed his reticence made it difficult for those not closely involved with him to be certain of his personal position in the many crises with which he had to deal. He was first and foremost a public servant of the highest quality and the utmost integrity. His personal interests always came second.

Armstrong was appointed MVO (1945), CB (1957), KCB (1963), and GCB (1968). He was admitted to the Privy Council in 1973 and created a life peer in 1975. He received honorary degrees from many universities, including Oxford (1971), Sheffield (1975), City (1974), and Heriot-Watt (1975); he was an honorary fellow of Exeter College, Oxford (1963), and of the Imperial College of Science and Technology, London (1977); and he was a trustee or member of many governing bodies.

In 1942 he married Gwendoline Enid, daughter of John Bennett, company director, of Putney; they had one son and one daughter. Armstrong died suddenly in the Radcliffe Infirmary, Oxford, 12 July 1980.

[Personal knowledge.]

EDWARD HEATH

published 1986

Herbert Henry

(1852–1928)

First Earl of Oxford and Asquith

Statesman, was born at Croft House, Morley, Yorkshire, 12 September 1852, the second son of Joseph Dixon Asquith, a nonconformist wool-spinner and weaver of that place, by his wife, Emily, daughter of William Willans, a wool-stapler of Huddersfield. His father died when he was eight years old, and his mother then went with her four children to live near her father at Huddersfield; there, and for a short time at a Moravian boarding-school at Fulneck, near Leeds, Asquith received his early education. In 1863 he was sent with his elder brother to live with relatives in London, and entered the City of London School, then situated in Milk Street, off Cheapside. He remained at this school for seven years and came strongly under the influence of Dr. Edwin Abbott, its most famous headmaster. Abbott early marked him out as a boy of brilliant promise with an especially precocious talent for speech-making, which was shown to great advantage at the school debating society. In 1870 Asquith proceeded to Balliol College, Oxford, having gained a classical scholarship at the age of seventeen. He more than fulfilled his school promise at Oxford where he obtained first classes both in classical moderations (1872) and *literae humaniores* (1874) and was awarded the Craven scholarship (1874), after being *proxime accessit* for the Hertford and the Ireland scholarships. Asquith was also in his last term president of the Oxford Union, where the fame of his exploits was handed on to many generations of undergraduates. Jowett, like Abbott, predicted a great career for him, and all his Oxford contemporaries were of the same opinion.

In 1874 Asquith was elected fellow of Balliol, the other fellowship of the same year being awarded to A. C. Bradley, professor of poetry at Oxford, 1901–1906. About the same time he entered as a student at Lincoln's Inn, and after a short residence at Balliol came to London, and for the next year was a pupil in chambers of the future Lord Justice Bowen, who confirmed what was now the usual opinion of his abilities. He was called to the bar in 1876. In 1877, in his twenty-sixth year, he married Helen, daughter of Frederick Melland, a well-known Manchester physician, and took up his residence at Eton House, in what used to be John Street, Hampstead. Asquith had early decided that his real career was to be in politics, and that the bar was to be only a means to that end. But in making his way at the bar he had six years of struggle and discouragement, in which he added to a slender income by lecturing and writing articles for the *Spectator* and

Economist. The rare briefs which came his way were well argued, but he lacked some of the superficial qualities which tell with juries and ensure quick success. It was not until 1883 that he began to make his mark at the bar, and then he caught the attention of (Sir) Robert Samuel Wright, afterwards a judge, at that time attorney-general's 'devil', and of Sir Henry James (afterwards Lord James of Hereford), for both of whom he 'devilled', and to whom he always acknowledged a great debt for help in these early years.

During this period Asquith devoted most of his leisure to politics, speaking for the Eighty Club at public meetings and engaging in debate at local parliaments as an ardent Gladstonian liberal. In 1886, being now fairly established at the bar, he decided to stand for parliament, and after a week's campaign was returned for East Fife, a constituency which remained faithful to him for thirty-two years. He at once made his mark in the House of Commons. His speeches were brief, pointed, trenchant, and admirably timed; it was said from the beginning that he spoke with the authority of a leader and not as a backbencher. During this parliament he concentrated on the Irish question, and distinguished himself as a vehement opponent of the coercive policy of Mr. Balfour, then chief secretary for Ireland. But his chief opportunity came in 1888 when he was appointed junior counsel for Charles Stewart Parnell before the Parnell commission—Sir Charles Russell being leader—and a brilliant cross-examination of one of the principal witnesses for *The Times* not only 'made' him at the bar but greatly enhanced his reputation in the House of Commons, where he made formidable use of the knowledge gained on the commission. From this time forward his legal practice increased by leaps and bounds, and his name became widely known in the country. He took silk in 1890.

As a tragic set-off to these successes came the loss of his wife, who died of typhoid fever in September 1891,when they were on holiday together at Lamlash in the Isle of Arran. 'To me', Asquith wrote to a friend some time afterwards, 'she was the gentlest and best of companions, a restricting rather than a stimulating influence, and knowing myself as I do, I have often wondered that we walked so evenly together. I was only eighteen when I fell in love with her, and we married when we were little more than boy and girl. In the cant phrase our marriage was a "great success"; from first to last it was never troubled by any kind of sorrow and dissension; and when the sun went down, it was in an unclouded sky.' Asquith was now left a widower with five young children (four sons and one daughter), and he had in front of him some of the hardest years of his life.

Up to the autumn of 1890, it was generally believed that the liberal party would come back to power with a large majority at the next election, but the Parnell divorce case in November of that year, and the complications which followed from it, blighted that prospect. Thus, when the election came in 1892, the party had a majority of only 40, with which to undertake the formidable task to which it was pledged of carrying a Home Rule Bill through parliament. That task was doomed to failure from the beginning, but, indomitable as ever, Mr. Gladstone was determined to try, and formed an exceptionally able Cabinet with a strong infusion of younger men. Abandoning his former objection to putting into a Cabinet men who had not served an apprenticeship as under-secretaries, he made Asquith home secretary, and no appointment received more general approval. Asquith thus became a Cabinet minister and the holder of the principal secre-taryship of state at the age of thirty-nine.

In lasting three years the liberal government outlived the most san-guine expectations of its friends, and at the end of that time Asquith was held to have justified and increased his reputation. He had shown firm-ness and good sense on such questions as the demand for the release of Irish dynamiters, the holding of public meetings in Trafalgar Square, and the Featherstone riots (August 1893); any one of these, if mishandled, might have put the government in jeopardy. He also left behind him an excellent administrative record, and steered an import-ant Factory Bill through the House of Commons in 1894 and 1895. His reputation was now firmly established as a debater in the house, and as an admirable speaker on platforms in the country. When parlia-ment was dissolved in 1895, he was generally regarded as a future prime minister.

In May 1894, while he was home secretary, Asquith married as his second wife Margaret (Margot), youngest daughter of Sir Charles Tennant, first baronet, a young woman well known in London society for her brilliant gifts and originality of mind and character. A selection (published in his biography) of the letters that he wrote to her before their marriage, reveals a deep and imaginative side of his character which he kept veiled from the public until the end of his life. The world said that they were unequally matched; but he remained as devoted to her to the end as she was to him, and was unqualified in his admiration of her gifts and in acknowledging the stimulus which she gave to his own less lively dis-position. There were five children of this marriage, of whom only two, a son and a daughter, survived infancy.

Asquith remained out of office for nearly eleven years—years of trouble and schism for the liberal party, from which at times it seemed doubtful if it could ever recover. The resignation of Lord Rosebery as leader of the party in 1896 was followed by the resignation of Sir William Harcourt from the same position in 1898. In the latter year Asquith was much talked of for the succession to the leadership, but he was resolved not to put himself into competition with Sir Henry Campbell-Bannerman, who had the claim of seniority, if willing to accept this 'bed of thorns', as Lord Rosebery called it. Asquith, moreover, was now busily engaged earning a large income at the bar, to which he had returned in defiance of the convention which was supposed to prevent an ex-Cabinet minister or, indeed, any privy councillor, from engaging in this profession, and he was not yet prepared to give his whole time to public affairs. He was, in fact, very often absent from the House of Commons in these days, and some said that he was tiring of politics.

That was never so, but politics were difficult and thorny enough for a liberal leader between the years 1899 and 1902. The Boer War which broke out in the autumn of 1899 deeply divided the party and its leaders. There were Little-Englanders, so called, who thought the War an iniquity and denounced it in unmeasured terms; there were 'Liberal-Imperialists' who thought it just and inevitable, at all events after President Kruger's ulti-matum. Asquith, although he had vigorously criticized the Chamberlain-Milner diplomacy which led up to the War, was of the latter opinion. This brought him into collision with Campbell-Bannerman who, although he admitted the inevitability of the War after the ultimatum, could never be brought to pronounce it just or, taking into consideration the whole course of events, unavoidable. Little-Englanders and Liberal-Imperialists composed their differences temporarily for the 'khaki' election of October 1900, in which both suffered equally, but the trouble broke out anew afterwards, and in June 1901 Asquith publicly protested against Campbell-Bannerman's use of the phrase 'methods of barbarism' as applied to the farm-burning practised by British troops in South Africa under the provocation of guerrilla warfare. Much recrimination followed, and the formation of the Liberal League by the Imperialist group in February 1902 seemed to indicate that the whole group was about to follow Lord Rosebery in the 'definite separation' which he had already announced on his own behalf. But by this time Asquith had come to the conclusion that the quarrel had gone too far, and in the next few weeks he used his in-fluence successfully to make peace.

The situation was eased by the ending of the War in May 1902, and before another year was out the conservative party, by its education policy and still more by raising the fiscal question, had done what liberals had failed to do for themselves—reunited the liberal party. From now to the end of the parliament, Asquith was foremost both in attacking the gov-ernment and in defending free trade; and the speeches which he made in the country were models of trenchant and lucid exposition of all aspects of the fiscal question.

Mr. Balfour's government resigned early in December 1905, and after ten and a half years of exclusion from office the liberal party again had an opportunity of forming a ministry. The circumstances at the moment were by no means auspicious. Lord Rosebery had just made a speech dissenting emphatically from the line taken by Sir Henry Campbell-Bannerman, with Asquith's consent, on the Irish question; and while the government was being formed a serious hitch occurred owing to the condition which Mr. Haldane and Sir Edward Grey sought to make that Asquith should be leader of the House of Commons while the new prime minister, Sir Henry Campbell-Bannerman, should accept a peerage and go to the Lords. Asquith, who had, in the meantime, accepted the office of chancellor of the Exchequer, was strongly opposed to any step which would lead to a crisis at that moment on an issue personal to himself; and when Campbell-Bannerman declined their condition, Haldane and Grey were persuaded to waive it, and to enter the government as secretary for war and foreign secretary respectively—appointments which were to be momentous in later years. At the election which followed in January 1906 the liberal party obtained an enormous majority mainly on the free trade issue, and for the next two years Campbell-Bannerman remained leader of the House of Commons, a position in which he greatly distinguished himself and—as no one acknowledged more generously than Asquith—belied all the fears that had been expressed about his capacity for leadership.

In these two years the struggle between Lords and Commons, which was to last continuously for the next five years, entered upon its first stage. The House of Lords either rejected or amended out of recognition the bills to which the liberal government attached most importance—education bills, land bills, franchise bills—and feeling ran high on this treatment of liberal legislation just after a great liberal triumph in the country. Asquith, as had been expected, proved the most formidable debater on the government side in these controversies; but his principal work was as chancellor of the Exchequer, and he was responsible for three budgets (1906, 1907, and 1908), the last of which he introduced after he had become prime minister. As a financier, he was orthodox, thrifty, and progressive. In his first budget he took off the 1s. per ton coal export tax, and reduced the tea tax from 6d. to 5d. In his second he established the difference between earned and unearned income for income-tax, and revised the whole system of grants in aid of local authorities, substituting equivalent grants for ear-marked taxes. In his third he made the first provision for old age pensions, at the same time reducing the sugar tax from 4d. to 2d. He took especial pride in having instituted old age pensions, and was able to claim that, in spite of this new demand on the Exchequer, he had reduced debt at the rate of £14–15 millions a year out of taxation.

Asquith

In February 1908 Campbell-Bannerman fell dangerously ill, and it soon became known that he was dying. His relations with Asquith had been intimate and affectionate, and Asquith on his side was reluctant to take any step which might be painful to him or retard the hope of his recovery, while it was yet possible to hope. The government was carried on with great difficulty in his absence during the next six weeks, and at the end of that time Campbell-Bannerman's doctors declared his resignation to be imperative. King Edward VII was then at Biarritz, and instead of returning to London, summoned Asquith to 'kiss hands' as prime minister at that French watering-place—a method of procedure which exposed him to no little criticism. Asquith departed for Biarritz on 5 April, 'kissed hands' on 6 April, and came back as prime minister the following day, with the list of his ministers approved. The most important changes which he made in the previous administration were the appointments of Mr. Lloyd George to be chancellor of the Exchequer, of Mr. Reginald McKenna to be first lord of the Admiralty, and of Mr. Winston Churchill to be president of the Board of Trade.

Never was a political succession less disputed than that of Asquith to the prime ministership in April 1908. There were no rivals in the field, and he came to the highest place by common consent. But no one at that moment thought it likely or, indeed, possible that he would hold this place for nearly nine years—the longest continuous period for which it had been held by one man since Lord Liverpool's resignation in 1827. In April 1908 the liberal tide was visibly ebbing from its high-water mark of 1906; almost all the legislation on which the party had set its heart had been brought to a standstill owing to the resistance of the House of Lords; and failing the means of overcoming this obstruction, the government was losing prestige in the country and seemed doomed, if it survived, to a sterile 'ploughing of the sands'. No one then foresaw that the House of Lords itself would provide the issue which would prolong the life of the government and keep the liberal tide flowing until the outbreak of the European War in 1914.

The issue arose out of finance. By the end of 1908, it had become clear that the large and unexpected increase in the German navy would require a corresponding effort on the part of the British government. The necessity was challenged by certain members of the Cabinet, who saw with dismay the prospect of the surplus which they had ear-marked for social reform being absorbed by the demands of the Admiralty. A sharp struggle followed, in which the Admiralty secured an even bigger programme than it had at first demanded; but the Cabinet decided that money should be found both for the construction of new ships and for the social programme which it had previously contemplated. The budget of 1909 which

Mr. Lloyd George introduced for this purpose, with its fourteen millions of extra taxation, may seem a modest effort to a later generation, but it led to a violent agitation, in which the proposed new land taxes were specially singled out for denunciation, and on the last day of November it was rejected by the House of Lords. This raised a constitutional question of the first magnitude. For at least 250 years it had been assumed by all parties that the power of the purse belonged to the House of Commons, and to that House alone; and it was clear that, if the House of Lords could establish its right to hold up supply, it would have acquired the power of dissolving parliament and bringing any government to which it objected to a standstill. In fact, the hereditary assembly would have the whip-hand of the elective.

Asquith immediately took up the challenge and appealed to the country. At the election which followed, in January 1910, the government secured a majority of 124—a majority large enough for ordinary purposes, but not large enough to overcome the opposition of the Irish if they carried their objection to certain taxes to the length of voting against the budget, when it was again presented to the House of Commons. For some weeks the fate of both the budget and the government was in doubt, but Asquith stood firm against any change to conciliate the Irish, and in the end the latter gave way and the budget was passed by a majority of 93 in the House of Commons on 27 April 1910, and accepted without a division by the House of Lords on the following day. But the liberal party was now unanimously of opinion that the government could not content itself with procuring the submission of the House of Lords on the one issue of the budget and continue to accept its unqualified supremacy over all other legislation. Simultaneously with the passing of the budget, Asquith had prepared and presented to the House of Commons a scheme for limiting the powers of the House of Lords by providing that a Bill which had been passed by the House of Commons in three successive sessions should, after a minimum period of two years from its first introduction, automatically become law in spite of its rejection in each of those sessions by the House of Lords. This was the plan which the liberal party had adopted in 1907, and it was now the party's unanimous demand that it should occupy the first place in the government programme.

It was evident from the beginning, however, that such a plan would not be accepted by the House of Lords except under pressure of a creation of peers, or the threat of such a creation, to overcome its resistance. No one saw this more clearly than King Edward, who had warned Asquith before the election of January 1910 that if the question of the House of Lords veto was raised in addition to that of the budget in the new house, he would not 'feel justified in creating new peers until after a second general election', at which the veto would be the sole and acknowledged issue. The natural sequence of events was broken by the death of King Edward in May 1910, and for the next few months Asquith endeavoured to reach a settlement of the House of Lords and other constitutional questions through a conference of the leaders of both parties. When this attempt broke down, he decided to dissolve parliament at once and to hold the second election on the House of Lords question for which King Edward had stipulated as the condition of using the royal prerogative to create peers. But before doing so he felt it necessary to satisfy himself that King George V would accept this second election as the final and sufficient test of the popular will, as presumably his father would have done. Accordingly, on 16 November, Asquith put the question to the king in an interview at Buckingham Palace, and obtained from him a 'hypothetical understanding', as he afterwards described it, that, if the government obtained 'a sufficient majority' at the coming election, he (the king) would create peers in sufficient numbers to overcome the resistance of the House of Lords, should it resist in the teeth of the popular verdict. It was agreed that this understanding should be divulged to no one except members of the Cabinet, unless it proved necessary to give effect to it in the new parliament.

Asquith always hoped that this necessity would not arise, and that, if the popular verdict was decisive, the House of Lords would bow to it without waiting for a creation of peers. In this way he hoped that the king would be kept out of the controversy which was bound to follow, if the understanding were made public either before the election or while the measure was being debated in the new parliament. To a considerable extent this hope was realized, but although the election of December 1910 gave the government a majority of 126, the House of Lords continued its resistance up to the last stages of the Parliament Bill which it amended in such a way as to defeat its principal objects. On 24 July, when the House of Commons met to consider the Lords' amendments, Asquith stood at the box for half an hour unable to make himself heard against the organized clamour of his opponents, and the house had to be content with learning the intentions of the government from the report of his undelivered speech in the next day's papers. It now became necessary to reveal that the king was prepared to use his prerogative if the peers persisted in their opposition, but even under this pressure the Bill was only passed by a majority of 17 after agitated debates in which Asquith was hotly assailed for having 'coerced the king'.

To the end of his life Asquith warmly repudiated this charge. The position was one, in his opinion, in which neither king nor minister had any option. The minister could not have undertaken another election without satisfying himself that, if a sufficient majority was obtained, the result would be decisive; the king could not, as the event proved, have obtained another minister who could have survived either in the existing parliament or in the new parliament. Opinions may differ as to the policy of the Parliament Act, but it is now scarcely disputed that the king's action was in strict accord with his constitutional duties and that Asquith, in peculiarly difficult circumstances, chose the method best calculated to keep the crown out of political controversy.

At the election of December 1910, Asquith made it clear that the removal of the absolute veto of the House of Lords was intended by the government to clear the way to other liberal legislation which, till then, had been obstructed by the peers; and in April 1912 he introduced a Home Rule Bill, proposing, for the third time since Mr. Gladstone's effort in 1886, to set up a subordinate parliament in Ireland. The accumulated bitterness of the party struggles of previous years now found vent in the opposition to this Bill. Before the year was out the protestant counties of Ulster, under the leadership of Sir Edward Carson and with the support of unionist leaders, began to drill and arm with a view to resisting the Bill if it became law, declaring this to be the only alternative remaining to them, now that the veto of the House of Lords was removed. This placed the government in extreme difficulty. It was warned that any legal proceedings which it might take would almost certainly be abortive, since in the heated state of opinion it was improbable that juries would convict; and Irish supporters of the government were strongly opposed to 'British coercion' being applied to any party in Ireland. Asquith held his hand, and during the next eighteen months endeavoured by all possible means to narrow down the field of controversy and bring the opposing parties to reason. The agitation continued unabated in the meantime, and among its more serious incidents was the intimation in March 1914 of a group of officers at the Curragh camp in Ireland, in answer to a question put to them by their commanding officer, that they would accept dismissal from the service rather than take part in the coercion of Ulster. Asquith was of opinion that such a question ought never to have been put to them, and that the whole matter had been seriously mishandled by the military authorities. The country and the House of Commons were greatly disturbed by this event, and in order to restore discipline and reassure the public, Asquith himself assumed the secretaryship for war and was actually serving in that capacity when the European War broke out (28 July).

After much patient negotiation, in which the king played a useful part, the Irish controversy was reduced to the question of the precise area to be excluded, and the conditions on which that area should vote itself out or vote itself in. This was submitted to a conference of party leaders at

Buckingham Palace on 14 July 1914, but even then the leaders failed to agree, and the future was still in doubt when the War came to suspend the controversy. The Home Rule Bill was passed into law in September 1914 after the War had broken out, but was accompanied by a suspensory Bill postponing its operations until the War was over. A parallel controversy went on during the same years about the Welsh Disestablishment Bill which was dealt with in the same way while the War continued, but was accepted afterwards by general consent.

During these years of agitating controversy between the male parties in the electorate, Asquith became a special target of the militant suffragists who were demanding votes for women and pursuing their campaign with acts of obstruction and violence. For the greater part of his life he was an opponent of women's suffrage, and he both spoke and voted against the resolutions and bills introduced into the House of Commons for the enfranchisement of women. His reasons were frankly sentimental. As his correspondence shows, he rated the capacity and intelligence of women very high, and had no more intimate confidante on serious matters than his wife and a few chosen women friends. But he considered that women in general would lose rather than gain by engaging in the rough and tumble of politics, and he saw no middle course between enfranchising them and admitting them to parliament, and for this final step he was not prepared. His opposition, however, as he explained to the house in one of the debates on the subject (6 May 1913) was 'not dogmatic or final'. He would withdraw it if, first, clear proof were given that an overwhelming majority of women desired to be enfranchised, and secondly, if it were shown that the absence of direct representation in the House of Commons caused the neglect by parliament of the special needs and interests of women. He considered that these conditions had been reasonably fulfilled by the experience of women's work in the War and the new position which they were evidently going to occupy in industry. The demand persisted, and there could no longer be any question of their special interest in legislation. Accordingly he supported their enfranchisement in the Act of 1918, and in the following year the removal of the bar to their sitting in parliament.

Grave and difficult as were the domestic controversies of these years, foreign affairs in the end overshadowed them all. Few British ministers can have had to face more, and more dangerous, crises in the same period of time as Asquith in the six years from the date on which he became prime minister to the outbreak of the European War. His complete accord during these years with Sir Edward Grey, the foreign secretary, he reckoned one of the most fortunate circumstances of his life, and the perfect partnership of the two men saved him from the friction so usual in the relations between prime minister and foreign secretary, and kept the government steadfast to a continuous line of policy. Asquith was anxious to find any means of conciliating Germany, but loyalty to the French *entente* and security against the challenge of the increasing German fleet he considered to be the two essentials of British policy. In the many struggles within his Cabinet about the increases in the British navy deemed necessary to meet the German competition, he was invariably a strong supporter of what the Admiralty thought necessary for safety, and he brought all the arts of persuasion to bear upon his colleagues who were unconvinced or reluctant. On the other hand, he was strongly opposed to scattering the resources of the country between army and navy in time of peace, and in a lively passage in his *Genesis of the War* (1923) has replied to the charge that he did not 'raise an army' on the continental model in the years before the War. He believed, as did most responsible men in both parties, that no government could have persuaded the British people to accept compulsory military service except under the pressure of extreme necessity, and he claimed for his government that in keeping the navy beyond challenge and maintaining the expeditionary force and territorial army, it had made a larger effort in naval and military preparation than any other government in the same space of time.

The successive crises arising out of the annexation of Bosnia-Herzegovina in 1908, the dispatch of the German warship *Panther* to Agadir in 1911, and the Balkan Wars of 1912–1913 tested the nerve of his government to the utmost, and not less because some of them coincided with the tensest moments in domestic affairs. The Agadir crisis, for example, ran side by side with the Parliament Bill in 1911, and while the Peers and Commons were at grips Asquith and his Cabinet had seriously to consider the possibility that in another week Great Britain would be plunged into war with Germany. In all these emergencies Asquith's steadiness and composure were of the highest value.

Asquith has left it on record in his *Memories and Reflections* (1928) that in the final crisis of July to August 1914 he started with five leading ideas on policy: (1) Great Britain has no obligations of any kind either to France or Russia to give them military or naval help; (2) Great Britain must not forget the ties created by her long-standing and intimate friendship with France; (3) it is against British interests that France should be wiped out as a great power; (4) Great Britain cannot allow Germany to use the Channel as a hostile base; (5) Great Britain has obligations to Belgium to prevent her from being utilized and absorbed by Germany. All five of these ideas had been embodied in the policy of Asquith's government in the previous years. In the Grey–Cambon correspondence of 1912 it was laid down for the information of the French that all final decisions rested with the British parliament. In the naval negotiations with Germany following the mission of Viscount Haldane to Berlin in the same year, a German formula which would have detached Great Britain from France and compelled her to remain neutral in the event of a German attack upon France was definitely declined, and in reporting the government's decision Asquith told the king that British interests alone, apart from consideration for France, required its refusal. The British documents in regard to the neutrality of Belgium further show that the British government made it quite clear that it would not be a party to the violation of Belgian territory by any power, and Marshal Joffre has revealed in his *Mémoires* that a French plan, which might have anticipated the German incursion by entering Belgian territory in advance of the Germans, had to be abandoned in November 1912 on that account. When the crisis came, all these ideas and motives worked together to the conclusion that honour and policy alike required British intervention; and Asquith himself never wavered in the view that a victory of Germany over France, leading, as it almost certainly would have done, to German control of Belgium and the Channel ports, and to a combination of hostile fleets in German hands, would leave Great Britain and the British Empire in a position of the gravest peril. His colleagues have left their testimony that when the final crisis came, his handling of the Cabinet was masterly. He knew where he would stand; but he knew also the importance of keeping the government united, and the unwisdom of forcing the hands of colleagues who shared his responsibility. By his patience and suasion he accomplished the feat, which at the beginning had seemed impossible, of bringing Cabinet and country to the all but unanimous conclusion that British participation in the War was a stern necessity.

Asquith's government, by common consent, handled the first stages of the European War with remarkable skill and success. The navy was at its stations at the critical moment; the six divisions of the Expeditionary Force were conveyed to France swiftly, secretly, and without a hitch. The plans devised in previous years to prevent panic and to enable business to continue worked with admirable efficiency. The appointment of Lord Kitchener as secretary for war was hailed as a masterstroke. But in Great Britain, as in other countries, both government and public were utterly unprepared for the prolonged and devastating struggle which followed. When the retreat from Mons had been retrieved by the victory of the Marne (September 1914), hopes ran high that the War would be 'over before Christmas', and the grim war of attrition which now set in presented all the governments concerned with unheard-of problems as to men, munitions, and supply. Within Asquith's government were influential men, especially Mr. Lloyd George and Mr. Winston Churchill, who believed that the war of attrition could be avoided by a 'more imaginative strategy' which would discover alternatives to an incessant hammering at trench barriers on the Western front; and Asquith himself made one exception—in favour of the Dardanelles expedition (February 1915)—to the belief which he otherwise strongly held that victory could only be attained by conquering the main German army in France. The Dardanelles expedition miscarried partly because an initial confusion between a purely naval and joint naval and military attack robbed it of the element of surprise, and partly because, when it had failed as a surprise, sufficient men and munitions could not be spared from the Western front to ensure its success.

The failure of the Dardanelles expedition in its initial stage coincided with an agitation on the subject of munitions on which Asquith had borne uncomplainingly much unfair criticism, and the two things together brought the purely liberal government, which had been in office since 1906 and had survived two general elections, to an end (May 1915). Asquith now formed a coalition Cabinet in which the principal unionist leaders and one member of the labour party (Arthur Henderson) were included.

For the purpose of the War the Coalition government was no improvement on its predecessor. The new men needed to be informed about everything from the beginning; all the parties expected to be represented on any body to which the conduct of the War was deputed; party feeling persisted and caused acute divisions on subjects like compulsory service and the treatment of the Irish question after the rebellion of Easter 1916. Asquith's official biography tells a story of incessant struggles on these and other questions within the Cabinet; and throughout its existence Mr. Lloyd George maintained a running fight with Lord Kitchener and the principal military authorities, demanding a complete change in the direction of the War, by which he meant the transfer of the chief part of the army from the Western to the Eastern front. Then, as later under his own government, this proposal encountered the all but unanimous opposition of the commanding officers, British and French. Both protested that the enemy would have the enormous advantage of interior lines against the long and uncertain communications of the Allies, to say nothing of the inadequacy of the ports and bases of supply and other geographical obstacles to campaigns in the East. The French especially were determined that none other than their own country should be the main theatre of war, while it was in the occupation of the enemy.

The French, nevertheless, made an exception to their own rule in favour of the Salonika expedition (October 1915), which proved a grave embarrassment to the British government. Asquith opposed it to the utmost of his power, but the French forced his hands, and by so doing compelled the evacuation of the Dardanelles, since troops could not be found simultaneously for both expeditions. The evacuation of the Dardanelles (December 1915) without the loss of a man was a great military feat, but in the public mind it set the seal of failure on the greatest military operation of the year 1915, and, combined with the ill success of the great offensives in France in the autumn of the same year, did much to sap the credit of the Coalition government.

Asquith met these troubles with his usual fortitude, and the next few months were occupied in preparing the Somme offensive and in instituting compulsory service which, after the failure of the Derby scheme of recruiting in the autumn of 1915, he thought inevitable. This, however, encountered fierce opposition from many different quarters, and once more it needed all Asquith's skill and patience to carry it through without breaking up his Cabinet. In the spring of 1916 came the Irish rebellion, which Asquith met characteristically by going to Ireland and informing himself about all aspects of the situation. He came back convinced that the only way to stem the tide of anti-British feeling was at once and without waiting for the end of the War to set up parliamentary Home Rule for the South of Ireland. In this he had the support of Mr. Balfour and Mr. Bonar Law, and even of Sir Edward Carson, but the opposition of other conservative members of the Cabinet, and especially of Lord Lansdowne, proved too strong and, to his great disappointment, he was compelled to drop the project.

In after years German soldiers confessed that the Somme offensive had played the principal part in exhausting the military power of Germany, but this result was not apparent at the time, and when, after heroic struggles and immense losses, the fighting died down in the autumn of 1916, the enemy seemed to be as firmly entrenched as ever on French soil. All the anxieties and disappointments of these times were now concentrated on Asquith, and he became the subject of violent and unscrupulous newspaper attacks which had the avowed object of driving him from office. He had from the beginning accepted the fullest responsibility for everything that went wrong, stood between the soldiers and impatient criticism at all critical moments, and scrupulously refrained from advertising his own activities or claiming credit for himself. These were conspicuous merits which won him the respect and confidence both of the soldiers in the field and of his intimate colleagues. But they left him exposed to critics who knew how to work on popular feeling against a man who never defended himself, and the legend that he was lethargic, that he was 'waiting and seeing' [see *Life*, i, 275, for the origin (1910) of the phrase], and even that he was 'sparing the Germans' obtained a wide vogue in the autumn and winter of 1916.

The cry now went up from these hostile quarters that Asquith should be displaced in favour of Mr. Lloyd George, who had long been pressing for a 'change in the direction of the War'. In the last days of November and the beginning of December 1916 a series of skilful manœuvres in which Sir Edward Carson, Lord Beaverbrook, and finally, though with some reluctance, Mr. Bonar Law, played the principal parts, led the unionist members of the Cabinet to transfer their support from Asquith to Mr. Lloyd George, and Asquith with all his principal liberal colleagues thereupon resigned (5 December 1916). Mr. Lloyd George proposed that the direction of the War should be taken out of the hands of the Cabinet and entrusted to a war council of four with himself as chairman and Asquith exercising only a shadowy and titular control as prime minister. Asquith was not unwilling to delegate some of his executive functions, provided that his final control was unimpaired, but conversations between the two men left it in extreme doubt whether this was Mr. Lloyd George's intention, and the group of newspapers which supported him made it quite clear that nothing less than Asquith's complete supersession was the object aimed at. Throughout this controversy Asquith had the support of all his liberal colleagues, and up to the beginning of December unionist ministers, with the exception of Mr. Bonar Law, had expressed a strong preference for his leadership. But at the critical moment a mistaken belief on his part that they had suddenly deserted him led to obscure cross-purposes between him and them, in the course of which they forced his hands by resigning. Whether the result would have been different if Mr. Bonar Law had acquainted Asquith with the resolution passed by unionist ministers at their meeting (Sunday, 3 December), and thus allowed him to explore the position for himself, has been much debated; but Mr. Bonar Law, for reasons which he thought good, withheld this resolution from Asquith, and the first war Coalition came to a close in a scene of confusion and misunderstanding. Mr. Lloyd George now succeeded Asquith as prime minister.

The change in the direction of the War which Mr. Lloyd George desired, namely, the transfer of the chief part of the British army from the Western to the Eastern front, proved as impossible under the new régime as under the old, and the next year (1917) was one of the blackest of the War for the Allies. As leader of the opposition, Asquith gave a general support to the government and refrained from any but the most moderate criticism; but in the following year an incident occurred which gravely affected his fortunes and those of the liberal party. This was the debate on the letter which General (Sir) Frederick Maurice, the director of military operations, Imperial General Staff, had addressed to the newspapers after the spring disasters of 1918, challenging the statements made by Mr. Lloyd George and other members of the government respecting the strength of the army in France at the time of the great German offensive in March 1918. On the appearance of this letter (7 May), Mr. Bonar Law, speaking on behalf of the government, had said that an impartial inquiry was necessary, and proposed that it should be undertaken by three judges. Asquith, who greatly objected to judges being invoked to decide questions which raised political issues, submitted an amendment in favour of a select committee of the House of Commons as the proper tribunal. Upon that Mr. Lloyd George announced that the government would regard a vote for this amendment as a vote of censure upon itself, and, withdrawing the proposal for inquiry, demanded a vote of confidence from the House of Commons there and then. Asquith persisted in his amendment, and in the division which followed he and 106 other liberals voted for it. No more was heard of this incident at the time, but in the following November, after the conclusion of the armistice, when the liberal and conservative leaders of the Coalition, Mr. Lloyd George and Mr. Bonar Law, decided to hold an immediate election, Asquith and the other liberals who had voted for his amendment found themselves branded as having conspired against the government at the most critical moment of the country's fortunes, and therefore as unworthy to be returned to parliament. Popular feeling ran so strongly at the time, and the joint appeal of the Coalition leaders had so destructive an effect on ordinary party loyalties, that the non-Coalition liberals were to all intents and purposes wiped out, and Asquith himself was defeated in East Fife—the constituency which up till then had returned him continuously for thirty-two years.

This method of electioneering, and the extravagant and embarrassing promises of indemnities and other punitive measures against the late enemy which accompanied it, found few defenders in subsequent years, but the result was decisive at the time. The independent liberals were reduced to 26 in number, and Asquith himself was out of parliament for the whole of the following year (1919). Although his services were available for the Peace Conference at Versailles, the prime minister refrained from including him among the British delegates. He bore these rebuffs with unfailing dignity and fortitude, and at the beginning of the following year (1920) a by-election at Paisley offered him the opportunity of returning to parliament. His campaign on that occasion is generally acknowledged to have been one of his finest oratorical efforts, and he used it to develop an all-round liberal programme and to state his views firmly about what he considered to be excessive and unworkable provisions in the peace treaties. He had by this time come to the conclusion that there was no solution of the Irish question short of Dominion Home Rule, and on that subject he declared himself uncompromisingly.

Returning to parliament, Asquith devoted himself mainly to the Irish question, and hotly denounced the method of reprisals adopted by the special force popularly called the 'Black and Tans', while again constantly urging the solution of Dominion Home Rule. The prime minister spoke of this as madness, and others called it 'treason', but Asquith was undismayed. The policy which he advocated was in fact adopted before the close of the year 1921. From that time onwards the Coalition rapidly disintegrated, and in the election which followed (November 1922), the conservative party, having thrown off Mr. Lloyd George, came back to power with Mr. Bonar Law as prime minister. There were 117 liberals of all sections (64 independents, and 53 followers of Mr. Lloyd George) in the new house, and a reunion between them was effected in the autumn of 1923, when Mr. Baldwin, who had become prime minister on Mr. Bonar Law's retirement in the previous May, suddenly dissolved parliament on the issue of free trade and protection. This reunion undoubtedly saved free trade for the time being, but it presented liberals with a very perplexing problem in the new parliament which met after the general election of December 1923. For although the conservatives were in a minority of nearly a hundred, labour, which was the next strongest party, with 191 seats, could only form a government with the support of liberals, who were 158 strong. Liberals, therefore, had to decide whether they should support labour in taking office, or support Mr. Baldwin in continuing in office, or take office themselves with the support of the conservatives.

There were not a few who urged Asquith to adopt the third course, and he received strong assurances of conservative support, if he would take it. But he was unhesitatingly for enabling labour to take office. He thought that it would be seriously harmful to the public interest and an incitement to class antagonism for the two 'middle-class' parties to combine together to deprive labour of an opportunity which either of them would have claimed as its right in like circumstances; he held it to be impossible for Mr. Baldwin, after he had told the country that he could not carry on without protection, to continue in office as if nothing had happened, when he had been refused permission to try that remedy; and he was not prepared either to enter into a coalition with conservatives or to take office depending on their support. His decision has generally been regarded as constitutionally correct, and in keeping with the instinctive sense of fair play characteristic of great parliamentary leaders; but the sequel was not a happy one for the liberal party. Fruitful co-operation between labour and liberal proved impossible; and after eight months the labour government came to an untimely end (October 1924) in what Asquith called 'two squalid crises, each of which could have been avoided, or at least circumvented, if they had played their cards with a modicum of either luck or skill'. In the election that followed, the strange incident of the 'Zinovieff' letter let loose a storm in the country which overwhelmed both liberal and labour, and Asquith himself was defeated when he presented himself for re-election at Paisley. Thus after thirty-eight years ended his career in the House of Commons.

The king immediately offered Asquith a peerage, and after a short period for reflection he accepted it and entered the House of Lords as Earl of Oxford and Asquith in 1925. He was created K.G. the same year. He remained leader of the liberal party for another eighteen months, but his last days in that capacity were clouded by differences with Mr. Lloyd George, arising first out of the Lloyd George fund and coming to a climax at the time of the General Strike (May 1926), when Mr. Lloyd George took action which, in Asquith's view, made an irreparable breach between them. In this view he was supported by nearly all his liberal colleagues, but the attitude of the rank and file of the party seemed to him ambiguous, and rather than face further dissensions he resigned his leadership in October 1926.

Asquith's health had already begun to fail, but in the next year he had a partial recovery and lived quietly, seeing his friends and working at his book, *Memories and Reflections*. His years of office had left him much impoverished, and for some time past he had turned to writing in order to supplement his income; in addition to many essays and addresses he produced two books, the *Genesis of the War* (1923) and *Fifty Years of Parliament* (1926), which are contributions of high value to history and autobiography. To the end he preserved the dignity, fortitude, and charity which had characterized him throughout his life. He died at his country home, The Wharf, Sutton Courtney, Berkshire, 15 February 1928, and having expressed a strong wish that there should be no public funeral, he was buried in the churchyard of that village.

It was said after his death that Asquith was the 'last of the Romans', and there is much in his character and career to justify that description. In his respect for institutions, his sense of decorum in public affairs, his dislike of mob-oratory and self-advertisement, his high sense of honour, he was in the line of classical English statesmanship. If circumstances made him leader in a great democratic struggle, he was, in his own view, defending the historic House of Commons against an innovation which, if not resisted, would have destroyed its prerogative, and he conducted the controversy on a high plane of serious argument. Like Mr. Gladstone he was defeated in his attempt to give Ireland parliamentary Home Rule, but his effort for a timely settlement on the lines then proposed may well seem conservative in contrast with the solution afterwards adopted. He had certain outward characteristics which lent themselves to the reproach of 'wait and see' which his enemies threw back at him, and his temperamental dislike of showy action undoubtedly was a drawback in war, when the public looks for dramatic qualities in its leaders. But the curtain is seldom lifted on the part which he played behind the scenes without showing him to have been prompt and decisive. He took the War Office into his own hands during the Ulster troubles, and returned to it again at a very critical moment in the War; he played a principal part in bringing Italy into the War; he went to Ireland himself after the rebellion. He was immovable in defence of soldiers in the field, or members of his Cabinet whom he thought unjustly blamed; he did unflinchingly many necessary but unpopular things, and bore the odium without complaint or explanation. In all these ways he earned the respect and trust of his colleagues, and conformed to the highest traditions of public life. In the end he showed certain signs of weariness after his long term of office and the incessant struggles and crises in which he had played the leading part, and he lacked the resilience to defend himself against the attacks which bore him down. But in the long period of his prime ministership he had played a continuous part in great and historic events such as had seldom fallen to any British statesman, and it may be said that only a man of commanding abilities, iron nerve, and high integrity of character could have sustained it.

Asquith's eldest son, Raymond, a man of exceptional brilliance, was killed in action in 1916, and he was succeeded as second earl by his grandson, Julian Edward George (born 1916).

Asquith was of middle height; his frame unathletic, but erect and firmly compacted. Spare till he was in the 'forties, in later life he filled out, and acquired in old age an ample habit of body. His face in early life was pale and ascetic, the eyes wide apart and if anything prominent rather than sunken, the nose substantial, the mouth full but firm; the whole dominated by a massive brow from which a wave of hair swept back. In middle age his complexion acquired a healthy red, the severe cast of feature yielded to a prevailing expression of serenity, the abundant hair silvered, yet his countenance still had austere phases. The mouth had contracted to the firm thin line which it tends to assume in lawyers; the forehead remained salient and formidable; and when he was speaking or under a high light which set off the modelling of the bones, his face could assume a sternness, an expression of command and of authority, which was at least as true a reflection of his character as the geniality which normally overlay them.

There are portraits of Asquith by Sir William Orpen in the Council Room, Lincoln's Inn; by Sir John Lavery at the Reform Club; by Solomon J. Solomon at the National Liberal Club, and by Fiddes Watt in Balliol College hall. The last was thought by his friends to be the best likeness. There are also various busts; one by Mrs. Clare Sheridan at the Oxford

Union; others at the City of London School, and in the Town Hall at Morley. Cartoons appeared in *Vanity Fair* 14 July 1904 and 17 March 1910. [*The Times*, 16 February 1928; J. A. Spender and Cyril Asquith, *Life of Lord Oxford and Asquith*, 2 vols., 1932; H. H. Asquith, *The Genesis of the War*, 1923, *Fifty Years of Parliament*, 2 vols., 1926, *Memories and Reflections, 1852–1927*, 2 vols., 1928, *Occasional Addresses, 1893–1916*, 1918; *Speeches by the Earl of Oxford and Asquith*, edited by J. B. Herbert, 1928; *The Autobiography of Margot Asquith*, 2 vols., 1922; J. A. Spender, *Life of Sir Henry Campbell-Bannerman*, 2 vols., 1923; A. G. Gardiner, *Life of Sir William Harcourt*, 2 vols., 1923; Lord Morley, *Recollections*, 2 vols., 1917.]

J. A. SPENDER

published 1937

ASSHETON Ralph

(1901–1984)

Second Baronet, and first Baron Clitheroe

Politician and businessman, was born at Downham 24 February 1901, the second of four children and only son of Sir Ralph Cockayne Assheton, first baronet, of Downham Hall, Clitheroe, and his wife, Mildred Estelle Sybella, daughter of John Henry Master, JP, of Montrose House, Petersham, Surrey. His family could trace its descent for more than a thousand years and had sent more than twenty of its members to the House of Commons since 1324. They were British landowners who, though never entering the highest ranks of nobility, had survived the Wars of the Roses and the English civil war, retaining and enlarging their estates. Assheton was educated at Eton and Christ Church, Oxford, where he obtained a second class in modern history in 1923. He was called to the bar at the Inner Temple (1925). He soon, however, felt the pull of the City and became a member of a firm of stockbrokers in 1927. Assheton was also a devout Anglican and represented the diocese of Blackburn in the Church Assembly from 1930 to 1950. He was also high steward of Westminster from 1962 to his death.

He had been an active Conservative at university and at a by-election in 1934 entered the House of Commons as member for Rushcliffe, Nottinghamshire. He soon made his mark by his knowledge of economics and finance. He was appointed parliamentary private secretary to W. D. Ormsby-Gore (later Lord Harlech), then minister of works and later at the Colonial Office (1936–8). This led to his being appointed a member of the royal commission on the West Indies (1938–9). On the outbreak of war Assheton was appointed parliamentary secretary to the Ministry of Labour and National Service, a post which he held until 1942, despite Sir Winston Churchill succeeding Neville Chamberlain as premier. In 1942 he was first promoted to parliamentary secretary to the Ministry of Supply and, from December, to financial secretary to the Treasury, 'the mounting block to the cabinet'. Assheton proved his worth dealing with the immense problems connected with wartime finance. He was sworn of the Privy Council in 1944.

In 1944, with a general election looming, Churchill asked him to become chairman of the Conservative and Unionist Party organization. During the war years the Conservative Party had declined in strength; there had been 400 agents in 1939, but by the time Assheton took over there were only 100. He fought hard touring the constituencies to revive Conservative philosophy very largely on a private enterprise and orthodox financial basis. None the less the Conservatives were defeated in 1945 and Assheton lost his own seat. He was, however, elected in the same year as Conservative member for the City of London and returned to the House of Commons as a front-bench speaker on financial and economic affairs. He also became chairman of the Public Accounts Committee (1948–50). When the City of London was disfranchised in 1950 he won back the Labour-held seat of Blackburn West for the Conservatives. He held the seat in 1951 and was generally expected to be included in the cabinet. In fact he was only offered the junior post of postmaster-general which he declined. He accordingly returned to the back-benches where he was chairman of the select committee on nationalized industries. Assheton was a strong supporter of the Suez group and in 1954 voted against the decision to withdraw from the Suez canal zone. In 1955 he retired from Parliament and accepted a hereditary peerage as first Baron Clitheroe. He succeeded to a baronetcy in the same year.

After this he devoted his career to business and held a large number of directorships, the most important of which were Borax Consolidated, the Mercantile Investment Trust, and a joint deputy chairmanship of the National Westminster Bank. He was a council member of the Duchy of Lancaster (1956–77) and was appointed KCVO in 1977. He continued to take a considerable interest in international affairs and more particularly those of Central Africa. He was a director of Tanganyika Consolidated and made a strong speech in the House of Lords urging support for Moise Tshombe's Katanga administration which the United Nations was seeking to integrate into the new Congo Republic (later Zaire). He showed himself a diligent landlord in Lancashire and took a keen interest in local affairs. He was lord lieutenant for Lancashire in 1971–6.

Assheton was very much what Sir Winston Churchill once described as 'an English worthy'. He had a keen intellect and great experience of financial and economic matters but he lacked the more theatrical gifts of politicians. His economic opinions were of an orthodoxy unfashionable until Margaret Thatcher's administration in 1979. He has been well described as 'the right man in the right place at the wrong time'.

In 1924 Assheton married Sylvia Benita Frances, daughter of Frederick William Hotham, sixth Baron Hotham. They had two sons and two daughters; one daughter died at birth. Assheton died 18 September 1984 at Downham Hall, and was succeeded in the baronetcy and the barony by his elder son, Ralph John (born 1929).

[Personal knowledge.]

JULIAN AMERY

published 1990

ASTOR Nancy Witcher

(1879–1964)

Viscountess Astor

Politician and hostess, was born 19 May 1879 at Danville, Virginia, the eighth, and fifth surviving, child of Chiswell Dabney Langhorne, Southern gentleman and Civil War veteran, who later made a fortune in railway development and bought an estate at Mirador near Charlottesville. Her mother, Nancy Witcher Keene, was of Irish extraction. The beauty of the second daughter, Irene, was immortalized by Charles Dana Gibson, the artist, whom she married.

Nancy herself was gifted with beauty, as well as wit and a good—although inadequately schooled—intelligence. In 1897 she was married, at the age of eighteen, to Robert Gould Shaw, by whom she had one son, but whom she divorced in 1903. This was a source of considerable embarrassment to her in her later career, when she was a vigorous opponent of divorce. In 1904 she came to England for the social and hunting seasons, and in 1906, after rejecting other suitors, married Waldorf (later second Viscount) Astor, who brought her immense wealth and lifelong devotion. They had four sons and one daughter.

Naturally religious, Nancy was converted in 1914 to Christian Science, which she thereafter practised and preached with missionary fervour, and to which she soon converted her friend Philip Kerr, later eleventh Marquess of Lothian. Her friendship with Kerr (always regarded as platonic) remained, until his death in 1940, the closest of her many friendships; and, since he was a fugitive from Roman Catholicism, it was probably under his influence that her natural Protestantism assumed an obsessively anti-Popish form.

In 1919 Waldorf Astor had to vacate his parliamentary seat—the Sutton division of Plymouth—on inheriting the peerage which he had not wanted his father to accept. In the resulting by-election Nancy, now Lady Astor, stood in his place and was returned as a Conservative supporter of the Lloyd George coalition. When she took her seat, 1 December 1919, she was the first woman to do so, since the Sinn Fein Countess Markievicz, elected in 1918, had disqualified herself by refusal to take the oath. To mark the historic occasion, Lady Astor was introduced by Lloyd George and Arthur Balfour, the only two members who had attained the rank of prime minister.

A more conventional woman might have shown her reverence for the ancient and illustrious men's club to which she had gained admittance by conforming very punctiliously to its rules and customs. But Lady Astor did not seek to prove herself the equal of her male colleagues, since it was her line that women were the superior sex. 'I married beneath me,' she used to say, 'all women do'—and in that spirit she made her presence felt in the House of Commons. Partly because she hated pomposity of any kind, and partly because her mind was rather disorderly, she was never a good parliamentarian in the traditional sense. Her interruptions, although often witty, were too frequent, and once, when she claimed to have been listening for hours before interrupting, a member exclaimed: 'Yes, we *heard* you listening!'

Yet her service in the House of Commons was by no means barren of achievement, and her best work was done during the early years. In 1923 she introduced and carried through all its stages her own private member's Bill raising, in principle, to eighteen the age qualification for the purchase of alcoholic drinks. Her husband then took charge of it in the Lords, and it became law. Her maiden speech had been in favour of Temperance, and her Bill gave practical, if limited, effect to her convictions. In addition, she championed a variety of women's causes: for instance, votes for women at twenty-one, equal rights in the Civil Service, and the preservation of the women's police force. She was also active on behalf of children, especially as a strong supporter and benefactress of the nursery schools of Margaret McMillan.

In 1931 she and her husband visited the Soviet Union with G. B. Shaw. Shaw returned an ecstatic admirer of Stalin, but the Astors were not blind to the atrocity of the Soviet regime. At home Lady Astor was one of those who vainly demanded more generous treatment of the unemployed.

She was instinctively anti-Nazi, never visited Hitler, and was, later, on his black list. All the same, she believed that the policy of appeasement was right and became one of its most conspicuous partisans—conspicuous mainly through the influence of the 'Cliveden set' myth. Cliveden was the Astors' magnificent home overlooking the Thames near Taplow, where they entertained liberally. The idea of a conspiratorial set meeting there to promote appeasement and a sell-out to Nazi Germany was a journalistic invention. It was demonstrably mythical since the outstanding feature of the Astors' hospitality was its open-endedness: no country house of the period had a more comprehensive clientele. Moreover, even among the Astors' intimate friends (naturally their most frequent guests) there were deep differences of opinion on foreign policy.

Churchill, however, was not one of their friends. Between him and Lady Astor relations were never good, although in 1940 she helped to make him prime minister by voting against the Government in the Norway division. During the war of 1939–45 the Astors dedicated themselves to Plymouth, she as one of the city's members of Parliament, he as its lord mayor for five successive years. They spent a lot of time at their house on the Hoe, which—with them in it—was damaged by high explosive and incendiary bombs. Lady Astor did much to sustain morale, not least by performing, for the benefit of people in air-raid shelters, the cartwheels with which she had amazed Edwardian house-parties when she was nearly forty years younger.

It is a virtual certainty, however, that she would have lost her seat in the Labour tide had she stood again in 1945, and it is possible that she would not have been asked to stand, for her parliamentary performance had deteriorated over the years. Her husband wisely persuaded her not to seek re-election. Resentful at being out of Parliament, she turned her resentment against him, with the sad result that their partnership was clouded during the years before he died in 1952. Surviving him by more than a decade, she died at her daughter's house, Grimsthorpe in Lincolnshire, 2 May 1964, and was buried with her husband at Cliveden.

Lady Astor was short and neat, but her air of alertness and challenge made her seem taller. Her eyes were blue, her colouring was fair, her nose and chin were strong and finely shaped, but without undue prominence. Her clothes were expensive, but she never wore bright colours, and in the House of Commons unfailingly wore a black coat and skirt with a white blouse and a black tricorn hat. A gardenia or sprig of verbena was usually in her lapel. Her finest qualities were courage, generosity, and zest; her principal defects insensitivity, prejudice, and a streak of cruelty. She was a curious mixture of religious maniac and clown, oscillating between the extremes of earnestness and levity. Moderation never came easily to her, yet paradoxically she always supported moderates in politics.

An oil painting of her by J. S. Sargent (1923) is in the National Portrait Gallery. There are three charcoal drawings of her by the same artist, two belonging to the fourth Viscount Astor, and one presented to the National Portrait Gallery by her son, Michael Astor. A picture by Charles Sims of her taking her seat in the House of Commons is on loan to the university of Virginia at Charlottesville, and a copy of this painting is in the Plymouth Art Gallery. A bust of her by K. de Strobl was presented by Shaw to the Palace of Westminster.

Lady Astor was appointed CH in 1937 and made an honorary freeman of Plymouth in 1959.

[Maurice Collis, *Nancy Astor*, 1960; Michael Astor, *Tribal Feeling*, 1963; Christopher Sykes, *Nancy: the Life of Lady Astor*, 1972; private information; personal knowledge.]

JOHN GRIGG

published 1981

ATTLEE Clement Richard

(1883–1967)

First Earl Attlee

Statesman, was born in London 3 January 1883, the fourth son and seventh child of Henry Attlee, a leading solicitor in the City, and his wife, Ellen, daughter of T. S. Watson, secretary of the Art Union of London. The Attlee family had lived near Dorking for generations as farmers, millers, and merchants, but by the middle of the nineteenth century were in the main solid and prosperous members of the professional class.

The Attlee house was in Putney; a country house in Essex was added in 1896. Attlee always said that his was 'a typical family of the professional class brought up in the atmosphere of Victorian England'. He was taught at home until he was nine, acquiring an abiding love of literature from his mother. Other teaching was done by a succession of governesses engaged for his sisters, one of whom had previously had (Sir) Winston Churchill in her charge. A preparatory school at Northam Place, Potters Bar, was then followed by Haileybury College. His record at both was undistinguished.

When he left Haileybury he was still immature and painfully shy, having made a mark only as an outstandingly good cadet.

He went up to University College, Oxford, in 1901 and spent three happy years there. He emerged with a deep love of literature and history (he obtained second class honours in modern history in 1904), a half blue for billiards, the sole game for which he had skill, and a lasting affection for his college and Oxford. Otherwise he was as conventional in general outlook and as Conservative in politics as he had been at Haileybury. He had already begun to eat dinners at the Inner Temple and was called to the bar in 1905.

In October 1905 Attlee's life took what proved to be a decisive turn when he paid his first visit to Haileybury House, a boys' club in Stepney, supported by his old school. He soon began to help regularly in the club and took a commission in its cadet corps. In 1907 he agreed to become manager of the club and went to live there. His home was in the East End for the next fourteen years.

By the end of 1907 he was a socialist, converted by his experience of life in Stepney and his reading of the works of John Ruskin, William Morris, Sidney and Beatrice Webb, and other apostles of socialism. In 1908 he joined the tiny Stepney branch of the Independent Labour Party. There was nothing unusual in such a conversion to socialism. Two of his brothers and several of his friends took the same path. What marked out Attlee was that he abandoned any idea of a regular career which might be combined with political agitation and social work on the side. His father's death in 1908 assured him of an income of £400 a year. It enabled him to abandon the law and was enough for his spartan tastes. He took a succession of ill-paid jobs connected with social work or politics: lecture secretary of the Webbs' campaign for the minority report of the Poor Law Commission, secretary of Toynbee Hall, lecturer at Ruskin College, Oxford, in 1911, and official explainer of the National Insurance Act of that year. At the instigation of Sidney Webb (later Lord Passfield), he became a lecturer in social administration at the London School of Economics in 1913. The other candidate was E. Hugh (later Lord) Dalton.

He thus had plenty of time for social work and socialist propaganda. As secretary of the Stepney branch of the ILP he was active in Labour's London organization and, his early shyness conquered, became an experienced, if not very effective, street-corner orator. By 1914, without any abandonment of his old friends and connections, his roots were deep in the East End and the growing Labour movement.

He had not, however, given up his voluntary commission in the cadets and within a few weeks of the outbreak of war, at the age of thirty-one, was a lieutenant in the 6th South Lancashire Regiment. He went with his battalion to Gallipoli and had two spells there, the second ending with command of the rearguard at the evacuation of Suvla Bay. He was in Mesopotamia in 1916, where he was badly wounded by a British shell and invalided home. After recovery he served with the Tank Corps for a year and was promoted to major in 1917. By the summer of 1918 he was back with the South Lancashires in France. During the advance to Lille he was injured and sent home, celebrating the armistice in hospital.

Attlee was unusual among the coming Labour leaders in having served as an active officer throughout the war. For many years he was most commonly known as 'Major Attlee', his vaguely military bearing and appearance, and the clipped anachronisms of his conversation, setting him somewhat apart from his contemporaries in the Labour Party. The war also gave rise to a keen interest in the theory of warfare; he was, for example, convinced that Churchill's strategic conception at Gallipoli had been sound.

Attlee returned to the London School of Economics and to political activity in the East End immediately after demobilization. In 1919 he was co-opted by Stepney Borough Council as mayor. Apart from the routine work of the Council his main concern was the high level of unemployment in Stepney. He helped to form an association of the Labour mayors of London boroughs and became its first chairman, leading a deputation to 10 Downing Street to appeal to Lloyd George for stronger measures to deal with unemployment in London.

Attlee continued, as an alderman, to be active in the affairs of Stepney until 1927. But marriage in 1922, the purchase of a house in an Essex suburb, and election as an MP brought to an end the years of absorption in the life of the East End. His main role became that of representing Stepney on many of the organizations set up to co-ordinate the work of the London borough councils; for some years he served as vice-president of the Municipal Electricity Authorities of Greater London.

When he was elected to the House of Commons in 1922 Attlee gave up his post at the London School of Economics and became, in effect, a full-time politician. His constituency, Limehouse, was one of the few safe Labour seats outside the mining districts. It was a fitting reward for all that he had done in the East End since 1907. Elsewhere, he was virtually unknown. Platform oratory was the route to reputation in the Labour Party and he had little talent for it.

He did, however, have some long-run advantages over the other middle-class and professional men who became Labour MPs in the elections of 1922 and 1923. His experience of working-class life was both extensive and first-hand and he had started at the bottom of the Labour movement. He had already begun to show, too, unusual effectiveness at the hard slog of committee work. His views were well to the left of his party's official policy. He was a member of a small 'ginger group' in the ILP in company with A. Fenner (later Lord) Brockway and R. Clifford Allen (later Lord Allen of Hurtwood), and also attracted by the guild socialism advocated by G. D. H. Cole.

Ramsay MacDonald was elected leader of the Labour Party after the election of 1922 and invited Attlee to be one of his parliamentary private secretaries. But the Parliament was short-lived. Stanley Baldwin (later Earl Baldwin of Bewdley) decided to seek a mandate for tariff reform and went to the country at the end of 1923. The upshot was a minority Labour Government which held office for ten uneasy months. Attlee served as under-secretary of state for war, under Stephen Walsh, a post which he found congenial.

Back in opposition, Attlee's contribution was largely confined to putting his party's case on the Electricity Bill (1926) and a Rating and Valuation Bill (1925) which was one of Neville Chamberlain's key reforms as minister of health. Attlee's growing reputation for competence at the detailed work of committees must have played some part in MacDonald's invitation in 1927 to serve as one of the two Labour members on a statutory commission for India, chaired by Sir John (later Viscount) Simon. For the next two years Attlee devoted himself to the political problems of India. The commission met considerable obstruction on its two visits to India and its report in 1930 was rejected by the leaders of the Congress and denigrated by their supporters in the Labour Party. Attlee himself always defended the commission's proposals for an extension of self-government in the provinces as going as far as was realistic at the time. Certainly his service on the Simon commission gave him a valuable insight into the problems of India.

After the election of 1929 MacDonald broke a promise that serving on the Simon commission would not affect Attlee's chance of a post in the event of Labour coming to power. His opportunity did not come until the spring of 1930 when Sir Oswald Mosley resigned from the chancellorship of the Duchy of Lancaster. Attlee succeeded him but with a considerably reduced brief. He assisted Addison with his Agricultural Marketing Bill, one of the Government's few parliamentary successes, and wrote a major memorandum on 'The Problems of British Industry' which, although it went unheeded by the Cabinet, was the first indication of his ability to analyse a problem and distil a course of action. In March 1931 Attlee was transferred to the Post Office which had gone to seed under Sir G. E. P. Murray, who had ruled it with an autocratic hand since 1914. Attlee set to with a will and inaugurated a number of reforms, the benefits of which largely accrued to Sir H. Kingsley Wood in the succeeding Government.

He was on holiday with his family in August 1931 when he was summoned to Downing Street and told, with the other non-Cabinet ministers, that the Labour Government was at an end and that MacDonald was forming a coalition Government. Attlee was never in any doubt about his own course of action in spite of his past association with MacDonald and a growing reputation for being not only middle-class but also middle-of-the-road. He had become increasingly disillusioned with MacDonald since joining the Government but the reasons for his staying with the Labour Party lay deeper, in the strength of his personal beliefs and his roots in the movement. He never changed his view that MacDonald had perpetrated 'the greatest betrayal in the political history of the country'.

Attlee survived the landslide of the 1931 election but with a majority at Limehouse of only 551. Labour, including the rump of the ILP, was reduced to 52 members. George Lansbury, the sole survivor of those who had sat in Cabinet, was elected leader of the parliamentary party and Attlee became his deputy. Sir R. Stafford Cripps completed a triumvirate; although solicitor-general in the Labour Government he had been in the Commons for little more than a year. The team of three worked harmoniously. Cripps provided the driving force and for a time Attlee was considerably influenced by him. But as Cripps moved further to the left, neither his views nor his crusade against Transport House were to Attlee's liking. Attlee was the last man to wish to split the Labour Party and his own ideas about policy were becoming increasingly balanced and eclectic. He expressed them in *The Will and the Way to Socialism* published shortly before the election of 1935.

The years from 1931 to 1935 were the making of Attlee. He was no longer confined to occasional parliamentary speeches on specialist topics but, as deputy leader, was called upon to cover the whole range of debate. In 1932 he filled more columns of *Hansard* than any other member and led the party for several months in 1934 when Lansbury fell ill. His own parliamentary style was steadily developing. His speeches lacked flourish to the point of being laconic but they were thorough and spiced with an occasional waspish sting. But none of this was enough to suggest that he was a potential leader of the party.

Lansbury resigned the leadership after his defeat at the Brighton conference in October 1935, a bare three weeks before the start of the election campaign. The parliamentary party had little choice but to appoint Attlee as leader. The *Manchester Guardian* reflected universal opinion; it observed, 'This is hardly more than an interim appointment.' Attlee worked hard in the campaign but made little personal impact on the electorate and the result, 154 seats to Labour, was a disappointment. In the contest for the leadership that followed the election the loyalty of his old colleagues, particularly the miners, from the previous Parliament and his reputation for rectitude were enough to ensure the defeat of Herbert Morrison (later Lord Morrison of Lambeth) and Arthur Greenwood, his rivals for the leadership. Even his modesty helped, for his approach to the tasks of leadership was the antithesis of the style which MacDonald had made suspect.

There was a full testing of Attlee in the years that followed. Few leaders have had a more difficult baptism. The Labour Party struggled to cope with its own divisions in the face of Hitler's challenge to the country's security and the seeming impregnability of the 'national' Government. Attlee largely concentrated on his role in Parliament. He recognized that he had no talent for the more flamboyant arts of leadership in opposition and that the constitution of the Labour Party provided little scope for the imposition of his views on others. In so far as he gave a lead it was, as he said, 'from slightly left of centre'.

With political passions running high his gift, as Dalton noted, was that he 'lowered the temperature'. This low-key approach was denounced as colourless and uninspiring by the militants of both Left and Right in the party. Nor did it make Attlee appear to the electorate at large as being of the stuff of which prime ministers are made. But if he did not inspire the Labour Party, he did nothing to divide it and it was this preservation of Labour's fragile unity which made it possible to seize the opportunity of 1940.

Attlee's approach stemmed from his deep understanding of the Labour Party as a loose alliance of divergent views and interests. He was fortunate in one respect. The shock of 1931 and the depth of the economic depression combined to remove most of the ambiguities that had characterized the party's domestic programme in the MacDonald era. By 1935 the Labour Party was firmly pledged to policies of socialist planning and public ownership. This measure of agreement was, however, obscured by a more fundamental debate, stirred by the political and economic crisis of the thirties, in which the defenders of parliamentary democracy came under increasingly heavy Marxist fire.

Attlee put his own views in *The Labour Party in Perspective* which he was invited to write for the Left Book Club in 1937. His intention, he wrote in the introduction, was 'to show the Labour Party in its historical setting as an expression in place and time of the urge for socialism, to show it as a characteristic example of British methods and as an outcome of British political instincts'. This belief in parliamentary institutions and the traditional ways of government was also exemplified in his support for Stanley Baldwin, for whom he had a lasting admiration, during the abdication crisis. They found themselves of one mind on the issue. Nor did Attlee doubt that he was expressing the views of the ordinary supporters of the Labour Party although not, as he noted later, 'of a few of the intelligentsia who can be trusted to take the wrong view on any subject.'

But as Germany grew more menacing, domestic questions gave way to the problem of how the challenge was to be met. Chamberlain, who became prime minister in May 1937, quickly dispelled the hesitations of the Baldwin Government by a forceful combination of policies of positive appeasement and moderate rearmament. The Labour Party found it difficult to make a coherent response. It had previously paid little attention to foreign policy. The split in World War I had been healed with the slogan, 'No more war' and the pull of the pacifists remained powerful. In May 1935 Attlee stated views to which the majority of Labour Party members would have subscribed: 'We stand for Collective Security through the League of Nations. We reject the use of force as an instrument of policy. We stand for the reduction of armaments and pooled security . . . Our policy is not one of seeking security through rearmament but through disarmament.' These policies of disarmament and collective security, tinged with pacifism, were slowly abandoned under the pressure of events. The occupation of the Rhineland, the Spanish civil war, and the Anschluss added substance to the arguments which Ernest Bevin and Dalton, in particular, had been advancing since Hitler's early days in power. Attlee himself denounced Chamberlain with vigour. When (Sir) Anthony Eden (later the Earl of Avon) resigned from the Foreign Office in February 1938 Attlee argued that the Government's policy was one of 'abject surrender to the dictators'. He attacked the Munich agreement as 'a tremendous victory for Herr Hitler' and pressed Chamberlain hard in the summer of 1939 to come to terms with the Soviet Union.

The key issue, however, was rearmament. In July 1937 the Parliamentary Labour Party finally decided to abandon its traditional vote against the defence estimates and to confine itself to abstention. Attlee voted against the change. It was not until after Munich that he began to accept the case for rearmament and when Chamberlain announced the introduction of conscription for military service in April 1939 Attlee attacked the measure as useless and divisive.

The Labour Party was so divided in its views that Attlee, as leader, was in a difficult position. Urged on by Bevin, the leaders of the unions were able to ensure, after 1937, that the official line was in support of rearmament. But the main movement of opinion among the rank and file was sharply to the left and looked to the Soviet Union for salvation. The middle path followed by Attlee sprang as much from conviction as from his conception of his role as leader. The conclusions that he had arrived at after World War I were not readily discarded and his hostility to

Chamberlain and his policies ran deep. In later years Attlee came close to admitting that the Labour Party had been in blinkers. His own comment on the vote against conscription is perhaps the best epitaph: 'Well, it probably wasn't awfully wise.'

Attlee was ill when war broke out. Two operations for prostate trouble kept him out of action for several months and Arthur Greenwood took over the leadership. It was not until the fiasco of the Norwegian campaign in April 1940 that the opportunity arose to topple Chamberlain.

After the debate on 7 and 8 May 1940 it was evident that he could not carry on without Labour support. When Attlee and Greenwood saw Chamberlain on 9 May, Attlee said that he would put two questions to the Labour National Executive Committee: (1) Are you prepared to serve under Chamberlain? (2) Are you prepared to serve under someone else? He telephoned the replies on the following afternoon: 'The answer to the first question is, no. To the second question, yes.' Chamberlain resigned within the hour. Churchill was summoned to the Palace and during the night he and Attlee agreed on the distribution of posts in a coalition government.

Attlee served in the War Cabinet as lord privy seal until February 1942. He then became secretary for the Dominions and, from September 1943, lord president of the Council. He was also deputy prime minister, at first *de facto*, but, from February 1942, with the formal title. At the highest level the war was run by the War Cabinet and two subsidiary bodies; military matters were dealt with by the Defence Committee, civil by the Lord President's Committee. Attlee alone served on all three bodies and did so for the life of the Government. But although he played his part on the Defence Committee, his main responsibility lay on the civil side where, by 1944, he was very much the committee workhorse of the coalition. Most of the key committees were chaired by him and by the end of the war he had earned a high reputation for the efficient and businesslike dispatch of business.

The day-to-day care of Government business in the House of Commons also fell mainly on Attlee and as deputy prime minister he took the chair at the War Cabinet and the Defence Committee when Churchill was absent from the country, as he increasingly was during the last two years of the war. These arrangements rested on a confidence and trust that lay at the heart of the coalition's high degree of harmony. Attlee's loyalty to Churchill never wavered for an instant, even in the dark days of 1941 and 1942.

From his central position in the machinery of government, Attlee was called upon to preside over much of the discussion of social reform that not only made the coalition one of the most considerable of all reforming governments but led to a consensus of view between the two parties and laid the framework for much of the work of Attlee's own administration. The war was fought on the home front with the weapons of economic control and social amelioration advocated by the Labour Party and it was evident by the end of 1943 that peace would bring further reforms: the implementation of the report of the committee on social insurance and allied services chaired by Sir W. H. (later Lord) Beveridge, the establishment of a National Health Service, and the carrying out of economic policies aimed at full employment.

Attlee was well suited by temperament and experience to soothe such strains as these great changes brought to the coalition. In backing proposals for reform he eschewed the socialist arguments and socialist labels which would have antagonized his Tory colleagues. The case was put in terms of national unity and what was needed to win the war. But it was not easy for Attlee to avoid offending Tories without outraging many of his own supporters who wished Labour to use its leverage in the coalition for more socialist purposes. Attlee's reply was that 'we cannot dictate to others the acceptance of our Socialist programme', but this realism was usually tempered with emphasis on how much had been gained by participation: 'The acceptance', as he said at West Hartlepool in January 1944, 'of so much of what our party has preached in the last thirty years.'

Attlee's wider responsibilities included the chairmanship of the committee on India and of committees dealing with the details of the post-war settlement in Europe. He opposed the Morgenthau plan to destroy Germany's industrial capacity although convinced of the need to enforce fundamental changes in its economic and social structure. He found himself very much in sympathy with Eden on more general questions and they combined on occasion to restrain Churchill, particularly when they thought him too influenced by Roosevelt. But the disagreements were minor and the bipartisan policy of the post-war years was forged during the coalition. No member of the Government was more hostile to Stalin than Attlee and he fully agreed with Churchill that long-term American participation in the peace settlement and the maintenance of the British Commonwealth were essential to counter the Russians and ensure stability.

Attlee's record during the war earned him little public reputation compared, for example, with Bevin and Morrison whose departments covered much of the home front. Within Whitehall, however, his standing grew as a chairman and conciliator of unusual quality. Churchill and he made an effective combination, of leader and chairman, which echoed that of Lloyd George and Bonar Law in the previous war. It also became increasingly clear that Attlee could not be lightly crossed; he could be devastating in his criticisms and his judgement, if sparsely offered, lacked neither crispness nor authority. It was an appreciation of these qualities, as he had seen them emerge during the war, that led Bevin to compare Attlee with Campbell-Bannerman as possessing 'that gift of character which enabled him to hold a team of clever men together'.

One of his Tory colleagues in the War Cabinet said subsequently that he could not remember Attlee 'ever making a point which I felt came from him as leader of the Labour Party' as distinct from his pressing for improvements in the lot of the working class and for effective preparation for the post-war period. It was this non-partisan approach to the coalition which led Aneurin Bevan to accuse Attlee of bringing 'to the fierce struggle of politics the tepid enthusiasm of a lazy summer afternoon at a cricket match'. Attlee's own view was that his biggest achievement had been 'to take a party intact into a coalition, to keep it intact for five years and to bring it out intact'.

In May 1945 Attlee accompanied Eden to the foundation conference of the United Nations in San Francisco. The prospect of a general election forced them to return early, but, on his way back, Attlee was able to meet Truman and found to his pleasure that they 'talked the same language'.

Churchill and Attlee would have preferred to continue the coalition until Japan had been defeated but opinion in both parties, especially on the Labour side, was in favour of a quick end. Churchill formed a caretaker Government and a general election followed immediately.

During the campaign Attlee established himself for the first time in the public eye. His broadcast in reply to Churchill's 'Gestapo' speech was a model of effective restraint and his campaign, for which he was driven about by his wife in their small family car, was in telling contrast to his opponent's almost regal style. He also emerged with credit from the one testing episode of the campaign, an attempt by Churchill and Beaverbrook to take advantage of some tiresome interventions by Harold Laski, the chairman of the Labour Party's National Executive Committee.

The result of the election, much to Attlee's surprise, was a Labour landslide with a majority over the Tories of 170. But he did not become prime minister without some exchanges in which, in Emanuel (later Lord) Shinwell's words, 'the brotherly love advocated by the movement was conspicuous by its absence'. Bevin's unwavering support ensured the defeat of a challenge by Morrison for the leadership and Attlee proceeded to form a strong and experienced Government. His first task, once the principal posts had been filled, was to return to the Potsdam conference with the new foreign secretary, Ernest Bevin.

Conservatives feared and socialists hoped that the election of 1945 presaged fundamental changes. The Labour Party's manifesto had declared, 'The Labour Party is a Socialist Party. Its ultimate aim is the establishment of the Socialist Commonwealth of Great Britain.' Attlee's own horizon was more restricted: to the implementation of the manifesto's specific proposals and the tackling of the problems which the post-war period would bring, particularly in economic policy and foreign affairs. During the war he and all his leading colleagues had participated in a gigantic exercise in planning and economic control so that, to a considerable extent, the election of 1945 signified not change but continuity. Nor, in spite of the dismay of defeat, did the Conservative Party lag far behind Labour. It was by 1945 already well on the way to embracing both the managed economy and the Welfare State. If Attlee presided over a revolution, therefore, it was, as he himself stressed, an extraordinarily quiet and peaceful revolution which had begun well before 1945 and was to lead more to consensus between the parties than to conflict.

The leading figures in the Government, Bevin, Morrison, Cripps, Dalton, and Bevan, formed an exceptionally able but difficult team, managed by Attlee with great skill. He was at his best when he could delegate substantial control of major areas of policy to ministers in whom he had complete confidence, as with Bevin at the Foreign Office and Cripps at the Treasury, and so be free to concentrate his own efforts on one or two key political problems and the general tasks of co-ordination and management. 'If you have a good dog, don't bark yourself' was a favourite Attlee proverb.

The backing of Bevin was proof against all intrigues but Attlee's authority over his principal colleagues and his more general mastery of the Cabinet sprang from his own qualities. He was a good judge of men and adept at managing them, rarely allowing his judgement to be clouded by personal prejudice. His integrity was accepted as being beyond question.

From the beginning Attlee succeeded in enforcing his own style on the working of his Government. He put high value on the bureaucratic virtues of formality, order, and regularity and in structure and method the Government conformed to them to an unusual degree. His own strong preference was for working through paper. Even at the highest level the circulation of boxes was the medium by which the work of the Attlee Government was mainly done. There was little of the informal and speculative discussion typical of Churchill's methods. The same puritanical concentration on the matter in hand characterized Attlee's running of the Cabinet and its committees. As he later remarked, 'I was always for getting on with the job.' Some indulgence was shown to senior ministers but short shrift was usually dealt out to anyone who had failed to master his brief or who attempted to read it. In summing up Attlee was invariably precise and succinct. Otherwise he said little and rarely took a vote. His aim was to make the Cabinet and its committees efficient machines for the dispatch of well-prepared business and to cut to the minimum their tendency to become talking shops.

The main defect of such methods was that Attlee remained remote from his party and the general public, and even from ministers who were not privy to the inner circle. The impression that he gave of a Victorian headmaster keeping his school under strict control was compounded by an inability to participate in the complimentary small-talk of politics, a consequence doubtless of his innate shyness. His considerable kindliness was invariably expressed by letter.

'The little man', as Bevin affectionately called him, had few of the attributes normally looked for in a political leader but this was of little significance while Bevin was attempting to forge a Western alliance or Cripps was embarking on his austere crusade. But when ill health compelled them to resign and Morrison proved a palpable failure at the Foreign Office, it was beyond Attlee's power to fill the gap. The Labour Party respected him to an unsurpassed degree but could not rise to him. Nor had he the gift, possessed by Bevin and Cripps, of rallying those outside the ranks of his own party even though his lack of partisan spite and devotion to the broad national interest came to be increasingly recognized. But as a catalyst among politicians engaged in the business of government Attlee has few rivals.

In domestic politics the first eighteen months or so of his office were almost untarnished honeymoon. The Opposition showed few signs of recovery and major legislation poured from Parliament at an unprecedented rate. Attlee was determined to push ahead and by the end of 1946, an *annus mirabilis*, acts had been passed nationalizing the Bank of England, the coal industry, civil aviation, and Cable and Wireless; there had also been a National Insurance Act, a New Towns Act, a Trade Disputes Act, an Act for the establishment of a National Health Service, and a host of minor measures. The legislation remains as a permanent memorial. It was passed in a period of optimism in politics and cheap money in the economy. The Japanese war ended with unexpected speed, taxation was cut, demobilization went smoothly with none of the unemployment that had been feared, and industry was turning over to peacetime production with remarkably little friction. The Welfare State was in an advanced state of construction and the nation was still proud of its rationing system and its sense of social discipline.

At this stage there was little public consciousness that there would be tight physical constraints on what could be done. J. M. (later Lord) Keynes, for example, wrote to Dalton about the latter's National Land Fund to say that he should have 'acquired for the nation all the coastline round the island at one stroke'. It was a time when anything seemed possible.

Attlee did not share this euphoria. He was shocked by the sudden ending of Lend-Lease in August 1945 and, while adamant that there was no alternative but to accept the terms on which the American loan was subsequently made, knew that the most severe difficulties would be likely to arise from the requirement to make sterling convertible within a year of the commencement of the loan.

In foreign affairs events at first appeared to match the fears that Churchill and Attlee had shared in the last months of the war. Stalin cemented his hold on Eastern Europe and was obstructive in Germany. Large Communist parties in France and Italy awaited his bidding. It was, however, the uncertainty engendered by American policy which most disturbed the Government.

Attlee did not doubt Truman's own goodwill but the negotiation of the loan and the passing of the McMahon Act by Congress in 1946 were jolting experiences and the American reaction to Russia seemed ambivalent and at times naïve. Relations between the two countries were further strained by Bevin's policy in Palestine, fully backed by Attlee, which American opinion thought pro-Arab and anti-Zionist.

A transformation of American policy began with the arrival of General Marshall at the State Department in January 1947. The Truman Doctrine which secured aid to Greece and Turkey, previously British responsibilities, was declared in March. A year later the Marshall Plan was launched and followed in 1949 by the setting up of the North Atlantic Treaty Organization. Together they ensured the economic recovery and political security of Western Europe. If the main influence bringing about the change was the effect of Stalin's obduracy on American opinion, the patient persuasion of Bevin and Attlee should not be discounted. In a relationship which Attlee called 'the closest of my political life' they were of one mind on the necessity of involving the United States in the defence of Western Europe.

Attlee's own most important contribution, and one with which his name will always be associated, was, however, the granting of independence to India. He acted in effect as his own secretary of state and all the major decisions bear his unmistakable stamp. He began with the intention of modifying the plan which Cripps had proposed to the Indians in 1942 but the failure of the Cabinet mission in 1946 convinced him of the need to take full account of the strength of the Muslim League and its determination to establish Pakistan. Viscount (later Earl) Wavell, who had been viceroy since 1943, was dismissed and replaced by Attlee's personal choice, Lord Louis Mountbatten, who was charged with the negotiation of independence within a time limit. The new viceroy arrived in India in March 1947 and acted with great speed and decisiveness. On the day of the declaration of Indian independence he wrote to Attlee, 'The man who made it possible was you yourself. Without your original guidance and your unwavering support nothing could have been accomplished out here.'

Attlee was also mainly responsible for the decision that Britain should manufacture her own atomic bomb. Concern at the narrowness with which American officials were interpreting the Quebec agreement for the exchange of atomic information led him to fly to Washington in November 1945. His discussions with Truman were cordial but the President was in the event unable to deliver even the little that he offered. The *coup de grâce* was delivered by Congress a few months later with the passage of the McMahon Bill. Attlee had no hesitation in deciding that Britain should make her own bomb: 'It had become essential. We had to hold up our position *vis-à-vis* the Americans. We couldn't allow ourselves to be wholly in their hands, and their position wasn't awfully clear always.' He also insisted on the maximum of secrecy. All but a few members of the Cabinet were kept in the dark, questions in Parliament discouraged, and large sums concealed in the estimates. 'The project', as Attlee put it, 'was never hampered by lack of money.'

The Government ran into its first major trouble early in 1947 when fuel supplies broke down in savage weather. For a time two and a half million men were out of work. During the following months the Cabinet was further shaken by a dispute over the nationalization of iron and steel and by an economic crisis. The nationalization of iron and steel was the only major item of the 1945 programme on which there had been no progress. Morrison, whose responsibilities included the co-ordination of economic policy, had always been lukewarm. With some encouragement from Attlee, he succeeded in negotiating an agreement with the leaders of the industry which fell well short of nationalization. But the compromise ran into trouble in the Cabinet, with Bevin, Cripps, and Dalton in opposition, and raised a storm in the party. Although Attlee took care to leave the running to Morrison, it was evident that he had made an error of judgement.

A growing exchange crisis came to a head in July when sterling became freely convertible, under the terms of the American loan. The Cabinet dithered for five weeks before suspending convertibility. His critics were confirmed in their view that Attlee, never at his best in discussions about finance, was losing his grip.

Foremost among these critics was Cripps who had some success in persuading one or two of his leading colleagues that Bevin should replace Attlee, with the latter taking the Exchequer. The attempt was doomed from the start by Bevin's response: 'What has the little man ever done to me?' But Cripps persisted. Although deserted by his fellow conspirators he went to see Attlee on 9 September. The interview began with Cripps suggesting that Attlee should give way to Bevin. It ended with Cripps agreeing to take on the new post of minister for economic affairs. Whatever the summer might have disclosed of Attlee's failings, his touch with men had not deserted him.

Dalton was compelled to resign in November as a consequence of a few indiscreet words to a journalist immediately before his budget speech. He was succeeded at the Exchequer by Cripps who thus came to dominate economic affairs and, to Attlee's immense relief, soon brought authority and purpose to domestic policy. Cripps's policies were hard and austere. Rations were, for a time, lower than they had been in the war. The housing programme was cut and the building of hospitals and roads brought al-most to a halt. The bombed wastes at the centre of cities became even more derelict. But the aim was clear: to bring the balance of payments into equilibrium and, in particular, to solve the problem of the dollar shortage while maintaining the benefits which the Government had earlier secured for the working class.

Attlee was content to leave the lead to Bevin and Cripps. In foreign affairs, the early work began to bear fruit. The Organization for European Economic Co-operation was set up and the Marshall Plan implemented in 1948, so providing the underpinning for Cripps's policies. The Russian challenge at Berlin was successfully met by the Anglo-American airlift and the North Atlantic Treaty Organization was established in 1949. But the growing movement in favour of a federal Western Europe was met by Bevin with a mixture of hostility and scepticism. Attlee was of the same mind. As he later wrote, 'Britain has never regarded itself as just a European power. Her interests are world-wide. She is the heart of a great Commonwealth and tends to look outwards from Europe.'

By the end of 1949, ten years of continuous office had taken its toll of the leading members of Attlee's Government. They had all suffered bouts of serious illness and Bevin and Cripps were soon to be forced to resign. It was also evident that the Government had little to offer by way of new ideas and policies once it had exhausted the capital of the 1945 manifesto. Cripps had successfully completed the transition from a war economy by marrying Keynesian techniques of budgetary manipulation to the system of rationing and controls inherited from the Churchill coalition but it could scarcely be argued that this was more than a temporary solution to the problem of how the economy should be run.

The inevitable consequence was an intensification of the ancient dis-pute between the left and right wings of the Labour Party. Attlee offered no lead, took no initiative. He increasingly concentrated his energies on contriving to achieve agreement in Cabinet and became even less disposed than before to contemplate crossing his bridges before he came to them.

Nevertheless, Attlee and his colleagues approached the general election in February 1950 with some confidence in spite of having been forced to devalue sterling in the previous autumn. No other industrial country in Europe had made a comparable recovery, the promises of 1945 had been broadly kept, and the working class, in particular, had much to be grateful for. The result was a disappointment, a majority of ten for Labour. Attlee, who had represented Limehouse since 1922, stood at West Walthamstow. He remained in office although no one expected that his Government would last more than a few weeks. In the event it survived for twenty difficult months. Few governments have achieved so little, been so battered by external circumstances, or suffered so much from internal disharmony. The Korean war, which began in June 1950 and brought in its train a massive rearmament programme, inflation, and a disruption of the balance of payments, was the main catalyst of disaster. Much of the ground that had been so painfully gained during the previous three years was lost. When Attlee's Government was defeated at the polls in October 1951, it ended as it had begun, running a war economy.

The strain on Attlee was considerable. The two mainstays of his Cabinet were forced to resign after long periods of ill health, Cripps in October 1950 and Bevin in March 1951. But he enjoyed something of a Roman triumph in December 1950 when, with Bevin too ill to fly, he decided suddenly to go to Washington because of a general worry that the Americans were intending to extend the Korean war and a particular fear, based on a misunderstanding, that Truman was contemplating the use of the atomic bomb. Morrison, who took Bevin's place, was a disaster at the Foreign Office; 'the worst appointment I ever made', was Attlee's conclusion. He was of necessity drawn into direct intervention in the conduct of foreign policy and it was largely due to his steadying hand that there was such a muted response to Musaddeq's expropriation of the Anglo-Iranian Oil Company.

Hugh Gaitskell succeeded Cripps at the Exchequer. There was no doubt about his competence but his promotion roused the resentment of Bevan who stood high in the party and had done well as minister of health. Attlee thought highly of Bevan's talents but had always found him difficult, in respect both of temperament and opinions, and had usually tried to deal with him through an intermediary. What he now had to face was not just personal animosity between the two men but a conflict between the standard bearers of the right and left wings of the party.

Matters came to a head with the preparation of the budget in April 1951. Gaitskell was determined to impose charges for a number of services which had previously been provided free in the National Health Service. Attlee was in hospital with a duodenal ulcer and Morrison, his deputy, made little attempt to confine the resulting conflict. When Attlee returned to duty, the breach was beyond repair. Bevan, (Sir) Harold Wilson, and John Freeman had already resigned and were soon leading a wide-ranging attack on the Government's policies.

A spurious unity was patched up for the election in October but the Labour Party entered it with considerable handicaps. Attlee was its sole leader with a reputation that still counted with the electorate and he campaigned with his wife in what had become his familiar style. He lost and Churchill took office but the total Labour vote was greater than that of the Conservatives and indeed the highest achieved by any party in any election.

The size of the vote was a remarkable indication of the loyalty which the Attlee Government aroused in its supporters. Labour's straightforward mixture of social concern and sensible pragmatism, exemplified by Attlee's own views, may not have been socialist enough to satisfy the Left or been a reliable pointer to the party's future but it satisfied its supporters. The main legacies of the Attlee Government were that it ensured the country's safety and initiated policies of welfare, full employment, and the budgetary control of the economy to such effect that Governments for the next twenty years had no alternative but to attempt to follow in its wake.

Attlee remained leader of the party for four more years. But they were years of frustration and anticlimax. In the House of Commons he continued to speak at a high level of statesmanship, particularly in support of the bipartisan policies in defence and foreign affairs of which he and Bevin had been the principal architects. But it was as leader of the Labour Party that he was judged and for much of this period the leadership was virtually in commission. The broad consensus of the 1940s had disappeared and divisions of opinion had inexorably hardened into faction. Attlee, bereft of the authority of a prime minister, found it hard to cope with the dissensions of Opposition and failed to regain his old touch with backbenchers and the rank and file of the party.

His aim, as it had been before 1939, was to hold the party together. Although unwilling to make any policy concessions to the left wing, he consistently opposed the hounding of Bevan and its other leaders which was enthusiastically led by Arthur Deakin, Bevin's successor at the Transport and General Workers' Union. But passions were too high and the division of opinion too deep for there to be a chance of more than a passing reconciliation. Attlee increasingly withdrew into silence and the anonymity of committee membership. As one of his colleagues put it, 'At the National Executive, he doodled where he should have led.'

The election of May 1955 was a dull affair. The result was a comfortable Conservative victory and it was evident that Attlee's retirement could not be long delayed. The candidates for the succession were Morrison, Bevan, and Gaitskell and by the autumn they were all in the field. But Attlee held on. The consequence, and almost certainly the intention, was that the prize went to Gaitskell. Attlee announced his retirement in a brief and unheralded speech at a regular meeting of the Parliamentary Labour Party on 7 December 1955. The Queen conferred an earldom on him; he had already been admitted to the Order of Merit in 1951.

Attlee was sworn of the privy council in 1935, was made CH in 1945, and KG in 1956. He became an honorary bencher (Inner Temple) in 1946 and FRS in 1947. He was awarded honorary degrees by many universities, and was made an honorary fellow of University College, Oxford (1942), Queen Mary College, London (1948), and LSE (1958).

Attlee's retirement was happy and busy. He travelled widely and wrote and lectured about politics with a frankness that surprised many of his former colleagues. His own stock rose as his virtues of integrity, fairness, and coolness in adversity came to be more widely appreciated. Even his habitual restraint and understatement, which had so often offended his supporters by making him appear remote and almost disinterested, appealed to a generation over-fed on political hyperbole.

Attlee is the leading example in modern times of a politician who achieves high office against all expectations, only then to reveal unsuspected talents. Before 1940 it was assumed that he held a short lease on the leadership of the Labour Party. Many of his colleagues still thought him unfitted for the premiership in 1945. Five years later there would have been little disagreement with Bevin's reported verdict, 'By God, he's the only man who could have kept us together.' Attlee's contribution doubtless lacked the ideas, stimulation, and flair, which are usually thought of as the stuff of leadership. He could act decisively, as he did with India, but he was in general content to wait until opinion had formed before he moved out to express it.

The qualities that made him indispensable and gained him the respect and loyalty of his colleagues were his sense of justice, his imperturbability in a crisis, his skill at the business of administration, and, above all, his adroitness in choosing and managing men. In the main, these are qualities not for opposition, but for office. They enabled Attlee to play a significant part during the war of 1939–45 and then to harness men of inherently greater ability and imagination into a team which effectively laid the foundations of post-war politics both at home and abroad.

Attlee was a solitary man but only in the sense that he had no political cronies. 'It's very dangerous', he said, 'to be the centre of a small circle.'

His gregariousness was expressed in other ways. He liked formal dinners and kept in close touch with the ramified Attlee family. The fortunes of his old friends of school, university, and army were followed in *The Times*; his daily recreation was then to solve the crossword. But his wife, to whom he remained devoted until her death in 1964, and his family, provided all the ordinary company and relaxation that he needed.

He married in 1922 Violet Helen, daughter of H. E. Millar, of Hampstead. They had three daughters and a son, Martin Richard (born 1927), who succeeded his father in the earldom. Attlee died in Westminster Hospital 8 October 1967.

There are portraits of Attlee by Flora Lion (1941); Rodrigo Moynihan (1948) in the Oxford and Cambridge Universities Club; G. Harcourt (1946) in the National Portrait Gallery; Cowan Dobson (1956); Lawrence Gowing (1963); and Derek Fowler, at Haileybury. There is also a bronze presentation medallion (1953), a bronze head by David McFall (1965) in the National Portrait Gallery, and a statue by Ivor Roberts-Jones in the lobby of the House of Commons (1979).

[Attlee's own writings, principally *As It Happened*, 1954; Kenneth Harris, a biography of Attlee in draft; Francis Williams, *A Prime Minister Remembers*, 1961; *The Times*, 9 October 1964; personal knowledge.]

Maurice Shock

published 1981

(1867–1947)

First Earl Baldwin of Bewdley

Statesman and three times prime minister, was born at Lower Park, Bewdley, 3 August 1867, the only son of Alfred and Louisa Baldwin. His father's folk had been for centuries Shropshire yeomen who had settled as ironmasters within the Worcestershire border. Alfred Baldwin was the head of an old-fashioned business of the patriarchal type, a model employer. Among his ancestors were country parsons and Quaker missionaries to the American colonies. Louisa, Stanley Baldwin's mother, was one of the remarkable children of the Rev. George Browne MacDonald, a Wesleyan minister of Highland stock which settled in Northern Ireland after the 'forty-five' and came under the influence of John Wesley.

MacDonald married Hannah Jones, of Manchester, but Welsh from the Vale of Clwyd. They had two sons and five daughters who survived infancy. Louisa's eldest sister Alice was the mother of Rudyard Kipling; Georgiana was the wife of Sir Edward Burne-Jones; Agnes of Sir Edward Poynter.

Stanley, an only child, was left much to himself and found his sustenance in the novels of Scott, the *Morte d'Arthur*, the *Pilgrim's Progress*, and the Lambs' *Tales from Shakespeare*. He was sent to Hawtrey's preparatory school, then in 1881 to Harrow, and in 1885 to Trinity College, Cambridge, where he was placed in the third class in the historical tripos in 1888. He entered the family business and (apart from a visit to the United States, significantly at a time when McKinley was running on the protectionist 'ticket') for four years, until his marriage, he lived at home at Wilden where his father had built a church, a school, and a vicarage. He learnt to know every man in the works, became a parish and county councillor, a magistrate, and a member of the Oddfellows' and the Foresters' friendly societies. A farm was attached to the works and he learnt about pigs and cows. His experience in industry was of a phase which was passing swiftly. 'It was the last survivor of that type of works, and ultimately became swallowed up in one of those great combinations.' In 1892 he married Lucy, the eldest daughter of Edward Lucas Jenks Ridsdale, of Rottingdean, a former assay master of the Mint. Three sons (the first stillborn) and four daughters were born to them.

In 1906 Baldwin unsuccessfully contested Kidderminster and blamed his defeat on the failure of the Conservative Party to help the trade unions by reversing the Taff Vale judgement. His father had been member for the Bewdley, or West, division of Worcestershire from 1892 and on his death in 1908 he was succeeded by his son who was unopposed. Stanley Baldwin held the seat until he went to the Lords in 1937. His maiden speech (June 1908) was in opposition to the coal mines (eight hours) bill. In the years which followed he spoke seldom and attracted little attention. Andrew Bonar Law had known Alfred Baldwin and on the formation of the War Cabinet in 1916 welcomed the son as his parliamentary private secretary. In June 1917 Stanley Baldwin became joint financial secretary to the Treasury with Sir Hardman Lever who was engaged in special duties in America and had no seat in the House. In the 'coupon' election in 1918 Baldwin was unopposed and was reappointed to his post at the Treasury. On 24 June 1919 there appeared in *The Times* a letter signed 'F. S. T.' (long afterwards revealed as an abbreviation for 'Financial Secretary to the Treasury') which appealed to the wealthy classes to tax themselves voluntarily and thus help to reduce the burden of war debt. The writer, having estimated his own estate at £580,000, had decided to realize 20 per cent and purchase £150,000 of the War Loan for cancellation. The secret of the writer's identity was well kept for some years, even from (Sir) Austen Chamberlain who was chancellor of the Exchequer at the time. It was the first revelation, though veiled, of Stanley Baldwin's unusual character.

In April 1921 Baldwin, who had been made a privy counsellor in the previous year, entered the Lloyd George Cabinet as president of the Board of Trade and piloted through Parliament the safeguarding of industries bill. In a Cabinet of 'first-class brains' he was inarticulate and uncomfortable. He was shocked by what he deemed the levity and cynicism of some of his colleagues and reflecting on his position while on holiday at Aix-les-Bains he wondered whether to resign. He was recalled to London (29 September 1922) at the time of the Chanak crisis. He was convinced that the country had been driven too near to the edge of war; and when he and other Conservatives realized that the party leaders—Austen Chamberlain, Balfour, and Birkenhead—were prepared to face a general election under Lloyd George, they rebelled. A Carlton Club party meeting (19 October) brought the coalition to an end by the resolution that the Conservatives should fight 'as an independent party, with its own leader and its own programme'. Baldwin's passionate speech revealed an intense distrust of Lloyd George: 'a dynamic force is a very terrible thing; it may crush you, but it is not necessarily right.' The speech not only carried the Carlton Club meeting but, after the general election which followed, brought Baldwin himself to the chancellorship of the Exchequer, 'the limit', he had said, of his ambitions.

His first major task was to arrange for the settlement of the American debt. He went to Washington (January 1923) with the governor of the Bank of England (Montagu, later Lord, Norman) and negotiated with Andrew Mellon who exacted terms more severe than were contemplated by Bonar Law, the British prime minister. Ultimately Baldwin agreed to recommend terms which would extinguish the debt in sixty-two years at an interest rate of 3% for the first ten years, 3½% thereafter, and 4½% for arrears. This was equivalent to an annual payment of £33 million for the first ten years, a tolerable sum in the view of the City. Unguarded words from Baldwin to newspaper reporters on his return home inflamed American opinion and made any reduction of the terms unlikely. On 31 January the Cabinet reluctantly approved them.

In the months which followed Bonar Law was a sick man and in April Baldwin came to lead the House of Commons. He had made a remarkable speech on the Address (16 February) revealing his unexpected recipe for 'salvation for this country ... Faith, Hope, Love and Work'. The speech left a deep impression on a House unaware of Baldwin's stature and in a country which recognized a new note in its counsels. In April Baldwin introduced a budget which was well received and on 20 May Bonar Law, a dying man, resigned. To the acute disappointment of Lord Curzon Baldwin, 'a man of the utmost insignificance', became prime minister on 22 May. But a week before Baldwin had been expressing the jocular hope of returning to Worcestershire 'to read the books I want to read, to live a decent life, and to keep pigs'. The premiership was uncovenanted. 'The position of leader came to me when I was inexperienced,' Baldwin told Asquith in 1926, 'before I was really fitted for it, by a succession of curious chances that could not have been foreseen. I had never expected it.' 'Presently', wrote a colleague, 'there shaped itself in his mind the idea of what a Prime Minister ought to be. It was, to begin with, to be as unlike Lloyd George as possible—plain instead of brilliant; steady instead of restless; soberly truthful instead of romantic and imaginative; English and not Welsh. ... Above all he must be patriotic; a lover of all his fellow-countrymen, of his country's history, of its institutions, its ancient monarchy, its great parliamentary tradition, its fairness, its tolerance. All these things were innate in his own disposition. But he steeped himself in them as the part which it was his duty to play as a Prime Minister, and they became more deeply ingrained in consequence.'

The seeming plainness and provincialism of Baldwin's character and his intense love of England were conveyed to the nation in a series of speeches which lodged him deep in its confidence. To an increasingly urban population he echoed a nostalgia for the English countryside from which it rooted, and he did this mainly in monosyllables. 'I speak', he said, 'not as the man in the street even, but as a man in a field-path, a much simpler person steeped in tradition and impervious to new ideas.' The elaborated ordinariness of a pipe-smoking premier matched the unadventurous public mood which welcomed 'a quiet man at the top'. Confidence may have been somewhat shaken when Baldwin returning from Aix met Poincaré in Paris (19 September 1923) and joined in a communiqué of surprising warmth considering the division of view about the occupation of the Ruhr and the payment of reparations. Baldwin never again willingly ventured into foreign affairs. Two months later confidence was certainly shaken when he suddenly plunged the country into a general election. It was a calculated—some thought an impetuous—decision to consolidate the still not reunited Conservative Party by outbidding Lloyd George, and to gain a mandate for protection which Baldwin held to be the essential remedy for unemployment. He felt it dishonourable to introduce a tariff policy without first consulting the electorate. 'I think Baldwin has gone mad', Birkenhead had written in August to Austen Chamberlain. 'He simply takes one jump in the dark; looks round; and then takes another.' Now, in their differing phraseology, Balfour and Curzon agreed with

Birkenhead's opinion. To Baldwin himself, however, the dissolution was 'deliberate and the result of long reflection'.

Instead of controlling a majority of 77 over all parties, the Conservatives were returned with 258 seats against Labour's 191 and the Liberals' 159. On Baldwin's defeat in the House, the King sent for Ramsay MacDonald and the first Labour Government took office. Baldwin's private secretary, Sir Ronald Waterhouse, retained the post under MacDonald, both retiring and incoming prime ministers agreeing that their positions would likely be reversed within nine months.

Despite the electoral set-back Baldwin was re-elected to the leadership of the Conservative parliamentary party and with the return of Birkenhead to the fold its formal unity was achieved. The Government fell on 8 October 1924. The ensuing election, in which the 'Zinoviev letter' played its part, sent back the reunited Conservatives, now supported by the Beaverbrook and Rothermere press, with a firm majority: 419 seats to Labour's 151 and the Liberals' 40. The Conservative leader became prime minister for the second time (4 November). Again might be noted a 'curious incoherence between Baldwin's political ideas and his actions and appointments'. Sir Arthur Steel-Maitland was appointed minister of labour, and to everyone's surprise, not least his own, (Sir) Winston Churchill went to the Exchequer. In his budget (28 April 1925) Churchill announced the crucial decision to return to the gold standard. In the previous month the prime minister had once more revealed his own unusual character, moved the House and impressed the country by closing a speech on the trade union (political fund) bill with the prayer 'Give peace in our time, O Lord': a note which he alone in public life would dare to strike and which put Baldwin once again in a position of unrivalled ascendancy as a national leader. 'There is only one thing', he had said in January, 'which I feel is worth giving one's whole strength to, and that is the binding together of all classes of our people in an effort to make life in this country better in every sense of the word. That is the main end and object of my life in politics.'

The industrial situation was difficult and in many speeches he pleaded for conciliation. When in July 1925 the miners were on the eve of forcing a general stoppage Baldwin resorted to a Royal Commission and a subsidy. In 1925 'we were not ready'. 'I still think', he wrote two years later, 'we were right in buying off the strike in 1925 though it proved once more the cost of teaching democracy. Democracy has arrived at a gallop in England and I feel all the time it is a race for life. Can we educate them before the crash comes?' The Government set about preparing and improving ad-ministrative measures with which to counter a strike on a national scale. The Samuel report on the coal industry was published on 10 March 1926 and while opposed to nationalization it advocated some wage reduction on condition that both sides accepted a policy of reorganization. Decisive leadership—but that was not in Baldwin's nature—might have secured the immediate adoption of the report. He went no farther than 'we accept the report provided that the other parties do so'. Indeterminate negotiations followed. The trade unions issued telegrams on Saturday evening, 1 May, instructing men 'not to take duty after Monday next'. The general strike began on 4 May and was called off on 12 May. The fairmindedness which Baldwin revealed in his broadcasts enormously contributed to this result. He was made, it was said, for the microphone, to which his delightful voice and intimate manner were remarkably attuned. He deprecated 'malice or vindictiveness or triumph' and pleaded for patience in re-building the prosperity of the coal industry. Exhausted by the strain of the crisis he had surmounted, Baldwin failed, when his influence was at its maximum, to follow through with an immediate attempt to pacify the industry. 'The Baldwin of 1926 stood on a moral level' to which it has been doubted that 'he ever returned. He might have done anything. He did nothing. And ever after he seemed to be trading on an accumulated fund of confidence which was never replenished.'

In 1926 he presided at his second Imperial Conference in London (his first was in 1923) and in August 1927 paid with the Prince of Wales a visit to Canada where he was received with enthusiasm and affection. In a series of speeches he did much to interpret Great Britain to Canada and was happy in his references to the historic traditions of her provinces.

In July 1928 the franchise was extended to women of twenty-one years and upwards on the same terms as men. The main domestic problem remained the burden of unemployment especially in the mining areas where millions were spent on 'uncovenanted' or 'transitional' benefit known as 'the dole'. There were demands for protection, subsidies, and the safeguarding of industry. Baldwin was pledged to resist any general measure of protection or taxes on food but encouraged a measure of safeguarding. His Government—in slack water—did not escape the de-terioration accompanying a safe majority; there were complaints of his indolence in Cabinet and even demands for his resignation. Yet he could point to Locarno abroad, and at home to a Local Government Act, a Pensions Act, an Electricity Act, a Franchise Act, a safeguarding policy, and to a million houses built. Nor could he be charged with failure to instruct the electorate: he made many political speeches and many on literary or historical subjects—the Bible, William Booth, the *Oxford Dictionary*, Mary Webb's novel *Precious Bane*, the *Boy's Own Paper*. In a political speech at Yarmouth (27 September 1928) he maintained: 'It is not wise in a dem-ocracy to go too far in front of public opinion. The British people are slow to make up their minds on a new question but they are thinking and thinking hard.' They may have been wondering too at the absence of leadership, as each member of the Cabinet seemed to go his own way with apparently nobody at the helm. The 'torpid, sleepy, barren' Government (as Lloyd George called it) was defeated at the general election of 30 May 1929. The Conservative Party paraded the uninspiring slogan 'Safety First' before the eyes of the new young voters, the Socialists issued a manifesto 'Labour and the Nation', and Lloyd George, spending his fund freely, announced that the Liberals could conquer unemployment. The poll gave Labour 288 members, Conservatives 260, and Liberals 59. Baldwin who had fully expected to return to Downing Street with a small but sufficient majority was again succeeded by Ramsay MacDonald, but his personal popularity was undiminished. 'The leader of the outgoing party', said *The Times*, 'remains in popular estimation the most generally trusted and acceptable personality in political life.' Honours were showered upon him. He had already been lord rector of the universities of Edinburgh (1923–6) and Glasgow (1928–31), and he now accepted the offices of chancellor of the universities of St. Andrews (1929) and Cambridge (1930) and became the first chairman of the Pilgrim Trust.

Baldwin did not court controversy and was seldom roused to take notice of it. In October and November 1929, however, he had rebuked in the House of Commons newspaper attacks upon him concerning his Indian policy. Now two newspaper proprietors, Lords Beaverbrook and Rothermere, were running an Empire Free Trade campaign. Baldwin was only in partial agreement. Overtures between November 1929 and March 1930 came to nothing. Then Rothermere overplayed his hand to the extent of demanding that he should be acquainted by Baldwin 'with the names of at least eight, or ten, of his most prominent colleagues in the next Ministry'. At a party meeting in the Caxton Hall (24 June 1930) Baldwin replied with unwonted force and passion to this 'preposterous and insolent demand', was given a vote of confidence with only one dissentient, and a thunderous welcome when he entered the House of Commons later in the day. But the campaign of abuse continued and he confronted it again in the same hall and with the gloves off (30 October) when by 462 votes to 116 he was confirmed in the leadership. It was a triumph of character, a character which appealed to a multitude of moderate citizens: 'the average voter upon whom his gaze was constantly fixed'.

He had chosen Lord Irwin (subsequently the Earl of Halifax) as viceroy of India in 1925 and unlike some of his party Baldwin was in full agreement with the policy which Irwin pursued and which culminated in his pledge of Dominion status made at the end of October 1929. In June 1930 the Simon statutory commission issued its report. The Round Table conference opened on 12 November 1930 but in December Churchill, speaking for the 'Diehards', dismissed the Indian claims as 'absurd and dangerous pretensions'. For some time, on both Empire Free Trade and India, it seemed that Baldwin was losing his hold over his party. In March 1931 he struck back and captivated the Conservatives by another speech on India which ranked among his finest parliamentary performances; and at the Queen's Hall (17 March) he replied fiercely to the press lords in phraseology more typical of his cousin Kipling than of his own familiar usages. When his lethargy was most exasperating and the mutiny of his followers most menacing Baldwin could produce—often at his wife's prompting—an energy and quality of speech which never failed to remind his grumbling party that he was its greatest electoral asset.

Meanwhile the Labour Government had its own troubles. The cost of unemployment insurance and the dole was mounting rapidly. The committee appointed with Sir George (later Lord) May as chairman to overhaul public expenditure proposed drastic reductions which divided and broke up the Labour Government. On 25 August 1931 a 'national' Government was formed, MacDonald remaining prime minister. Baldwin became lord president of the Council. At the general election which followed (27 October) the coalition Government secured over 550 seats, 471 of which were held by Conservatives. Had Baldwin wished to press his own claims to be prime minister again, it is now known that he could have done so successfully; he was content to serve as lord president for four years, a position not inconsistent with the exercise of considerable influence in the Cabinet and commanding authority over his party. An import duties bill imposing a general tariff and setting up an Import Duties Advisory Committee (1 March 1932) marked the definite return to the protectionist era for which Baldwin had always yearned. In July and August he presided with patience and good temper at the imperial economic conference at Ottawa. The free trade members of the coalition who had threatened resignation as early as January 1932 could no longer 'agree to differ' and resigned.

Japan's successful aggression in Manchuria revealed, early in 1932, the impotence of the League of Nations in the Far East with two Pacific powers absent, Russia and the United States. In Europe the appointment of Hitler as German chancellor in January 1933 was a prelude to a series of explosions. This country was profoundly pacifist and its obstinate faith in disarmament was demonstrated in the East Fulham by-election (October 1933) by a marked turnover of votes to Labour. Baldwin looked back on this event in a speech to the House on 12 November 1936: 'My position as the leader of a great party was not altogether a comfortable one. I asked myself what chance was there—when that feeling that was given expression to in Fulham was common throughout the country—what chance was there within the next year or two of that feeling being so changed that the country would give a mandate for rearmament? Supposing I had gone to the country and said that Germany was rearming and that we must rearm, does anybody think that this pacific democracy would have rallied to that cry at that moment? I cannot think of anything that would have made the loss of the election from my point of view more certain.' He was to pay dearly for this disclosure in after years: for his 'appalling frankness' was to be quoted against him, not always with much care about its original context. The Putney by-election (November 1934) again saw a marked reduction in Conservative support. Although Baldwin had told the House (30 July 1934) that the air arm had abolished old frontiers—'When you think of the defence of England you no longer think of the chalk cliffs of Dover; you think of the Rhine'—he sounded no urgent alarm, when introducing a measure of rearmament, at the growth of German air power and his advisers were slow to give credence to the reports of this growth which were reaching them. He deprecated panic; he saw 'no risk in the immediate future of peace being broken'. In November he admitted that looking ahead 'there is ground for very grave anxiety' but maintained that 'It is not the case that Germany is rapidly approaching equality with us.' By May 1935 he admitted frankly that his estimate of the future situation in the air had been 'completely wrong'.

Ramsay MacDonald, deserted by his old friends and associates, dependent therefore on reluctant Conservative support and primarily interested in establishing peaceful foreign relations, was betraying increasing signs of declining powers. At last in June 1935 he exchanged places with Baldwin who became prime minister for the third time at the age of nearly sixty-eight. Baldwin took the fruitful course of sending Sir Philip Cunliffe-Lister (subsequently the Earl of Swinton) to take charge of the Air Ministry, and inviting Churchill—his fiercest critic—to join the committee on air defence research. In March 1935 the Government had issued a white paper (Cmd. 4827) which not only proposed an expansion of the Air Force but gave the Government power to take preliminary steps in regard to all the forces on which a subsequent policy of rearmament was based. This was eight months before the general election. It was an early step in the educational process which Baldwin believed had to be gradual. Doubtless he remembered his precipitancy in 1923.

Meanwhile Churchill had not been Baldwin's critic on the subject of rearmament only. There was also India. 'He had gone about threatening to smash the Tory party on India', said Baldwin, 'and I did not mean to be smashed.' On 4 December 1934 Baldwin at a Conservative central council meeting made it clear that he accepted the white paper (Cmd. 4268) of 1933 and the report of the joint select committee of both Houses (November

1934). The Government of India bill was published 24 January 1935 and on the second reading (11 February) Baldwin, having been urged to consolidate the party, showed himself once again 'the most powerful man in the House of Commons'. The bill received the royal assent on 2 August 1935.

The League of Nations Union, the chief propagandist body in Britain, conducted a ballot which in June 1935 revealed a vote of 10½ millions (over 90 per cent of those who voted) in favour of an all-round reduction of armaments by international agreement. At the general election which followed in November, while the Government supported a new defence programme, both parties protested their pacific intentions and placed the support of the League Covenant in the forefront of their platforms. To the Peace Society (31 October) Baldwin, who even when electioneering—and it proved an electoral asset—tended to speak rather as a national than a party leader, managed to have arms and the League in one and the same breath: 'We mean nothing by the League if we are not prepared, in the end, and after grave and careful trial, to take action to enforce its judgement. . . . Do not fear or misunderstand when the Government say that they are looking to our defences. . . . I give you my word that there will be no great armaments.' Baldwin was returned with 430 supporters against an opposition of 184.

On 11 September the foreign secretary (Sir Samuel Hoare, subsequently Viscount Templewood) in a speech at Geneva had conveyed the impression that this country was embarking on a vigorous League policy which might not stop short of war on the Abyssinian issue. There was clamour for sanctions against Italy. Baldwin's view was that 'real sanctions mean war'; so sham sanctions were imposed, futile because they omitted a ban on oil. In December Hoare initialled in Paris an agreement with Pierre Laval, the French prime minister, for a proposed settlement of the Abyssinian war by the cession of Ethiopian territory to Italy. A surprised Baldwin acquiesced, but the country, still in the exalted mood of Hoare's Geneva speech, apparently endorsed by the general election, compelled the prime minister, not for the first time in his experience, to reverse his engines. He disavowed his foreign secretary. Hoare resigned and many thought that Baldwin should have resigned also. He made lame, uncomfortable speeches. His lips, he said, were sealed: a remark which the cartoonists were to remember.

The king died in January 1936 and Baldwin was deprived of a steady source of strength, if George V himself had sometimes (so it would seem from his biographer) been impatient with his prime minister's 'deft quietism'. The months which followed were heavy with trouble: the occupation of the Rhineland, the fall of Abyssinia, rioting in Palestine, civil war in Spain. The Government issued another white paper on 3 March (Cmd. 5107) admitting that conditions in the international field had worsened and that the level of national armaments continued to rise all over the world. It announced that the prime minister had presided over the defence policy and requirements sub-committee and had subjected the armed forces to a prolonged and exhaustive examination. As was to be expected, it stressed the importance of retaining the goodwill of industry. The new policy introduced 'the first real measure of expansion'.

On 7 March Hitler reoccupied the Rhineland. Sir Thomas Inskip (later Viscount Caldecote), not Churchill, was appointed minister for the co-ordination of defence. On 6 April, but six months after the election, the prime minister was forced to obtain a vote of confidence: yet 'the honours of the day were with Churchill and Austen Chamberlain.' Even Baldwin's skill in Parliament seemed to be deserting him. There was a budget leakage which distressed him greatly. He seemed overwhelmed by domestic and international problems, and by midsummer he appeared to have reached the end of his tether. He grew more and more depressed and towards the end of July his doctor, Lord Dawson of Penn, ordered him to take three months' complete rest. When he returned to Downing Street on 12 October he was able to handle with freshness and vigour what became known as the abdication crisis which arose out of the decision of the new King, Edward VIII, to marry Mrs. Wallis Simpson, an American citizen who had divorced one husband and was on the eve of divorcing a second. Thanks to the voluntary discretion of the British press the matter had only reached a small fraction of the public but it was well known abroad. The prime minister's first interview with the King on the subject was on 20 October when he found his mind irrevocably fixed on marriage. On 2 December the silence of the press unexpectedly ended and an intense emotional release of comment followed. The suggested device of a 'morganatic' marriage was given short shrift by the Cabinet, still shorter by the Dominions, and was not pressed by the King. There was talk for a moment of a 'King's party', but receiving no support from the King himself it swiftly passed. Nor was there deep discord in Parliament or in the country. Baldwin knew his provinces. In announcing to the House of Commons (10 December) that the King had renounced the throne, Baldwin told the story of his conversations with him in a speech simple, direct, dignified, and compelling assent. Baldwin throughout the whole episode had revealed a sureness of judgement which immeasurably enhanced his prestige. It was the second crisis in which he became the incarnation of the national will. Baldwin will go down to history as the prime minister who steered the country successfully through the general strike and the Empire through the royal abdication.

Baldwin was now in his seventieth year and had already indicated Neville Chamberlain as his successor. On 5 May 1937 he delivered his last set speech in the Commons—an appeal for peace in the mining industry, then threatened with stoppage—and on 27 May he announced the Government's proposal to increase from £400 to £600 the salaries of members of Parliament. On 28 May, a fortnight after the coronation of King George VI, he went to the Palace to tender his resignation, fourteen years to the day since he had been elected leader of the Conservative Party in succession to Bonar Law. His Majesty bestowed on him a knighthood of the Garter and on 8 June he became an earl. Baldwin was worn out and suffering from increasing deafness. He resolved to make no political speeches, neither to speak to the man at the wheel nor to spit on the deck. By 1939 he was well enough to visit Toronto and New York where he delivered addresses on his favourite subjects, democracy and citizenship. Then came the war and he withdrew to Astley Hall, his Worcestershire home, where he lived quietly, reading few newspapers, listening regularly to the radio news, delving among family archives, re-reading Scott, Jane Austen, Wordsworth, and Hardy, or scanning a new book sent to him by its author. He was often in pain from arthritis and limped with the aid of a stick. He went rarely to London and refused invitations to broadcast on the war effort lest he should stir up controversy. He was aware that he was widely supposed to be responsible for all that had happened since 1931 'by people who have no historical sense'. On 12 September 1942 he and Lady Baldwin celebrated their golden wedding. She, who shared his faith and was his perfect sympathizer, died in June 1945. He followed on 14 December 1947 and his ashes were laid with his wife's in Worcester Cathedral. He was succeeded by his elder son, Oliver Ridsdale, Viscount Corvedale (1899–1958), author and Labour politician, who became governor and commander-in-chief of the Leeward Islands (1948–50).

In appearance, Baldwin was a sturdy countryman of medium height, broad-shouldered, with mobile countenance, sandy, shaggy eyebrows, and sandy hair parted in the middle and well smoothed down. His eyes were blue, his hands broad and sensitive. He had a shrewd, quizzical expression and a musical voice which carried well. He was a lover of books, the friend of scholars, and an inveterate smoker. During his political life he played neither tennis nor golf but, until crippled in his later years, he was always an enthusiastic walker, with a great affection for the atmosphere and simple fare of old country inns.

For fourteen years (1923–37) Baldwin dominated the British political scene and at the coronation in 1937 he 'almost divided the cheering with the royal pair themselves'. Already in 1922 'probably the best-liked man in the House', from then onwards he revealed an extraordinarily acute sense of the House of Commons over which he was increasingly to exercise his own 'sedative authority'. Whenever possible he avoided the direct debating speech: preferring rather to lower the temperature by a disarming, even 'appalling', frankness; but on occasion—which he made great—he could 'conceive and be delivered of a powerful oration' and 'the ironmaster turned goldsmith'. His speeches usually transcended the bounds of party; many were lay sermons with the emphasis upon the eternal commonplaces. One colleague noted that 'he was not so effective on the platform as in the House of Commons, but there he obtained for several years such ascendancy that, if a member interrupted him, it seemed almost like brawling in church'.

He was happier as prime minister than as a departmental head because he had little capacity for detail or quick decision. Mastering figures, of the unemployed in Great Britain, or of rearmament in Germany, was not his forte and his uneasiness about both problems did not result in active and positive measures to tackle them. He trusted to goodwill in industrial relations which perhaps had changed—like industry itself—more than Baldwin realized. As one Labour member said to him after Baldwin's moving speech in the Macquisten debate (6 March 1925), 'It was true, prime minister, every word was true. But those times have gone.' He had little interest in foreign affairs and was never quite willing to face the growing German problem frontally. His chosen biographer has suggested that 'the nerve, injured in October 1933, the East Fulham nerve, never quite healed: he was afraid of the pacifists: . . . Andhe was not sure of himself. He could never master the logistics . . . of defence. All his shortcomings combined to keep him off that ground—his indolence, his lack of scientific interest, his indifference to administrative concerns.' He conceived his function to be that of a non-intervening chairman. He was neither vain nor arrogant nor was he easily impressed and he could escape from high politics with disconcerting suddenness into talk of cricket or clouds or flowers or other irrelevance. He was genuinely modest and never quite got over his surprise at being elevated to the premiership. A political career he regarded as akin to that of a Christian minister: he was a religious man with a serious view of life. Withal he was (to Churchill) 'the greatest party manager the Conservatives had ever had' and, by a genius for waiting on events, he reformed them as a party and kept them in power for a generation in the knowledge that, however much they might worry about the direction, Conservatives were unlikely to drop a pilot who went too slowly; and after 1923 Baldwin was never again in danger of moving too fast. Nor, in the event, was any party likely to jettison a leader with so singular a capacity to garner the suffrages of the doubting voter. 'My worst enemy', it was

Baldwin's pride to maintain, 'could never say that I do not understand the people of England': especially middle-class England.

His lethargy was often a mask to cover impulsive, emotional, and exhausting spurts of nervous energy. The long spells on the front bench sniffing the order paper, contemplating his finger tips or reading Dod's *Parliamentary Companion*, or again, solving crossword puzzles or playing patience in the Long Gallery at Chequers (he claimed not to be able to think in 10 Downing Street), or on holiday at Aix: all were indispensable modes and means of recuperation. He was incapable of prolonged continuous effort. His exasperating indecisions were charmed away by his sweetness of temper, his rapid and pungent conversation, and the unexpected turn of his humour. Reverie to him was not a vacuum but a refreshment. 'There is a cloud round my mind, it takes shape, and then I know what to say' was his own explanation. 'Baldwin', said Lloyd George, 'is one of us. He is a Celt.' If so, he persuaded the English (having early persuaded himself) that he was a typical Englishman. He had no time for foreigners and in a series of farewell speeches reviewing his political career he made no mention whatever of international problems. For intellectuals of all parties he had a profound contempt. 'Use your commonsense: avoid logic: love your fellow men: have faith in your own people, and grow the hide of a rhinoceros' was his advice to the political man. He saw his role as that of a national statesman as much as that of the accomplished if idiosyncratic party leader he evidently was. 'I sometimes think', he said in a broadcast (5 February 1935), 'that, if I were not the leader of the Conservative Party, I should like to be the leader of the people who do not belong to any party.' If he dined with the Tories, he smoked with the trade-unionists. Labour members he treated with marked respect and sympathy. His long hours in the House held the hope that the Labour Party would choose the parliamentary way, to which he was devoted, in the belief that it would fulfil their purposes when their inevitable turn came. He sought to diminish class hatred, to retain national unity and to take the bitterness out of political life. 'The reason for his long, tenacious, successful hold over the electorate', one of his juniors has conjectured, 'is probably to be found in the simple fact that he was, fundamentally, a nice man; and the country knew it.' At the first Trinity Commemoration dinner (13 March 1948) after Baldwin's death, Dr. G. M. Trevelyan, master of his old Cambridge college, made this his epitaph: 'Stanley Baldwin was an Englishman indeed, in whom was much guile, never used for low or selfish purposes. In a world of voluble hates, he plotted to make men like, or at least tolerate, one another. Therein he had much success, within the shores of this island. He remains the most human and lovable of all the Prime Ministers.'

There are busts of Baldwin, by Lady Kennet at Bewdley Town Hall, by Sir Alfred Gilbert at Shirehall, Worcester, by Newbury A. Trent (1927) in the possession of the third Earl Baldwin who has also a small portrait by Seymour Lucas (1910). A portrait by R. G. Eves (1915) is in the possession of Lady Huntington-Whiteley, one by (Sir) Oswald Birley was with the second Earl Baldwin, and a portrait by Thomas Monnington is at Trinity College, Cambridge; another by Francis Doddis at Rhodes House, Oxford (Baldwin was from 1925 a Rhodes Trustee). The National Portrait Gallery has a portrait by R. G. Eves and a chalk drawing by Sir William Rothenstein.

[*Lord Baldwin, a Memoir*, published by *The Times*, 1947; Nourah Waterhouse, *Private and Official*, 1942; Winston S. Churchill, *The Second World War*, vol. i, 1948; Trinity College, Cambridge, *Annual Record*, 1948; *Cambridge Journal*, November 1948; *Listener*, 15 February 1951 and 1 January 1953; G. M. Young, *Stanley Baldwin*, 1952; Harold Nicolson, *King George V*, 1952; D. C. Somervell, *Stanley Baldwin*, 1953; L. S. Amery, *My Political Life*, vol. ii, 1953; private information; personal knowledge.]

THOMAS JONES

[Robert Blake, *The Unknown Prime Minister, The Life and Times of Andrew Bonar Law*, 1955; A. W. Baldwin, *My Father: The True Story*, 1955; C. L. Mowat in *Journal of Modern History*, vol. xxvii, Chicago, 1955; Lord Percy of Newcastle, *Some Memories*, 1958; Lord Vansittart, *The Mist Procession*, 1958.]

published 1959

BALFOUR Arthur James

(1848–1930)

First Earl of Balfour

Philosopher and statesman, was born at Whittinghame (now Whittingehame), East Lothian, 25 July 1848, the eldest son and fourth child of James Maitland Balfour, of Whittinghame, by his wife, Lady Blanche Mary Harriet, second daughter of James Brownlow William Gascoyne-Cecil, second Marquess of Salisbury. His paternal grandfather, James Balfour, younger son of John Balfour, of Balbirnie, after making a fortune as a contractor in India, had purchased the Whittinghame estate; and this passed in due course to his father, James Maitland Balfour, a country gentleman, sometime chairman of the North British Railway, and a member of parliament for Haddington district 1841–1847, but a man of no great mark. Through his paternal grandmother, Lady Eleanor, daughter of James Maitland, eighth Earl of Lauderdale, he was descended from William Maitland, of Lethington; from his mother he inherited the blood of William Cecil, Lord Burghley; but, while these sixteenth-century sources of political ability deserve mention, it might be as difficult to trace any resemblance between his character and that of either of those statesmen as between his career and one or other of theirs.

By common consent his mother's influence, accentuated as it may have been by his father's premature death in 1856, was supreme in Balfour's early education, for the boy was beyond doubt deeply impressed by a personality at once profoundly religious and brilliantly amusing. Handicapped by short sight and delicate health, he owed less perhaps to Eton, where nevertheless he came under the influence of William Johnson (Cory), or even to Cambridge, where from 1866 to 1869 he was a fellow-commoner of Trinity College, than to a home circle of which the indigenous distinction, so to speak, of his brothers and sister, Gerald, the scholar and statesman, Frank, the biologist [see Balfour, Francis Maitland], and Eleanor (Mrs. Sidgwick), subsequently principal of Newnham College, was presently increased by that of his brothers-in-law, Henry Sidgwick, the moral philosopher, and John, third Lord Rayleigh, the physicist. In such company Balfour, who secured no more at the university than a second in the moral sciences tripos, shone indeed, but as no bright particular star; and many who saw the modesty of his first beginnings failed wholly to foresee the brilliancy of his final ends. His mind was perhaps too independent for a curriculum; and he was in any case always more interested in finding truth for himself than in learning what others had supposed it to be. 'For the history of speculation', he declares, 'I cared not a jot. Dead systems seemed to me of no more interest than abandoned fashions. My business was with the groundwork of living beliefs; in particular with the goodness of that scientific knowledge whose recent developments had so profoundly moved mankind' [*Theism and Humanism*, p. 138]. It followed that his writings showed something less of contact with the old masters and something more of conflict with current theories than was consistent perhaps with the most enduring work. If he thought in any man's tradition, it was in that of Berkeley, of whom he published a study (published originally in the *National Review*, March–April 1883, reprinted in *Essays and Addresses*), and whose lucid style and exquisite dialectic seems to anticipate his own. In the harmonies of his thought and language may be caught, indeed, an echo of the eighteenth century, as was proper enough in one whose considered preference [see his essay 'The Nineteenth Century' in *Essays and Addresses*, 1905, pp. 315 ff.] was for that epoch and whose love of music was stimulated to the uttermost by the oratorios of Handel, a composer possessed, so he maintains in one of his most graceful essays, of 'a more copious, fluent and delightful gift of melody' than any other [*ibid.* p. 169]. His natural taste was, in truth, for a time characterized by 'unity and finish'; and he clung to its legacy, finding Scott and Jane Austen, Coleridge and Wordsworth, Keats and Shelley to be better companions than authors of more recent repute—than Dickens and Thackeray, than Carlyle with his 'windy prophesyings' or Mill with his 'thin lucidity'. What, intellectually, he was not, was a mid-Victorian. No child of the late 'forties more instinctively reverted to the serene mentality of an earlier period; no man of the early 'seventies prepared himself with less effort to assimilate the scientific knowledge of a later one. He was all his life intermittently concerned to formulate the rational grounds of faith in such a manner as to bring metaphysics back into the scales of common thought and so to recover for physics its proper weight, and no more, in the balances. Two things helped him in this endeavour—a mind untiringly interested in scientific development, of which he kept abreast not by experiment but by reading, discussion, and inquiry, and a style, never trite or precious, but illustrating with no little charm and liveliness the virtue of putting the right word in the right place, and rising in such a passage as that upon the prospect of man in a purely physical universe to an impressive and moving eloquence. The passage mentioned shows, indeed, in the opinion of competent judges, his literary power at its highest, and as such merits quotation here:

'We survey the past', he wrote, 'and see that its history is of blood and tears, of helpless blundering, of wild revolt, of stupid acquiescence, of empty aspirations. We sound the future, and learn that after a period, long compared with the individual life, but short indeed compared with the divisions of time open to our investigation, the energies of our system will decay, the glory of the sun will be dimmed and the earth, tideless and inert, will no longer tolerate the race which has for a moment disturbed its solitude. Man will go down into the pit, and all his thoughts will perish. . . . Matter will know itself no longer. Imperishable monuments and immortal deeds, death itself, and love stronger than death, will be as though they had never been. Nor will anything that *is* be better or be worse for all that the labour, genius, devotion and suffering of man have striven through countless generations to effect.' [*Foundations of Belief*, pt. I, c. I.]

For all the patent grace and power of such digressions Balfour's real achievement as a metaphysician is not easy to determine, and none the more that his fame as a statesman tended to advertise his work with the vulgar and to depreciate it with the elect. The former took him at his word and proclaimed him without further ado a philosopher; the latter dismissed him without too much consideration as an amateur. His strong conflict was with naturalism; his contention, that the foundations of natural science are no firmer than those of theology, and even perhaps not so firm; his thesis, that Theism clears, instead of confusing counsel. He pushed home these opinions with much ingenuity and without any undue apparatus of technical phraseology; yet the public was long in understanding him. The title of his earliest book—*A Defence of Philosophic Doubt* (1879)—suggested to those who had not assimilated its contents that he was a philosophic doubter; and, though this was far from being the fact, it was nevertheless true that the position there taken up as regards theology fell something short of that adopted later in his *Foundations of Belief* (1895) and his Gifford lectures on Theism (1915 and 1922–3).

Very briefly Balfour's argument was this. The theory of knowledge underlying the scepticism of science in regard to religion should in any dispassionate mind produce a similar scepticism as regards science itself. By its attacks upon religion the scientific mind has in fact manufactured a boomerang; and this point was brought out with all Balfour's dialectical ability. It was, however, as he maintained in a reply to his critics delivered near the end of his life before the British Academy [see *Proceedings* of the British Academy, 9 December 1925], a complete misconception of his meaning to suppose that he had tried to destroy rational values by insinuating philosophic doubts. The aim of his criticism was quite other. 'The sceptic says', he urged, 'that, as we can prove nothing, we may believe anything. I say that, as we believe a great deal and intend to go on believing it, we should be well advised to discover on what assumption we may believe it most reasonably.'

'All men, including all philosophers, are', Balfour maintained, 'believers'; and his aim was fearlessly to recognize that all constructive thought rests upon a foundation of faith and is not on that account insecure. A body of beliefs, he pointed out, that can neither be proved nor ignored nor rejected forms the pre-supposition of what is termed scientific knowledge—the belief, for example, in the existence of others as distinct from ourselves, in our power to communicate with them, in our mental resemblance to them, in our occupation of the same physical universe with them, and so forth. Our awareness of other minds, he argued by way of illustration, is not direct but dependent upon observation of or conjecture about their associated bodies. Though 'inevitable' it is not 'self-evident', is entangled with admissions of faith and theories of knowledge, and lies beyond the sphere of intuitive assurance. Such perceptions, for the rest, are 'no trustworthy purveyors of information about the character of physical reality'. They cannot be treated as a product of evolution, and, if we are to suppose our beliefs upon the way to truth, we are obliged to assume 'a Power transcending the physical universe'. Carrying the attack upon philosophic naturalism into its citadel, Balfour drove home the point that, if naturalism were true, then 'all the convictions we entertain and all the reasoning by which they are supported must be completely dependent on the preterrestrial distribution of electric charges—entities which are guided by nothing more intelligent than the blind forces of attraction or repulsion and do nothing more purposeful than radiate energy at random through the depths of space.' 'Theories', he submitted, 'which give this account of their origin are well on the way to suicide.' Only let the same rights be conceded by science to the values of goodness and beauty that it is accustomed and compelled to claim for truth, and, not only is the case for naturalism gone, but the whole sphere of human experience is welded into a more coherent whole.

Such then was the line of argument, such the pathway of thought that Balfour, had he been left to make a life for himself, would, according to his own belief, have pursued and elaborated. Even as things turned out, his metaphysic possesses for the intellectual development of his age something of the value of a bee-line. Physical science was in fact moving towards a position scarcely distinguishable from philosophic doubt in respect of its theory of knowledge, though neither with his speed nor by his methods. And psychology was presently to sharpen the point of his criticism by raising doubts whether reason can by any rational process clear itself from the suspicion of springing in the last resort from unreasoning impulse. It deserves perhaps to be added that the value of Balfour's apologetic did not go without recognition in the English Church. 'As Lord Balfour argues in his Gifford Lectures', observes Dr. Inge,'what makes Naturalism untenable is that the higher values cannot be maintained in a naturalistic setting. . . . This is the chief argument in his book, and I think it is valid' [W. R. Inge, *God and the Astronomers*, p. 230].

The influence that diverted Balfour's energies from philosophy to politics was that of his uncle. At the suggestion of Lord Salisbury [the third Marquess,] he stood for the borough of Hertford and in 1874 entered parliament as a supporter of Disraeli's last administration. So far as the subtlety and versatility of his mind allowed of a party label, he was a conservative, as well by choice as by tradition. 'Conservative prejudices', he is reported to have said to Alfred Lyttelton, the best-loved of his men friends, 'are rooted in a great past and Liberal ones planted in an imaginary future.' His political talent, however, was of slow growth. His first election-address was without facility and his first parliamentary speech long in coming. He felt diffident and unambitious. But also a far-reaching shadow fell at this time across his path.

In the opening of the year 1875 occurred the death of Miss May Lyttelton, the sister of the remarkable band of brothers who made in their time the fame of their family. Only a month or so earlier Balfour after no little delay had, if not formally, at least in effect, become engaged to her; and this tragic sequel to a reciprocated affection, though it did not absolutely close the door on thoughts of marriage, left him half-hearted or hesitating; and in the event he remained a bachelor.

It was so often discussed, even by some who were well acquainted with him, whether, behind Balfour's easy charm of manner and perfect appearance of interest, there lay any great strength of human feeling, that a word on this point seems to be required. Those who knew him best knew best how deeply he could be moved and how inexhaustible could be his solicitude and his sympathy. A dread, rather than a defect of emotion, explains some part of what was said to the contrary; natural reserve, coupled with a profound dislike of any sort of insincerity in matters of the deepest moment, much of the rest. Yet it may be true to add that in his general attitude towards human life and its conditions there was something less both of passion and compassion than might have been looked for in a man of such fine perception and delicate discernment. 'Philosophy can clip an angel's wings', and seldom if ever in his essays or his speeches does he indicate sensibility to the tears of things or lend words to the stammering tongue of humanity. This limitation, whatever its cause, goes some way to explain why, for all his long lifetime of service, his personality never quite captured the public imagination. His appeal was essentially to the few and not the many, to the salon and to the senate rather than to the street: and on more than one critical occasion he showed a lack of what goes by the name of the 'common touch'.

Though his abilities were such as to have made his reputation in any but a jacobinical society, it must be reckoned a circumstance very favourable to Balfour's career that the public life of the country at the time of his entry into politics was still strongly coloured by aristocratic influences. The landed aristocracy among whom his inheritance placed him had not yet lost its consequence, and the intellectual aristocracy towards which his talents drew him was still gaining in power. But if he found a congenial society, he as certainly founded, though without conscious effort, a congenial clique. The memory of the 'Souls' is intimately associated with his name. They formed a coterie for which it might be difficult to find a parallel in English history. Free from any disastrous exclusiveness either social or conversational, interested in really interesting things, alive to the claims of art and not dead to those of morals, blending politics with fashion and fashion with philanthropy, they contrived, without incurring too much ridicule, to sacrifice to Beauty, Truth, and Goodness against a background of west-end dinner-parties and great English country-houses. Of this circle of clever men and often brilliant and beautiful women

Balfour seemed made to be the *arbiter elegantiarum*. The intellectual grace of his appearance, the charm of his manner, the play of his mind, the liberality of his views, the lightness of his touch, all contributed to make him the cynosure of a set whose day-dreams of chivalry and fair women found some sort of expression in the collection of Burne-Jones's paintings that he hung in his London house; whilst his own shattered romance, impoverishing though some felt it to have been to the full development of his character, left him the freer to form and cultivate those great friendships with women which claim some mention in any sketch of his life. Lady Oxford, herself an early friend, has picked out three of these for special notice—those with (Mary) Lady Wemyss, Lady Desborough, and (Alice) Lady Salisbury—and the justice of this choice will be generally agreed to.

An incomparable guest in many well-known houses, an engaging host in his own, a much-prized member of many eminent institutions and learned societies; president of the British Association (1904), of the British Academy (from 1921), of the Psychical Research Society, of the Synthetic Society, and, it might even be claimed, potentially of the Royal Society, since in 1920 he was approached, though without success, on the subject; honorary fellow of his college; chancellor of Cambridge (1919) and Edinburgh (1891) universities; foreign member of the French Academy; Romanes lecturer at Oxford; Gifford lecturer; member of the Order of Merit, and wherever he was, an outstanding figure, exceptionally gifted both as talker and listener, in the conversation piece, Balfour enjoyed a social prestige perhaps unequalled by any statesman since the days of Fox. Of all the eminent men of his day he was possibly the one whom the majority of cultivated people would have preferred to meet and whose opinion in difficult issues they would have been inclined to follow. His indirect influence, imponderable though it is, upon the 'social tissue' of his time was thus certainly large; and the depth of his interests was shown in the breadth of his hospitalities. The doors of Whittingehame, where autumn after autumn he was accustomed to entertain a large family circle with the aid of his devoted sister, Miss Alice Balfour, were thrown open to an assortment of visitors as varied as Bergson, the philosopher, Wilfrid Ward, the Catholic apologist, and Mr. and Mrs. Sidney Webb, the Fabian socialists; whilst with some of his direct opponents in parliament—with Asquith, with Haldane, and with Morley—his relations approximated to friendship.

A lively interest in games and music added pleasing traits to a figure in every aspect possessing the charm of the amateur and eluding the provincialism of the expert; and the great worlds of learning and of leisure marked with equal satisfaction the versatile politician listening rapt to an oratorio of Handel, or celebrating victory, not undemonstratively, at the close of an Eton-and-Harrow cricket match. For the rest, golf and lawn-tennis, which he continued to play almost to the close of his life, rounded off the tale of Balfour's recreations.

There can be little doubt that the exceptional position which he occupied in the intellectual and social life of his time tended on the whole to fortify Balfour's influence in politics; and the growth of the one needs to be remembered in considering the advance of the other, with which this account will now be exclusively concerned. In the course of a six-months' tour round the world with her brother, Spencer, after Miss Lyttelton's death, Balfour visited the United States, Australia, and New Zealand. His parliamentary career opened with his return. In 1876—on 10 August— picking his occasion so as to test his powers before the smallest possible audience, he made his maiden speech on the subject of Indian currency with the House in committee. In 1877 he recommended the grant of university degrees to women. In 1878 he produced his first attempt at legislation by the introduction of a Burials Bill which, however, was 'talked out'. It is, perhaps, of more consequence that in this year he became Salisbury's parliamentary private secretary and in that capacity attended the Congress of Berlin (June–July 1878). It was, however, the conservative disaster at the general election of March 1880 that first brought him into notice. He had retained his seat at Hertford, though only by a small majority, and in the new parliament became associated with the meteoric 'Fourth Party', sometimes described, but not altogether correctly, as 'a party of four', since Balfour's real allegiance remained with his uncle, who presently succeeded Beaconsfield in the conservative leadership.

The Irish question was at this time fast becoming the central issue in politics; and on 16 May 1882 Balfour spoke with telling effect on the so-called Kilmainham Treaty, stigmatizing it, to Gladstone's indignation, as 'an infamy'. Though his speaking lacked fluency, his power of argument made from that date a growing impression. His speech in favour of a conservative amendment requiring a two-thirds majority before the new expedient of the closure could be employed was particularly remarked, and the more that it brought him into conflict with Lord Randolph Churchill, the Fourth Party leader. A deeper rift, however, between these associates presently appeared. The interregnum as regards leadership had plainly to be terminated if the conservatives were to regain power. Churchill saw this, as he also saw that power itself was destined to pass from parliament to the constituencies; and, in the guise of the champion of 'Tory-Democracy', he attempted to transfer the seat of party sovereignty from the Central Committee, of which Salisbury defended the traditional rights, to the National Union of Conservative Associations. During the struggle Balfour, as the friend of one protagonist and the nephew of the other, occupied a mediatorial position, not without adding to his own consequence in conservative counsels; and this consequence was further augmented by the fact that the motion which brought about the downfall of Gladstone's administration was planned in his house, no. 4 Carlton Gardens (June 1885). In the formation of the so-called 'ministry of Care-takers' which followed, he seems to have given further assistance in dealing with Churchill, who went to the India Office, whilst he himself became president of the Local Government Board, an appointment that he filled for six months without any particular distinction.

At the ensuing general election (December 1885) Balfour was returned in East Manchester, for which constituency he sat continuously until 1906. The liberals, however, were in general victorious. Gladstone, for reasons tactically prudent, if morally questionable, had made no clear declaration of policy about Ireland before the polling, and a short period of confusion, during which Balfour as his uncle's nephew became the recipient of confidences both from Gladstone and Joseph Chamberlain, resulted. The first Home Rule Bill was, however, eventually introduced in April 1886 only to be rejected by the House of Commons in June. A general election followed; and a clear majority against Home Rule was returned, though no majority was secured by any single party. In the ensuing conservative administration, which depended upon liberal-unionist support, Balfour filled the recently created post of secretary for Scotland. The crofters' agitation against rent was at that time at its height. He dealt firmly and effectively with the Scottish Land League which was active in Skye and elsewhere; the secret of his success, if there was one, lying in his resolve to recover for the law its lost prestige. In November 1886 he was given Cabinet rank, and in March 1887 he was offered the Irish chief-secre-taryship. He hesitated, consulted Sir William Jenner about his health, which was passed as sufficient, and finally accepted. The country saw with something like stupefaction the appointment of the young dilettante to what was at the moment perhaps the most important, certainly the most anxious office in the administration. Salisbury knew, however, very well what he was about.

The celebrated Irish 'plan of campaign' for the reduction of rents by the intimidation of landlords had at this juncture already been launched, and an Irish Crimes Bill, to run for a term of unlimited duration, had been drafted in reply (March 1887). Balfour, whilst yielding to liberal sentiment by abandoning the proposed removal to England of the venue of trials by jury, took power to 'proclaim', or in other words to suppress, the National League in any district where he thought this desirable, and made use of these powers in August 1887. But the real tug-of-war came in September with the prosecution, under the Crimes Act, of William O'Brien. Violence was met with force; and the sanguinary result, though only two rioters appear to have been killed, won for the Irish chief secretary the title of 'Bloody Balfour'.

The 'resolute government' which was the foundation of Lord Salisbury's Irish policy achieved its purpose; and the Crimes Act was eventually suspended in every district of Ireland. Constructive measures were not, however, wanting. A Light Railways Act was passed with especial reference to the west of Ireland (1889). A Congested Districts Board was set up to deal with the difficulties of the poorer parts of the country (1890). A Land Purchase Act (1891) attempted to encourage peasant proprietorship and to reduce the scandal, by no one resented more deeply than by Balfour, of the unjust or absentee landlord. And a Catholic college, endowed by the state except only in respect of the teaching of dogmatic theology, would, but for the opposition that it aroused in different quarters, have formed another feature of Balfour's administration. His personal triumph was indubitable. He had put his views into effect in spite of the resistance of what at the end of his life he declared to have been 'in some respects the most brilliant parliamentary party which the British system of representative government has ever produced' [*Chapters of Autobiography*, p. 191]. But if the tactics and eloquence of the Irish were well calculated to bring out Balfour's political ability, their 'miscellaneous scattering of violent adjectives', as Lady Oxford has called it [*More Memories*, p. 99], was not less well calculated to make his political fortune. The House admired the fine courage, the imperturbable temper, the exquisite irony which he opposed to the terrorism and invective of his opponents; and upon the death of Mr. W. H. Smith in October 1891 the leadership in the Commons, with the office of first lord of the Treasury, fell to him almost as a matter of course. Mr. Goschen was the only possible alternative, but for various reasons not an acceptable one. An interesting situation had now arisen with uncle and nephew respectively in command of the conservative forces in their different Houses; and it was none the less interesting that nothing like it had occurred, unless in the case of Pelham and Newcastle, since, under another queen, Burghley and Cecil had held the chief offices of state. The combination worked well and was not without its bearing upon the fact that the opening of the twentieth century saw the prime minister still a member of the House of Lords.

Balfour, however, was not at his best in the early days of his leadership. He gave the impression of being a less hard worker than his immediate predecessor; and he certainly did not think more about politics outside working hours than he must. But, if sometimes a hesitating speaker, he showed himself no less a master of debate—as distinct, that is, from eloquence—in a House which still contained Gladstone, than a master of the subject which now had Gladstone's and indeed all men's attention. It is, of course, impossible to trace in detail his tactical moves in the great parliamentary game. It must suffice to say that at the general election of July 1892, when the Gladstonians were returned to power, Balfour kept his seat by a reduced majority; that, after a period of opposition, during which Gladstone's second Home Rule Bill was defeated in the Lords, the unionists came back in July 1895 with a majority of over 150; and that in the coalition government which followed, Balfour again became first lord of the Treasury with the leadership in the Commons. His work in this capacity was heavy, various, and of varying merit. In 1896 he piloted into port an Irish Land Bill and an Agricultural Derating Bill, but the Education Bill of that year suffered shipwreck, not without reflecting upon his political management nor, it might be added, without causing him to reflect upon the educational complexities that had led to his failure. In 1897 a Workmen's Compensation Act and in 1898 an Irish County Councils Act were the principal features of unionist policy. Then in October 1899 came the Boer War.

In regard to South African affairs Balfour showed in private some disposition to sympathize with the Jameson Raid (December 1895), to criticize the handling by Mr. Chamberlain of the diplomatic negotiations which preceded the outbreak of war, and to condemn Sir Redvers Buller's conduct of the military operations. These views naturally found no public utterance; and indeed his loyalty to Chamberlain at this time was the making of their subsequent good relations. His individual contribution to the prosecution of hostilities must be sought in his serenity and decision in council—a serenity and decision of particular value during the crisis, which eventuated in the dispatch of Lord Roberts to take over the supreme command (December 1899). On the platform, however, Balfour, failing not for the last time to catch the public mood, did himself less than justice; and to the anxious eyes of the crowd his nonchalance looked too much like flippancy. Yet upon no man's mind was the great lesson of that war more deeply impressed; and a searching and continuous attention to the problem of military efficiency forms thenceforward a marked feature of his political activity.

At the so-called 'khaki' election of October 1900, which resulted in the return of the unionists with a slightly reduced but still very powerful majority, Balfour nearly trebled his own figures at East Manchester. He was nearing the apex of his fortunes, and when, in July 1902, after the conclusion of peace, Salisbury resigned the premiership, the succession fell to him with the full assent of the Duke of Devonshire and of Chamberlain.

The recognition of his qualities was ample; yet his position from the first was as much weaker than his uncle's as a majority inherited is a worse title to power than a majority newly won at the polls. Moreover, even as Balfour came into office, the seeds of his difficulties were being sown. The Imperial Conference, that year assembled, passed a resolution in favour of granting preferential duties to the Colonies; and Chamberlain, before he left for a visit to South Africa at the close of the year, sought a Cabinet decision on the issue. The policy agreed upon was to maintain the existing shilling duty upon corn but to remit it in respect of the Empire. Mr. C. T. (afterwards Lord) Ritchie, however, whom Balfour had made his chancellor of the Exchequer, was temperamentally antipathetic to his chief and dogmatically attached to free trade. His budget speech (23 April 1903) revealed his sentiments; and his budget proposals repealed the corn-duty. Feeling rose quickly. Balfour tried to allay it by suggesting that the duty might be reimposed as part of some larger policy. But Chamberlain, though not apparently with deliberate purpose, brought the issue to a head by a speech at Birmingham on 15 May; and the battle was joined between the tariff reform and free trade sections of the unionist party. In these circumstances Balfour's attitude was governed by two considerations, the one, to keep the party together, and the other, to secure what he defined as 'liberty of fiscal negotiation'. As his memorandum on the subject shows, he believed that retaliatory duties against the foreigner would promote freedom of trade; and for the imposition of these he held the country to be already prepared. Before, however, the grant of preferential treatment to the Colonies, involving as it must some taxation of food, was made, he considered that a period of propaganda was required; and he attempted, therefore, to treat 'preference' as for the time outside the sphere of practical politics.

These views were not deficient in lucidity; nor was Balfour lacking in firmness in his handling of the situation. Reluctantly convinced, however, by the pressure put upon him that tariff reform must be withdrawn from the category of open questions, he insisted still that his own policy as regards 'preference' must prevail amongst the members of his administration. Chamberlain made no complaint of this procedure but was not himself more willing to forgo the advocacy of preferential tariffs than were Ritchie, Lord George Hamilton, and Lord Balfour of Burleigh to abandon their opposition to retaliatory duties. The disruption of the Cabinet became, therefore, inevitable; and Balfour determined that neither body of dissentients from his own views should gain any advantage from it. But, whilst parting with the extremists, he continued to do his utmost to minimize the party cleavage. He attempted, and for a short time successfully, to retain the Duke of Devonshire, a free-trader; and on the other hand, whilst accepting Joseph Chamberlain's resignation, he made it clear to him that he intended Austen Chamberlain to be Ritchie's successor at the Exchequer. Then, on 14 September, at a meeting of the Cabinet, at which his memorandum *Economic Notes on Insular Free-Trade* (subsequently published) formed the chief item on the agenda, he—in Devonshire's phrase—'summarily dismissed' Ritchie and Balfour of Burleigh. To his regret a speech of his at Sheffield (1 October) caused Devonshire's resignation to follow.

Balfour's administration now entered upon its most difficult phase. The party friction, adversely affected by his own unfortunate, though unavoidable, absence from the debate on the royal address in February 1904, developed rapidly; and the division-lists discovered a wide rift in the unionist ranks. He attempted to mark time, going only so far in the October of that year as to say that, if returned to power, he would summon a colonial conference of which the recommendations were only to be adopted if approved at another election. But, if Balfour had the caution of Fabius Cunctator, Chamberlain had all the energy of an old man in a hurry; and the nation watched with growing impatience the two years' delay in giving battle.

Balfour's procrastination was doubtless due in part to his perception that there were other things besides tariffs to be considered. His administration was, in fact, making its mark both in domestic and foreign policy to a degree but little observed; and he was anxious, so far as possible, to consolidate its achievements. In the military reconstruction which the lessons of the South African War had rendered necessary, he had interested himself, as well in regard to general matters, as more particularly in regard to the rearming of the field artillery with the eighteen-pounder gun (December 1904) and the formation of the Committee of Imperial Defence (December 1902–March 1903), of which he gave some account in speeches at Liverpool (13 February) and in the House of Commons (5 March). Both these preoccupations found full justification a decade later; and the Committee, providing as it does for a consultative, non-party council of experts and statesmen assisted by a secretarial staff, has long taken its place amongst British political institutions. Its fortunes, however, like those of the gun, were none too well assured even so late as the date of Balfour's resignation in 1905. Evolved from the old Defence Committee of the Cabinet and entrusted with the continuous survey of defensive problems of a mixed political, military, and naval nature, it must always be reckoned a remarkable proof of his patriotic foresight. For the first time in history the leaders of rival political parties were enabled to associate in the work of public defence without the difficulties of public debate or the obscuries of private conference.

Balfour

The liquidation of the South African War formed another of Balfour's anxieties. Whilst the situation there, as the liberals saw, eventually demanded the bold generosity of a grant of self-government—a grant which, when the time for it came, he made the mistake of opposing with vigour—the introduction of Chinese labour on the Rand, unavoidable though it seems to have been in the actual circumstances, stood in some need of defence against doctrinaire denunciation. Again, in the matter of education the Bill, which Balfour had introduced in March 1902 and carried largely by his own efforts to the statute book against a great clamour of opposition, led by Mr. Lloyd George within and by Dr. John Clifford without the House, required the undenominational criticism of time to establish its merits. With the possible exception of the Licensing Act of 1904, into which also he put much personal work with a view to securing both the reduction of licences and the equitable compensation of publicans, it was perhaps the most important piece of legislation that Balfour was ever directly concerned with; and its provisions, controversial as they appeared to be at the date of their enactment, have survived, broadly speaking, a quarter of a century of widespread change. Conceived in conjunction with Sir Robert Morant and designed to secure to every parent, so far as possible, the kind of religious teaching he desired for his child, the new settlement provided rate-aid for voluntary schools, whilst substituting a committee of the county council for the former school board as the local education authority. Though the actual issue has largely lost interest, Balfour's defence of his action, published among his *Essays and Addresses* under the title of 'Dr. Clifford on Religious Education', may still be read with pleasure. It is a small masterpiece of very delicate and finished irony, and shows, perhaps better than anything else that he wrote, what he was capable of in this vein.

It was, however, in regard to foreign policy that Balfour most feared a change of government. His experience of foreign affairs dated back to the days when his uncle during illness or absence would entrust him with their temporary conduct. The inception of the Franco-British *entente*, which followed quickly upon Salisbury's retirement, represented, however, a striking departure in policy from nineteenth-century tradition. Balfour and the foreign secretary, Lord Lansdowne, appear, it is true, to have envisaged the diplomatic understanding with France rather as a method of settling old disputes than of providing new defences; and it was only after they had left office that military conversations between the Powers concerned were formally initiated. The fact remains that it was Balfour's administration which for better or worse abandoned the time-honoured plan of an England holding the diplomatic balances in Europe by virtue of sea power for that of an England with its weight, both naval and military, thrown into one of the scales. A memorandum of Balfour's, furnished at Mr. Winston Churchill's request to Sir Edward Grey in 1913, shows, however, that he fully realized the dangers involved in the policy of an *entente*, and would have preferred a defensive alliance governed by the principle that the fulfilment of its pledges could not be claimed unless the party claiming were ready to submit a case for arbitration. This preference for clear rather than obscure commitments was exemplified in Balfour's treatment of the Far-Eastern alliance with Japan which he had inherited and was resolved, if possible, to renew before quitting office. The outbreak of war between Russia and Japan in 1904 merely intensified his purpose, since he wished to demonstrate Great Britain's fidelity as an ally whilst the outcome was still uncertain. Negotiations for the renewal of the Anglo-Japanese Agreement of 1902 were therefore initiated in the beginning of 1905 and carried to a successful conclusion in the following summer. Any project for a better understanding between Britain and Russia became dormant in these circumstances. The countries were, in fact, in consequence of the Dogger Bank incident, within an ace of war in October 1904. Balfour's private correspondence with Lansdowne indicates, moreover, a grave suspicion of Russian designs in India and an almost uncanny intuition of such a deal between Russia and Austria in the Near East as was later concluded at Buchlau (1908). His personal orientation, in the strict sense of that word, was therefore only towards Japan, whilst his occidentation, if the word may be allowed, was as certainly towards the United States. He was able before the end of his life to give effect to both these feelings in the Washington Naval Agreement of 1921, though the resulting collapse of the Anglo-Japanese alliance showed clearly enough that it was not possible for England, at any rate at that time, to look both to the East and to the West.

As the year 1905 drew to a close, it became increasingly obvious that the tale of Balfour's administration was told and that the nation had tired of the telling. By November, in default of a fiscal truce within the party, he was ready to make an end, and, after considering the respective merits of dissolution and resignation, elected for the latter. On 4 December he resigned the premiership—an office for which he had provided a constitutional recognition and official precedence previously unknown. For three years and a half he had served as the prime minister of a sovereign whose great qualities were too different from his own to make close sympathy or understanding easy.

The storm now fell in full strength upon a minister whose record in regard to national defence was little known, in regard to education widely resented, and in regard to foreign policy imperfectly understood. Even amongst his supporters Balfour's governing resolve to avoid the mistake of Peel and to maintain at all costs the unity of his party was taken for evidence of vacillation. Two incidents had further accentuated the general discontent with his administration. His imprudent extension of the term of office in India of Lord Curzon eventuated in an unseemly dispute between the viceroy and Lord Kitchener; and his reluctant assent to George Wyndham's wish to have Sir Antony (afterwards Lord) Macdonnell appointed as undersecretary in Ireland resulted, unfairly enough, in his being himself charged with deserting a friend.

In the general election of January 1906 the conservative disaster at the polls was complete. Balfour himself was defeated at East Manchester by nearly 2,000 votes; and his following in the House was reduced to a very small remnant. A safe seat, however, was offered him as member for the City of London, and on 12 March he returned to the House, where in spite of the historic attempt of the new prime minister (Sir H. Campbell-Bannerman) to discredit him ('enough of this foolery') his ascendancy in debate was quickly regained. An exchange of letters with Chamberlain reaffirmed fiscal change as the first plank in the unionist platform, but into a detailed programme of economic policy Balfour wisely refused to be drawn. He recognized in the increased representation of labour in parliament the advent of a new era; and he saw the supreme business of his party as that of enabling the ship of state to ride the coming storm. Whilst conservative dissatisfaction with his leadership culminated in the cry that 'Balfour must go', that leadership was directed towards the preservation of a common front in both Houses against legislation calculated, as he saw, to force the question of the House of Lords into the forefront of the battle. He is thus to be found putting up a good fight in the Commons against the Education Bill of 1906, the Licensing Bill of 1908, and the budget of 1909, holding as he did that the rights of parents in regard to religion were attacked by the first, the rights of property by the second, and the rights of the constitution, through the insertion of land valuation clauses in a Finance Bill, by the third. In due course he approved the rejection of the budget by the peers (November 1909) and defended their action as 'abundantly justified'.

The general election of January 1910 which followed, made the Irish nationalists masters of the situation. Resolutions, however, restricting the veto of the House of Lords so as to allow of the passage of a Home Rule Bill were only just carried and the delayed Finance Bill passed, when the death of King Edward VII in May 1910 changed the mood of the nation. The inception of a new reign invited a party truce; and a conference of party leaders met on 17 June and sat until 10 November. Of this conference Balfour was a leading member; and his ability made a deep impression even upon his opponents. The apparent issue upon which the negotiation broke down lay between the liberal plan of resorting to a general election in the event of an irreconcilable difference between the two Houses over constitutional questions and the conservative preference for a referendum. Balfour, however, would, it appears, have yielded the point, if all possible Home Rule bills, and not only the forthcoming one, had been placed within the scheduled category of constitutional measures compelling an appeal to the constituencies.

Towards the close of the conference and on Mr. Lloyd George's initiative, Balfour entered upon an informal, secret negotiation for a settlement of the outstanding political issues in the national interest by the formation of a coalition government. Whilst not altogether unsympathetic, Balfour, haunted as he was by the spectre of Peel, eventually refused to entertain a scheme involving so large a sacrifice of party principles and so great a breach of party ties. To the charge, subsequently brought against him by Mr. Lloyd George, of having made a great refusal he might, perhaps, have replied that he had avoided a great betrayal. A reference to the experienced judgement of Mr. Akers-Douglas had in fact confirmed his opinion that the project was not only impracticable but rendered impossible by the initial difficulty of forming a coalition ministry to put it into effect.

The constitutional battle was therefore resumed. In November 1910 the prime minister, Mr. Asquith, obtained from King George V a pledge to create a sufficiency of peers to carry the Parliament Bill in the event of a favourable response at the polls and, with this pledge in his pocket, appealed to the country. In Balfour's view no guarantee of the sort was constitutionally required until a constitutional crisis had actually arisen and unless the sovereign had no alternative ministry, and, when in July 1911 he learnt that the king's pledge had already been obtained, he summoned a 'shadow' cabinet to consider the situation. Some of his colleagues were for resistance to the Bill; others for surrender. The split spread to the party; and a 'die-hard' revolt was added to a tariff reform division.

Concerned with practical consequences and anxious always to save the Crown from criticism, Balfour had little sympathy with those who regarded the issue as one of high principle and were resolved to die fighting. As he saw things, their action was merely theatrical since they were powerless to stop the impending change in the status of the Upper House and could only aggravate its incidents. The 'die-hards' were, however, unconvinced and carried their opposition to the Bill to a division (10 August). Balfour suffered so keenly from this rejection of his advice as to feel that it put a term to his leadership. At Bad Gastein, which he visited in August, he reviewed the position; in September, upon his return to England, he discussed it with the party organizers; in October he took his decision; and in November he resigned.

Balfour

The effect of this step was striking. Freed from the trammels of circumstance, his high character, his vast ability, his rare distinction quickly stood out; and as a statesman he now began to receive the recognition which had been refused him as a leader. It happened that the Irish question was once again in the centre of the political stage. There were none on either side of the House who could rival him in knowledge and experience of it, and there were few anywhere who understood so well as he how far beyond any liberal solution of the problem the passions, now fiercely clashing, had carried the issue. He did what he could in a crisis not of his making, recommending the division of Northern and Southern Ireland; emphasizing the view in his *Nationality and Home Rule* (1913) that the Irish national spirit would rest content with no half-measures of separation; advising the opposition not to incur responsibility, by any amendment of the government's amending Bill, for the delimitation at the eleventh hour of a boundary between North-East Ulster and the rest of Ireland; and even holding himself in readiness, should the king desire to take a last opportunity of testing English opinion, to resume office, with or without Lord Rosebery as his colleague, in a 'ministry of Caretakers'.

It was just at this juncture that the outbreak of the European War (28 July 1914) suppressed all smaller quarrels. Balfour turned his mind at once to the new issues. He gave his assurance of support to the bolder section of the Cabinet in the hour of decision, accepted, at the king's wish, when England became involved in the conflict, a seat on the committee of the Prince of Wales's Fund for the relief of distress; resumed, at the prime minister's request, membership of the Committee of Imperial Defence; and assisted in the preparation of plans for dealing with the civil population in the event of coastal raids. From November 1914 he attended the meetings of a 'war-council' or 'inner cabinet' convened by the prime minister at 10 Downing Street, thus involving himself in responsibilities scarcely compatible with the position of an ex-minister in opposition. This state of things was, however, of no long duration. Shortage of munitions and dissensions at the Admiralty led in May 1915 to the formation of a Coalition government, in which Balfour became first lord of the Admiralty, the only 'heavy administrative office', so he told the prime minister, for which he could usefully be responsible.

Mr. Lloyd George in his *War Memoirs* [vol. ii, p. 1017] has conveyed the impression that the minister whom he afterwards placed at the head of the Foreign Office was incompetent for the work of the Admiralty. This was not the opinion of those who saw Balfour there at close quarters. Behind characteristically indolent postures he brought to bear upon the issues submitted to him so penetrating a judgement that it was possible for the secretary at that time to the department to assert that 'at the Admiralty it was felt that, if Balfour personally did not favour any particular action or policy, there was no need for further inquiry.' His speech introducing the navy estimates (7 and 8 March 1916) showed according to the same authority 'as much knowledge of the important questions of naval administration as the speeches of any of his predecessors with more advantages on their side of time and political conditions'. It showed, too, incidentally and in reference to Mr. Churchill a mastery of debate and delicacy of sarcasm equal to anything he had displayed in his prime.

Balfour, in fact, though he attempted no departmental reorganization, believing as he did that the existing system worked well if wisely handled, dealt effectively in a series of board meetings with various matters of naval policy requiring regulation and decision, and quickly restored serenity to a department distracted by the differences between his predecessor, Mr. Churchill, and Lord Fisher. Two considerable events fell within his term of office—the withdrawal from Gallipoli, the wisdom of which he had doubted, and the battle of Jutland (31 May 1916). The former was faultlessly executed. The *communiqué* in which he announced the news of the latter drew, however, much criticism upon his department. Drawn up in his hand and but slightly modified after consultation with his naval advisers, it was dispatched, notwithstanding statements to the contrary, without reference to the secretary to the Admiralty or to Mr. Churchill, and gave the public, as he always maintained it should have done, the unvarnished truth, yet at the same time certainly disseminated a false impression of disaster that was only by degrees removed as the sufficiency of the naval success became plain. A lull followed the engagement, but the German submarine menace was none the less growing; and in November 1916 Balfour created a special department to deal with it. Both Mr. Asquith and Sir Edward Grey, however, were anxious for some change of personnel in the naval membership of the Admiralty Board, and before the fall of the first Coalition, Admiral Jellicoe had been appointed to succeed Sir Henry Jackson as first sea lord. Whether this new combination of talent would have resulted, as one well-qualified observer believed, in a more rapid suppression of the submarine attack cannot be determined, for the downfall of the Asquith administration was coincident with it.

Balfour had nothing to do with organizing the cabal which ousted Asquith from power, but he seems to have taken no exception to it, and his decision to give it countenance was momentous for England and, still more, for Europe. A certain modesty and moral simplicity characteristic of him were apparent in his conduct. In his view the sole question to be considered was how the War might be most efficiently carried on and, once he had satisfied himself that Mr. Lloyd George was of all men available the best qualified for the task, he was characteristically indifferent to all personal considerations, such as that minister's recent but unsuccessful attempt to remove him from the Admiralty. His assistance was undoubtedly essential to the formation of the new Coalition, for without it the administration must have lacked sufficient support in influential conservative quarters. In the new distribution of departments he was given the Foreign Office. His presence there had the greater consequence that, with the break-up of the Asquith government, British counsels had lost the diplomatic experience and moderation both of Lansdowne and of Grey.

The association between the new prime minister, Mr. Lloyd George, and the foreign secretary, which during the late crisis had issued in a marked personal sympathy, was as the meeting of two currents, one turgid and strong, the other refined to a crystal clarity. It was easy to see from the first that the prime minister had planned such a dyarchy in foreign affairs as had not previously been known to the constitution. An amateur foreign office, irreverently termed the 'garden-suburb', arose in the precincts of 10 Downing Street; and by this means Mr. Lloyd George exercised a direct as well as indirect and constitutional influence upon foreign affairs. Balfour's importance to the prime minister and ready access to his presence modified the immediate effect of such a system, but its ultimate consequences were apparent at the Peace Conference, where Balfour's position contrasted unfavourably with that of Castlereagh at Vienna or Salisbury at Berlin.

The change of government meanwhile afforded no spectacular successes. During 1917 the submarine trouble grew at sea, differences between the prime minister and the generals accentuated the difficulties of carrying on hostilities, and the land operations were overshadowed by the slaughter at Passchendaele (August). The entry of the United States into the War, which came early in the year, needed, however, only to be developed to make victory sure. Balfour, to his lasting distinction, seized a diplomatic opportunity which he of all men living was best qualified to use. On 14 April 1917, after ascertaining that his visit would be welcome to President Woodrow Wilson, he sailed for the United States at the head of a diplomatic mission. His enthusiasm for an understanding between the two Anglo-Saxon peoples put a spur to his tact and ability. He made good friends with Wilson, charmed the Americans generally by the grace of his manners, and delivered memorable speeches both before Congress and at Washington's grave. His diplomatic achievement was consummated by the intimation, unofficially conveyed to the president, of the existence of those secret treaties with Russia and Italy which ran counter to the principle of nationality and so to American policy. In brief his mission had secured a success which stood the Allies in good stead as American credit, shipping, and soldiers became increasingly needful, whilst on a longer view it seemed to have laid the foundation of just such a fusion of Anglo-Saxon sentiment as Balfour had long had at heart.

In foreign policy in general Balfour's achievement is less assured. Both the progress of the War and the versatile energy of the prime minister drove him continuously towards those very things which his memorandum for the Cabinet of 4 October 1916 (published in Lloyd George's *War Memoirs*, vol. ii, pp. 884–886) shows that he had wished to avoid, namely, the humiliation of Germany, the dissolution of the Dual Monarchy, and the peril of a pan-German state incorporating or seeking to incorporate a purely German Austria. A stronger diplomacy might perhaps have made more of the Austrian peace move (1917), a subtler one might perhaps have gauged the Bolshevist mentality better; and some uncertainty of aim may be inferred from the countenance, long unsuspected, which he gave to the publication, if not the contents, of the famous 'peace letter' of Lord Lansdowne of November 1917 by referring its writer to Lord Hardinge, at that time permanent under-secretary for foreign affairs. It might indeed be difficult to say whether his foreign policy was in the tradition of the old Europe or of a new order founded, at least in theory, upon nationality, democracy, a league of nations, and an open diplomacy. Salisbury's large wisdom and Mr. Lloyd George's vivacious versatility seemed to dispute possession of a mind constitutionally cool and unfailingly receptive.

One decisive move which he himself rated as his great achievement, did, however, characterize Balfour's tenure of the Foreign Office. Ever since a conversation with Dr. Weizmann at Manchester during the throes of the general election of 1906, he had been keenly interested in Zionism; and intercourse with Mr. Justice Brandeis in America had strengthened his faith in its political value. In November 1917 he triumphed over opposition both within and without the Cabinet and issued the so-called Balfour Declaration in favour of a Jewish national home in Palestine. The project finally took shape at the Peace of Versailles. Under a British mandate from the League of Nations the Jews were established in the Holy Land on equal terms with the existing inhabitants, and, though Arab feeling was aroused to such a degree as to endanger Balfour's personal safety when he visited Damascus in 1925, the experiment proved so popular among the Jews that at the hour of his death Jewry mourned him with honours perhaps never before accorded to a Gentile.

'It was not so much the war as the peace that I have always dreaded', Balfour told Lady Wemyss on the evening before he left for the Peace Conference at Paris in January 1919. The two English ministers were lodged in the Rue Nitot, the prime minister on the first, the foreign secretary on the second floor. During the inaugural period of the Conference the two ministers sat alike in the so-called 'council of ten', which contained both the heads and the foreign ministers of the five great, victorious delegations. This period, which lasted for a month from the middle of January 1919, closed with the temporary absence of President Wilson in America, Lloyd George in England, and Clemenceau in bed, and was followed by an interval of three weeks (16 February–8 March) during which Balfour dominated the situation. He altered it vastly for the better, so much so indeed that Clemenceau on recovery named him the Richelieu of the Congress. 'Whereas in the middle of February', remarks Mr. Churchill, 'the work of the Conference was drifting off almost uncontrollably into futility, all was now brought back in orderly fashion to the real' [W. S. Churchill, *The Aftermath*, vol. v, p. 190]. Its commissions, spurred on by this new pressure, had, in other words, got through their work and reported. On the return of Mr. Lloyd George, however, and in consequence of a leakage of information, a 'council of four' was superimposed, with the foreign secretary's full approval, upon the original council of ten. From that time Balfour, whilst as foreign minister he retained his seat on the latter (known thenceforward as the 'council of five') and both by reason of the proximity of his lodgings to those of the prime minister and his prominence on the British Empire Committee remained acquainted with the general course and conduct of the negotiations, no longer participated in the principal discussions and was not in every case made aware of impending decisions, even when of grave moment. The extent to which he thus abrogated his office may be inferred from a statement which he made towards the close of the Conference to his colleague, Lord Robert Cecil, to the effect that, not having been consulted on some point or another, he should not defend the Peace Treaty, which, he added, was not of his making. But even if this *obiter dictum* ought not to be pressed, though in fact it does not lack corroboration, as evidence of his secondary position, the extraordinary circumstance that the Foreign Office apparently worked on the assumption that a peace was to be negotiated, whereas in the event the terms intended for negotiation were dictated without serious discussion or amendment, would still indicate, conclusively enough, the limitations of his influence. To such a degree, then, but at such a price may Balfour's direct responsibility be reduced for a treaty which cannot readily be reconciled with the British tradition of 1814, the British purpose in 1914, the conditions of the Armistice, the aspirations of a League of Nations, or his own, in general, conciliatory dispositions. Had he, however, been in a position to insist upon the conclusion which he desired, of a preliminary agreement imposing a naval and military, and perhaps outlining a territorial, settlement, and had he also concerned himself more with the economic and financial aspects of the peace to be negotiated, the outcome might, perhaps, have been happier.

The signing of the treaty with Germany on 28 June 1919 left Balfour again at the head of the British delegation; and the Treaty of St. Germain with Austria, which followed on 10 September, was his particular contribution to the settlement. Prejudiced by certain previous decisions of the council of four, it cannot be said to have avoided the danger that he had early signalled of a small Austria exciting sentiments both of affinity and cupidity in a great German neighbour. In the retrospect, indeed, Balfour was accustomed to defend the geographical aspect of the peace terms in general by arguing that the frontiers approved could not in practice have been bettered. His apologists may, however, prefer to dwell upon the terrific strain that his office had imposed upon a man now over seventy. There can in fact be little doubt that he felt the conduct of foreign affairs, involving as it did at Paris a social side which he was not the man to wish to avoid, to be getting beyond his strength; and this notwithstanding that, when he left for Paris, Lord Curzon had been inducted as acting foreign secretary at Whitehall. With the conclusion of the Austrian treaty he resigned (24 October 1919), retaining a place in the Cabinet as lord president of the council.

Balfour's association with foreign affairs was, however, by no means finished. In November 1921 he figured as leading British delegate at the Washington Conference which resulted in a Five-Power treaty for a measure of naval disarmament and a Four-Power compact of good understanding in the Pacific, but which also eventuated in the termination of the Anglo-Japanese Alliance of 1905. Then, in August 1922, he gave his name to the British note which he had drafted recommending a general cancellation of war debts as part of a general settlement. And finally, in the October following, as British representative at Geneva, he carried, largely by his own efforts, a scheme, which was successfully put into effect, for the financial rehabilitation of Austria under the auspices of the League of Nations. It might be added that a few weeks earlier he had taken together with Mr. Lloyd George and Mr. Churchill the grave responsibility of issuing a *communiqué* committing Great Britain to resist the crossing of the Straits at Chanak by the Turkish forces.

The same year 1922 brought him, in March, the K.G. and, in May, an earldom. He elected to call himself Earl of Balfour and, as a second title, Viscount Traprain. Thenceforward he figures as an elder statesman, yet—although the fall of Mr. Lloyd George, by whom he stood, a little rushed perhaps by circumstance, in the political crisis of 1922, threw him for a time out of office—not as one on the retired list. As lord president of the Council he was included in Mr. Baldwin's second administration from 1925 to 1929 and in that capacity took occasion to show his abiding sense of the overshadowing importance of physics in relation to politics by the foundation of the Committee of Civil Research, a body conceived on the same lines as the Committee of Imperial Defence but designed to give to men of science direct access to ministers as well as to co-ordinate scientific investigations throughout the Empire. But of his imperialist outlook those years contained another proof. The so-called Balfour Definition (1926)—embodied in the report of the Inter-Imperial Relations Committee of which he acted as chairman—gave expression to the view that positive ideals and free institutions formed the basic principle of the British Empire and so paved the way for the Statute of Westminster (1931) which recognized the equal status, both in domestic and foreign affairs, of the Colonies with the mother-country. Here was evidence enough that the eye of his mind was not dimmed, even if his bodily strength had abated. Yet there were some who thought that his career should have been earlier closed, some, not without influence in the matter, who would have liked to see him end his life, as but for the War he had himself dreamed that he might do, as head of his old Cambridge college. So graceful a tribute to his life-long interest in all that made for education might, had circumstances allowed it to take effect, have saved him from any ministerial association with the grant of Home Rule to Ireland; an association plainly inconvenient, to say no more, and imperfectly explained away by the fact of his absence in America at the date of its occurrence.

Balfour died at Fisher's Hill, his brother's house near Woking, 19 March 1930, and was buried at Whittingehame with the rites of the Church of Scotland, to which, though without any exclusive attachment—for he was a communicant also in the Church of England—he belonged. His metaphysical studies had satisfied him that personal immortality was implicit in the very structure of man's being. Not less did his patriotic achievement satisfy his contemporaries that political immortality was assured to the spacious record of his life. Yet his place amongst his compeers is no easy one to determine. He was a first minister in King Edward VII's piping times of peace, first lord of the Admiralty when the drums of war were beating at their loudest, foreign secretary at the greatest peace congress, or more strictly conference, the world has ever seen; yet it would be too much to say that he shone with Pitt's beacon-light, burned with Chatham's incandescent fire, or got Europe back to work with Castlereagh's laborious patience. Accomplished parliamentarian as he was, he had neither Canning's gift of speech nor Peel's grand manner. A conservative leader, and very loyal to his trust, he made no such impression, as Salisbury's, of sagacious strength or, as Disraeli's, of romantic vision. His political genius was in fact essentially transitional, evolutionary, and in that sense creative; nor, if it had been other, could he have worked so well in turn with Salisbury, with Chamberlain, and with Lloyd George. It was of a piece with this that he rose by opposing in Ireland the very principle of nationality which he ended by advocating in Palestine and saw in these apparently contrary purposes his own two chief achievements. Yet this seeming inconsequence was not in his case incompatible with a deeper intellectual integrity. For the rapier with which he had first opened the world's oyster seemed, when laid aslant the imperial and constitutional problems of his time in later life, to turn to a fine edge of light cutting their knots and tangles. The native propensity towards mediation which set a limit to his powers of leadership, increased the range and finish of his thoughts; and in a period of unexampled change and far-reaching confusion his serene and luminous cast of politics frequently exemplified the instinctive courtesy of an even mind observing the golden mean. In no derogatory sense, then, he possessed, as John Morley noticed, something in common with Halifax, the 'trimmer'—the Halifax, that is, of Macaulay's portrait with 'his keen, sceptical understanding, inexhaustibly fertile in distinctions and objections; his refined taste; his exquisite sense of the ludicrous; his placid and forgiving, but fastidious temper, by no means prone either to malevolence or to enthusiastic admiration', the Halifax of whom Walter Raleigh, the critic, observed that 'his importance may well be measured by this, that it never depended on the office that he held.' Yet when all the claims of contrast and comparison have been satisfied, Balfour remains, in the eyes at least of many who knew him, a unique figure—one of those rare men, indeed, about whom it may be said without rhetorical exaggeration that neither his own generation nor another will look upon his like again.

There are several portraits of Balfour at Whittingehame—by George Richmond in the 'seventies, by Ellis Roberts in 1890, by P. A. László in 1908, by Sir William Rothenstein in 1923, by Sir James Guthrie in 1927. The Carlton Club contains a full-length portrait painted in 1908 by J. S. Sargent; Trinity College, Cambridge, a portrait in his D.C.L. robes by László, and Eton College one by Fiddes Watt. A bust by Onslow Ford is also at Whittingehame. A cartoon appeared in *Vanity Fair* 27 January 1910.

[Balfour was succeeded as second earl by his only surviving brother, Gerald William (born 1853). Blanche E. C. Dugdale, *Arthur James Balfour, First Earl of Balfour*, 2 vols., 1936, written with intimate knowledge based upon the author's contemporary memoranda. Balfour's own *Chapters of Autobiography* (edited by Mrs. Dugdale), 1930, though only a fragment put together in his last illness, has also great importance for the student of his life and character. His *Essays and Addresses*, 1893 (3rd edition 1905) and his *Essays Speculative and Political*, 1920, contain autobiographical matter and illustrate the development of his views. The student of his philosophy will need to consult his *Defence of Philosophic Doubt*, 1879 (new edition 1920), his *Foundations of Belief*, 1895 (8th edition 1901), and his *Theism and Humanism* and *Theism and Thought*—the Gifford lectures which he delivered in 1915 and 1922–1923 respectively.

Estimates of and allusions to Balfour can be found in such contemporary biographies and recollections as Lady Gwendolen Cecil's *Life of Robert, Marquis of Salisbury*, vols. iii and iv, 1931 and 1932; J. L. Garvin's *Life of Joseph Chamberlain* vol. iii, 1934; *War Memoirs of David Lloyd George*, vols. i–iv (to 1917), 1933–1934; Sir Austen Chamberlain's (forthcoming) *Memoirs*; (Margot) Countess of Oxford and Asquith's *Autobiography*, 1922, and *More Memories*, 1933; Viscount Esher's *Journals and Letters*, ed. M. V. Brett, vols. i and ii, 1934. Sir Ian Malcolm, who was one of Balfour's political secretaries, published in 1930, *Lord Balfour: A Memory*, which deserves notice, as does an article in *Ten Personal Studies*, 1908, by Wilfrid Ward. The present Lord Rayleigh has dealt with the scientific aspect of Balfour's activities in a short obituary notice prepared for the Royal Society, and reprinted under the title *Lord Balfour in his relation to Science*, and Mr. John Buchan (Lord Tweedsmuir) with his literary style in an article in *Homilies and Recreations*, 1926. For the episode of the Lansdowne 'peace letter' of 1917 see *The Nineteenth Century and After*, March 1934 (article by Lord Lansdowne); and in regard to Balfour and the Peace Conference Mr. Harold Nicolson's *Peacemaking 1919*, 1933, will be found useful.]

ALGERNON CECIL

published 1937

BALL Sir (George) Joseph

(1885–1961)

Intelligence officer, party administrator, and business man, was born in Luton 21 September 1885, the son of George Ball, bookstall clerk, of Salisbury, and his wife, Sarah Ann Headey. He was educated at King's College School, Strand, and at King's College, London. After leaving college he worked as a civilian official in Scotland Yard, and he was called to the bar with first class honours by Gray's Inn in 1913. He was a keen footballer, playing centre-half for the Casuals till an injury prevented him. He was a good shot and an expert fly-fisher. On the outbreak of war he joined MI5, and was appointed OBE in 1919. He remained in the service until 1927 when he was persuaded by J. C. C. (later Viscount) Davidson, chairman of the Conservative Party, to join the party organization as director of publicity. Major Joseph Ball, as he then was, proved to be a notable asset, along with Sir Patrick Gower, also diverted by Davidson from government employment. Years later in 1955 Davidson said 'he is undoubtedly tough and has looked after his own interests . . . On the other hand he is steeped in the Service tradition, and has had as much experience as anyone I know in the seamy side of life and the handling of crooks.' One of Ball's successful clandestine efforts was to insert agents in the Labour Party headquarters and in Odham's Press which did most of the party's printing. In this way he managed to secure both Labour reports of political feeling in the country and also advance 'pulls' of their leaflets and pamphlets; it was thus possible for the Conservatives to reply suspiciously instantaneously to their opponents' propaganda. Not surprisingly Ball was closely involved in assisting Stanley Baldwin to deal with the parliamentary debate in 1928 on the affair of the Zinoviev letter which had occurred four years earlier. Baldwin was able to emerge triumphantly. It is not known whether Ball played any part in the original episode.

In 1930 in the aftermath of the loss of the general election, Davidson created the Conservative Research Department and made Ball its director under the chairmanship first (briefly) of Lord Eustace Percy and then of Neville Chamberlain to whom Ball is said to have taught the art of fly-fishing. Chamberlain respected Ball's knowledge, discretion, and reliability, later using him in 1938 as an intermediary with Count Grandi, Italian ambassador in London, in order to bypass the foreign secretary, Anthony Eden (later the Earl of Avon). Ball was appointed KBE in 1936.

Ball was a very able director. He did much to lay the foundations for the success of the Conservative Party's Research Department after World War II and he recruited for it many young men of high calibre, among others Henry Brooke (later Lord Brooke of Cumnor) and Frank Pakenham (later the Earl of Longford) who, however, later moved to the Labour Party. Ball retired in 1939. From 1940 to 1942, reverting to his earlier profession as an intelligence officer, he served as deputy chairman of the Security Executive.

After the end of the war Ball entered the world of business, becoming chairman of Henderson's Transvaal Estates and five subsidiary companies, and also of Lake View & Star. He was a director of Consolidated Goldfields of South Africa and of the Beaumont Property Trust. He was chairman of the Hampshire Rivers Catchment Board 1947–53. He died in London 10 July 1961.

Moving for most of his life in the shadow of events and deeply averse to publicity of any sort he gave very little away, and the formal accounts of his career, whether written by himself or others, are curt and uninformative. He was, however, a quintessential *eminence grise*, and his influence on affairs cannot be measured by the brevity of the printed references to him. Alan Hugh Ball, his son by his wife, Mary Caroline, became a director of Lonrho Ltd.

Bevan

[*The Times*, 12 July 1961; Robert Rhodes James, *Memoirs of a Conservative*, 1969; L. Chester, S. Fay, and H. Young, *The Zinoviev Letter*, 1967; John Ramsden, *A History of the Conservative Party*, vol. iii, *The Age of Balfour and Baldwin 1902–48*, 1978.]

ROBERT BLAKE

published 1981

BEVAN Aneurin

(1897–1960)

Politician, was born 15 November 1897 in Tredegar, Monmouthshire, the sixth of the ten children, seven of whom survived, of David Bevan and his wife, Phoebe, daughter of John Prothero, blacksmith. David Bevan was a miner, a Baptist, a regular reader of Blatchford's *Clarion*, a lover of music and of books: a gentle, romantic man who had more cultural influence on his son than the elementary school in which Bevan was a rebellious pupil and acquired little but the ability to read. A stammer which he later persevered to overcome probably had some part in his hatred of school; his immense desire for knowledge had hardly developed when at thirteen he left; thereafter he had to educate himself. The Workmen's Library was well stocked with 'the orthodox economists and philosophers, and the Marxist source books'. But it was not in Nye Bevan's undisciplined temperament to become a Communist. Until the failure of the general strike of 1926 he believed that industrial action would bring the workers to the promised land of which he dreamed as he roamed the Welsh mountains, disputed with his friends, or declaimed the poetry which he loved.

Meantime Bevan had gone into the pits. He became an expert collier and almost equally expert at making trouble for his employers: by 1916 he was chairman of his lodge. He was exempt from military service on account of an eye disease and became well known in Tredegar and beyond for his opposition to what he considered a capitalist war. In 1919 the South Wales Miners' Federation sent him to the Central Labour College in London for two years which were probably not quite the waste of time he thought them: his horizons widened and his debating skill improved.

Bevan returned in 1921 to Tredegar and his conflict with the owners who had resumed control of the mines after the war, despite the Sankey recommendation of nationalization. It was not perhaps surprising that Bevan could find no work. His meagre unemployment benefit was stopped when his sister began to earn, and when his father fell ill with the chest disease which was to kill him he received no sickness benefit until his son fought the case. Bevan's enforced familiarity with the intricacies of sickness and unemployment benefit was at the disposal of all who cared to consult him. To keep his position in the mining industry he worked for some months as a checkweighman until the pit closed down and he was once more on the dole. Then in 1926 he became disputes agent for his lodge at a salary of £5 a week. In the long conflict with the owners in that year he showed himself an efficient organizer of relief; made fighting speeches at special national conferences of the Miners' Federation in July and October; yet a month later opposed Arthur Horner by recommending negotiation before the drift back to work should bring about the disintegration of the Federation.

In the following year the local guardians who were deemed to have been too generous with poor relief were replaced by commissioners: 'a new race of robbers' whom Bevan never forgot or forgave. He realized now that power to redress the miseries of the unemployed in the South Wales coalfield must come through political action. Already a member since 1922 of the Tredegar urban district council, in 1928 he was elected to the Monmouthshire county council and in 1929 was returned to Parliament as Labour member for Ebbw Vale, a seat which he retained until his death. For all his turbulence, his highly independent outlook, his criticism of his own leaders, Bevan remained to the last convinced that only through Parliament and the Labour Party could he achieve his aims.

Throughout the early thirties unemployment was a major issue on which Bevan had plenty to say and he soon became known in Parliament as an attacking speaker of considerable if erratic brilliance, marred by a vituperative inability to keep his temper. He was prominent in opposing non-intervention in the Spanish civil war, and as foreign affairs became of increasing concern found himself allied with Sir Stafford Cripps whom he supported in his unity campaign of 1937 and as a founder of and regular contributor to *Tribune*, which he was himself to edit in 1942–5. Early in 1939 he was expelled from the Labour Party for supporting Cripps in his Popular Front campaign, but he was readmitted in December.

The outbreak of war meanwhile had brought Bevan new fields of discontent. His opposition to the Government throughout the war earned him notoriety and suspicion and Churchill's description of him as 'a squalid nuisance' probably reflected the opinion of the man in the street. Yet his complaints had some basis: Churchill, he maintained, was conducting a one-man government; furthermore, was no strategist. Bevan pressed for an early second front; and later mistrusted the 'Big Three' conferences as ignoring the claims of lesser countries and preventing the post-war development of a western Europe strong enough to stand between the opposing American and Soviet powers. He came into conflict with Ernest Bevin over his treatment of the coalmining industry, and in 1944 was nearly expelled again from the Labour Party for his violent opposition to a regulation imposing penalties for incitement to unofficial strike action in essential industries: 'the disfranchisement of the individual'. He was asked for, and gave, a written assurance that he would abide by standing orders. At the Labour Party conference of December 1944 he was elected for the first time to the national executive; and in the Labour Government of the following year C. R. (later Earl) Attlee made him minister of health and housing. He was then sworn of the Privy Council.

The National Health Service Act of 1946 provided free medical and dental care for all who cared to avail themselves of it and in the event ninety-five per cent of the nation did. The scheme derived from a number of sources but Bevan included such daring ideas as the nationalization of the hospitals, to be run by regional boards, and the abolition of the sale of general practices. The service was to be financed from general taxation. There followed two years of negotiation with the doctors before the scheme came into effect in 1948. The battle was fought on the grand scale. Yet Bevan displayed more patience and flexibility than were usually at his command in bringing to a successful outcome a cause which was very dear to his heart and was certainly his finest achievement. He was ably assisted by his permanent secretary, Sir William Douglas. With the minister of national insurance Bevan was also responsible for the National Assistance Act of 1948 which completed the break-up of the Poor Law and introduced a comprehensive scheme of assistance and welfare services. Housing he tackled with schemes for the repair of war damage, for prefabricated houses, and for large subsidies to local authorities to enable them to provide houses to rent to people in the lower income groups.

For all his achievement, Bevan was still an uncertain asset to his party. He was apt to get carried away by his own rhetoric: his 'lower than vermin' onslaught on the Tories in July 1948 did him more harm than it did the Tories who were estimated by Harold Laski, no friend of Bevan, to have gained some two million votes thereby. It was seized upon by the British press, still smarting from Bevan's attack upon it as 'the most prostituted in the world'. With his own Government Bevan was increasingly out of sympathy, mainly over armaments expenditure and Ernest Bevin's policy of alliance with the United States and the containment of Russia. It was unfortunate that Cripps, to whom Bevan was much attached and who could exercise a moderating influence upon him, fell ill and resigned in October 1950. In January 1951 Bevan moved to the Ministry of Labour, only to resign in April when he came into conflict with Hugh Gaitskell over the latter's proposal to introduce certain charges into the health service. Harold Wilson and John Freeman also resigned: the armament programme, it was thought, would impoverish the country. In the election of constituency members to the national executive in October Bevan headed the poll, with Mrs. Barbara Castle second and two other supporters gaining places: a shift of opinion within the Labour Party noted perhaps by the electorate which returned the Conservatives to power at the general election later in the month.

For the remainder of his life Bevan was in opposition. *In Place of Fear* (1952), his only book, set out his belief in democratic socialism 'based on the conviction that free men can use free institutions to solve the social and economic problems of the day, if they are given a chance to do so'. He deplored American foreign policy and discounted Russia's military aims. For a time it seemed that Bevan would bring about a split in his own party by the growth of the 'Bevanite' group within it. At the Labour Party conference of 1952 six Bevanites were elected to the national executive with Bevan again at the head of the poll. But at a subsequent meeting of the parliamentary Labour Party in October Attlee successfully moved a resolution calling for the abandonment of all unofficial groups within the party. The Bevanites protestingly complied, but the philosophy of 'Bevanism' remained. At the ensuing annual elections of the parliamentary party Bevan unsuccessfully challenged Herbert Morrison (later Lord Morrison of Lambeth) for the deputy leadership; but he was elected to the shadow Cabinet. This position he resigned in April 1954 when he attacked Attlee's approval of S.E.A.T.O. In the summer he went with Attlee in a Labour Party delegation to Russia and Red China. But in March 1955 he was again defying his leader in the House: this time over the use of nuclear weapons in the event of hostilities, even if not used by the aggressor. The party whip was withdrawn and his expulsion from the Labour Party sought, but again Bevan gave an assurance of conformity. Once again a general election was in sight and again Labour lost. When Attlee resigned in December, Bevan unsuccessfully challenged Gaitskell for the leadership, although he outstripped Morrison; then he stood for the deputy leadership, only to be defeated by James Griffiths. But in October 1956, by a narrow majority over George Brown, he attained the post of party treasurer which he had failed to wrest from Gaitskell in the two preceding years.

In Gaitskell's shadow Cabinet Bevan was entrusted with first colonial, then foreign, affairs: an attempt to close the ranks in which Bevan saw that he must co-operate if Labour were to return to power, even if he regarded Gaitskell as 'a desiccated calculating machine'. On colonial problems, Malta, Cyprus, Kenya, and during the Suez crisis, Bevan spoke with skill and moderation for the Opposition. Although he urged the banning, by agreement with Russia and America, of nuclear and hydrogen bomb tests, at the party conference of 1957 he helped to defeat a motion demanding that Britain should make a unilateral renunciation of such bombs, saying that it would send a British foreign secretary naked into the conference chamber. His standing within his party became more secure and in October 1959 he was elected unopposed as deputy leader of the parliamentary party; he continued as party treasurer. His speeches had become persuasive rather than aggressive, but were delivered with all the old felicity which, despite the hatred and fear he could engender, had made him generally considered the best speaker, after Churchill, to be heard in the House. If a touch of melancholy was to be detected now, it might be attributed to the trend of international affairs and to the decline of his own physical powers. After some months of illness he died at his home at Chesham, Buckinghamshire, 6 July 1960.

With Bevan's passing some of the colour and much of the passion went out of politics. He fought vehemently, with deadly invective, but with gaiety and wit as well, for his beliefs. Not everybody shared them, least of all within his own party where he was strongly opposed by the trade-unionists. He was essentially an original—complex, baffling, and infuriating, especially when he gave way to indolence or showed a tendency to disappear at times of crisis; but the sincerity and stature of the man were not in doubt. If on occasions he could be a menace to, he also vitalized, the Labour Party and enlarged and influenced its thinking. He was sustained throughout by Jennie Lee, herself a staunch left-wing member of the Labour Party, later to hold office, whom he married in 1934; they had no children. Art, literature, and music, as well as politics, contributed to the richness of the domestic life which they enjoyed, for preference in the country. Bevan always hated London and indeed would personally have fitted better into a more exotic background than the British, although politically he would have been unlikely to survive. A large man whose thatch of black hair silvered elegantly early, he was immensely alive, exercising a personal magnetism which made it difficult even for those who most detested his views to resist his charm. The very large congregation which attended the memorial service in Westminster Abbey was a tribute to the affection and respect in which he had come to be held.

[Aneurin Bevan, *In Place of Fear*, 1952; Jennie Lee, *This Great Journey*, 1963; Michael Foot, *Aneurin Bevan*, vol. i, 1897–1945, 1962; Vincent Brome, *Aneurin*

Bevan, 1953; Mark M. Krug, *Aneurin Bevan: Cautious Rebel*, 1961; Francis Williams (with Earl Attlee), *A Prime Minister Remembers*, 1961; *The Times*, 7 July 1960; private information.]

HELEN M. PALMER

published 1971

BEVIN Ernest

(1881–1951)

Trade-union leader and statesman, was born 7 March 1881 in the small Somerset village of Winsford on the edge of Exmoor, the illegitimate son of a forty-year-old village midwife named Mercy Bevin who had separated from her husband, William Bevin, some years before and at the time of Ernest's birth described herself as a widow. It was a period of acute rural depression and she sometimes found it difficult to keep a roof over her family's head. She worked as a domestic help on local farms and in the village public house as well as village midwife, but was several times forced to apply for parish relief. She died after months of illness when Ernest, youngest of her six sons, was eight. He never knew who his father was. After his mother's death Bevin was given a home by his half-sister Mary and at the age of eleven, after reaching Standard IV at the Hayward Boys' School in Crediton and getting his labour certificate, was found work as a farm boy at a wage of 6s. 6d. a quarter, living in. He could read, write, and do simple arithmetic. That was the end of his formal education.

Although in some ways he remained a countryman all his life, Bevin had no liking for farm life and when he was thirteen he joined two of his brothers who had found casual work in Bristol. A succession of blind-alley jobs followed. He was kitchen boy at a cheap eating-house, a van boy, a page boy at a restaurant, conductor on the horse trams, until in 1901 he became van driver with a mineral water firm. He was soon earning 25s. a week in wages and commission which he later increased to nearly £2 by working longer hours and extending his round. Although he was an unskilled man this put him on the level of a skilled artisan in regular employment and he seemed perfectly content to remain at this level. In other ways, also, the job suited him. Once he had climbed on his two-horse dray at six o'clock in the morning he was on his own in the open air for the rest of the day, a tough, barrel-chested figure of a man, well able to look after himself in a fight or an argument. From the comparative security of this employment Bevin in his early twenties began his lifelong partnership with Florence Anne Townley (died 1968), the daughter of a wine taster at a Bristol wine merchants; they had one daughter.

Bevin had a hard boyhood and youth. He was often hungry, and later claimed that he sometimes had to steal for food. But his struggles left no personal scars and their importance lay far more in their representative than in their personal quality: they gave him a permanent sense of identification with all those others in the working class whose experience had been much the same. He had many of the qualities of a captain of industry. But unlike many self-made men of the Victorian age he never had any wish to climb out of his own class. He preferred, instead, to help it to rise and to rise with it.

His mother, who had been the one sure centre of affection in his early life, had been a keen Chapel woman, a Methodist when Methodism was as much a social as a religious creed, a vehicle of dissent against the massed forces of Church, State, and landlord. Bevin turned naturally to the Chapel in Bristol. He joined the Manor Hall Baptist Mission and had some thought of becoming a minister or even a missionary. He attended the Quaker Adult School and other discussion and study classes and as with many other early labour and trade-union leaders non-conformity provided the nursery of political action and the bridge to socialism. His interests turned gradually from Chapel to politics: he joined the Bristol Socialist Society, affiliated to the Social Democratic Federation, and became an active speaker and organizer in its ranks, and, after 1908, in the Right to Work movement which developed as a result of mounting unemployment. In November of that year he led a procession of 400 unemployed men into morning service at the cathedral to draw attention to their plight. In 1909 he was defeated as a socialist candidate for the city council. In June 1910 a strike at Avonmouth which later spread to the whole of the Bristol docks pushed Bevin in a new direction. Most of the dockers were organized in the Dock, Wharf, Riverside and General Workers' Union. The carters, many of whom worked out of the docks, were unorganized. However, they could not escape the implications of the dockers' struggle, especially when attempts were made to use them as strike breakers to load and unload ships at the docks. Harry Orbell, a local organizer of the Dockers' Union (later its national organizer), who knew of Bevin's activities in the Right to Work committee, persuaded him to bring the carters together. A carmen's branch of the Dockers' Union, with Bevin as its chairman, was formed in August 1910, and Bevin, although he could not know it, prepared to enter upon his kingdom. In the spring of 1911 he climbed down from his mineral water van for the last time and became a full-time official of the Dockers' Union.

The union had been born out of the great London dock strike of 1889 led by Ben Tillett, Tom Mann, and John Burns. Bevin's contribution to the trade-union movement was something very different from the passion and demagogy of a man such as Tillett. He brought it massive self-confidence, great negotiating ability, and a conviction of the need for centralized authority. None of these qualities had shown themselves in Bevin earlier: they grew out of his first years as a trade-union official when the failure of a series of dockers' and seamen's strikes called by the loosely organized Transport Workers' Federation forced him to go back to the grass roots of trade-union organization. As he stumped Wales and the west country trying to rebuild the branches he learnt the vital importance of carrying the rank and file with him in every decision. He absorbed also another lesson which remained with him throughout his trade-union life: that numerical strength without central authority is illusory.

By 1913 he had become an assistant national organizer and in 1914 one of the union's three national organizers. Because of his direct personal links with the local secretaries and branch officials and their personal loyalty to himself he held the most important strings of union power in his hands. To him trade-unionism was essentially an instrument to enable workers to meet employers as equals in the negotiating chamber. But because he learned his business of leadership when conciliation was out of fashion on both sides, his public character had a curious duality. Capable of great suppleness in negotiation and sensitive to the mutual interests which made industrial co-operation desirable, he presented in public an image which was dogmatic, overbearing, uncompromising, and egotistical. In negotiation he was a realist who understood the need for compromise. On the public platform he permitted himself every licence of venom, innuendo, and the grossest partiality.

This duality of posture stood him in good stead. Among the rank and file it gave him a reputation for left-wing iconoclasm, valuable to those who wish to push their way to the front in the Labour movement, while in private negotiations his realism won many practical advantages for his members. Both sides of this personality were evident during the war of 1914–18. He had no doubt where the sentiments of the great mass of the workers lay and spat scorn on the pacifism of the politicians of the Independent Labour Party. But he found it possible to be equally contemptuous of trade-union leaders like Arthur Henderson and J. R. Clynes who 'betrayed their class' by joining a Lloyd George government, while he himself took an active and forceful part in the work of joint committees to secure the efficient use of manpower.

In 1915 for the first time Bevin was a delegate of his union at the Trades Union Congress and in the winter of 1915–16 he went as a fraternal delegate to the annual convention of the American Federation of Labor. It was his first journey abroad and his visit broadened his outlook and stimulated his imagination. In the summer of 1916 he was elected to the executive council of the Transport Workers' Federation. When the war ended Bevin had become an important trade-union official of the second rank. He was one of his union's permanent delegates to the Trades Union Congress and Labour Party conferences and its representative on close to a dozen committees set up by the ministries of Labour and Reconstruction. Moreover, without ever loosening his strong emotional link with the rank and file he had become a disciplined administrator with a remarkable talent for absorbing documents and sifting evidence.

In the general election of 1918 Bevin was defeated as the Labour candidate for Central Bristol. In 1920 he became assistant general secretary of his union. In that year he became a national figure for the first time, as the 'Dockers' K.C.' when he persuaded the dockers instead of striking to submit a claim for 16s. a day to a court of inquiry under the new Industrial Courts Act. He won their case by brilliant advocacy, at one stage producing before the court a number of plates on which were set out the derisory scraps of food on which dockers would have to move seventy-one tons of wheat a day on their backs if the court accepted as adequate the family budgets advanced by the employers supported by the professional witness of (Sir) A. L. Bowley. Bevin's national status was confirmed by his leadership in the Council of Action which successfully boycotted the sending of arms to Poland for use against the Russian revolutionary armies.

The collapse of the Triple Alliance of miners, railwaymen, and transport workers on Black Friday, 15 April 1921, endorsed all Bevin's earlier suspicions of the fragility of alliances without central command. He was already engaged on the complex and often tortuous negotiations designed to replace the Transport Workers' Federation with its loose alliance of autonomous unions by a compact structure of which his own union should be the centre. The Transport and General Workers' Union which merged fourteen unions with a combined membership of 300,000 came into being on 1 January 1922 with Bevin as general secretary. It was a monolithic achievement ruthlessly secured. Tillett, nominally Bevin's superior in the hierarchy of the Dockers' Union, was swept aside and turned into an ineffectual pensioner after being allowed to believe almost to the very end that he would be president of the new organization, although Bevin had decided at an early stage that he would have to be sacrificed in a deal with one of the other unions. The withdrawal of the union from the Transport Workers' Federation brought about the disappearance of the latter, a blow from which its secretary Robert Williams never recovered. The fate of neither man moved Bevin to any compunction any more than did that of

George Lansbury when years later Bevin used all the force he could command to destroy Lansbury's influence in the Labour movement over the issue of sanctions against Italy over Abyssinia.

Had Bevin turned to Communism in the twenties as some militant trade-unionists were tempted to, the history of British Labour might have taken a different course. But for all his ruthlessness and concern for power Bevin could never have been a Marxist and was indeed to become British Communism's most implacable enemy. He never lost the saving grace of human involvement. When he talked of the working class as 'my people' he did not think of an economic class, the proletariat, but of individual men and women who seemed to him the salt of the earth. To him the trade-union movement was not a tool to be used in the pursuit of an ideology. It was the living embodiment of the best hopes and truest comradeship of ordinary men and women who had given him their trust and to whom he had given his loyalty, and he was only happy when he could feel he was referring back to them. Thus the constitution of the Transport Workers' Union with almost as many checks and balances as the American Constitution which he much admired was meticulously designed to create a chain of command going right back to the individual members in the branches, while providing for a national leadership with power to act decisively at times of crisis. It was in some ways a cumbersome constitution and more democratic in theory than in practice, for it required an active participation which only a minority was ready to give. At the beginning it drew its strength much more from Bevin's own character than from any formal safeguards. But it stood the test of time.

The pattern of union advance on which Bevin had set his hopes was interrupted by the general strike of 1926. The failure of that strike, in which Bevin's working-class loyalties were deeply committed but which ran counter to his strongest convictions about the proper use of industrial power, confirmed him in his belief that industrial animosities, if allowed to continue at their former level, must prove self-destructive to both sides and that the best hope of advance for the workers lay in negotiation from strength rather than in industrial conflict. The number of unions absorbed by his union had reached 22 by the end of 1923. By the end of 1926 this had been increased to 27. In 1929 the hundred-thousand-strong Workers' Union was added. From this powerful base Bevin, a member of the general council of the T.U.C. since 1925, set himself to secure a change in the whole climate of industrial relations.

In this he had the strong support of Walter (later Lord) Citrine, the general secretary of the T.U.C. These two were cast in very different moulds and there was little personal sympathy between them. But they saw industrial problems in the same terms and together helped to bring about a decisive shift towards industrial conciliation, beginning with the Mond-Turner talks in 1928. It was in this year that Transport House was opened, as the headquarters not only of Bevin's union but of the T.U.C. and the Labour Party, and an example of Bevin's imaginative thinking.

Bevin was also branching out in other directions. He travelled abroad as a trade-union delegate to international conferences and to the I.L.O. and began to take a perceptive interest in foreign affairs. He became a member of the Macmillan committee on finance and industry appointed by the MacDonald government and with J. M. (later Lord) Keynes as a fellow member he acquired a shrewd—and highly critical—understanding of the operations of international finance and the working of the gold standard. He was a member of the Economic Advisory Council and of the T.U.C. economic committee. He was instrumental in turning the *Daily Herald*, founded by Lansbury, subsequently owned by the trade unions, but too much of a narrowly based official organ, into a successful popular newspaper under the joint ownership of the T.U.C. and Odhams Press. Although still suspicious of politicians and declining in November 1930 an invitation to go to the House of Lords, he began to play a much more active political role, especially after Ramsay MacDonald, whom he had never trusted, became the head of a 'national' government and Labour suffered the electoral disasters of 1931. Bevin himself was defeated at Gateshead. He was among the first to recognize the threat of Nazism and among the most powerful opponents of pacifism in the Labour Party, urging the case for rearmament at Labour conference after conference and at the meetings of the National Council of Labour. In 1936–7 he was chairman of the T.U.C. In 1938 he made a tour round the world and the knowledge which he gained of Canada, Australia, and New Zealand in-spired him with the idea of the British Commonwealth as the nucleus of a new League of Nations with an economic basis.

Bevin was now generally accepted as one of the most powerful of Labour leaders not only on the industrial but also on the political side. Although his power came in part from the size of the block vote he commanded at Labour Party conferences it derived even more from the natural authority of his personality. He was not by any standard a great orator but his utterances had a raw strength which compelled conviction. The very clumsiness of his sentences, his contempt for syntax and the niceties of pronunciation, the harshness of his voice and the powerful emphasis of his gestures seemed when he was speaking to a mass audience to make him the embodiment of all natural and unlettered men drawing upon wells of experience unknown to the more literate. To watch him advance to the rostrum on such occasions in his thick-soled boots with his customary rolling walk and hear him begin to speak after a long slow look around his audience which seemed to say, 'now you are going to hear one of yourselves', was to be brought up against something resembling a force of nature: implacable, confident, yet often lit by flashes of imagination which outspanned and transcended the ordinary limitations of debate. There was, of course, a good deal of the actor in all this; and he had an actor's sense of occasion and timing. But what counted most in the end was the hard content of what he had to say. It was the broad and penetrating sweep of his judgement and the force of his personality which gave him his great influence, no less than the proven strength of his position as a trade-union leader.

All these qualities converged when in May 1940 Bevin became wartime minister of labour and national service. He was member of Parliament for Central Wandsworth (1940–50) and East Woolwich (1950–51) but he was never wholly at home in the House of Commons. He came to it too late. He was nearly sixty when he entered it as a minister—and from a background to decision-making very different from that of political debate. But his impact upon the War Cabinet, which he entered in October 1940, was, as the *Manchester Guardian* reported, 'as decisive for the ends he set himself as was that of Winston Churchill as war-time Prime Minister'. Nor would many of those in a position to assess what he accomplished dissent from the *Guardian*'s further judgement that 'the work he did in mobilising the manpower and the industrial resources of the country could have been done with equal efficiency, sure judgment and resolute purpose by no other man.' The eight months which preceded the Churchill administration had been for Bevin, as for many others, a period of frustration, anxiety, and suspicion. He had always distrusted Chamberlain, and his animosity, which had long roots in the past, was confirmed by what seemed to him Chamberlain's failure to understand the spirit in which the majority of the British people had gone to war and his patronizing attitude to the trade unions. The only minister with whom he found it possible to establish friendly relations during this period was, to his surprise, Churchill. There was long political enmity between them but this was submerged in their appreciation of each other's understanding of the need for total war.

Despite the shortage of armaments and equipment of all kinds there were more than a million workers unemployed in April 1940. When Bevin became minister of labour and national service he claimed responsibility for all manpower and labour questions, including the right to examine the use made of labour and if necessary withdraw it. He was given, although he did not ask for it, power to conscript and direct labour, and for some time was criticized for his reluctance to use this power. He believed that compulsion hastily used would produce grievance which could lead to bad workmanship and he preferred to wait until the necessity for compulsion was fully accepted by the working class. To obtain the support of both sides of industry he called a meeting of the National Joint Advisory Council of sixty industrialists and trade-union leaders and asked them to appoint a committee of seven trade-union leaders and seven employers to advise on all problems arising from the legislation which had given effect to his powers—greater than those ever previously vested in any man in peace or war. On the same day he met the Engineering and Allied Employers' Federation, the Amalgamated Engineering Union, and the two big general workers unions and began negotiating agreements permitting the breakdown of skilled jobs in factories and the introduction of large numbers of unskilled and semi-skilled workers, including women. This he followed with the appointment of a Labour Supply Board—two trade-unionists, two managers—which until March 1941 met daily under his chairmanship to see that labour was made available wherever it was needed. Subsequently (Sir) Godfrey Ince was director-general of manpower. Bevin also set up a factory and welfare division of the Ministry under Ince which concerned itself not only with working conditions but with the living conditions, feeding arrangements, and leisure of the workers.

Within a week Bevin had transformed the whole industrial atmosphere. His reputation as a wartime minister of labour does not, however, rest solely or even primarily on the speed with which he acted, although this made a substantial contribution to industrial morale. There was no aspect of industrial affairs he did not touch upon. By the middle of 1943 he had so organized the mobilization of labour that there had been an expansion of three and three-quarter million in four years of those serving in the armed forces, civil defence, or industry. The armed forces had increased by nearly four million and the munitions industries by two; there had been a transfer of more than three and a quarter million workers from the less essential industries. This vast disruption of the ordinary life of the communitywas carried through not only with a speed and efficiency completely unmatched in any of the dictatorships, but with a remarkable lack of industrial trouble. The time lost by industrial stoppages was eventually reduced to rather less than one hour per worker per year. The elaborate organization he built was always touched with humanity. When there were criticisms of the call-up of women who had never done outside work in their lives he could snap, 'It never hurt anyone to work'; but when there were complaints of absenteeism because girls stayed home from the factories when their sweethearts were on leave from the forces, he retorted, 'That's not absenteeism, that's human nature'; and he saw to it that there was a proper system of leave in all factories for such occasions. To him the workers were 'my people'. To them he was 'Ernie' and he knew by instinct what their reactions would be to the demands placed on them. He made some mistakes, among them the too hurried withdrawal of labour from the mines after the fall of France which the later direction of 'Bevin boys' underground did little to correct, although it was dear to his heart because he hoped it would not only ease an emergency but help to break down class barriers. Yet when the scale of his activities is taken into account, the proportion of failures was amazingly small.

These activities were, of course, directed first and foremost to winning the war. But he was also determined to establish a new framework of co-operation in industry and permanently raise the status of the industrial and agricultural worker. 'They used to say Gladstone was at the Treasury from 1860 to 1930', he said jokingly. 'I'm going to be at the Ministry of Labour from 1940 to 1990.' The long-term impact of his policies may in the end be seen in the acceptance of joint machinery for industrial relations by both sides of industry. The efficiency and fairness of the demobilization procedures at the end of the war and the avoidance of the economic dislocation and industrial strife that had followed the war of 1914–18 were a tribute to his foresight. At the end of May 1945 Churchill offered Bevin the C.H. for his 'remarkable work at the Ministry of Labour', but this Bevin declined saying that he desired no special honours for doing his job, like thousands of others, in the interests of the nation.

Bevin had come to be regarded as one of the most helpful members of the Government, not only by reason of his work as minister of labour but as a leading member of the lord president's committee on the civilian and economic resources of the country, as chairman of the Production Executive, and as a member of many other committees. In the last two years of the war, as his own departmental pressures decreased, he had applied himself vigorously to questions of post-war reconstruction such as ways of implementing the Beveridge report and he had strongly supported the Education Act of 1944. He was also deeply interested in international relationships and had become a close student of the foreign telegrams which flowed across his ministerial desk. His first ambition when Labour won its victory at the polls in 1945 was, however, for the Treasury. He had greatly developed the interest in monetary and economic policy he had first acquired as a member of the Macmillan committee, and was full of ideas for making the Treasury a much more creative force in the national economic life. Attlee considered offering Bevin the chancellorship and Hugh (later Lord) Dalton the Foreign Office; indeed he actually discussed this with both of them. Further thought over a solitary lunch persuaded him, however, that Bevin would be better at the Foreign Office for two reasons. The first and most important was that Attlee had become convinced that with the end of the war in Europe, Soviet Russia would become tough, aggressive, and unco-operative and that Bevin was temperamentally the more suited of the two to meet this situation and also more likely by reason of his standing in the Labour movement to carry the party with him in doing so. The second was that he had decided to invite Herbert Morrison (later Lord Morrison of Lambeth) to be lord president of the Council and leader of the House of Commons with a general oversight of home affairs and thought it better in view of the personal antipathy between Bevin and Morrison—particularly on Bevin's side—to keep the two apart.

It was, therefore, Bevin who accompanied Attlee to the adjourned Potsdam conference as foreign secretary. There, according to James Byrnes the United States secretary of state, the first impact he made was 'so aggressive that both the President and I wondered how we would get along with this new Foreign Secretary'. However, it did not take Byrnes long in his own words 'to learn to respect highly his fine mind, his forthrightness, his candour and his scrupulous regard for a promise'.

In the Foreign Office itself there were many who at first feared that they had been given into the untutored hands of a clumsy Visigoth. These anxieties departed as they got to know him. In the Office itself he became one of the most admired and best loved of foreign secretaries—a response to his humanity and his loyalty to and concern for his staff touchingly demonstrated on his seventieth birthday when every member of the Foreign Office from the permanent under-secretary to the messengers and junior typists each contributed sixpence—the dockers' tanner—to give him a birthday party to which much to his joy they all came, an event unique in Foreign Office history.

But although he sought advice from his permanent officials he made his own decisions and formed his own policy: there was never a man less run by his department. He had hoped and had publicly declared at the pre-election Labour Party conference that in dealing with Russia it would be possible for 'Left to speak to Left'. He even hoped that there might be some residue of gratitude for his part in preventing the sending of arms to aid the anti-Bolshevik forces at the end of the first world war. He proved mistaken in both beliefs as Attlee—more shrewd in his judgement of Soviet ambitions—had from the first assumed would be the case. Nine months of arduous negotiations on peace treaties with Italy and the German satellite countries and for a more permanent settlement with Germany than had been reached at Potsdam convinced Bevin that although broad agreement between Britain and the United States was possible on most matters despite differences in detail, Russia saw in European disorder the best opportunity for ideological and territorial expansion. He believed that behind this lay suspicions of western motives and fears of capitalist attacks that had a certain historical justification and tried to allay them in a personal meeting with Stalin in Moscow by offering to extend the wartime Anglo-Russian Treaty into a fifty-year alliance. But although Stalin at first expressed some interest every effort to negotiate such a treaty failed and Bevin found himself increasingly forced to the opinion that Stalin was determined to exploit Britain's post-war weakness and American preoccupation with domestic problems to expand Communist power right across Europe.

The extent to which Britain was at this time the primary and for long periods the sole target of Soviet attack both at the United Nations and in Turkey, the Dardanelles, Northern Persia, Greece, Trieste, and in the Middle East has often been forgotten. But it forced Bevin to concentrate all the power he could command on confining Soviet expansion until America could be persuaded to commit her weight in the political and ideological struggle. His forces were small. Indeed, along with the wartime prestige Britain still enjoyed they rested very largely on Bevin's own character and his refusal to admit even to himself how slight was his freedom of manœuvre. He was urged by many on the democratic Left, hostile to what they regarded as his too great dependence on America, to seek to build a 'third force' of western European powers standing apart from and between the great power blocs of the United States and the U.S.S.R. and acting as a counter-balance to both. For a time he was drawn to the idea. It fitted in with many of his socialist conceptions. But the socialist idealist was over-ruled by the trade-union realist. He remembered the collapse of the paper forces of the Transport Workers' Federation and the Triple Alliance and came to the conclusion that however numerically impressive it might seem on paper a third power would lack both the cohesion and the resources to fill the power gap. In any event the American presence in Europe was already a fact and as such was capable ultimately, if properly deployed, of restoring in a way nothing else would the balance of power jeopardized by British weakness and Soviet ambition. For the time being, however, American public opinion was still resistant to the idea of any further involvement in Europe. Moreover a sizeable official opinion inclined to Harry Hopkins's view that no basic conflict existed between Russian and American interests and to Admiral Leahy's much-canvassed judgement that Britain was 'prostrate economically' and 'relatively impotent militarily' and that the Soviet Union must therefore be accepted by the United States as the 'unquestioned, all powerful influence in Europe'.

In these circumstances Bevin saw his responsibility as that of holding the line until such time as the United States could be awakened by a clear issue to the real situation, fully knowing that it was a gamble in which time and

his own resources were running out. In February 1947 he judged the time
and the issue had arrived in Greece where for two years of civil war Britain
had accepted alone the responsibility for meeting and holding Communist
pressure. Now as mounting pressure coincided with the first signs, as he
judged, of American disillusionment with Russia he instructed the British
ambassador to deliver a memorandum to General Marshall, the secretary
of state, informing him that Britain's economic position would no longer
allow her to act as the main reserve of economic and military support for
Greece or Turkey and that if America agreed that their freedom from
Soviet control was essential to western security she must be prepared to
step in. The immediate effect of this memorandum on American official
opinion was of shock and anger. But sixteen days later came the 'Truman
doctrine' declaring security throughout the whole of the eastern Mediterranean to be an American interest. Judged by the developing consequences of this doctrine Bevin's carefully timed stroke can be seen as one
of the most decisive diplomatic acts in modern history.

Satisfied that the inevitable British withdrawal from areas of traditional
British influence would no longer leave a power vacuum which could
tempt the Soviet to dangerous adventures, Bevin turned his attention to
building a pattern of European alliances which would enable western
Europe to play its full part in western security. The treaty of Dunkirk with
France (March 1947) was the first substantial brick in this structure. It was
followed a year later by a treaty of mutual assistance binding together
Britain, France, Belgium, Holland, and Luxembourg. The shock to
American opinion of the Communist coup in Czechoslovakia in 1948
enabled Bevin to achieve his larger purpose of widening this alliance into a
North Atlantic Treaty of which the United States and Canada would be a
part. The treaty was signed 4 April 1949.

The creation of N.A.T.O. came as the climax of Bevin's efforts. But it
was not his only achievement. More than any man—including even
Marshall himself—he was responsible for the development of Marshall Aid
to Europe. When Marshall made his Harvard speech in June 1947 suggesting that if the European nations would organize themselves for
mutual help American economic aid for reconstruction might be forthcoming he had, as he subsequently stated, no clear plan in mind; and
indeed nearly three weeks later the U.S. secretary to the Treasury was still
denying that the speech had any special significance. It was Bevin's response which brought the speech to life—within a matter of hours he had
not only cabled Britain's appreciation of the offer and readiness to take it up
but had set in motion the machinery necessary to create the Organization
for European Economic Co-operation. He hoped it would be possible to
bring the U.S.S.R. and satellites in too and with Marshall's agreement

invited Molotov to meet the French foreign minister and himself in Paris to discuss their participation. Although Molotov came, the talks were without result; not for lack of trying on Bevin's part.

It can be argued that in doing everything he could to bring America into Europe Bevin helped to make inevitable the division between East and West. But this division was not of his making. It was a fact of Soviet immediate post-war policy to which he had to reconcile himself and was nowhere more apparent than in Germany whose problems occupied so much of Bevin's time. The alternative to American co-operation in Europe was Soviet hegemony over most of the Continent and having once convinced himself that this was the major post-war danger he played his cards with stubborn skill, although his hand was weak and he knew that he would be bitterly attacked by many on his own side. The objectives he set himself he achieved, even if he was never able 'to go down to Victoria Station and take a ticket to where the hell I like without a passport'.

Nor was he always so successful elsewhere. He hoped to bring both stability and economic progress to the Middle East. One of his first policy declarations when he went to the Foreign Office was a memorandum declaring Britain's interest to be peasants not pashas. But Britain no longer had the economic strength to prime the pumps for the reconstruction policies he dreamed of and he himself underestimated the forces of revolutionary nationalism that the war had helped to set in motion in the Arab world. Sometimes he seemed too ready to dismiss those who would not fit into his larger plans as no better than break-away unions. He was essentially a pragmatist and pragmatism was not enough, although it is difficult to see what else he could have done with the resources he had. He tried desperately hard to find a Palestine solution acceptable to both Jews and Arabs. He failed partly because he underestimated the passions on both sides and partly because his efforts, although supported by the U.S. State Department, were continually undermined by the pressures of American domestic policy on the President. He did not hide his anger, believing—perhaps optimistically—that with American backing he might have achieved an agreement which would have met the reasonable claims of Jewry without permanently antagonizing their Arab neighbours and have enabled Jewish skill and intelligence to assist in raising the level of life throughout the Middle East. Failure was, perhaps, inevitable. It was in the end sharpened by his impatience in handing over the problem to the United Nations and pulling out the British administration when a decision was imposed which he thought to be wrong.

Looking at the whole field of foreign affairs his total achievement must, despite his failures, be judged remarkable and Bevin himself a great foreign secretary. He was moreover the strong man of the Government and

Attlee's closest and most loyal associate with a powerful voice in all major decisions. Bevin had three careers: trade-union leader; wartime Labour minister; foreign secretary. He was nearly sixty when he embarked on the second and entered the House of Commons for the first time; and only six years short of his death when he went to the Foreign Office. To each he brought integrity, loyalty, and a powerful and imaginative mind. In each his impact was massive and creative. He grew with each demand made upon him and in whatever situation he found himself had in the highest degree that quality which Goethe once thought was to be noted in the English: 'The courage they have to be that which Nature made them.' 'A turn-up in a million' was Bevin's own description of himself.

In March 1951 Bevin became lord privy seal but his health was rapidly declining and he died in London 14 April 1951. His ashes were buried in Westminster Abbey.

Bevin was sworn of the Privy Council in 1940, elected an honorary fellow of Magdalen College, Oxford, in 1946, and received honorary degrees from Cambridge and Bristol. Busts by E. Whitney Smith went to Transport House, the Ministry of Labour, and the Foreign Office; by Sir Jacob Epstein to the Tate Gallery; the National Portrait Gallery has a portrait by T. C. Dugdale.

[Francis Williams, *Ernest Bevin*, 1952; Alan Bullock, *The Life and Times of Ernest Bevin*, 2 vols., 1960–67; personal knowledge.]

FRANCIS-WILLIAMS

published 1971

BIRCH (Evelyn) Nigel (Chetwode)

(1906–1981)

Baron Rhyl

Economist and politician, was born in London 18 November 1906, one of two sons (there were no daughters) of (General Sir) (James Frederick) Noel Birch, GBE, KCB, KCMG, and his wife Florence Hyacinthe, the daughter of Sir George Chetwode, sixth baronet, and sister of (Field-Marshal Lord) Chetwode. Educated at Eton, he became a partner in the stockbroking firm of Cohen Laming Hoare. A skilful operator, especially in the gilt-edged market, he acquired at an early age a sufficient fortune to assure him independence. He joined the Territorial Army (King's Royal Rifle Corps) before 1939 and served in World War II on the general staff in

Britain and the Mediterranean theatre, attaining the rank of lieutenant-colonel in 1944.

He was elected to Parliament for Flintshire in 1945 and quickly made a formidable reputation on the Conservative opposition benches for his mordantly witty interventions and speeches and for his advocacy of strictly honest public finance and his critique of the prevalent Keynesian trend. On forming his government, in November 1951 (Sir) Winston Churchill appointed him—some believed as a result of mistaken identity—not, as was expected, to a financial post but as parliamentary under-secretary at the Air Ministry and subsequently at the Ministry of Defence (from the end of February 1952).

He attained ministerial rank in October 1954 as minister of works where he enjoyed, as he said, 'gardening with a staff of three thousand' and deserved to be remembered for his insistence upon retaining the trees in Park Lane when it was widened. He served in the government of Sir Anthony Eden (later the Earl of Avon) as secretary of state for air from December 1955; but the first appointment in his special field came only when Harold Macmillan (later the Earl of Stockton) made him economic secretary to the Treasury—technically a demotion—in January 1957.

Birch supported and encouraged the chancellor of the Exchequer Peter (later Lord) Thorneycroft in evolving a theory of inflation which was the recognizable forerunner of the monetarism of later decades, and when Thorneycroft failed to obtain from his cabinet colleagues the restraint in public expenditure he considered essential, Birch joined him and the financial secretary (J. Enoch Powell) in the triple resignation on 6 January 1958 which Macmillan, in a jaunty phrase which became famous, dismissed as 'a little local difficulty'.

Though he never held office again, Birch exercised great influence on economic and financial questions and continued to castigate what he regarded as the lax and inflationary proclivities of Macmillan's government. When Macmillan was about to be toppled by the scandal of the 'Profumo affair', Birch demanded his resignation in a philippic long famous for its closing phrase from Robert Browning's 'The Lost Leader', 'Never glad confident morning again', which went down in parliamentary memory along with his exclamation to a full House on the announcement of the resignation of E. H. J. N. (later Lord) Dalton: 'They've shot our fox!' The failing eyesight which increasingly inhibited Birch's other activities did not interfere with his stream of contributions to economic debate, which, though meticulously prepared, were invariably delivered without a note.

Birch, who once accused the Treasury of 'the reckless courage of a mouse at bay', was representative of a distinctive element in the House of Commons after World War II. He combined with personal courage, independence, and integrity an understanding of public finance and economic affairs acquired and perfected in the practical life of the City. He was appointed OBE in 1945 and admitted to the Privy Council in 1955.

Having continued from 1950 to represent West Flint, where he resided at Saithailwyd ('seven hearths') near Holywell, he went to the House of Lords in 1970 as a life peer, Lord Rhyl. He married in 1950 Esmé Consuelo Helen, OBE, daughter of Frederic Glyn, fourth Baron Wolverton. There were no children. He died 8 March 1981 at Swanmore, Hampshire.

[Personal knowledge.]

J. ENOCH POWELL

published 1990

BONHAM CARTER (Helen) Violet

(1887–1969)

Baroness Asquith of Yarnbury

Political figure, was born in Hampstead, London, 15 April 1887, the fourth of the five children and the only daughter of Herbert Henry Asquith (later first Earl of Oxford and Asquith) and his wife, Helen Kelsall, daughter of Frederick Melland, a well-known Manchester physician. The youngest child, Cyril, became Lord Asquith of Bishopstone.

Her mother died of typhoid fever in 1891, when Violet was four. In 1894 her father married Margaret (Margot), daughter of Sir Charles Tennant. There were two surviving children of this second marriage, one of whom, Anthony, achieved prominence in the film world. In 1892 Asquith became home secretary in Gladstone's last administration. Violet Bonham Carter often said she could not remember a time when she did not hear talk of politics. Her devotion to her father, and after his death in 1928 to his memory, was absolute. Some of the fiercest battles she fought in later years were in defence of his conduct as wartime prime minister. She would not let even trivialities go unchallenged. A powerful controversialist with a biting wit, she excelled in curt ridicule. As with all other causes she took up, she would never compromise or give up a battle.

Violet Asquith had no English schooling. Educated privately and unsystematically by a series of governesses, she read English literature widely and was taught French and German. Finished, as the term was, in Dresden and Paris, she returned to England with a full knowledge of both languages and of their literatures. However politically busy, she always made time for reading. Some of her warmest friendships were based on a shared love of the classics.

But her overriding interest was in public affairs. From the time of her mother's death her father treated her as an adult. She could remember how on his return from the House she would ask him 'Did Mr Gladstone speak?' and 'What did the Irish do?'. He gave her careful answers. When she was eighteen he was appointed chancellor of the Exchequer in Sir Henry Campbell-Bannerman's Government. He became prime minister (1908) in the month of her coming of age. She was with her father when the suffragettes stopped his car and lashed at both of them with dog whips. She had been also with him throughout the 1906 general election that produced the Liberal landslide. She won her own political spurs in the Paisley by-election of 1920 that returned Asquith to Parliament after his defeat at East Fife in the 'khaki election' of 1918. She was his most effective platform supporter.

Fourteen years earlier she had met the other immortal 'whom I was blessed to call my friend'. In the first volume of *Winston Churchill as I Knew Him* (1965), a work which, alas, she never finished, she described how at a dinner party in the early summer of 1906 she found herself seated next to a 'young man who seemed to me quite different from any other young man I had ever met'. She was nineteen, Churchill was thirty-one. These were the years when she made her early contacts with famous men—Grey, Balfour, Morley, Lloyd George, Kitchener, and others. But the relationship with Churchill became a thing apart. She had too strong a mind to follow him blindly. There were periods of disagreement which Churchill resented. But throughout almost sixty years the friendship held to the day of Churchill's death.

Violet Bonham Carter—she married in 1915 (Sir) Maurice Bonham Carter (died 1960), her father's principal private secretary; they had two sons and two daughters (one of whom, Laura, married Joseph Grimond, who became the leader of the Liberal Party)—must, however, be seen in her own right, not merely as an accompanist to others more famous. She was the last Asquithian Liberal. Her bitterness towards Lloyd George never diminished. But her father's death closed for her the aftermath of the Edwardian age. Soon thereafter Britain was faced with problems and menaces which the first three decades of the century were thought to have banished. In October 1931 she declared in favour of the 'national' Government brought into being by the perilous state of the nation's finances. Inherently against both Conservatives and Socialists she regarded this as merely an emergency measure. She was president of the Women's Liberal Federation twice (1923–5 and 1939–45). In 1945 she accepted an invitation to succeed Lord Meston, who had died in 1943, as president of the Liberal Party Organization, an office which she held until 1947—the first woman to do so.

In the general election of 1945 she gave one of the Liberal Party's broadcasts, ridiculing Churchill's efforts to panic people with 'the threat of Mr Attlee and the Gestapo'. She stood for Wells in that election, coming bottom of the poll, behind Lt.-Col. D. Boles, a Conservative who had won the seat unopposed in a by-election in 1939, and C. Morgan, the Labour candidate. She tried again in 1951, standing as Liberal candidate for Colne Valley. This time she had Conservative support, the local Conservative association being split. Unfortunately for her her opponent was one of the most attractive members of the Labour Party, William Glenvil Hall. He won by a majority of 2,189 in a poll of over 58,000. Finally she entered Parliament as a life peeress, Baroness Asquith of Yarnbury, in 1964. Although she had never sat in the Commons and was then seventy-seven, she immediately engaged in the work of the House of Lords, her last speech being about Biafra.

This was highly characteristic. Violet Bonham Carter's horizon was never insular. She knew Europe well; moreover, she had visited Egypt in her twenties and the Middle and Far East in her seventies. She also crusaded for the League of Nations from its conception, and was a member of the executive of the League of Nations Union until 1941. In May 1933 she vigorously attacked Franz von Papen who, having made a deal with Hitler, had forced Hindenburg to appoint the Führer chancellor, and had himself taken office as vice-chancellor. She was an active supporter of Churchill's anti-Nazism in the 1930s, joining him and Sir A. Sinclair (later Viscount Thurso) in their campaign to create a Ministry of Supply. She became a vice-chairman of the United Europe Movement in 1947. She was, in addition, a delegate to the Commonwealth Relations Conference in Canada in 1949, and president of the Royal Institute of International Affairs 1964–9. Letters to *The Times* concerning international as well as domestic causes often had her as one of their signatories, and unfriendly fun was sometimes made of this. But if occasionally her zeal did outrun her discretion, of her passionate care for fundamental freedoms and her sympathy for suffering people in all nations there was no doubt.

The general election of 1945 briefly interrupted one of Violet's most fruitful services to the nation. When Churchill, on becoming prime minister in 1940, restored to the BBC its full muster of seven governors—at the outbreak of war Neville Chamberlain had left only Sir (George) Allan Powell, the chairman, and C. H. G. Millis, the vice-chairman, in office—he appointed Violet Bonham Carter as one of them. Under the stresses of war, a novel situation for every broadcasting organization, the BBC had become apprehensive, narrow, and inhibiting to the point of intolerance. With (Sir) Harold Nicolson and J. J. Mallon as her supporters, Violet Bonham Carter swung a hesitant board behind a new director-general committed to freeing the BBC from its political and psychological straitjacket and to enlarging its provision for information and culture. She had to resign from the board to fight the Wells seat in 1945, was re-appointed on her defeat, and finished her term of office in 1946. She was also a member of the royal commission on the press (1947–9), a governor of the Old Vic from 1945, and a trustee of the Glyndebourne Arts Trust from 1955.

In 1963 she became the first woman to give the Romanes lecture at Oxford; she spoke on 'The Impact of Personality on Politics'. It was a historic and memorable occasion. Starting with her personal experiences, she ended with a denunciation of 'the fallacy of Historic Fatalism'. 'In all ages great human beings have overcome material odds by the inspiration they have breathed into their fellow men.' She was also a speaker at the Royal Academy dinner in 1967, the first time in over a century and a half that women had attended. She had a pure carrying voice, which she was able to modulate with thrilling effect. She depended on gestures hardly at all, and indeed, she seemed frail to carry such a load of conviction. When she died, the tribute to her from Jeremy Thorpe, the Liberal leader—'The Party has lost its greatest orator'—was valid beyond politics.

Violet Bonham Carter never thought of herself as an orator. Her voice was a minor weapon in her lifelong battle for her beliefs. Her major one was the alliance of cogency and passion. She exemplified the dictum of William Hazlitt: 'The seat of knowledge is in the head, of wisdom, in the heart.' Her lifetime covered the rise, zenith, and nadir of the Liberal Party of her youth. Her first reported speech was in aid of funds for Liberalism when she was twenty-two. Never did she lower her flag. She was still fighting gallantly, if rather forlornly, at the end. She was appointed DBE in 1953, and received an honorary LLD from Sussex University in 1963. She died in London 19 February 1969.

A portrait of her by (Sir) William Orpen, the gift of the House of Commons on her marriage in 1915, is in the possession of her son, Raymond. Her elder son, Mark, has a water-colour portrait by E. Barnard (1910). A bust by Oscar Nemon (1960–9) is in the National Portrait Gallery.

[Violet Bonham Carter, *Winston Churchill as I Knew Him*, 1965; *The Times*, 20 February 1969; personal knowledge.]

WILLIAM HALEY

published 1981

BOYLE Edward Charles Gurney

(1923–1981)

Third Baronet, and Baron Boyle of Handsworth

Politician, was born at 63 Queen's Gate, Kensington, 31 August 1923, the elder son and eldest of three children of Sir Edward Boyle, second baronet, barrister, and his wife, Beatrice, daughter of Henry Greig, of Belvedere House, Kent. He was the grandson of Sir Edward Boyle, Conservative MP for Taunton in 1906–9, who was created the first baronet in 1904. He was educated at Eton where he was captain of Oppidans, editor of the *Eton Chronicle*, and president of the Political Society. Journalism and politics remained two of his abiding interests. He succeeded his father as baronet in 1945. Towards the end of World War II he served for a short period in the Foreign Office, after which he went up to Oxford as a scholar of Christ Church where he read history. He played an active part in Conservative undergraduate politics and was elected president of the Union in the summer of 1948. Even at that time he was considered to be exceptionally mature, a charming and persuasive, though not a rhetorical, speaker, and one who was likely to make his mark in the outside world. He left Oxford in 1949 with a third class degree, disappointing to him and at first sight somewhat surprising. His intellectual characteristics, however, comprised a wide breadth of interest, a remarkable store of information, and a phenomenal memory for everything which he encountered, but his was not a mind full of innovative ideas or of penetrating analysis. His strength lay in his deep-seated and moderate convictions which guided him all through his life.

It was, no doubt, because he was so impressively grown-up that he was selected to fight a by-election in the Perry Bar division of Birmingham in 1948 whilst still at Oxford. Having lost the by-election he fought the same seat in the 1950 general election when he again lost. Meantime he had become a journalist and was assistant editor of the *National Review* under John Grigg. Later in that year he was elected to the House of Commons for the Handsworth division of Birmingham at the age of twenty-seven, the youngest member in the House. His ability and steadfastness were soon recognized by his appointment the following year as parliamentary private secretary to the under-secretary for air. In 1954 he received his first government post as parliamentary secretary to the Ministry of Supply, after which the whole of his parliamentary life until he left the House of Commons in 1970 was spent on the front bench either in government or in opposition, with one short exception after his resignation at the time of Suez.

In 1955 he became economic secretary to the Treasury and from then on it was economic affairs and education which he enjoyed in politics above all else. A heavy responsibility was placed upon him by the budget of R. A. Butler (later Lord Butler of Saffron Walden) in the autumn of 1955. Butler himself was overstrained by the illness and death of his wife. His emergency budget had been whittled down by the cabinet to the point where it was doubtful whether it was worth the trouble it caused. No one, however, had the strength to call a halt to it. Boyle defended it tirelessly in the Commons, in particular the proposition that it was possible to reduce inflation by increasing indirect taxation, thus putting up prices, a proposition which became colloquially known as 'Boyle's Law'.

When Sir Anthony Eden (later the Earl of Avon) announced his decision to use British forces in Egypt, Boyle resigned, though without great fuss. He thought the policy was both dishonourable and doomed to failure. When Harold Macmillan (later the Earl of Stockton) became prime minister in January 1957 he began to heal the wounds in the Conservative Party caused by the Suez adventure by inviting both Julian Amery and Edward Boyle to take office in his government. Boyle became parliamentary secretary to the Ministry of Education, but returned to the Treasury as financial secretary after the general election of October 1959. There he strongly supported proposals for indicative planning and an overall incomes policy. In 1962 he was appointed minister of education and became a member of the cabinet. He was successful in expanding and bringing up to date the educational system. Always an admirer of Butler, he continued to develop the approach set out in the Butler Education Act of 1944.

When the responsibility for science was moved from the lord president of the Council to the enlarged Department of Education and Science in 1964, Quintin Hogg (later Lord Hailsham of St Marylebone) became secretary of state for the new department, and Boyle was made minister of state with special responsibility for higher education. He retained his seat in the cabinet and in no way resented his change of status at the department, for the new structure was one that he had himself urged upon the government.

After the defeat of the Conservative Party in the general election of 1964, Sir Alec Douglas-Home (later Lord Home of the Hirsel) made Boyle shadow home secretary. Here he was unhappy, feeling that his own moderate views on home affairs were all too often in conflict with the more right-wing views of many members of his party. He became opposition front bench spokesman for education and deputy chairman of the party's advisory committee on policy a few months later in February 1965. As leader of the Conservative Party, Edward Heath made a number of attempts in 1965 to persuade Boyle to move to other front-bench positions to enable him to widen his experience in preparation for the highest offices in government. However, he repeatedly refused and in 1970 retired from Parliament in order to devote more time to what had now become his overwhelming interest, education, and in a role where he could express his views and implement his policies without constant interference from those taking part in the political battle. He became vice-chancellor of the University of Leeds in the same year.

Whilst still in Parliament in the second half of the sixties, he had engaged in many additional activities, becoming a director of Penguin Books (1965), a member of the Fulton committee on the Civil Service (1966–8), and pro-chancellor of the University of Sussex (1965–70). After he moved to Leeds his main activity outside the university was as chairman of the top salaries review board. Here he was noted for the fairness and firmness with which he dealt with the intractable problems which arose between governments and the public services during the 1970s. He felt deeply that the constant attacks on public servants from the press and politicians were unjustified and deeply damaging to the national interest. He went to great pains to ensure that those working in the public service received the honourable recognition which was their due, expressed not only in words but in their remuneration.

The early years of Boyle's vice-chancellorship of Leeds University covered that difficult period during the first half of the 1970s when the majority of students on both sides of the Atlantic were opposed to the continuation of the war in Vietnam and, in particular, to those governments which appeared to be supporting it or conniving at it. Boyle's diplomatic touch, administrative skills, concern for the welfare of both teachers and students alike, and above all his energy and humanity in keeping in continuous contact with all aspects of university life enabled him to maintain a reasonable stability where many others failed. Everyone knew that he cared little about himself and his personal position, but that he was determined to maintain the standards of his university in the interests of the future of the students for whom he was responsible. In 1977–9 he was chairman of the committee of vice-chancellors and principals. He found these dignitaries more difficult to handle. He was most happy when he was moving among his own students in his own university.

Boyle was a genial host and a stimulating conversationalist. He had a great love of music, which he shared with Edward Heath, who visited him on the evening before his death. Although he did not play any instrument himself, he possessed a fine collection of gramophone records and a profound knowledge of music and musicians. He was a regular opera goer, favouring particularly Glyndebourne in the summer. He was an admirer of Gabriel Fauré about whom he had collected papers for a book which, alas, was never written. To this Dictionary he contributed the notice of Reginald Maudling. In his early days he was a high Anglican but over his last twenty-five years he moved further and further towards agnosticism.

Boyle, who received honorary degrees from the universities of Leeds (LLD, 1965), Southampton (LLD, 1965), Aston (D.Sc., 1966), Bath (LLD, 1968), Heriot-Watt (D.Litt., 1977), Hull (D.Litt., 1978), and Sussex (LLD, 1972) was also an honorary freeman of the Clothworkers' Company (1975) and a freeman of the City of London, a charter fellow of the College of Preceptors, and an honorary fellow of the Royal College of Surgeons of England (1976). Boyle was admitted to the Privy Council in July 1962 and received a life peerage in 1970. He became a Companion of Honour at a special investiture ceremony at Buckingham Palace on 30 June 1981, shortly before his death.

He died in the vice-chancellor's lodge at Leeds on Monday 28 September 1981 after a prolonged illness, at the early age of fifty-eight. He was unmarried and was succeeded in the baronetcy by his brother, Richard Gurney Boyle (born 1930).

[Private information; personal knowledge.]

EDWARD HEATH

published 1990

BRACKEN Brendan Rendall

(1901–1958)

Viscount Bracken

Politician and publisher, was born at Templemore, county Tipperary, 15 February 1901, the younger son of J. K. Bracken, of Ardlaugh House, Kilmallock, and Templemore, county Tipperary, a builder and monumental mason, and one of the leading spirits in reviving the Gaelic games at Thurles. Brendan lost his father when he was very young and his mother moved to Dublin, where he attended the Christian Brothers' School. But she found him hard to manage, and sent him to the Jesuit College, Mungret, near Limerick, from which he ran away, about the time of his fifteenth birthday. His mother then shipped him to Australia in 1916, although she had no connections there except a priest, brother of Patrick Laffan, a builder, whom she was soon afterwards to marry as her second husband.

Bracken was put on a sheep station in New South Wales, but soon displeased his employer by his addiction to reading instead of sheep tending. The Brigidin nuns nearby at Echuca were kind to him, and let him read the books in the convent library. But he had an unhappy time until he made his way to Sydney. There he sought more congenial work, offering himself to the Christian Brothers as a teacher, and obtaining employment on the diocesan newspaper, to secure advertisements. From this precarious life he made his way back to Ireland in 1919, after the war had ended. He found that his mother had married Laffan and he was not wanted at home, but that he had a small legacy of a few hundred pounds. With this he made his way for the first time to England. It was the time of the Black and Tans, but he represented himself not as coming from Ireland, or as a Catholic, and of a strongly nationalist family, but from Australia, where, he said, his parents had perished in a bush fire.

He applied to various public schools, and had the good fortune to secure admittance to Sedbergh, where he was one day to become chairman of the board of governors. He was nineteen but represented himself as sixteen. He stipulated what subjects he wished to study—history and languages—and paid his own fees in advance. But his money ran out after two terms, and he then secured teaching posts, first in Liverpool, then in a preparatory school at Bishop's Stortford. This second move had the great advantage of bringing him near London. He made the acquaintance of J. L. Garvin who introduced him to Oliver Locker-Lampson, then the owner of the *Empire Review*, for which Bracken undertook to gain subscriptions. It was about this time that he met (Sir) Winston Churchill, to whom he was to attach himself for the rest of his life. Garvin recommended him and he worked for Churchill in his unsuccessful election campaign at Leicester (1923), and in the by-election for the Abbey division of Westminster (1924), and those who were with him remember him as a colourful figure, tall, red-haired, vigorous, with a great power of invective.

The turning-point of his fortunes came in 1924 when he met the head of the publishers Eyre & Spottiswoode, Major Crosthwaite Eyre, a retired Indian Army officer who had married Miss Eyre and was looking for young talent. He recruited Bracken to help with an illustrated monthly of which Hilaire Belloc was the editor. From this small beginning, Bracken emerged in 1925 as a director of the firm, and proved himself full of ideas and drive, with an excellent business judgement. He persuaded Eyre &

Spottiswoode to acquire the *Financial News*, to give him a share of the equity, and to let him run it. This was the first of a number of successful newspaper and periodical enterprises. He founded the *Banker*, a handsomely produced monthly, and, as editor, used his position to secure the entrée to City institutions. He acquired the particular friendship of Sir Henry Strakosch, with whom in 1929 he joined in the control of *The Economist* with a special constitution guaranteeing the editor's independence. He acquired control of the *Investors Chronicle* and the *Practitioner*, an old-established medical journal. All these prospered, but it was the *Financial News* which established him, and enabled him to secure adoption, with the support of Churchill, then chancellor of the Exchequer, as Conservative candidate for North Paddington, for which he was duly returned in 1929. In the Parliaments of the thirties he made himself, in Stanley Baldwin's phrase, 'the faithful Chela' of Winston Churchill, in those years in which Churchill was not only out of office but very much out of favour with the Conservative Party. Bracken, like Churchill, was a staunch imperialist, opposing the government of India bill, and the foreign policy pursued by Baldwin and Chamberlain.

When on the declaration of war Churchill was called to office at the Admiralty, Bracken went with him as his parliamentary private secretary; and when, in May 1940, Churchill formed his own wartime coalition government, he brought Bracken with him, still as his P.P.S., to No. 10. Bracken, who was sworn of the Privy Council in June, asked for nothing higher than, as he put it, 'to stand round and collect the coats'; but he was in his element at the centre of power throughout the war, one of the two or three men closest to Churchill, sitting up with him in the small hours, and living at 10 Downing Street or its annexe. He went out of his way to ease Churchill's burdens and to take the strain from 'the Boss' as he genially called his master. The extent of his influence cannot easily be estimated, but certainly he prompted many of Churchill's appointments, and the disposal of patronage, not excluding appointments in the Church of England which interested him more than they did the prime minister. He had a wide knowledge of English journalism, and particularly cultivated the Commonwealth and American correspondents whose goodwill was so important to Britain at that time. This paved the way for his appointment as minister of information in 1941, a post in which he won golden opinions from Fleet Street for his direct and informal manner. He was fortunate to come to the Ministry when it was beginning to settle down after an uncertain start. He was one of the three political chiefs of the Political Warfare Executive. He deserves great credit for the vitality and imagination which he brought to the Ministry and for lifting it out of the disregard into which it had fallen. At the end of the war Bracken was made first lord of the Admiralty in Churchill's caretaker government; and when he lost his seat in the general election of 1945, he was promptly found the safest of seats at Bournemouth.

He pursued his business interests as thoroughly as ever, and became chairman of the amalgamated *Financial Times* and *Financial News*, and contributed for many years every Monday a weekly column under the pen-name 'Observer' on 'Men and Matters' in the City. After his death the new offices of the paper were named in his honour Bracken House. He founded *History Today* as a monthly periodical under the wing of the *Financial Times*. His friend Strakosch had arranged for him to become his successor as chairman of the Union Corporation, a large mining and financial house operating in South Africa, and he did so in 1945. When Churchill returned to power in 1951, Bracken declined office in the Government, but in 1952 accepted a viscountcy, although he never took his seat in the House of Lords. In his later years he became increasingly interested in public schools: Trinity College, Glenalmond, and Ampleforth, as well as his old school Sedbergh for which he built a fine school library, to which he bequeathed his own excellent collection of books on English literary and political history of the last two centuries.

He was a man of much architectural and artistic taste, who formed close friendships with the leading figures in the world of architecture and art, and was instrumental in many good aesthetic causes. He avoided publicity, especially for his benefactions. In the last ten years of his life his health deteriorated and he spent long periods abroad. Finally he developed cancer of the throat which he faced with great fortitude, until he died in London 8 August 1958. Such a volume of tributes was paid to him by contemporaries of distinction that they were collected in a book. But he ordered all his papers to be destroyed, so that there should be no biography.

There is an old Irish proverb 'From the fury of the Brackens, good Lord deliver us' and Brendan Bracken, inexhaustibly voluble, was an overpowering figure, who stormed his way to commercial and political success. Arriving with neither connection nor wealth, he established himself before he was thirty as a well-placed director and member of Parliament, imposing himself at his own valuation. He was impervious to rebuffs, and he disregarded the conventions: arriving at parties to which he had not been invited, or changing his place at the dinner table to talk to those to whom he wished to talk. If these habits made him many enemies, there was also about him a warm-heartedness, a generosity, an imaginative sympathy, and a readiness to take trouble over individuals, however lowly placed, which won him a great deal of affection. He was a gifted phrasemaker, a ceaseless talker, with unlimited powers of invention, but also with an immense range of information, not always exact, but always delivered with an extreme self-assurance, very galling to those who knew better but lacked his overriding personality. He never married, and bequeathed a large part of his wealth, proved at over £145,000, to Churchill College, Cambridge, where there is a charcoal drawing by Robert Lutyens in the Bracken Library. There is a bust by Uli Nimptsch at Bracken House.

There are many references to Bracken in works on Churchill, notably Lord Moran's *Winston Churchill: The Struggle for Survival, 1940–65* (1966).

[Private and family information; personal knowledge.]

DOUGLAS WOODRUFF

published 1971

BRIDGES Edward Ettingdene

(1892–1969)

First Baron Bridges

Public servant, was born at Yattendon Manor in Berkshire, 4 August 1892, the third of the three children and the only son of Robert Seymour Bridges, later poet laureate, and his wife, (Mary) Monica, daughter of the architect Alfred Waterhouse. His education followed a classical pattern, which equipped him admirably for the career which he was to adopt in later life. In 1906 he went to Eton; and in 1911 he entered Magdalen College, Oxford, where he gained a first class in *literae humaniores* three years later. He had intended to read history after his first degree; and, to the end of his life, the interests and concerns of scholarship claimed a large part of his affection. But the war abruptly ended any thought of an academic career. He joined the 4th battalion of the Oxfordshire and Buckinghamshire Light Infantry and served as adjutant and captain until he was wounded on the Somme in March 1917; and, after being awarded the MC, he held a temporary post in the Treasury until he was fit to return to active service.

At the end of the war he passed the Civil Service examination and returned to the Treasury as an assistant principal. Although he was a fellow of All Souls from 1920 to 1927, he seems finally to have decided to resist Aristotle's injunction that the contemplative life should be rated more highly than the practical; and the next twenty years were spent in learning the ways of Whitehall and acquiring that expert knowledge of the machinery of government which was to serve him so well during the culminating years of his career. At that date the Treasury was responsible not merely for budgetary and financial policy but also for the administration of the public service; and Bridges' early years in Whitehall were devoted to learning the intricacies of principle and practice which governed the control of numbers, grading, and conditions of service in the increasingly complex machine of modern government. The skill which he acquired in these matters was reinforced by successive appointments to several departmental inquiries and royal commissions (including the royal commissions on police powers, 1928–9; the Civil Service, 1929–31; and lotteries and betting, 1932–3); and by a subsequent period of attachment to the Estimates Committee of the House of Commons.

In 1934 he became an assistant secretary; and in 1935 he was appointed to be head of the Treasury division which controlled expenditure on the supply and equipment of the armed forces. It was in the following three years that his powers of organization first became fully apparent. The need for greatly enlarged expenditure on rearmament had at last been acknowledged; and the normal criteria implied by orthodox Treasury doctrine were required increasingly to defer to that need. But economic solvency was no less vital to the nation's survival; and in so reshaping the machinery of Treasury control as to maintain a reasonable balance between those conflicting claims on national resources Bridges showed a pragmatic flexibility of judgement which was to become his most outstanding characteristic.

In 1938 he succeeded Sir Maurice (later Lord) Hankey as secretary to the Cabinet, the Committee of Imperial Defence, the Economic Advisory Council, and the Ministry for the Co-ordination of Defence. The cumulative burden of these appointments was eased when (Sir) Winston Churchill became prime minister and the responsibilities which Bridges had inherited from Hankey were divided. Sir H. L. (later Lord) Ismay, who had been deputy secretary of the Committee of Imperial Defence under Hankey, was appointed an additional member of the Chiefs of Staff Committee in 1940 and became, in effect, the prime minister's principal staff officer when Churchill succeeded Neville Chamberlain. It was Ismay, therefore, who carried, throughout the war, the immense burden of acting as the unique link between Churchill and the chiefs of staff, both in the formulation of global strategy and in the conduct of major military operations. To Bridges fell the less glamorous, but no less vital, task of harnessing the whole of the intricate machinery of government to serve the war effort. The conflict was so different from the war of 1914–18, both in nature and scope, that he had little in the way of precedent to guide him. But to each task—whether the concise recording of the discussions and decisions of a Cabinet which would meet at any hour of the day or night; or the creation of new and unorthodox administrative machinery to deal with the wholly unforeseen problems which the war created; or the mobilization of the morale of a public service required to work for long periods under almost intolerable conditions of strain—he brought the same indomitable energy, the same fixed determination to master the odds against him. It was typical of this quiet but resolute confidence that, at an early stage in the war, he should have found time to arrange for the commissioning of its official history, a work which, as he realized, would not be finished until many years after the war had ended. And the same concern for the longer term was evident, on a larger scale, in the care which he brought to the creation of machinery, notably the Ministry of Reconstruction, to prepare for the eventual transition from war to peace.

Initially, Bridges' relations with Churchill were not wholly easy. The prime minister was wary of an official recruited from the ranks of the Treasury, which he regarded as at least partly responsible for the pre-war procrastination in mobilizing the country to meet the growing Nazi menace. But he quickly came to realize the superb administrative ability of his Cabinet secretary. And he would surely have agreed that his success in guiding the nation to ultimate victory owed not a little to the untiring service of Bridges and Ismay, who, although men of very different temperaments, shared a common devotion to their great leader and shouldered, between them, the immense responsibility of translating the inspired poetry of his directives into the plain prose of effective action. Bridges has left his own testimony to the great prime minister in his contribution to *Action This Day* (a collection of memoirs by six public servants who worked closely with Churchill during the war, edited by Sir John Wheeler-Bennett, 1968); and it is matched by Churchill's generous, and illuminating, tribute to Bridges in *Their Finest Hour* (volume ii of *The Second World War*, 1949), where he describes him as 'a man of exceptional force, ability, and personal charm, without a trace of jealousy in his nature. All that mattered to him was that the War Cabinet Secretariat as a whole should serve the prime minister and War Cabinet to the very best of their ability. No thought of his own personal position ever entered his mind, and never a cross word passed between the civil and military officers of the Secretariat.'

But Bridges did not serve only on the home front. His concerns and responsibilities extended to the oversight of the whole of the intricate network of international relationships which sustained the British war effort after the United States and the Soviet Union entered the war. The negotiation of the Lend-Lease agreements, the organization of supplies to the Russian theatre, the creation of such novel posts as British ministers resident in North and West Africa, the preparation of complex and sensitive briefs for the British teams at the critical Allied conferences at Yalta and Potsdam—all these required his attention; and all benefited from his experience of brigading diverse, and not always harmonious, interests into a common purpose.

As a result, when Sir Richard Hopkins retired as secretary to the Treasury in 1945 and Bridges was appointed by Attlee to succeed him, he brought to the post an unrivalled knowledge of the changed position which Britain would henceforward occupy in an international community which had itself changed, in some ways beyond recognition, since 1939. This was particularly true of British relations with the United States. Bridges never had any doubt about the primacy of this relationship in any realistic inventory of British interests; and it was he who, at the turning point in the negotiation of the vital post-war American loan to Britain, was dispatched to Washington to break the deadlock which had developed between the two parties about its precise terms and conditions. Two years later, when it became necessary for the United Kingdom to suspend the convertibility of sterling which it had been one of the main purposes of the loan to promote, it was again Bridges who finally persuaded a reluctant chancellor of the Exchequer that this step was inevitable. In each case he achieved his end not by any display of economic or financial expertise, which he gladly left to others, but by a genuine comprehension and acceptance of the altered status of Britain in the world, combined with the kind of irresistible common sense best exemplified by the question which was, for him, the acid test of any decision—'Have you a better alternative?' It was a test before which, more often than not, the experts fell silent.

He brought a second category of experience from his wartime service to the administration of post-war Britain—a knowledge, acquired at first hand, of the resourceful flexibility of the British administrative machine under pressure, coupled with a shrewd appreciation of the constitutional and practical limits to that flexibility. In 1945 new prophets were abroad in the land, J. M. (later Lord) Keynes, Sir W. H. (later Lord) Beveridge, and a whole generation of scientists and technologists, to whom the war had given enhanced status. These prophets preached novel, and not always consistent, doctrines. But they had a willing audience in a public which was anxious to end the austerity of the past six years and had been encouraged to believe that the new doctrine of economic growth would enable them to move forward into a world of full employment and a rising standard of living. By one means or another the Government of the day was expected to realize these aspirations as rapidly as possible; and it fell to Bridges to devise the machinery which would enable it to discharge this task. As early as 1942 he had subscribed to the view that, if the machinery of government was to match the problems of the post-war world, it would need to be overhauled well before the war ended. But his approach to the problem was essentially pragmatic—difficult questions, he once wrote, are solved 'by good sense, not by definition'; and he had no enthusiasm for an inquiry on the model of the committee on the machinery of government chaired by Lord Haldane at the end of World War I, purporting to be based on logical principles of administrative methodology, which, if correctly applied, would impose order and coherence on the most in-tractable administrative confusion. He was concerned to produce a ma-chine which would work effectively in the actual conditions of a post-war world as he foresaw them; and his contribution to the deliberations of the committee chaired by Sir John Anderson (later Viscount Waverley), which was established in 1942 to review the machinery of government against the day when peace would return, was determined largely by his realization of the unprecedented scope and nature of the problems which the war would bequeath to the years thereafter. When Bridges took charge of the Government Organization Committee towards the end of 1946, he knew that one of its most urgent tasks would be the construction of integrated administrative machinery capable of formulating the national economic plan proposed by the Labour Government and operating the controls required by that plan within the constraints of Britain's post-war balance of payments and the novel disciplines imposed by the new international economic and commercial order. He brought to the task a fund of massive common sense, combined with an unrivalled knowledge of what the machinery of Whitehall could, and could not, do. And, as he led the public service through the successive economic crises of 1947, it was very clear that he had no equal in promoting the kind of interdepartmental col-laboration which was to play an increasingly important part in post-war administrative history.

But, although he was inevitably concerned with immediate problems for some years after the war, the longer-term future of the public service had its fair share of his attention and concern. He realized, almost in-stinctively, what needed to be done. Professional economists and statist-icians were introduced into the Treasury for the first time; departments were encouraged to draw more readily on scientific advice and to include scientists and technologists among their regular staffs; following on the recommendations of the committee chaired by Ralph Assheton (later Lord Clitheroe), systematic schemes of training for civil servants were intro-duced and their pay and conditions of service were progressively improved; and, within the necessary limits of financial prudence, the Treasury was encouraged to adopt a liberal attitude to its functions of financing the universities and exercising the State's new patronage of the arts. By the time of his retirement in 1956 Bridges had laid the foundations of the public service as it was to be in the second half of the twentieth century; and the achievements of later reforms, notably those recommended by the committee on the Civil Service chaired by Lord Fulton (1966–8), would have been impossible without his pioneering work. In 1964 he published a book on the workings of the Treasury.

If, untypically, Bridges had looked back and tried to evaluate the result of his years in Whitehall, he would certainly have disclaimed any pretension to radical greatness. He was essentially an unassuming man, who disliked the affectation of importance in others as intensely as he would have despised it in himself. He had a great sense of fun and a keen sense of the ridiculous; and he often took an impish delight in deflating the more pompous members of the official community. But it was always done without malice or rancour; and it reflected an impatience with anything that was superficial or irrelevant to the task in hand rather than any assumption of moral or intellectual superiority. His own principles were high and strongly maintained; and the habit of his daily life was simple and unaffected. But he made no attempt to impose his personal views on others; and he ruled Whitehall by example rather than by precept. It was essentially an example of strenuous endeavour. He was a tireless worker, who brought to every task an intense concentration of effort to establish the facts of a situation, to judge the direction in which they pointed, and to ensure that the conclusion of the debate which they had occasioned was promptly and effectively translated into action. His style of administration did not conform with the conventional ideal of an effortless superiority which transacts business from a clear desk by vigorous delegation with the minimum of personal intervention. He was an artist rather than a craftsman; and he established his mastery over his material by immersing himself in it and moulding it to his purpose rather than by subordinating it to any specific technique or expertise. This did not always make for economy of effort; and his light would often be burning in Whitehall long after all others had been extinguished. But he set an example of sustained expenditure of strength and stamina which evoked an instant response from all who worked for him; and the unfaltering leadership which he provided during the darkest days of the war attracted a respect and affection transcending the normal loyalties of Whitehall.

He remained, however, an essentially private individual, who had few close friends outside his family and guarded the intimacy of his personal life very jealously. He retained a devoted memory of his father and spent much of his spare time ordering his letters and papers. But he seldom spoke of him and made no attempt to claim any share in his reputation. The integrity of his own character was his sufficient reward; and the homespun virtue, which he wore like a piece of honest, durable, worsted cloth, was his surest cloak against the wind and weather of the world of public affairs.

Retirement in 1956 brought a change in the pattern of his life but no relaxation in his service to the public interest. He was chairman of the National Institute for Research into Nuclear Energy from 1957, of the Fine Arts Commission from 1957 to 1968, of the British Council from 1959 to 1967, and of the Pilgrim Trust from 1965 to 1968. In 1963 he was appointed to preside over the commission on training in public administration for overseas countries. From 1945 to 1965 he was a member of the governing body of Eton; and he was also much concerned with higher education, being chairman of the board of governors of the London School of Economics and Political Science from 1957 to 1968, chancellor of Reading University in 1959, chairman of the Oxford Historic Buildings Fund in 1957, and from 1960 to 1962 chairman of the commission appointed at Cambridge to study the relationship between the colleges and the university.

Bridges' work was rewarded by many honours. He was appointed GCB (1944), GCVO (1946), privy councillor (1953), baron (1957), and KG (1965). He received honorary degrees from the universities of Oxford, Cambridge, London, Bristol, Leicester, Liverpool, Reading, and Hong Kong; he was elected to a fellowship of the Royal Society in 1952, an honour which gave him particular pleasure; and he was an honorary fellow of All Souls and Magdalen Colleges at Oxford, of the London School of Economics and Political Science, and of the Royal Institution of British Architects.

In 1922 Bridges married Katherine ('Kitty') Dianthe Farrer, daughter of the second Baron Farrer. They had two sons and two daughters. Bridges died at the Royal Surrey County Hospital, Guildford, 27 August 1969, and was succeeded by his elder son, Thomas Edward (born 1927).

A portrait of Bridges by Allan Gwynne-Jones was exhibited at the Royal Academy Summer Exhibition in 1963.

[Lord Bridges in *Action This Day*, ed. Sir John Wheeler-Bennett, 1968; Sir John Winnifrith in *Biographical Memoirs of Fellows of the Royal Society*, vol. xvi, 1970; personal knowledge.]

BURKE TREND

published 1981

BROOK Norman Craven

(1902–1967)

Baron Normanbrook

Secretary of the Cabinet, was born in Bristol 29 April 1902, the son of Frederick Charles Brook, assessor of taxes, and his wife, Annie Smith. He was educated at Wolverhampton Grammar School and Wadham College, Oxford, where he obtained a first in honour moderations in 1923 and a second in *literae humaniores* in 1925; he became an honorary fellow in 1949.

He chose the Civil Service as his career; and from the moment of his entry into the Home Office in 1925 it was clear that he possessed exceptional administrative ability. It was almost inevitable that he should be selected, in 1938, to become principal private secretary to Sir John Anderson (later Viscount Waverley), who was then lord privy seal and later home secretary; the link between the two men which was thus established remained a firm bond in the subsequent years when Brook continued to serve Anderson as his personal assistant when he was lord president of the Council from 1940 to 1942.

The next steps followed logically when Brook became successively one of the deputy secretaries of the Cabinet, with special responsibility for the co-ordination of the civil aspects of the war effort, and (1943–5) permanent secretary of the Ministry of Reconstruction, which was concerned with elaborating, in anticipation of the end of the war, detailed plans for the eventual restoration of the civil life of the country. When Brook became secretary of the Cabinet at the beginning of 1947 in succession to Sir Edward (later Lord) Bridges he was thus in a unique position to observe, for the next sixteen years, the extent to which those plans were brought to fulfilment or were forcibly modified by the series of economic crises which confronted Britain in the post-war years. In 1956 he became joint permanent secretary of the Treasury and head of the Home Civil Service, an office which he combined with that of secretary of the Cabinet until he retired from the public service at the end of 1962.

This bare recital of the successive stages of Brook's career illustrates the common thread which links all of them in a continuous and consistent experience. Each of them was essentially regulatory, rather than innovative, in character; each entailed the reconciliation of multiple and differing views rather than the pursuit of a single, undivided, purpose. It was in the exercise of a function of this kind that Brook excelled. His natural disposition was that of the co-ordinator, seeking to transcend departmental boundaries and to elicit from the conflict of disparate purposes the measure of agreement which would most nearly accord with the basic policy of the government of the day and would be most likely to promote the interests of the country as a whole. All that survives of such work is the final product—the memorandum of proposals as finally submitted to the Cabinet and the record of the Cabinet's subsequent discussion and decision. There is little, if any, evidence of the earlier stages, often difficult and protracted, in which differences of departmental view were laboriously argued out and the conflict of competing claims was gradually reduced, even if not completely resolved. But it was in this area of management that Brook's penetrating intellect and cool judgement were unequalled and commanded a respect which was not accorded to any of his contemporaries.

The skill and patience which he brought to this daily round of painstaking and unspectacular administration sprang from a twofold root. By temperament, he was disciplined and austere; and his classical education reinforced an instinctive belief that dispassionate reason should be capable of reducing the most intractable conflict and confusion to an orderly and acceptable solution. But at a deeper level of conviction he was concerned to defend the concepts of Cabinet government and collective ministerial responsibility as he interpreted them in the context of a system of parliamentary democracy. In such a system a government must so manage its affairs that the Cabinet must be able to present to Parliament, at any moment, a united front against any challenge, whether to their policies as a whole or to the actions of only one of their number. So, and only so, can the liberty of the subject be defended against attack, whether by external aggression or by domestic tyranny. If so, however, the apparatus of central administration must clearly be devised to serve this purpose as efficiently as possible. The refinement of the machinery of government was one of Brook's most dominant concerns. His approach was essentially that of a pragmatist, whose period of office as secretary of the Cabinet covered a time of momentous changes. The great programmes of social and economic reform which were introduced in the years immediately after the war; the construction of the post-war partnership between Europe and the United States of America which found its most significant expression in the North Atlantic Treaty Organization; and the gradual replacement of a colonial Empire by a Commonwealth of independent nations united only by a common acceptance of the British sovereign as its head—all of these carried far-reaching implications for Britain. In each case the major decisions of policy involved were necessarily reserved to the Cabinet as a whole. But a mutiplicity of more detailed questions had inevitably to be delegated to a rather lower level, to a body of committees designed to relieve the Cabinet of as much as possible of the burden of discussion and analysis.

Brook brought clear and concise ideas to the elaboration of the committee system, derived from his experience of its very successful operation during the war, when speed was of the essence of decision. He maintained that a Cabinet committee was invested with executive authority by implied devolution from the Cabinet; and it could, and should, take firm decisions on that basis. But its proceedings should conform to certain principles designed both to protect the Cabinet's own supremacy and to maintain the doctrine of collective responsibility. Its chairman should always, if possible, be a minister who was himself a member of the Cabinet and could judge the point at which the committee should report to senior colleagues, whether for approval or for further instructions. Its membership should be carefully chosen in order to ensure that those departments whose interests were directly engaged should be fully represented but that the committee as a whole should remain sufficiently compact to deal with its business with dispatch. Its discussions should be as thoroughly prepared, as efficiently conducted, and as accurately recorded as those of the Cabinet itself.

To serve the Cabinet and its committees there had to be an effective administrative apparatus, responsible for circulating the relevant papers in good time, for arranging and recording discussions, and for ensuring the prompt and efficient implementation of decisions. The Cabinet Secretariat owed much to the care and time which Brook devoted to these purposes. Always an economical administrator, he was concerned that it should remain small and compact and that its members should be encouraged to work quickly and—as he himself worked—with the minimum expenditure of words. He wrote well and easily, but without great colour or emphasis. His prose was lean and muscular; eschewing rhetoric and emotion; and designed to reduce the most heated and confused exchanges to a record of orderly, logical, objective discussion. This was what was required for the efficient dispatch of government business; and this overriding purpose should not be obscured or obstructed by undue consideration for individual views and personal preferences which were merely ephemeral interest and of no relevance to the final decision.

It was a severe process of redaction; and when the official records are opened future historians and biographers may regret that they are so spare and undramatic in their descriptions of the nature of the major crises of government and the reactions of those who took part in the momentous discussions involved. But in other respects their profession owes Brook a considerable debt. Although the monumental *Official History of the*

Second World War was not finally complete when he retired, the great bulk of it was published during his period of office; and each of its successive volumes, whether in the military or the civil series, passed under his watchful and exacting scrutiny before it was released. Authors and editors alike paid tribute to the generous spirit in which he made time, among many weightier preoccupations, to deal with their problems, to help them with their researches, and to ensure, so far as he could, that their work measured up to his own high standards of historical accuracy.

He was no less helpful to former ministers who wished to publish their memoirs. It was consistent with his basic conviction about the true nature of responsibility in a democratic society that he should vigorously defend the right of those who had been personally and publicly accountable to Parliament to publish their own version of affairs while no less firmly deprecating any corresponding claim by civil servants who had discharged only an advisory function and were constitutionally entitled to expect their ministers to shoulder the blame for failure no less than to accept the credit for success. The criterion of propriety in such matters was already changing in Brook's last years; but however much fashions of literary discretion may change, Brook would certainly have held that the maintenance of a proper balance between public order and personal liberty in a democratic society requires both a generous measure of freedom of speech for those who carry ultimate political responsibility and a reasonable degree of reticence on the part of those whose function is essentially non-political in any party sense.

He brought this concept with him when, in 1956, he became the official head of the Home Civil Service; and in the following years, until his retirement, he was well placed to affirm throughout the whole public service the high standards of professional efficiency and personal integrity which he had maintained when he was the secretary of the Cabinet. But he continued to hold the latter office as well; and the combination of two such exacting responsibilities prevented him from giving to the public service as much attention as he would have wished. He introduced no major reforms in public administration; and when he retired the radical review of the public service which was eventually undertaken by the Fulton commission still lay several years ahead. But he foresaw the tendencies very clearly and he did much, within the existing framework of the Service, to improve its processes of recruitment and training and to modernize its methods of work.

Perhaps his most significant, although also least definable, contribution to the development of the machinery of government was made in a wider field, which was always very close to his heart. For sixteen years he acted as secretary to successive meetings of Commonwealth heads of government and served their members with the same loyalty and efficiency with which he served the members of British governments. He watched the development and enlargement of the modern Commonwealth with keen interest, wasting no time or tears on sentimental regrets for a fading imperial past but seeking strenuously to ensure that the basic community of purpose which had animated the Commonwealth from the outset, together with the relationship of easy and informal friendliness among its members, should not be diluted or destroyed by its progressive enlargement. It was the essence of the Commonwealth, as he envisaged it, that it should have neither constitution nor rules of procedure, that it should take no formal decisions and reach no necessary conclusions. This unique forbearance enabled it, against all reasonable expectations in an age of increasing self-determination, to ventilate differences of view, and not infrequently to reach broad agreement, on issues which would have proved intractable by a more self-conscious and organized procedure; and Brook, as he marshalled its agenda and recorded its debates, could rightly claim that the continuing allegiance which it commanded was perhaps the most eloquent tribute to the principle of free and rational discussion between equal partners to which his own professional life had been dedicated.

His last years were overshadowed by illness; and, although he found that his duties as chairman of governors of the BBC (1964–7) presented administrative problems which to him were novel and intensely interesting, the oversight of an independent corporation, inevitably and rightly concerned with debatable issues, was liable from time to time to take him closer to the area of public controversy than his naturally reticent temperament found wholly congenial. But he strove unremittingly to uphold the standards of propriety and impartiality which his years in Whitehall had instilled so deeply in him.

His appearance reflected his character: correct, sober, and unostentatious, even in moments of leisure and relaxation. He discouraged informality in greeting and address; and his manner was one of rather intimidating reserve. But, as acquaintance deepened into friendship, he revealed himself as a kindly and generous host, with a ready wit and a keen sense of social enjoyment. At home, as at his office, he was essentially the craftsman; and the woodwork which was his favourite hobby was the occasion of many simple jokes about his skill as a Cabinet maker. These he endured with the same slightly impatient tolerance with which he observed the other frailties of mankind.

Brook married in 1929 (Ida) Mary ('Goss'), daughter of Edwyn Alfred Goshawk. She died in 1981. He was appointed CB (1942), KCB (1946), GCB

(1951), and was sworn of the Privy Council in 1953. He was created a baron in 1963. He had no children and the title became extinct when he died in London 15 June 1967.

[Private information; personal knowledge.]

Burke Trend

published 1981

George Alfred

(1914–1985)

Baron George-Brown

Politician, was born 2 September 1914 in Peabody Buildings, Lambeth, London, the elder son and eldest of the four children of George Brown, grocer's packer and later van driver, of London, and his wife, Rosina Harriett Mason. He was educated at Gray Street elementary school and West Square Central School in Southwark. He became a choirboy at the church of St Andrew-By-the-Wardrobe, and in later life remembered Father Sankey, the priest there, and some of his schoolteachers as people who had greatly influenced him. Although his family would not have ranked among the very poorest in London he was, from an early age, acquainted with hardship. This experience, combined with the strong trade-union loyalty of his father and the spiritual element contributed by school and church, produced a man who was to become a champion of the underprivileged and a figure in world politics.

Leaving school at fifteen, Brown became a fur salesman for the John Lewis partnership and then secured a job with the Transport and General Workers' Union. In his spare time he was politically active, especially in the Labour Party League of Youth. In 1937 he married Sophia, a book sewer, daughter of Solomon Levene, bookbinder, and his wife, two outstanding figures in East London Labour politics. There were two daughters of this marriage, and Brown became a grandfather in his early fifties. In 1939 he made his first speech at a Labour Party conference, attacking Sir R. Stafford Cripps. His trade-union work during the war brought him into touch with agricultural workers and George Dallas, a veteran of the Agricultural Workers' Union, helped him to become parliamentary candidate for Belper, for which constituency he was elected in 1945. He became at once parliamentary private secretary to George Isaacs, the

139

minister of labour, and in 1947 was taken on, still as PPS, by E. H. J. N. (later Lord) Dalton, chancellor of the Exchequer. While in this position he became involved in a plot to put Ernest Bevin in the place of C. R. (later Earl) Attlee as prime minister. The plot failed—Bevin himself would have none of it—but in October 1947 Attlee promoted Brown to be a junior minister of agriculture and fisheries. In 1951 the resignation of Aneurin Bevan produced several ministerial changes and George Brown became minister of works in April and a privy councillor. A few months later, however, the defeat of the Labour government moved him to the opposition benches.

The years of opposition, 1951–64, were hard on Labour MPs. Parliamentary salaries were inadequate, and strife within the party created an atmosphere of discouragement. Despite his rapid rise to the front rank, Brown considered leaving Parliament and resuming trade-union work, but financial help from Cecil King of the *Daily Mirror* made it possible for him to stay at Westminster. He was elected to the shadow cabinet and became spokesman on defence. His ability as an administrator and a debater was widely recognized. His style was sometimes elevated by passionate belief, sometimes degraded by ill-temper, so that he accumulated both admirers and enemies. His famous quarrel with the Russian leaders Khrushchev and Bulganin when they were the Labour Party's guests at dinner can be regarded as a sturdy defence of democracy, or an ill-timed discourtesy, or both. In 1960, on the death of Aneurin Bevan, he was elected deputy leader of the Labour Party and firmly supported the leader, Hugh Gaitskell, in the struggle against unilateral nuclear disarmament. On Gaitskell's death in 1963 Brown was deeply disappointed at being defeated (by 144 votes to 103 in the final ballot) by Harold Wilson (later Lord Wilson of Rievaulx) in the election for the leadership: but he set to work to co-operate with Wilson in making plans for the expected Labour government.

Accordingly, Labour's victory in 1964 meant that George Brown became secretary of state for economic affairs, charged with the task of creating a new department which would plan the nation's economy. He was successful in recruiting people of great ability, and a national plan was drawn up which the National Economic Development Council was, with difficulty, persuaded to accept. It was buttressed by a declaration of intent on productivity, prices, and incomes, in which employers and trade unions—again, persuaded with difficulty—accepted the view that incomes and prices depend on productivity and could not be left to conflicting bargaining power. Regional planning councils were set up to work out the application of the plan throughout the country.

In 1966 a sharp balance of payments crisis obliged the government to choose between devaluation of the pound or a stern package of deflationary measures. Brown recognized that deflation would have meant the destruction of much of the work of the new department, but he was overruled by the cabinet. His decision to leave the government, however, was met by an appeal from over 100 Labour MPs and, after piloting through Parliament a measure for the statutory control of prices and incomes, he moved to the Foreign Office in August 1966.

The nineteen months which Brown spent as foreign secretary were packed with difficult problems. He had always followed closely the problems of the Middle East, and, after the 1967 war, was able, with the help of Lord Caradon, to draft the Security Council resolution 242 which set out the principles on which a settlement might be based; but the contending parties refused to put it into practice. He had also taken a keen interest in the approach of the United Kingdom to the European Economic Community; he and Harold Wilson visited all the Community countries, seeking agreement, but were frustrated by General de Gaulle's veto. At one point he seemed close to securing agreement between the USA and the USSR on Vietnam, but this also failed at the last moment. In March 1968 he came into conflict with Harold Wilson, whose conduct of the government seemed to him too autocratic, and the long-suffering prime minister accepted his resignation from the cabinet, which Brown had offered once too often.

His memoirs, entitled *In My Way*, published in 1971, help us to see what he sought to do in the two high offices which he held. In both, he was disappointed in his main objective: but it is noteworthy that innovations which he made in the relations between government and industry, and in the organization of the Foreign Office, have left their mark. His ability was universally recognized, but his explosive temperament, often aggravated by alcohol, hampered his performance.

After his resignation Brown continued, as deputy leader, to work in the Labour Party, and he toured the country vigorously in the 1970 election campaign. It is possible that he did this to the neglect of his own constituency and so contributed to his defeat at Belper. He was then created a life peer, as Lord George-Brown, having changed his surname by deed poll, but his interest in politics declined. In 1972 the University of Milan awarded him the Biancamano prize for his work for Europe, and his efforts for peace in the Middle East were recognized by conferment of the Order of the Cedar of Lebanon (1971). He took up a number of business appointments which involved frequent visits to the Middle East. In 1976 he left the Labour Party after a disagreement on the question of the 'closed shop' and founded a social democratic organization; this however was overshadowed by the Social Democratic Party. By 1980 his health had begun to deteriorate, and he and his family saw less of each other. He went to live in a Cornish village, and, after a lengthy illness, died 2 June 1985 in the Duchy Hospital, Truro, of a liver complaint. Despite the disappointments of his last years he will be remembered as one whose faith and energy did much to raise the Labour Party to influence and power.

[*The Times*, 4 June 1985; George Brown, *In My Way*, 1971 (autobiography); private information; personal knowledge.]

MICHAEL STEWART

published 1990

BUTLER Richard Austen

(1902–1982)

Baron Butler of Saffron Walden

Politician, was born at Attock Serai in the Punjab, India, 9 December 1902, the eldest of a family of two sons and two daughters of (Sir) Montagu Sherard Dawes Butler and his wife, Anne Gertrude Smith. His father, who had passed top into the Indian Civil Service, was a member of a remarkable academic dynasty (since 1794) of Cambridge dons, which included a master of Trinity, two headmasters of Harrow, and one of Haileybury. He later became governor of the Central Provinces and, finally, of the Isle of Man. His mother, warm, sympathetic, and encouraging, and to whom Butler was always devoted, was one of ten talented children of George Smith, CIE, a Scottish teacher, journalist, and editor in India. She was the sister of Sir George Adam Smith.

When Butler was six, he fell from his pony and broke his right arm in three places, an injury which was aggravated by a hot-water bottle burn. The arm never fully recovered, and successful games playing was thus ruled out though he became a keen shot. Returning to be educated in England, Butler attended the Wick preparatory school at Hove. Having rebelled against going to Harrow because of a surfeit of Butlers there and having failed a scholarship for Eton, Butler (by now known as 'Rab' as his father had intended) went to Marlborough. After a final year learning modern languages which were better taught than the classics he had earlier endured, Butler went to France to improve his French with the Diplomatic Service in mind. He won an exhibition to Pembroke College, Cambridge—the money was needed—which after a first class in the modern and medieval languages tripos (1923) was converted into a scholarship. He became secretary of the Union as a Conservative. An unsuccessful love affair and a mainly nervous collapse did not stop him becoming president of the Union (1924). In his fourth year Butler gained a first in history (1925) and a fellowship at Corpus Christi College.

While an undergraduate he had met Sydney Elizabeth Courtauld, a capable, strong-minded girl, who became his wife in April 1926. Her father, Samuel Courtauld, an industrialist, settled £5,000 a year on Butler for life tax free. This financial independence enabled him to decide on a parliamentary career, though his father told him that strong personal executive decisions were not his forte and he should aim for the speakership. While the honeymooners went round the world, the Courtauld family secured for them a fairly safe seat, Saffron Walden in Essex, and on their return Butler was duly selected without the complication of competing candidates. He had a comfortable victory in the general election of 1929 and held the seat until his retirement in 1965. Before the election he had become private secretary to Sir Samuel Hoare (later Viscount Templewood), and he soon became known to the party hierarchy. His first notable public act was a sharp exchange in *The Times* with Harold Macmillan (later the Earl of Stockton), who was advised to seek 'a pastime more suited for his talents' than politics.

In the national government in 1931 Hoare became India secretary and Butler his parliamentary private secretary. At the second Round Table conference, Butler was deeply impressed by M. K. Gandhi, the current hate figure of many Conservatives and of his father. After a tour of India, Butler became Hoare's under-secretary in September 1932. His support of constitutional reform and knowledge of the Indian scene made him a natural choice, even though he had been in Parliament only three and a half years and was easily the youngest member of the government. India was the issue on which (Sir) Winston Churchill was challenging Stanley Baldwin (later Earl Baldwin of Bewdley), and in the Commons Butler compared himself to 'the miserable animal', a bait 'in the form of a bullock or calf tied to a tree awaiting the arrival of the Lord of the Forest'. Yet he was never devoured by Churchill and proved himself Hoare's able lieutenant in defending the India Bill during the fierce two-and-a-half-year war waged against it by the Conservative right wing.

The Butlers had since 1928 lived in the constituency first at Broxted and then at Stansted Hall, Halstead, where their three sons and a daughter were largely brought up, and where in 1935 Baldwin came for the weekend and Churchill was invited. They also had a flat in Wood Street, London, until they moved to 3 Smith Square in 1938. They entertained generously in both London and the country.

Neville Chamberlain's accession to the premiership in May 1937 brought Butler a welcome release from the India Office but not a department of his own. However, his stint as parliamentary secretary at the Ministry of Labour gave him a useful acquaintance with the depressed areas and with mass unemployment. After nine months he went to the Foreign Office as under-secretary of state in February 1938. With the foreign secretary, the first Earl of Halifax, in the House of Lords he was once again prominent—in the long run, indeed, too prominent. The policy of appeasement cut across the Conservative Party much more deeply than India or unemployment, and, when Churchill took over, Butler was on the wrong side of the divide. Appeasement was held against him in a way it was not against those more minor supporters of the Munich agreement, Lord Dunglass (later Lord Home of the Hirsel) and Quintin Hogg (later Lord Hailsham of St Marylebone).

Butler was an enthusiastic Chamberlainite and like Chamberlain regarded Munich not as a means of buying time but as a way of settling differences with Adolf Hitler. He was disposed, however, to interpret Benito Mussolini's invasion of Albania as a general threat to the Balkans, until Chamberlain told him not to be silly and to go home to bed. Butler remained an appeaser down to the outbreak of war, opposing the Polish alliance signed on 25 August 1939 because it would have 'a bad psychological effect on Hitler'. After Chamberlain's fall he, together with Alec Dunglass and two friends, drank to 'the King over the water' and described Churchill as 'the greatest political adventurer of modern times'.

Despite his conspicuous identification with the *ancien régime*, Butler survived Churchill's reconstruction of the government in May 1940. 'I wish you to go on', Churchill told him, 'with your delicate manner of answering parliamentary questions without giving anything away'; the prime minister also expressed appreciation of having been asked to 'Butler's private residence'. The Foreign Office was now a backwater, whose calm was only disturbed by Butler's imprudent conversation about peace with the Swedish minister in June 1940, which Churchill thought might indicate a lukewarm attitude to the war if not defeatism. Bombed out of both Smith Square and his father-in-law's house, Butler went for a time to stay in Belgrave Square with (Sir) Henry Channon, his parliamentary private secretary since 1938.

Butler remained at the Foreign Office against his wishes when Sir Anthony Eden (later the Earl of Avon), whom he did not admire, succeeded Halifax in December 1940. But in July 1941 after nine years as an under-secretary he became president of the Board of Education. Even further removed from the war than the Foreign Office, education was nevertheless a political minefield and had seen no major reform since 1902. Ignoring Churchill's warnings not to stir up either party politics or religious controversy, Butler decided on comprehensive reform. Although in the end he had to exclude the public schools, every child was given the right to free secondary education and, to make that right a reality for the poor, provision was made for the expansion of both nursery and further education and for the raising of the school leaving age. All Butler's formidable diplomatic and political skills were needed to secure the agreement of the churches and the acquiescence of Churchill. The 1944 Education Act was Butler's greatest legislative achievement and was deservedly called after him.

Butler became chairman of the Conservative Party's post-war problems central committee in 1941, and in November 1943 he joined the government's reconstruction committee. The only leading Conservative clearsighted enough to oppose an early election, he became minister of labour in Churchill's 'caretaker' government in May 1945. After the electoral defeat in July—Butler's own majority fell to 1,158—Churchill made him chairman both of the Conservative Research Department and of the highpowered industrial policy committee. From these two positions Butler exerted the major influence in reshaping Conservative policy, and, even more than Macmillan, was chiefly responsible for the civilized conservatism of the post-war party. In 1947 the industrial policy committee produced the *Industrial Charter*, which, Butler later wrote, was 'an assurance, that in the interests of efficiency, full employment, and social security, modern Conservatism would maintain strong central guidance over the operation of the economy'. Mass unemployment was to be a thing of the past; as Butler put it, those who advocated 'creating pools of unemployment should be thrown into them and made to swim'. The right wing regarded Butler's efforts as 'pink socialism', a recurring charge under various names in his later career. He himself believed that, without the rejection of unemployment and the acceptance of the Welfare State, the spectre of the thirties would not be exorcized and the Conservative Party would remain in opposition.

Contrary to the general expectation and his own, Butler became chancellor of the Exchequer in October 1951 and inherited the usual economic crisis. He tackled it by import controls and the resurrection of monetary policy. The cabinet rejected, however, his plan for a floating exchange rate, a decision which Butler both then and later regarded as a fundamental mistake. Butler's first two budgets were popular and successful, expansion and the promotion of enterprise being his general themes, and such was his standing that in September 1952 in the absence of both Churchill and Eden he was left in charge of the government. The same happened for a longer period in the summer of 1953 when, with Eden ill in Boston, Churchill was felled by a stroke. The gravity of Churchill's illness, concealed by his entourage, was known to Butler; this was perhaps the first occasion on which he could have become prime minister had he striven for the job. He had no such thoughts and ran the government well. Since Marlborough, painting had been Butler's chief hobby; after the war he occasionally painted with Churchill, once being commanded by him to 'take the mountains', while his leader would 'take the sea'. Butler thought their paintings were of about the same standard.

At the Treasury Butler, who was one of the two best post-war chancellors, had two special difficulties. Sir Walter Monckton (later Viscount Monckton of Brenchley) had been made minister of labour by Churchill to conciliate the unions, and conciliation entailed conceding excessive wage claims, sometimes in concert with the prime minister and without consulting the chancellor. The second was the Conservatives' pledge to build 300,000 houses a year, which Macmillan, the minister of housing, never allowed the chancellor or the cabinet to forget. In consequence, too many of the nation's resources went into the housing drive. In 1954 Butler's third budget was, as he said, a 'carry-on affair' with few changes, but later in the year he predicted the doubling of the country's standard of living within twenty-five years.

In December 1954 his wife died after a long and painful illness. His grief and the loss of her influence as well as the effects of three gruelling years affected Butler's political judgement. His troubles were in any event growing: inflation and balance of payments difficulties necessitated a 'stop', and in February 1955 Butler raised the bank rate and brought back hire-purchase restrictions. Nevertheless he produced an electioneering budget, taking 6d. off income tax. That was his first mistake. After the election Eden invited him to give up the Treasury, but Butler refused, which was his second mistake. A run on the pound compelled an autumn budget whose unimaginativeness underlined the errors of its predecessor—his third mistake. In December 1955 Eden decided to replace Butler with Macmillan, who showed by his stipulated terms that he was determined also to replace Butler as Eden's heir apparent. Butler consented to become merely lord privy seal and leader of the House—his fourth and biggest mistake. He needed a change, but ministerial power in British politics rests with the big departments and for Butler to allow himself to be left without a department was a gratuitous act of unilateral disarmament.

Though Macmillan was to the left of him on economics, there was no issue on which Butler was, in the eyes of the Conservative Party, seen to be right wing. Many Conservatives saw him as a 'Butskellite'. Hence he was always more popular in the country than in his own party. His appearance was not charismatic, with his damaged arm, his sad, irregular features, and his clothes, described by Channon as 'truly tragic'. But behind it there was a Rolls-Royce mind and a sharp sardonic wit which he enjoyed exerting at the expense of his colleagues. He was the master of many types of ambiguity—'my determination is to support the prime minister in all his difficulties' or 'there is no one whose farewell dinner I would rather have attended'—and occasionally the cause of ambiguity in others. His famous saying that Eden was 'the best prime minister we have' was put to him as a question to which he rashly assented. Butler had a strong vein of innocence, rare in sophisticated politicians. He was also abnormally good-natured and inspired great affection.

Butler was ill when President Nasser of Egypt nationalized the Suez Canal Company in 1956 and was in no danger of being infected by the collective reaction. He missed the first cabinet meeting at which the fatal route to Port Said was mapped and he was not included in the Egypt committee that Eden set up, though he occasionally attended it. His freedom from departmental responsibilities would for once have been an advantage, but cool, detached advice was not what Eden wanted. Over Suez Butler's predicament was acute. Far too intelligent to accept Eden's likening of Nasser to Mussolini, he had nevertheless an 'appeasing' past to live down. Believing that party and public opinion required action of some sort, Butler also believed that Britain should act in accordance with international law.

Hence Butler was in a similar position to John Foster Dulles, the American secretary of state, and was driven to similar deviousness: as the international position altered, different expedients had to be produced to prevent Eden launching an attack on Egypt. But what was permissible in Dulles, trying to divert an ally from folly, looked less so in the cabinet's nominal number two seeking to restrain his leader, sick and unbalanced though Eden was. Butler would probably have done better to state his position unequivocally or to keep quiet or to resign; doubts were not enough. Even so, if he had succeeded, as his phrase went, in keeping Eden 'in a political strait-jacket' he would have done the prime minister and the country a great service. But by October Butler had run out of strait-jackets, and he used the wrong tactics for defeating the Anglo-French-Israeli plan. Instead of joining with Monckton in direct opposition to a grubby conspiracy which was bound to fail, Butler implausibly advocated an open attack on Egypt by the three countries which would have been scarcely less disastrous. After the UN had voted for an emergency force and an Israeli-Egyptian cease-fire seemed imminent, Butler tried to prevent the Anglo-French invasion as it was by then redundant; and when two days later Eden told the cabinet that a cease-fire was essential, Butler like Macmillan strongly supported him.

Butler's deviousness over Suez was honesty itself compared with the duplicity of Eden and some colleagues; and he was more consistent than Macmillan whose fire-eating bellicosity first drove Eden on towards destruction and who then suddenly demanded peace. Yet Butler ended up by pleasing virtually no one, and his varying indiscretions to different back-bench groups gave the impression that he was not playing the game. Others were playing a deeper one.

Eden's retreat to the West Indies to recuperate left Butler to do the salvage work at the head of a weak and divided government. Butler was at his best but gained no credit for limiting damage that he had not caused. Instead he incurred odium for unpopular though necessary decisions, made at Macmillan's insistence, over Britain's unconditional withdrawal from Egypt. In consequence, when Eden finally resigned in January 1957, Butler had no chance of succeeding him. The cabinet voted over-whelmingly for Macmillan, and back-bench soundings gave a similar result. Churchill, too, recommended Macmillan. Eden gave no advice to the Queen: he disliked both men although he preferred Butler. Butler took his defeat well. Macmillan refused him the Foreign Office, and Butler did not insist, accepting the Home Office while remaining leader of the House. At least he now had a department. He also, as under Churchill and Eden, had the government to run from time to time. When Macmillan in 1958 went on his Commonwealth tour after settling his 'little local diffi-culties' over the resignation of his entire Treasury team in January, Butler was left, as he said, 'to hold the baby'. As usual he held it well, and this time was popular. As home secretary he was a reformer, which was less popular.

After the October 1959 election Butler became chairman of the Con-servative Party in addition to being home secretary and leader of the House. Other than demonstrating that there was almost no limit to his capacity for transacting public business—at which he was indeed the unrivalled master—there was little point in Butler's new job. It was in any case scarcely compatible with his existing ones. His leadership of the House entailed trying to get on with the opposition in the Commons, while his chairmanship of the party entailed attacking the opposition in the country. Further, as home secretary, Butler was intent on penal re-form, while many of his party faithful were intent on the return of flogging. However Butler was always adept at squaring circles, and he squared those three. Much more important to him than the acquisition of offices was his wedding, in the presence of the couple's ten children, in October 1959 to a relative by marriage of his late wife, Mollie, widow of Augustine Courtauld, polar explorer, and daughter of Frank Douglas Montgomerie, of Castle Hedingham, Essex. The marriage was strikingly happy and gave Butler renewed strength. He was an outstanding home secretary, making few mistakes in handling a notoriously tricky department and initiating much useful legislation. He beat the flogging lobby and passed a major Criminal Justice Act; he reformed the laws of gambling, public houses, prostitution, and charities; and also passed in 1962 the Bill to curb immigration which had been prepared by Churchill's government and successively deferred.

In October 1961 Butler lost two of his offices, retaining only the Home Office, and was made overseer of the common market negotiations which in practice meant little. In March 1962 Macmillan, tired of the squabbling between the Colonial and Commonwealth Offices, formed a new central Africa department and persuaded Butler to take charge of it. This was a real job, if a thankless one; characteristically, Butler merely added it to his other one. But in the cabinet massacre of July 1962 he lost the Home Office and was left with his central African responsibilities with the honorific title of 'first secretary of state' plus the intimation that he would be serving as deputy prime minister. Macmillan was thus able both to heap burdens on to the good-natured Butler and to strip him of them again almost at will. For nearly all his long parliamentary career Butler had been a minister: this gave him a unique experience of administration but made him too addicted to Whitehall ever to think of withdrawing. He had, too, the character and quality of a great public servant.

Macmillan weakened his government by banishing Butler from the home front. Yet the government gained in Africa. At the Victoria Falls conference in July 1963 Butler achieved the seemingly impossible feat of an orderly dissolution of the Central African Federation without conceding full independence to Southern Rhodesia.

Butler made no attempt to take advantage of Macmillan's considerable troubles in the first half of 1963, and the prime minister's revived fortunes had persuaded him to fight the next election, when his prostate operation altered that decision. Butler was yet again asked to deputize. Yet Macmillan was determined to prevent Butler succeeding him and played an unprecedented part in choosing his own successor. At first he supported Hailsham and then switched to Home. Even more important, he devised a procedure under which he kept control of events. In acquiescing, the leading cabinet ministers, Butler above all, were markedly trusting or negligent. And after fudged consultations with cabinet ministers by the lord chancellor, Lord Dilhorne, who produced an idiosyncratic reading of the results, and with MPs by the whips, some of whom knew the answer they wanted and went on till they got it, and after some apparent refining of the figures by the chief whip, Sir Martin (later Lord) Redmayne, Macmillan adjudged Home the winner.

This decision was leaked on 12 October 1963, the day before Macmillan was to see the Queen. That evening a meeting of cabinet ministers at Enoch Powell's house telephoned Butler urging him to fight. Hailsham did the same very strongly. Butler's response was merely to ask the lord chancellor the next morning to call a meeting of all the leading candidates. Home felt like withdrawing, but was dissuaded by Macmillan who ignored the opposition to his 'compromise' choice and did not change his intended advice to the Queen. Shortly afterwards Home was on his way to the palace where he was asked to see if he could form a government. Even then Butler could have prevailed: both Hailsham and Reginald Maudling had agreed to serve under him, he had much cabinet support, and his wife was urging him on. But his heart was not in the fight, and after reserving his position he became foreign secretary on 20 October. Perhaps, as his father had long ago told him, he could not take strong personal executive decisions. Perhaps, like his old chief in 1940, Halifax, he did not really want the job. More likely he was inhibited by fears of splitting the party; and Home had been a friend since their Chamberlain days. Whatever the truth, his forbearance did not help the Conservatives. The supporters of both Butler and Hailsham thought their man would win the election of 16 October 1964, and both were probably right. Home just lost it. In his farewell message to the party conference, Macmillan hailed the coming into existence of 'the party of our dreams', which accepted a 'pragmatic and sensible compromise between the extremes of collectivism and individualism'; at the very same time he was blocking the man who was at least as responsible as himself for the existence of such a party, thus ensuring that the dream was short-lived. The 1964 election was crucial. A Conservative victory would have consolidated such a party and probably produced a Labour realignment. Defeat led to the later polarization of the parties and an abandonment of Macmillan's 'compromise'.

The rest, politically, was for Butler anticlimax. The job he had wanted in 1957 and 1960 no longer presented much of a challenge. He ran the Foreign Office easily, but had no opportunity or inclination to do anything of note. Had the Conservatives won the election, he would not have been reappointed. Butler was given no part in the election preparations and only a bit part in the election itself, though he gave one rather unfortunate interview. After the election he lost his chairmanship of the Conservative Research Department. Home offered him an earldom which he refused; in 1965 the new prime minister, Harold Wilson (later Lord Wilson of Rievaulx), offered him the mastership of Trinity College, Cambridge, which he accepted. He then accepted a life peerage in 1965 and took his seat on the cross-benches. Butler was the first non-Trinity man to become master for 250 years, and his appointment was at first not wholly welcome in the college. Nevertheless he and his wife were pre-eminently successful there, and in 1972 91 out of 118 fellows present voted for the maximum extension of Butler's term of office. In 1971 he published his autobiography. Lively, wise, and relatively accurate, *The Art of the Possible* was a strong contrast to the multi-volume efforts of Eden and Macmillan and was one of the very few political autobiographies to enhance its author's reputation. This was followed in 1977 by *The Conservatives*, a history of the party, which Butler edited and introduced. In the same year he retired from Trinity.

His son, Adam, was a member of the 1979 Conservative government, but Butler like Macmillan had no great liking for the new Conservative regime. In February 1980 he defeated in the Lords the government's proposal to allow local authorities to charge for school transport, which he saw as a breach of the 1944 Act's promise to provide free secondary education for all. Butler's portrait was painted by Margaret Foreman for the National Portrait Gallery, where he was last seen in public. He finished *The Art of Memory* (1982) which was little more than a footnote to its predecessor and was published after his death. He died 8 March 1982 at his home in Great Yeldham, Halstead, Essex.

Butler was sworn of the Privy Council in 1939, and was appointed CH in 1954 and KG in 1971. He was awarded honorary degrees by thirteen universities (including Oxford and Cambridge, both in 1962), and elected an honorary fellow of Pembroke College, Cambridge, in 1941, Corpus Christi College, Cambridge, in 1952, and St Antony's College, Oxford, in 1957. He was rector of Glasgow University (1956–9), high steward, Cambridge University (1958–66), chancellor of Sheffield University (1960–78), chancellor of Essex University from 1962, and high steward, City of Cambridge, from 1963. He was president of the Modern Language Association and of the National Association of Mental Health from 1946, and of the Royal Society of Literature from 1951. He was given the freedom of Saffron Walden in 1954.

[R. A. Butler, *The Art of the Possible*, 1971, and *The Art of Memory*, 1982 (autobiographies); Anthony Howard, *Rab*, 1987; Molly Butler, *August and Rab*, 1987; Robert Rhodes James (ed.), *Chips, The Diaries of Sir Henry Channon*, 1967; John R. Colville, *The Fringes of Power*, 1985; private information; personal knowledge.]

IAN GILMOUR

published 1990

Sir Henry

(1836–1908)

Prime minister, born at Kelvinside House, Glasgow, on 7 Sept. 1836, was second son, and youngest of the six children of Sir James Campbell, Knt., of Stracathro, co. Forfar, by his wife Janet, daughter of Henry Bannerman, a Manchester manufacturer; her mother's brother was William Motherwell, the Scottish poet. The future prime minister assumed the additional name and arms of Bannerman in 1872 under the will of his maternal uncle, Henry Bannerman, of Hunton Court, near Maidstone, Kent.

Sir Henry's grandfather, James Campbell, came from Inchanoch, in Menteith, to Glasgow in 1805, and began business as a yarn merchant; his second son James (the prime minister's father), then a lad of fifteen, becoming a tailor, and William, his fourth son (afterwards of Tullichewan, co. Dumbarton), a draper. In 1817 these two brothers founded the great Glasgow firm of J. & W. Campbell, wholesale drapers and warehousemen. The father was a strong conservative, stood in that interest as parliamentary candidate for Glasgow in 1837 and in 1841, without success, and as lord provost of Glasgow (1840–3) was knighted on the birth of prince Albert Edward, afterwards King Edward VII (9 Nov. 1841). He bought the estate of Stracathro in 1848.

The elder son, James Alexander Campbell of Stracathro (1825–1908), conservative M.P. for the universities of Glasgow and Aberdeen (1880–1906), succeeded his father in 1876, and was made a privy councillor in 1898. He died on 10 May 1908.

Sir Henry was educated at Glasgow High School, and then at Glasgow University (1851–3), where in 1853, the same year in which Edward Caird, afterwards Master of Balliol, won the Latin medal, he won, among other things, the Cowan gold medal for the best examination in Greek. In 1883 his university, on the installation of John Bright as lord rector, conferred upon him the honorary degree of LL.D., and at the time of his death in 1908 he was liberal nominee for the lord rectorship. From Glasgow he went to Trinity College, Cambridge, where, taking a double degree—as twenty-second senior optime in the mathematical tripos, with a third class in the classical tripos—he graduated B.A. in 1858 and M.A. in 1861. He took no part in the debates at the union. After leaving Cambridge he joined his father and uncle's prosperous business in Glasgow, in which he became and remained a partner until 1868. He was one of the original members of the first Lanarkshire rifle volunteers, and commanded his company (M company, known as 'Campbell's Corps', the members being drawn exclusively from the employees of Messrs. J. & W. Campbell & Co.) at the royal review at Edinburgh on 7 Feb. 1860.

In April 1868 he contested the Stirling Burghs against John Ramsay of Kildalton. Both candidates were liberal, Campbell the more advanced of the two. He declared himself 'a warm adherent of the party of progress', advocating national education, the repeal of university tests, administrative reform of the army and navy, Irish church disestablishment, and land reform. Ramsay defeated him by 565 to 494 votes. He fought Ramsay again at the general election which followed the 1868 Reform Act, and won the seat on 19 November, polling 2192 votes against Ramsay's 1670. He sat for the Stirling Burghs uninterruptedly until his death. His opponent subsequently sat for the Falkirk Burghs from 1874 to 1886.

In the new parliament of 1868 Campbell soon identified himself with the more independent and advanced supporters of Gladstone's first administration, advocating the reform of endowed schools in Scotland, compulsory attendance at parochial schools, the abolition of university tests, the application of the representative principle to county government, the infusion of new blood into Oxford and Cambridge, the abolition of hypothec, and the cause of the tenant farmer. His political ability was recognised by his appointment, in November 1871, as financial secretary to the war office, of which Cardwell was then the head. He retained the post until the fall of the administration in February 1874.

During the years of liberal opposition, from 1874 to 1880, Campbell-Bannerman took little part in general debate, but intervened regularly in the discussion of army votes and the affairs of Scotland. He characterised the bill for the abolition of patronage (1875) as a political device to strengthen the established church at the cost of the other presbyterian churches.

In March 1880 parliament was dissolved, Lord Beaconsfield's government was defeated, and in April Gladstone formed his second administration. Campbell-Bannerman returned to his former post at the war office, of which Childers was then the chief, and he held the office till May 1882. Then, in succession to Sir George Trevelyan, who was transferred to the Irish chief secretaryship on the murder of Lord Frederick Cavendish, he became secretary to the admiralty. Lord Northbrook, the first lord, was in the House of Lords, and Campbell-Bannerman represented the department in the House of Commons. In October 1884, again in succession to Sir George Trevelyan, he was appointed chief secretary for Ireland (without a seat in the cabinet), while Lord Spencer was still lord-lieutenant. The office was one of danger and difficulty, and Campbell-Bannerman was held at the time to be the only man who ever actually enhanced his political reputation by its tenure. He discharged his duties with imperturbability and good humour, and Ireland grew more peaceful. Parnell wrote of him 'as an Irish secretary he left things alone—a sensible thing for an Irish secretary' (see Barry O'Brien's *Life of Parnell*). According to Mr. Tim Healy he 'governed Ireland with Scotch jokes'; Mr. T. P. O'Connor likened him to a 'sandbag'. During his short tenure of the Irish secretaryship it was announced that some provisions of the Crimes Act would be re-enacted, and an Irish land purchase bill was promised; but the life of the government came to an end in June 1885, and Campbell-Bannerman retired from his Irish office after holding it for only eight months.

In February 1886, on the fall of Lord Salisbury's first administration, Campbell-Bannerman became secretary of state for war in Gladstone's third government, entering the cabinet for the first time, together with Lord Herschell, Mr. John, afterwards Viscount, Morley, and Mr. Mundella. Home rule for Ireland, which was the chief measure before the cabinet, met with Campbell-Bannerman's approval. On 8 June the proposals of the government were defeated in the House of Commons by 343 to 313, ninety-three liberals voting against the bill (Morley's *Gladstone*, iii. 341). Gladstone dissolved parliament, was defeated at the polls, and Lord Salisbury accepted office for a second time. For six years (1886–92) the liberal party remained in opposition. During the period Campbell-Bannerman actively supported Gladstone in fighting the cause of Ireland and home rule. In 1887 he moved an amendment to Mr. A. J. Balfour's Irish land bill, to the effect that no bill of the kind was satisfactory which did not provide for revision of the judicial rents. In the course of the Irish controversy he described the process of adopting home rule as 'finding salvation', and he invented the term 'Ulsteria' for the peculiar blend of Orange bigotry and Irish toryism which he imputed to the Irish opponents of home rule.

During the agitation for improved national defence in 1888–9 he maintained a critical attitude, strongly opposing any diminution of civilian control of the army, and any attempt to place that control entirely in the hands of military advisers. In June 1888 he served with Lord Randolph Churchill, W. H. Smith, and others, under the chairmanship of Lord Hartington (afterwards eighth duke of Devonshire), upon the royal commission appointed to inquire into the civil and professional administration of the naval and military departments. The commission reported finally in February 1890 (C. 5979 of 1890), when Campbell-Bannerman, who had been unable to take part in the consideration of the second portion of the report, added a memorandum expressing his general acquiescence in its tenor and his cordial concurrence in its principal recommendation, 'that the secretary of state should be advised by a council of military officers, who should be the heads of several military departments'. He at the same time strongly dissented 'from the further proposal to create a new department—that, namely, of chief of the staff'. He reasoned that the innovation was unnecessary, and likely to re-introduce the evils incidental to the office of commander-in-chief which the new council of general officers was designed to replace (10 Feb. 1890).

Lord Salisbury dissolved parliament in 1892, and his government was defeated at the polls. Thereupon Gladstone formed his fourth adminis-tration (July 1892), and Campbell-Bannerman joined the cabinet in his former post of secretary of state for war. He was a member of the cabinet committee which drafted the second home rule bill, which passed the House of Commons, but was decisively rejected by the House of Lords. When Lord Rosebery succeeded Gladstone as prime minister on 3 March 1894, Campbell-Bannerman retained his office. He was an active admin-istrator. Under his régime at Pall Mall there was established a forty-eight hours week (or an average of eight hours a day) in the ordnance factories at Woolwich Arsenal and he justly anticipated no necessity for 'a reduction in wages' (see *Hansard*, 5 Jan. 1894). He also arranged for the delicate matter of the retirement of the duke of Cambridge from the office of commander-in-chief, and tactfully effected the step without disturbing the good relations which had always existed between the duke and himself. But he doubted the wisdom of offering the duke a special pension which was offered him later by the conservative government, and the duke declined the offer on the ground of this difference of view. On the day of Campbell-Bannerman's announcement of the duke's retirement (21 June 1895) Mr. St. John Brodrick (afterwards secretary of state for war and Viscount Midleton) moved a reduction of Campbell-Bannerman's salary on the ground that the reserves of cordite and other small arm ammu-nition were inadequate. Campbell-Bannerman admitted that the reserves did not exceed 100,000,000 cartridges. The government was defeated by seven votes in a small house, 132 against 125; Lord Rosebery, the prime minister, resigned next day. A lack of harmony between Lord Rosebery and some of his colleagues partly prompted so serious a treatment of the adverse division. Harcourt, in announcing to the House of Commons Lord Rosebery's resignation and the queen's acceptance of it, said: 'The division of last Friday night upon the army vote for the war office was a direct vote of censure upon the secretary of state for the war department, than whom I will take on me to say there is no more able, more respected, or more popular minister.' Campbell-Bannerman received the G.C.B. on leaving office. The adverse vote had little positive justification. As Campbell-Bannerman subsequently explained (cf. speech at Newport, 30 Nov. 1903), expert opinion proved it inexpedient to keep in stock any large supply of cordite, then a new explosive in an experimental stage, which was easily and rapidly manufactured as the need for it arose.

Meanwhile in 1895, when Mr. Peel resigned the speakership of the House of Commons, Campbell-Bannerman frankly confessed to a wish to succeed him. The conservatives were prepared to acquiesce in his selection, in view of his fairness and impartiality. But his colleagues were unwilling to lose him, and he was persuaded to concur in the selection of William Court Gully, Viscount Selby.

Lord Salisbury accepted office on 23 June 1895 and formed an administration. Parliament was dissolved on 8 July, and a majority of 152 was returned to support the new conservative government. Campbell-Bannerman, speaking at Blairgowrie on 12 Dec. as one of the liberal leaders, announced that so long as the Irish declared by constitutional methods that they were in favour of self-government, liberals would be bound to support their demand.

Before the end of the year South African affairs became a predominant political interest. Dr. Jameson's abortive raid into the territory of the Transvaal Republic, and his surrender after two days' fighting at Krugersdorp (1 Jan. 1896), roused in the more advanced section of the liberal party a suspicion that Mr. Chamberlain, the colonial secretary, was implicated in the affair. Campbell-Bannerman, Sir Michael Hicks-Beach, then chancellor of the exchequer, Sir William Harcourt, Henry Labouchere, John Ellis, and others, were, on 14 Aug. 1896, appointed members of a select committee of inquiry into the circumstances of the raid. This South African committee sat to take evidence from January to June 1897. The majority report of 14 July, which was signed by both Campbell-Bannerman and Harcourt, while condemning Cecil Rhodes and two of his associates in general terms, exonerated the imperial and South African governments of all complicity. In the House of Commons both Campbell-Bannerman and Harcourt frankly defended the report when it was impugned by a member of their own party, Mr. Philip Stanhope (afterwards Lord Weardale), whose amendment of dissent was rejected by 333 to seventy-four. A bitter feeling against both Rhodes and Mr. Chamberlain ran high in the left wing of the liberal party, but no other conclusion than that which Campbell-Bannerman and his colleagues reached was justified on a temperate review of the material evidence.

As far back as 1894, when the resignation of Gladstone disclosed differences of opinion within the liberal party, Campbell-Bannerman was named by competent observers as a probable future leader. He had enjoyed much administrative experience, and held alike the peculiar confidence of his colleagues and the esteem and goodwill of the House of Commons. But he had made no impression on the public outside the house, and many of his colleagues stood far higher in popular favour. A continuance of personal dissensions among the leaders of his party during the long unionist régime gradually brought him to the first place. On 6 Oct. 1896 Lord Rosebery resigned his leadership on the ground of 'internal difficulties', the want of 'explicit support' from any quarter, and 'apparent difference with a considerable mass of the party on the Eastern question' (Turkey and Armenia). Thereupon Harcourt naturally succeeded to the leadership. But Lord Rosebery still had his followers in the House of Commons, and Harcourt's authority was often called in question. On 14 Dec. 1898 Harcourt retired from the leadership of a party which he described as 'rent by sectional disputes and personal interests'. Mr. John Morley approved Harcourt's action, and declared 'that he, too, could no longer take an active and responsible part in the formal councils of the heads of the liberal party' (17 Jan. 1899). There seemed to be fundamental divergences of view within the party touching the whole field of foreign, colonial, and Irish politics. In this critical embarrassment the liberal party elected Campbell-Bannerman as its leader in the House of Commons. Lord Kimberley now led the liberals in the House of Lords since the withdrawal of Lord Rosebery. At a meeting held at the Reform Club on 6 Feb. 1899, which was attended by 143 members of parliament, the choice of Campbell-Bannerman was unanimously adopted. The names of Sir Henry Fowler and Mr. Asquith had been previously suggested and had been withdrawn. The new leader promised 'to bring all his powers to his task' and to give 'the government a watchful and active, and not a violent and reckless, opposition'. He still adhered to his home rule convictions, but laid on them a qualified stress. On 21 March, at the meeting of the National Liberal Federation at Hull, he declared that it was impossible to make home rule the first item of the liberal programme, but added 'we will remain true to the Irish people as long as the Irish remain true to themselves.'

The South African policy of Mr. Chamberlain, which culminated in war at the end of 1899, was the first great question with which Campbell-Bannerman in his new capacity had actively to deal. His attitude was from the outset clear and firm; it did not, however, succeed in winning the support of the whole party. On 17 June 1899, in a speech delivered at Ilford, before hostilities broke out, he declared that 'he could see nothing in what had occurred to justify either warlike action or military preparation.' With this view Lord Kimberley, the liberal leader in the House of Lords, associated himself (*Hansard*, 28 July). At the opening of the autumn session (17 Oct.), when the war had just begun, Campbell-Bannerman at once offered to facilitate the grant of supplies 'for the prosecution of the war'. But in speeches at Manchester (14 Nov.) and Birmingham (24 Nov.) he continued to criticise the conduct of the government before the war in mixing up negotiations with military preparations 'in such a manner as to prejudice greatly the chances of a peaceful solution'. After the grave reverses at Stormberg (10 Dec.), Magersfontein (12 Dec.), and Colenso (15 Dec.), Campbell-Bannerman, speaking at Aberdeen (19 Dec.), deprecated 'doubt or despondency', and urged the nation to brace itself 'more earnestly to the task before us'. At the same time he repeated that 'Mr. Chamberlain is mainly answerable for this war.' When the military situation improved next summer, he laid it down as England's first duty to aim, 'after the security of the imperial power', at 'the conciliation and the harmonious co-operation of the two European races in South Africa, and to restore as early as possible' to the conquered states the 'rights of self-government' (Glasgow, 7 Jan. 1900). From this aim he never swerved.

On 25 Sept. 1900 parliament was dissolved, and the country returned Lord Salisbury's government again to power with a majority of 132. The 'khaki' election, as it was called, was won on the plea that the war was finished, and that the government responsible for it should finish their task and be responsible for the settlement after the war. Yet the war dragged on for another twenty months. Throughout this period Campbell-Bannerman consistently advocated conciliatory and definite terms of peace. On 10 Dec. 1901 Lord Rosebery (at Chesterfield) expressed concurrence with him on this point, and Campbell-Bannerman thereupon invited Lord Rosebery anew to co-operate with his former colleagues; but Lord Rosebery preferred an attitude of detachment, and Campbell-Bannerman thenceforth pursued his own line, even at the risk of prolonging existing party dissensions.

On the methods which were adopted in the field during the later stages of the difficult warfare, Campbell-Bannerman declared his views without shrinking. On 6 Dec. 1900, in the House of Commons, he extolled the humanity and the generosity of the British soldier and the British officer, expressing his entire disbelief 'in the stories that have been told on both sides of discreditable, irregular, and cruel outrages'. Subsequently he urged (at Peckham, 7 Aug. 1901) the need of making 'even the stern necessities of war minister to conciliation', and both denounced and promised to 'continue to denounce all this stupid policy of farm-burning, devastation, and the sweeping of women and children into camps'. To this promise he remained faithful, with the emphatic approval of one important section of liberal opinion, and with the no less emphatic disapproval of another important section.

On 31 May 1901, at a liberal meeting in Edinburgh, he had acknowledged the existence of differences in the opposition ranks about the war, but claimed that at any rate they were united, with a few insignificant exceptions, against 'the most unwise as well as the most unworthy policy of enforcing unconditional surrender upon those who were to be their loyal and contented subjects in the new colonies'. A fortnight later (14 June), at a National Reform Union banquet given to Harcourt and himself, he used a phrase which obtained much currency and moved applause and resentment in almost equal measure. The government had lately described the war as 'not yet entirely terminated'. Campbell-Bannerman added the comment, 'A phrase often used is that war is war: but when one came to ask about it one was told that no war was going on—that it was not war. When was a war not a war? When it was carried on by *methods of barbarism* in South Africa.' Three days later (17 June) in the House of Commons he supported Mr. Lloyd George's motion for the adjournment of the house in order to call attention to the concentration camps in South Africa, and while he deprecated the 'imputation of cruelty, or even indifference, to officers or men', he repeated his application to 'the whole system' of the term 'barbarous'. Renewed signs of party discontent followed these deliverances. Mr. Haldane refused to support the motion, and with Mr. Asquith, Sir Edward Grey, Mr. Lawson Walton (afterwards attorney-general), Mr. Robson (afterwards solicitor-general), and nearly fifty liberals, walked out of the house before the division. There seemed a likelihood of an open breach on the part of the dissentient section of the party. On 2 July, speaking at Southampton, Campbell-Bannerman described the position of the party as 'critical'. But on 9 July, at the Reform Club, 163 liberal members of the House of Commons, of all sections, including Sir William Harcourt, Mr. Asquith, and Sir Edward Grey, expressed unanimously continued confidence in Campbell-Bannerman's leadership. Later in the year (25 Oct. 1901) Campbell-Bannerman hopefully appealed to true liberals throughout the country for unity. Passing to another controverted topic, on which there was not universal consent in the liberal ranks, he declared that he was 'as strongly as ever in favour of giving self-government to Ireland'. 'There is no actual alliance', he added, with the Irish party, but he hoped for a cordial co-operation. The declaration checked for a time the movement towards unity. A liberal imperial council had been in existence to maintain within the party the views of Lord Rosebery on imperial and Irish questions. On 27 Feb. 1902 it was decided to reconstitute the council with its old aims as the Liberal League. Campbell-Bannerman saw no reason for such a step (speech, National Liberal Club, 5 March). He denied that there were personal differences among the leaders. The war was a transient interlude, and the only final solution of either the South African or the Irish question lay in the liberal principle of assent. In Lord Spencer, who spoke at Eastbourne on the same day, Campbell-Bannerman found a whole-hearted adherent.

The terms of peace in South Africa were announced on 2 June. On 11 July Lord Salisbury, prime minister, resigned, and on 14 July Campbell-Bannerman in the House of Commons, on behalf of the house as a whole, congratulated Mr. Balfour on filling the vacant place. Through the session he steadily opposed the government's chief measure, the education bill, which he called the bill of the church party. It was finally passed in an autumn session (December 1902), in spite of nonconformist opposition and some dissatisfaction among liberal-unionist supporters of the government. Next year the liberal party's position was immensely improved by a schism which rent the government and its supporters. The healing of internal differences among the liberals was greatly facilitated by the perplexity and division which Mr. Chamberlain's announcement at Birmingham of his new fiscal programme (May 1903) created in the unionist ranks. Without delay Campbell-Bannerman made strategic use of his new opportunity. On the adjournment for the Whitsuntide recess (28 May) he denounced the government for their 'cuttle-fish' policy in raising a new issue, which he characterised on 9 June as a proposal to tax anew the food of the people. He laid stress on Mr. Chamberlain's statement that it was the question on which the next general election was to be fought. In the autumn the resignations of Mr. Chamberlain, Mr. Ritchie, the duke of Devonshire, and other prominent members of the government illustrated practically the disintegrating tendency of the fiscal policy. At Glasgow, on 6 October, Mr. Chamberlain explained his proposals at length, and Campbell-Bannerman, at Bolton (15 Oct.), retorted by denouncing as a wicked slander on the mother country and the colonies alike the assertion that the empire could only be saved from dissolution by a revolution in fiscal policy. On the new free trade issue Lord Rosebery declared that all liberals were united (7 Nov.). Thereupon Campbell-Bannerman renewed his former advances; but Rosebery's reply was very cautious, and no further attempt was made to close the breach between the two.

The reconstructed government's difficulties grew rapidly. At the end of 1903 resolutions were adopted by the Transvaal legislative council for the importation of Chinese indentured labour, and they were sanctioned by the home government. Liberals at once contended that slavery was revived, and the plea found support in the constituencies. Yet henceforth, both in parliament and outside, the paramount political issue was fiscal reform. On that theme Campbell-Bannerman and his colleagues concentrated most of their energy. On 1 Aug. 1904 he moved a vote of censure upon the government, because three members of the government had accepted office in the Tariff Reform League, which advocated preferential duties and therefore the taxation of food. Next year his position was strengthened when the National Union of Conservative and Constitutional Associations at Newcastle formally adopted fiscal reform as a plank in the party platform, and Mr. Balfour's appeal to the party on the same evening to unite on a practical fiscal policy failed to conciliate unionist free traders. Meanwhile on all political topics Campbell-Bannerman was now sedulously defining his position and developing a programme, with a view to the increasing likelihood of the party's return to power. He criticised Arnold-Forster's army reforms (14 July 1904); he advocated the encouragement of small holdings, better security for the farmer, and the provision of cottages (26 Oct.); he urged the payment of members and of election expenses (17 Nov.), and in a speech at Dunfermline (8 Dec.) he discussed comprehensively education, licensing, housing, rating, and the poor law. On two questions he pronounced himself with growing precision and emphasis inside and outside the house, viz. the extravagance of the government and the need of retrenchment in public expenditure, and the curbing of the veto of the House of Lords. He still adhered to 'the policy of thorough and fundamental alteration in the whole system of Irish government'; he was there treading on slippery ground, even on the eve of victory. Differences in the unionist cabinet over Irish administration had given new life to the home rule controversy (March 1905), and the uncompromising restatement by Campbell-Bannerman of his views seemed to threaten a renewal of the old liberal schism. On 23 Nov. 1905 he made at Stirling a plain declaration in favour of home rule. Two days later, on 25 Nov., Lord Rosebery, at Bodmin, said he would not fight under that banner. On 27 Nov. Sir Edward Grey, at Newcastle-under-Lyme, expressed the view that if a liberal majority were obtained at the next general election it would be obtained on other issues than home rule, and it would not be fair to use the votes to reverse the anti-home rule verdict of 1895. This view was assented to by two other prominent liberal leaders, by Mr. Asquith on 28 Nov. and on 30 Nov. by Mr. James Bryce. An accommodation was reached on these lines. For the sake of the unity of the party, Campbell-Bannerman tacitly accepted the understanding that the consideration of home rule was postponed for the present. The proper solution of the Irish question was, Campbell-Bannerman finally declared (12 Jan. 1906), to refer purely Irish affairs to an Irish parliament; but he did not believe there would be any opportunity for such a scheme in the near future.

On Monday, 4 Dec. 1905, Mr. Balfour resigned, and on the following day Campbell-Bannerman was invited to form a government. Lord Kimberley had died in 1902, Harcourt on 1 Oct. 1904. Lord Spencer, Kimberley's successor as leader of the liberal party in the House of Lords, had been generally designated as the next liberal prime minister, but he had fallen seriously ill on 13 Oct. 1905. Campbell-Bannerman's claim as leader of the party in the House of Commons was therefore unquestioned. He brought to the great office imperturbable good temper, a strong sense of humour, personal popularity, much administrative experience and earnest convictions of the advanced liberal stamp. Campbell-Bannerman formed a ministry which was representative of all sections of the party. Mr. Asquith became chancellor of the exchequer and Mr. John Burns was chosen to be president of the local government board, being the first labour member of parliament to receive cabinet rank. In accordance with the rule observed by the liberal government of 1892–5, but discarded by Lord Salisbury and his successor, Mr. Balfour, Campbell-Bannerman made acceptance of office by those invited to join the government conditional on the resignation of all public directorships held by them. Mr. Balfour had already arranged that any new prime minister should be accorded by royal warrant a high place of precedency in ceremonial functions. Hitherto the office had not been formally recognised in the official table of precedency. Accordingly Campbell-Bannerman was the first prime minister to receive this formal recognition, and he was admitted to the fourth place among the king's subjects, the archbishops of Canterbury and York and the lord chancellor alone preceding him.

The new government at once dissolved parliament, and the general election followed in January 1906. Campbell-Bannerman's seat was not contested, owing to his opponent's illness, and he was free to speak elsewhere during the campaign. The main issues which he placed before the electors were free trade and the stopping of Chinese labour, which he had already promised in a speech at the Albert Hall on 21 Dec. 1905. He also undertook to revise drastically the Education and Licensing Acts of the late government. The result of the general election was startling. The unionists suffered a net loss of 214 seats—213 to the liberal and labour parties, and one to the nationalists. Wales did not return a single unionist. Scotland only returned twelve, out of a total of seventy-two members. London (including north and south West Ham and London University— sixty-two seats in all) returned twenty unionists, as compared with fifty-four in 1900. The rout of unionism was complete.

The liberals numbered 377, the labour members 53, and the nationalists 83, while the conservatives were only 132 and the liberal unionists 25. Independently of the Irish party the liberal and labour parties had a majority of 273 over the unionists. Not since the election of 1832, after the first reform bill, when the liberals numbered 486 against 172 conservatives, were the liberals in so strong a position. The first king's speech of Campbell-Bannerman's administration (19 Feb.) promised legislation on most of the lines to which the recent declarations of himself and his colleagues committed them. They pledged themselves at once to a policy of retrenchment and to a new education bill for England and Wales. Without directly raising the home rule issue, they announced undefined plans for associating the people of Ireland with the conduct of Irish affairs. Throughout the session Campbell-Bannerman took an active part in debate. At the outset the procedure of the House of Commons was revised with a view to economising the time of the house, and a Scottish grand committee was set up to deal with Scottish business (9 April). In South African affairs Campbell-Bannerman showed special resolution. While bringing Chinese labour to an end, he boldly insisted on establishing without delay full responsible government in the newly conquered Transvaal and Orange Free State colonies and on revoking the plan of the late government for giving a preliminary trial to a very modified scheme of representative government. The opposition declared this step unduly venturesome, but Campbell-Bannerman carried with him his colleagues and his party. After a committee had gone out to South Africa and had reported on the electoral basis of the constitution to be granted to the two new colonies, he announced the main provisions of the new responsible constitution on 31 July. The three domestic measures which mainly occupied the time of parliament were the education bill for the public control of all public money spent on education and for the abolition of religious tests for teachers, the trades disputes bill for extending the rights of trades unions in trades disputes, and the plural voting bill for disallowing more votes than one to any voter. The discussion of these bills was prolonged through an autumn session. All passed the House of Commons by great majorities, although the trades disputes bill excited misgivings among some supporters who thought the prime minister was making unwise concessions to his labour allies. 'C.-B. seems', wrote the duke of Devonshire, 'prepared to go any lengths.' In the House of Lords all three bills were strongly opposed. The trades disputes bill was freely amended by the lords, but somewhat ironically they abstained from insisting on their amendments, and the bill became law. The plural voting bill was summarily rejected. Much negotiation took place over the lords' amendments to the education bill, but no compromise was reached, and the bill was dropped on the final adherence of the lords to their demand that in all non-provided schools denominational teaching should continue independently of the local authority. In the House of Lords the duke of Devonshire and the bishop of Hereford supported the government. Campbell-Bannerman on 20 Dec. laid the blame for the failure of the bill on Mr. Balfour, and argued that the lords' amendments would perpetuate and extend the very system which the bill was designed to abrogate.

But the action of the lords raised far larger issues than details of the education question. Campbell-Bannerman at the same time as he announced the withdrawal of the education bill charged the upper house with neutralising and thwarting and distorting 'the policy which the electors have shown they approve'. He warned the lords that the resources neither of the British constitution nor of the House of Commons were exhausted, and 'that a way must be found, by which the will of the people, expressed through their elected representatives in this house, will be made to prevail'.

In matters of foreign policy Campbell-Bannerman devoted his efforts to advocating arbitration for the settlement of international disputes, to urging the policy of limiting armaments by negotiation with rival powers, and to encouraging liberal sentiment in foreign countries. On 23 July 1906 there assembled in London the fourteenth inter-parliamentary conference, which was attended by members of the Russian duma, the newly instituted Russian parliament. Before the opening of the conference the duma was dissolved by the Tsar. Campbell-Bannerman, who was present to welcome the conference, referred to the incident in the memorable words 'La duma est morte: vive la duma!' Speaking in the house (5 March 1906), he favoured the two-power naval standard, with the qualification that close alliances with the greatest naval powers might make its maintenance needless. His hopes of reducing armaments were not realised.

In the vacation of 1906 Lady Campbell-Bannerman died at Marienbad, and although the prime-minister's political energy seemed unimpaired during the following autumn session and at the opening of the new session, he never recovered from the blow. The anxiety in which her ill-health had long involved him had intensified the strain of public life. But his sense of public duty was high. When parliament met on 12 Feb. 1907, he repeated his determination to bring the conflict with the lords to a decisive end. The king's speech contained the sentence: 'Serious differences affecting the working of our parliamentary system have arisen from unfortunate differences between the two houses. My ministers have this important subject under consideration with a view to a solution of the difficulty.' A final handling of the problem was, however, postponed. The government prepared to devote their strength to Ireland—to 'measures for further associating the people of Ireland with the management of their domestic affairs'. These words were identical with those used in the former king's speech. The government's hope was to conciliate by a moderate policy those of their party who distrusted a thorough-going policy of home rule. The effort failed. A plan of creating a series of Irish councils was rejected by the Irish members, and was consequently dropped. The prime minister pointed with greater pride to a reduction of nearly 2,000,000*l*. on the navy estimates (5 March). On the eve of the Hague peace conference of May 1907 he contributed to the 'Nation' newspaper an article entitled 'The Hague Conference and the Limitation of Armaments' (*Nation*, 7 March 1907), in which he urged his favourite plea. But the pronouncement excited mistrust in Germany, and on 30 May the German chancellor, Prinz von Bülow, announced that Germany would refuse to discuss at the conference the arrest of armaments.

The session of 1907 bore fruit in Mr. Haldane's army scheme, the Criminal Appeal Act, the Deceased Wife's Sister's Marriage Act, and the Small Holdings Act for England and Wales. Two government bills adopted by the commons, the land values (Scotland) bill and the small landholders (Scotland) bill, were rejected by the lords in August. Meanwhile, Campbell-Bannerman, after three days' debate, carried by 434 to 149 the motion 'That in order to give effect to the will of the people as expressed by their elected representatives, it is necessary that the power of the other house to alter or reject bills passed by this house should be so restricted by law as to secure that within the limits of a single parliament the final decision of the commons shall prevail' (26 June).

There was no autumn session, but Campbell-Bannerman was not free from public business. Speaking in Edinburgh (5 Oct.) he said that the dominant political fact of the day was that the government, though powerful in the House of Commons and in the country, lived on sufferance; and he recapitulated the serious grievances of the commons against the lords. In November the German emperor and empress paid a state visit to King Edward VII, which required Campbell-Bannerman's constant attendance. He left Windsor early on 13 Nov. for a luncheon at the Guildhall in honour of their imperial majesties, and the same evening spoke at the Colston banquet at Bristol. An attack of heart failure took place in the night. Recovery seemed rapid. He presided at several meetings of the cabinet before the end of the month; but acting on medical advice, he spent the next eight weeks at Biarritz (27 Nov. 1907 to 20 Jan. 1908).

On his return journey Campbell-Bannerman stayed a few days in Paris, and had interviews with the prime minister, M. Clemenceau, and M. Pichon, the French foreign minister. He was not in his place in parliament when the session opened on 29 Jan. In the king's speech an announcement of the re-introduction of the two Scottish bills rejected by the House of Lords was the only reminder of the constitutional struggle with the lords. A promise of old age pensions and of an Irish universities bill was the most important item in the government's programme. Campbell-Bannerman came to the house on 4 Feb. to move in vigorous language an address to the king on the assassination of King Carlos and the duke of Braganza, and to express sympathy with the royal family of Portugal. On 12 Feb. he moved the 'guillotine', or an 'allocation of time' motion, providing for the rapid passage through the House of Commons of the two Scottish bills.

He did not reappear in parliament. He had become 'father of the House of Commons' on 22 May 1907, when George Henry Finch, M.P. for Rutland (since 1867), died. He had sat nearly forty years continuously for the Stirling Burghs when his parliamentary career ended.

Campbell-Bannerman stayed at home on 13 and 14 Feb. on grounds of fatigue. On 15 Feb. a sharp attack of influenza supervened, and he never recovered his strength. On 4 March King Edward VII, whose relations with him during his period of office had been very cordial, called to see him before leaving for Biarritz and saw him alone for some time. On 4 April he resigned his office, and was succeeded by Mr. Asquith. He died of heart failure at 9.15 a.m. on 22 April at his official residence, 10 Downing Street. By his own desire he was buried at Meigle, by the side of his wife (28 April), the first part of the service taking place on 27 April in Westminster Abbey. On the same day the House of Commons re-assembled after the Easter vacation, and it adjourned out of respect for him, after impressive tributes had been paid to his memory. Mr. Asquith, his successor, called attention to his modest estimate of himself, to his sensitiveness to human suffering and wrong-doing, to his contempt for victories won in any sphere by mere brute force, and to his almost passionate love of peace, combined with personal courage—'not of a defiant and aggressive type, but calm, patient, persistent, indomitable'. 'He was', Mr. Asquith continued, 'the least cynical of mankind, but no one had a keener eye for the humours and ironies of the political situation. He was a strenuous and uncompromising fighter, a strong party man, but he harboured no resentment. He met both good and evil fortune with the same unclouded brow, the same unruffled temper, the same unshakable confidence in the justice and righteousness of his cause.'

Campbell-Bannerman's career as leader lasted rather more than nine years. At the outset his opportunity, unsought by himself, was due to the withdrawal of senior and more prominent colleagues. He was twice unanimously elected leader.

For seven years in opposition he led his party fearlessly and cheerfully through its darkest days; restoring confidence by his sagacity and determination; turning to good account the errors of his opponents; developing a frankly progressive programme; and finally undertaking without hesitation to form a government in which he successfully combined all the elements of strength in his party. When the time came, his original selection as leader as well as his authority as prime minister were emphatically ratified at the polls by the liberal victory of 1906, which Gladstone's greatest triumphs never approached. The new House of Commons revealed his strong personal popularity with his party; and though his term of office as prime minister ended in little more than two years, it will be memorable for the grant of self-government to South Africa and for his House of Lords policy subsequently embodied in the Parliament Act of 1911.

A man of ample means and many social interests, a good linguist and a born raconteur, he found his chief recreation in European travel, in his books, and in entertaining his friends. It was his habit for many years to spend a portion of the autumn recess at Marienbad for his wife's health. He was not an orator. But as a widely read scholar he was scrupulous and even fastidious in the choice of language, and his speeches, which he carefully prepared, were admirable in form. As a rule he spoke from copious notes. Though this somewhat marred his delivery, he was effective and ready in debate, and a strong and successful platform speaker. His shrewd wit, which was always good humoured, his courage, and sincerity never failed. He was a warm supporter of women's suffrage.

In 1880 he purchased Belmont Castle, near Meigle, which had been the abode of James Steuart Mackenzie, and known as Kirkhill where the bishop of Dunkeld occasionally resided. Campbell-Bannerman thoroughly restored the house, which had been greatly injured by fire while in possession of Lord Wharncliffe, from whom Campbell-Bannerman bought it. In 1907 he was made both hon. D.C.L. of Oxford and hon. LL.D. of Cambridge. He was known familiarly both inside and outside the House of Commons as 'C.-B.'.

In 1860 he married Sarah Charlotte, daughter of Major-general Sir Charles Bruce, K.C.B. Lady Campbell-Bannerman died at Marienbad on 30 Aug. 1906, without issue. She was a woman of great spirit and of fine feeling and discernment, was the constant companion of her husband, and shared all his interests. For many years before her death her health was indifferent, and she lived much in retirement. Campbell-Bannerman's heir was James Hugh Campbell (*b* 1889), grandson of his elder brother.

There are portraits of Campbell-Bannerman in the National Liberal Club, by Mr. John Colin Forbes; in the Reform Club, by Mr. J. H. F. Bacon, A.R.A.; and in the National Portrait Gallery, Edinburgh, by Sir James Guthrie, P.R.S.A.; all were painted while he was prime minister.

A monument to him was voted by parliament. It was placed in Westminster Abbey in 1912; the design includes a bust by Mr. Paul Raphael Montford, who has since been commissioned to execute a full-length statue, to be erected at Stirling.

[Private information; personal knowledge; *The Times*, 23 April 1908; Lucy's *Diaries of Parliament*; Holland's *Duke of Devonshire*, 1911; Hansard's Debates.]

JOHN SINCLAIR

published 1912

Hugh Richard Heathcote Gascoyne-
(1869–1956)

Baron Quickswood

Politician and provost of Eton, was born at Hatfield 14 October 1869, the fifth and youngest son of the third Marquess of Salisbury. Educated at Eton and University College, Oxford, he laid the foundation of a life devoted to Anglican principles and Conservative politics in a family circle and historic house consecrated to both. Tradition has it that before he was seven he had indicted his nurse as a Socinian and admitted that for long he himself had not been quite orthodox.

Equipped with a first class in modern history and a prize fellowship at Hertford (1891), he prepared to take holy orders like his brother William, later bishop of Exeter. Instead he was persuaded to become assistant private secretary to his father, who simultaneously held the offices of prime minister and foreign secretary. This apprenticeship led in 1895 to his election as Conservative member of Parliament for Greenwich, a seat he held until his advocacy of free trade helped to ensure his defeat in the general election of 1906. Religion, nevertheless, remained the mainspring of his life; and even had the tenacity of his Conservative beliefs not deterred him from crossing the floor of the House in the wake of his lifelong friend (Sir) Winston Churchill, the strength of nonconformity in the Liberal Party would no less surely have repelled him from so drastic a change of political faith. So his allegiance rested with the Tories and in 1910 he secured a congenial seat as burgess for the university of Oxford which he retained until 1937. He received an honorary D.C.L. (1924) and was an honorary fellow of Hertford, Keble, and New colleges.

Cecil was perhaps the most accomplished classical orator of his generation. He was handicapped by a frail physique, restless mannerisms, and a voice pitched too high for sonority. But Lord Curzon, himself a majestic exponent of the art of eloquence, was not alone in holding that Cecil's words combined 'the charm of music with the rapture of the seer'. His most memorable speeches were delivered during debates on the education bill in 1902 and on the Welsh Church bill in 1913. The intensity of his beliefs sometimes provoked him to less edifying interventions and the hysterical animosity which he and his friends bore against Asquith for daring to lay hands on the constitution in the Parliament bill of 1911 earned them the style of 'Hughligans'.

Although well past the age of forty and never in robust health, Cecil joined the Royal Flying Corps in 1915. His intrepid manœuvres while learning to fly eventually brought him his pilot's wings—on condition that he never again made a solo flight. In 1918 he was sworn of the Privy Council, an exceptional honour for a back-bench parliamentarian whose independence of mind and reverence for individual liberty unfitted him for the discipline of office.

During the years between the wars his interest was captured increasingly by the Church Assembly, which he had helped to create. As in the Commons, he relished an arena where Christian principles as he saw them could be defended by forensic logic and an artful grasp of procedure. In 1927, however, and again in 1928 he unexpectedly failed to persuade the Commons to accept the revised Prayer Book. Too often in controversy he spoke with the tongue of an ecclesiastical lawyer, not of an angel. The subtle magic of his eloquence fascinated as of old but did not convince; and many who thought themselves no less loyal churchmen than Cecil found his interpretation of Christian doctrine so rigid as almost to exclude the charity of Christ. In 1933–4 he exercised his authority in Anglican affairs by successfully challenging the right of a bishop (A. A. David) to admit Unitarian ministers to the pulpit of a cathedral. A later demand that the Church Assembly should pass a measure prohibiting the use of the marriage service to all divorced persons was overwhelmingly rejected.

In 1936 he was appointed provost of Eton in succession to M. R. James. He delighted in the services in college chapel and as its ordinary would preface his sermons with the words, 'I speak as a layman to laymen without the authority of the priesthood', then go on to be very authoritative indeed. His tall swaying figure surmounted by a green eyeshade, his incisive and often provocative commentary on biblical texts, and his oblique anti-clericalism will all be remembered. So too will his destructive *obiter dicta* on talks to the boys by distinguished visitors. 'I hope I am not boring you', one of them said nervously in the middle of an address. 'Not yet', the provost replied with a tigerish smile. He regarded the war as a vulgar intrusion on well-established routine and scorned to abandon his habit of dining in knee-breeches. As chairman of the governing body he amused some of his colleagues and exasperated others by insisting that under its statutes Eton was responsible only for educating the boys, not for providing air-raid shelters for their protection. The relentless analysis of a medieval schoolman to which he subjected human problems was not always appreciated. But fellows, masters, and boys alike loved him for the ingenuity of his fancy and the felicity of his phrase.

'Linky' Cecil, who had been best man at Churchill's wedding in 1908, was touched when in 1941 the prime minister recommended him for a peerage. He took the title Baron Quickswood but did not often speak in the Lords. Three years later he retired from Eton. 'I go to Bournemouth in lieu of Paradise', he told the assembled school, and there he bore the growing infirmities of age with cheerful courage. His last act before he died there, 10 December 1956, was to dictate a characteristic letter in support of the local Conservative member of Parliament whose political opinions he had not always shared but whose freedom of action he felt to be intolerably threatened by pressure from the constituency association.

Although Cecil never married and had no house of his own until appointed to Eton, he enjoyed unbroken domestic happiness. For most of his life he lived at Hatfield in rooms set aside for his private use. He took his meals, however, with the rest of the family, who readily forgave his unpunctuality in return for the sustained conviviality of his talk. At night he would retire early to read and to meditate. Unhappily he committed little to print except a small volume entitled *Conservatism*, published in the Home University Library in 1912 and embodying a personal creed which remained unchanged to the end of his days. Pageantry and ceremonial appealed to him as reminders of the past. To aesthetic experience, however, he was immune and when a friend once drew his attention to a glorious sunset he replied, 'Yes, extremely tasteful.' Until well into middle age he was an occasional but adventurous rider to hounds. A portrait by Sargent is at Hatfield and another by P. A. de László at Church House, Westminster.

[*Eton College Chronicle*, 7 February 1957; private information.]

KENNETH ROSE

published 1971

CECIL   Robert Arthur Talbot Gascoyne-
(1830–1903)

Third Marquis of Salisbury

Prime minister, the lineal descendant of Robert Cecil, first earl of Salisbury, was born at Hatfield on 3 Feb. 1830. His father, James Brownlow William Gascoyne-Cecil, second marquis (1791–1868), held the offices of lord privy seal and lord president of the council in the conservative administrations of 1852 and 1858 respectively, and assumed by royal licence the surname of Gascoyne before that of Cecil in 1821 on his marriage to Frances Mary, only child and heiress of Bamber Gascoyne (1758–1828), M.P. for Liverpool

1780–96, whose grandfather, Sir Crisp Gascoyne, was lord mayor of London in 1753. Cecil's mother was the friend and frequent correspondent of the first duke of Wellington. Of Cecil's brothers, the elder, James, Viscount Cranborne (1821–1865), who became blind at an early age, was an historical essayist of some power and a member of the Société de l'histoire de France and corresponding member of the Société de l'histoire de Belgique and of the Institut Génevois; and the younger, Lt.-col. Lord Eustace Cecil (*b* 1834), was surveyor-general of the ordnance (M.P. 1865–85) in the conservative administration (1874–80). His elder sister, Lady Mildred, married Alexander Beresford-Hope, member for Cambridge University; the younger, Lady Blanche, married James Maitland Balfour of Whittinghame and was the mother of Mr. Arthur James Balfour, Salisbury's successor in the premiership, of Francis Maitland Balfour, and of Mr. Gerald William Balfour.

Cecil was at Eton from 1840 to 1845, and at Christ Church, Oxford, from 1847 to 1849. At Oxford he obtained the honorary distinction of a fourth class in mathematics. During Michaelmas term 1848 he was secretary and during Easter term 1849 treasurer of the Oxford Union. Subsequently in 1853 he was elected to a fellowship at All Souls College. Private memoranda show that he experienced the impact of the Oxford movement (e.g. 'Every virtue is a narrow mountain ridge with a valley of sin on each side'), though in these notes on religious and ethical subjects (written *c* 1853–4) he maintains throughout a critical and sometimes hostile independence of judgment. After leaving the university he went between July 1851 and May 1853 to Australia—at the time considerably agitated by the recent gold discoveries—and visited the mines near Melbourne. On his return in 1853 he was elected in the conservative interest M.P. for Stamford, which he continued to represent until his succession to the peerage. His election address exhibits the readiness to abide by the *fait accompli* (in this case the abolition of the corn laws) which was one of his most salient characteristics. He made his maiden speech in Parliament on 7 April 1854, opposing the second reading of the Oxford University Bill (which embodied the recommendations of the recent commission) on the ground that endowments ought either to continue to be applied to those purposes for which they had been bestowed or else to revert to the donor's heirs. This speech in defence of property was followed within the year by speeches on religious education and foreign affairs. It was along these three lines of political thought that his mind was principally to travel.

The ability which he had shown led to his being selected on 17 July 1855 on behalf of the opposition to second the previous question after John Arthur Roebuck had moved his famous vote of censure upon the late ministry of Lord Aberdeen, which had been responsible for the conduct of the Crimean war. The previous question was carried. On this occasion Cecil gave indirect support to Palmerston's government. Three years later he was amongst those who combined to defeat the same administration upon its Chinese policy. Palmerston was however returned at the ensuing general election of 1857. In the new parliament Cecil introduced a bill to substitute the use of voting-papers for personal attendance at the polling booths, urging that such a measure would prevent both disorder and intimidation, but the proposal had no success. He also entered upon a vigorous resistance to the abolition of compulsory church rates, which was prolonged until 1868, when, seeing that further opposition was hopeless, he supported the measure in a moderate form (speech, 19 Feb. 1868).

On 11 July 1857 he married Georgina Caroline, the eldest daughter of Sir Edward Hall Alderson, baron of the exchequer, and a woman of great ability. Owing to his father's disapproval of the union, his married life was started on a very limited income, and he was at this time partly dependent upon his pen. He wrote for 'Bentley's Quarterly Review' (1859) and for the 'Saturday Review' (the property of his brother-in-law, Alexander Beresford-Hope) between 1857 and 1865, and in 1860 he began the long series of articles in the 'Quarterly Review'—thirty-three in all—which are perhaps the best mirror of his mind. In 1858 he contributed an article called 'Theories of Parliamentary Reform' to the volume of 'Oxford Essays' for that year. It is remarkable (i.) for its frank recognition of the utilitarian as the only genuine standpoint in modern politics; (ii.) for its definite abandonment of the feudal basis of the older toryism; and (iii.) for the selection of persons of substance as the class whose position and privileges it was the particular business of the conservative party, in the interest of equity, to defend. His distrust of democracy was in fact laid not in any distrust of the poorer classes as such—he regarded them as neither better nor worse than other men (speech in the House of Commons, 27 April 1866)—but in the belief that the law ought not to expose them to predatory temptations, which poverty encouraged and wisdom was not present to resist, nor to strip their more fortunate neighbours of that influence which was the 'single bulwark' of wealth against the weight of numbers. The conclusion therefore was, that 'we must either change enormously or not at all'. Since symmetrical constitutions like that of Sieyès were opposed to human nature, since an educational franchise could not be constructed so as to embody any logical principle, since a wide or 'geographical' franchise imperilled property, the writer expressed himself in favour of leaving things where they were. Reform, however, was in the air, and as soon as Derby took office on the fall of the Palmerston administration in 1858 a reform bill was adumbrated, which Disraeli introduced in the following year with a view to settling the question on conservative lines. Cecil spoke on 21 March 1859 in favour of the clause depriving the forty-shilling freeholder, who voted in a borough, of the vote for the county which he had possessed as well. But the new government fell without being able to carry the measure, and from July 1859 to 1866 the conservatives were once more in opposition.

This period was 'the most interesting stage in Cecil's career' (Traill). Inside Parliament he was making a name by incisive attacks upon the liberal government. He crossed swords with Gladstone both by supporting the action of the House of Lords in refusing to repeal the paper duties (1860–1) and by opposing the taxation of charitable corporations (1863), and it was his motion charging the vice-president of the council with the mutilation of the reports of school-inspectors, which brought about the resignation of Robert Lowe (afterwards Viscount Sherbrooke) in 1864. By his speech of 8 Feb. 1861 on Villiers's motion for a committee to inquire into the relief of the poor he revealed an interest in and knowledge of social problems, and by that of 7 April 1862 a considerable mastery over finance. Outside Parliament his articles in the 'Quarterly Review' were making an effect upon a public opinion still responsive to such influences. Their trenchancy was such that both Russell and Gladstone paid them the compliment of uncomplimentary references (see *Quarterly Review*, July 1860, p. 292, and July 1866, p. 266), and they still constitute a formidable and independent criticism of the conduct of the leaders of both parties during the period as well as a lively review of the problems and politics of the time. Singularly free of literary artifice as well as of literary allusion, seldom if ever attaining any great height of eloquence, their style has long been recognised as a rare model of restrained, pungent, and vigorous English.

The Russell ministry fell in June 1866 owing to the opposition of the whigs and conservatives to their reform bill, and Cecil (who by the death of his elder brother on 14 June 1865 had become Viscount Cranborne and his father's heir) was appointed to the Indian secretaryship in the Derby government and sworn of the privy council (6 July 1866). Within a week of taking office it fell to his lot to bring in the Indian budget, and the ability which he displayed added considerably to his credit. Otherwise his nine months' administration was uneventful. In the counsels of the cabinet, however, he played an important part. The July riot in Hyde Park converted the parliamentary agitation for a reform bill into a popular movement, and Disraeli resolved to anticipate his opponents in giving effect to it. He hoped to do so without losing the support of his more conservative colleagues, and two bills, one to establish in the boroughs a conditional household suffrage, the other a 6*l.* rating franchise, were submitted to the cabinet. On 23 Feb. 1867 Disraeli contrived by a judicious manipulation of statistics to get the more radical measure for household suffrage provisionally accepted by the whole cabinet. During the following day, however, which was Sunday, Cranborne had leisure to examine the figures more particularly, and by the evening had reached the conclusion that he could not support the measure. On the Monday morning he tendered his resignation to Derby, who was to address a party meeting the same afternoon. Peel and Carnarvon followed suit. To avoid a schism the ministry fell back, at the last minute, on the less violent project. But this manœuvre had no success with the House of Commons, and ten days later (4 March) Derby allowed his dissentient colleagues to withdraw, and proceeded with the household suffrage reform bill, which in due course became law, though not until it had been shorn of all its anti-democratic checks. Its passage was the occasion of some of Cranborne's most biting oratory and of the most famous of his 'Quarterly Review' articles—'The Conservative Surrender'—in which he pressed home the great outrage upon political morality committed by the conservative leaders. A private letter (printed in the *Life of Lord Coleridge*, ii. 156) shows that he was near abandoning public life on the ground that his 'opinions were of the past', and that the new constitution should be worked by those who believed in it. In any case the scene of his activities was bound to change, for the death of his father on 12 April 1868 had made him a member of the House of Lords. His last speech in the lower house was delivered on 30 March in opposition to Gladstone's motion for the disestablishment of the Irish Church.

He continued his defence of that church establishment in the upper house, and counselled the lords to reject Gladstone's bill which temporarily suspended the exercise of the Irish crown patronage. This course was taken, and the question referred to the constituencies, which returned a substantial liberal majority. A bill to disestablish the Irish Church was then sent up to the lords. Prior to the general election (speech in House of Lords, 26 June 1868) Salisbury had laid down, in words often quoted since, what he conceived to be the function of the peers in the modern state. They must secure for the country, he said, an opportunity of expressing its 'firm, deliberate, and sustained conviction', whenever that opportunity was denied to it by the lower house. After that opportunity had once been secured, they must abide by the result whichever way it might go. He re-affirmed this doctrine after the general election in an impressive speech, advising them to pass the second reading of the bill (17 June 1869). 'It is no courage', he said, 'it is no dignity to withstand the real opinion of the nation. All that you are doing thereby is to delay an inevitable issue—for all history teaches us that no nation was ever thus induced to revoke its decision—and to invite besides a period of disturbance, discontent, and possibly of worse than discontent.' In the ensuing division he went so far as to vote for the bill, which was passed. Difficulties, however, arose between the two houses in respect to the lords' amendments, but these were eventually overcome, mainly by the exertions of Archbishop Tait, but to some extent by his own (*Life of Tait*, chap. 19).

Towards the two other great Acts of this Parliament—the Irish Land Act and the Education Act of 1870—he showed a spirit of benevolent criticism and amendment, and his severest language was reserved for Gladstone's arbitrary abolition of army purchase. That step would produce, he said characteristically, not (as Cardwell had claimed) 'seniority tempered by selection' but 'stagnation tempered by jobbery'. His other activities included the introduction of a measure in March 1869 to carry over into the succeeding session bills which had been passed in one house and had lacked time to reach the other, as well as of a limited owners improvements bill, designed, in the interest of cottagers, to shift the financial burdens of administering an estate from the life-tenant to the corpus of the property. He failed, however, to carry either of them; nor did Russell's life peerage bill, which he supported, fare any better. He was equally unsuccessful in his resistance to the Universities Tests Abolition Act in 1871, and the lords, who on his advice had inserted in the bill a clause imposing a pledge on tutors, deans, and divinity lecturers to teach nothing contrary to the teaching of the Old and New Testaments, did not insist upon this amendment. A special importance attached to his opinion, as on 12 Nov. 1869 he had been elected to the chancellorship of Oxford University, vacant through Derby's death. He held that dignified office for his life, but took little active part in the university's affairs. In 1876 he made an unsuccessful attempt to get rid of 'idle fellowships'. At his instigation the universities' commissions were appointed in 1877, and on their recommendation important changes were introduced into academic organisation. One reform limited the tenure of prize fellowships to seven years. Salisbury, however, though he approved the report of the commissioners, held aloof from university contentions.

His activities were, indeed, by no means confined to politics. On 16 Jan. 1868 he had been elected to the chairmanship of the Great Eastern railway, which he retained until 1872, and under a special act of parliament he became during part of 1871–2, in conjunction with Lord Cairns (who afterwards bore witness to the admirable character of his work), arbitrator of the disordered affairs of the London, Chatham and Dover Railway Co. But in spite of his political pessimism and discouragement, political interests remained dominant in his nature. In October 1869 he had contributed a striking article to the 'Quarterly' on 'The Past and the

Future of Conservative Policy'. He started from the thesis that the religious motive in politics, which has hitherto repressed the class motive, had passed away with the struggle over the Irish Church. The contest of the future would be a contest about material things. The new electorate was incontestably liberal. The conservatives therefore could not look for power at all and only for office on the same ignoble terms as those upon which they had obtained it for three short periods during the previous twenty years—that is to say, by allying themselves with the radicals to the discomfiture of the whigs. They would do better to look to nothing but their character and be guided by no rule except that 'of strict fidelity to conviction'.

The diagnosis seemed plausible, but it was nevertheless to prove false. The liberal ascendancy could not survive five years of drastic legislation, and Disraeli returned to office in Feb. 1874. Salisbury resumed his place at the India office—an event which caused some surprise, as his relations with the leader of his party had long been of the coldest nature. In the later years of the administration these became, however, much more cordial, and Salisbury paid a sympathetic tribute to Beaconsfield on the occasion of the latter's death on 19 April 1881. His conviction and commonsense had, meanwhile, been brought once more into contrast with the opportunism of the prime minister on the introduction of the public worship regulation bill (1874), when Disraeli played upon the protestant sentiment of the country and took occasion to describe his colleague, who had shown a just appreciation of the futility of the proposed measure, as 'a great master of gibes and flouts and jeers'. It was in criticising this bill that Salisbury defined his conception of the Church of England, over whose establishment and privileges he was ever on the guard. 'There are', he said, 'three schools in the church, which I might designate by other names, but which I prefer to call the sacramental, the emotional, and the philosophical. ... They arise, not from any difference in the truth itself, but because the truth must necessarily assume different tints as it is refracted through the different media of various minds. But it is upon the frank and loyal tolerance of these schools that the existence of your establishment depends.'

At the India office Salisbury's administration was marked by his refusal to check the export of corn during the famine in Bengal, contrary to the advice of the lieut.-governor, Sir George Campbell. 'The difficulty', he told the House of Lords, was 'not to procure grain but to bring the supplies to the houses of the starving population.' The event justified his policy. In this case Lord Northbrook, the governor-general, had seen eye to eye with him, but there was a difference of opinion between them about the advisability of appointing a mixed commission to try the Gaikwar of Baroda, which Northbrook aggravated by altering some of the customs duties without reference to the secretary of state. Afghan frontier policy proved a more serious source of friction. Northbrook belonged to the old 'Lawrence' school of administrators, who were satisfied with the existing northwest frontier, and desired to avoid interference with the Amir. Salisbury, on the other hand, was of opinion that 'a diplomatic invasion' of Afghanistan by Russia was taking place, and must be resisted by the establishment of a British agent at Herat. This 'forward policy' was inaugurated by Lytton, who replaced Northbrook in April 1876. Salisbury defended it, as well as his personal integrity in respect of it, in a speech in the House of Lords on 10 Dec. 1878. Of a Russian military invasion of India he made light, advising one who feared it 'to use large maps' (11 June 1877). But he maintained that, unless we took our precautions, there was a danger that the Russians might at some convenient moment prompt the Afghans to embarrass us upon the frontier:—'Russia can offer to the Afghans the loot of India; we, if we desired to make a competing offer, can promise nothing—because there is nothing in Turkestan to loot' (*Quarterly Review*, April 1881, p. 548).

It was not, however, from the India office that he was principally to oppose Russian designs and to win in the Tsar's eyes the character of being 'l'ennemi acharné de la Russie' (*Life of Lord Randolph Churchill*, p. 719). The Eastern question, owing to a rebellion attended by Turkish atrocities in Bulgaria and the adjacent provinces, had become acute in 1876, and a conference between the great powers was arranged to meet in Constantinople. Salisbury was sent out in December as British plenipotentiary. His purpose was to secure so far as possible both the integrity of Turkey and the safety of its Christian subjects. Instead of any occupation of Bulgaria by Russia he brought the Powers to agree upon the appointment of an international commission to re-organise the territory with the support of six thousand Belgian troops, in the intention of placing it, together with Bosnia and the Herzegovina, under the control of governors nominated by the Sultan and approved by the Concert. To these terms, however, the Porte obstinately and unexpectedly refused its assent, and Salisbury returned to England in the end of Jan. 1877. War between Russia and Turkey followed in April, and the Russians were within reach of Constantinople by the end of the year. On 6 Dec. Cranbrook records in his diary, 'Salisbury is bent upon England having a share, if there should be a break up in the East, and evidently has no desire that Turkey should stand.' The treaty of San Stefano (3 March 1878), however, put Russia clearly in the wrong, inasmuch as it was a violation of the integrity of Turkey, guaranteed by England, France, and Austria in 1856. The British government accordingly required all the terms of that armistice to be submitted to a

European conference. The Russian reply reserved to Russia the right of excluding from discussion whatever clauses of the treaty it chose. This brought the two Powers to the brink of war, and Derby, who was constitutionally unprepared for that contingency, resigned the foreign secretaryship, under some misapprehension, however, as to the exact intentions of his colleagues, which resulted in a regrettable passage at arms in the House of Lords with his successor (see *Life of Lord Cranbrook*, ii. 77). Salisbury was appointed to the vacant office on 1 April 1878. His qualifications for filling it included, besides his recent mission to Constantinople, a prolonged study of foreign affairs, of which the evidence is to be found as well in early speeches (e.g. House of Commons, 7 June 1855) as in some of his articles contributed to the 'Quarterly Review' ['Lord Castlereagh' (Jan. 1862); 'Poland' (April 1863); 'The Danish Duchies' (Jan. 1864); 'Foreign Policy' (April 1864)]. He brought to his work a clear conception both of the character and aim of English diplomacy, which is best stated in his own language. 'In our foreign policy', he said at Stamford in 1865, 'what we have to do is simply to perform our own part with honour; to abstain from a meddling diplomacy; to uphold England's honour steadily and fearlessly and always to be rather prone to let action go along with words than to let it lag behind them' (Pulling's *Life and Speeches of Lord Salisbury*, i. 68). Five years before (*Quarterly Review*, April 1860, p. 528) he had approved (in contrast to the then existing policy of non-interference) the 'traditional' part which England had played in Europe—'England did not meddle with other nations' doings when they concerned her not. But she recognised the necessity of an equilibrium and the value of a public law among the states of Europe. When a great Power abused its superiority by encroaching on the frontier of its weaker neighbours, she looked on their cause as her cause and on their danger as the forerunner of her own.'

It was in accordance with these precepts that a day after (2 April 1878) he took over the foreign office he issued the 'Salisbury Circular', requiring that all the articles of the treaty of San Stefano should be submitted to the proposed conference, declaring emphatically against the creation of a 'big' Bulgaria, and arguing that, even though the Turkish concessions to Russia might be tolerated individually, taken together they constituted a serious menace to Europe. One of Salisbury's successors at the foreign office has pointed to this despatch as the masterpiece of Salisbury's diplomatic work (Lord Rosebery, speech at the Oxford Union, 14 Nov. 1904). It is at any rate remarkable for its promptitude, its lucidity, and its firmness, and it undoubtedly secured for the government a large measure of public support. England was clearly in earnest, and subsequent secret negotiations between Salisbury and Shuvalov, the Russian ambassador, resulted in an agreement to divide the proposed province into two parts—that south of the Balkans to be administered by a Christian governor, nominated by the Sultan. Through the treachery of Charles Thomas Marvin, a foreign office copyist, the terms of this agreement appeared in the 'Globe' newspaper, and Salisbury's denial in the House of Lords of the authenticity of the statements, thus disclosed at a momentous diplomatic crisis, is the most debatable incident in a singularly honourable career. The secret convention with Russia, balanced by the 'Cyprus' convention with Turkey, secured the semblance of a diplomatic success for England at Berlin, and Salisbury, who in company with Lord Beaconsfield, the prime minister, represented this country at the congress (13 June–13 July 1878), returned bringing in the famous phrase 'peace with honour'. His services were rewarded with the garter, almost the only distinction which he was ever induced to accept (30 July 1878). A well-known epigram of Bismarck—'The old Jew means business, but his colleague is lath painted to look like iron'—may have strengthened the idea that Salisbury was at this time something of a tool in the hands of his chief. It is unlikely, however, that, when the diplomatic history of this period comes to be more fully told, this verdict will be endorsed.

The principal provisions of the treaty of Berlin were that the Slavonic settlement of the Eastern question, embodied in the idea of a 'big Bulgaria', should be abandoned; that Austria, for which Salisbury, like his diplomatic model, Castlereagh, entertained a peculiar regard, should be entrusted—and this was done at his particular instance—with the administration of Bosnia and the Herzegovina; that Russia, who obtained Batum (together with Kars and Ardahan), should make of it 'a free port, essentially commercial'. The Cyprus convention transferred to England the protectorate of that island, so long as Russia retained the cities just named and on the understanding that if the Porte carried out the reforms desired in Armenia England should guarantee its Asiatic dominions. It is evident, therefore, if the history of the last thirty years be interrogated, that the diplomacy of 1878, whatever its immediate merit, has produced no lasting triumph. The cession of Cyprus did not result in any immunity of the Armenians from Turkish misgovernment, nor even, as was perhaps dreamed of, in the creation of an English sphere of influence in the Euphrates valley: the Russian port of Batum has been closed and fortified: Bosnia and the Herzegovina were annexed by Austria with the utmost cynicism when at length in 1908 the opportunity offered: and Bulgaria and Eastern Roumelia were united by Prince Alexander in 1885, if not actually with Salisbury's *post factum* approval, at least without any active resistance on his part; though, as he was careful to point out (Newport speech, 7 Oct. 1885), the Bulgaria thus formed was not the 'big Bulgaria' of the San

Stefano treaty, nor was it evolved under Russian influences. About the underlying principle of the English policy—the maintenance of Turkey— he was himself eighteen years later, in the height of the Armenian atrocities, to encourage the gravest doubt. The defence of the Berlin Treaty, he told the House of Lords on 19 Jan. 1897, lay in its traditional character, not in its inherent excellence. 'The parting of the ways was in 1853, when the Emperor Nicholas's proposals were rejected. Many members of this house will keenly feel the nature of the mistake that was made, when I say that we put all our money upon the wrong horse. It may be in the experience of those that have done the same thing, that it is not very easy to withdraw from a step of this kind, when it has once been taken, and that you are practically obliged to go on. All that Lord Beaconsfield did was to carry out the policy which his predecessors had laid down. I am acquainted with Lord Beaconsfield's thoughts at that time; he was not free from misgiving; but he felt that the unity of the policy in this great country was something so essential, and that the danger of shifting from one policy to another without perfectly seeing all the results to which you would come was so paramount, that he always said that the policy of Lord Palmerston must be upheld. He still entertained hopes, which I did not entertain in quite the same degree. But those hopes have not been justified.'

The brilliant effect of the Berlin Congress was even more evanescent than its provisions. Two years later the conservatives were put in a minority by the election of 1880. Beaconsfield only survived his defeat by about a year, and at his death (19 April 1881) Salisbury was chosen (9 May) to lead the opposition in the House of Lords, Sir Stafford Northcote continuing to do so in the House of Commons, and the party being left without any recognised leader in the country. The years of this 'dual control' are perhaps the least effective of Salisbury's life. His great ability was not yet fully realised, and he had still to make himself a name for sagacity and moderation. Irish questions, involving the larger issue of interference with the established rights of property, were dominant, and much of his activity was devoted to opposing the Irish legislation of the government, represented by the land bill of 1881 and the arrears bill of 1882, which he did with partial success by means of amendments instead of open resistance. To the bill of 1884 introducing household suffrage in the counties he only offered opposition contingent on the refusal of the government to make public the complementary redistribution of seats bill. A compromise, which involved a constitutional innovation, was however eventually arrived at. Salisbury and Northcote were taken into counsel by the ministry, and, to the profound indignation of some members of the conservative party, their leaders privately negotiated the provisions of a redistribution bill, on the understanding that the House of Lords would pass the franchise bill (extending the vote to nearly twice as many persons as was done in 1867), without forcing an appeal to the country.

The domestic policy of the liberals was not easy to attack from any popular standpoint, but their conduct of affairs in the Sudan, in Egypt, in Afghanistan, and in Ireland gave Salisbury the opportunity for trenchant criticism. Northcote, on the other hand, as Lord Randolph Churchill was at pains to show, possessed little aptitude for turning occasion to advantage, and when the government fell on 12 June 1885, Salisbury, who had been Beaconsfield's choice (*Life of Lord Cranbrook*, ii. 149), and during the last year had been more and more taking the lead (*ibid.* p. 215) was summoned by the queen. With reluctance he accepted office on 23 June. He was embarrassed as well by his unwillingness to take precedence of Northcote as by Churchill's refusal to serve, if Northcote retained the leadership in the commons, but the pressure put on him by the queen, by the party itself (*Life of Lord Randolph Churchill*, p. 332), and by the exigencies of the political situation (*Life of Sir Stafford Northcote*, ii. 210) overcame his disinclination. He decided to take the foreign office himself, thus associating it with the premiership for the first time since it had been a distinct office. To Northcote, who went to the House of Lords as earl of Iddesleigh, he made over the post of first lord of the treasury, which had hitherto gone with that of prime minister. Sir Michael Hicks Beach became leader of the House of Commons.

With the assistance of Lord Dufferin, the Indian viceroy, Salisbury carried forward the Afghan frontier negotiations, which had been interrupted by the Penjdeh incident. All danger of war with Russia was removed by the protocol of 10 Sept. 1885, securing the Zulfikar pass to the Amir, though the final delimitation of the boundary between the Hari Rud and the Oxus was not completed until the treaty of St. Petersburg in July 1887. The eastern frontier of India was similarly secured against French influences by the annexation of Burmah. Other activities included the raising of a long-delayed Egyptian loan and, by a curious irony, the diplomatic support of Prince Alexander's action in uniting Eastern Roumelia to Bulgaria. Salisbury's foreign policy appeared very able to his contemporaries. Cranbrook thought it had secured a European reputation to its author, and Gladstone said that he could not object to one item in it (*Life of Lord Cranbrook*, ii. 239).

In Parliament Salisbury promoted and passed a bill for the housing of the working classes (based upon the report of a commission for which he had moved on 22 Feb. 1884), by which landlords were penalised for letting insanitary tenements and the local government board empowered to pull down dwellings unfit for habitation. It was a type of the only kind of ordinary legislation in which he really believed [... 'Those matters on which parties do not contend we hold ... to be so far from objectionable that they and they alone are the proper work of Parliament, and that it is detained from its normal labours by the perpetual intrusion of revolutionary projects' (*Quarterly Review*, Oct. 1873, p. 556)]. There is no dispute as to its salutary effect upon urban slums.

More sensational matter, however, occupied the public mind, as Ireland continued to be in a state of unrest. Salisbury dealt with the question at some length on 7 Oct. 1885 at Newport, and from the elaborate disquisition on local government which the speech contains it has been argued that his mind was at this time oscillating towards a home rule policy. This passage of the speech is, however, followed by an explicit repudiation of the federative principle in connection with Ireland, and in his private correspondence there is nothing to show that he ever contemplated anything more than the measure of Irish local government which in fact he afterwards granted. Any shadow of plausibility which the charge possesses is derived solely from the fact that Carnarvon, the lord-lieutenant of Ireland, had (with his previous assent and subsequent approval, but without the knowledge of the cabinet) held a secret conversation with Parnell in which, according to Parnell's but not Carnarvon's account, Carnarvon used words favourable to an extensive measure of home rule.

The general election of December 1885 left the Irish the real masters of the field, since neither side could retain office without their aid. In the course of the next month Gladstone matured his home rule convictions, thus attracting the Irish vote at the same time that the conservatives, contrary to the wishes of Carnarvon, whose resignation was, however, made in accordance with a previous understanding on grounds of health, were repelling it by the project of a coercion bill. The government was defeated on 27 Jan. 1886 and Salisbury resigned on the 28th. Gladstone resumed office, and introduced his first home rule bill in the following April, but the conservatives, materially aided by the secession of Hartington, John Bright, and Mr. Joseph Chamberlain, effected its defeat on 8 June. Parliament was dissolved, and the question referred to the country. In strong contrast to Gladstone's sentimental appeal for justice to Ireland Salisbury had declared (15 May 1886, speech at Union of Conservative Associations) for 'twenty years of resolute government', introducing this statement of policy with the ill-judged remark, not to be forgotten or forgiven, that some races, like the Hottentots and the Hindus, were unfit for self-government. The electorate returned a majority of 118 for the maintenance of the union. In the hope of including liberal-unionists in the administration, Salisbury expressed his readiness to leave the premiership to Hartington, but the offer was declined. He therefore took office on 26 July 1886, and formed a conservative ministry dependent on a unionist majority. He himself became first lord of the treasury; Iddesleigh foreign secretary under his supervision; and Lord Randolph Churchill, chancellor of the exchequer and, through Sir Michael Hicks Beach's self-abnegation, leader of the House of Commons. Churchill, whose speeches were perfectly attuned to the ear of the new electorate, and who by virtue of them had become the best known of the unionist leaders, was not slow to try conclusions with the premier. He had already, in 1884, made a vigorous though, on the whole, unsuccessful attack upon his chiefs with the view of democratising the party organisation, and his attitude had facilitated the passage of the franchise bill through the commons. In the next year he had made his power felt by compelling the withdrawal of Northcote to the House of Lords, and he now took exception to Iddesleigh's foreign policy, threatening to resign unless the military estimates which that policy necessitated were reduced. Deeper differences lay in the antagonism between the spirit of the new tory democracy, of which Churchill was the exponent, and that of the old conservatism of opinion and method, which Salisbury represented. The prime minister made no effort to retain his rebellious lieutenant at the price of concession, and Churchill left the government in December 1886. Salisbury, after again ineffectually offering to serve under Hartington, induced George Joachim (afterwards Lord) Goschen to fill the breach and take the exchequer, and in the ensuing shuffle of places, necessitated by the transfer to W. H. Smith of the treasury with the leadership of the house (*Life of Lord Cranbrook*, ii. 273), himself took the foreign office, a little brusquely, out of Iddesleigh's hands into his own. It must be remembered, however, that Iddesleigh had volunteered to resign, and had refused any other office.

Subsequent events showed that the cabinet had disliked Churchill's dictation more than his policy. Not only the service estimates of Goschen's budget, but the greatest legislative achievement of the administration (the Local Government Act, 1888) and the new Closure Act regulating parliamentary procedure were framed in accordance with his ideas. But the prime minister, even though he had in his own department been content with less interference in the Near East than had commended itself to Iddesleigh, could never be induced to recall him (*Life of Lord Randolph Churchill*, p. 776).

More lasting interest attaches to Salisbury's African policy. By granting a royal charter to the British East Africa Co. (1888), lately founded by Sir William Mackinnon, he recovered for England the hold over the upper sources of the Nile which Iddesleigh by an agreement with Germany in

1886 had nearly lost. It was not, however, until 1890 that, after the fall of Bismarck, the Kaiser relinquished any claim to this region and to Uganda, and acknowledged a British protectorate over Zanzibar. In return for this Salisbury gave up Heligoland and, to the dismay of constitutional theorists, invited the consent of parliament to the surrender (see Anson's *Law and Custom*, ii. 299). It was characteristic of his diplomacy that he never regarded concessions—'graceful concessions', as his critics called them—as a heavy price to pay for a good understanding, and there is little doubt that, in the belief that the Triple Alliance furnished the best guarantee for European peace, his policy was at this time governed by the idea of a good understanding with Germany. But beyond a good understanding he was not disposed to go. Like all the great English foreign ministers from Wolsey downwards, he saw that England's true function and strength consisted in maintaining the balance of power. The charter granted to the British East Africa Company was followed in 1889 by one in favour of the British South Africa Company which, under the guidance of Cecil Rhodes, was to colonise what is now Rhodesia. This occasioned trouble with the Portuguese, who raised a shadowy claim to Matabeleland. Salisbury sent an ultimatum to Lisbon, requiring their withdrawal from the British sphere of influence. Portugal was obliged to yield, and shortly afterwards a treaty delimiting the frontiers of Rhodesia was concluded. Trouble had also arisen with France in the same region in 1888, but in 1890 the French protectorate in Madagascar was acknowledged by England in return for a recognition of the English protectorate in Zanzibar. At the same time the British sphere of influence in Bornu was admitted and the French were compensated with the sands of the Sahara. It is plain that here, as well as in respect of the agreements with Germany and Portugal, British diplomacy had got the best of the bargain, and these bloodless African settlements are probably the most enduring monument of Salisbury's skill.

To return to home affairs. In 1888 the prime minister himself introduced in the House of Lords a life peerage bill, empowering the crown to create fifty peers for life, selected from the superior ranks of judges, officers in the army and navy, civil servants, and diplomatists as well as from among ex-colonial governors. The bill passed its second reading, but was then withdrawn. In 1891 the government passed a Free Education Act, which Salisbury had foreshadowed in 1885 (Newport speech), when he argued that since the state had made education compulsory, it was not fair that the very poor should have to find the money for it. But it was neither by this non-controversial act nor by that introducing local government in 1888 that the government was judged. It had been constituted upon the Irish issue, and Irish affairs played a conspicuous part in its history. The appointment of the Parnell commission Salisbury supported on the ground that it was most nearly analogous to the practice adopted by the House of Commons in respect of exceptional cases of bribery and some other matters (speech in the House of Lords, 10 August 1888). The discretion which Mr. Balfour showed in defending the Crimes Act of 1887, and the indiscretion which brought Parnell into the divorce court in 1890, enabled the ministry to fulfil its natural term of office.

At the general election of 1892, however, Gladstone was returned with a coalition majority of forty, and Salisbury gave place to the liberal leader. Gladstone introduced his second home rule bill, which, on Salisbury's advice, was rejected by the House of Lords. The new government retained office, however, under Lord Rosebery's leadership, until its defeat in 1895, when Salisbury formed a coalition ministry with Devonshire and Mr. Chamberlain (June 1895). At the ensuing general election he secured a majority of 152, and the country, in accordance with his ideas, entered upon a seven-year period of singularly unobtrusive but not unimportant legislation, which included such measures as the Workmen's Compensation Act (1897), the Criminal Evidence Act (1898), and the Inebriates Act (1898) (see for a useful list of laws passed Mee, *Lord Salisbury*, Appendix II). His special activities, however, lay at the foreign office, which he again combined with the premiership. Between 1895 and 1900 England found herself on the brink of war with each of the four great powers of the world, but no war occurred. The first crisis was produced by President Cleveland, who in his message to the United States Congress on 17 Dec. 1895 declared that Salisbury's refusal to agree to arbitration in the matter of the boundary between British Guiana and Venezuela amounted to a violation of the Monroe doctrine, and asked leave to appoint a boundary commission, whose finding should be enforced by the Republic. Salisbury took no immediate notice of this intemperate action, which roused American feeling to fever-point, but, when the clamour began to subside, supplied to the United States Commission, without prejudice, papers setting out the British case. That case was in fact so strong that the international tribunal, which in the end determined the dispute, decided almost wholly in its favour. A reaction in favour of England had meanwhile set in in America. Salisbury was careful to encourage it, by refusing to consent to European intervention in the Spanish-American war of 1898; thus reversing the traditional English policy of keeping Cuba out of the hands of a first-class power. He spared no effort to bring about a good understanding between the two Anglo-Saxon communities. Even though his project of a general treaty of arbitration was thrown out by the United States Senate in 1897, he continued to manifest goodwill by the surrender of the British rights in Samoa, including the harbour of Pago-Pago in 1899, while by the abrogation (Hay-Pauncefote treaty, 1901) of that part of the Clayton-Bulwer treaty of 1850 which stood in the way of a canal at Panama under American control, he allowed the United States to strengthen further their dominant influence over Central America.

The crisis in Anglo-German relations was destined to leave more durable memories. Within three weeks of Cleveland's message (on 3 Jan. 1896) the German Emperor despatched a telegram to President Kruger of the South African Republic congratulating him in imprudent language on the suppression of the Jameson Raid. English feeling rose high, but Salisbury contented himself with a naval demonstration in home waters which was probably so calculated as to produce an effect also in America.

At the close of the next year he suffered in the Far East what were perhaps the only considerable diplomatic reverses in his career. He was not able to prevent either the Germans from acquiring from China the lease of Kiao-Chau or Russia that of Port Arthur in 1897; nor was he prepared to resent the Russian representation that the presence of two British ships at the latter harbour, where they had a treaty right to be, had 'produced a bad impression at St. Petersburg'. Wei-hai-wei, which he secured for England as a set-off against these cessions to Russia and Germany, has admittedly proved to be a place of no strategic value. On the commercial side, however, his policy was successful. He checked the attempt of Russia to secure exclusive trading rights—in violation of the Treaty of Tientsin (1858)—within her recognised sphere of influence in Manchuria, and he obtained an undertaking from China not to alienate the Valley of the Yangtse, where British interests pre-eminently lay. This insistence upon the policy of the open door was followed by a very remarkable development of British enterprise in China.

His Far-Eastern policy, besides, must not be viewed alone. A dispute with France was already on the horizon. Early in 1897 a French expedition under Major Marchand had left the Congo, and the French flag was planted at Fashoda on the Upper Nile in July 1898. From this place Sir Herbert (Lord) Kitchener dislodged it shortly after the battle of Omdurman. The action was deeply resented in France, but Salisbury declined any compromise, and boldly faced the likelihood of war. The French eventually gave way, and relinquished any claims in the Sudan by the declaration of 21 March 1899. It is significant of Salisbury's far-sightedness that a secret agreement with Germany about Portuguese Africa was being concluded, when Marchand was discovered at Fashoda.

His most characteristic work is however to be found in his Near-Eastern policy. In 1897 the Armenian massacres had aroused great indignation, which was fostered by Gladstone. Salisbury, however, was not to be moved. He fully admitted the legitimacy of the feeling against Turkish rule; he solemnly warned the Sultan of the ultimate fate of misgoverned countries; but he steadily maintained that to endanger the peace of Europe for the sake of avenging the Armenians was not to be thought of. Hence he declined to act without the approval of the greater Powers—of the 'Concert of Europe', an expression which in his time became very familiar. And though nothing was effected in Armenia, the use of this cumbrous instrument of diplomacy was vindicated in Crete, where, after the Greco-Turkish war of 1897, an autonomous constitution was established in 1899 by the pressure which the Concert under his leadership brought to bear upon the Porte. His support of arbitration was of a piece with his support of the Concert, and the English deputation to the Hague Conference, which followed upon the Tsar's Rescript (1899), proved perhaps the most efficient of those sent to it.

Meanwhile events in South Africa had brought England into open war with the Boer republics there, as a result of long pending disputes between the Boer rulers and British settlers. It was something of an irony that the largest army England had ever assembled should have been put into the field under the administration of a man who so earnestly laboured for peace. But to the charge that he ever wavered in his belief in the justice and necessity of the South African war he returned an indignant denial (speech at Albert Hall, 7 May 1902). He firmly refused to entertain any idea of foreign mediation (statement in the House of Lords, 15 March 1900), and his diplomacy was probably never more skilful than during that period of acute European Anglophobia. But his pre-occupation with foreign affairs had necessarily restricted his activity as prime minister, and at the re-constitution of the ministry in Nov. 1900, after the 'khaki' election of that year had confirmed him in power by a majority of 134, he took the sinecure post of lord privy seal and resigned the foreign office to Lord Lansdowne, retaining, however, a special supervision over its business so that the Anglo-Japanese Treaty of 1902 was concluded under his eye. His health had been failing for some time, but he regarded it as a matter of duty to retain the premiership until the war was finished. During that interval Queen Victoria died on 22 Jan. 1901. His personal devotion to her had been one of the deepest springs of his energy, and she had compared him with Peel and spoken of him as a greater man than Disraeli (Boyd-Carpenter, *Some Pages of my Life*, p. 236). He was closely associated with some of the leading events in the great movement which gave lustre to the latter part of her reign. The Royal Titles Act making her Empress of India had been carried during his tenure of the India office. Both her jubilees fell within his premierships. The first Colonial Conference in 1887 was inaugurated under his administration. The ideal of pacific imperialism was one which he endeavoured to impress upon his countrymen, and with which he believed the future of his country to be closely bound up, though with characteristic caution he deprecated any factitious attempt to quicken or consolidate imperial sentiment. Almost his last public utterance (Albert Hall, 7 May 1902) was a warning not to hurry the affections of the mother-country and her daughter states. 'They will go on', he told his audience, with a touch of mysticism very seldom to be found in his language, 'in their own power, in their own irresistible power, and I have no doubt they will leave combinations behind them which will cast into the shade all the glories that the British Empire has hitherto displayed. But we cannot safely interfere by legislative action with the natural development of our relations with our daughter countries. . . . There is nothing more dangerous than to force a decision before a decision is ready, and therefore to produce feelings of discontent, feelings of difficulty, which, if we will only wait, will of themselves bring about the results we desire.'

Peace was concluded with the Boers on 31 May 1902, and on 11 July he tendered his resignation. He had regarded it as a matter of public duty to see the war ended, and would thus, but for King Edward's illness, have attended the coronation ceremony of that year. His premiership had lasted through a total period of thirteen years and ten months, a tenure exceeding in duration by sixteen months that of Gladstone. On his recommendation his place as prime minister was filled by his nephew, Mr. A. J. Balfour, already first lord of the treasury and leader of the House of Commons. Salisbury died at Hatfield, a year after his retirement, on 22 Aug. 1903. In accordance with his wishes he was buried beside his wife (20 Nov. 1899) to the east of Hatfield church; in this last point, as throughout his life, avoiding publicity so far as he was able. Parliament voted a monument to him in Westminster Abbey.

Owing to his great reserve, his character, so lovable to those few who knew him well, remained to the end something of an enigma to his countrymen. They were sensible of a sort of massive wisdom in his presence, and they came to trust him completely, because he was so evidently indifferent to all the baser allurements of place and power. But they hardly realised either the large simplicity of his nature or the profundity of his religion. His life, it was said, had been 'a consecrated one'. Each day at Hatfield was in fact begun in the chapel. The very deep belief in the greatness of goodness, which appears in his tribute to Dr. Pusey (speech at Arlington Street, 17 Nov. 1882), and in his constant insistence upon the superiority of character over intellect, was fortified as well as balanced by a very keen perception of the impenetrable mystery of the universe. He was to the end of his life, as his library and laboratory bore witness, a close student of science as well as of theology. These, though dominant and, as it sometimes seemed during his lifetime, conflicting interests, were curiously blended in the address on 'Evolution' which, as president of the British Association, he delivered at Oxford in 1894. He shows himself there as jealous for the honour of science that no guesses, however plausible, should be taken for solid proof of the theory of natural selection, as, for the honour of theology, that nothing should be allowed to overthrow the argument from design. The address (although one at least of its principal arguments—that correlating the antiquity of man with the rate of the cooling of the earth's crust—is no longer in date) exhibits a wide range of reading and reflection just as the brilliant article on 'Photography' (*Quarterly Rev.* Oct. 1864) exhibits great power of lucid exposition and of practical foresight, but it must nevertheless remain doubtful whether he possessed any real talent for original scientific work. The article 'On Spectral Lines of Low Temperature' (*Philos. Mag.* xlv. 1873, pp. 241–5) does not make for an affirmative conclusion. His early bent was towards chemistry, but he became much interested in electricity later in life.

Theology, science, and history filled his leisure moments. There seemed to be no inclination for any of the thousand forms of recreation which men ordinarily affect. He was accustomed to pass part of the year near the sea, sometimes at Walmer, which came to him in 1895 with the lord wardenship of the Cinque Ports, more usually at his villa in France, first at Puys near Dieppe and afterwards at Beaulieu on the Riviera. He was an interested observer of French developments and a careful student of French thought; his keen taste in literature made him a reader of the finely cut work of Mérimée and Feuillet. Yet no man was less of a doctrinaire. He considered questions on their merits, not in the light of *a priori* ideas. Politics, as he said, speaking on the question of hostile tariffs, were no exact science (speech at Dumfries, 21 Oct. 1884). He was all in favour of promising experiments, provided they were undertaken with caution. His mind was, indeed, of the broad English pattern; he enjoyed the poetry of Pope; he possessed an English contempt for the impracticable. The unfailing resolve to keep within the limits of the actual and the possible was, it has been said, at the root of the most familiar of his characteristics—his so-called cynicism—if cynicism be 'the parching-up of a subject by the application to it of a wit so dry as to be bitter' (Lord Rosebery, speech at the Oxford Union, 14 Nov. 1904). But also his cynicism was a continual protest against sentiment, for he dreaded more than all things the least touch of cant.

It is of a piece with this that the note of passion is wanting in his eloquence, for his emotion, instinctively repressed, seldom stirs the polished surface of his language. No great passage of oratory, no vivid imaginative phrase, keeps green the memory of his speeches. It is something of a satire upon this master of satire, that he is best remembered by certain casual and caustic comments, which criticism denominated 'blazing indiscretions'. His diplomatic caution and his extreme courtesy seemed to slacken in his public speeches, and he occasionally expressed himself before popular audiences with a humour as reckless as it was shrewd; not that he was, as was sometimes alleged, a blue-blooded aristocrat of the traditional type, but that he cordially detested all the plausible manœuvres by which party-managers set themselves to catch the vote of an electorate. He regarded democracy as inimical to individual freedom. A belief in letting men alone to develop their own thoughts and characters was native to his nature and at the heart of his creed. His relations with his colleagues, like his relations with his children, were characterised by this intense dislike of interfering with others. His conservatism itself rested upon the old conviction that by means of well-contrived checks and balances our ancestors had provided for the utmost possible freedom of the subject compatible with the maintenance of society. He desired to see the state just and not generous. And though his mind was too tenacious of experience, too intensely practical to allow of his making any very original contribution to conservative theory, his presentment of that theory was singularly penetrating. Whilst he saw 'the test-point of conservatism' in the maintenance of an hereditary second chamber (*Quarterly Rev.* July 1860, p. 281) he found 'the central doctrine of conservatism' in the belief 'that it is better to endure almost any political evil than to risk a breach of the historic continuity of government' (*ib.* Oct. 1873, p. 544). In regulating the franchise, he maintained that only a material and not any spiritual nor philosophic conception of the state was in point, and he vindicated the analogy between the state and a joint-stock company with singular ingenuity by an appeal to 'natural rights'. 'The best test of natural right is the right which mankind, left to themselves to regulate their own concerns, naturally admit' (*ib.* April 1864, p. 266). He was thus the inveterate enemy of the alliance of 'philosophy and poverty' against 'property'. He believed that the remedy for existing discontents—so far as they were susceptible of remedy at all—lay in the encouragement of forces diametrically opposed to free thought and legislative confiscation—that is in dogmatic religion and in production stimulated by security. He was a merciless querist of the radical idea of progress (*ib.* 'Disintegration', Oct. 1883, p. 575). After the more definite conservatism of his youth had become a lost cause, he urged the need of restoring 'not laws or arrangements that have passed away, but the earlier spirit of our institutions, which modern theory and crotchet have driven out. ... The object of our party is not and ought not to be simply to keep things as they are. In the first place the enterprise is impossible. In the next place there is much in our present mode of thought and action which it is highly undesirable to conserve. What we require in the administration of public affairs, whether in the executive or legislative department, is that spirit of the old constitution which held the nation together as a whole, and levelled its united force at objects of national import instead of splitting it into a bundle of unfriendly and distrustful fragments.'

Above all things, then, he was a patriot. His conservatism, trenchant and thorough as it was, merged in a larger devotion to his country. The bitterest moment of his career (1867), when public life seemed to be slipping from his grasp, evoked the loftiest of his utterances: 'It is the duty of every Englishman and of every English party to accept a political defeat cordially and to lend their best endeavours to secure the success, or to neutralise the evil, of the principles to which they have been forced to succumb. England has committed many mistakes as a nation in the course of her history; but their mischief has often been more than corrected by the heartiness with which after each great struggle victors and vanquished have forgotten their former battles, and have combined together to lead the new policy to its best results' (*ib.* Oct. 1867, p. 535). Here was the secret spring of his greatness, and it enabled him to hold back the forces he feared for a full decade. For, though his special talent lay in the sphere of foreign affairs, he ranks with the greatest of prime ministers. He thrice led his party to decisive victory at the polls, and held the first place in the state for a longer period than any prime minister of the nineteenth century save one, Lord Liverpool. He retired in the enjoyment of the unabated confidence of the country. For seven years he held a coalition together in office, though the combination had shown symptoms of splitting before his ministry was formed (*Life of the Duke of Devonshire*, ii. 267–9), and a split at once followed the withdrawal of his influence. In all his nearly fourteen years of office only one member of his cabinets resigned on principle, and this was a man constitutionally unfit for cabinet government. Curiously enough it is Lord Randolph Churchill's son who has drawn attention to Salisbury's exceptional capacity for managing that machine (Winston Churchill's *Life of Lord Randolph Churchill*, p. 602).

In his relations with the rank and file of his party Salisbury was perhaps less successful. Though he was a most considerate host, society bored him; the ready word, the genial interest in unknown men's endeavour were not his to give; and he was frequently charged with availing himself too exclusively of the ability that lay close at hand. For all that something akin to reverence was felt for his person and his opinion. Like Pitt, one of the two statesmen on whom he formed himself, he seemed towards the end to move in an atmosphere of splendid aloofness from common cares and aims. Yet it is rather to the character which he drew of

Castlereagh that the student of his life and work will turn for a concluding sentence: 'He was that rare phenomenon—a practical man of the highest order, who yet did not by that fact forfeit his title to be considered a man of genius.'

Among the honours bestowed on him he received, besides the Garter, the G.C.V.O. from King Edward VII on 22 July 1902. He was lord warden of the Cinque Ports and constable of Dover Castle from 1895 (installed 15 Aug. 1896); one of the Elder Brethren of Trinity House; high steward of Westminster and Great Yarmouth; and from 1868 to 1876 chairman of the Hertfordshire quarter sessions. Academic distinctions included a D.C.L. at Oxford (1869), a LL.D. at Cambridge (1888), and an hon. studentship of Christ Church (1894).

There are portraits of him (1) by G. Richmond (1872) at Hatfield, of which there is a replica at All Souls' College, Oxford; and (2) by the same artist (1887) at Windsor; (3) by Millais (1882) in the possession of the Hon. W. F. D. Smith; (4) by Watts (1884) at the National Portrait Gallery; (5) by Sir H. von Herkomer (1893) at the Carlton Club; and (6) by Anton von Werner as a study for the head in the picture of the Berlin Congress painted for the German Emperor. This portrait is in the possession of the present marquis of Salisbury. There is also in Lord Salisbury's possession a well-known crayon head by Richmond, which was done between 1865 and 1868. A statue of him by Sir G. Frampton stands just outside Hatfield Park gates, and another by Mr. H. Hampton at the foreign office. Both of these are posthumous. In the last year of his life he sat for the bust, by Sir G. Frampton, now in the debating hall of the Oxford Union Society. There is also a bust of him by W. Theed, jun. (1875), at Hatfield House. The monument near the west door of Westminster Abbey was designed by Mr. Goscombe John, who is now (1912) executing one for Hatfield church.

Of his sons, the present Lord Salisbury, who succeeded to the title, has been under-secretary of state for foreign affairs (1900–3), lord privy seal (1903–5), and president of the board of trade (1905); Lord William, the rector of Hatfield, is an hon. canon of St. Albans and chaplain to the King; Lord Robert, a K.C. and M.P. (1906–10 and 1911); Lord Edward, D.S.O., is under-secretary for finance in Egypt; Lord Hugh has been M.P. for Oxford University since 1910.

[Pending the appearance of the authoritative *Life of Salisbury* by Lady Gwendolen Cecil, that by H. D. Traill (1890), though it closes in 1886, remains the best. S. H. Jeyes's *Life and Times of the Marquis of Salisbury* (4 vols. 1895–6) carries the story up to 1895. F. S. Pulling's *Life and Speeches of the Marquis of Salisbury* (2 vols. 1885) and H. W. Lucy's *Speeches of the Marquis of Salisbury* (1885) will also be found useful. *The Third Salisbury Administration*, by H. Whates (1900), gives a full account of the activities of his government between 1895 and 1900. There are numerous other lives of him of no great value, among which that by F. D. How (1902) may be mentioned. Scattered references to his work and character appear in the biographies of his colleagues and contemporaries, viz. in those of Lord Cranbrook (Hon. A. E. Gathorne-Hardy), Lord Iddesleigh (Andrew Lang), Lord Randolph Churchill (W. S. Churchill), Bishop Wilberforce (R. Wilberforce), Duke of Devonshire (B. Holland), and Mr. Alfred Austin's Autobiography.

The two most suggestive things that have appeared about him are Lord Rosebery's tribute at the unveiling of his bust at the Oxford Union (14 Nov. 1904) and an anonymous article signed 'X' in the *Monthly Review*, Oct. 1903. The latter, which is of an intimate character, was written by Lord Robert Cecil, K.C. In the *Quarterly Review* Oct. 1902 and Jan. 1904 are articles dealing respectively with his foreign policy and with his connection with the *Review*. The student will, however, find in Salisbury's own contributions to that periodical, of which a complete list is subjoined, the most valuable of all the sources of information about him. These contributions were:—1860: April, The Budget and the Reform Bill; July, The Conservative Reaction; Oct., Competitive Examinations. 1861: Jan., The Income Tax and its Rivals; April, Lord Stanhope's Life of Pitt, i. and ii.; July, Democracy on its Trial; Oct., Church Rates. 1862: Jan., Lord Castlereagh; April, Lord Stanhope's Life of Pitt, iii. and iv.; July, The Bicentenary; Oct., The Confederate Struggle and Recognition. 1863: Jan., Four Years of a Reforming Administration; *April, Poland. 1864: *Jan., The Danish Duchies; *April, The Foreign Policy of England; July, The House of Commons; Oct., Photography. 1865: Jan., The United States as an Example; April, Parliamentary Reform; July, The Church in her Relations to Political Parties; The Elections. 1866: Jan., The Coming Session; April, The Reform Bill; July, The Change of Ministry. 1867: Oct., The Conservative Surrender. 1869: Oct., The Past and the Future of Conservative Policy. 1870: Oct., The Terms of Peace. 1871: Jan., Political Lessons of the War; Oct., The Commune and the Internationale. 1872: Oct., The Position of Parties. 1873: Oct., The Programme of the Radicals. 1881: April, Ministerial Embarrassments. 1883: Oct., Disintegration.

The three articles marked * were republished in 1905 in a volume as 'Essays: Foreign Politics'.]

ALGERNON CECIL

published 1912

CHAMBERLAIN (Arthur) Neville
(1869–1940)

Statesman, was the youngest of three members of his family who, in two successive generations, played great parts at the highest level of British statesmanship. He was born at Edgbaston, Birmingham, 18 March 1869, the only son of Joseph Chamberlain, by his second wife, Florence, daughter of Timothy Kenrick, of Birmingham. His half-brother (Sir Joseph) Austen Chamberlain, being set apart for a political career, passed from Rugby to Cambridge. Neville, who was to go into business, returned home from Rugby and took commercial courses at Mason College, which was afterwards converted into Birmingham University. There he studied metallurgy and engineering design. From Mason College he entered the office of a firm of accountants where his mental alertness and quick mastery of financial problems were soon noted.

In 1890 Joseph Chamberlain bought 20,000 acres on the island of Andros in the Bahamas where he was advised that sisal could be profitably grown. There Neville went at the age of twenty-one (November 1890) to take charge of the development of the estate. For seven years he planned and toiled in the attempt to bring the enterprise to success. It was a life of extreme hardship, and all in vain: the soil was too thin for the crop. In the complete social isolation of those years, he found comfort in books, reading steadily and well in history, biography, and science. While his character was strengthened, the extreme loneliness of the life must have intensified the natural shyness and reserve which handicapped him for a time when he entered public life.

Back at Birmingham in 1897, Chamberlain began the business career which for many years absorbed all his energies. Although he then had no ambition for a parliamentary career, he was an ardent politician with a lively interest in local public affairs. No one could be of the household of Joseph Chamberlain and remain indifferent to the problems of government or to the individual's civic responsibilities. But his father and brother were fully occupied by their public duties and, after the loss of precious time in the Bahamas, Neville felt that he must concentrate on business until he had established an independent position. He soon became one of the outstanding figures in the industrial life of Birmingham and took an active part in the proceedings of the influential chamber of commerce. At the same time his lifelong interest in health questions was stimulated by work for the General Hospital, of which he became chairman. His life was broadening as Joseph Chamberlain's had done a generation before. There is, indeed, a remarkable resemblance between father and son, not only in the several main stages of their careers—business, city government, parliament, Cabinet—but (allowing for the seven lost years) in the timing of them.

Chamberlain was elected to the Birmingham city council in 1911, the year of his marriage to Annie Vere, daughter of Major William Utting Cole, 3rd Dragoon Guards, of Woodhay House, Newbury, who became an unfailing help in all phases of his public as of his private life. To city government he brought new vitality and enterprise. Under his chairmanship of the town planning committee, two Birmingham schemes for planning in built-up areas were the first to be sanctioned in this country. A still more notable personal achievement was the establishment in 1916, against the strong opposition of banking interests, of the first municipal savings bank. Although it succeeded beyond expectation, it remains the only municipal institution of its kind in the country.

Chamberlain's very exceptional record in city government was noted outside Birmingham and soon widened his responsibilities. In 1915 he was appointed a member of the Central Control Board (Liquor Traffic). A hapless experience in national war administration followed. In December 1916 Lloyd George, who had just succeeded Asquith as prime minister, proposed to relieve the strain on manpower by voluntary recruitment of labour for war industries. Chamberlain was made director-general of national service to organize and direct the work. In order that he might give his full time to the post, he resigned the lord mayoralty of Birmingham, to which he had been elected for a second term in the previous month. His efforts were fruitless. Within a few days of the appointment Lloyd George conceived a dislike of him and he was left without authority or equipment for his difficult task. He said afterwards that he was without instructions and without powers. After seven months of futility he resigned and returned to Birmingham.

This unhappy episode was a turning-point in Chamberlain's life. He was not the man to sit down quietly under failure that was not due to fault of his own. His mind was at last fixed on a career in national politics and, at the general election of December 1918, he was returned to the House of Commons as conservative member for the Ladywood division of Birmingham. He was then in his fiftieth year: there is no other instance of a prime minister who entered parliament so late.

For four years Chamberlain supported the coalition government of which his brother Austen was a leading member. He spoke seldom but always well. Voice, pose, and a lucid and incisive style recalled memories of his father. He was chairman of several departmental committees but rejected a suggestion of Bonar Law that he should accept government office; he no longer had any confidence in Lloyd George and would not serve under or with him. On the Irish 'treaty' of December 1921 he supported the government.

When the coalition fell in October 1922, Chamberlain was on his way home from a holiday in Canada. For the first time he and his brother were in different camps. Austen was the chief defender of the coalition at the Carlton Club meeting (19 October) which destroyed it; and he continued for a time longer his co-operation with Lloyd George. Bonar Law pressed Neville to join the new government and, having become definitely anti-coalition, he accepted office as postmaster-general. At once the prime minister was greatly impressed by his sound judgement and fine administrative gifts. Promotion came swiftly, and he rose easily to each successive post. There were four posts in a little over a year (1922–1924): after the Post Office, the paymastership-general, the Ministry of Health (where he passed an important housing bill), and the chancellorship of the Exchequer. He was sworn of the Privy Council in 1922.

In his first term at the Treasury (1923–1924), Chamberlain was a chancellor without a budget. Baldwin, who succeeded Bonar Law as prime minister in May 1923, having announced a policy of tariff reform, decided—against the advice of most of his colleagues, including Chamberlain—to appeal to the country in the autumn. The conservative majority was lost and, with liberal help, Ramsay MacDonald formed the first labour government in January 1924.

It was a sharp disappointment to Chamberlain that when the conservatives secured a great majority in the following October, the party was once more committed against a general tariff. Baldwin offered him the Exchequer again but he preferred to return to the Ministry of Health; Mr. Churchill, who had just rejoined the conservative party, went to the Exchequer. His first budget provided the finance of the widows, orphans, and old-age pensions bill. This measure was suggested to Baldwin by Chamberlain while in opposition in 1924 and it was he who piloted the bill through the House in 1925.

Chamberlain's four and a half years (1924–1929) at the Ministry of Health raised the department's status and his own. Masterly conduct of the difficult Rating and Valuation Act of 1925 (which gave relief to agriculture and industry) put him in the first rank of parliamentarians. By securing the full co-operation of private builders as well as of the local councils, he solved the immediate housing problem: nearly a million houses had been built when he left office. In 1929 he passed the very important Local Government Act which reformed the Poor Law (boards of guardians were abolished) and recast the financial relations of the State and local authorities.

At the general election of May 1929 Chamberlain was returned for the Edgbaston division of Birmingham, and held the seat until his death. With labour in office again, he, at Baldwin's request, turned his attention to the re-organization of the conservative central office. A research department was set up and at once gave special consideration to the question of tariffs. The party leadership also came under review and, as chairman of the central office, he presented a critical memorandum which Baldwin so much disliked that for a short time it was thought that he would resign.

In the financial crisis of August 1931, which destroyed the labour government, it was Chamberlain who, until Baldwin returned from abroad, represented the conservative party in negotiations preceding the formation of the provisional all-party government. In that he was again minister of health, but he succeeded Philip Snowden as chancellor of the Exchequer when the government was reconstituted in November after the general election, and he held the office for five and a half years. Drastic economies were necessary for several years before normal expenditure and revenue could be balanced. Throughout that trying period he directed policy with courage and sound judgement. Upon him also fell the brunt of negotiation and decision on war reparations, war debts, and Empire trade policy, this last being dealt with at the memorable Imperial Economic Conference held at Ottawa in 1932.

Although, in the general election, the government was not committed on the fiscal question, Chamberlain secured Cabinet approval for a general tariff which, at a common standard of 10 per cent., was more for revenue than protection. The free trade system, initiated eighty-six years before with the repeal of the Corn Laws, was thus ended in 1932; and the settlement has not since been seriously challenged. In the same year a great saving in debt charges was effected by the conversion of £2,000,000,000 of the 5 per cent war loan to a 3½ per cent stock.

By 1935 there seemed to be a good prospect of substantial tax reductions; but hope of that vanished when, in the following year, the government proposed an expenditure of £1,500,000,000 on rearmament within five years. This had been delayed to the point of danger, partly because of hostile public opinion, partly because a disarmament policy was still being pursued in the League of Nations, and partly because the financial crisis in the early 'thirties was held to be, for the time, more important. As soon as that anxiety was relieved Chamberlain's was the chief political initiative in increasing the air estimates in 1934. He thought that Baldwin exaggerated the strength of labour opposition in the country and he desired to make rearmament the main issue at the general election in 1935.

Dangers multiplied. Italy invaded Abyssinia in October 1935; Hitler's aggressions had already begun; the Spanish civil war broke out in July 1936; the Japanese menace continually disturbed the Far East. Foreign affairs occupied more and more of the time of the Cabinet, and Chamberlain took an active part in the discussions. Labour party hostility to him, which reached the depth of bitterness after the Munich conference of 1938, was intensified in the Abyssinian war when, quite wrongly, he was widely regarded as pro-Italian and anti-League of Nations. He had been in fact a stout upholder of the League and in the Abyssinian crisis was ready, if the French had been willing to co-operate, to prevent or stop war. He supported League sanctions against Italy, and called for their abandonment only when their failure was manifest.

In the summer of 1936 Baldwin, worn by the labours and anxieties of the time, decided to resign the premiership after the coronation in the following May. There was no rival to Chamberlain as his successor and, within the inmost circle of high politics, it was known for months before that he would be the next prime minister. It was with the warm approval and goodwill of all his colleagues that he entered upon the office on 28 May 1937.

Chamberlain had thus been able to ponder, months in advance, over the grave responsibilities awaiting him. The paramount, inescapable problem now was national defence. German militarism, and its aggressive political direction, menaced the peace of the world. Great Britain was unprepared to meet it: and danger was so near that it had become imprudent to reveal her military weakness. The labour party's opposition to rearmament still continued.

The position was one of extraordinary difficulty. British and French military weakness was an incitement to German aggression, and prejudiced every effort by negotiation to stop the drift towards war. Could Germany and Italy be brought back into the comity of nations? In no other way could war be averted. It was the way which for nearly two years Chamberlain resolutely pursued. He knew the difficulties and, in particular, was not unaware of the sinister qualities of Hitler and Mussolini. But the pacification of Europe, which was the aim of his policy, could not be achieved without their collaboration, and not to seek it was to admit failure which he would not do while any hope of success remained. He often said that he would take no responsibility for war until he had done everything possible to prevent it.

Conversations with the Berlin government were opened in the early days of the new premiership. The German foreign minister accepted an invitation to come to London in June; but events in the Spanish civil war angered Hitler and the visit was never paid. Chamberlain then turned to

Rome. Through the foreign secretary, Mr. Eden, he sent a message to Mussolini who, in a friendly reply, suggested the expansion of the Anglo-Italian 'gentleman's agreement' of the previous January. It was arranged to begin negotiations in September, but here also the Spanish war barred the way.

In November direct contact with Hitler came about in a curious manner. Lord Halifax, who was a master of foxhounds as well as lord president of the Council, went to Berlin for a national hunting exhibition. While there he was invited to meet the Führer at Berchtesgaden. They had what Lord Halifax called a 'free, frank, informal and confidential talk'. There was in this no movement away from France, whose government was at once informed of what happened. M. Chautemps, the premier, and M. Delbos, the foreign minister, came to London for discussion of the European situation; and, shortly afterwards, M. Delbos exchanged views with von Neurath in Berlin. The way appeared to be clearing for Anglo-German negotiations. Sir Nevile Henderson, the British ambassador in Berlin, came to London for consultation and returned with full instructions. At the same time von Ribbentrop, already counted an enemy of Great Britain, was appointed foreign minister in the German government. A month passed before Hitler received the ambassador. He was, Henderson reported, in a bad temper, very angry with British newspapers, and resentful of any criticism of his relations with Austria.

Hitler's designs upon Austrian independence alarmed Mussolini who at this turning-point (February 1938) informed the British government that he was ready to open discussions covering all matters in dispute between Great Britain and Italy. Chamberlain felt that if this offer were spurned the Hitler-Mussolini association would be strengthened and the risk of war increased. Mr. Eden objected to the procedure proposed on the ground that there should be no negotiation with Italy until she had withdrawn a substantial part of her forces from Spain. Chamberlain's undertaking that no agreement should take effect until that condition was complied with did not satisfy the foreign secretary; and, after close discussion at three meetings of the Cabinet, he resigned on 20 February. Lord Halifax succeeded him at the Foreign Office, and negotiations with Italy began at once. Three weeks later Hitler invaded Austria, destroyed its government, and proclaimed it a province of the German Reich. British protests, ignored in Berlin, were repeated in parliament: Chamberlain spoke of the profound shock to the friends of peace and the setback to hopes of international co-operation. The Germans gave a general undertaking that there would be no further aggression, and a particular assurance that they had no designs against Czechoslovakia. But confidence was everywhere weakened.

The British Cabinet considered the position and, on 24 March, Chamberlain gave to the House of Commons a detailed review of the country's liabilities abroad. As to Czechoslovakia, he quoted with approval a statement made by Mr. Eden, when foreign secretary, that 'nations cannot be expected to incur automatic military obligations save for areas where their vital interests are concerned.' But that, Chamberlain continued, must not be interpreted as meaning that Britain would in no circumstances intervene. Ought Britain to assure France forthwith of full military support if she were called upon, by reason of German aggression, to go to the aid of her ally, Czechoslovakia? The Cabinet had decided against that but, said Chamberlain, 'legal obligations are not alone concerned and, if war broke out . . . it would be well within the bounds of probability that other countries besides those which were parties to the original dispute would almost immediately become involved. This', he added, 'is especially true in the case of two countries like Great Britain and France, with long associations of friendship, with interests closely interwoven, devoted to the same ideals of democratic liberty and determined to uphold them.'

While the labour opposition condemned this speech, Mr. Churchill welcomed it as 'a very considerable advance on any previous declaration'. In effect, he said, there was evidently a defensive alliance with France and he was for declaring it openly and making it effective by a military convention. This view was not accepted. The Dominion governments approved the policy announced, but they did not wish to widen their obligations; and it would not have been easy at that time, nor even when events became more critical later in the year, to bring them into war on any issue which had then arisen in central Europe.

Within Czechoslovakia the situation rapidly worsened throughout the summer. Discontent among the three million Germans in the Sudeten border districts was whipped by Nazi agents into fierce agitation. Concessions by the Prague government were met by demands for more and still more. Border 'incidents', invented or distorted, were reported with provocative headings in all the German newspapers. The position was already dangerous when, towards the end of July, Chamberlain persuaded Lord Runciman to go to Prague as mediator. After weeks of negotiation with both sides he submitted a plan of home rule for the Sudeten areas on the Swiss cantonal model, and it was accepted by the Czech government. It was too late. Henlein, the Sudeten leader, threw off disguises and was seen to be Hitler's tool. The orders now came direct from Hitler. At Nuremberg, on 12 September, he demanded self-determination for the Sudetens and promised them the support of the Reich. Powerful German forces were ready for action. Lord Runciman could do no more and returned to London on 16 September.

The French government had approved the Runciman mission. France was pledged by treaty to defend the Czechs against aggression. At Lanark on 27 August, Sir John Simon, speaking for the government, repeated Chamberlain's declaration of 24 March which was, in effect, that if France were involved in war with Germany because she went to the aid of the Czechs, Britain would be at the side of France. Nevile Henderson also repeated this in an official communication to the German foreign minister. But France was unready. Many French newspapers, of all parties, favoured the German minority claims and blamed the Czech government for dilatoriness. Public opinion generally was apathetic. After information that the German army was ready to strike, the French Cabinet met on 13 September and the announcement was made that 'more reserves may be called up.' It was evident that France would not then fulfil her treaty obligations to the Czechs. M. Daladier, the premier, afterwards said that he suggested to Downing Street some 'exceptional procedure'.

Chamberlain had already considered what, in such a situation, his exceptional action should be. On the evening of 14 September the world was startled by the news that he had just sent a message to Hitler proposing that they should meet the next day to discuss a peaceful settlement. Hitler agreed, and on Thursday, 15 September, Chamberlain flew to Berchtesgaden. His action was everywhere approved. Hitler demanded an immediate assurance that the British government accepted the principle of self-determination for the Sudeten Germans. Chamberlain said that he would consult the Cabinet about that if Hitler gave an assurance that Germany would, meantime, refrain from hostilities. The assurance was given.

Chamberlain returned to London on the Friday, the same day that Lord Runciman arrived from Prague. The Cabinet sat for five hours on the Saturday, and on the Sunday there were long discussions with M. Daladier and M. Bonnet, the French foreign minister. It was then announced that the two governments were 'in complete agreement'. The demand for self-determination had been conceded. British labour leaders condemned the decision and sought common action against it with French labour only to find that their French friends were not prepared to risk a war to preserve the integrity of Czechoslovakia.

On Thursday, 22 September, Chamberlain met Hitler a second time, at Godesberg, and was able to tell him that self-determination was accepted not only by Britain and France but also by Czechoslovakia. Moreover, arrangements for the transfer of territory had already been worked out. Hitler denounced these arrangements as dilatory and said that the German flag must fly over Sudetenland within a few days. Having considered this overnight, Chamberlain sent a letter to Hitler, protesting against any threat of force and adding that the Czechs could not withdraw their armed forces so long as they were faced with the prospect of invasion. Hitler replied a few hours later with a violent attack on the Czechs. Germany's decision was irrevocable. Chamberlain's curt rejoinder was that he proposed to return home at once. He asked for a memorandum and a map showing the areas in which it was proposed that plebiscites should be taken. These were not received and at half-past ten that night he saw Hitler again. He was then shown the memorandum. It provided for Czech evacuation of the Sudeten frontier districts within forty-eight hours. This moved Chamberlain to anger. He called it an ultimatum. Talk continued for several hours without removing the deadlock. But Hitler did say that 'this was the last of his territorial ambitions in Europe, and that he had no wish to include in the Reich people of any other race than the Germans'. On Saturday, 24 September, Chamberlain returned to London.

Before the Godesberg conference ended, the Prague government was informed that the British and French governments could no longer take the responsibility of advising it not to mobilize. French opinion stiffened and M. Daladier said that if Czechoslovakia were attacked France would take measures to help her. The Czech government rejected the German terms. War appeared to be certain. British military and civil defence preparations were pressed forward with all speed.

But Chamberlain refused to abandon his peace efforts. On 26 September he sent Sir Horace Wilson to Berlin with a letter to Hitler suggesting that German and Czech representatives should together consider how the territory to be ceded should be handed over. The letter was delivered to Hitler the same day by Sir Horace and the British ambassador. Next morning Sir Horace saw Hitler again and gave him this message from the British prime minister: 'If, in pursuit of her treaty obligations, France became actively engaged in hostilities against Germany, the United Kingdom would feel obliged to support her.' 'It is Tuesday to-day', Hitler retorted, 'and by next Monday we shall be at war.' But he replied to the prime minister with an assurance that the Czechs' fears were groundless and that their 'economic organism' would be stronger than before. Chamberlain thereupon appealed to him not to risk a world war when settlement was within reach in a few days. At the same time he asked Mussolini to support his proposal for further negotiation; and the Duce asked Hitler and Ribbentrop to delay action for twenty-four hours.

The next afternoon, Wednesday, 28 September, the prime minister reported to the House of Commons. From no quarter was there any ray of hope that war would be averted. The speech, heard in sombre silence, was near its end when a note from Lord Halifax was passed along the Treasury bench and handed to Chamberlain who read it and, with scarce a pause, announced that Hitler had invited him to a conference at Munich on the following day. Mussolini and Daladier were also invited. 'I need not say what my answer will be', he added. The relief was indescribable. For the moment differences were forgotten, and the goodwill of the whole House was with him as he left for the last stage of these momentous events.

Many people, perhaps most, failed to apprehend the limited range of the Munich conference. Settlement was possible only on the basis of self-determination, which meant the cession of the Sudeten districts in which Germans were a majority of the population. That had already been agreed: it was Hitler's assumption of the rights of a victor in war that the Czechs, supported in this by Great Britain and France, found intolerable. In a few hours at Munich the Godesberg terms were so modified that the Czech government accepted them. The evacuation of the Sudeten areas, which was to have been completed on 1 October, was extended over ten days. It was agreed that the limits of the territory to be occupied by the Germans after the first four days should be defined by an international commission. An international force was to occupy the plebiscite areas. Hitler withdrew his demand that the evacuating Czechs should take none of their goods with them. The release of Germans from the Czech army was to be completed, not in one day but in four weeks; and a right of option into or out of the transferred territories might be exercised at any time within six months after the date of the agreement. So, for the time, was peace saved.

The agreement was signed at 12.30 a.m. on Friday, 30 September. Later the same morning Chamberlain saw Hitler for the last time and they both signed a declaration which, taken at its face value, was of immense importance. The agreement on Czechoslovakia just signed was said to be 'symbolic of the desire of our two peoples never to go to war again'; and 'the method of consultation shall be the method adopted to deal with any other questions that may concern our two countries.' This document had been prepared by Chamberlain in advance, with the thought in his mind that, if it were violated, it would effectually damn Hitler. A similar declaration, on behalf of Germany and France, was signed in Paris several weeks later.

In the evening of 30 September Chamberlain was welcomed back to London by vast crowds of cheering people. The newspapers of all parties on the Saturday and Sunday acclaimed him as the saviour of peace: the British press had never been more united on any great public occasion. The churches were crowded at services of thanksgiving. From all parts of the world messages of congratulation poured into Downing Street. The statesmen of the Dominions and Colonies were fervent in their praise. 'A great champion has appeared in the lists', General Smuts said at Johannesburg. . . . 'He risked all and I trust he has won all.'

But there was criticism, much of it strident and bitter, in the House of Commons during the four days' debate in the following week. With a few notable exceptions, the labour party was solidly hostile; and a small conservative minority which condemned the Munich settlement included Mr. Churchill. Yet nearly every speaker swelled the chorus of praise of the prime minister's courageous struggle for peace. All deplored the terms of settlement. The government's justification was put in one sentence by Sir John Simon: 'How many amongst us are there who, if we could undo what was then done, would reject the settlement to which the prime minister put his hand on Friday, and instead—because it was the only alternative—would fling the world into the cauldron of immediate war?' Chamberlain said: 'By my action I did avoid war. I feel equally sure that I was right in doing so.'

On 6 October, by 366 votes to 144, the House of Commons declared confidence in the government. There was no division in the House of Lords, and the speeches there, spread over three days, nearly all supported Chamberlain's policy. It was remarkable, moreover, that in the French Chamber the Munich settlement was approved, except for the communists, by an all but unanimous vote.

Chamberlain had the support of a great majority of the nation. He said in the Commons debate that he would not snatch party advantage by capitalizing the thankfulness for peace; he would not advise an early general election unless some new issue arose which required a fresh mandate from the country, or he lost the confidence of his supporters. One other sentence showed that on the morrow of Munich he realized the grave uncertainties of the future. 'It is possible', he said, 'that we may want great efforts from the nation in the months to come, and if that be so the smaller our differences the better.' He had insisted that rearmament would be pressed forward.

The European prospect worsened throughout the autumn. A dreadful pogrom against Jews in Germany horrified civilized people everywhere. Hatred of Hitler and his works spread among all classes in Britain. But Chamberlain would not yet abandon his peace efforts: if there was to be war let the country be ready for it. He could not, of course, persist in his attempt to turn the Germans from their evil ways and, at the same time, tell the world what he thought of their leader. The restraints which his policy imposed were misunderstood, and the prejudice against him, fostered by political opponents, deepened from this time on.

With Italy relations had temporarily improved. The negotiations that followed Mr. Eden's resignation soon led to a comprehensive agreement. It was approved by the House of Commons on 2 May 1938. The condition that it should not take effect until there had been a substantial withdrawal of Italian forces from Spain was, however, insisted upon and the agreement did not come into full operation until November. In January 1939 Chamberlain and Lord Halifax went to Rome for discussions with the Italian government, but without any fixed agenda and the visit had no lasting effect.

In the same month, at Birmingham, Chamberlain spoke of political tension in Europe. There was talk of German designs on the free city of Danzig which was in the Polish customs system; but Ribbentrop countered that with the assurance at Warsaw on 26 January enmity no longer existed between Germans and Poles. This was the prelude to a war of nerves against the Czechs. President Hacha was summoned to Berlin on 14 March and there bullied hour after hour until he signed a document in which he 'placed the fate of the Czech people in the hands of the Reichsführer'. Czechoslovakia was simultaneously invaded and, in a few hours, the Prague Cabinet surrendered.

The policy of appeasement was dead—'wantonly shattered', Chamberlain said at Birmingham. Hitler stood before the world a man forsworn, whose word no one could trust, from whose lawless aggression no neighbour of Germany was safe. The Poles at once consulted the British and French governments, and a provisional understanding was reached. On 31 March Chamberlain announced in the House of Commons that Britain and France would give all the support in their power to Poland if her independence were threatened while negotiations were in progress.

Even before that announcement there were more aggressions: Hitler had seized Memelland from Lithuania and demanded the incorporation of Danzig in the Reich. On Good Friday, 7 April, Italy invaded Albania, three days after an official denial that military action was intended against that country. The British government thereupon gave assurances of support to Greece and Rumania, and made a long-term agreement with Turkey.

As early as March it was found that Poland and Russia could not be brought into one alliance. But obviously Britain's new agreements in Europe would be strengthened by a good understanding with the Soviet government. Anglo-French negotiations to secure it were begun at Moscow early in the summer. One obstacle was Russia's demand that Britain should recognize her annexation of the three Baltic republics, Latvia, Estonia, and Lithuania. This could not be squared with the British policy of protecting small nations against aggression. Yet on 24 May Chamberlain told the House of Commons that he hoped for early and full agreement. Discussions continued, and at the beginning of August British and French military missions went to Moscow. As this was done on Russia's invitation, a painful shock was caused by the announcement on 21 August that she had signed a non-aggression pact with Germany.

German propagandist reports that Britain would now abandon Poland were at once denied by Chamberlain. If the need arose, he said, British forces would be fully engaged in support of our Allies. Yet he continued the most strenuous exertions to prevent war and intensified these efforts when, in the last week of August, the hour of decision was felt to be near. But Hitler was bent on war, and on the morning of Friday, 1 September, German armies invaded Poland. British and French demands for suspension of hostilities being ignored, Chamberlain, at 11.15 in the morning of Sunday, 3 September, broadcast from 10 Downing Street the announcement that 'this country is at war with Germany. ... It is the evil things we shall be fighting against—brute force, bad faith, injustice, oppression and persecution—and against them I am certain that right will prevail.' France declared war on Germany six hours later.

Chamberlain's wish that the war-time government should represent all parties was thwarted by the refusal of the labour leaders and of liberals led by Sir Archibald Sinclair to serve under him. But there were some notable recruits, Mr. Churchill and Mr. Eden among them. Emergency measures were passed quickly with the support of all parties.

The opening stages of the war were very different from what had been expected. U-boat attacks on British and Allied shipping began on the first day but many months passed before enemy air raiders bombed London, and there were only minor clashes between the opposing armies on the Franco-German frontier. After the quick defeat of Poland, there were no important land operations until the invasion of Denmark and Norway on 9 April 1940. As the British fleet, owing to air attacks, could not remain in the Skagerrak, there was no effective check upon enemy reinforcements for Norway, and the small British forces landed to help the Norwegian defence were mostly re-embarked within two or three weeks.

This was the first and not the worst British disaster in the war but it made a greater impression upon parliament than any that followed. On 7 and 8 May the withdrawal from Norway was debated in the House of Commons. In the division forced by the labour party the government was given a majority of 81—the figures were 281 to 200—but 40 ministerialists were in the minority and many abstained. Chamberlain thereupon considered his position and, when he was informed on 10 May that labour members still refused to serve under him, he at once tendered his resignation and advised the King to commission Mr. Churchill to form a new administration. The change was announced in a broadcast by Chamberlain that night.

Chamberlain joined the new government as lord president of the Council and for several months worked in full harmony with his successor. In August he underwent an operation which was believed to be successful and he resumed his official duties, but only for a short time: illness returned and on 1 October he resigned from the War Cabinet, knowing that his public life was over. Titular honours (including the Garter) he declined, preferring to remain plain Mr. Chamberlain. He was a freeman of Birmingham; the freedom of the City of London death prevented him from accepting, and the scroll was presented to Mrs. Chamberlain in 1941. Honorary degrees were conferred upon him by the universities of Oxford, Cambridge, Birmingham, Bristol, Leeds, and Reading; and he was elected a fellow of the Royal Society (1938). He died at Highfield Park, Heckfield, near Reading, on 9 November. His ashes were interred in Westminster Abbey. His son and daughter survived him.

Chamberlain's career has some remarkable features. Coming to parliament in his fiftieth year, without a reputation in national politics, he excelled in every office entrusted to him and was given the premiership for the best of all reasons, because he was the most trusted man in his party. He owed nothing to social influence. He was temperamentally unfitted for the arts of self-advertisement. The lucid speech of which he was a master was on simple, straight lines: and the style was the man. On the business side of the premiership he was exceptionally efficient. Occasionally his appointments to government office were criticized, but his leadership of the Cabinet was strong and masterful; and his colleagues knew that in all affairs that came before them he was animated by a lofty sense of public duty. To this all his varied interests were subordinate. Gardening and bird life attracted him all through his life. Music was a joy to him and he did much to foster public interest in the art. Family love and loyalty were deep and strong. His leadership of the conservative party did not mean repudiation of essentials in the radical faith in which he was brought up, and it was a grief to him that war prevented far-reaching social reforms upon which his heart was set. The failure to maintain peace was not, however, a complete failure; for, as Mr. Churchill said on the first day of the war, his resolute struggle for peace was of the highest moral and practical value and secured 'the wholehearted concurrence of scores of millions of men and women whose co-operation was indispensable'.

Of portraits of Chamberlain, one, by Sir William Orpen, is in the possession of Mrs. Chamberlain; another, by Oswald Birley is in the Birmingham Art Gallery; and a third, by James Gunn, is at the Carlton Club.

[Keith Feiling, *The Life of Neville Chamberlain*, 1946; private information; personal knowledge.]

W. W. HADLEY

published 1949

CHAMBERLAIN Joseph

(1836–1914)

Statesman, was born at Camberwell Grove, London, 8 July 1836. His father, Joseph Chamberlain, was the master of the Cordwainers' Company, with which his family had been connected for four generations, carrying on the business of wholesale boot and shoe manufacturers in the same house and under the same name for one hundred and twenty years. His mother was Caroline, daughter of Henry Harben, a provision merchant in London. In 1850 Joseph, who was their eldest son, was sent to University College School; but after a short stay, during which he showed no little promise, he was put into his father's business at the age of sixteen. Two years later an opening occurred to expand the business of Mr. Nettlefold, screw-manufacturer, the brother-in-law of Mr. Chamberlain senior, at Birmingham, and Joseph was sent there to represent his father's interests. He remained an active member of the firm for twenty years, displaying such business capacity that he was able to retire at the early age of thirty-eight with a substantial income. His relations with his employees were always of a most friendly character; and when a charge of ruthlessness was afterwards made by a political opponent regarding his dealings with the smaller manufacturers, the accuser, after careful inquiry, acknowledged the complete untruth of his allegations.

Chamberlain's apprenticeship in public speaking was served in the Birmingham and Edgbaston Debating Society. He became in 1869 a member of the city council, and in 1870 of the first school board. Politics appealed to him from the first. An intimate friend has asserted that, at the outset, it was uncertain whether foreign policy would make him a tory, or home affairs a radical; and at the election of 1859 he canvassed on behalf of the opponent of John Bright, because he was opposed to Bright's pacificism. But very soon the impulse of social reform drove him to radicalism. It was on the subject of education that his interest was first excited. He became chairman of the National Education League of Birmingham in 1868. At the time education in Birmingham was at a low ebb; and both by agitation and by practical experiment Chamberlain sought to find a remedy. He started classes at his own works, and taught history, French, and arithmetic in connexion with a Unitarian Sunday school; whilst, simultaneously, he flung himself into the campaign for a national system of education. He held the Church of England to be the enemy; and, when Mr. W. E. Forster's Bill of 1870 was found to contain provisions which seemed to encourage the maintenance of the denominational system, he attacked it with great bitterness. He had become, in March 1870, the chairman of the National Education League, and voiced with extreme vigour the case of the nonconformists.

But education was only one plank in the platform of social reform, and there were other questions, less controversial, upon which Chamberlain was able to give the lead not only to his adopted city but to England at large. He became mayor of Birmingham in 1873, and was re-elected in 1874 and 1875. If he was a radical, he maintained it was because political means were necessary to deal effectually with the evils standing in the way of social reform. Ignorance, and the existence of insanitary and disgraceful housing, were the two main evils. But, whilst free education could only be secured by act of parliament, the improvement of sanitary conditions lay with the municipalities themselves; and here there can be no question of the results achieved by Chamberlain. They included the purchase by the Birmingham corporation of the gas-works, water-works, and sewage farm, the destruction of the slums in the heart of the city, and the provision of artisans' dwellings. He worked for the extension of free libraries and art galleries, and sought in every way to make Birmingham a place in which its inhabitants should take a civic pride. Nor were his interests confined to Birmingham. At the close of 1874 he arranged a conference of municipal authorities and others interested in the sanitation of large towns, in order to create a sound public opinion on the subject. It took place in January 1875 and was a starting-point in the development of municipal social reform.

Holding the view that legislation was needed for effecting improvements, it was natural that Chamberlain should seek a yet wider field for his activities. In 1874 he stood for parliament unsuccessfully at Sheffield; but, at a by-election in 1876, he became the colleague of Bright in the representation of Birmingham. From this time till the final split over Home Rule, Chamberlain was closely associated with (Sir) Charles Dilke. Forming a close offensive and defensive alliance, they agreed that neither should accept office unless the other was also satisfied. In 1877 Chamberlain reorganized the liberal party in the constituencies by forming large local associations on a representative basis, and federating these in a central organization. He thus became the Carnot of the liberal victory of 1880. But Mr. Gladstone did not at first intend to admit either Dilke or Chamberlain to the Cabinet, his personal sympathies being with the more moderate type of liberal. His hand was forced, however, by Dilke, who refused to join the ministry unless either Chamberlain or he became a Cabinet minister. Queen Victoria raised strong objections to Dilke, because of the line which he had taken on grants to the royal family; and thus Chamberlain, though in his earlier years he had seemed to coquette with republican views, and though at the time his parliamentary reputation was less than Dilke's, became president of the Board of Trade, whilst Dilke was put off with the subordinate office of under-secretary of state for foreign affairs. When, at the end of 1882, room was at last found for Dilke in the Cabinet, there was at first some question of Chamberlain taking the vacant office of chancellor of the duchy of Lancaster, so that Dilke should go to the Board of Trade. The Queen was unwilling to have Dilke as chancellor of the duchy, and, indeed, afterwards showed some reluctance to accept Chamberlain. The difficulty was met by Mr. J. G. Dodson (afterwards Lord Monk-Bretton) exchanging the Local Government Board for the duchy, so that Dilke might fill his place. The episode, however, enabled Chamberlain to show the staunchness of his friendship. 'Your letter', he wrote to Dilke on 13 December, 'has spoilt my breakfast. The change would be loathsome to me for more than one reason and will give rise to all sorts of disagreeable commentaries. But if it is the only way out of the difficulty, I will do what I am sure you would have done in my place and accept the transfer.'

The intimate letters of Chamberlain to Dilke reveal the absence of sympathy between Chamberlain and most of his colleagues in the ministry of 1880–1885. In any case, in the words of Dilke, 'the holding of strongly patriotic and national opinions in foreign affairs, combined with extreme radical opinions upon internal matters, made it difficult to act with anybody for long without being attacked by some section with which it was necessary to act at other times, and made it difficult to form a solid party.' But the special circumstances regarding Ireland and foreign and colonial questions made the situation still more difficult. As to Ireland, Chamberlain distrusted and disliked a policy of coercion. He had an uneasy conscience at having accepted it in 1880; at the same time he was at a loss for an alternative. He recognized in October 1881 that Parnell had now got beyond the radicals. The Irish leader was demanding 'no rent' and 'separation'; and Chamberlain was not prepared to say that the refusal of such terms as these constituted an Irish grievance. His own inclination was to stand aside and let the coercionists and Parnell fight out their quarrel; but this was now impossible. Altogether it was an awkward situation, and he did not see his way out of it.

The imprisonment of Parnell shortly followed (October 1881), but no improvement took place in the situation. Accordingly, the pressure of the radicals caused another change of policy. It was reported that Parnell was in a more pliant mood, and Chamberlain, 'taking his life in his hands', with the approval of Gladstone, entered into negotiations, the outcome of which was the so-called Kilmainham Treaty (2 May 1882). Parnell promised, if released, to advise payment of rent and the cessation of outrages. The absence of a public promise, however, diminished the force of this undertaking. Parnell and two other members of parliament were thereupon released, W. E. Forster in consequence resigning the post of Irish secretary. Dilke and Chamberlain had expected that the latter would be Forster's successor, and the appointment of Lord Frederick Cavendish took them by surprise. Again, after the murder of Lord Frederick (6 May), Chamberlain would have accepted the post, had it been offered him, with the intention of attacking the whole Dublin Castle system. But Gladstone had no desire to see Chamberlain Irish secretary, nor did he desire an Irish secretary who would be a Cabinet minister.

Chamberlain never wavered in his belief in the necessity of an Irish Local Government Bill; and a speech in which he compared the position of England and Ireland with that of Russia and Poland (February 1883) showed his discontent with the existing state of things. The pressure of foreign and domestic questions for a time diverted attention from Ireland; but in 1885 Chamberlain, in despair of a solution, suggested that Parnell or some other Irishman should become chief secretary. At the same time he proposed a more practicable plan. He advocated the creation of a system of representative county government. In addition to elected county boards, there should be a central board for all Ireland, in its essence municipal and not political, mainly executive and administrative, but with the power to make by-laws, raise funds, and pledge public credit, in such modes as parliament should provide. The central board should take over primary education, poor law, sanitary administration, and the control of public works, without dealing, however, in any way with the administration of justice, police, or prisons. It should not be elected directly by the Irish people, but chosen by the county boards. The scheme had the approval of the Irish bishops, and Parnell, according to Captain O'Shea, promised to give it his support, and not to obstruct a limited Crimes Bill. It obtained the half-hearted approval of a committee of the Cabinet; but, on being submitted to the full Cabinet, met with defeat. All the peers, except Lord Granville, voted against it; all the commoners, except Lord Hartington, were in its favour. As the Cabinet broke up (9 May) Gladstone said to a colleague, 'Ah, they will rue this day.'

Meanwhile drafts not only of a Coercion Bill but also of a Bill for Land Purchase came before the Cabinet. The latter Bill, however, was dropped for the time being, on the protests of the radical members of the Cabinet; nevertheless, Lord Spencer, the viceroy, remained convinced of its necessity; and Gladstone, under the impression that the objections of Chamberlain and Dilke would be met if, under the Bill, funds were only provided for a single year, gave notice of its introduction. But Chamberlain had not moved from the position that there should be no Land Purchase

Bill, unless it was accompanied by a Bill for Local Government. He and Dilke, therefore, sent in their resignations. They afterwards agreed to suspend them; so that their resignations had not taken effect when the government was defeated in the House of Commons (8 June 1885). The situation is made clear by a letter from Chamberlain to Gladstone (21 May 1885): 'I doubt very much if it is wise or was right to cover the serious differences of principle that have lately disclosed themselves in the Cabinet. I think it is now certain that they will cause a split in the new parliament, and it seems hardly fair to the constituencies that this should only be admitted after they have discharged their function, and are unable to influence the result.'

But it was not only on Irish and domestic questions that the Cabinet was divided. On foreign and colonial questions also there was much difference of opinion. With regard to the Transvaal, Chamberlain had no doubts respecting the wisdom and justice of the policy that prevailed; but as to Egypt his position was much less easy to summarize. On the one hand he maintained that strong measures were called for after the Alexandria massacre (11 June 1882), earning thereby Lord Granville's description of him as 'almost the greatest Jingo' in the Cabinet. On the other hand he was determined that Great Britain should not become the tool of the bondholders' interests. He wrote a memorandum to this effect in October 1882. Our first duty, he insisted, was to our principles and to our supporters and not to other powers; and, if the powers insisted on financial control, we should at least identify ourselves with the legitimate aspirations of Egyptian national sentiment. When, in April 1884, the relief of General Gordon was under consideration, Chamberlain agreed with Dilke and Hartington that, whether Gordon had acted against his instructions or not, an expedition for his relief was necessary. As early as February Chamberlain had proposed to telegraph to Sir Evelyn Baring (afterwards Earl of Cromer), giving him authority to concert measures with Sir Evelyn Wood for the relief of the beleaguered garrisons in the Sudan. But Gladstone and Granville broke up a meeting of the Cabinet, so as to prevent the adoption of this policy. Still, though differences in the Cabinet might delay an expedition till it became useless, they could not prevent it. Dilke and Chamberlain were consistently in favour of relieving Gordon, though Chamberlain strongly opposed the grandiose campaign of Lord Wolseley, believing that a small striking force of picked men was all that was required to avert the coming tragedy. He did not intend to be forced any further in the direction of a protectorate. He was in favour of an international guarantee of the neutrality of Egypt, and was ready to declare that country bankrupt. Two subjects, he wrote to Dilke, occupied the time of successive Cabinet councils, the finances of Egypt, and

Gordon; but, whereas the former took up some two or three hours, the latter received about five minutes at the fag-end of business. Thus neither by what it did nor by what it left undone did the Egyptian policy of the Gladstone ministry of 1880–1885 win the approval of its radical members.

Chamberlain was even less in sympathy with the prevailing tendencies in other parts of the world. In 1883 a committee of the Cabinet was appointed to deal with affairs on the west coast of Africa; and this committee, according to Dilke, by its delays and hesitations, lost England the Cameroons. 'The Cameroons!' wrote Chamberlain to Dilke in September 1884, 'It is enough to make one sick. As you say, we decided to assume the protectorate eighteen months ago. If the Board of Trade or the Local Government Board managed their business after the fashion of the Foreign Office and the Colonial Office, you and I would deserve to be hung.' If he had had the direction of affairs, he would have demanded explanations from Germany regarding New Guinea; and he shared Dilke's resentment at the policy of truckling to Germany, which was adopted in the case of Samoa and of Zanzibar and East Africa.

Nevertheless, while these causes of dissatisfaction were at work, Chamberlain was proving his capacity in his own special department, where his business experience stood him in good stead. In the session of 1880 he had in charge two measures relating to merchant shipping, the one concerning grain cargoes, the other the payment of seamen's wages. In 1881 he was responsible for an Electric Lighting Bill, which entitled municipalities, with the consent of the Board of Trade, to adopt electric lighting, without the cost and trouble of a private Act of parliament. An Act of 1883 effected a valuable reform in the law of bankruptcy, by subjecting the accounts of trustees to the control of an independent authority, and by setting on foot a searching inquisition into the conduct of insolvent debtors. The Act has been improved by subsequent legislation, but at the time was recognized by lawyers and business men as marking a great advance. The Patent Act of 1883 made easier the road for the inventor, by reducing greatly the scale of provisional fees and subsequent payments. More generally interesting and more adapted to the temperament of a fighting politician was the Merchant Shipping Bill of 1884, directed against shipowners who insured unseaworthy vessels beyond the value of the ships or of their cargoes. In a speech at Newcastle in January 1884 Chamberlain asserted that in the preceding year one seaman in every sixty had met his death by violent means; three thousand five hundred men had thus come to a premature end, many of them in the prime of life and many of them leaving behind them widows and orphans. So strongly did he feel on the subject that, when parliamentary reasons dictated the withdrawal of his measure, he at once proffered his resignation; which, however, he afterwards withdrew in view of the need of a united front until the question of the vote for the agricultural labourers should be finally settled. Moreover, he was able to secure the appointment of a royal commission, which in the end bore good fruit; for subsequent Acts accomplished most of the objects at which the Bill of 1884 had aimed. As an instance of Chamberlain's courage may be noted the fact that at Hull (6 August 1885) he stood on the same political platform with Samuel Plimsoll whose name was anathema to all shipowners.

On the question whether the Bills for equalizing the county and town franchise and for redistribution should be introduced simultaneously, Chamberlain strongly supported the view that the measures should be kept separate, and that no more than a promise of a Redistribution Bill to follow should at the time be given. While the question remained open his relations with Lord Hartington were far from friendly, and Gladstone's mediation was necessary. It seemed to Dilke that Chamberlain was anxious to make Hartington resign on the question of the franchise. For the time being Chamberlain was full of wrath against the House of Lords; and, whilst his friend Dilke was working for a peaceful solution of the Redistribution question with Lord Salisbury, he himself was busy denouncing the iniquities of the Upper House.

The violence of Chamberlain's language at this time gave grave offence to the Queen, who made Gladstone's life a burden by her strictures on the indiscretions of this *enfant terrible* of the Cabinet. In a dramatic speech at Birmingham on 5 January 1885, Chamberlain confessed his faith in the doctrine of 'ransom' for private property. After explaining how, as a radical minister in a liberal government, he had at times to reserve and even to sacrifice his opinions, he went on to ask what was to be the nature of the domestic legislation of the future? It would be more directed to social objects than had hitherto been the case. How to promote the greater happiness of the masses of the people, how to increase their enjoyment of life, this was the problem of the future. Private ownership had taken the place of communal rights, and this system had become so interwoven with our habits that it might be very difficult, and perhaps impossible, to reverse it. But then, what ransom would property pay for the security it enjoyed? Society was banded together in order to protect itself against the instincts of those of its members who would make very short work of private ownership if they were left alone. That was all very well, but society owed to these men something more than mere toleration in return for the restraints which it placed upon their liberty of action.

But in the same speech there were utterances more in keeping with Chamberlain's future career. 'If, however', he said, 'occasion should come to assert the authority of England, a democratic government, resting on the confidence and support of the whole nation and not on the favour of a limited class, would be very strong. It would know how to make itself respected, how to maintain the obligations and honour of the country. I think foreign nations would be very ill advised if they were to assume that, because we are anxious to avoid all cause of quarrel with our neighbours, we are wanting in the old spirit of Englishmen, and that we should be found very tolerant of insult, and long-suffering under injury.' Again: 'We are not unmindful of our obligations. If foreign nations are determined to pursue distant colonial enterprises, we have no right to prevent them. ... But our fellow-subjects may rest assured that their liberties, their rights, and their interests are as dear to us as our own; and if ever they are seriously menaced, the whole power of the country will be exerted for their defence, and the English democracy will stand shoulder to shoulder throughout the world to maintain the honour and integrity of the Empire.' In further speeches he emphasized the necessity of enlarging the programme of the liberal party. Free education, the provision of healthy dwellings and fair rents in the large towns, and compulsory powers for local authorities to acquire land at a fair price, that is to say, the price which a willing purchaser would give to a willing seller in the open market—these were the objects at which to aim. Payment of members, the abolition of plural voting, and a revision of the existing system of taxation were also urgent reforms. He told the Eighty Club (April 1885) that to a large and ever-increasing number of persons politics was the science of social happiness, as its half-sister, political economy, was the science of social wealth; and the inferences to be drawn from the statement were sufficiently obvious.

These utterances from a Cabinet minister caused a flutter in the ministerial dovecots, and Gladstone sent a grave remonstrance regarding the 'unauthorized programme', which Chamberlain interpreted as a dead set against himself. He saw, however, that he had gone too far, and excused himself on the ground that the present was an exceptional moment, new political vistas having been opened by the recent measure of reform. Moreover, his actual proposals had not been extravagant; he only demanded a revision of taxation, which Gladstone himself had advocated, and the extension of the powers of local authorities, on lines already conceded in Ireland. It was, perhaps, not so much the proposals themselves as the manner in which they were advocated, that deeply shocked the political feelings of men of the type of Goschen. Lord Fitzmaurice has described Chamberlain's proposals as 'innocuous and almost meaningless'; and in fact many of them became law under subsequent unionist legislation.

Chamberlain

Strong as were Chamberlain's views on social reform, he was no less firm in his determination to uphold the supremacy of the imperial parliament in regard to Ireland. When the liberal ministry of 1880 had come to its somewhat inglorious end, and the conservative government, which succeeded it, seemed to be coquetting with the idea of Home Rule, the situation became more strained; both because Parnell saw his opportunity of playing upon the needs of the rival parties, and because the apparent movement in the mind of the conservative ministry led Gladstone to believe that Home Rule was within the range of practical politics. For the moment, however, other questions than that of Ireland occupied Chamberlain's attention. With regard to the future, the radicals were not willing to be mere lay figures in a Cabinet of Goschens; and, if a liberal government attempted to do without them, they were determined to make trouble. Gladstone, however, recognized the importance of placating the redoubtable radical leader, and summoned him to Hawarden for a friendly discussion (8 October 1885). Three points were indispensable, in Chamberlain's opinion, to the programme of a liberal government: first, the granting of authority to local bodies for compulsory expropriation; secondly, a readjustment of taxation (as had been foreshadowed in Gladstone's election address); and thirdly, a recognition of the right of a Cabinet minister to support free education, notwithstanding that the other members of the ministry might not share his views. The questions of the future of the House of Lords and of church disestablishment he was willing to leave for decision to the future. According to Gladstone, he and Chamberlain were pretty well agreed on the subject of Ireland. But the latter insisted that he had always excluded Home Rule as impossible, proposing a Local Government Bill which he thought Parnell might accept. The impression left on Chamberlain was that Gladstone had as yet no definite plan. If he got a majority, his first effort would probably be to find a *modus vivendi* by entering into communications with Parnell. A little later Chamberlain was made uneasy by a note from Gladstone, confessing a presentiment that the Irish question might elbow out all others. He was further alarmed by a report from another source that Gladstone was trying to get Parnell's ideas in detail. 'It is no use', he wrote. After the liberals had gained their Pyrrhic victory at the general election of December 1885, and Gladstone had outlined an 'admissible plan' of Home Rule, Chamberlain commented: 'My view is that Mr. G's Irish scheme is death and damnation; that we must try and stop it; that we must not openly commit ourselves against it yet; that we must let the situation shape itself before we finally decide; that the Whigs are our greatest enemies, and that we must not join them if we can help it.'

On 26 December, in a very interesting letter, Chamberlain proposed a new solution of the Irish difficulty. His own inclinations were still in favour of the extension of local liberties on municipal lines; but the fatal objection was that the nationalists would not accept such a solution. Apparently the only logical alternative was separation, with its attendant dangers. Between these lay 'the hazy idea of Home Rule', which would mean an independent Irish parliament; while all guarantees and securities, whether for the protection of minorities or for the security of the Empire, would prove altogether illusory. To this he would prefer separation, towards which, indeed, Home Rule was but a step. There still remained the possibility of an arrangement which might secure the integrity of the Empire, whilst allowing Irishmen to manage Irish affairs in their own way. He then suggested a scheme of federation, involving separate parliaments for England, Scotland, Wales, Ulster, and South Ireland. To make the scheme workable it would be necessary to set on foot a supreme court, to decide the limits of the powers of the several local legislatures. Such changes had no terrors for a radical such as he was, but was it conceivable that such a clean sweep could be made in order to meet the Irish demand for Home Rule? The obvious answer to this question decided Chamberlain's future policy. In the general confusion of affairs, of one thing he was certain. He would sooner that the tories remained in office for the next ten years than agree to what he thought would be the ruin of his country. Nevertheless, it was his friend and follower, Jesse Collings, who moved the so-called 'three acres and a cow' amendment which gave the tory government its quietus; it resigned on 28 January 1886.

Chamberlain believed that he ought to accept, for the time being, a post in the new liberal ministry; though he recorded another protest against Home Rule in a letter to Gladstone. He would have preferred to become secretary for the Colonies. Gladstone's surprised comment: 'Oh! a Secretary of State!' bears out the assertion of Lord Randolph Churchill that Gladstone never really understood Chamberlain's capacity till he faced him as a foe. There was some question of Chamberlain going to the Admiralty; but he finally became president of the Local Government Board, though 'not very willingly'.

Starting under such auspices, it was not likely that the ministry would long remain united. Chamberlain intended to resign on the proposal of a Land Purchase Bill, but it was not till after a discussion in the Cabinet on the question of Home Rule that he finally left the government (15 March). On 21 April he justified his action before a meeting of Birmingham electors; after the Redistribution Act he had in 1885 become member for West Birmingham. 'Fifteen or sixteen years ago', he said, 'I was drawn into politics by my interest in social questions . . . and from that time to this I have done everything that an individual can do. I have made sacrifices of money and time and labour, I have made sacrifices of my opinions to maintain the organization and to preserve the unity of the liberal party.' Home Rule, he urged, now blocked the way of social reform, and the persistency of Parnell and the pliancy of Gladstone had altered the whole course of British politics. But Chamberlain knew that he must walk warily; and, after a destructive analysis of the two measures, he was careful to explain that as far as the Home Rule Bill was concerned his opposition was conditional. If the representation of Ireland were preserved on its present footing, the imperial parliament thus maintaining its control over imperial taxation in Ireland, and if there were conceded to Ulster a separate assembly, he might be able to support the measure. But these were not matters for committee; and on the answer to them depended his vote.

The speech was a great personal triumph, and although Mr. Francis Schnadhorst, the master of the 'caucus', had thrown in his lot with Gladstone and did what he could to thwart Chamberlain, the meeting passed, almost unanimously, a vote of confidence. The news of Dilke's intention to vote for the second reading was a great blow. 'The party', Chamberlain wrote, 'is going blindly to its ruin; and everywhere there seems a want of courage and decision and principle which almost causes one to despair.' For him the retention of the Irish representatives at Westminster was the touchstone. With their removal, separation must follow; with their retention, some system of federation might be possible. He would vote against the second reading, unless the ministry gave definite pledges on this point. 'The present crisis', he added, 'is, of course, life and death to me. I shall win if I can; if I cannot, I will cultivate my garden. I do not care for the leadership of a party which shall prove itself so fickle and so careless of national interests as to sacrifice the unity of the Empire to the precipitate impatience of an old man, careless of the future in which he can have no part, and to an uninstructed instinct which will not take the trouble to exercise judgement and criticism.' In a subsequent letter (6 May) Chamberlain made an illuminating admission: 'I do not really expect the government to give way, and, indeed, I do not wish it. To satisfy others I have talked about conciliation and have consented to make advances, but on the whole I would rather vote against the Bill than not, and the retention of the Irish members is with me only the flag that covers other objections.' On 26 May he wrote: 'I shall fight this matter out to the bitter end, but I am getting more and more doubtful whether, when it is out of the way, I shall continue in politics. I am wounded in the house of my friends, and I have lost my interest in the business.' Nevertheless, he threw out in parliament on 1 June the suggestion of yet another scheme, under which the position of Ireland with regard to the imperial parliament should be that of a Canadian province to the Dominion; but there was no support for this proposal.

On 7 June came the defeat of the Home Rule Bill by a majority of thirty; Chamberlain, along with Bright, voting against it. Various motives have in the past been ascribed to him. It has been supposed that he desired to oust Gladstone from the leadership. But the leadership was already, as it seemed, assured to him in the near future. The defection of the whigs under Lord Hartington must have inured to the benefit of the radical wing of the liberal party; Gladstone was a very old man, and Chamberlain was marked out as his natural successor. Chamberlain sacrificed this prize by voting with the whigs, who had been his special aversion, and with the tories, who had regarded him as Jack Cade; he risked political extinction sooner than comply with the demands of Parnell. Nevertheless, considering his past, considering the nature of his relations with most of the dissentient liberals, who, like Lord Hartington, had merely reached a goal to which for a long time they had unconsciously been moving, it was natural that Chamberlain should, for some time, retain hopes of reunion with his old associates; and the Round Table Conference at the beginning of 1887, attended by Sir William Harcourt, (Lord) Morley, and Lord Herschell from the one side, and by Chamberlain and Sir George Trevelyan from the other, was an attempt to find a *modus vivendi* between men who were in fact fundamentally at issue. In this state of things, a provocative letter by Chamberlain in *The Baptist* merely killed what could never have survived. The resignation of Lord Randolph Churchill (December 1886) had seriously affected Chamberlain's position. The tory democracy of Churchill attracted him; and the idea of organizing, along with Churchill, a new national party occurred to him, though he soon recognized its impossibility. Still, he thought that the tory government was doomed, and formed the gloomiest anticipations of the probable result of another general election, with coercion again to the fore.

Chamberlain's mission, however, to the United States to negotiate a treaty regarding the North American fisheries (November 1887–March 1888) gave him a few months' peace from party politics. The Bayard-Chamberlain Treaty of 15 February 1888 sought to make a satisfactory settlement of the questions relating to the interpretation of the Convention of 1818. That Convention gave, to a limited extent, the same territorial advantages over certain portions of the island of Newfoundland and of Canada as were given under the Treaty of 1783, and in return secured the renunciation by the United States of the liberty of their fishermen to enter on any other portion of the recognized waters of British North America, except for certain specified purposes. The Treaty was rejected by the American Senate in the following August. Nevertheless, when the Hague Tribunal arbitrated on the meaning of the Convention of 1818, the basis of their settlement was the same as that adopted in the Bayard-Chamberlain Treaty. Moreover, the *modus vivendi* which was continued after the failure of the Treaty removed all causes of irritation between the United States and Canada; and Sir Charles Tupper, the Canadian commissioner, bore witness to the tact, ability, and firmness with which Chamberlain met and overcame all but insurmountable difficulties. The visit served to strengthen those feelings of friendship towards the United States which so profoundly influenced his later policy.

After Chamberlain's return to British politics there was a noticeable movement in the direction of support to the conservative government. He was found jeering at the 'crazy-quilt' of Lord Randolph's professions, and supporting the ministry against his attacks. The return to power of a Home Rule ministry in August 1892 further tended to unite all enemies of Home Rule; and no one worked more ably or persistently against the measure of 1893 than Chamberlain.

In other directions Chamberlain's views were crystallizing. A visit to Egypt in 1889 had deeply impressed him with the benefits accruing to that country from the British occupation, and had led him to modify his earlier opinions. In a speech urging the retention of Uganda (20 March 1893) he anticipated his future rôle as colonial secretary. He laid stress on the need for following in the footsteps of our ancestors, who had not been ashamed to 'peg out' claims for posterity, thereby creating that foreign trade without which the population of Great Britain would starve. Very characteristic of the future colonial secretary was his defence of Captain Lugard, whose pledges for the continuance of the protectorate were then in danger of being repudiated by the Gladstone Cabinet: 'Captain Lugard was on the spot—Let me say in passing that I sometimes think we do not do justice to our bravest and noblest citizens. Any man, who reads his accounts impartially, will agree in this, that he was at all events a man of extraordinary power, capacity, tact, discretion, and courage.' Equally characteristic was the statement: 'Make it the interest of the Arab slave-traders to give up the slave trade, and you will see the end of that traffic. Construct your railway and thereby increase the means of traffic and you will take away three-fourths, if not the whole, of the temptation to carry on the slave trade.'

Such being the bent of his mind, it was natural that, after the electors in July 1895 had completely vindicated the action of the House of Lords in rejecting the Home Rule Bill of 1893, Chamberlain should have chosen the office of secretary of state for the Colonies when he joined Lord Salisbury's government. He informed a supporter that he had accepted the Colonial Office with two objects: first, to see what could be done to tighten the bond between Great Britain and the self-governing Colonies; and, secondly, to attempt to develop the resources of the Crown Colonies, and to increase the trade between them and Great Britain. In a speech (22 August 1895) he described the British tropical colonies as possessions in which it would be necessary to sink British capital. In small things no less than in great, the Colonial Office felt the hand of its new master. It was cleaned up and refurnished, and the maps were brought up to date. A circular of November 1895 instituted an inquiry into the extent of foreign competition in colonial markets, and the reasons for its existence. In the same spirit a Commercial Intelligence Branch of the Board of Trade was opened some four years later, and four trade commissioners were appointed. In the same year (1899) the Treasury was authorized by act of parliament to advance to certain Crown Colonies a sum of nearly three and a half million pounds at $2^3/4$ per cent repayable in fifty years. Although Chamberlain was by no means the first British minister to show interest in the material development of the Crown Colonies, none before him displayed such energy and capacity in the task. Like many other colonial secretaries, on his assumption of office he found the West Indies in a lamentable plight. The royal commission of 1896 considered the causes of West Indian depression to be permanent, inasmuch as they were largely due to the system of foreign sugar bounties which was not likely to be abandoned. Nevertheless the energy of Chamberlain achieved the apparently impossible; and the Brussels Convention (3 March 1903) abolished, for the time being, the bounty form of protection. Meanwhile, in consequence of the report of the royal commission, a department of agriculture for the West Indies was set on foot, an example that has been followed in Africa and the Far East. West Indian interests were further benefited by an arrangement (April 1900) with Messrs. Elder, Dempster & Co. for a fortnightly service of steamers between England and Jamaica. At the same time Chamberlain's handling of the Jamaica constitutional question in 1899 proved that he could be as firm as he was sympathetic.

Nor were Chamberlain's sympathies confined to the West Indies. No one was quicker to realize how essential to the complex life of the modern world is the supply of tropical products; and he at once saw that the policy already adopted of placing the scientific resources of Kew at the disposal of the West Indies was capable of unlimited extension, with the object of making the Empire, as far as possible, self-sufficient.

Perhaps, on this side of his work, Chamberlain's most unchallenged title to fame was the campaign which he waged on questions of health in tropical countries. In 1897 he realized the necessity of scientific inquiry into the causes of malaria, and of special education for the medical officers of

Crown Colonies. He followed eagerly on the trail which had been blazed by Sir Patrick Manson. A circular was issued in 1898, addressed to the General Medical Council and the leading medical schools in Great Britain, which urged the necessity of including tropical diseases in the medical curriculum. A special school of tropical medicine was set on foot in connexion with the Albert Dock branch of the Seamen's Hospital. The Treasury contributed half the cost; and the colonial governments were asked to concur in arrangements for the training of their medical officers at this school. A little later Chamberlain wrote to Lord Lister, inviting the co-operation of the Royal Society in a thorough investigation into the origin, the transmission, and the possible prevention and cure of tropical diseases, especially of the malarial and black-water fevers prevalent on the West African coast. The Royal Society gave a ready response; so that within a year of an address by Sir P. Manson, which gave a lead to the profession, both a school of tropical medicine and a systematic inquiry into the nature of malaria had become accomplished facts. Nor was this all. Another school of tropical medicine was founded in Liverpool, which also owed its origin to the initiative of Chamberlain. Improvements were effected in the form of the medical and sanitary annual reports from the Crown Colonies; and the enlargement of the British pharmacopoeia, so as to adapt it to Indian and colonial needs, received the powerful support of the Colonial Office. Unofficially, also, Chamberlain was able to leave his mark on this side of the work, as the establishment of the Colonial Nursing Association was mainly due to him and to Mrs. Chamberlain.

Turning to a wholly different subject, we note that under Chamberlain the British possessions in West Africa were extended by the effective occupation of the territories behind the Gold Coast and Lagos, and by the placing of the Royal Niger Company's territories under the control of the Colonial Office (1900). Chamberlain also gave his strong support to the federalizing of the protected Malay States and to the extension of their railway system.

But, valuable as was his work for the benefit of the Crown Colonies, it is in his relations with what are now known as the Dominions that Chamberlain is chiefly remembered. As early as 1888 he had told a Toronto audience that the federation of Canada might be 'the lamp to lighten our path' to the federation of the British Empire. Soon after he came to the Colonial Office the Jameson Raid (December 1895), and the events that followed in South Africa, obliged him to concentrate his attention, for the most part, on that one subject. But the symptoms of general European hostility which followed that unfortunate episode served to point the moral: 'Let us do all in our power by improving our communications, by developing our commercial relations, by cooperating in mutual defence;

and none of us will ever feel isolated . . . and in the time to come, the time that must come, when these colonies of ours have grown in stature, in population, and in strength, this league of kindred nations, this federation of Great Britain, will not only provide for its own security, but will be a potent factor in maintaining the peace of the world' (21 January 1896). In too confident a mood he seemed to think that the opportunity had already arrived for consolidating the scattered parts into 'a great self-sustaining and self-protecting empire'.

But the South African difficulty, though it might suggest such ideals, prevented any immediate attempt at their realization. Chamberlain had already given a proof of his mettle in one sharp encounter with President Kruger. The president, in 1895, closed the Vaal drifts in pursuance of his policy of obtaining for the Delagoa Bay Railway Company the monopoly of conveying overseas goods into the Transvaal. Chamberlain, having first obtained an assurance that the government of Cape Colony was pre-pared to share equally in the expense of any military operations that might be necessary, sent an ultimatum to the president, and the drifts were promptly reopened. But the after-effects of the Jameson Raid undoubtedly made Chamberlain's position more difficult. During the anxious years that followed he was assailed with great bitterness. He was accused of com-plicity in the Raid; and after his solemn denial had been unanimously accepted by the House of Commons committee which dealt with the matter, it was still insinuated that there was more behind, which should have been divulged. In fact, Chamberlain's prompt and immediate action in denouncing the Raid before he knew of its failure, is sufficient proof that he could not have had previous knowledge regarding it. There may have been some confusion between a rising of the Johannesburg Uitlanders, which was expected in England, and the Raid, which was a bolt from the blue. In any case, the atmosphere of suspicion and hate, which the Raid created, made almost hopeless the attempt to secure civic rights for the Transvaal Uitlanders. Moreover, the attitude of the high commissioner, Sir Hercules Robinson (afterwards Baron Rosmead), who concentrated all his efforts on securing lenient terms for the prisoners, made still more difficult the task of the colonial secretary. An ultimatum might lead to war; and such a war, he told the House of Commons on 8 May 1896, would be in the nature of a civil war—long, bitter, costly, leaving behind it the embers of strife, which generations might not extinguish. But success in dealing with the Jameson trouble had both hardened Kruger's heart and increased his confidence in his own wisdom; whilst the Raid had aroused a strong nationalist spirit throughout Dutch South Africa. An agreement which was practically an offensive and defensive alliance between the Orange Free State and the Transvaal (1897) was a serious menace to British interests, and the temporary eclipse of Cecil Rhodes made the English in Cape Colony as sheep without a shepherd.

The appointment, in 1897, of a high commissioner—Sir Alfred (afterwards Viscount) Milner—who combined strength with caution, gave the colonial secretary an adviser in whom he could place complete confidence. Read now, the controversy between the Transvaal and British governments on the question whether the Republic was a sovereign state, and whether foreign arbitration was admissible, may seem academic. But the practical interests of many British subjects were deeply involved; whilst there were additional complaints—of the dynamite monopoly, of maladministration in Swaziland, and of other grievances. For a year Milner remained silent, studying the situation. When he spoke, it was to counsel the Dutch in Cape Colony to warn their kinsmen in the Transvaal against any fatal rashness. Henceforth, though Chamberlain was always ready to interfere if necessary, British policy was mainly directed by the man on the spot. It was the fashion amongst a certain school of radicals to regard Chamberlain as a firebrand, who was only kept in order by the influence of his more moderate colleagues. If his speeches showed moderation it was assumed that this was only because Lord Salisbury was holding him back. There appears, however, not to be a tittle of evidence for such a reading of the history.

In any case, the Bloemfontein Conference (May–June 1899) was an honest attempt on the part of the British authorities to reach a *modus vivendi* on the questions at issue. Its starting-point was as follows: On 4 May Milner, in a powerful and plain-spoken telegram, stated the case for intervention. 'The true remedy', he said, 'is to strike at the root of all these injuries, the political impotence of the injured. What diplomatic protests will never accomplish, a fair measure of Uitlander representation would gradually but surely bring about.' 'The case for intervention', he insisted, 'is overwhelming. . . . The spectacle of thousands of British subjects kept permanently in the position of helots, constantly chafing over undoubted grievances and calling vainly to Her Majesty's government for redress, does steadily undermine the influence and reputation of Great Britain and the respect for the British government within the British dominions.' Chamberlain's considered reply, sent on 10 May, covered the whole ground. After summarizing the details of the Uitlanders' grievances, the most serious of which affected their 'personal rights' placing them 'in a position of political, social, and educational inferiority to the Boer inhabitants of the Transvaal, and even endangering the security of their lives and property', the dispatch finally stated the conclusions at which the British government had arrived. Recognizing the exceptional circumstances of the case, they had, since February 1896, intentionally refrained from any pressure on the government of the South African Republic, except in cases where there had been a distinct breach of the Convention of 1884. Reluctant as they were to depart from this attitude of reserve and expectancy, still, 'having regard to the position of Great Britain as the paramount power in South Africa, and the duty incumbent on them to protect all British subjects residing in a foreign country, they cannot permanently ignore the exceptional and arbitrary treatment to which their fellow-countrymen and others are exposed, and the absolute indifference of the government of the Republic to the friendly representations which have been made to them on the subject'. 'With the earnest hope of arriving at a satisfactory settlement and as a proof of their desire to maintain cordial relations with the South African Republic', the British government proposed that a meeting should be arranged between President Kruger and Sir Alfred Milner at Pretoria. Meanwhile, the idea of a conference was already in the mind of leaders of the Dutch in Cape Colony and the Orange Free State; and the Bloemfontein Conference, which lasted from 31 May to 4 June, was welcomed by moderate men of all parties. The question was complicated by Kruger's desire to offset any concessions he might make with regard to the franchise by gains in other directions; and by Milner's insistence that there were other questions, besides the franchise, about which it might be necessary to make complaints. On the main subject of the Conference Milner proposed as a settlement a five years' retrospective franchise, and a substantial increase in the number of seats in the Volksraad to be allotted to the Rand. On the third day of the Conference a counter-scheme was put forward by Kruger, which included a six months' notice of intention to apply for naturalization; naturalization after two years' continued registration; and the right to the franchise after continuous registration for five years after naturalization. It proved impossible to arrive at an agreement, and the Conference came to an end.

It is easy to maintain that the Bloemfontein Conference broke down on petty points; but, in fact, throughout the negotiations Kruger never showed that spirit of conciliation without which paper concessions would have proved practically worthless. No one recognized more clearly than Chamberlain how great a calamity would be a war in South Africa, of the nature of a civil war; but the question was whether the situation had not become so serious that even war might be the less of two evils. Moreover, if the British government had really aimed at putting an end to the Republic, they would not have counselled measures that would have secured to it a new lease of life.

Even after the failure of the Bloemfontein Conference Chamberlain did not behave as if the door was finally closed to a settlement. In the words of

Lord De Villiers, he 'held out an olive branch' by proposing a joint inquiry into the franchise proposals. The Dutch members of the Cape ministry were strongly in favour of the acceptance of the offer, and the European governments gave similar advice; but Kruger's mind was apparently made up, and a peaceful issue had become impossible. The conciliatory attitude of Chamberlain was all to no purpose. When he offered, as part of a general settlement, to give a complete guarantee against any attack upon the independence of the Republic, either from within any part of the British dominions, or from the territory of a foreign state, the only reply was a curt ultimatum demanding that the points at issue should be settled by arbitration, and that the troops on the borders should be withdrawn, the reinforcements removed, and the troops on the high seas forbidden to land. It is true that Chamberlain's dispatch had also contained the warning that Kruger's attitude made it necessary to consider the whole situation afresh, and that final proposals would be made after such consideration. But this warning can hardly be said to excuse the curt and peremptory tone of Kruger's ultimatum.

From this time the sword had to decide the issue, and a minister, however active and able, was forced to play a secondary part. In the darkest hour of the War, however, Chamberlain never lost heart or courage. 'Never again', he said on 5 February 1900, 'shall the Boers be able to erect in the heart of South Africa a citadel from whence may proceed disaffection and race animosities; never again shall they be able to endanger the paramountcy of Great Britain; never again shall they be able to treat an Englishman as if he belonged to an inferior race'; and in a powerful dispatch of July 1900, which tore in pieces the analogy set up by the Cape ministry between the situation at the time of the Canadian rebellion and the situation in South Africa, we may recognize Chamberlain's handiwork. There was, moreover, much in the attitude of the other colonies to give consolation. These had shown their sympathy with the wrongs of the Uitlanders and with the cause of Great Britain by deeds as well as by words. The Australian colonies sent during the War no fewer than 15,502 men to South Africa; New Zealand sent 6,129, and Canada 5,762. There was force in Chamberlain's boast that these young nations were beginning to recognize the duties and responsibilities, as well as the privileges, of empire.

With the coming of peace more direct opportunities for statesmanship presented themselves. Few now will question that Chamberlain's visit to South Africa at the end of 1902 was a very wise move. No secretary of state had before this time visited a British colony in connexion with political questions; but there was enough of the old radical left in Chamberlain for this not to stand in his way. It seems clear that his influence and persuasive powers helped forward a reconciliation between the rival races and parties in Cape Colony; and this reacted favourably upon the general South African situation. Nor was he less successful in his dealings with the Boers of the Transvaal. In open discussion with their leaders he did much to clear the air of dislike and suspicion. 'The terms of Vereeniging', he told them, 'are the charter of the Boer people, and you have every right to call upon us to fulfil them in the spirit and in the letter; and, if in any respect you think we have failed, or that in the future we do fail, in carrying out these terms, bring your complaints to us, and they shall be redressed.' Again: 'In the terms of peace it was promised that Dutch education should be given to the children of all parents who desired it; that promise we will keep.' 'What are the qualities', he asked, 'which we admire in you? Your patriotism, your courage, your tenacity, your willingness to make sacrifices for what you believe to be right and true. Well, those are the qualities which we desire to imitate; and which we believe we shall.' He looked forward with confidence to the day when Boer and Briton would be one free people, under a common flag. It must be noted that these sentiments represented no new doctrine on the part of Chamberlain. During the heat of the War, when racial and political animosities were at their height, he had written (2 August 1900): 'It is the desire of Her Majesty's government that the inhabitants of these territories, assuming that they peaceably acquiesce in British rule and are ready to co-operate, irrespective of race, in maintaining the peace and furthering the prosperity of the country, should, as soon as circumstances permit, have all the advantages of self-government similar to that which is enjoyed by the inhabitants of the Cape Colony and Natal.' At the same time it was obvious that there would have to be a period of Crown Colony government, between the annexation and the grant of full self-government. Chamberlain does not, however, seem to have recognized the expediency of a period of representative, without responsible, government, such as that afterwards set on foot by Alfred Lyttelton.

Nor were Chamberlain's utterances less successful when addressed to the capitalists of the Rand. An eyewitness has testified that a speech of his at Johannesburg actually persuaded an audience, that had come with intent of refusing, to promise a loan of thirty million pounds, the proceeds of which should be paid to the British government, as a contribution to the cost of the War. It is true that this loan was never raised, bad times and a shortage of labour having disappointed the high hopes raised by the British successes. But such failure cannot be laid to the charge of the colonial secretary.

In dealing with the Rand magnates, Chamberlain was no less open than when dealing with the Boer leaders. Already the demand was beginning to be made for Asiatic labour, and his remarks on the subject are significant, in the light of its future history. 'It is clear to me, and no doubt to you', he said at Johannesburg (17 January 1903), 'that an overwhelming popular opinion in this very colony is opposed to such a solution. You have first to convert the people. Then you will have seen that the other great colonies of the Empire, that the opinion of the mother country itself, regard a step of this kind as retrograde and dangerous. And, lastly, if these difficulties are removed, there are serious practical obstacles in the way, which will meet you at the outset, and which, I think, justify my opinion that it would be very long indeed, even if all other difficulties were removed, before you would obtain any reliable supply from the sources which have been suggested.'

Another proof of Chamberlain's moderation was his vetoing, in 1902, the suspension of the Cape Colony constitution as proposed by the English party in the House of Assembly, although the line taken by Sir Wilfrid Laurier at the Imperial Conference of that year may have influenced his decision. Whilst emphasizing his desire for South African federation he recognized, in a dispatch of 23 February, that nothing could be worse than federation forced upon a people before they had time thoroughly to grasp its meaning and to understand how it would affect them personally in their several states, and to come to something like a general conclusion on the subject. The harvest could not yet be reaped; but, when the Union of South Africa came into being, it owed something at least to the seed sown by Chamberlain.

He had already done good work in the cause of federation by piloting the Commonwealth of Australia Bill through the House of Commons (1900). In his attempt to maintain unimpaired the appellate jurisdiction of the Privy Council, he may have exaggerated its importance as a bond of imperial union; and the conclusion finally reached, which was that no appeal should be allowed in cases in which the question at issue was the limits *inter se* of the constitutional powers of the commonwealth and those of any state or states, or the limits *inter se* of the constitutional powers of any two or more states, without the leave of the commonwealth high court, was, in fact, a 'confession of failure'. Nevertheless, the birth of the Commonwealth of Australia seemed a distinct step forward in the direction of Chamberlain's ideals.

With his return from South Africa in March 1903, Chamberlain entered upon the last stage of his political life. During the South African War a tax of one shilling a quarter on imported corn had been imposed, which produced some two and a half million pounds a year without apparently affecting the price of bread. Chamberlain was in favour of retaining this small tax with the view of giving a rebate to imperial wheat; and he was bitterly disappointed by its abolition during his absence in South Africa. He was under the impression that, before his departure for South Africa, his policy had received the assent of the Cabinet with the exception of the chancellor of the exchequer, Mr. C.T. (afterwards Lord) Ritchie. The absence at the time of Cabinet ministers and other circumstances prevent certainty on the subject. Later, Chamberlain wrote to the Duke of Devonshire (21 September): 'For my part I care only for the great question of imperial unity. But for this ... I would not have taken off my coat. ... While I was slaving my life out, you threw it (my policy) over as of no importance; and it is to this indifference to a great policy, which you had yourselves accepted, that you owe the present situation.' On 9 September 1903 he wrote to the prime minister, Mr. Balfour, recognizing that as an 'immediate and practical policy' the question of preference to the Colonies could not be pressed with any success at the time, and saying that, as colonial secretary, he stood in a position different from any of his colleagues and would justly be blamed if he accepted its exclusion from the programme of the government. He therefore tendered his resignation so that he could, from outside, devote his attention to explaining and popularizing those principles of imperial union which his experience had convinced him were essential. It was not, however, till 16 September that the prime minister reluctantly acquiesced in this decision.

Chamberlain, while in the unionist government, was mainly preoccupied with colonial questions. He had not, however, altogether forgotten his zeal for social reform, and the Workmen's Compensation Act of 1897 was mainly due to his efforts. The weakest side of his statesmanship was, perhaps, shown in his excursions into the field of foreign policy. His attack upon Russia in 1898, with its remark that 'who sups with the devil must have a long spoon', cannot have made easier the path of Lord Salisbury's diplomacy. Nor was his grandiose scheme for an alliance between Great Britain, Germany, and the United States (1898–1901) likely, in the circumstances, to meet with success. Its object, the prevention of a great European war, was assuredly worth the price of granting a free hand to Germany in Asia Minor, and, if the negotiations had been left in the hands of Count Hatzfeldt, a conclusion might have been reached; but, with the Kaiser's jealousy and dislike of England, with the narrow persistence of Herr von Holstein, the permanent head of the German foreign office, in regarding the proposal as an opportunity to exact the hardest terms from the needs of Great Britain, and with Prince Bülow's subserviency to his royal master, the attempt was apparently from the first foredoomed to failure. It is a proof, however, of Chamberlain's flexibility of mind, since in March 1896 he had seemed to Count Hatzfeldt 'especially hostile to Germany and German interests'.

Whatever were the immediate circumstances of Chamberlain's resignation, in any case views were developing in his mind that foreshadowed a revolutionary change of policy. It must be remembered that, although it was easy enough to put side by side, as has been done, conflicting statements of his economic views at different periods, he had never, in theory or in practice, belonged to the Manchester school of free traders, to whom free trade was but one item in a general creed of *laissez-aller* and anti-socialism. From his first entrance into politics he had advocated a modified form of state socialism. He had, indeed, accepted free trade as part of the orthodox faith of a good liberal; but during those years he had failed to realize the importance of the imperial factor in the decision of the question. It was the consideration of this factor that accounted for his change of policy. On the fiscal side he had for some years been in favour of some kind of imperial *Zollverein*, and in 1896 he had protested against the proposal that, while the Colonies should be absolutely free to impose what protective duties they pleased, our whole system should be changed, in return for a small discrimination in favour of British trade. The foreign trade of Great Britain was so large and that of the Colonies comparatively so insignificant that a small preference would give a merely nominal advantage; he did not think the British working classes would consent to make so revolutionary a change for what would seem to them an infinitesimal gain. Even as late as the opening of the Imperial Conference of 1902 he declared: 'Our first object is free trade within the Empire.'

But during the sitting of this conference the conviction was borne home to him that an imperial *Zollverein* was, for the time being, an impossibility; whilst the need for closer union became more and more urgent. Unless such union could be achieved between the component parts of the Empire, he thought that separation must sooner or later be the end. The enthusiasm aroused throughout the Empire by the South African War had seemed to give him his opportunity, and at the Imperial Conference he had suggested 'a real council of the Empire to which all questions of imperial interest might be referred. Such a council would be at first merely advisory; but its object would not be completely secured until it had attained executive functions and perhaps some legislative powers.' It was the chilling reception accorded to this suggestion, and the failure of the attempt to organize closer union on the lines of imperial defence, which led him to seek elsewhere for bonds of union. A statement made in October 1903 throws light on the trend of his political development. Discussing the subject of a federal council he said: 'The Colonies want to know what it is they are to discuss before they come to your council. When you have got a commercial union, there will be something to discuss. ... You cannot approach closer union by that means (a federal council). I tried next in connexion with imperial defence. Again I was beaten by the difficulties of the situation; but I did not on that account give it up, and I come back therefore to this idea of commercial union, which will bring us together, which will necessitate the council, which council may in time do much more than it does in the beginning, and may leave us, though it will not find us, a great united, loyal, and federated Empire.' A little later he declared: 'I hope to lay firm and deep the foundations for that imperial union which fills my heart when I look forward to the future of the world.'

Welcoming the statement made by an opponent in the press that the real issue in question was between imperialism and 'Little Englandism', Chamberlain nailed his colours to the mast as a convinced imperialist (Liverpool, 27 October 1903). He would never have raised the question, as he avowed next day, if he had not been moved by his own personal experiences, and by the responsibilities which he felt he had towards the Colonies. If he had not felt, in connexion with that experience and responsibility, that the whole future of the Empire depended upon a readiness to review the past history, he would have left the subject, so far as it concerned the immediate interests of Great Britain, to younger men. But a constructive policy was essential, and during his long stay at the Colonial Office he had had more opportunities than most men to meet and consult with distinguished colonial statesmen, and he had found that this matter of closer union was much in their thoughts. 'I found very soon that these men agreed that all progress must be gradual, and that the line of least resistance would be a commercial union on the basis of preference between ourselves and our kinsmen.' Starting from different premises, he arrived at the same conclusion as Adam Smith, that the British Empire was a potentiality, a project of empire, not an empire—'a loose bundle of sticks'—bound together by no tie but that of sentiment and sympathy. In the same speech he spoke of the sacrifices by which the Empire had been created; and a sympathetic critic may regret that more stress was not throughout laid on the necessity of sacrifice for the attainment of great objects. But it must be remembered that Chamberlain was an old campaigner in politics, and if, in the course of his appeal to the British voters, he seemed sometimes to be absorbed in considerations other than those which had launched him on his adventure, he perhaps only followed in the usual steps of the practical politician. Whilst his resignation gave him complete liberty of action, matters were not made easier for him by the hesitating attitude of some of his old colleagues, and especially of the prime minister, Mr. Balfour. Moreover, the ministry had become unpopular by reason of the Education Act of 1902, of which Chamberlain strongly disapproved, though he was too loyal to express his views openly.

The effect of all this was to make him concentrate more and more upon the one object, of bringing the British people round to his views of tariff reform. He had, in any case, a difficult task before him. Arrayed against him were the political and economic beliefs of the majority of educated Englishmen; whilst vague memories of 'the starving 'forties' made any kind of protection suspect to the labouring classes.

Still, whether we agree or disagree, we must recognize the strength of Chamberlain's convictions; and it was fitting that the last words in his three years' campaign, which ended on 9 July 1906, should have been these: 'The union of the Empire must be preceded and accompanied by a better understanding, by a closer sympathy. To secure that, is the highest object of statesmanship now at the beginning of the twentieth century; and, if these were the last words that I were permitted to utter to you, I would rejoice to utter them in your presence and with your approval. I know that the fruition of our hopes is certain. I hope I may live to congratulate you upon our common triumph; but, in any case, I have faith in the people. I trust in the good sense, the intelligence, and the patriotism of the majority, the vast majority of my countrymen. I look forward to the future with hope and confidence, and

"Others I doubt not, if not we, The issue of our toil shall see".'

But it was not given him to see the issue of his toil. Only two days later (11 July), a sudden attack cut him off, for his remaining years, from active life. He did not, indeed, lose the control of his faculties, but the aphasia which had come upon him made further public life impossible. He died at Highbury, Birmingham, 2 July 1914. A funeral in Westminster Abbey was offered, but the family preferred that he should be buried near his home.

Turning from the statesman to the man, we find a unanimity of opinion among those who knew Chamberlain intimately. If, in Lord Morley's words, he had the 'genius of friendship', he had no less the genius both of family and of official life. Chamberlain was married three times: first, in 1861 to Harriet (died 1863), daughter of Archibald Kenrick, of Berrow Court, Edgbaston; secondly, in 1868 to Florence (died 1875), daughter of Timothy Kenrick, of Birmingham, and a cousin of his first wife; thirdly, in 1888 to Mary, only daughter of William Crowninshield Endicott, a distinguished American judge and statesman, belonging to a family well known in New England history. Chamberlain had become engaged to Miss Endicott when he was working on the fisheries commission, but the marriage could not be announced or take place until after the American presidential election, for fear of prejudicing the chances of the democrats. By his first wife Chamberlain had one son (Joseph) Austen, and one daughter; by his second, one son (Arthur) Neville, and three daughters. He was a devoted husband and father, and perhaps one of the happiest moments of his life was when Mr. Gladstone gracefully alluded to the merits of his elder son's maiden speech; when he and Mr. Ritchie both resigned in 1903, it must have been some consolation that the latter was succeeded by the same son, (Sir) Austen Chamberlain, as chancellor of the exchequer. Mr. Neville Chamberlain, also, entered the Cabinet as chancellor of the exchequer in Mr. Baldwin's ministry in 1923.

Although on one occasion Chamberlain lamented the loss of a university education, the loss was made up by intercourse with the best books and with a few choice spirits at Birmingham. According to Mr. T. H. S. Escott, the writer who, more than any other, formed his mind and style, was the French publicist, Paul Louis Courier. Lord Morley, who went abroad with him frequently, bore witness to his interest in pictures, buildings, and history. In 1896 he was elected lord rector of Glasgow University, and delivered a characteristic address on patriotism, in which he protested his faith in one race and one nation: 'I believe that with all the force and enthusiasm of which democracy alone is capable they will complete and maintain that splendid edifice of our greatness.' Further, he was in a yet closer way connected with the university of Birmingham, the foundation of which in 1900 was largely due to his efforts; he became, as was meet, its first chancellor.

Chamberlain belonged to a Unitarian family, and seems always to have remained faithful to the creed of his fathers. Lord Morley has given a vivid picture of him as a companion, 'alert, not without a pleasant squeeze of lemon, to add savour to the daily dish'. Spare of body, sharp and pronounced in feature, careful of dress, Chamberlain looked ever ready. Caricaturists everywhere fixed eagerly on the monocle in his eye and the rare orchid bloom, culled from his favourite greenhouse, habitually worn in his button-hole. No physiognomy was better known to contemporaries, either at home or abroad. Gladstone, who was by no means a friendly critic, bore witness to Chamberlain's merits in serious discussions. What impressed Froude about him was that he knew his own mind. There was no dust in his eyes; and he threw no dust in the eyes of others. He was naturally open and spontaneous; and, in Lord Morley's words, 'when he encountered a current of doubt, dislike, suspicion, prejudice, his one and first impulse was to hasten to put his case, to explain, to have it out.' He was a hard hitter, and not always careful to remember that others were more thin-skinned than himself, but he was of a nature essentially generous and forgiving. After a temporary quarrel with Lord Randolph Churchill, at the time of the Aston riots (1884), he wrote to Lord Randolph who was starting for India, a characteristic letter, burying the hatchet, which received a cordial response. He seems to have been totally devoid of jealousy; and he carried loyalty to those who had once obtained his confidence to its extreme limits. With these qualities he naturally attracted friendship; and his relations with men so different as were Dilke, Churchill, Morley, and Balfour, were the best witness to that attraction. 'To him', again in Lord Morley's words, 'the friend was not merely a comrade in a campaign. He was an innermost element in his existence; whilst, if he stood by his friend, he counted on his friend to stand by him.'

The same loyalty that endeared him to his friends called forth the devoted attachment of his official subordinates. Lord Milner described him as an incomparable chief. He always, if possible, consulted those who served under him. He gave the fullest consideration to all their representations. He went thoroughly into every aspect of the case, for he was a most industrious minister; and finally, he laid down firmly and deliberately the policy which he wished to be followed, leaving a large latitude to those who had to work it out. Sir Harry Wilson, who was principal private secretary to Chamberlain from 1895 to 1897, has also described his methods of dealing with business. His 'minutes' were almost invariably concise, and always strictly to the point. While he generally accepted the advice of his under-secretaries, often making illuminating additions to their drafts, he sometimes reversed their conclusions, though not without full discussion. The vigour of his methods is attested by the fact that, at the time of the Jameson Raid, he made a personal invasion, at one o'clock a.m., of the office of the Eastern Telegraph Company, to discover why an important telegram had not been delivered. Through his whole life he justified the words of his son: 'He never rested. To his last day he seemed too young to leave things as they are.' When party animosities are forgotten, men will probably recognize the truth of the Earl of Balfour's testimony—'He was a great statesman, a great friend, a great orator, a great man.'

Chamberlain's speeches are contained in the following editions: C. W. Boyd, *Mr. Chamberlain's Speeches*, 2 vols. (1914); H. W. Lucy, *Speeches, with sketch of Life* (1885); *Speeches on Home Rule and the Irish Question, 1881–1887* (1887); *Foreign and Colonial Speeches* (1897); *Imperial Union and Tariff Reform 15 May–4 November 1903* (2nd edition, 1910). He was the author of *Patriotism* (1897) and of a preface to *The Radical Programme* (1885). He also wrote the following articles in the *Fortnightly Review: The Liberal Party and its Leaders*, and *The Next Page of the Liberals* (1874); *The Right Method with the Publicans*, and *Lapland and Swedish Licensing* (1876); *Free Schools, Municipal Public-Houses*, and *The New Political Organization* (1877); *The Caucus* (1879); *Labourers' and Artisans' Dwellings* (1883). In the *Nineteenth Century* he wrote: *Shall we Americanise our Institutions?* (1890); *The Labour Question* (1892); *A Bill for the Weakening of Great Britain* (1893); and in the *New Review, Municipal Reform* (1894).

The chief portraits of Chamberlain are those by Frank Holl (1886), by J. S. Sargent (1896), by Sir H. von Herkomer (1903, *Royal Academy Pictures*, 1904), and by C. W. Furse (1904, unfinished owing to the artist's death). A bust in Westminster Abbey was unveiled on 31 March 1916 by Lord Balfour, and another, executed by F. Derwent Wood in 1915, belongs to the Corporation of the City of London (*Royal Academy Pictures*, 1915).

[*The Times*, 4 July 1914; Stephen Gwynn and Gertrude Tuckwell, *Life of Sir Charles W. Dilke*, 2 vols., 1917; Lord Morley, *Recollections*, 2 vols., 1917, and *Life of William Ewart Gladstone*, 2 vols., 1905; Winston S. Churchill, *Lord Randolph Churchill*, 2 vols., 1906; Bernard Holland, *Life of Spencer Compton, Eighth Duke of Devonshire*, 2 vols., 1911; G. M. Trevelyan, *Life of John Bright*, 1913; Lord Edmond Fitzmaurice, *Life of Granville George Leveson Gower, Second Earl Granville*, 2 vols., 1905; Hon. A. R. D. Elliot, *Life of George Joachim Goschen, First Viscount Goschen*, 2 vols., 1911; E. A. Walker, *Lord De Villiers and his Times, South Africa 1842–1914*, 1924; A. G. Gardiner, *Life of Sir William Harcourt*, 2 vols., 1923; N. M. Murrell Marris, *Joseph Chamberlain, the Man and the Statesman*, 1900; S. H. Jeyes, *Mr. Chamberlain; his Life and Public Career*, 2 vols., 1904; Alexander Mackintosh, *Joseph Chamberlain; an honest biography*, 1906; Louis Creswicke, *Life of Joseph Chamberlain*, 4 vols., 1904; H. von Eckardstein, *Lebenserinnerungen*, translated by George Young as *Ten Years at the Court of St. James, 1895–1905*, 1921; Sir Willoughby Maycock, *With Mr. Chamberlain to the United States and Canada, 1887–1888*, 1914; Sir C. Tupper, *Recollections of Sixty Years*, 1914; Sir C. Bruce, *The Broad Stone of Empire*, 2 vols., 1910; A. W. W. Dale, *Life of R. W. Dale of Birmingham* (3rd ed.), 1899; R. Barry O'Brien, *Life of Charles Stewart Parnell*, 2 vols., 1898; W. Basil Worsfold, *Reconstruction of the New Colonies under Lord Milner*, 2 vols., 1913; R. Jebb, *The Imperial Conference*, vol. i, 1911; L. C. A. Knowles, *The Industrial and Commercial Revolutions in Great Britain during the Nineteenth Century*, 1921; '*The Times' History of the War in South Africa*, edited by L. C. M. S. Amery, vols. i and vi, 1900–1909; Sir Sidney Lee, *Life of King Edward VII*, vol. i, 1925; Articles on Chamberlain in the *United Empire*, vol. viii, pp. 102–11, 1917; by T. H. S. Escott in *Britannic Review*, vol. vii, pp. 321–41; and by M. Woods in *Fortnightly Review*, August 1914; *Parliamentary Papers*; *Hansard's Parliamentary Debates*; *Die Grosse Politik der Europäischen Kabinette 1871–1914*, vol. xi, 1923; E. Fischer, *Holstein's Grosses Nein. Die Deutsch-Englischen Bündnisverhandlungen von 1898–1901*, 1925.]

Hugh Egerton

published 1927

CHILDERS Robert Erskine
(1870–1922)

Author and politician, was born in London 25 June 1870, the second son of Robert Caesar Childers, the Pali scholar, by his wife, Anna Mary Henrietta, daughter of Thomas Johnston Barton, of Glendalough House, co. Wicklow. From his father, the pioneer of Pali literary studies in England, who died of consumption, hastened by devotion to his beloved studies, at the early age of thirty-eight, Childers seems to have inherited his extraordinary powers of concentration on his work; from his mother, his intense love of Ireland, fostered by the fact that until his marriage Glendalough House was his only real home. He was educated at Haileybury and at Trinity College, Cambridge, taking the law tripos and his B.A. degree in 1893, and from 1895 to 1910 was a clerk in the House of Commons. Quiet and reserved in appearance, even in his early days he showed a singular power of rising to the occasion. At Cambridge his remarkable elocutionary efforts as a candidate for the presidency of the *Magpie and Stump* are still remembered as the occasion of the most delightful 'rag' there within living memory. Soon after he left Cambridge he began spending a large part of his holidays, either alone or with a friend or two, navigating some tiny little yacht through the storms of the Channel or the North Sea, or threading his way through the complicated shoals of the German, Danish, or Baltic coasts.

When, at the end of 1899, the call came for volunteers in the South African War, Childers was among the first to join the City Imperial Volunteer battery of the Honourable Artillery Company. As a result of this experience there came from his pen a vivid personal record of the war, *In the Ranks of the C.I.V.* (1900); he was also responsible, as a collaborator, for the official volume, *The H.A.C. in South Africa* (1903). But his most popular and lasting book, *The Riddle of the Sands* (1903), was the outcome of his yachting expeditions to the coast of Germany. The story, told with even more charm than his narrative about the C.I.V., and based on exact topographical observations of this coast, was a purely imaginary account of preparations for a German raid on England; but it at once touched the prevalent feeling of suspicion as to German plans, and became even more popular when it was republished in August 1914. In September 1903 he went to Boston with the Honourable Artillery Company on a visit to the Ancient and Honourable Artillery Company of Massachusetts, an offshoot of the London body, the first visit in peace time of an armed body of British soldiers to the United States. In the course of the celebrations he happened one day to sit next to Miss Mary Alden Osgood, of Boston: the two fell in love at first sight, and on 5 January 1904 were married at Boston. On his return to London in that month they established themselves in a Chelsea flat. Of this marriage Childers wrote some years later that it was 'the most wonderful happiness that I know'; indeed, in all his subsequent activities he and his wife were as one mind and soul. Two sons were born to them.

Childers's next literary work was vol. v of *The Times' History of the War in South Africa* (1907)—a task which suggested to him a campaign against antiquated uses of cavalry, through his volumes *War and the Arme Blanche* (with a preface by Lord Roberts, 1910) and *German Influence on British Cavalry* (1911). His summer holidays were, as before, spent yachting, chiefly in the Baltic in the yacht *Asgard*, modelled on the lines of Nansen's *Fram* by Colin Archer, of Larvig; the yacht was one of his wedding presents. In all these trips he was accompanied by his wife, who, though crippled, soon became almost as expert in seamanship as he was himself.

Meanwhile Childers's attention had been more and more concentrated on Irish affairs. Of unionist stock, he came back from the South African War with a growing inclination to liberalism; but in 1902 he still could write, 'I am not a Home Ruler.' It was not until 1908 that, after seeing much of Sir Horace Plunkett's work in Ireland, he wrote in a private letter, 'I have come back finally and immutably a convert to Home Rule.' Thenceforward he thought of little else but Ireland. In 1910 he resigned his clerkship in the House of Commons in order to devote himself to political work, appearing for a short time as liberal candidate for Devonport, a constituency which was little suited to him, and which he relinquished before the election came on. In London he joined a committee to discuss *Home Rule Problems* (the papers, including one of his, read before this committee being published under this title in 1911); and in his own book, *The Framework of Home Rule* (1911), he went farther than most Englishmen of the time in advocating full dominion status for Ireland. In July 1914, after the passage of Mr. Asquith's Home Rule Bill and the subsequent failure of the government to prevent the arming of the Ulster Volunteers, Childers and his wife undertook, on behalf of a small Anglo-Irish committee, to carry a cargo of arms in his yacht *Asgard* into Howth harbour, five miles north of Dublin, for the use of the National Volunteers—a task which he accomplished with complete success.

Immediately afterwards the European War broke out. Childers, with his knowledge of the German coast as displayed in *The Riddle of the Sands*, was naturally pitched upon by the Admiralty for reconnaissance work on the seaplane carrier H.M.S. *Engadine*. As an R.N.V.R. officer he took part in the Cuxhaven raid (November 1914), and during the rest of the War was

employed as an intelligence officer and in training officers for reconnaissance work in the Royal Naval Air Service. He also did staff work at
the Admiralty, and at the end of the War made an important report on the
effects of enemy bombing on protected buildings. He was several times
mentioned in dispatches, was promoted lieutenant-commander, and
eventually, on amalgamation of the Naval Air Service with the Royal Air
Force, held the rank of major; for his services in the War he received the
D.S.C.

At the outset of the War Childers had joined up enthusiastically, in the
belief that the rights of nationality promised by the Allies would be extended to Ireland; moreover, in 1917 he was seconded for service on the
secretariat of the Irish Convention, which, however, failed to secure
agreement on Home Rule. Bitterly disappointed in 1918 by the continued
delay in giving any form of self-government to Ireland, he determined, on
his demobilization in March 1919, to devote the rest of his life to securing,
no longer dominion status, the time for which he believed had passed, but
complete independence for Ireland as a republic. With this object, in the
same year he accompanied the Irish republican envoys sent by Arthur
Griffith to Paris to put the case for Ireland before the Versailles Conference, and in the following December settled with his family in Dublin in
order to work in the Irish republican ranks. He wrote continually in the
English, Irish, and foreign press to protest against the Dublin Castle
methods of government and against the employment of the 'Black and
Tans', some of his articles being reprinted as a pamphlet, *Military Rule in
Ireland* (1920). In May 1921 he was elected to the self-constituted Dail
Eireann as member for county Wicklow and was appointed minister of
propaganda. After the truce of July in that year he went with Eamonn De
Valera on the first delegation to London and was principal secretary to the
subsequent Irish delegation which negotiated the Treaty with the British
government (October–December 1921). But by this time Childers had
become irreconcilable to any form of treaty which did not recognize an
Irish republic, and in the Dail debates on the articles of agreement he
vehemently opposed Arthur Griffith and Michael Collins, who were for
acceptance of the Treaty.

After the establishment of the Irish Free State government, Childers
joined the Republican army, and while actually serving in mobile columns
in the south edited and published the Republican organ *Poblact na h-
Eireann*. On 10 November 1922 his old home, Glendalough House, where
he had taken passing refuge, was surrounded by Free State soldiers; he had
a pistol, but did not fire it, as one of the women of the house threw herself
between him and the soldiers. He was arrested, and court-martialled in
Dublin on 17 November by a court which he refused to acknowledge; and

on 24 November he was shot at Beggar's Bush barracks by a firing party, with each member of which he had first shaken hands.

At the time Childers's name was branded on both sides of the Channel as that of a traitor and renegade to both Ireland and England. But no one who knew the man believed that, whatever might be thought of his judgement, he had a particle of meanness or treachery in his nature, or that the course of action which he had adopted was based on anything but the prompting of his conscience and sense of honour. By his friends Childers will always be remembered as a man of indomitable courage, of winning modesty, of extraordinary generosity and, in his earlier and happier days, of a most engaging sense of humour.

[Basil Williams, *Erskine Childers* (a pamphlet privately printed), 1926; private information; personal knowledge.]

B. WILLIAMS

published 1937

CHURCHILL Randolph Frederick Edward Spencer-

(1911–1968)

Journalist and MP, was born at Bolton Street, London, 28 May 1911, the only son and second of four children of (Sir) Winston Leonard Spencer-Churchill, later prime minister, and his wife Clementine Ogilvy Hozier (later Baroness Spencer-Churchill). He was educated at Eton and Christ Church, Oxford. He was a loquacious and precocious boy, drinking double brandies at the age of eighteen—a habit which did not change over the years. His father disapproved, but told a visitor: 'Modern young people will do what they like. The only time parents really control their children is before they are born. After that their nature unfolds remorselessly petal by petal.' Relations between Winston and Randolph were always uneasy, the father alternately spoiling and being infuriated by the son. They accompanied each other in reasonable harmony on Winston's visit to Canada and the USA in 1929, but Randolph displeased his father soon afterwards by leaving Oxford without a degree in order to become a journalist. He was at an early age a fluent writer and speaker, and a vigorous, if at times embarrassing, supporter of his father's cause.

In February 1935, without consulting his father, he stood at a by-election in Wavertree as an independent Conservative against the India Bill, thus splitting the party vote and letting in Labour. In the general election that autumn he stood, this time as official Conservative candidate, for West Toxteth. He lost, and lost again at a by-election in February 1936 in Ross and Cromarty against Malcolm MacDonald, the National Government candidate and dominions secretary—another embarrassment for his father who was then angling for a cabinet post. In 1940, thanks to the party truce, he was elected for Preston, but lost in the election of 1945.

During World War II he was a major in the 4th Queen's Own Hussars, serving on the general staff (intelligence) at GHQ Middle East. In January 1944 he was parachuted into Yugoslavia as a member of the (Sir) Fitzroy Maclean mission to support General Tito. He was joined by Evelyn Waugh and F. W. F. Smith, second Earl of Birkenhead. His loquacity maddened his colleagues. There is a story that they bet him a substantial sum that he could not read a certain number of books of the Bible without talking. Well before the end of Genesis he exclaimed 'Christ! This is exciting' and lost his bet, but never paid.

After two more unsuccessful attempts to get into Parliament in 1950 and 1951 he took to authorship, though continuing as a lecturer, journalist, and broadcaster. His ambition was to write the life of his father. The trustees who owned the papers were not too sure. He decided to show that he was a serious biographer by writing the life of E. G. V. Stanley, seventeenth Earl of Derby. It is a reputable if rather dull book, but Lord Derby was a dull man. It was published in 1959 and the trustees gave their consent. Churchill assembled a team of ever-changing research assistants—their position was neither easy nor well paid—at his house, Stour in East Bergholt, Suffolk. In 1964 he wrote *The Fight for the Tory Leadership*, a very pro-Macmillan account of the accession of A. Douglas-Home (later Lord Home of the Hirsel) to the premiership. He was blown out of the water on 17 January 1964 by Iain Macleod, who had just become editor of the *Spectator*, in one of the most famous and devastating articles that has ever appeared in that journal. For once Randolph had no comeback. The first volume of his father's biography appeared in 1966, *Youth 1874–1900*; the second, *The Young Statesman 1901–1914*, a year later, along with five companion volumes of documentation (1967–9). He had set the pattern for a major biographical achievement but he died prematurely. The work was carried to completion by one of his leading research assistants, Martin Gilbert. The eighth and final volume appeared in 1988.

Slim, blond, and good-looking in his youth, he became somewhat bloated in middle age, and his potations did not improve his appearance. Conversation with him could be exciting and enjoyable, but one was uneasily aware of potential explosions. He was not liked in his father's wartime entourage: 'I thought Randolph was one of the most objectionable people I had ever met', wrote Sir John Colville, one of Winston's private secretaries. The shadow of a famous father can often damage a competitive son.

He was twice married: in 1932 to Pamela Beryl, daughter of Edward Kenelm Digby, eleventh Baron Digby; they had one son. The marriage was dissolved in 1946 and in 1948 he married June, daughter of Colonel Rex Hamilton Osborne, of Little Ingleburn, Malmesbury, Wiltshire; they had one daughter. The marriage was dissolved in 1961. Churchill died at Stour 6 June 1968.

[Randolph Churchill, *Twenty-one Years*, 1965; Martin Gilbert, *Churchill*, 1971–88, seriatim; Mark Amory (ed.), *The Letters of Evelyn Waugh*, 1980; Sir John Colville, *The Fringes of Power*, 1985; private information; personal knowledge.]

ROBERT BLAKE

published 1993

COOPER Alfred Duff

(1890–1954)

First Viscount Norwich

Politician, diplomatist, and author, was born at 9 Henrietta Street, Cavendish Square, London, 22 February 1890, the fourth child and only son of (Sir) Alfred Cooper by his wife, Lady Agnes Cecil Emmeline Duff, sister of the first Duke of Fife. His father, who came of a family long established in Norwich, was a popular and successful London surgeon. His mother had been twice previously married. While still a child he acquired from his sisters a love of poetry, a gift for memorizing, and the habit of declamation. He was educated at Eton where he achieved no special prominence and after a year abroad went up in 1908 to New College, Oxford.

His mother by then had retired into secluded widowhood and his three sisters had married. His Eton friend, John Manners, introduced him to Clovelly Court, near Bideford, where he stayed every summer from 1908 to 1914, and where he met the more gifted and vigorous of his contemporaries. They cured him of a tendency to dilettantism and aroused in him the ambition to secure the richest prizes which life had to offer. This ambition was not, it is true, very apparent during his first two years at

Oxford. He made a few pugnacious speeches in the Union, profited much from the guidance of his tutor, H. A. L. Fisher, but in the end obtained only second class honours in history (1911).

After two years spent mainly in Hanover and Paris he passed into the Foreign Office in October 1913. Many of his dearest friends, including John Manners, were killed during the early stages of the war and it irked him to be tied to a civilian job. In July 1917 he obtained his release from the Foreign Office and, after a period of training, joined the 3rd battalion of the Grenadier Guards in time for the offensive. On 21 August 1918, in the Battle of Albert, known as 'the battle of the mist', he led his platoon with such skill and gallantry that he was cited in dispatches for 'splendid leading' and was appointed to the D.S.O. On demobilization he returned to the Foreign Office.

In 1919 he married Lady Diana Olivia Winifred Maud Manners, daughter of the eighth Duke of Rutland, and one of the most beautiful women of her time. In her he found a dazzling and valiant companion, who watched over him with intelligent devotion until his death. At their house at 90 Gower Street, where they lived for seventeen years, they would entertain the survivors of his own generation together with some of their older friends, such as Augustine Birrell, Edwin Montagu, Maurice Baring, Hilaire Belloc, Lord Beaverbrook, and (Sir) Winston Churchill. Duff Cooper's ambition to enter Parliament was stimulated by these associations and by the fact that, on being appointed private secretary to the parliamentary under-secretary in February 1922, he was regularly attending debates in the House of Commons. The difficulty was finance. In 1923, however, Lady Diana obtained a rewarding contract to play the leading part in *The Miracle* in New York. On 31 July 1924 Duff Cooper, who had never been a natural civil servant, resigned from the Foreign Office and in October of that year he was elected Conservative member of Parliament for Oldham. On 15 December he delivered an impressive maiden speech which immediately placed him in the forefront of the back-benchers. In January 1928 he was appointed financial secretary to the War Office, but lost his seat in the general election of 1929. He was consoled by the birth of his son, John Julius, on 15 September 1929. He devoted the leisure to working on his biography of *Talleyrand* which, when published in 1932, earned universal acclaim.

In March 1931 a by-election occurred in the St. George's division of Westminster. Certain Conservatives, with the encouragement and support of Lord Rothermere and Lord Beaverbrook, decided to put up an independent candidate as a protest against Baldwin's leadership of the party. Duff Cooper volunteered to stand as the official Conservative. After a spirited campaign, which attracted much public attention, he won by

5,710 votes and retained the seat until he resigned it in 1945. In September 1931 he resumed his former post as financial secretary to the War Office; in June 1934 he was promoted to financial secretary to the Treasury; in November 1935 he became secretary of state for war and a privy counsellor.

During the abdication crisis in 1936 Duff Cooper was one of the two cabinet ministers whom, with Baldwin's approval, King Edward VIII consulted. Realizing that His Majesty's resolve could not be shaken, Duff Cooper begged him to postpone his marriage for a year and meanwhile to be crowned. The King felt it would be wrong to go through so solemn a ceremony as the coronation without letting his ultimate intentions be known: this advice he therefore rejected.

In May 1937, when Chamberlain succeeded Baldwin as prime minister, Duff Cooper was, to his surprise and pleasure, offered the post of first lord of the Admiralty. Meanwhile he had been able to complete his life of *Haig*, undertaken at the request of the executors, in two volumes (1935–6). Duff Cooper enjoyed being first lord. He got on well with the naval staff, he grappled with the problem of the Fleet Air Arm, and he strove to put the navy in readiness for a war which he saw to be inevitable. Chamberlain, with whom he was never on terms of ease or confidence, did not support these endeavours. Duff Cooper, having abandoned his initial trust in the League of Nations, had fallen back on the two classic principles that Great Britain must be the 'natural' enemy of any power seeking to dominate the Continent, and that it was a mistake to have more than one major enemy at a time. Thus, although he was not opposed to an agreement with Italy, he was convinced that any compromise with Hitler would prove unworkable. When, therefore, the Czechoslovak crisis arose in the autumn of 1938, he found himself at variance with Chamberlain and the majority of his colleagues. It was with difficulty that he obtained their approval to the mobilization of the Fleet which took place on 28 September. When two days later Chamberlain returned from Munich, bringing with him the terms of his agreement with Hitler, Duff Cooper was unable to share the general relief and jubilation. On 3 October, in a speech which shocked the country and profoundly impressed the House of Commons, he demonstrated that the Munich agreement was meaningless and dishonourable. Even among those who were most pained by this opinion there was admiration for his moral courage.

Immediately on his resignation he accepted an offer from Lord Beaverbrook to write a weekly article for the *Evening Standard*. Although he did not always share the political views of Lord Beaverbrook, he was accorded complete independence on the condition that the editor need not publish, although he must pay for, any article of which he disapproved.

The winter of 1939–40 was devoted to an extended lecture tour in the United States. When in May 1940 (Sir) Winston Churchill succeeded Chamberlain, Duff Cooper was given the post of minister of information. On 26 June 1940 after the fall of France, he flew with Lord Gort on a forlorn hope to Rabat with the intention of establishing contact with those French ministers, such as Georges Mandel, who were credited with the wish to continue resistance in North Africa. The French authorities had orders to prevent any such meeting, if necessary by force: Duff Cooper returned to London with his mission unaccomplished. In July 1941 he left the Ministry of Information with a sigh of relief and became chancellor of the Duchy of Lancaster. In August he left for the Far East on behalf of the War Cabinet to examine and report on the arrangements for consultation and co-ordination between the various British authorities, military, administrative and political, in those regions. After Pearl Harbor he was appointed resident cabinet minister at Singapore and authorized to form a War Council, but the appointment of Sir A. P. (later Earl) Wavell as supreme commander very shortly afterwards made his post redundant. He arrived in England in February 1942 to find that his name had been associated with responsibility for the Singapore collapse. He consoled himself for this unfairness by working hard as chairman, from June, of the cabinet committee on security and by writing a romantic study of King David (1943).

In January 1944 he arrived at Algiers as British representative with the French Committee of National Liberation established in North Africa under General de Gaulle. In September 1944 his mission moved to Paris and on 18 November he presented his letters of credence as British ambassador. During their three years' residence at the embassy Duff Cooper and Lady Diana sought by their tact and hospitality to heal the wounds left by the war and the aftermath of Vichy. Duff Cooper's aim had always been to secure a treaty of alliance: at first his efforts were hampered by the incompatibility existing between de Gaulle and Churchill: it was not until March 1947 that the treaty was finally signed by Bidault and Ernest Bevin at Dunkirk. When, at the end of 1947, he lost his post as ambassador he had the satisfaction of knowing that the main purposes of his mission had been achieved. He was appointed G.C.M.G. in 1948 and raised to the peerage as Viscount Norwich, of Aldwick, in 1952.

The remainder of his life after his retirement was devoted to literature and to entertaining his friends at his house at Vineuil near Chantilly. His ingenious fantasy *Sergeant Shakespeare* as well as a selection from his poems were published in 1949. In 1950 came his novel *Operation Heartbreak*. His remarkable autobiography *Old Men Forget* appeared in 1953. A few weeks later, on 1 January 1954, he died when on a voyage to the West Indies. His body was landed at Vigo and buried at Belvoir Castle, the home of his wife's family.

Duff Cooper possessed a striking personality. Although too reserved to win popularity, and too proud to court it, he influenced his contemporaries by the force of his courage, the vigour of his principles, and the distinction of his mind, his manners, and his discourses. He was choleric in argument and pugnacious in debate; yet in his later manhood he was never, as some imagined, a fanatical conservative, since he regarded as 'barbarians' all extremists, whether of the Right or the Left. Although his political ambitions waned in middle life, he never lost his zest for literature, travel, conversation, shooting, wine, and the society of gifted and beautiful women. 'Life has been good to me', he wrote in the last paragraph of his autobiography, 'and I am grateful.'

He was succeeded by his son John Julius (born 1929) who entered the Foreign Service and resigned in 1964. A portrait of Duff Cooper by Sir John Lavery, painted in 1919, is at the Château de St. Firmin, Vineuil, Oise. There is a memorial tablet in the crypt of St. Paul's Cathedral.

[Duff Cooper, *Old Men Forget*, 1953; Diana Cooper, *The Rainbow Comes and Goes*, 1958, *The Light of Common Day*, 1959, and *Trumpets from the Steep*, 1960; private information; personal knowledge.]

HAROLD NICOLSON

published 1971

CRAIG James

(1871–1940)

First Viscount Craigavon

Statesman, was born at Sydenham, a suburb of Belfast, 8 January 1871, the youngest of the six sons of James Craig, J.P., of Craigavon and Tyrella, co. Down, a successful business man in Belfast, by his wife, Eleanor Gilmour, daughter of Robert Brown. Educated at a private school at Holywood in county Down and afterwards at Merchiston Castle, Edinburgh, he became a stockbroker.

After the South African war, in which he served with distinction, Craig turned to politics, and at the general election of 1906, after an unsuccessful candidature in North Fermanagh (1903), he was elected member for East Down and held the seat until 1918. He was member for Mid-Down from 1918 to 1921. His sagacity, honesty of purpose, and courage were fully recognized at Westminster, and he served as parliamentary secretary to the Ministry of Pensions (1919–1920) and as parliamentary and financial secretary to the Admiralty in 1920–1921. He resigned on becoming, in June of the last-named year, under the Government of Ireland Act of December 1920, the first prime minister of Northern Ireland. Thenceforth he sat as one of the members for county Down in the parliament of Northern Ireland.

Craig's time at Westminster was mainly occupied in a struggle against the Irish separatist movement, which was relegated to the background in the general election of 1906 and by the majority given then to the liberals in the House of Commons. But the constitutional crisis following on the rejection of the finance bill of 1909 by the House of Lords, involved two appeals to the electorate (January and December 1910), the outcome of which was to make the nationalist vote a decisive factor in parliament. Thereupon the liberal government committed itself to another home rule bill, and in the bitter struggle which followed Craig took a leading part as the chief lieutenant of Sir Edward Carson, the Ulster leader.

Both leaders knew well the difficulties and dangers of the task that lay ahead, but they also knew that the loyalists of Ulster would never surrender their birthright as citizens of the United Kingdom. Ulster people were convinced that home rule for Ireland would lead to an Irish republic, disloyal to the Empire, and that Ulster's industries would be seriously affected by legislation promoted by men unacquainted with its industrial affairs.

Between the two leaders it was agreed that Carson would mainly devote himself to upholding Ulster's interests at Westminster and on public platforms throughout the kingdom, and that Craig would chiefly deal with organizing the means of resistance which, it was felt, must be adopted. The intention was that if the home rule bill became law, Ulster should be held in trust, in the King's name, until the Act was repealed. To this end a provisional government, with a judiciary, was planned, the Ulster Volunteer Force was brought into existence and armed, and the Ulster Covenant was signed (28 September 1912) by almost half a million people who pledged themselves to shirk nothing which might be required to prevent dismemberment of the kingdom.

In 1914 there followed a crisis of supreme gravity marked by the gun-running incident at Larne (24 April), but the war of 1914–1918 supervened, and at Carson's call the Ulster Volunteer Force, to the military qualities of which Kitchener afterwards paid tribute, became the Ulster Division and won undying glory in France.

Meanwhile the home rule bill had been placed on the Statute Book, but with a stay on its operation. With the advent of peace, however, the Irish question (complicated by the Sinn Fein rising at Eastertide 1916) again became a very dangerous issue, and after the provisional 'settlement' of 1920, promoted by Lloyd George as head of the coalition government, had been repudiated by the Southern Irish, the 'treaty' of 6 December 1921 led to immediate 'opting out' by Northern Ireland. Craig, a baronet since 1918, remained prime minister of Northern Ireland. He faced a task of great difficulty. The members of his government had to be chosen for the most part from men with no former parliamentary experience; a new police force had to be brought into being; and order established. Lawlessness was rampant at the time, murder and outrage of almost daily occurrence, and ministers carried on their work at great personal risk. In an attempt to make government impossible, nationalists boycotted the new parliament and the new Royal Ulster Constabulary Force and demanded a revision of the Ulster boundary. In due course a boundary commission was set up by the British government but its report was never published, the *status quo* being maintained as a result of a financial deal between the ministers of London and Dublin.

For nineteen years, until his death, Craig, who was raised to the peerage as Viscount Craigavon, of Stormont, co. Down, in 1927, remained prime minister of Northern Ireland, slowly and surely steering the small ship of state into relatively calm waters, and setting himself to strengthen its defences against future storms. During his premiership parliament passed many measures such as those maintaining social services similar to those in Great Britain, providing for improved housing and drainage, and creating a new educational system, as well as legislation designed to further the establishment of new industries and improve the agricultural position.

As parliamentarian and statesman, Craigavon possessed qualities of a very high order. He was a man of undaunted courage, high character, sound judgement, and devotion to duty, and his powers of leadership were conspicuous. He was a great organizer. He trusted his colleagues and his colleagues trusted him.

Craigavon died suddenly at Glencraig, co. Down, 24 November 1940, and was buried in the grounds of the parliament with the establishment of which his name is peculiarly connected. The aftermath of his work has been described in Mr. Churchill's commentary on the part played by Ulster since the outbreak of war in 1939. 'Only one great channel of entry remained open. That channel remained open because loyal Ulster gave us the full use of the Northern Irish ports and waters, and thus ensured the free working of the Clyde and the Mersey. But for the loyalty of Northern Ireland and its devotion to what has now become the cause of thirty governments or nations, we should have been confronted with slavery and death, and the light which now shines so strongly throughout the world would have been quenched.'

Craig married in 1905 Cecil Mary Nowell Dering, only child of Sir Daniel Alfred Anley Tupper, an officer of the King's household, and had twin sons and a daughter all of whom survived him. He was succeeded as second viscount by his elder son, James (born 1906). He was sworn of the Irish Privy Council in 1921, and of that of Northern Ireland in 1922. He received the honorary degree of LL.D. from Queen's University, Belfast, in 1922, and that of D.C.L. from Oxford in 1926.

A statue of Craigavon by L. S. Merrifield was placed in the Northern Ireland House of Commons at Stormont in 1945.

[*The Times*, 25 November 1940; Hugh Shearman, *Not an Inch. A Study of Northern Ireland and Lord Craigavon*, 1942; St. John Ervine, *Craigavon, Ulsterman*, 1948; personal knowledge.]

JOHN M. ANDREWS

published 1949

CRIPPS Sir (Richard) Stafford

(1889–1952)

Statesman and lawyer, was born at Elm Park Gardens, London, 24 April 1889, the fifth child and fourth son of Charles Alfred Cripps (later first Lord Parmoor), and his wife, Theresa Potter. His mother, whose sister Beatrice became Mrs. Sidney Webb, died when Stafford Cripps was four. Yet her influence remained with him all his life. In a remarkable letter left for her husband when she realized death was imminent she wrote, 'I should like the children brought up as much as possible in the country, and to be educated much in the same style as their father was. I should like their living to be of the simplest, without reference to show or other follies. I should like them trained to be undogmatic and unsectarian Christians, charitable to all churches and sects studying the precepts and actions of Christ as their example, taking their religious inspiration directly from the spirit of the New Testament.'

This charge the father faithfully carried out as well as the further precept, 'You will teach my children to love only what is true, and ever to seek further truth, and make it known to others, whatever career they may choose.' All his life Stafford Cripps was never consciously to depart from these standards. From his father's side came a bent towards public service for its own sake. It was always strongly reinforced by powerful but simple religious beliefs. The combination of Potter and Cripps blood merged in Stafford Cripps to produce the highest possible ideals in personal and public life.

Cripps showed early brilliance. The papers which won him from Winchester a natural science scholarship to New College, Oxford, in 1907 were so remarkable that the professor of chemistry at University College, London, Sir William Ramsay, who had been asked to scrutinize, persuaded Cripps to prefer the better equipped laboratories at University College. This resulted in Cripps being part author of a paper on the properties of the inert gas xenon which was read before the Royal Society when he was twenty-two. Undoubtedly he could have become an eminent chemist. But the legal and political pulls in his family, which echoed his own inclinations, drew him to the bar, to which he was called by the Middle Temple in 1913.

Medically unfit for the army, for which he volunteered after the outbreak of war in 1914, Cripps worked as a lorry driver in the Red Cross. After a year, because of his knowledge of chemistry, he was recalled from France to work in munitions. As assistant superintendent of the explosives factory at Queensferry he learned and contributed much. Through his gift for administration and capacity to work long hours and master intricate problems he made Queensferry the most efficient of all the munitions factories. It was largely because of the reputation he won there that (Sir) Winston Churchill appointed him minister of aircraft production in the war of 1939–45.

The work at Queensferry was hard. It was made harder by Cripps's zeal and energy. His inherent ill health grew far worse and he was never again to be fully fit. By the end of the war the doctors had despaired of conventional remedies. This prompted Cripps to turn to nature cures, vegetarianism, teetotalism, and the like. By such means he effected a considerable improvement in his health. What others often put down to crankiness was the product of trial and error in an attempt to ease his chronic physical disabilities. He went to bed early and was usually at work by six in the morning or before. This gave him half a day's advantage over his rivals and colleagues in any field throughout his life: one of the reasons for his rapid progress at the bar. But his successes did not come from energy and long hours alone; he had one of the most acute minds of his generation. He could rapidly comprehend complicated matters so that within a few hours he would understand almost as much of them as the experts. His clarity of thought enabled him to set out any proposition with striking lucidity and logic.

Cripps

Four years after his return to the bar in 1919 Cripps appeared for the Duff Development Company against the Colonial Office. His mastery of constitutional law, his ability to confound expert witnesses from their own writings, and his success in making the Colonial Office pay £387,000 established him in the legal profession as almost unbeatable when it came to digesting masses of complicated documents and evidence. Not only the defeated Colonial Office, but other important authorities and institutions, began to seek his aid; and his reputation advanced rapidly particularly in patent and compensation cases. When he appeared for the London County Council before the Railway Rates Tribunal in a matter which lasted from May 1924 to October 1926, his comprehensive understanding of the 39,000 questions put to expert witnesses on highly technical matters enormously impressed Herbert Morrison (later Lord Morrison of Lambeth) and formed in his mind the aim to persuade Cripps to join the Labour Party. In 1927 Cripps became the youngest K.C. But his enthusiasms outside his practice were not yet attracted to politics. Instead he spent much time on 'the World Alliance to promote international friendship through the Churches', of which he was for six years treasurer. By 1929 Cripps with his characteristic impatience had become bored by the lack of results achieved.

In that year his father and Sidney Webb, his uncle by marriage, were both members of Ramsay MacDonald's Cabinet but it was as much due to Morrison's influence as to his family's that Cripps joined the Labour Party. In 1930 he became solicitor-general and was knighted, and in January 1931 he was elected Labour member for East Bristol. When the 'national' Government was formed in 1931 MacDonald asked him to continue as solicitor-general. Cripps at the time was in a sanatorium at Baden. His delay in replying led to speculation that he was going to accept and there may have been some hesitation in Cripps's mind. In the event he declined and rapidly hurled himself with the same missionary enthusiasm that he had devoted to the World Alliance into propagating socialism. From being not even a member of the Labour Party a few years earlier, he shot right through it in terms of ideals and policies and almost out the other side. Morrison was astonished by the extremism of his protégé. Always irritated by delays, Cripps's logical mind concluded that if socialism were the right answer to economic and social problems it had better be brought in at once, lock, stock, and barrel, with barely a transitional period. He was a leading member of the Socialist League, a militant group within the Labour Party. Among other things he proposed the abolition of the House of Lords, the introduction of a dictatorial Emergency Powers Act to forestall sabotage by financial interests in the event of another Labour Government and, in 1934, he remarked 'there is no doubt we shall have to overcome opposition from Buckingham Palace.' This last observation produced alarmed disclaimers from the Labour leaders but in the public mind Cripps was confirmed as an out-and-out revolutionary while becoming a hero to Labour Party militants of the left wing.

It was not surprising that with his temperament he found the Labour Party in Parliament and outside an ineffectual organization. In 1936 he was a prime mover of the United Front designed to combine the Labour Party, the Communists, and the Independent Labour Party, and radicals in the Liberal Party into one organization. A new journal, *Tribune*, was launched in 1937 to further the cause. Shocked at his willingness to work with Communists the Labour Party executive declared that any member who appeared on the same platform as a Communist or a member of the I.L.P. would be automatically expelled. Despite various protests from Cripps this decision was upheld by the 1937 annual conference which at the same time re-elected Cripps to the national executive.

In the autumn of 1938 Cripps began to advocate an even wider grouping to remove Neville Chamberlain's government from office. This was a Popular Front which was to include Conservatives as well. When he proclaimed his programme for a Popular Front campaign and refused to withdraw it at the request of the national executive he was expelled from the Labour Party in January 1939. He was not readmitted until 1945. During this period considerable criticism was levelled at him by trade-unionists and other sober Labour Party stalwarts on the grounds that he abused his privilege of a rich man by spending considerable sums on internal propaganda in the Labour Party which were denied to the ordinary person. There was also complaint that he professed extreme socialism to assuage his own feelings of guilt at being richer than others, to the detriment of the Labour Party. At the same time Cripps was winning many friends. His handling of the inquiry into the Gresford Colliery disaster of 1934, in which he appeared without fee for the North Wales Miners' Federation, endeared him for ever to the miners, who were prepared to forgive what they regarded as his eccentricities. He had, too, a peculiar gift for inspiring loyalty in those younger than himself. The public picture of a Robespierre was belied by the private charm and kindliness. Nor, apart from his enforced carefulness in diet, did he live in any particular discomfort. He had an agreeable country house and farm and did not wear a hair shirt. Nor was he a non-smoker.

Just after the war broke out in 1939 Cripps embarked on a world tour with some assistance from Lord Halifax, then foreign secretary, who admired his honesty of purpose. This journey was of great importance to his future career. He visited India for the first time and was attracted by its people and leaders and infused with a desire to promote Indian independence and to help solve India's problems. He also visited Moscow and formed the view that it was possible to prevent Germany and the Soviet Union actually becoming major allies despite the non-aggression pact of August 1939. On his return to England he urged on all and sundry the need to try and draw Russia away from Germany. Churchill, who had just taken over as prime minister, was so taken by his arguments that he promptly sent him as ambassador to Moscow where Cripps arrived in June 1940.

He remained for nearly two years in Russia where he suffered considerable disillusion; in this he was not alone. Whatever outbursts he had allowed himself he was always a firm believer in the democratic processes and it was a surprise to him to find that the Soviet leaders paid no more regard to a socialist believer in democracy than to a capitalist. It was impossible for him to form any special relationship and he was often not only frustrated but irritated by the long months of idle helplessness. He could not claim to have advanced Anglo-Russian friendship at all up to the time of the German invasion of Russia on 22 June 1941—when Cripps happened to be in London, where he was sworn of the Privy Council. He immediately went back to Moscow and organized the pact of mutual assistance signed on 12 July 1941. When he returned to Britain in the following January he found that he had acquired an unexpected and barely deserved aura of success: the public enthusiasm for the new Russian ally had washed over on to Cripps. The remarkable broadcast which he made when he finally returned from Moscow confirmed this feeling and made him such a popular figure that there was even some talk of his being a potential replacement for the prime minister.

Churchill made him leader of the House of Commons as well as giving him a seat in the War Cabinet as lord privy seal in the month after he returned from Russia. Perhaps for the same reason Churchill allowed him to go on a one-man mission to India in an attempt to secure Indian support for the war with a promise of full self-government after it ended. L. S. Amery, secretary of state for India, subsequently remarked that it was thought better that Cripps should fail than that he should. Cripps very nearly succeeded and remained always convinced that it was M. K. Gandhi, who sabotaged the hopes of success, after taking no part in the official discussions himself. Consequently Cripps put the utmost emphasis on Gandhi's being completely involved in any future discussions.

The failure in India produced a fall in popular esteem, and there were differences of opinion with Churchill which brought Cripps near to resignation. He relinquished the leadership of the House and left the War Cabinet in November 1942, to become minister of aircraft production, a post in which he was extremely successful, until the German war ended in

1945. That probably prompted C. R. (later Earl) Attlee to make him president of the Board of Trade in the post-war Labour Government. With his usual long working days and grasp of detail Cripps crashed into Britain's economic problems. He saw clearly what would have to be done and that it would be unpopular. He endeavoured to alleviate the unpopularity by making regular and clear expositions of the country's need to increase exports and production. Nobody at that time could compare with him in his ability to force the House of Commons and the nation to listen to dry unpalatable economic facts and to be moved by his presentation of them, although he never had any gift for literary phraseology or oratorical language.

Cripps went with two other cabinet ministers on the cabinet mission to India in 1946. He was the mission's directing force, working with all his powers of persuasion and energy to bring Congress and the Moslem League to agreement. The cabinet mission plan, with all its complicated essentials drafted by Cripps himself in one morning before breakfast, was the basis of all subsequent political discussion. That it failed was due to Congress withdrawing its initial acceptance although the Moslem League had agreed to it. Yet Cripps's knowledge of the situation and perseverance did much to bring both sides to a realization of Britain's determination to withdraw and to the necessity which lay upon them of coming to terms.

In October 1947 Cripps, who had begun to dominate the home economic front, was appointed minister for economic affairs. When, in a few weeks' time, Hugh (later Lord) Dalton was forced to resign as the result of a budget indiscretion, Cripps was the natural successor as chancellor of the Exchequer. With things going from bad to worse as a backwash of the war, Cripps instituted in the beginning of 1948 a voluntary wage freeze. Without legislation to back him, by his mental, almost spiritual, force and the strength of his moral integrity, he compelled the trade-union leaders to comply. He promised them that he would likewise make private industry accept a dividend limitation and in 1949 he was able to announce that 93 per cent of business firms had not only agreed to hold their dividends but were in fact doing so. Cripps held the front for two years with no better weapon than the strength of his personality. During this period he probably had more power over the economy than any other single minister before. Despite his efforts, in September 1949 he was obliged to announce the devaluation of the pound. When he explained his reasons to Churchill, then leader of the Opposition, immediately before the announcement, the wartime leader complimented him on his courage and congratulated him for doing exactly the right thing. Cripps was the more distressed, therefore, when Churchill in the House of Commons and

Cripps

elsewhere pointed to Cripps's earlier statements that there was no intention to devalue the pound and said that he could no longer be trusted as chancellor and should resign. To Churchill this was the small change of politics. To Cripps, who believed passionately in truth, it was grievous abuse and later that year he declined to accept an honorary degree from the hands of Churchill as chancellor of Bristol University. Cripps was able to demonstrate that there was no intention to devalue at the time he had made his various disclaiming statements. It was only the suddenly worsening dollar crisis that had forced the measure on him.

Cripps's frail constitution was now letting him down more and more frequently. In the summer of 1950 he was compelled to go for medical treatment to Switzerland. On 20 October 1950 he resigned in a state of almost complete exhaustion. Held so high in the world's regard it was strange, though touching, that he was hurt by the omission of King George VI to offer him one word of thanks for the work he had done when he tendered his resignation. But Cripps had established a firm place in the regard of his countrymen who trusted him because they believed that his clearly expressed Christian principles were not a sham but a reality which moved into every action and word. Although he acquired the sobriquet 'Austerity Cripps', because he was obliged to make the nation tighten its belt in order to survive the arduous post-war years, it was soon realized that he never believed in austerity for austerity's sake and that his toughness had been right and justified.

In October 1951 Cripps returned from Switzerland to his home in the Cotswolds but at the beginning of 1952 he had once more to go back to Switzerland where there was a recurrence of the spinal infection which finally killed him on 21 April 1952, three days before his sixty-third birthday. His ashes were buried in the Cotswold village of Sapperton.

For the whole of his public life Cripps leant heavily on his wife, Isobel, daughter of Commander Harold William Swithinbank, of Denham Court, Bucks., whom he married in 1911. She was appointed G.B.E. in 1946. She shared with Cripps the same simple Christian faith and was always at his side wherever he went. Without her help his health would have been even worse than it was throughout his life and undoubtedly he would have done far less work. Her creation of a happy home atmosphere was more important to him, in constant need of rest from the exactions he placed upon himself, than for most men in public life. They had three daughters and one son, John Cripps, who contributes two notices to this Supplement.

Cripps was a fellow of University College, London (1930), rector of Aberdeen University (1942–5), and was elected F.R.S. in 1948. He was appointed C.H. in 1951.

A bust by Siegfried Charoux is in the possession of the family; another by (Sir) Jacob Epstein is in St. Paul's Cathedral.

[Colin Cooke, *The Life of Richard Stafford Cripps*, 1957; Eric Estorick, *Stafford Cripps*, 1949; private information; personal knowledge.]

WOODROW WYATT

published 1971

CROSLAND (Charles) Anthony (Raven)
(1918–1977)

Politician and writer, was born 29 August 1918 at St. Leonard-on-Sea, Sussex, the only son and the second of three children of Joseph Beardsel Crosland, CB, under-secretary, War Office, and his wife, Jessie Raven, lecturer in Old French at Westfield College, University of London. He was educated at Highgate School and, as a classical scholar, at Trinity College, Oxford, where he obtained a second class in classical honour moderations in 1939. His university years were interrupted by World War II, in which he served from 1940 to 1945. He was commissioned in the Royal Welch Fusiliers in 1941, transferred to the Parachute Regiment in 1942, and subsequently served in North Africa, Italy, France, and Austria. His most notable military exploit was to land by parachute on the casino at Cannes, during Operation Anvil in the summer of 1944.

At Oxford he had a notable career, both academically and as an undergraduate politician. He lost interest in classics and turned to philosophy, politics, and economics (primarily economics). After his return to the university in 1946, he secured a first class in PPE in 1946 and was elected a lecturer and later a fellow in economics at Trinity. He held this position from 1947 to 1950, and in 1966 became an honorary fellow. Before the war he was an active and orthodoxly Marxist member of the Labour Club. In the early months of the war, however, he found himself increasingly out of sympathy with its fellow-travelling and neutralist line, and in May 1940 he joined with others to lead the successful breakaway of the Democratic Socialist Club, which was much closer to the national Labour Party position. He was elected treasurer of the Union Society, but was defeated for the presidency. Six years later, however, on his return from the army, he redressed this set-back and secured the higher office.

Crosland was an imposing undergraduate, apparently self-confident, irreverent, and even glamorous, with striking good looks, intellectual assurance, a long camel-hair overcoat and a rakish red sports car. Later, as a young don, he with one or two contemporaries formed something of a cult group, of which the distinguishing characteristic was the unusual combination of hard intellectual endeavour and undisciplined, even rather riotous, relaxation. Crosland was, and remained, a puritan (his family were Plymouth Brethren) shot through with strains of self-indulgence.

In 1950, at the age of thirty-one, he was first elected an MP, for the constituency of South Gloucestershire, which he was able to win for the Labour Party and hold for the next five years because it contained a good deal of Bristol suburb as well as south Cotswold countryside. He gave up his Oxford fellowship a few months later, and never returned to professional academic life, although he remained very much an intellectual in politics. In the House of Commons he had a considerable, although not perhaps a remarkable, success. He was an economic specialist, and a close friend and assistant of Hugh Gaitskell, who for most of that period was shadow chancellor of the Exchequer. In 1952 Crosland married Hilary Anne Sarson, of Newbury, the daughter of Henry Sarson, a member of the vinegar family, but the marriage was short-lived and was finally dissolved in 1957.

Before the 1955 general election the boundaries of South Gloucestershire were redrawn in a way unfavourable to Labour, and Crosland decided to seek another seat. This was a mistaken move, for the one which he found, Southampton, Test, produced a larger Conservative majority than the one he had left. He was not, however, greatly disconcerted by his exclusion from Parliament, for although devoted to politics in a broader sense, he regarded the trappings and life of the House of Commons with some indifference.

He had other things to do. In 1953 he had already published his first book, *Britain's Economic Problem*. This was a lucid but fairly conventional analysis of the country's post-war trading difficulties. By 1955 he was already well into a much more original and substantial work, which he completed in the next year and published in the autumn of 1956. *The Future of Socialism* was well received at the time, but only gradually, over the next decade or so, achieved its position as the most important theoretical treatise to be written from the moderate left of British politics in the twenty-five post-war years. It assumed the triumph of Keynesianism, and with it a future of broadening abundance and the withering of the Marxist class struggle. It disputed the importance of nationalization and challenged the bureaucratic socialism of the Fabian tradition of Sidney and Beatrice Webb: 'Total abstinence and a good filing system are not now the right sign-posts to the socialist Utopia; or at least, if they are, some of us will fall by the wayside.' It was at once libertarian and strongly egalitarian.

It saw no conflict which could not be resolved by the flowing tide of continuing economic growth. It was in the mainstream of the optimism, many would now say the complacency, of the English liberal tradition. It influenced a generation.

Political theory having been disposed of with imagination, even if not total prescience, Crosland showed his practical sense by devoting the next two years to acting as secretary (under Gaitskell's chairmanship) to the independent committee of inquiry into the Co-operative Movement and writing a good report. Then he re-entered the House of Commons in 1959 as member for Grimsby, the constituency which he represented for the remaining seventeen and a half years of his life. He was quickly involved in all the Labour Party disputes which followed that lost election, urging Gaitskell on in the argument over 'clause four' (the nationalization clause in the Party's constitution), supporting him against unilateral disarmament, sharply disagreeing with him over his reticence towards Macmillan's initiative for British entry to the European community. Even apart from the European issue, however, he was in no way a client of his leader. He had too strong a personality and too critical a judgement for that. In some ways Gaitskell sought him more than he sought Gaitskell, and he was less thrown by Gaitskell's early death in 1963 than were some others in the circle. In the election to the leadership which followed he supported James Callaghan, who ran a bad third, rather than George Brown (later Lord George-Brown) who was the candidate of the majority of the 'Gaitskellites'.

In 1964 Crosland married again and also entered government for the first time. His second marriage was to Mrs Susan Barnes Catling, daughter of Mark Watson, of Baltimore, Maryland, who subsequently (under the name of Susan Barnes) became a prolific writer of skill and perception; unlike the first marriage, it was a great and continuing success and brought Crosland two step-daughters. His initial government post was minister of state in the newly-created Department of Economic Affairs, but after only three months he filled an unexpectedly early Cabinet vacancy and became secretary of state for education and science. He was admitted to the Privy Council in 1965.

The combination of these events, some close observers felt, produced a considerable change in Crosland's personality. He had a happier and more rounded life, and became more benign. He also became more of a party politician, more stirred by ambition, less the uninhibited and fearless commentator. He was a successful departmental minister, a master of various subjects, but occasionally lacking in decisiveness, always believing that a decision had so carefully and logically to be thought through that he sometimes missed the moment at which to make it. His popular impact was also limited, and, surprising though this may seem in retrospect, he was frequently confused in the public mind with Richard Crossman.

He stayed at education for two and a half years and then became president of the Board of Trade in 1967, hoping that this would lead on to the Exchequer. When the vacancy in the chancellorship occurred a few months later and this did not follow, he was deeply disappointed. His relations with Harold Wilson (later Lord Wilson of Rievaulx) were not close, and in the autumn of 1969 there was some doubt about his survival in the government. But he was too able a man to lose and for the last few months of that government occupied a co-ordinating role over unmerged departments as secretary of state for local government and regional planning.

There followed nearly four years in opposition. He worked hard as a party spokesman, published another book, *Socialism Now*, in 1974 (which, like its 1962 predecessor, *The Conservative Enemy*, was a collection of political essays, but more circumscribed in scope by his housing and local government responsibilities) but surprised and disappointed many of his friends by failing to vote with sixty-eight Labour MPs in favour of Britain's entry to the European community in the decisive division of October 1971; he did not vote against, but abstained. This probably accounted for his poor result in the deputy leadership election of 1972.

In the 1974 Wilson government he was secretary of state for the environment, essentially the same job but with a different name, tighter control over his subordinate ministers, and a more senior position at the Cabinet table than he had occupied in 1969. His experience as an upper middle rank departmental minister was unrivalled. The great offices of state continued to elude him. He responded by being increasingly effective in his department, and by exercising more authority in the Cabinet than in the previous government, while moving consciously away from the right and towards the centre of the party. In March 1976, when Harold Wilson resigned as prime minister, Crosland was determined to contest the succession. He ran fifth of five candidates, securing only seventeen votes. Yet the contest did not damage him. He succeeded to the Foreign Office in the new Callaghan administration with an unimpaired authority, and had he lived might well have been a stronger rival to Michael Foot in 1980 than Denis Healey proved to be.

He was foreign secretary for only ten months. Although he had always tried to think and write in an internationalist context, his experience was insular. He was unacquainted with the intricacies of foreign or defence policy. He was impatient of many of the nuances of the game. He knew foreign sociologists rather than foreign statesmen. Yet, after a hesitant start, he impressed most of his officials and his foreign colleagues by his authority, his wit, and his intellect. His personality, if not his fame, was a match for that of his principal confrère, Henry Kissinger. He was no longer the glamorous *enfant terrible* of his Oxford days, or even the adventurous thinker of *The Future of Socialism*. He was not old, but he had become a little tired in body, heavy and hooded-eyed, yet mordant of phrase, contemptuous of pomposity, and capable of a still dazzling charm.

He was pleased to be foreign secretary, but he still wanted, as ten years before, to be chancellor of the Exchequer, and devoted some of his over-taxed and waning energy to preparing for that job which he was never to hold. This was a last but typical manifestation of the paradox of Anthony Crosland. His intellect was one of the strongest in post-war British politics, and he fortified it by exceptional powers of application. But it was weakened by some uncontrolled demon of discontent, which marred his satisfaction in his own particular roles of excellence. He died at Oxford 19 February 1977, in office and at the age of fifty-eight, six days after a massive cerebral haemorrhage.

[Susan Crosland, *Tony Crosland*, 1982; personal knowledge.]

ROY JENKINS

published 1986

CROSSMAN Richard Howard Stafford

(1907–1974)

Journalist, diarist, and politician, was born 15 December 1907 in Bayswater, London, the third of six children (three boys and three girls) of (Sir) (Charles) Stafford Crossman, of Buckhurst Hill House, Essex, and his wife, Helen Elizabeth, daughter of David Howard, DL. His father, appointed to the bench in 1934, was an industrious Chancery barrister of strictly conservative disposition; there was little rapport between the cautious parent and his ultimately rebellious middle son. There was never any doubt, however, that more than any of the other five children Crossman inherited his father's intellectual ability and academic bent: at the age of twelve, like his father he won a scholarship to Winchester. His school career, which ended with his becoming prefect of hall and winning a scholarship to New College, Oxford, was conventionally successful but his father's hope that his son would follow him into the law did not survive Crossman's own declaration that, if so, he would want to be 'a famous criminal advocate'—an aspiration that caused his father, as a bencher of

Lincoln's Inn, such pain that he readily accepted his son's alternative ambition to become a don.

Having again followed in his father's footsteps by taking first classes in both classical honour moderations (1928) and *literae humaniores* (1930), Crossman was duly offered a fellowship by his own college in 1930. To ease the transition from junior to senior common room, a condition was that he should first spend a year abroad. Crossman elected to go to Germany and, given the rise of Hitler at the time, it turned out to be a fateful choice. Though he had hitherto taken little interest in politics, his year in Germany awakened a political appetite in Crossman that was to remain unabated for the rest of his life. He also met in Berlin a twice-married German Jewess, Erika Simon (née Landsberg), who in 1931 became his first wife.

Back in Oxford Crossman soon made his mark, lecturing to crowded houses in the Examination Schools and acquiring renown as a brilliant tutor with a special gift for the toughest sort of dialectic. His technique of teaching is probably best preserved in the books he wrote at the time—*Plato Today* (1937), *Socrates* (1938), and *Government and the Governed* (1939). By the time the latter two were published he had already left the university—though he retained his links with the city through his leadership from 1936 to 1940 of the Labour group on the Oxford City Council, to which he had first been elected in 1934.

The occasion of Crossman's departure from New College lay in a development in his private life. In 1937 he was married for the second time—on this occasion to the divorced wife (Inezita Hilda Baker, née Davis, who died in 1952) of one of his own colleagues in the New College senior common room. But the cause of his wanting to get away from Oxford had deeper roots than this personal difficulty. By the mid 1930s he had become an active participant in Labour politics, nationally as well as locally; along with Hugh (later Lord) Dalton and a few others he was a lonely champion of British rearmament in the Labour Party. In 1937 he unsuccessfully fought a by-election in Labour's interest at West Birmingham and a year later was adopted as the party's prospective candidate for the then single seat of Coventry.

In the ordinary course of events, Crossman could have expected to enter the House of Commons in 1940 at the latest. But the outbreak of war, and the extension of the 1935 Parliament, meant he had to wait another five years. He initially used the waiting time in Workers' Educational Association lecturing and political journalism (becoming an assistant editor of the *New Statesman* in 1938)—but in 1940 he was drafted into the Ministry of Economic Warfare by Hugh Dalton to organize the British propaganda effort against Hitler's Germany. Of the official view of his performance in this role one piece of contemporary evidence survives in the Public Record Office. It is the final character assessment written on him in 1945 by Sir Robert Bruce Lockhart, his immediate superior, who said that he lacked team spirit and defied regulations but his energy and agility of mind made a notable contribution to political warfare. 'I have no hesitation in saying that his virtues greatly outweigh his faults. In other words, if he doesn't win a prize for good conduct, he certainly deserves a commendation for distinguished service.' During 1944–5 Crossman was assistant chief of the Psychological Warfare Division, SHAEF.

The antithesis noted by Lockhart was to run right through Crossman's career and, no doubt, does something to explain why he languished for nineteen years on the back-benches before being appointed to any ministerial office. Elected Labour MP for Coventry East in 1945, a seat which he held until 1974, he was offered no front-bench post throughout the six years of the Attlee government. The nearest he ever came to official favour was when he was nominated by Ernest Bevin, then foreign secretary, to serve in 1946 as a member of the joint Anglo-American Palestine commission. The report, providing for further Jewish immigration into Palestine to an upper limit of 100,000 European refugees, was however far from welcome to Bevin who blamed Crossman for it, even aiming his famous 'stab in the back' reference at the following year's Labour Party conference directly at him.

Denied any regular chance to display his gifts within the House of Commons, Crossman turned to the party conference, being elected to the party's national executive committee in 1952 and staying on it for the next fifteen years. A founder member of the original Bevanite rebellion of 1951, he remained a formidable and influential lieutenant to Aneurin Bevan until the latter's resignation from the shadow cabinet in 1954 when he, virtually alone among the Bevanites, defended the right of Harold Wilson (later Lord Wilson of Rievaulx) to take Bevan's place at the shadow cabinet table. Although his attitude made him very unpopular with his left-wing colleagues, it proved a shrewd investment for the future—providing, indeed, the foundation for his subsequent close association with Harold Wilson whose campaign for the leadership, following the death of Hugh Gaitskell in January 1963, he effectively managed.

With Gaitskell, Crossman's relationship, though personally cordial enough (they had been at Winchester and New College together), had tended to be politically bumpy. Only with Wilson's election to the leadership in February 1963 did Crossman at last become an integral part of the Labour leadership team. In 1964 he made an important contribution to constitutional debate by his controversial introduction to a new edition of Bagehot's *The English Constitution*. Appointed to the front-bench as opposition spokesman on higher education and science, he had confidently expected to be made secretary of state for education and science when Harold Wilson formed his first government in October 1964. Instead, as a result of a last-minute switch, he was sent to the Ministry of Housing and Local Government, where he proved a strong, if turbulent, head. His effectiveness at the dispatch box persuaded the prime minister in August 1966 to promote him to lord president of the Council and leader of the House of Commons—a post in which he started promisingly, originating the Commons departmental select committees, but finished somewhat frustratedly, even having to watch from the sidelines as his own pet scheme for the reform of the House of Lords foundered in face of a parliamentary filibuster by Labour and Conservative back-benchers alike. Crossman's last two years as a Cabinet minister (from November 1968 to June 1970) were spent at the newly created mammoth Department of Health and Social Security, where he worked hard and conscientiously to weld together two former disparate ministries, though perhaps without conspicuous success. He also had to endure the ultimate disappointment of seeing his national superannuation plan (a subject to which he had given his sporadic attention from 1957 onwards) fail to come into law as a result of Harold Wilson's defeat in the election of 18 June 1970.

For most politicians leaving Cabinet office at the age of sixty-two, their careers are effectively over. If it was not so in the case of Crossman, this had little to do with the post he immediately took up—that of being editor of the *New Statesman*, a reversion that had been privately promised to him, regardless of the election result, the previous October. It was a job that Crossman had always hankered after—at one stage, in 1955, even at the price of giving up his parliamentary career. But the reservations registered at that time by the paper's editor, Kingsley Martin, proved in the event to be fully vindicated. True, in 1955, when he left the paper's staff to become a twice-weekly political columnist for the *Daily Mirror*, he was only forty-eight and might still have had the capacity to subordinate his own personality to that of the paper; but by 1970 it was much too late. The gap in age, celebrity, and sheer intellectual fire-power between Crossman and the rest of his staff proved too great to bridge: the following twenty-one months, until his somewhat brutal dismissal by the *New Statesman*'s board in March 1972, were to prove unhappy ones both for him and the paper.

The circumstances of Crossman's departure hurt him deeply—but, ironically, they gave him the opportunity for the triumphant coda to his career. From his days on the opposition back-benches in the early 1950s to his years in the Cabinet between 1964 and 1970, he had regularly kept a full political diary recording not only his own daily activities but also his reflections on the entire British political process. Leisure and the relaxed setting at his Oxfordshire farm inherited via his father-in-law (following his third and very happy marriage in 1954 to Anne Patricia, daughter of Alexander Patrick McDougall, farmer), enabled him to prepare the diaries for publication. Having already undergone a major operation at the beginning of 1972, he knew that time was not on his side—but before his death in 1974 he had the satisfaction of handling the first page proofs of what eventually was to be a three-volume work, *The Diaries of a Cabinet Minister* (1975, 1976, and 1977), subsequently to be followed by an additional volume, *The Backbench Diaries of Richard Crossman* (1981). The publication of the first volume of the *Diaries* was preceded by a great legal battle: the Labour attorney-general of the day vainly sought an injunction before the lord chief justice to prohibit their distribution in book form, even after they had been successfully serialized in the *Sunday Times* for nine consecutive weeks.

Crossman did not live to see this battle but he would have been highly gratified at the result. Although frequently criticized for inconsistency, one principle to him was as constant as the northern star: he never wavered in his belief that democracy must mean that people were entitled to know just how the decisions were reached that were taken in their name. In the earliest of all his books, *Plato Today*, published when he was only twenty-nine, he had made his subject wonder out loud whether parliamentary democracy was not in essence 'a sham, a gaily-painted hoarding behind which are kept hidden the government and the machinery of the state'. That was a paradox that he continued to tussle with until the day he died—and, with his well-known iconoclasm, he would have delighted in the fact that, through his *Diaries*, his own doubts were passed on to a succeeding generation. He died at his home at Prescote Manor 5 April 1974, being survived by his wife and a son and a daughter. There were no children of his previous marriages. Crossman was appointed OBE in 1945 and sworn of the Privy Council in 1964.

[R. H. S. Crossman, 'My Father', *Sunday Telegraph*, 16 December 1962; Susan Barnes, 'The Man Who Thinks Out Loud', *Sunday Times*, 29 November 1970; Kingsley Martin, private memorandum, 1955; James Fenton, 'Mr Crossman's Dogsbody', *New Review*, November 1976; BBC 2 'Reputations' script, 'Richard Crossman: Chronicler of the Cabinet', *Listener*, 5 April 1979; Janet Morgan, editor's introduction, *The Backbench Diaries of Richard Crossman*, 1981; private information.]

ANTHONY HOWARD

published 1986

CURZON George Nathaniel

(1859–1925)

Marquess Curzon of Kedleston

Statesman, was born at Kedleston Hall, Derbyshire, 11 January 1859. He was the eldest of the eleven children, four sons and seven daughters, of the Rev. Alfred Nathaniel Holden Curzon, fourth Baron Scarsdale, rector of Kedleston, by his wife, Blanche, daughter of Joseph Pocklington Senhouse, of Netherhall, Maryport, Cumberland. His father was of a reserved disposition, and his mother died when he was sixteen. The formative influences in his early life were those of his governess, Miss Paraman, and a private schoolmaster of the name of Dunbar. The discipline of Miss Paraman, at times ferocious, her exaggerated insistence on precision of detail, her morbid parsimony, her frequent injustice, while strengthening the combative qualities in Curzon, did not encourage the more gentle or elastic elements in his nature. At the age of ten he left the bleak nurseries of Kedleston for the private school of the Rev. Cowley Powles at Wixenford in Hampshire. Here again he was exposed to a strong and violent nature, and the harsh lessons learned from Miss Paraman, which during the holidays that lady would instil anew, were confirmed for him by the cramming of the assistant master, Mr. Dunbar. His capacity for acquiring knowledge was fully displayed during his three years at Wixenford. He became head of the school, and in his last term he carried off five prizes. Already at the age of twelve his letters had a touch of Gibbon.

In 1872 Curzon left Wixenford for Eton, where he remained until 1878. His first tutor was Mr. Wolley Dod; during his later years he was under the charge of Mr. E. D. Stone. His career at Eton was one of almost unbroken success. By 1877 he had risen to the position of captain of the Oppidans, was a member of 'Pop', had carried off seventeen prizes and been 'sent up for good' twenty-three times, was on the 'select' for the Newcastle scholarship, and was president of the Literary Society.

The precocity of Curzon at Eton had manifested itself in many forms. The influence of Oscar Browning, who took him in the holidays to France and Italy, developed an early taste for history and for the historical, rather than the aesthetic, aspects of art. Already as an Eton boy he had begun, with that acquisitive instinct which never left him, to collect objects of interest and value. His love of rhetoric, both oral and written, was much encouraged by his proficiency in the Literary Society and at 'Speeches', and from his Eton days dated his abiding delusion that words, as the vehicle of thought, were more important than the thought itself. The doctrine of precision inculcated by Miss Paraman and Mr. Dunbar thus fused, towards his seventeenth year, with the doctrine of verbal elegance inculcated by Oscar Browning.

While still at Eton Curzon became absorbed, as the result of a chance lecture by Sir James Stephen, with a passion for the magnificent mystery of the East. The cold religion of Kedleston Hall had appealed only to his sense of fear and doom. This was no small constituent in his character, and there was always about him a touch of Calvinism. But the emotional aspects of his religion, which might in other circumstances have driven him towards the Roman Catholic Church, blended with his passion for travel and his almost mystic acceptance of the Oriental. Curzon's enthusiasm for Asia was, in its essence, a reaction against the chill protestantism of Kedleston. In other words it was a 'religious' passion.

In 1878 Curzon was assailed by the first symptoms of that curvature of the spine which was to torment him till the day of his death. His natural tendency to self-pity may at moments have tempted him to exaggerate the grave physical disability under which he suffered. It would be a mistake, however, to underestimate the effect upon his career and character of his spinal weakness. The presence of pain, always imminent and at times acute, was largely responsible for the tenseness of his mental energy, for that lack of elasticity which hampered his splendid activities of mind and soul. The steel corset which encased his frame and gave to his figure an aspect of unbending perpendicular, affected also the motions of his mind: there was no middle path for him between rigidity and collapse. Conversely, his determination not to be classed as a cripple led him to perform prodigies of industry which were often unnecessary and sometimes harmful. Finally, as is often the result of spinal afflictions, his disabilities, while constituting a constant drain upon his nervous system, affected him with abnormal suspicion of his fellow men.

In October 1878 Curzon went up to Balliol College, Oxford. Although he had failed to obtain a scholarship, a reputation for great gifts, fortified by even greater self-assurance, had preceded him. Less than a month after his arrival at Oxford he was declaiming to the Union upon the Afghan question, and within a few weeks he was the leading spirit in the group of young conservatives who formed the Canning Club. His friendships with St. John Brodrick (afterwards Lord Midleton), Lord Wolmer (afterwards Lord Selborne), and Lord Cranborne (afterwards Lord Salisbury) date from this period. His tutors were R. L. Nettleship and the benign and absent-minded Strachan-Davidson. In January 1880 he came of age. In May of that year he was elected president of the Union and gained a first class in honour moderations. On securing the secretaryship of the Canning Club he exercised over the meetings and minutes of that society an autocracy which filled his contemporaries with admiration and alarm. In 1882 he obtained a second class in *literae humaniores*: his mortification was intense. 'Now', he exclaimed, 'I shall devote the rest of my life to showing the examiners that they have made a mistake.' At Balliol the unctuous adulation of Oscar Browning had been succeeded by the penetrating criticism of Jowett. The master suggested that Curzon should try to be less precocious, less prolix, less exclusive. His precocity in fact distressed his friends as much as his fluency: they feared that both these qualities might lead him to 'a superficiality of heart and mind'. But Curzon's only remedy for his lack of intellectual profundity was his great capacity for taking trouble. His political convictions during his Oxford period were those of tory democracy seasoned by a strong flavour of imperialism.

On leaving Oxford in 1882 Curzon joined Edward Lyttelton in a journey to Greece. The deference paid to his companion as being the nephew of Mr. Gladstone was somewhat irksome to Curzon, and he always retained a marked distaste for the Greek nation. In January 1883 he was in Egypt, visiting the battlefield of Tel-el-Kebir, genially assisting Lady Dufferin in her charity fêtes, and writing his Lothian prize essay in a dahabeeyah. In April he was in Constantinople, and in May, while stopping at Vienna, he learned that he had won the Lothian prize. He returned in delight to England. Further academic honours were still to come. In October 1883 he was elected a fellow of All Souls College, and in the same autumn he gained the Arnold essay prize. By these successes he felt that he had compensated for the mortification of his second in 'Greats'.

During 1884 Curzon, whose allowance from his father was far too meagre for his needs, endeavoured to increase his income by writing frequent articles for the reviews on current political questions. He had, while in Egypt, acquired some local knowledge of the Egyptian question, and this knowledge was of use to him in his journalistic work. He was at the same time adopted as prospective conservative candidate for South Derbyshire, and his first public speeches were devoted to the Egyptian problem.

The spring of 1885 was marked by a visit to Tunis, and by that strange meeting with General Boulanger which Curzon himself has admirably recorded in his *Tales of Travel* (1923). On 8 June 1885 Mr. Gladstone's administration was succeeded by that of Lord Salisbury. The new prime minister invited Curzon to become his assistant private secretary; but at the general election of that autumn Curzon was defeated for South Derbyshire by 2,090 votes in a poll of 10,280. On 1 February 1886 Mr. Gladstone returned to power pledged to the Home Rule Bill. Curzon decided to stand for the Southport division of Lancashire, and at the ensuing general election of June 1886 he was elected by a majority of 461 votes.

Curzon, as has been said, was at the outset of his career a believer in tory democracy. At Bradford in 1886 he came out openly as the pupil of Lord Randolph Churchill, whom he proclaimed to be 'instinct with life and fire'; he even clamoured for the reform of the Church and of the House of Lords. He happened, however, to be present at Hatfield on 20 December 1886 when the news was received of Lord Randolph's resignation, and the 'thanksgivings and hosannas' which arose on that occasion convinced him that, if there had been a mutiny, it would be preferable that there should be 'a solitary mutineer'. They also convinced him that, for a public man, it was sometimes a mistake to resign. From that moment tory democracy ceased to have any very potent attraction for Curzon: he spoke and wrote thereafter of 'respect for such institutions as reconcile a historic grandeur with the ability to meet the requirements of the age'; and his activities centred from that moment on obedience to Lord Salisbury, an intense interest in foreign and colonial policy, and the enjoyment of the social amenities of London.

'Society', wrote Curzon about this time, 'is passing through a phase of worshipping intellect.' Much has since then been written both about the Crabbet Club and the 'Souls'. The former, under the eccentric aegis of Wilfrid Scawen Blunt, was a real stimulus. Curzon much enjoyed the annual symposia at Crabbet Park. The identity of the 'Souls', or 'the gang', as they called themselves, remains more questionable; their frontiers were fluid and undefined. Curzon was always fond of society and could prove the most genial of hosts: the hauteur of his platform and House of Commons manner, and the subsequent pomposity of his vice regal state, blinded many people to his convivial side, to the fact that, even if he possessed small wit and an uncertain sense of humour, he yet possessed a boundless sense of fun. In some ways Curzon never grew up; in other ways he never was a boy. For even in the early 'eighties he saw himself as the man with a career.

On 31 January 1887 Curzon delivered his maiden speech in the House of Commons. He spoke on the Irish question, and allowed himself to criticize Lord Randolph Churchill. The speech erred on the side of excessive proficiency: it was too polished, too eloquent, and too long. On 25 March his second speech, although 'a shade too petulant', was better received. During the spring of this year he gained for himself, at Manchester and elsewhere, a reputation as a platform speaker. There were those, indeed, who saw in Curzon the successor of Lord Randolph Churchill, but in actual fact his ambitions were not confined to Westminster.

Curzon

The period of Curzon's great journeyings began in August 1887. It is convenient to anticipate the chronological narrative and to deal with these journeys by themselves. They can be summarized as follows: (1) 1887–1888: Canada — Chicago — Salt Lake City — San Francisco — Japan — Shanghai — Foochow — Hong-Kong— Canton — Singapore — Ceylon — Madras — Calcutta — Darjeeling — Benares — Agra — Delhi — Peshawar — Khyber Pass; (2) 1888–1889: St. Petersburg — Moscow — Tiflis — Baku — Askabad — Merv — Bokhara — Samarkand — Tashkent; (3) 1889–1890: Persia; (4) 1892: United States — Japan — China — Cochin China — Siam; (5) 1894: the Pamirs — Afghanistan — Kabul — the course of the Oxus. Apart from numerous articles in *The Times* and the reviews, the results of these travels were embodied in three books of importance, *Russia in Central Asia* (1889), *Persia and the Persian Question* (1892), and *Problems of the Far East* (1894). The industry, knowledge, and convictions embodied in these remarkable volumes rapidly earned for Curzon the reputation of being one of the leading authorities on Asiatic affairs. His Persian book, for instance, constitutes even to-day the most comprehensive textbook yet written upon that country. It may be true that much of its practical value and accuracy was due to the collaboration of (Sir) A. Houtum-Schindler, but the fact remains that Curzon's own knowledge was detailed and illuminating, and that it was his own genius for presentation which enabled him to transmute an inchoate mass of information into a form at once lucid, readable, and concise. It will be observed also that each of his journeys had drawn him in the end to the confines of India. By the age of thirty-five he had thus acquired an unequalled personal knowledge of the countries bordering upon British India. He had spoken face to face with Nasr-ed-Din of Persia; he had slept in satin sheets as the guest of Abdur Rahman of Afghanistan; he had seen the weakness of the French administration in Indo-China; he had gauged the inevitability of Russian infiltration on the north. His fervent, almost religious, faith in the imperial destiny of England had been confirmed for him upon the Yangtze and in the defiles of the Khyber Pass. Curzon had never been one of those who believed in the 'sordid policy of self-effacement'. His five great journeys rendered him at once a xenophobe and a nationalist. The rule of India and the defence of India became for him at once an ambition and a cause. It is not to be wondered at that the House of Commons thereafter appeared to him of minor importance.

The year 1889 and the early part of 1890 were spent in travelling. During the summer season of 1890 Curzon met, in a London ballroom, Mary Victoria Leiter, the daughter of an American millionaire, Levi Zeigler Leiter, of Chicago. She was a woman of outstanding beauty and great sweetness of character. They were not, however, engaged until the spring of 1893, and their engagement was not announced until Curzon's return from his expedition to Afghanistan and the Pamirs in March 1895. The following month they were married in Washington. It is impossible to exaggerate the humanizing effect exercised by this beautiful and unselfish woman upon Curzon's character. She became, indeed, the moral centre of his life.

During the intervals of this romance Curzon's career was centred upon his great voyages and the composition of the books and articles which they entailed. It was while he was intent upon the preparation of his book on Persia that he was offered, in November 1891, the post of under-secretary at the India Office. He had set his hopes on the under-secretaryship for foreign affairs, which had just been offered to and accepted by Mr. J. W. Lowther. The new post was almost as good, and his disappointment was allayed. Curzon entered the India Office with some trepidation. He adopted an attitude of 'virginal modesty' towards the permanent officials. But Lord Salisbury insisted, now that Curzon was a member of the administration, on certain modifications being introduced into the manuscript of his work on Persia. The passages regarding Nasr-ed-Din Shah were watered down, and in May 1892 the book was published. It met with an appreciative reception, but its permanent value was not fully realized at the time.

In March 1892 Curzon piloted the India Council Bill through the House of Commons. At the general election of July 1892 he retained his seat for Southport, but in the following August Lord Salisbury's government was defeated, and nine days later Curzon, again a private member, left England for Siam. The years 1893 and 1894 were occupied by his fierce battle with the authorities for permission to visit Afghanistan, and crowned by his final visit to Kabul and his repeated interviews with Abdur Rahman—'a great man and almost a friend'.

The year 1895 marked the end of Curzon's deliberate voyages of information: it also marked the beginning of his married life. Profiting by his wife's fortune he ceased to be the restless and often impoverished bachelor, and became the prosperous nobleman, renting castles in Scotland, country houses, and a mansion in Carlton House Terrace, purchasing works of art, and indulging his passion for stateliness. He began also early in 1895 to take his parliamentary career with greater seriousness. On Lord Wolmer's succession to the earldom of Selborne in May 1895 Curzon joined with St. John Brodrick in raising the constitutional issue whether a member of the House of Commons was obliged, on succeeding to a peerage, to take the Chiltern Hundreds. The issue was settled against him by the committee of privileges. On 24 June 1895 Lord Salisbury returned to office. He himself assumed the post of foreign secretary and offered Curzon the post of parliamentary under-secretary for foreign affairs. Curzon thus became charged with the duty of representing the Foreign Office in the House of Commons. The importance of his functions was signalized by his being sworn a member of the Privy Council at the early age of thirty-six.

Curzon's three years' service as under-secretary to Lord Salisbury were not wholly to his liking: by temperament he was ill suited to subordinate positions, and Lord Salisbury was too apt to ignore his under-secretary and to forget that he required information. Curzon, moreover, was a believer in dynamic diplomacy; he regarded the British Empire as 'a majestic responsibility' rather than as 'an irksome burden'; he desired the Empire to be 'strong in small things as in big'; and he regarded Lord Salisbury's policy of conciliating the concert of Europe as one of 'throwing bones to keep the various dogs quiet'. He thus saw himself obliged to accept, and even to defend, what he regarded as a policy of undue passivity in such matters as the Armenian atrocities, Venezuela, and the Cretan question. These subjects were, however, outside the Asiatic orbit, and as such possessed for him no intensely personal interest; similarly, his emotions were not stirred by the Jameson Raid or by the Kaiser's telegram to President Kruger. The German menace was for Curzon a purely European matter, and as he was no specialist on Europe it left him unmoved. It was otherwise with the French encroachments in Siam: he had been there; he had even seen the futility of French administration in Cochin China; on the Siamese question he felt very deeply indeed. Even more intense were his feelings on the subject of Kiao-chow. He urged that the occupation of that harbour by Germany in November 1897 would have as its corollary a Russian occupation of Port Arthur and a war in which he felt that Great Britain should take the side of the Japanese. In this, viewed as a matter of immediate expediency, Curzon was right; as also he was right in forcing on the Cabinet the lease of Wei-hai-wei. But a man of wider vision might have foreseen that it was not for a country possessing vast Asiatic responsibilities to desire or to assist the defeat of a Western by an Oriental power.

Confronted as he was by the well-informed criticism of Sir Charles Dilke and Henry Labouchere, Curzon did not find his task of defending Lord Salisbury in the House of Commons by any means a superficial one. The industry and the informative material which he brought to his speeches, while it sometimes irritated, also impressed. Labouchere might complain of his manner of 'a divinity addressing black-beetles', but the reputation of the under-secretary during these three years was established not only in the House but with the general public. He became, if not a popular, at least a public, figure: on his return to the House after a severe illness in the spring of 1898 he was greeted with sympathetic applause; his name and his features became familiar in the London press; and it was with no surprise that the public learned, on 10 August 1898, that this young man of thirty-nine had been chosen to succeed Lord Elgin as viceroy of India. On 11 November he was created Baron Curzon of Kedleston in the Irish peerage; he was unwilling to accept an English barony since he desired, so long as his father lived, to keep open the door of re-entry into the House of Commons. On 15 December he left England; on 30 December he landed at Bombay; and on 3 January 1899 he reached Calcutta and formally entered upon his term of office.

The seven years (December 1898 to November 1905) of Lord Curzon's vice-royalty fall into two main periods, divided from each other by the great Durbar of 1903. During the first period, in spite of the 'mingled bewilderment and pain' which he caused the local officials, he was admired in India and supported at home. During the second period his popularity in India began to wane, whereas his differences with 'the officials who rule and over-rule from Whitehall' became increasingly bitter.

On landing at Bombay Curzon created a good impression by his announcement that he 'would hold the scales even' between the manifold nationalities and interests committed to his rule; and that this was no figure of rhetoric was amply demonstrated by his firm attitude in the 'Rangoon outrage' of the following September, when he risked the resentment of British military circles by publicly disgracing a regiment in which an assault upon a native woman had occurred. On reaching Calcutta he at once proceeded to cut through the red tape which impeded administration. His constant battle against the departmental file earned him the name of 'a young man in a hurry', and within a few weeks of his arrival he had reversed the decision of the permanent officials in two important cases. He refused to sanction the Calcutta Municipal Act, which appeared to him to have been drafted 'partly in panic and partly in anger'. He further insisted on the imposition of countervailing duties to protect the sugar industry from the competition of bounty-fed sugar from other countries. He then turned his attention to external or frontier affairs. He at once curtailed the expenditure which it was proposed to devote to a policy of adventure upon the North-West Frontier, and decided in favour of retirement to defended positions covered by a screen of tribal levies. The administrative questions arising out of the political control exercised by the Punjab government were deferred for subsequent examination.

In the Persian Gulf Curzon was more adventurous. He concluded with Sheikh Mubarak of Koweit a treaty under which the latter agreed not to surrender his territory to any third power. He also obliged the sultan of Muscat to cancel a lease which he had accorded to the French government for the establishment of a coaling-station. Both these acts were high-handed. Sheikh Mubarak's own title to Koweit was at least questionable; and by the treaty of 1862 France was entitled to equal rights with Great Britain in Muscat. It is possible that in regard to Muscat the political agent went farther than Lord Curzon intended. In any case Lord Salisbury found himself exposed to embarrassing protests from the French ambassador. The government at home was therefore far from enthusiastic on receiving Curzon's famous dispatch of 1899 in which he claimed that the Persian Gulf, even at the risk of war, should be closed to all intruders.

On reaching Simla in the spring of 1899 Curzon, released from the social obligations of Calcutta, entered upon months of intensive labour. He endeavoured in vain to induce the home government to reduce the status of the Madras and Bombay presidencies; he waged renewed war on the departmental machinery; he flung himself with lavish energy into the question of famine relief; he completed the draft of the Calcutta Municipal Bill, although not in a form to satisfy native opinion; and he composed an encyclical on the duties of Indian ruling princes, which, while intended to discourage all 'absentee interests and amusements', was drafted in so hectoring a tone as to cause widespread consternation and alarm. It was doubtless in order to soothe the feelings which he had thus unintentionally inflamed, that Curzon set about drafting schemes for an imperial cadet corps in which Indian princes and gentlemen would have the opportunity of holding commissions.

The second year of Curzon's viceroyalty was darkened by the menace of a second famine, but the rains broke at the very moment when he journeyed to Guzerat for the purpose of himself supervising a campaign of relief. His timely arrival was taken by the natives as a sign of his miraculous powers. The second summer at Simla was devoted mainly to a study of the administration of the North-West Frontier, and after a stiff struggle with the local authorities he induced the home government to sanction the creation of a new North-West Frontier province under a chief commissioner responsible only to the government of India. This innovation was bitterly resented by Sir William Mackworth Young, the lieutenant-governor of the Punjab, and the altercations which ensued 'embittered and rendered miserable' Curzon's life at Simla.

In the autumn of 1900 Curzon visited Bombay and Madras, and at the former place made a speech regarding the need of 'consulting and conciliating public opinion in India' which caused great, if transitory, satisfaction in Indian circles. The Simla season of 1901 was one of feverish and excessive activity. Lady Curzon had returned to England on account of her health, and the viceroy endeavoured by vast personal labour to numb his own loneliness. He plunged into an intensive study of the land assessment of India and produced a report thereon which was a model of detailed and lucid exposition; he re-examined every aspect of the educational problem, and himself arranged, and subsequently presided over, a great educational congress held in September. In spite of the enormous energy and vast knowledge which Curzon brought to this task, the educational problem was not, in fact, much advanced during his viceroyalty, although the main issues were formulated and the office of director of education established. After a short holiday in Burma Curzon returned to Calcutta, where he found both the Afghan and the Tibetan questions causing anxiety. In October 1901 the Amir Abdur Rahman had been succeeded by Habibullah, and Curzon endeavoured to induce his old acquaintance to visit him in India. The hesitation displayed by the new amir to accept this pressing invitation caused Curzon a certain amount of uneasiness. In Tibet also the Dalai Lama was proving recalcitrant: Curzon was indignant 'that a community of unarmed monks should set us perpetually at defiance', and suggested to the home government that an armed mission should be sent to Lhasa; the government, which had its hands full with the South African War, did not respond to this suggestion. In February 1902 Curzon visited the Khyber Pass, and in March he proceeded to Hyderabad, where he managed to conclude with the Nizam the basis of a settlement of the Berar question. This diplomatic adjustment, which removed a long-standing source of grievance between the Nizam and the government of India, was subsequently embodied in the treaty of 5 November 1902. It was hailed by Curzon as 'the biggest thing I have yet done in India'.

The spring and summer of 1902 were mainly occupied with the gigantic preparations for the Durbar of 1903. Curzon, who had a passion for organizing all forms of pageantry, took an autocratic interest in the arrangements, and there is evidence of constant friction between him and the home government on the question of expense. A further and even more acrimonious conflict with the India Office arose from Curzon's refusal to defray from Indian revenues the expenses of the Indian mission to King Edward VIIth's coronation. A third dispute arose over his desire to announce as a 'boon' at the Delhi Durbar a general remission of taxation. The Cabinet at home considered such a promise would furnish an awkward precedent, but Curzon threatened to resign if his views were not accepted. A private telegram from St. John Brodrick warned him that such a threat might be taken seriously; he therefore, with resentment in his soul, agreed to accept a compromise. The closing months of 1902 were further embittered by what became known as the IXth Lancers incident. Curzon, having reason to suppose that officers of this regiment had endeavoured to hush up the circumstances of an assault by two troopers on a native, ordered an investigation, and as punishment stopped the leave of all officers. This action was much resented in military circles, and a demonstration in favour of the IXth Lancers at the Durbar review in January 1903 was exaggerated in England as evidence of Lord Curzon's growing unpopularity.

The Durbar of January 1903 marked the summit of Lord Curzon's viceregal splendour. From that moment the clouds began to gather. Lord Kitchener had arrived in India as commander-in-chief in November 1902; but before his final conflict with that masterful personality other and less pregnant issues had arisen between Curzon and the government at home. He had urged a forward policy in Afghanistan and Tibet: the home government desired to enter into no further commitments. Curzon also considered that Indian revenues were being unduly drawn upon in order to maintain troops in South Africa, a matter in which India could have only a contingent interest. Lady Curzon urged her husband to resign. 'Don't', she wrote to him, 'let us stay until the *joie de vivre* has died in us.' Curzon, unfortunately, did not follow this advice: his term of office was due to expire in January 1904; he hoped for a renewal; and the moment passed when resignation would have been dignified.

At Simla once again in the late spring of 1903 Curzon developed a passion for internal reforms, and commissions were constituted to deal with irrigation, railways, agricultural banks, and police questions. His financial reforms were already bearing fruit, and his currency reforms were widely applauded. His great work for Indian historical monuments, his restorations at Delhi and Agra, were already a source of personal satisfaction. Whatever Curzon may or may not have done in the administrative field, he set his stamp for ever upon the art and archaeology of India. The Victoria Memorial Hall at Calcutta was entirely due to his initiative and energy. Meanwhile the government at home had at last lent ear to his warnings about the Persian Gulf: not only did Lord Lansdowne himself make a public pronouncement that the British government would not tolerate any Russian encroachments in Southern Persia, but the viceroy was authorized to pay a state visit to the Persian Gulf. This visit, accompanied by every evidence of naval supremacy, took place in November 1903. From that moment, until the accession of Reza Khan to the throne of the Kadjars, British predominance in the Gulf remained unquestioned.

In January 1904 Curzon completed the first five years of his term of office. An extension of the period had been announced in the previous August: instead, however, of accompanying Lady Curzon to England on leave of absence, he decided to remain for a few months in India. His main occupation was the study of the partition of the Bengal province. His success in settling the Berar incident had convinced him that greater efficiency of administration could be secured by splitting up the more unwieldy provinces and creating smaller administrative districts from the parts thus detached. The scheme was sanctioned by the secretary of state in June 1905, and the formation of a new province, comprising 106,000 square miles with a population of eighteen million Moslems and twelve million Hindus, was formally inaugurated.This action, which was interpreted by the Bengalis as a revenge on the viceroy's part for the congress movement, cost him his popularity with that 'Indian opinion' which he had been the first to recognize and proclaim.

On 30 April 1904 Curzon sailed for England on leave of absence. Lord Ampthill remained in charge as acting governor-general. Curzon was offered and accepted the lord wardenship of the Cinque Ports and entered with enthusiasm on the tenancy of Walmer Castle. This enthusiasm was quickly damped: Lady Curzon fell ill at Walmer, and Curzon himself condemned it as 'an ancestral dog-hole'. Meanwhile, the India Office had at last sanctioned the mission of Sir Francis Younghusband to Tibet, and in September 1904 a treaty was extracted from the Tibetans. Curzon did not consider the terms of the Lhasa convention an adequate compensation for the effort made. His difference of opinion with St. John Brodrick on these matters did not improve their relations, and he was also angered at discovering that, in his absence, Lord Kitchener had addressed to the Committee of Imperial Defence a long memorandum condemning the system of dual control in force in the Indian army.

The Indian army possessed, in fact, two heads, the commander-in-chief and the military member of the viceroy's council. The latter not only dealt with administrative matters, but was the sole channel through whom the commander-in-chief had access to the viceroy. It often happened, moreover, that the military member, while possessing these supervisory powers over the commander-in-chief, was his military junior. The anomalies of this position had impressed Lord Kitchener soon after his arrival, but Curzon had urged him to wait for a year before formulating his objections. The relations between the two men, during 1903, had been wholly amicable: Kitchener knew that it was Curzon himself who had pressed for his appointment. Curzon welcomed in Kitchener a reforming zeal equalled only by his own. It was thus during the summer of 1904, when Curzon was absent in England, that Kitchener first launched his attack. The government of Lord Ampthill could not support Kitchener's contention that the position of the military member should be rendered subsidiary to that of the commander-in-chief. Kitchener thereupon threatened to resign, and the home government, fearing that so dramatic a resignation would be unpopular in the country, asked Curzon for advice. Imagining that he would be better able to manage Kitchener himself, Curzon advised the home government to call for a report from the government of India and thus to postpone the issue until he himself had returned to Calcutta.

Curzon left for Bombay on 24 November 1904 and reached Calcutta on 13 December. Lady Curzon, who was seriously ill, did not accompany him: it would have been better if he had listened to her premonitions against his return. The dispatch calling for a report left London on 2 December 1904. On its receipt, Curzon asked for the comments both of Lord Kitchener and the military member. The latter defended the existing dual system; the former insisted that both functions should be fused in that of the commander-in-chief. Curzon then drew up his own minute of 6 February 1905, in which he decided in favour of the maintenance of the present dual system, mainly on the ground that the concentration of such powers in the hands of the commander-in-chief would create a military autocracy subversive of the supreme control of the civil government. On 10 March the matter came before the council: Curzon's opinion was endorsed by all the civilian members; Kitchener read a brief statement regretting that he was in a minority of one and refusing to discuss the matter further. The results of this meeting were conveyed to the India Office in a dispatch of 23 March. Kitchener at the same time took steps to see that his own views were placed before the home government and press. St. John Brodrick, faced with this deadlock, appointed a committee. The committee recommended a compromise by which the military member would in future deal only with the quasi-civilian side of army administration and be called the 'member in charge of the department of military supply.' All purely military matters would be under the commander-in-chief, who would have direct access to the viceroy and government. This compromise, under the style of a 'decision', was communicated in the India Office dispatch of 31 May 1905. On 25 June Curzon induced Kitchener to agree to some modifications in the compromise which would give the government of India a 'secondary military opinion' or, in other words, would enable the supply member also to be consulted on military matters. The home government was so startled by Kitchener's acquiescence in this modification that it asked for confirmation. This was given, and on 14 July the government telegraphed accepting the agreed modifications and congratulating Curzon on the settlement reached. Two days later Curzon heard that the new supply member had been chosen by the India Office without his being consulted. He had himself wished to propose (Sir) Edmund Barrow, to whom Kitchener had also agreed. Curzon telegraphed urging this appointment: it was refused, and Curzon tendered his resignation. On 22 August 1905 his resignation was accepted; it had, in fact, been published in London the day before, together with the announcement of Lord Minto's appointment as his successor. Curzon remained on in India in order to receive the Prince and Princess of Wales on 9 November. He left India, an angry and embittered man, on 18 November 1905.

It will be seen that Curzon's resignation came about, not as a result of the main conflict between himself and Kitchener, which had in fact been settled by a compromise, but on the subsidiary question whether his own nominee or that of the India Office should be selected as supply member of the viceroy's council. The home government, as is clear from its almost disappointed surprise when Kitchener agreed to Curzon's eleventh-hour modifications, had in fact determined that so turbulent a viceroy should be removed. It is indeed probable that the embittered relations which by then existed between Curzon and Brodrick rendered impossible all hope of smooth co-operation. The manner of his dismissal was, however, unnecessarily discourteous, and there was some foundation for Curzon's subsequent complaint that the Balfour-Brodrick combination had treated him with 'tortuous malignity'. There is a certain irony in the fact that the day after Curzon's return to London witnessed the fall of the Balfour administration and the return to power of a liberal Cabinet under Sir Henry Campbell-Bannerman.

There followed a period of eleven years' political disappointment and domestic sorrow. Curzon received no public recognition for his work in India. He retired in anger and mortification to the South of France. On 18 July 1906 Lady Curzon died. Curzon shut himself up with his three young daughters in Hackwood Park, Basingstoke, a prey to despair. In 1907 he was elected chancellor of Oxford University, and tried to find alleviation for his sorrows in the question of university reform. He visited Oxford in person and resided for some weeks at the Judge's Lodgings in St. Giles. His aim was to avoid a governmental commission into university finance by the passage of reforms from within. He succeeded in staving off a government inquiry for many years. During a visit to South Africa in 1909 he prepared with his own hand a long memorandum on university reform entitled *Principles and Methods of University Reform*. This was considered by the university authorities in April 1910, and a final report was ready by August of that year. Further reports followed until the outbreak of war put an end to all subsidiary efforts. Curzon's ardour in the cause of Oxford became his greatest solace during those lonely and inactive years.

Curzon refrained, largely in deference to the wishes of King Edward VII, from re-entering party politics, and did not seek re-election to the House of Commons. In January 1908 he entered the House of Lords as an Irish representative peer, and in February of that year he made a spirited and informed attack upon the Anglo-Russian convention of 1907. In the same year he was elected lord rector of Glasgow University. He flung himself with enthusiasm into Lord Roberts's agitation for universal military training, and he opposed Mr. Asquith's threats to the privilege of the House of Lords, urging his fellow members to fight to the last ditch.

When he realized, however, that the liberal government was in deadly earnest, he had the wisdom to retreat, and it was Curzon's sensible advice which largely decided the debate of 8–10 August 1911 and secured for the liberal government a bare majority in support of its proposals.

Curzon's main activities during these years were not, however, of a political nature. His election in May 1911 as president of the Royal Geographical Society gave him an occasion for displaying his organizing talent, and within a few years he had collected sufficient money to purchase the fine premises in which the society is now housed. As a trustee of the National Gallery he drafted a report which to this day forms the main charter both of that gallery and of the Tate Gallery. His interest in architecture was also a great resource. He was elected an honorary fellow of the Royal Institute of British Architects, and his restoration of Tattershall Castle in Lincolnshire and subsequently of Bodiam Castle in Sussex (both of which he bequeathed to the nation) showed that his zeal for the preservation of ancient monuments was not confined to India. In November 1911, as a coronation honour, Curzon was created Earl Curzon of Kedleston, Viscount Scarsdale (with reversion to his father and heirs male), and Baron Ravensdale (with reversion to his daughters and heirs male). It was activities and honours such as these which, after a lapse of shrouded years, again rendered his name familiar to his countrymen. A second period of important public service was about to open before him.

On 27 May 1915, with the formation of the Coalition Cabinet, Lord Curzon was given the office of lord privy seal. He was not, however, accorded any important functions, and was, in fact, excluded from the war committee, established in the autumn of that year, until July 1916. He was bitterly opposed to the evacuation of Gallipoli, and addressed to his colleagues a cogent and vivid note protesting against any policy of retreat. He was strong also in pressing for compulsory service, and it was largely owing to his insistence that the national register was instituted in 1915. So deeply did he feel on this subject that when the Garter was offered him at the end of December 1915 he refused to accept this long-coveted honour until Mr. Asquith had pledged himself to introduce the Compulsory Service Bill into the House of Commons.

Early in 1916 Curzon was placed in charge of the Shipping Control Committee, and quickly realized that a drastic restriction of imports was essential if tonnage supplies were not to be exhausted. Throughout the year he struggled in vain to impose his opinion on the Cabinet, but it was only in March 1917 that his views were adopted and the necessary legislation passed. He also became president of the Air Board (May 1916), an organization established for the purpose of conciliating the conflicting requirements in aviation of the War Office and the Admiralty. He pressed strongly for the creation of an Air ministry, but it was not until January 1918 that his opinion prevailed.

With the fall of Mr. Asquith in December 1916 Curzon became a member of the inner War Cabinet under Mr. Lloyd George. In January 1917 he married, as his second wife, Grace, daughter of Joseph Monroe Hinds, at one time United States minister in Brazil, and widow of Alfred Duggan, of Buenos Aires. Once again 1 Carlton House Terrace became a social centre, and the loneliness of Curzon's middle age was succeeded by a second period of domestic happiness. He was intensely active. As member of the War Cabinet, leader in the House of Lords, and lord president of the Council, he could no longer complain of insufficient employment. Between December 1916 and November 1918 the Cabinet held as many as five hundred meetings, and at each of these Curzon would express his views with his customary trenchancy and conviction. He opposed, although in vain, the policy of Great Britain assuming any commitments towards the Jews in Palestine; he was, on the other hand, a strong supporter of a forward policy in Mesopotamia and of the creation of an Arab state. He was a bitter opponent of the Montagu-Chelmsford report (1918), feeling that it would lead to parliamentary government in the Indian Empire and thus shatter the basis of British rule. In this he showed some inconsistency, since it was he himself who had inserted into the announcement of 20 August 1917 the promise of 'the progressive realization of responsible government' in India. Nor was it in regard to India alone that Curzon found difficulty in reconciling his position as one of the leaders of the conservative party with his functions as the spokesman of a government pledged to liberal concessions. The Dublin rising of April 1916 revived the Home Rule controversy which had been shelved in September 1914. Curzon as a professed, although not convinced, unionist considered for a moment whether he should resign: he accepted instead the chairmanship of a Cabinet committee which prepared the draft of a bill for an Irish settlement. Mr. Lloyd George summarily rejected this draft in favour of his own scheme for an Irish Convention, and it fell to Curzon not merely to swallow this affront but to defend the Convention in the Upper House. Neither the Irish Convention nor the subsequent committee established under (Viscount) Long achieved a solution of the Irish problem, and in June 1918 Curzon had the melancholy satisfaction of announcing to the House of Lords that, in view of the spread of rebellion in Ireland, the government had been impelled to suspend all further proposals for Home Rule.

Curzon had never been a protagonist in the Irish question, and his subservience to Mr. Lloyd George in Irish matters, while it distressed his unionist friends, was no betrayal of deep personal conviction. His conduct in regard to the question of women's suffrage did, however, entail grave personal inconsistency, and contributed largely to his loss of prestige with the conservative party. For since February 1912 Curzon had been president of the Anti-Suffrage League, and when, in 1917, the House of Commons conferred the franchise upon women by a majority of 385 to 55 votes, the League looked to its president to oppose the Bill in the House of Lords. Curzon at this juncture did not manifest that firmness of decision which his rigid manner had led his supporters to expect. While leaving the Anti-Suffrage League under the impression that he would speak and vote against the Bill, he deserted it on the second reading and voted against Lord Loreburn's amendment on the ground that it would be imprudent for the Upper House to defy so strong a majority in the House of Commons.

With the conclusion of the Armistice in November 1918 it fell to Curzon to deliver a speech of victory in the House of Lords, and he was also charged with the task of organizing the peace celebrations. Meanwhile, Lord Balfour had accompanied Mr. Lloyd George to the Peace Conference in Paris, and Curzon was invited to take charge of the Foreign Office at home. From January to October 1919 he assumed the invidious role of foreign minister *ad interim*, and watched with growing dismay and resentful impotence what he felt to be the reckless policy pursued by Mr. Lloyd George in Paris. On 24 October 1919 Lord Balfour resigned the post of foreign secretary and Curzon was appointed in his place. But disillusionment was in store for him. Ever since the days when he had chafed under the dilatory caution of Lord Salisbury, Curzon had dreamed of the time when he himself would control the levers of British foreign policy. That time had now arrived; the levers were there, to all appearances under his hand: but the machine had altered and did not respond. Other hands than his were in control. The irony of it was that this functional change in the machine of imperial policy was brought home to him upon that very stretch of line with which he himself was most familiar. The end of the War saw British troops in occupation of large sections of Persian territory, and the general call for retrenchment and demobilization necessitated their recall. Curzon insisted, however, that the occasion should be seized to place British relations with Persia on a durable basis. After protracted negotiations a treaty was signed in August 1919 which placed Great Britain in control of the Persian army and finances. Curzon failed to realize the artificial nature of this agreement and acclaimed it as an outstanding triumph. The treaty in fact was never put into effect: no sooner had British troops evacuated Persian territory than the nationalists and the Majlis pronounced that the treaty had been secured by force and bribes, and refused to accept it. In February 1921 the nationalist government in Persia concluded with the Russian Soviet government a treaty diametrically opposed to that signed only eighteen months before between Vossuq-ed-Dowleh and Sir Percy Cox. The funeral oration of that instrument was preached by Curzon on 26 July 1921.

The failure of the Persian treaty appears to have shaken Curzon's confidence in the stability of his old Asiatic landmarks. In dealing with the Egyptian question he displayed a greater understanding of the postwar mentality of the East. In November 1919 the Milner commission had been dispatched to Egypt with the task of considering how the protectorate established in 1915 could be reconciled with the movement for self-government headed by Zaghlul Pasha. In the spring of 1920 the Milner report was submitted to Lord Curzon; it avowedly exceeded the terms of reference under which it had been framed. Curzon was quick to recognize the fact that Lord Milner had been wise in exceeding his instructions, and he agreed to receive an Egyptian mission under Adly and Zaghlul Pashas and to negotiate a treaty of alliance to supersede the existing protectorate. The mission arrived in June 1920, and by August of that year the heads of agreement had been initialled. In February 1921 these heads of agreement were approved by parliament, and an invitation was addressed to Egypt to send a mission to London with full powers to conclude a definitive treaty. This mission, under the leadership of Adly Pasha, arrived in July. In the interval, however, an Imperial Conference had been held in London, and great stress had been laid by the dominion delegates upon the importance of maintaining British control over the Suez Canal. The attitude of the Cabinet was thus less conciliatory than it had been at the time of the Zaghlul conversations of the previous year. Curzon was unable to induce his colleagues to consent to any terms which Adly could accept; the latter returned to Egypt without his treaty and immediately resigned. The British authorities at Cairo thereupon imposed martial law and deported Zaghlul. Curzon was able to assure the Cabinet that his own worst prognostications had been fulfilled.

This unsatisfactory situation continued till January 1922. Lord Allenby, the high commissioner, then suggested to Curzon the basis of an arrangement under which Sarwat Pasha would be prepared to form a ministry. The essence of this arrangement was that the protectorate should at once be abolished and Egypt be recognized as an independent kingdom. Curzon was able to induce the Cabinet to agree to this proposal, and a unilateral manifesto was thus published abolishing the protectorate while insisting upon certain reserved points. Under these reservations Great Britain safeguarded her position in regard to the Sudan, the Suez Canal, and the protection of Egypt against external interference. On 14 March 1922 the House of Commons approved this manifesto.

A more intense difference of opinion arose between Curzon (who was created a marquess in June 1921) and Mr. Lloyd George in regard to the Graeco-Turkish question. During the Paris Conference Curzon had repeatedly warned Mr. Lloyd George of the danger of any delay in concluding peace with the Turks, and of the more specific danger of allowing the Greeks to land at Smyrna. His own solution was the simpler one by which the Turks would be turned out of Europe and the Greeks would not be allowed into Asia. It is impossible here to trace the stages which led to the Treaty of Sèvres, the Kemalist movement in Turkey, the defeat of Venizelos in Greece, the return of King Constantine, and the final Greek debacle of August 1922. It may be said in general that Curzon's advice was not followed and that he was frequently not consulted in matters of policy, but that his assistance was evoked in meeting the difficulties to which the policy adopted gave rise. His renewed attempts to come to an agreement with the French in order to secure a basis for joint mediation between Greece and Turkey were constantly negatived by the intervention of Mr. Lloyd George, and thereby the conviction gained ground both in Paris and Athens that the ostensible impartiality of Curzon was but a cloak for the encouragement secretly given by the prime minister to Greece. This duality of purpose and lack of centralized responsibility led even to disorganization within the Cabinet at home. In 1922 Edwin Samuel Montagu, secretary of state for India, authorized the viceroy to publish a pro-Turkish manifesto destined to appease the feelings of the Khalifat agitators. He was obliged to resign, but the spectacle of a Cabinet thus disunited and undisciplined in matters of foreign policy left Curzon embarrassed and weakened in face of M. Poincaré who, on assuming office in January 1922, embarked upon a concentrated and deliberate policy of siding with the Turks.

The inevitable crisis arrived in the early autumn of 1922. The Kemalist army, having flung the Greeks into the sea, now faced the Allied forces guarding the neutral zone of the Straits. At a Cabinet meeting of 15 September it was decided that the British forces at least should maintain their positions on the Asiatic side, although it was realized that M. Poincaré might well hold other views. On the following day, after Curzon had left London for Kedleston, certain members of the Cabinet, without his knowledge or consent, issued a *communiqué* in which the possibility of war with Turkey was foreshadowed. On 18 September Curzon returned to London, pointed out that this *communiqué* would enrage M. Poincaré, and insisted on proceeding alone to Paris to soothe the feelings of the French. On the following day M. Poincaré as a rejoinder to the *communiqué* withdrew the French detachment at Chanak on the Asiatic shore of the Dardanelles, leaving the British detachment to face the Kemalists alone.

On 20 September Curzon reached Paris and after a series of scenes with M. Poincaré, one of which reduced the British foreign secretary to tears of rage, reached an agreement under which an armistice was to be negotiated with the Kemalists at Mudania.

Public opinion at home had been deeply alarmed by the Chanak crisis, and Mr. Lloyd George's position, in view of the disaster attending his phil-Hellene policy, was seriously shaken. Mr. Winston Churchill invited the leading members of the Coalition Cabinet to dinner at his house, and it was then decided that the Coalition should ask for an immediate dissolution and appeal to the electorate for a new lease of power. Curzon agreed to this procedure. On 15 October, however, Mr. Lloyd George, in spite of Curzon's entreaty, delivered an anti-Turkish speech at Manchester, and at the same time the foreign secretary was apprised of a further flagrant instance of negotiations conducted by the prime minister's secretariat behind his back. This incident convinced him that it would no longer be possible to support Mr. Lloyd George's Coalition: he refused to attend a second dinner party given by Mr. Churchill to the Coalition ministers; and on 19 October a meeting at the Carlton Club led to the fall of the Coalition Cabinet and the formation of a conservative ministry under Mr. Bonar Law. In this ministry, which was confirmed by the general election of 15 November 1922, Curzon retained the post of foreign secretary.

Within a few days Curzon was on his way to the European Conference at Lausanne. His complete domination of that assembly constitutes one of the most remarkable episodes in his career. The French and Italians imagined that British prestige had been so irretrievably shaken by the Greek disaster that it would be safe to leave to Curzon the invidious role of registering the defeat which Europe had suffered at the hands of Turkey. This was a miscalculation on their part. The retention of Chanak by Great Britain, in contrast with Poincaré's policy of retreat, had done much to inspire the Turks with respect for British determination. Curzon's own magnificent equipment of knowledge and rhetoric strengthened this impression. During the eleven weeks of the first Lausanne Conference he succeeded in impressing his personality upon Ismet Pasha and in securing his assent to the political clauses, and above all to the 'freedom of the Straits', which constituted the main British desiderata. Upon the question of Mosul the Turkish delegation found Curzon adamant, and his firm attitude on this point, in contrast with the weakness of the Cabinet at home, forced the conference to defer the matter for subsequent consideration. After the conference had been sitting for ten weeks the French realized that, whereas England had obtained as much as she had hoped for, the important financial, economic, and capitulatory chapters of the treaty, in which they themselves were mainly interested, had made no progress at all. On 30 January 1923 they issued through the Havas agency a statement to the effect that they did not consider the treaty as by then drafted to be more than 'a basis of discussion'. The Turks immediately refused to sign the treaty in the form which it had then reached. On the night of 4 February Curzon made a final appeal to Ismet Pasha to sign the treaty, and, on his refusal, broke off negotiations and left Lausanne on that very evening by the Orient express. It is true that he had not secured a treaty of peace: but he had secured those portions of it which were of chief interest to his own country, and he had broken off negotiations, not on a purely British issue, but on questions which were of equal, or even greater, interest to the Italians and French. Above all, he had restored British prestige in Turkey. The abortive Conference of Lausanne was the most striking of his diplomatic triumphs.

In dealing with Asia, even with the new Asia of post-war nationalism, Curzon had all the confidence of expert knowledge. His handling of European diplomacy was less certain and far less self-assured. For years the British and the French governments had envisaged the problems of security and reparation from a different standpoint. Much bickering had ensued. On 11 January 1923, while Curzon was still at Lausanne, these differences were brought to a head by M. Poincaré's occupation of the Ruhr Valley. During the period of *rupture cordiale* which then ensued between London and Paris, Curzon showed considerable skill in maintaining the British policy of benevolent neutrality, and it was his speech in April 1923 which formed the germ of what subsequently developed into the schemes of General C. G. Dawes and Mr. O. D. Young for reparation payments. For it was in this speech that the proposal of a jury of impartial experts was first mooted.

On 21 May 1923 Mr. Bonar Law, whose health had long been causing anxiety, resigned. On the following day Curzon, who was spending Whitsuntide at Montacute House, a seat which he had rented in Somerset, received from Lord Stamfordham, the king's private secretary, a letter asking for an immediate interview. He journeyed to London in the triumphant certainty that he had been designated as Bonar Law's successor. Lord Stamfordham informed him on his arrival that the king had decided to send for Mr. Stanley Baldwin. For several hours Curzon remained in a state of collapse under the crushing blow of this bewildering disappointment. He contemplated complete retirement from public life. His abiding sense of public duty asserted itself, however, and on the following day he wrote to Mr. Baldwin promising his support. Few actions in his public life were more magnanimous.

On resuming work at the Foreign Office Curzon embarked upon two acute controversies. He had never approved of Mr. Lloyd George's policy of recognizing the Soviet government in Russia, and by the early summer of 1923 it was clear that the trade agreement of 1921 had failed to work. Curzon prepared a long and detailed indictment of Russian evasions of that agreement and presented his demands in the form of an ultimatum. Somewhat to his own surprise the Soviet government replied giving him satisfaction on most of the points raised. His persistent endeavours to mediate between France and Germany met with less success: while urging the German government to abandon passive resistance, he endeavoured to obtain from the French their consent to an impartial inquiry into Germany's capacity to pay reparations; his failure to move M. Poincaré led to much acrimonious correspondence and to embittered interviews with the French ambassador. Realizing that further progress was impossible, Curzon caused a detailed statement of the British point of view to be prepared in the form of a note to the French and Belgian ambassadors. This note was delivered on 11 August 1923 and was thereafter published. The storm of indignation provoked in Paris by this indictment left Curzon unaffected: he journeyed to Bagnoles to nurse his phlebitis in peace.

In the autumn of 1923 Mr. Baldwin, against Curzon's urgent advice, decided to appeal to the electorate on the issue of protection. The government was placed in a minority and on 23 January 1924 Mr. Baldwin resigned. When the conservatives returned to power in November of the same year, Curzon was not invited to resume the post of foreign secretary. Once again he determined to retire from politics and to devote his closing years to the reconstruction of Kedleston. He was persuaded, however, to afford the government the moral support of his presence, and with great public spirit he again accepted the post of lord president of the Council.

In March 1925, while staying the night at Cambridge, Curzon recognized symptoms of grave internal disorder. He was taken next day to London and on 9 March an operation was performed. On 20 March he died. On 25 March his coffin was taken to Westminster Abbey, and on the following day he was buried by the side of his first wife in the church at Kedleston.

Curzon left three daughters by his first wife. In default of male heirs the marquessate became extinct on his death. He was succeeded in the viscounty of Scarsdale by his nephew, Richard Nathaniel (born 1898), and in the barony of Ravensdale by his eldest daughter, Mary Irene (born 1896).

Few men have experienced such extreme vicissitudes of triumph and defeat. Viceroy at thirty-nine, at forty-six it was his fate to be excluded from politics for eleven years; foreign secretary at a triumphant moment of his country's history, it fell to him not to fortify victory but to protect lassitude; and the supreme prize of his ambition was dashed at the last second from his lips. He acquired great possessions and resounding titles;

he left his mark upon the art and literature of his country; and yet he achieved successes rather than success. Had his will been as forceful as his intellect, his determination as constant as his industry, he might have triumphed over his own anachronisms. But the tense self-preoccupation of the chronic invalid robbed him of all elasticity, and he failed to adapt himself to the needs of a transitional age which did not like him and which he did not like. He will live less by his achievements than by his endeavours: he will live as a man of great ambition, and some egoism, who was inspired by a mystic faith in the imperial destiny of his country, and devoted to that faith unexampled industry, great talents, and an abiding energy of soul.

The painted portraits of Lord Curzon are cold and statuesque representations, none of which is really life-like. The best, by J. S. Sargent (1914), is at the offices of the Royal Geographical Society, Kensington Gore. Another portrait, by P. A. de László (1913), is at All Souls College, Oxford, and copies of this are at Eton College and in the Carlton Club. The statues in Carlton Gardens, London, and at Calcutta bear little resemblance to the original. Curzon's personal appearance is better observed in the many photographs reproduced in published works.

[*The Times*, 21 March 1925; Lord Ronaldshay (now Marquess of Zetland), *Life of Lord Curzon*, 3 vols., 1928; H. Caldwell Lipsett, *Lord Curzon in India, 1898–1903*, 1906; Lord Curzon, *Speeches, 1898–1905*, 4 vols., Calcutta, 1900–1906, *British Government in India*, 2 vols., posthumous, 1925, *Bodiam Castle, Sussex*, 1926, *The Personal History of Walmer Castle and its Lords Warden*, 1927, *Tattershall Castle, Lincolnshire*, 1929; Winston Churchill, *The World Crisis, 1911–1914*, 1923; Wilfrid Scawen Blunt, *My Diaries*, 1919 and 1920; Lady Oxford, *The Autobiography of Margot Asquith*, 1922; private information; personal knowledge.]

HAROLD NICOLSON

published 1937

DALTON (Edward) Hugh (John Neale)

(1887–1962)

Baron Dalton

Labour politician, was born at Neath, Glamorganshire, 26 August 1887, the eldest child of Canon John Neale Dalton by his wife, Catharine Alicia, elder daughter of Charles Evan-Thomas, JP, DL, of the Gnoll House, Neath, and sister of Sir Hugh Evan-Thomas; there was also a daughter, and another son who died at birth. Hugh Dalton's father had been tutor to Prince Edward, and to Prince George, afterwards King George V, whose friend and counsellor he remained throughout his life, serving as his domestic chaplain from 1892. He was a canon of St. George's Chapel, Windsor, from 1885 until his death in 1931; chaplain-in-ordinary to the sovereign in 1891–7, and thereafter deputy clerk of the closet. He was appointed KCVO in 1911.

Hugh Dalton was educated at Summer Fields, Oxford, and Eton, where he became captain of his house. He went up to King's College, Cambridge, where he won the Winchester reading prize and was classed junior optime in part i of the mathematical tripos (1909); he went on to read economics in his fourth year, studying under A. C. Pigou and J. M. (later Lord) Keynes, and obtained a good second in part ii of the economics tripos (1910). At Cambridge he became a close friend of Rupert Brooke, and a somewhat romantic socialist through his strong adolescent dislike of unfair privilege; his socialism was fermented by a visit of Keir Hardie shortly after Dalton had joined the Fabian Society. In 1911 he won the Hutchinson research studentship to the London School of Economics and began to work on a thesis on 'Some aspects of the inequality of incomes in modern communities'. He also joined the Middle Temple, and was called to the bar in 1914. On the outbreak of war in that year he joined the Inns of Court OTC; he served in France in 1916–17, and was then transferred to an artillery regiment on the Italian front for a year and a half. He was de-mobilized early in 1919 and in the same year published his first book, *With British Guns in Italy*.

He then returned to the London School of Economics, where he lectured on economics under Professor Edwin Cannan, completed his thesis, which was published in 1920, and obtained his D.Sc. (1921). He also took tutorial classes in economics for the Workers' Educational Association. He was Sir Ernest Cassel reader in commerce (1920–5) and reader in economics (1925–36) at London University, and was a member of the Cambridge University statutory commission in 1923–5. In 1923 he published his classic, *Principles of Public Finance*, based on orthodox pre-Keynesian economics; there followed the publication of *Towards the Peace of Nations* (1928) and *Practical Socialism for Britain* (1935). It was not until after 1937 that he became an ardent Keynesian.

Dalton entered politics in 1922 equipped for his way through life, as he said, with 'good physical health . . . great stamina, a strong voice, a strong temper, strong views, some obstinacy . . . a capacity for friendship on equal terms . . . and an abiding loyalty to firm friends'. By 1924 he had fought three general elections and two by-elections as Labour candidate, winning a seat at Peckham in that year. He was chosen as prospective candidate for

Bishop Auckland in 1928, but the sitting member died in December while Dalton was still member for Peckham; so his wife stood in his stead and won the seat in February 1929 to 'keep it warm' for him. In the general election later that year Dalton won Bishop Auckland himself with an overall majority for Labour of 3,700. On the formation of a Labour Government by Ramsay MacDonald, Dalton was delighted at his appointment as parliamentary under-secretary to Arthur Henderson at the Foreign Office; he was devoted to Henderson, and glad of the opportunity to advance the cause of disarmament and the League of Nations.

However, Dalton declined to serve in MacDonald's 'national' Government of 1931, and lost his seat in the ensuing general election. He travelled extensively during the next four years, visiting Russia, Italy (where he had a cordial interview with Mussolini, claiming to have been a soldier of the Italian 'unconquered army'), France, and Germany, where he was appalled by the Nazi treatment of his Jewish academic friends. Later he visited Australia and New Zealand, which he loved.

In the general election of 1935 Dalton regained Bishop Auckland with a Labour majority of 8,086. As Opposition spokesman for foreign affairs in the House of Commons he spoke frequently and, convinced of Hitler's menace, fought hard to stop his party's voting against all Service estimates, in which he succeeded in 1937. By that time he had gained stature in the Labour Party, of which he was chairman in 1936–7. In 1935 he had been top of the constituency votes for the national executive, to which he was first elected in 1926 and on which he served without a break from 1928 to 1952.

When war broke out in 1939 Dalton was prominent in support of policies which (Sir) Winston Churchill also advocated; in 1940 he was appointed minister of economic warfare in the coalition Government, and was sworn of the Privy Council: he chose Hugh Gaitskell to be his principal private secretary, and John Wilmot (later Lord Wilmot of Selmeston) as parliamentary private secretary. In addition, Dalton had the task of setting up the Special Operations Executive—the secret organization for subversion and sabotage and the strengthening of guerrilla and resistance movements in occupied countries—with which Churchill invited him to 'set Europe ablaze'. He appointed (Sir) Frank Nelson to 'build up the new machine', and battled—often successfully—against suspicion and even hostility from the Foreign Office and the Services.

His organizational abilities were recognized by Churchill who promoted him to the presidency of the Board of Trade in February 1942, although, as Dalton said, 'Handing over S.O.E. twanged my heart-strings'. The Board of Trade was at that time 'a rag-bag of problems with no connecting thread', containing, among others, the Department of Overseas Trade, the Mines Department, and the Petroleum Department. At first Dalton's main preoccupation was with the fuel shortage, and after four months' intense and patient consultation his recommendations were finally adopted and a Ministry of Fuel and Power was set up, to which those responsibilities were transferred. In that short time he had done much for the coal industry, especially in regard to miners' wages and in ensuring government control (with owners, miners, and others) through a National Coal Board. His major achievement was to forearm against post-war unemployment by steering new factories into the 'distressed' (renamed 'development') areas. He used the allocation of building licences and compulsory consultation with industrialists to 'take the work to the worker'; his white paper also included important provisions for powers of compulsory purchase, and financial aid. These measures were embodied in the distribution of industry Bill, which Churchill's caretaker Government saw through its final stages, the royal assent being received on the very day the wartime Parliament was dissolved.

In the 1945 general election Dalton held Bishop Auckland with an increased majority of 8,860. In the ensuing Labour Government, the prime minister, Clement (later Earl) Attlee, gave Dalton the Treasury, Ernest Bevin the Foreign Office, and Herbert Morrison (later Lord Morrison of Lambeth) the lord presidency of the Council with leadership of the House of Commons.

Dalton's first act as chancellor of the Exchequer was to appoint Keynes as his personal adviser and give him the arduous job of negotiating an American loan to replace 'lease-lend', which he believed could save the country from mass unemployment and starvation. Dalton steered both the loan agreement and the Bretton Woods agreement through the House of Commons in December 1945. In his first budget—October 1945—he cut income tax by a shilling in the pound, raised surtax, and cut excess profits tax. In his second budget, April 1946, he remitted purchase tax on some household necessities, made a start in the repayment of post-war credits, substantially raised estate duties, making provision for the transfer of land and historic houses to the National Trust and similar bodies, and carried £50 million from the sale of war stores to a National Land Fund for the purchase of beautiful tracts of land on behalf of the nation, an issue on which, as an inveterate hiker, he felt strongly. He also allocated generous sums for the 'development' areas, for many forms of welfare, and for education, especially the universities. In the nationalization programme to which the Labour Government was committed, he was responsible for the nationalization of the Bank of England (1946)—which made it a public board independent of the Treasury in most monetary affairs—and for the Borrowing (Control and Guarantees) Act of 1946, which regulated new issues. On Treasury advice he did not set up a National Investment Board, as he had intended, but only a consultative National Investment Council, which had no powers at all.

But Dalton's popularity as chancellor did not last long. Trouble came in 1947, which he described as 'annus horrendus' as compared with the 'annus mirabilis' of 1946. He had been encouraged by Keynes to pursue cheap money—dear money would have added to inflation—and with the continuation of strict rationing, cheap money was a tenable policy. But Keynes was no longer there to help, and Dalton carried cheap money too far: it was a great achievement to have financed the floating debt at ½%, but he put too much faith in the official control of the gilt-edged market through the government broker. Advised by the Treasury and Bank of England, he decided to call in 3% Local Loans stock and replace it with an undated 2½% Treasury stock (thereafter called 'Daltons'). This proved more than the market was prepared to accept, having just digested a 2½% savings bond issue redeemable in eighteen to twenty-one years. The new 2½% Treasury undated stock only held its issue price for a very short time in February 1947 and was then heavily sold, falling to a substantial discount.

After this market disaster came the coal fuel crisis (when electricity was cut off for several hours a day), and a worsening balance of payments. To no avail Dalton had begged his ministerial colleagues to reduce their expenditure. In April 1947 he introduced his third budget, which did little to help, since it still adhered to cheap money. In July–August a sterling crisis broke, and the convertibility clause of the American loan agreement had to be suspended. By now overworked and overstrained with worry, Dalton prepared his fourth budget in November 1947. On his way into the chamber of the House of Commons to deliver it, he was questioned by a well-known lobby correspondent of the *Star*. Thinking that he spoke in confidence and that his questioner would continue on his way to the press gallery to listen to his speech, Dalton briefly outlined his proposals. They appeared prematurely in the guise of a forecast in an edition of the paper on sale before the proposals were announced just after 4 o'clock by Dalton. On discovering his error of judgement next morning, Dalton immediately offered his resignation which Attlee reluctantly felt obliged to accept. His place at the Treasury was taken by Sir Stafford Cripps.

Dalton rejoined the Cabinet in June 1948 as chancellor of the Duchy of Lancaster, and went to Paris in November as head of the British delegation to the conference which in the following year provided the constitution for the new Council of Europe. He served on its Consultative Assembly in 1949 as deputy leader of the Labour section under Morrison, and as leader in 1950. He was well equipped for the task, as he was fluent in French and

Italian (an unusual accomplishment for a Labour minister), but he did not disguise his dislike of the Germans, and his love of the Poles and of all Slavs and Latins. After the general election of 1950 he was made minister of town and country planning (in 1951 enlarged into local government and planning), an office he accepted because of his interest in the new towns and parks; but his ministerial career came to an end—although he retained his seat in the Commons—after Labour's defeat in the general election of October 1951. He won Bishop Auckland yet again in the general election of 1955 (with a reduced majority), but withdrew from the shadow Cabinet and urged other veterans in the party to do the same; in 1957, shortly after his seventieth birthday, he announced that he would not stand at the next election, which took place in 1959. He received a life peerage in 1960. He published the last of the three volumes of his memoirs, *High Tide and After*, in 1962; the earlier volumes were *Call Back Yesterday* (1953) and *The Fateful Years (1931–1945)* (1957).

Dalton was master of the Drapers' Company in 1958–9, as his father and other members of his family had also been, taking much interest in its affairs. He was an honorary fellow of LSE, and the universities of Sydney, Manchester, and Durham awarded him honorary degrees; he had also been elected an honorary bencher of the Middle Temple in 1946.

Dalton was for many years one of the 'big five' in the Labour Party with Attlee, Bevin, Morrison, and Cripps; he did much to help transform the party by attracting and promoting the talent of younger men such as James Callaghan, Hugh Gaitskell, Anthony Crosland, Denis Healey, and Douglas Jay, who gave it a non-Marxist egalitarian but pragmatic socialism. He was essentially patriotic, rooting out pacifism from the party before 1939 and, with Bevin, steadily opposing Marxist infiltration. He was one of the few Labour leaders who had actually fought for his country on the battlefields of Europe, and he loved the virile young men who had done the same and had voted Labour. Apart from the miners of Bishop Auckland, whom he represented for twenty-six years in all, many others were grateful to him too, not least for extending the national parks and forests which he loved. He was perhaps too emotional, but there were many who valued his loyal friendship and generosity, especially the young; tributes were also paid to his buoyant optimism and exuberance of spirits—not to say panache—with matching drive and decision and a 'big booming voice' which, as Queen Victoria had remarked when he was only four years old, was 'just like his father's'. He excelled as a teacher, being scrupulously fair, and wrote good English easily, with brevity and clarity—an advantage to any politician. In appearance he was rather ungainly: over six feet tall, with long legs and short arms; he had piercing light-blue eyes, which he turned up to heaven when he talked, and a great bald domed head; but his smile was warm and friendly, his expression one of cheerful benevolence, and in youth he had been decidedly handsome.

In 1914 Dalton married Ruth (died 1966), daughter of Thomas Hamilton-Fox, a business man; they had one daughter who died in 1922, aged four and a half. Dalton died in London 13 February 1962, after a lengthy illness.

[*The Times*, 14 and 20 February 1962; *Manchester Guardian Weekly*, 15 February 1962; Hugh Dalton, *Memoirs*, op. cit.; Nicholas Davenport, *Memoirs of a City Radical*, 1974; personal knowledge.]

NICHOLAS DAVENPORT

published 1981

D'AVIGDOR-GOLDSMID Sir Henry Joseph

(1909–1976)

Second Baronet

Politician and bullion broker, was born at Somerhill, Kent, 10 June 1909, the elder son (there were no daughters) of (Sir) Osmond Elim d'Avigdor-Goldsmid, first baronet (created 1934) and his wife, Alice, daughter of Joseph Landau, of Warsaw. Osmond d'Avigdor had assumed by royal licence the name and arms of Goldsmid on succeeding to the Goldsmid settled estates in 1896. 'Harry', as he was always called, united both in blood as well as name the vitality, attitudes, and temperaments of two Jewish banking dynasties—the Goldsmids, established and respected in London since the late eighteenth century, and the d'Avigdors, brilliant sensitive sophisticates from Nice.

He had himself an almost Renaissance range and depth of abilities—intellectual, artistic, political, social, soldierly, and financial: a commanding personality and appearance; wit, bravery, patriotism, a sense of public and Jewish service, and a capacity for friendship and family life. He was capable of swift changes of mood: he could be impatient, he could not tolerate fools, he was easily bored. Despite all his talents things did not come easily to him: he was introspective, self-doubting, and drove himself by sustained self-discipline.

He was educated at Harrow and at Balliol College, Oxford. He obtained second class honours in philosophy, politics, and economics in 1931. In Oxford he met a number of gifted contemporaries in the literary world, forming friendships that lasted for the rest of his life. On leaving Balliol he went into the family firm of Mocatta and Goldsmid, bullion brokers. In business his honesty, shrewdness, prudence, and judgement of people brought him success. He was also to be an able manager of the large family estates which he inherited. In 1940 his father died and he succeeded to the title.

In the same year he married Rosemary Margaret, former wife of Sir Peter James Cunliffe Horlick, third baronet, and daughter of Lt.-Col. Charles Rice Iltyd Nicholl. He was already serving in the Royal Armoured Corps (the Royal West Kent Regiment) having got himself transferred from staff duties. Overcoming a strong sense of fear he led a reconnaissance unit during the campaign in north-west Europe with courage and resourcefulness, and was wounded. He won the MC (1945) and two mentions in dispatches, and was appointed to the DSO (1945). He ended the war with the rank of major.

Between 1945 and 1955 he worked as a bullion broker with Mocatta & Goldsmid, and served in local government in Kent, rising to be leader of the Conservatives on the county council.

Entering politics as Conservative member for Walsall in 1955, he became devoted to and beloved by his constituents, to whom he was endlessly patient and helpful. In the House of Commons he was rapidly accepted as a financial authority and rose to the chairmanship of important all-party committees, including the select committee on public expenditure. On two occasions, by short, moderate, rational speeches, he effectively demolished efforts to outlaw the Jewish ritual method of slaughter. He was parliamentary private secretary (1955–6) to Duncan Sandys (later Lord Duncan-Sandys) when minister of housing. He was no orator, but was widely liked and respected. Why he never became a minister is a mystery. Perhaps he was too successful to be invited to junior office; perhaps his uncompromising and fearless opinions and his contempt for mediocrity made him seem too mature for team work. He resigned his seat at the 1974 election.

In parallel with his business and his political lives he was active in public service—JP (1949), high sheriff of Kent (1953), deputy lieutenant (1949). He inherited from his father a strong sense of Jewish community service. For twenty-five years he was president of the Jewish Colonization Association, set up and endowed by Baron de Hirsch in 1892 to spend its revenue to establish and train Russian Jews as farmers in South America. Judging that, had Israel then existed, it would have been there that the baron would have wished to establish Jewish farming communities, d'Avigdor-Goldsmid, over time, redeployed the main efforts of the JCA from the Americas to Israel. His was a notable, strong, and effective presidency. He was also chairman of the Anglo-Israel Chamber of Commerce and chairman of both Bank Leumi (UK) and of the Anglo-Israel Bank. He accepted the caretaker chairmanship of Pergamon Press which he worked effectively to re-establish from 1969 to 1971 in close co-operation with Robert Maxwell, the ousted former chairman who rejoined the board as a non-executive director and eventually reassumed his old post.

At his fine inherited home at Somerhill in Kent d'Avigdor-Goldsmid established a warm and strong family and social life with his wife and their two daughters. It was there that he increased his family collection of paintings and books, wrote his contributions to the *Times Literary Supplement* and other book reviews, entertained a wide circle of friends, built up a stable, and made himself a bold rider to hounds. But it was there also that the zest for life left him when his beloved elder daughter Sarah died in a sailing accident at sea in 1963. Though he forced himself to carry on his activities, and though his sparkle and wit sometimes returned, he never recovered.

He was a man of rich and varied gifts; high principle; public spirit; a proud independence of character and judgement; and a brilliant intellect— with a keen eye for the ridiculous. Despite all his achievements his potential was never fully realized. In 1974 he became an honorary freeman of Walsall. He died in Eaton Mansions, London, 11 December 1976 and was succeeded in the baronetcy by his brother, Major-General James Arthur d'Avigdor-Goldsmid (born 1912).

[*The Times*, 13, 14, and 15 December 1976; private information; personal knowledge.]

KEITH JOSEPH

published 1986

DEAKIN Arthur

(1890–1955)

Trade-union leader, was born at Sutton Coldfield, Warwickshire, 11 November 1890, the son of a domestic servant, Annie Deakin. At the age of ten he moved with his mother and stepfather to Dowlais in South Wales where he started to work for the steel firm, Guest, Keen, and Nettlefolds, at the age of thirteen, for four shillings a week. He joined the National Union of Gas Workers and came under the influence of Keir Hardie, then member of Parliament for Merthyr Tydfil of which Dowlais was a part. In 1910 Deakin moved to Shotton in North Wales and took a job with another steel firm as a roll turner. For a brief spell he was a member of the Amalgamated Society of Engineers but in 1911 he moved over to the expanding, heterogeneous Dock, Wharf, Riverside, and General Workers' Union which gave ample scope to his incipient qualities of leadership. Within three years he was an active lay member and in 1919 he became a full-time official of the union. Until that year he belonged also to the small British Roll Turners' Society of which for a brief period he was general secretary. When in 1922 the Dockers' Union became part of the Transport and General Workers' Union, Deakin became assistant district secretary for the North Wales area where the high unemployment of the next ten years strongly conditioned his subsequent attitudes and responses. In 1919 he became an alderman of the Flintshire County Council and in 1932 its chairman.

In 1932 Deakin moved to London where until 1935 he was national secretary of the General Workers' trade group of the Transport and General Workers' Union. He toured the country examining the problems of his group and so impressed Ernest Bevin, the general secretary of the union, with his organizing ability that in 1985 he was appointed assistant general secretary. He worked closely with Bevin through a difficult time for the union, for in 1938 some of its members seceded to form a union for busmen; and Bevin himself was showing signs of strain from overwork.

When in 1940 (Sir) Winston Churchill invited Bevin to become minister of labour in the wartime coalition Government, Deakin took Bevin's place in the union and continued as acting general secretary until Bevin retired from union office in March 1946, when Deakin was elected general secretary in his place, with a majority of 59,105 votes over the combined votes of the other five candidates.

Although from 1940 until 1946 Deakin was the formal head of his union, the largest in Britain and one of the largest in the world, his work was done in the shadow of Bevin whose reputation among the ordinary members was almost legendary and who never effectively relinquished his control of union activities. Deakin himself was essentially a Bevin creation and perhaps the most loyal supporter of a man upon whom he modelled himself to the extent of copying some of his public mannerisms. On the General Council of the Trades Union Congress where he took Bevin's place, he was a useful but not an influential member. The Council had been dominated by Bevin and its general secretary, Sir Walter (later Lord) Citrine; with Bevin's departure Citrine remained firmly in control, unaffected by Deakin's presence. Deakin became a member of the Government's War Transport Council and of the committee established to advise the Production Executive. In one respect he achieved notoriety during the war. When he visited Sweden in 1943 as a fraternal delegate to the Congress of the Swedish Transport Workers' Union he conferred with a Finnish trade-union leader on the possibilities of negotiating a peace treaty; for this he received much adverse publicity.

A new phase in Deakin's career began in 1946 when he became leader of his union in his own right. After the resignation of Citrine from the Trades Union Congress and a period of uncertainty in the leadership of the movement, the position gradually clarified and settled and by 1948 Deakin had emerged as the most dominant figure in British trade-unionism and an influential one also in the international movement. He retained his trade-union and political influence until his death which took place on 1 May 1955 while he was addressing a May Day rally in Leicester.

Like so many men who find themselves thrust into positions of power and responsibility, Deakin developed to meet the situation. People who knew him under Bevin could never have imagined his filling the role which he subsequently attained in post-war Britain. A Labour Government was in office and the country faced extreme economic difficulties. Both factors demanded that trade unions break with their traditional attitudes. They required a close collaboration with the Government and the acceptance of attitudes about productivity and profits which unions had traditionally rejected. After an initial hesitation, Deakin gave the Government his unconditional support. He urged unions to try to increase productivity and advocated a policy of wage restraint. He possessed a deep loyalty to the labour movement which was epitomized for him by the Labour Government. In his eagerness to support the Government he stifled much useful criticism of its activities, for he disliked anything which could be misconstrued by the general public or used for political purposes. He was more than an advocate. As far as he could he applied the policy of wage restraint in his own union and incurred the displeasure of some of his more militant members. But if he thought his policy was right no amount of criticism would deter him. At times he risked the unity of his organization and faced large-scale unofficial strikes rather than make expedient concessions. No Government could have had a more loyal supporter.

Deakin travelled widely as a member of the international committee of the Trades Union Congress and as the most prominent representative of his own union. He was a member of the executive board of the World Federation of Trade Unions and did much to heal the breach between its Communist and non-Communist members. During his tenure as chairman of the board, however, he led a walkout of the non-Communist delegates and helped to form the International Confederation of Free Trade Unions in 1949. Thereafter he became uncompromisingly anti-

Communist in his attitude towards foreign affairs, national domestic affairs, and the running of his own union which in 1949 he persuaded to ban Communists from holding office.

The attitude of Deakin towards Communists was in part a reflection of his attitude towards opposition. He believed in the sanctity of majority decisions and was intolerant of those who opposed them. He attacked minorities in his union and in the Labour Party with invective and organizational measures. He would defy procedures and conventions to get his own way and was often accused by his antagonists of being a dictator. By his public manner, outspoken, brusque, and intolerant, and by his manner of handling internal union affairs, he lent support to the accusation. The administrative problems of his union increased as it expanded from 743,349 members in 1940 to 1,305,456 in 1955 and by and large Deakin coped with them. But he possessed a vital reluctance to delegate authority and maintained a strict control over even the smallest administrative detail in his union's head office. He would sometimes speak on behalf of his union without consulting the general executive council which constitutionally controlled him. Deakin believed in positive leadership. 'I cannot and will not be a cipher', he told his members. Yet all the time he was aware of the source of his power and always made sure that on the major issues he had the majority of his ordinary members behind him. He was sentimental about his relations with the lay members of his union. Nothing hurt him more than the suggestion that he was out of touch with them. A cartoon which depicted him with his head in the clouds caused him considerable anger. He did much to improve contacts between officials and lay members and saw the development of educational provisions within the union as a means to this end. His union introduced pioneering training schemes for shop stewards and branch officials and under his guidance the education department became large and influential.

The public image of Deakin lent itself to caricature. He dressed flamboyantly, smoked large cigars, and courted publicity. But in essential ways both the public image and the caricatures gave a misleading impression. Deakin was modest and shy. He lived quietly and modestly in a small semi-detached house in a north London suburb where his evenings, when free from union business, were spent at home with his wife. He did not drink alcohol and was a member of the Primitive Methodist Church. He did not make friends easily and found communication on an individual level difficult. But those with whom he had a close relationship came from various walks of life and different political affiliations. In this respect he was paradoxical. He tended to be distrustful of Labour Party politicians and his personal relations with them were uneasy, whereas he could get on very well with self-made employers and with Conservative politicians. Thus he found it easy to make the transition from a Labour to a Conservative Government in 1951. But he never transferred his distrust of Labour politicians to the party itself and he disapproved of those trade-union leaders who moved into industrial management.

Deakin was often accused of seeking honours, yet he twice refused a knighthood. He was appointed C.B.E. in 1943 and C.H. in 1949, and was sworn of the Privy Council in 1954; these he regarded as honours to the labour movement rather than to himself.

In 1914 Deakin married Annie, daughter of Robert George, of Connah's Quay, Flintshire; they had two sons.

[*The Times*, 2 May 1955; V. L. Allen, *Trade Union Leadership*, 1957; personal knowledge.]

V. L. ALLEN

published 1971

DE VALERA Eamon

(1882–1975)

Prime minister and later president of the Republic of Ireland, was born in New York 14 October 1882, the only child of a Spanish father, Vivion Juan de Valera, artist, and an Irish mother, Catherine (Kate), daughter of Patrick Coll, a farm labourer of county Limerick. His father died when he was two. His mother took him home to Ireland in 1885 before returning to America. He was brought up on the small farm of his mother's brother Patrick Coll. He obtained his education the hard way. He went to the village school at Bruree, a more advanced school in Charleville, to which he frequently had to walk seven miles a day, and thence as a lay boarder at the age of sixteen to Blackrock College in Dublin. Two years later he secured a place at University College, Blackrock. By the age of twenty he had acquired the passion for mathematics which remained with him to the end of his days. At twenty-one he obtained a teaching appointment at Rockwell College near Cashel. In 1904 he gained a pass degree in mathematical science in the Royal University of Ireland. Later he became a professor of mathematics in the training college of Our Lady of Mercy, Carysfort, Blackrock.

He came to acquire a lifelong interest in the Irish language of which he knew little as a boy. Among his teachers was a young woman about four years older than himself, Sinéad Flanagan, who had already won a gold medal in a major competition. She was the daughter of Laurence Flanagan, of Carbery, county Kildare. Their marriage on 8 January 1910 in St. Paul's Church, Arran Quay, Dublin, was to prove the happiest of partnerships. Mrs de Valera was a woman of strong personality and literary gifts, but she dedicated herself to her husband and their seven children (five sons, one of whom was killed in a riding accident in 1936 at the age of twenty, and two daughters).

In 1913 a Home Rule Bill had been passed through the British House of Commons, but overwhelmingly rejected by the Lords. It could not become law until summer 1914. The Ulster Protestants set up a provisional government and organized full-scale military resistance. De Valera was crucially affected by these developments. In November 1913 a public meeting was held in Dublin to found a volunteer force in the South in reply to the Ulstermen. De Valera attended, joined the Volunteers, and committed himself irrevocably to a share in the armed conflict which he thought was inevitable.

He became a wholehearted and efficient Volunteer. He was in no way concerned with the decisions which led to the 1916 rising, but in that traumatic week his military performance was impressive. He expected the death sentence but he was not among the first to be court-martialled, and his sentence was commuted to life imprisonment. He was saved by the delay and a change in government policy, not, as is sometimes said, because of his American birth. After the executions it was natural that he should be looked on as the senior commander. In various British prisons he exhibited a marked gift for leadership. Along with other prisoners he was released by a general amnesty in June 1917. Soon after his release he won a memorable by-election in East Clare on a policy of complete and absolute independence for an Irish Republic. At a convention on 25 October 1917, in the Mansion House, Dublin, he was elected as president of Sinn Fein. By now he was becoming a thorn in the British side. In May 1918 he was rearrested and imprisoned in Lincoln Gaol, from which he made a sensational escape in February 1919. By this time a republic had been declared in Ireland and an alternative and 'illegal' system of government established. De Valera, the newly elected president, remained in hiding till he set off for the United States in June 1919. He did not return to Ireland until December 1920, by which time the guerrilla war of independence was reaching a climax. One purpose of his visit, that of raising funds, was achieved most successfully; the wider propagandist purpose, less obviously. But at least the Irish case was placed fairly and squarely before the American people, and identified henceforward with that of other struggling nations, India and Egypt among them.

Back in Ireland at the end of 1920, de Valera was once again in hiding. During the first half of 1921 the British government fluctuated between a policy of stepping up coercion and putting out fresh feelers. On 23 June King George V, opening the new Stormont parliament, set up under the 'Partition Act' of 1920, made a historic plea for reconciliation. The next step was to hand de Valera a letter which invited him to a conference in London with Lloyd George and Sir James Craig (later Viscount Craigavon), prime minister of Northern Ireland. De Valera could on no account accept a parity between his position and that of Craig. But the latter in any case refused. A truce was negotiated. De Valera went to London and had several meetings with Lloyd George. There was no meeting of minds personally or politically. De Valera reaffirmed the Irish demand for a republic Lloyd George offered dominion status, an immense advance compared with the Act of 1920, or the Home Rule Bill of 1912, but hedged round with significant qualifications.

The Irish Cabinet found the Lloyd George terms quite unacceptable. De Valera now worked out the notion of external association, of which much would be heard later and which to the end of his life probably expressed his own conception of the best Anglo-Irish relationship. Ireland would not be a dominion or a member of the Commonwealth, but a friendly country externally associated with the latter. After prolonged correspondence five Irish delegates came to London in October 1921. Two months of intense negotiations followed. A treaty was signed in the small hours of 6 December 1921. The Irish Free State would be established as a dominion, and thus after 750 years the British occupation of twenty-six counties would be ended.

De Valera had not gone to London for these negotiations—a decision which was to have fateful consequences. To the end of his life he was anxious to defend his decision at considerable length. But in essence he had believed at the time that he would be able to exercise a stronger influence if he stayed in reserve. In the event he misjudged his control over the delegates, especially Arthur Griffith and Michael Collins. At the crunch, under threats of 'immediate and terrible war' they signed the treaty without referring back to him. A nominally republican delegation agreed to an arrangement in which a republic could have no place. In the light of his declared convictions, de Valera had little option but to repudiate the document. The Dáil however supported the treaty by 64 votes to 57. He was supplanted as president and became an unofficial leader of the opposition. Many republicans prepared to resist the treaty in arms. A civil war followed inexorably. De Valera was bitterly attacked by the treaty party in Ireland and by almost everyone of influence in England for causing the civil war. It is fairest to conclude that once he had repudiated the treaty there was nothing which he could do to avert the tragedy. The republicans were totally defeated. De Valera who had been on the run made a spectacular reappearance at Clare in the general election of 1923. He was not released until nearly a year later (July 1924). His fortunes seemed to be at a nadir, his career quite possibly at an end.

But he had never ceased to plan a political resurrection for the republican cause. In 1926 he launched a new party, Fianna Fáil. Initially their elected deputies declined to take their seats in the Dáil because of the required oath of allegiance to the British Crown. But in 1927 de Valera made a much derided volte-face, doing the right thing it must seem now, but showing far less consistency than usual. On 12 August 1927 the Fianna Fáil deputies took their seats in the Dáil. In the general election of 1932 they increased their seats from 57 to 72. This did not give them an overall majority but an arrangement with the Labour Party enabled de Valera to form a government. At the age of fifty, after an interval of ten years, he was once again the official leader of the Irish people.

The pre-war years, 1932–9, were disfigured by the economic dispute with Britain which ended in a kind of draw with the agreement of 1938. De Valera and his eventual successor, Sean Lemass, made a virtue of necessity and introduced measures of self-sufficiency which were in any case in line with Fianna Fáil and Sinn Fein thinking. On the constitutional front de Valera's largest personal achievement was the new constitution of 1937. In social policy it gave expression to Catholic social teaching. The special position of the Catholic Church in Ireland was emphasized, but Protestant and Jewish Churches were explicitly mentioned. Protestants at the time were pleased, but many years later the special position accorded to the Catholic Church came to seem sectarian and the clause in question was repealed.

The name of the state was changed from Irish Free State to Eire. The Anglo-Irish side of the constitutional revolution has been well summed up by Professor P. N. S. Mansergh—'Taken together, the External Relations Act and the new Constitution destroyed the dominion settlement of 1921. Relations with Britain and the Commonwealth had been taken out of the Constitution, where Mr de Valera felt that they had no place, and had become matters of external policy for the Government of the day. This was the most significant development in the whole period' (1926–39). (N. Mansergh, 'The Implications of Eire's Relationship with the British Commonwealth of Nations', *International Affairs*, January 1948.) After the agreement of 1938, and six years of neutrality in the war, it was manifest to all that total independence for the twenty-six counties had been secured. Under the agreement of 1938, de Valera secured what he had hardly hoped for, the return of 'the ports'—that is to say the renunciation by Britain of the naval and air facilities in certain Irish ports enjoyed under the treaty. De Valera and Neville Chamberlain, the British prime minister, struck up a remarkably cordial relationship. If war had not come so soon, an effective defence arrangement might have led to a united Ireland. In retrospect, de Valera dwelt occasionally on this 'might have been'.

In the event, war came all too rapidly. De Valera instantly proclaimed neutrality. The British representative in Dublin, Sir John Maffey (later Lord Rugby) privately advised the British Cabinet that no government could exist in Ireland that 'departed from the principle of neutrality.' In various secondary ways de Valera made his neutrality highly benevolent to the Allies; it will always remain a matter of dispute as to how far the Allied cause was damaged by the non-availability of the ports. At the beginning of the war Churchill showed an interest in recovering the facilities by force. Sir John Maffey, who maintained throughout the war an excellent relationship with de Valera, played a notable part in defeating any such initiative. At different times during the war the Germans, the British, and the French brought extreme pressure to bear, but de Valera maintained his iron nerve throughout six desperately anxious years. Perhaps the most successful address he ever delivered was a radio reply to Churchill at the end of the war. Churchill had boasted of the restraint and poise which the British government had shown in not laying violent hands on Ireland. De Valera's speech was moderate and conciliatory, but contained the telling question 'could he [Mr Churchill] not find in his heart the generosity to acknowledge that there is a small nation . . . that could never be got to accept defeat and has never surrendered her soul?' Never had he spoken so clearly for the nation and never had the nation been so proud of him. Churchill privately conceded that de Valera had the better of the exchanges.

After the war, the independence of the twenty-six counties was not in dispute. But, although large numbers of southern Irishmen had served often with distinction in the British forces, this could not weigh against Britain's conviction that her foothold in the North had been essential to survival and victory. Partition was thus more firmly entrenched than ever. In the general election of 1948 de Valera was not surprised to be defeated by a rather strange combination of Fine Gael, traditionally more pro-British than Fianna Fáil and Clann na Poblachta, a new radical republican party, under the charismatic Sean MacBride. The new government proceeded to sever the last link with the Commonwealth by repealing the External Relations Act which de Valera had sedulously preserved. De Valera acquiesced but he did not pretend that he would have proceeded along these lines. The change was announced in the clumsiest way possible. The British responded by strengthening their guarantee to Northern Ireland.

De Valera was returned to power in 1951, but was out of office from 1954 to 1957. In the latter year, aged seventy-five, he came back with the first overall majority since the wartime election of 1944, but by 1959 he recognized that the time had come to hand over to a younger generation and to repair as president to 'The Park' where he served for fourteen years, a model of mellow dignity. One great regret in old age was his failure to make any headway with the ending of partition. From 1920 onwards he had insisted that 'Ulster must not be coerced', that force, in other words, must be renounced, in seeking to achieve Irish unity. It sometimes seemed that the distinctiveness of the Northern Unionist culture never fully came home to him. They were all Irishmen and equally dear accordingly. He persisted in the belief that the Gaelic Ireland which he had tried so hard, though with limited success, to establish in the twenty-six counties, would itself be instrumental in promoting Irish unity. Not many today would share that opinion. On the other hand, the modern notion that a united Ireland should be of a federal rather than a unitary character was completely in line with his later thinking.

In international affairs, one speculates wistfully about what he could have achieved if he had been at the head of a great state instead of a small nation. He was by chance president of the council of the League of Nations in 1932, the same year that he became head of the Irish government. He made a profound impression on that occasion. His opportunities of exercising widespread international influence were afterwards limited, but in his dealings, usually at a disadvantage with world leaders, he proved himself fully their equal. Churchill who at one time had no good word to say of him came to recognize at the end his pre-eminent quality.

Eamon de Valera was six feet one inch in height and looked even taller by reason of his upright carriage. His athletic frame was that of a man who had once played in a Munster trial at rugby football. His features were strongly developed, his eyes were dark and deep set behind the spectacles he had worn since he was a youth. He never lost his passion for mathematics. For many years before his death he was virtually blind. For most of his life he was involved in bitter controversy, but no one ever denied the dignity and courtesy of his bearing. His religious devoutness would be hard to parallel among statesmen. Once installed in the president's residence he visited the oratory five times a day. He had long been a daily communicant. But he was no Catholic bigot. It was Daniel O'Connell who said 'I take my religion from Rome, but my politics from Ireland'. It was a phrase de Valera himself might have coined. In the civil war of 1922–3 the Irish bishops condemned the side that he was nominally leading. At the end of his life he was at pains to point out to more than one visitor that he had *not* been excommunicated. He had taken the matter up with the pope of the day a few years after the civil war and found that the pope agreed with him. He was asked 'what would you have thought if the pope had disagreed with you?' He replied with his familiar dead-pan humour 'I should have considered that His Holiness was misinformed.' One of his chaplains, later a bishop, is on record as saying of him: 'He would have made a good Protestant.'

Though he was a man of subtle mind and complex personality, he stood through life for simple conceptions: religion, the family, democracy, law and order, fair dealing between nations, justice for the oppressed. In all these respects, he left an indelible mark on the state which he did so much to create and foster.

He died in Dublin 29 August 1975 at the age of ninety-two. His personality had dominated the Irish scene for nearly sixty years. No Irishman in this century, or indeed any other, has achieved so prolonged an eminence in his lifetime.

[The Earl of Longford and Thomas P. O'Neill, *Eamon de Valera*, 1970; private information; personal knowledge.]

FRANK LONGFORD

published 1986

DILKE Sir Charles Wentworth

(1843–1911)

Second Baronet

Politician and author, born on 4 Sept. 1843 in the house in Sloane Street, London (No. 76), which his father had occupied and in which he himself lived and died, was elder son of Sir Charles Wentworth Dilke, first baronet. Charles Wentworth Dilke, the antiquary and critic, was his grandfather. His mother, Mary, daughter of William Chatfield, captain in the Madras cavalry, died on 16 Sept. 1853. His younger brother was Ashton Wentworth Dilke, M.P. for Newcastle-on-Tyne from 1880 until his death in 1883.

Dilke, after being educated privately, became in 1862 a scholar of Trinity Hall, Cambridge—his father's college. There (Sir) Leslie Stephen was his tutor. He graduated LL.B. as senior legalist, i.e. head of the law tripos, in 1866, and proceeded LL.M. in 1869. He was an active member of the Cambridge Union, serving twice as vice-president and twice as president. He was an enthusiastic oarsman and rowed in his college boat when it was head of the river. That recreation he pursued all his life. In later years he built himself a bungalow at Dockett Eddy near Shepperton and spent much of his time on the water. He was also a keen and capable fencer and frequently invited his friends to a bout with the foils at his house in Sloane Street. He was called to the bar at the Middle Temple on 30 April 1866, but never practised.

In 1866 Dilke left England for a tour round the world, beginning with a visit to the United States. Here he travelled alone for some months, but was subsequently joined by William Hepworth Dixon, editor of the 'Athenæum', the paper of which his father was proprietor. The two travelled together for some time, visiting the Mormon cities of Utah, but they parted at Salt Lake City, Dixon returning to England and Dilke continuing his journey westward, visiting San Francisco on his way to Panama. Thence he crossed the Pacific and visited all the Australasian colonies in turn. He returned home by way of Ceylon, India, and Egypt, reaching England at the end of 1867. In the following year he published the results of his studies and explorations in English-speaking and English-governed lands in a work entitled 'Greater Britain: a Record of Travel in English-speaking Countries during 1866 and 1867'. The book immediately achieved an immense success, and passed through four editions. The title, a novel and taking one, was Dilke's invention (see Murray's *New Eng. Dict.*), and the whole subject as treated by Dilke was as new as its title. 'The idea', wrote Dilke in the Preface, 'which in all the length of my travels has been at once my fellow and my guide—a key wherewith to unlock the hidden things of strange new lands—is a conception, however imperfect, of the grandeur of our race, already girdling the earth, which it is destined, perhaps, to overspread.' Thus, while Dilke was an advanced radical through life, he was also from first to last a convinced and well-informed imperialist.

In 1868 the first general election took place under the Reform Act of the previous year. Dilke was selected by the radical party in the newly constituted borough of Chelsea, to which two members were allotted, as one of its two candidates. His colleague was Sir Henry Hoare, and their opponents were (Sir) William H. Russell and C. J. Freake. Dilke headed the poll on 17 Nov. with 7374 votes, Hoare receiving 7183, and Russell only 4177. He at once attracted the favourable notice of the party leaders and was chosen to second the address at the opening of the session of 1870. He joined the extreme nonconformists in opposition to Mr. Forster's education bill, and moved the amendment which the government accepted for the substitution of directly elected schoolboards in place of committees of boards of guardians. To the normal articles of the radical creed, Dilke added republican predilections, and he frankly challenged the monarchical form of government on many public platforms. He questioned whether monarchy was worth its cost. His statement at Newcastle on 6 Nov. 1871, in the course of an elaborate republican plea, that Queen Victoria paid no income tax excited a bitter controversy. At Bristol, Bolton, Derby, and Birmingham he pursued the propaganda, often amid scenes of disturbance. Heated protests against his attitude were raised in the House of Commons, where he moved on 19 March 1872 for a full inquiry into Queen Victoria's expenditure. His confession of republican faith was then echoed by Auberon Herbert, who seconded his motion. A passionate retort followed from Gladstone, the prime minister. Sir Wilfrid Lawson and another were the only members who voted in support of Dilke's motion, for which he and Herbert told. Sharply opposed at Chelsea on the score of his advanced opinions at the next election in 1874, he yet was the only one of three liberal candidates who was elected. He polled 7217 votes, and the conservative candidate was returned as his colleague.

In 1869, on the death of his father, Dilke succeeded to the baronetcy and also to the then lucrative proprietorship of the 'Athenæum' and of 'Notes and Queries'—the former purchased and edited by his grandfather and the latter established by him in 1849—and to a part proprietorship of the 'Gardeners' Chronicle'. He always took an active interest in the conduct of the 'Athenæum' and frequently contributed to its columns, though except during the occasional absence of the responsible editor he never edited it himself. He collected for the press his grandfather's 'Papers of a Critic' (1875), chiefly contributions to the 'Athenæum'. In 1872 he married Katherine Mary Eliza, only daughter of Captain Arthur Gore Sheil.

Meanwhile he was a frequent visitor to Paris, where he became intimate with Gambetta and other republican leaders. He spoke French fluently, though not perhaps quite with the accent of a Parisian. French influence was apparent in his second literary venture, which was published anonymously in 1874. A thin brochure bound in white, it was entitled 'The Fall of Prince Florestan of Monaco'. It told the story of a light-hearted prince, educated at Eton and Cambridge, who was unexpectedly called to the sovereignty of Monaco. He at once set to work to put in action the liberal and reforming ideas he had imbibed at Cambridge, and soon found himself at loggerheads with his subjects, who were all catholics and led by a Jesuit priest. Foiled in his projects of reform, he abdicated and returned to Cambridge. The story was brightly written and displayed no little satiric humour—which spared neither Dilke himself nor his radical contemporaries. It showed in Dilke a mood of genial banter and shrewd detachment from popular shibboleths which was otherwise so little in evidence that few suspected its existence. The book passed through three editions and was translated into French. Perhaps it was better appreciated in France than in England.

In 1874 Dilke's first wife died after giving birth to an only son, Charles Wentworth Dilke, subsequently the third baronet. Next year Dilke made a second tour round the world, now visiting China and Japan, and thenceforth for many years he spent much leisure at a modest villa which he purchased near Toulon. At the same time during his second parliament (1874–80) he greatly improved his position. He became an effective speaker, and won the ear of the House of Commons (Lucy's *Diary of Parliament*, 1874–80, pp. 307–10). His radicalism lost nothing of its strength on shedding its republican features. He made an annual attack on unreformed corporations. On 4 March 1879 he seconded (Sir) George Trevelyan's resolution for extending the county franchise to the agricultural labourer, and on 31 March he moved on behalf of the liberal party a vote of censure on the government's South African policy. To the cause of Greece he proved himself a warm friend. At the general election of April 1880, Dilke for the third time headed the poll at Chelsea with 12,408 votes, carrying the second liberal candidate (Mr. J. B. Firth) in with him with 12,040 votes.

Before Gladstone returned to power in 1880, Dilke was an acknowledged leader of the radical section of his party. Mr. Joseph Chamberlain, M.P. for Birmingham since June 1876, was his chief colleague. Gladstone, however, was very slowly persuaded of the importance of the radical leaders. At first 'he never dreamed of them for his cabinet'. When at length he sent for Dilke while forming his administration, he was annoyed by Dilke's refusal 'to serve unless either himself or Mr. Chamberlain were in the cabinet'. In the end, despite Dilke's superior position in public esteem, Mr. Chamberlain entered the cabinet as president of the board of trade, and Dilke remained outside as under-secretary to the foreign office (cf. Morley, *Life of Gladstone*, ii. 630).

Dilke's knowledge of foreign affairs was exceptional, and as representing the foreign office in the commons with his chief, Lord Granville, in the lords, he enjoyed an influence little short of that of a cabinet minister not yet of the first rank. Of prodigious industry, he conducted the parliamentary business of his department with assiduity, courtesy, and discretion. In 1881–2 he served as chairman of a royal commission for the negotiation of a commercial treaty with France in conjunction with commissioners of the French government. He spent many months over this business, which was conducted in London and in Paris. Early in 1880 his growing reputation had led the Prince of Wales (afterwards Edward VII) to seek his acquaintance and a close intimacy between them lasted through the next four years. They met in Paris as well as at home, and at Paris, by the prince's request, while the commercial negotiations were in progress, Dilke invited his close friend Gambetta to join them at breakfast (24 Oct. 1881).

On Forster's retirement from the Irish secretaryship in April 1882 Dilke was offered the post, but he declined it on the ground that it did not carry with it a seat in the cabinet. Towards the close of the year the cabinet was partially reconstructed, and Dilke at last obtained a place in it as president of the local government board (8 Dec.). At the statutory election at Chelsea he was returned without a contest. There were rumours of reluctance on Queen Victoria's part to assent to Dilke's appointment, which great firmness on the part of the prime minister was needed to dispel (*Annual Register*, 1882, p. 180). In the House of Commons there was now a general belief that he was destined before long to lead his party (cf. Acton's *Letters to Mary Gladstone*). An indication of the public confidence which he commanded was shown by the bestowal on him of the freedom of the borough of Paisley (1 Nov. 1883). He had long given close attention to the problems of local government, and his tenure of office as president of the board was marked by much important legislation. In 1884 he presided as chairman over the royal commission on the housing of the working classes, of which the Prince of Wales, Lord Salisbury, and Cardinal Manning were members. He also took an active part in the negotiations which were initiated in that year by Queen Victoria between government and the opposition in the controversy over the Franchise Act of 1884 and the attendant redistribution of seats. By virtue of his office and by reason of what Lord Morley in his 'Life of Gladstone' called his 'unrivalled mastery of the intricate details' of the whole question of redistribution, he took charge of the redistribution bill and conducted it through the House of Commons with exceptional skill. On 18 Jan. 1884 Dilke, Lord Granville, and Lord Northbrook met General Gordon with Lord Hartington and Lord Wolseley at the war office and they decided on behalf of the cabinet to send Gordon to the Soudan.

In 1885 the Gladstone ministry, externally weakened by the miscarriages of its Egyptian policy, and discredited by its failure to rescue Gordon, was also distracted almost to dissolution by internal dissensions arising out of its Irish policy. New bills for a partial renewal of the expiring Coercion Act, for land purchase and for local government in Ireland were before the cabinet early in 1885. Dilke and Mr. Chamberlain recommended a central administrative board, and resisted the other proposals without effect. On 19 May Gladstone announced in the House of Commons a land purchase bill. Thereupon Dilke and Mr. Chamberlain tendered their resignations. They were requested to reconsider them (Morley's *Gladstone*, iii. 194). But that necessity was spared them. An unexpected defeat on a proposed increase in the beer duties under the budget gave the whole cabinet an opportunity, which they eagerly welcomed, of resigning (8 June 1885). Neither Dilke nor Mr. Chamberlain had favoured the increase of the beer duties. He and Mr. Chamberlain projected under Parnell's auspices a tour in Ireland for the autumn. But Parnell's negotiations with the new conservative lord-lieutenant, the earl of Carnarvon, led him to withdraw his support, and the visit was abandoned. Dilke never again held office under the crown.

Dilke's fall was sudden and tragical. In August 1885 Mr. Donald Crawford, liberal M.P. for Lanark, filed a petition for divorce against his wife on the ground of her alleged adultery with Dilke. Mrs. Crawford was a sister of the wife of Dilke's only brother Ashton, and with her family he was on intimate terms. On the announcement of the charge, Dilke denied its truth in an open letter to the liberal association of Chelsea. The association accepted his disclaimer. He stood for the constituency—now a single member division—at the general election in Dec. 1885 and was returned by 4291 votes against 4116 cast for the conservative candidate. The divorce suit was heard on 12 Feb. 1886, when Mr. Crawford obtained a decree nisi against his wife, solely on the evidence of her confession. Dilke offered to deny on oath in the witness-box Mrs. Crawford's story, but his counsel declined to call him and his friends unwisely dissuaded him from insisting on being called. The outcome of the suit was equivocal. The case against Dilke was dismissed, but Mrs. Crawford's guilt was declared proven on her own evidence, which inculpated none but him. In public opinion Dilke was not cleared of the allegations against him.

Meanwhile Dilke was not included in Gladstone's third administration (Feb. 1886), but he attended parliament as usual, and voted for Gladstone's home rule bill (7 June). His liberal friends at Chelsea expressed sympathy with him, and he stood again at the general election of July 1886. But he was defeated by 176 votes. His connection with the constituency was thus severed after eighteen years. Mainly owing to Dilke's representations to the queen's proctor, the divorce case was re-opened before the decree nisi was made absolute. The queen's proctor did not intervene directly on Dilke's behalf, and the application of both Dilke and Mrs. Crawford to plead in the suit was refused—in Dilke's case on the ground that he had not given evidence at the first hearing (30 June). The second hearing began on 16 July 1886. Dilke and Mrs. Crawford both gave evidence at length and sustained a searching cross-examination. Mrs. Crawford acknowledged that she had committed adultery with a man not mentioned in her original confession, but withdrew none of her former charges against Dilke, and added odious details which were regarded by believers in Dilke's innocence to be inventions directed solely to prejudice. Dilke absolutely denied all the accusations. Finally the jury found that the original 'decree was obtained not contrary to the facts of the case and not by reason of material facts not having been brought before the court'. Public opinion for the most part took this finding as a verdict against Dilke and regarded it as just. Dilke, however, maintained from the first and through the rest of his life the attitude and demeanour of an innocent man, and many, though not all, of his friends avowed and manifested their unshaken confidence in his honour and veracity.

Dilke bowed at once to the decision. To the electors of Chelsea he announced his withdrawal from public life; he pointed out the legal disadvantages under which he laboured at the second trial in being denied the status of a party to the proceedings, and at the same time he reasserted his innocence.

At the opening of these difficulties, on 3 Oct. 1885, Dilke married at Chelsea Emilia Francis, widow of Mark Pattison. The marriage was singularly happy, and Dilke owed much to her affection and belief in his innocence. Although saddened, he was not soured nor corrupted by his political and social eclipse.

On his retirement from parliament in 1886 Dilke returned with great zeal and industry to the study of those larger English and imperial problems which had engaged his attention at the outset of his career. In 1887 he published 'The Present Position of European Politics' (translated into French) and in 1888 'The British Army'. In 1890 appeared his 'Problems of Greater Britain' in two volumes, designed as a sequel to his earlier work on 'Greater Britain'. It was a treatise on the present position of Greater Britain in which special attention was given to the relations of the English-speaking countries with one another and to the comparative politics of the countries under British government. Foreign travel varied his occupation. He paid at least one annual visit to Paris, where his French friends always welcomed him with enthusiasm. In the autumn of 1887 he made a journey through the Near East, visiting Greece, the cause of which he had always championed, and Constantinople, where he was entertained by the Sultan. In the winter of 1888–9 he was the guest of Lord Roberts, commander of the forces in India, and attended with his host the military manœuvres of the season.

In 1892 Dilke returned to public life as member of parliament for the Forest of Dean. The electors had convinced themselves of his innocence. He beat his conservative opponent after a contest by a large majority. He represented that constituency till his death, fighting the elections of 1900 and Jan. and Dec. 1910, but being returned without a contest in 1895 and 1906. Henceforth a private member, he did not speak frequently in the House of Commons. He confined himself almost entirely to industrial questions, to foreign and imperial affairs, and to the larger questions of policy involved in the navy and army estimates. On these subjects his authority was recognised, but his position in the house remained one of some aloofness. He enjoyed, however, the complete confidence of the labour party. He continued his literary work, publishing in 1898 a little volume on 'Imperial Defence' in co-operation with Mr. (now Professor) Spenser Wilkinson; and yet another work on the British Empire in the same year. Although he hospitably entertained his friends, he continued to be little seen in society. In Oct. 1904 the death of his wife gravely disabled him, and he prefixed a touching memoir to a work of hers, 'The Book of the Spiritual Life', which appeared in 1905. In 1906 he served as chairman of the select committee on the income tax and drafted its report, some of the recommendations of which were subsequently embodied in legislation. In 1910 his health began to fail. After the exhausting session of that year he fought with success the general election of Dec. 1910 in the Forest of Dean. But he was unequal to the effort. He returned in Jan. 1911 from a brief vacation in the South of France only to die. He died of heart failure at his house in Sloane Street on 26 Jan. 1911, and his remains were cremated at Golder's Green. He was succeeded in the baronetcy by his only son.

A portrait of Dilke by G. F. Watts was left to his trustees for presentation to a public institution. It is now on loan at the National Portrait Gallery. A caricature portrait appeared in 'Vanity Fair' in 1871.

Dilke owned a valuable collection of works of art, and he dedicated those which were of historic interest to public uses. He left by will the portrait by Watts of John Stuart Mill to the Westminster city council; the portrait by Madox Brown of Mr. and Mrs. Fawcett, and the portrait by Frank Holl of Mr. Joseph Chamberlain, to the National Portrait Gallery; the portrait of Gambetta by Alphonse Legros went to the Luxemburg Museum in Paris. Most of the relics of Keats, which he inherited from his grandfather, were bequeathed to the Hampstead public library. His literary executor, Miss Gertrude Tuckwell, his second wife's niece, was warned, in preparing his political papers for the press, against seeking the assistance of 'anyone closely connected with either the liberal or conservative party'. His pictures by old masters, water-colour drawings, tapestries, and miniatures were sold by auction at Christie's on 7–8 April 1911. The 'Athenæum' and 'Notes and Queries' were, in accordance with the powers given by the trustees under Dilke's will, transferred in 1911 to the printer and publisher, Mr. John Collins Francis.

[Authorities mentioned in the text; obituary notices in the press, especially *The Times*, 27 Jan. 1911; Dilke's publications; Herbert Paul's *History of Modern England*; personal knowledge and private information.]

J. R. THURSFIELD

published 1912

DUTT (Rajani) Palme
(1896–1974)

British communist leader, was born at Cambridge 19 June 1896, the younger son (there was also a daughter) of Upendra Krishna Dutt, a Bengali, who had come to study medicine in England, became a surgeon, and settled in Cambridge. Dutt's mother, Anna, was Swedish, Palme being the family name which he subsequently added; and the family home in Cambridge was inevitably the meeting place for visiting Indian nationalist leaders. Dutt was educated at the Perse School, Cambridge, and he won a scholarship to Balliol College, Oxford, where he took up residence in the autumn of 1914. In 1916 he took a first class in classical honour moderations and in the following year he was sent down for a speech to a private meeting of a students' society giving a Marxist analysis of the war and of the approaching Bolshevik revolution, and was imprisoned as a conscientious objector on socialist grounds. He returned to Oxford in 1918 to take the final school of *literae humaniores* and obtained an outstanding first. After a very short period in teaching he joined the Labour Research Department in March 1919—G. D. H. Cole was honorary secretary—and worked first on home affairs and then in September 1919 became responsible for a new international section. He remained with the Department until he began publishing *Labour Monthly* in July 1921.

Dutt had become a foundation member of the Communist Party in 1920 although still a member of the 'left-wing committee' of the Independent Labour Party. His *Labour Monthly*, for which he wrote the 'Notes of the Month' for over fifty years, was to become essential reading for working-class militants in the inter-war years; and it probably did more to inculcate an anti-imperialist Marxism than any other journal of the period. Dutt's own anti-colonial interests were, not surprisingly, centred upon India. Although only a young man his outstanding intellectual qualities were quickly recognized and his place in the leadership of the British Communist Party was important from the middle twenties. In 1922 he was one of a three-man commission on the 'Bolshevization' of the British Communist Party; and although he spent some of the middle years of the twenties outside Britain, for health reasons, he was always in close touch with British politics. In particular he developed a close relationship with Harry Pollitt with whom he was intimately involved in the bitter struggles within the British Communist Party concerning the application to Britain of the 'class against class' tactic. The sixth world congress of the Comintern in 1928 elaborated its 'social-fascist' analysis and Dutt, Pollitt, and R.

Page Arnot were in the minority of those who supported the new line. When the Comintern imposed its will upon the British Communist Party, Pollitt became general secretary and Dutt a member of the Politburo; and for the next three decades these two dominated the CPGB. The only partial break in the partnership was in the autumn of 1939 when Pollitt could not accept the Comintern's change of policy that the war was an imperialist war; and Dutt took over the position of general secretary until the Nazi invasion of Russia in 1941, when the Comintern's policy was again reversed. Dutt's own position followed the new line and his *Britain in the World Front* (1942) reflected the new, unswerving support for the alliance against Germany. In 1945 Dutt stood, unsuccessfully, as the Communist candidate in Sparkbrook, Birmingham, and in 1950 for Woolwich East. For the next decade and a half until his retirement in 1965 Dutt was vice-chairman of the British CP; and during the most serious crisis in the history of the CP—that which followed the revelations in the secret speech of Khrushchev at the twentieth congress of the Russian Communist Party in 1956—Dutt was the most unyielding defender of the Stalinist position.

Palme Dutt's political ideas and allegiances were formed by the Bolshevik revolution of 1917, and further developed within the Comintern under Stalin. Dutt became the outstanding interpreter in the English-speaking countries of Stalinism. He was also the foremost writer in English of anti-colonialism and anti-imperialism of an orthodox Marxist, i.e. Stalinist, position. His first important study, *Modern India*, published in Bombay in 1926 and the next year in England, led to a major debate within the Comintern. Dutt had argued that despite distortions due to imperialist control, India and other Asiatic countries were undergoing rapid industrial development. This became known as the theory of 'decolonialization' and was vigorously attacked by the Russian-controlled Comintern secretariat. After being severely criticized by Comintern speakers, there was no further occasion—in public that is—when Dutt revealed any disagreement with the policies and tactics of the International Communist movement that derived from Moscow.

His general political influence in Britain and the countries of the British empire before World War II was considerable. It was especially important in India and upon the Indian Left well beyond the communist groups. He knew for instance Jawaharlal Nehru well from the later 1920s.

In addition to his 'Notes of the Month'—each a substantial essay on current political issues—Dutt wrote a number of books and many pamphlets. *Fascism and Social Revolution* (1934), *India Today* (1940), and *The Crisis of Britain and the British Empire* (1953) were among his most important writings. His work, immensely erudite, logically argued, and often offering subtle and interesting insights, suffered from two serious disabilities, and these became more evident as he got older. The first was his unswerving devotion to the political strategy and tactics of the Comintern, and to the end of his days Dutt remained a Stalinist; and the second was the absence of any serious and sustained critique of his work within the British Communist Party. His theoretical writing, notably after World War II, became increasingly inadequate and unsubstantial. With his immense intellectual gifts Dutt remains an individual exemplar of the tragedy of Stalinism in its impact on the international working-class movement. In 1962 he became an honorary doctor of history at Moscow University, and in 1970 he received the Lenin centenary medal.

In 1922 he married Salme (died 1964), daughter of Ernst Murrik, of Karkski, Estonia. She had come to Britain as a representative of the Communist International in 1920. There were no children of the marriage. Palme Dutt died in London 20 December 1974.

[*The Times*, 21 December 1974; *Labour Monthly*, February–June 1975; *Labour Research*, February 1975; personal knowledge.]

JOHN SAVILLE

published 1986

EDEN (Robert) Anthony

(1897–1977)

First Earl of Avon

Statesman, was born at Windlestone Hall near Bishop Auckland in County Durham 12 June 1897, the third of the four sons and fourth of the five children of Sir William Eden, seventh baronet of the first creation and fifth of the second, who owned an estate of some 800 acres. Eden's mother was Sybil Frances, daughter of Sir William Grey (1818–1878), great-niece of the prime minister, the second Earl Grey, and a distant cousin of Edward, Viscount Grey of Fallodon. Her grandmother was Danish, descended from a family, one of whose forebears had been a general in the Thirty Years' War. The Eden baronetcy of the first creation dated back to 1672 and two of the sons of the third baronet were given peerages which still exist, Auckland and Henley. Eden was thus closely connected on both sides with the traditional landed governing class. Sir William Eden was an irascible eccentric given to furious outbursts of uncontrolled temper which terrified his children. A description of him is given in *The Tribulations of a Baronet* (1933), by Eden's brother Timothy. Of his mother Eden enigmatically wrote in his autobiography *Another World 1897–1917* (1976): 'I think my mother preferred the simpler relationship which existed between donor and recipient to the more complicated one between mother and child.'

He went to Sandroyd School in Surrey at the age of nine and to Eton four years later, making little impression on either. He remembered his school-days with no pleasure. He spent much of his holidays in France and Germany and spoke fluent French—perhaps the only twentieth-century prime minister to do so, apart from Harold Macmillan (later the Earl of Stockton). He was still at Eton when World War I began. His second brother was interned in Germany at once, and within three months his eldest brother, John, was killed. His father died in February 1915. Greatest tragedy of all—his younger brother Nicholas to whom he was devoted, a midshipman of only sixteen, was killed at the Battle of Jutland in the summer of 1916. Meanwhile Eden had joined the King's Royal Rifle Corps in September 1915. His connection with the Rifle Brigade was something which he never forgot. He became adjutant of his battalion in 1917 and was awarded the MC that year for rescuing his sergeant under fire. In 1918 at the age of twenty he was made brigade-major, the youngest in the British Army.

Demobilized with the substantive rank of captain in 1919 he decided to complete his education at Christ Church, Oxford. He read Persian and Arabic, with a view to a career in the Diplomatic Service, and obtained first class honours in 1922. He took no interest in the politics of the Oxford Union, though he was persuaded by one of the local Conservative agents to speak from time to time in Oxfordshire villages. His principal hobby was art. He and Lord David Cecil founded the short-lived Uffizi Society. Sir William Eden, in between bouts of rage, had been a discerning collector of the modern pictures of his time. His son was to find in the same pursuit a welcome distraction from the strains of public life. On leaving Oxford he felt too impatient to face the slow course of promotion in the Diplomatic Service. He saw a quicker route to the top via politics. He stood as Conservative candidate in the general election of November 1922 for the unwinnable seat of Spennymoor in County Durham but in 1923 he was adopted for the safe constituency of Warwick and Leamington. In the election of that December he was opposed by an orthodox Liberal and a highly unorthodox Labour candidate, Frances, Countess of Warwick, former mistress of King Edward VII and mother-in-law of Eden's sister. Eden won easily and retained his seat through eight subsequent elections till his retirement from politics. In the same year he married Beatrice Helen (died 1957), daughter of Sir Gervase Beckett, created a baronet in 1921, banker and chairman of the *Yorkshire Post*, a staunch Conservative organ which gave helpful publicity to Eden's early speeches and writings.

Eden's maiden speech on 9 February 1924 seems surprisingly aggressive, given his later reputation for diplomacy. It was a vigorous defence of air-deterrence sprinkled with gibes against the pacifism of some of the Labour government's supporters. Eden specialized in defence and overseas policy but after the Conservative victory of October 1924 he became parliamentary private secretary (unpaid) to Godfrey Locker Lampson, a junior minister in the Home Office. In 1925 he obtained leave of absence for five months to go on a tour of the Empire partly financed by the *Yorkshire Post* for which he wrote articles converted into an unmemorable book, *Places in the Sun* (1926), with a foreword by Stanley Baldwin (later Earl Baldwin of Bewdley) for whom he had a genuine admiration. In *Facing the Dictators* (1962) he wrote 'No British statesman in this century has done so much to kill class hatred.' In July 1926 Eden was made parliamentary private secretary to the foreign secretary, Sir Austen Chamberlain. This was an important step in his career.

In 1929 Labour won the election. Eden survived in his constituency, though winning on a minority vote for the first and last time. In opposition he constituted part of a small 'ginger group' which held weekly dinners and included Oliver Stanley, William Ormsby-Gore (later Lord Harlech), Walter Elliot, and W. S. Morrison (later Viscount Dunrossil). They were left of centre and supporters of Baldwin whose position seemed precarious. The events of late August 1931 which resulted in Ramsay MacDonald forming a coalition government gave Eden an opening. The foreign secretary was a Liberal, Rufus Isaacs, first Marquess of Reading, and Eden became his parliamentary under-secretary; he was thus the sole official voice of the Foreign Office in the House of Commons. The situation lasted only two months but enhanced his political stature. A general election in October produced a landslide victory for the national government. In the reconstructed Cabinet Sir John (later Viscount) Simon was foreign secretary. He liked Eden who reciprocated at first but later found his chief less congenial. Eden's position was decisively enhanced by his role in the abortive world disarmament conference of 1932–4 where he had to speak at length.

At the end of 1933 he was made lord privy seal, though not in the Cabinet and with the same Foreign Office duties as before. In February 1934 he represented the Foreign Office on a visit to Paris, Berlin, and Rome, trying to 'sell' the government's new memorandum on disarmament. He met Hitler and Hindenburg in Berlin, and Mussolini in Rome. Hitler made a favourable impression on him. At a meeting in Berlin a year later they discovered that in 1918 they had been opposite each other on the western front. The French ambassador who overheard the conversation said to Eden: 'And you missed him? You should have been shot.' Mussolini too impressed Eden. There seems no truth in the story that they took against each other from the start. The negotiations, however, came to nothing and the disarmament conference expired in April. Later that year Eden won diplomatic laurels as rapporteur for the League council after the assassination in Marseilles of King Alexander of Yugoslavia and the French foreign minister Barthou. He gained further prestige by skilful handling of the Saar plebiscite. Early in 1935 he visited Moscow. He was the first British minister to be received there since the revolution. He was not deceived by Stalin 'whose courtesy', he writes, 'in no way hid from us an implacable ruthlessness.'

When in June 1935 Baldwin succeeded MacDonald Eden entered the Cabinet as minister without portfolio for League of Nations affairs. The new foreign secretary was Sir Samuel Hoare (later Viscount Temple-wood). Eden had misgivings about this arrangement, only accepting on the understanding that it would be temporary. His relations with Hoare proved, however, to be friendly, and their differences over policy have been much exaggerated. The question of the day was the action to be taken by the League of Nations against Mussolini's contemplated invasion of Abyssinia. Eden was in favour of a compromise, like Hoare and the rest of the Cabinet. But, also like Hoare, he believed that sanctions, or the threat of them, could be a serious deterrent to Mussolini, if France co-operated. It was soon clear that France, under Pierre Laval, would not. The difficulty was that the peace ballot and the Conservative programme in the general election held on 14 November made a deal with an obvious aggressor very difficult. Eden was not an ardent 'sanctionist.' He regarded Hoare's famous speech on 11 September to the League Assembly as going too far, but the Italian invasion early in October convinced him that the League should apply sanctions including oil, in order to encourage Mussolini to negotiate.

The plan which Hoare put to Laval on his ill-fated visit to Paris with Sir Robert (later Lord) Vansittart on 7 and 8 December 1935 gave away more of Abyssinia to Mussolini than Eden expected—but not much more. Neither he nor his colleagues appreciated that compromise with Italy would be regarded as surrender to an aggressor and cause a furore in Britain. Hoare who had never seriously exceeded his brief was forced to resign. Eden was in Geneva during the crisis. Baldwin summoned him on his return and asked him whom he would like to see as foreign secretary. He dismissed the name suggested and then said: 'It looks as if it will have to be you.' In this somewhat unflattering way Eden was appointed on 22 December to an office that he was destined to hold, though not continuously, for longer than anyone else in the twentieth century, apart from Edward Grey.

At thirty-eight he was the youngest foreign secretary since Lord Granville. He was also the best looking since Palmerston. Slim, debonair, well dressed, wearing the hat named after him, and talking with the clipped yet languid accents of the Eton and Christ Church of his day, he might have stepped out of a play by (Sir) Noël Coward. He seemed more like a man of fashion than a serious public figure. The appearance was deceptive. Eden was a tireless worker, and he drove his secretaries and assistants hard. Behind an urbane manner he was both tough, and sensitive. He stood up for his rights in no uncertain fashion, putting Sir N. F. Warren Fisher in his place when that formidable head of the Civil Service claimed that ambassadorial appointments had to be submitted through him for approval by the prime minister. Eden replied that the foreign secretary might consult the prime minister but that he recommended appointments to the King on his own responsibility. His parliamentary under-secretary was Robert Cecil, Viscount Cranborne, later fifth Marquess of Salisbury who had much influence on him at this time and whose judgement he greatly respected.

Eden's first tenure of the Foreign Office lasted little over two years. The features of it were the triumph of Mussolini in Abyssinia, the reoccupation of the demilitarized Rhineland by Hitler, the outbreak of the Spanish civil war, and a growing crisis in the Far East. There was little Eden could do about Abyssinia without French co-operation. When he pressed for oil sanctions in February 1936, Flandin, the new French foreign minister, asked him on 3 March what Britain's reaction would be if Italy withdrew from Locarno and the Germans moved into the demilitarized zone. Eden could not answer, and four days later this was what Hitler did. In fact Eden had no intention of upholding every clause of the Versailles settlement. He was in favour of conciliating Germany. The problem was to placate France while securing a deal with Hitler that would stabilize Europe and protect British interests. In these matters Eden was fully supported by Baldwin and the Cabinet. The fact remained that both dictators had won their immediate aims. On 10 June Neville Chamberlain, without consulting Eden, referred to continuance of sanctions as 'the very midsummer of madness', and they were dropped a few weeks later.

In mid-July 1936 civil war broke out in Spain. Eden was convinced that neutrality was the only safe course and that it was vital to limit intervention by other European powers. He succeeded in keeping Italian interference within bounds and in preserving the British naval position in the Mediterranean. He effectively scotched the Italian threat to Spain's territorial integrity. But the price was the loss of any chance to reconstruct the Stresa Front (Britain, France, and Italy) and thus put a curb on German expansionism. The emerging threat of simultaneous hostilities with Germany, Italy, and Japan worried others more than Eden himself who seems at this time to have been curiously optimistic about the state of Britain's defence. The creation of the Rome–Berlin axis in November 1936, followed closely by the anti-Comintern pact between Germany and Japan, emphasized this danger which became even greater when Italy joined the pact a year later. Eden did, however, achieve two notable diplomatic successes which had their effect in World War II—the Montreux convention with Turkey on 20 July and the Anglo-Egyptian treaty on 26 August. He put relations between Britain and those two countries on a friendly footing that was to be of much importance during the next decade.

On 28 May 1937 Neville Chamberlain succeeded Baldwin as prime minister. Eden had got his way on most matters under Baldwin, but, ironically, he welcomed the more active successor whose positive views were in the end to drive him into resignation. Their differences were more over method than content. Both were against the policy advocated, though not always consistently, by (Sir) Winston Churchill—collective security involving continental commitments which had little chance of acceptance by Parliament at that time. Eden, unlike Churchill who now saw Hitler as a real threat, regarded Mussolini with greater dislike. But Chamberlain and Eden believed in 'appeasement' of the dictators in the sense, as Eden points out, of the Oxford Dictionary's first definition—'to bring to peace, settle strife etc.' Where they differed was on emphasis, conditions, and timing. The precise course of their increasing divergence is impossible to chart. In retrospect Eden made much of a private message sent by Chamberlain to Mussolini without consultation on 27 July but he did not complain at the time. The first major quarrel was over the visit to Germany of the first Earl of Halifax in November 1937. Chamberlain's idea was to use the opportunity of an invitation to Halifax from Goering to an international sporting exhibition for informal talks with Hitler. Eden at first agreed but changed his mind after learning that the talks were to be in Berchtesgaden, not Berlin—which made it look as if Halifax was 'running after' Hitler. He was suffering from influenza but hastened to see Chamberlain and protest both about the visit and the delay in rearmament which worried him far more than it had a year earlier. He became so excited that Chamberlain urged him to 'go back to bed and take an aspirin'. The visit took place without notable result. No immediate breach occurred and the two men were agreed on getting rid of Vansittart whose voluble anti-Germanism had become a liability. He was replaced by Sir Alexander Cadogan early in 1938.

Two episodes brought their differences to a head. On 13 January 1938 while Eden was on holiday in the South of France Chamberlain without consulting him politely rejected a secret proposal from Roosevelt to summon the diplomatic corps in Washington and launch an international peace plan. Apprised by Cadogan Eden returned two days later, justifiably furious at being bypassed, the more so since the deadline for reply was not till 17 January. He sent off a telegram reversing Chamberlain's message. When they met he threatened resignation and Chamberlain gave way. Roosevelt, however, for reasons still obscure, dropped the proposal.

The second episode was the final straw. Chamberlain wished to concede *de jure* recognition of Italy's annexation of Abyssinia and to open formal diplomatic conversations with the Italian government on Spain. Eden was not in principle against *de jure* recognition but he was irritated by his knowledge that Chamberlain was conducting personal diplomacy behind his back through Austen Chamberlain's widow who was living in Rome. He was convinced that conversations should not be opened until Mussolini gave a tangible sign of good faith by beginning to withdraw his 'volunteers' from Spain. This time Chamberlain refused to compromise and Eden resigned on 20 February after protracted efforts by the prime minister and the Cabinet to persuade him to remain. Cranborne and J. P. L. Thomas (later Viscount Cilcennin), his parliamentary private secretary, resigned with him. Halifax was appointed the new foreign secretary.

No resignation since that of Lord Randolph Churchill has been the subject of greater controversy. Did Eden expect to bring down the government? Was he in a state of nervous exhaustion? What were the real differences of policy? His detractors played them down, alleging vanity and wounded *amour propre*. There was also talk about poor health, but it had no substance. Eden was certainly sensitive about his position. He was under pressure from Cranborne, Thomas, and others to stand up for his office and some of his friends believed that his departure would break up the government. But there was a genuine divergence between him and Chamberlain about conversations with Mussolini though it concerned tactics not strategy. It would be wrong to categorize him as in any sense a Churchillian at this time. For example his speech in the Munich debate was far more conciliatory than Churchill's and although the so-called 'Eden Group' of some twenty MPs, like Churchill's friends, abstained in the division, there was no liaison between them. Later events should not be allowed to disguise the fact that Eden and Churchill were rivals for the succession to Chamberlain if events obliged the latter to retire.

When war broke out on 3 September 1939 Chamberlain dealt a blow to Eden's chances by appointing Churchill to the small War Cabinet as first lord of the Admiralty and offering Eden the Dominions Office without a seat in the Cabinet. Eden accepted patriotically but unhappily. Both Churchill and Halifax were now ahead of him. Even when Churchill succeeded Chamberlain in May 1940 Eden still remained outside the War Cabinet, though he was given the more important office of war secretary and Churchill told him that 'the succession must be mine' declaring that he did not intend to linger like Lloyd George after the war ended. Eden was closely involved in all the major decisions arising from the fall of France. He was most reluctant to release the French prime minister from his pledge not to conclude a separate peace. He was almost certainly right, but he did not get his way. However, he successfully resisted Churchill's wish to remove Sir John Dill and Sir Archibald (later Earl) Wavell from their respective posts of CIGS and C-in-C Middle East. In October Eden went out to Cairo. He was opposed to the diversion of troops to meet Mussolini's attack on Greece, deeming Egypt to be the vital place. On this he was overruled by Churchill who, however, offered him, rather surprisingly, the Middle East Command which he firmly declined. The post that he really wanted became vacant with Halifax's departure to Washington as ambassador. On 23 December Eden was appointed foreign secretary for the second time and was to retain the post till the Labour victory of 1945. He now at last entered the War Cabinet.

Early in 1941 he reversed his previous attitude towards Greece and pressed for sending more troops and supplies. He feared a deal between the Greeks and the Axis powers which might prevent Yugoslavia and Turkey coming out on the side of Britain—a prospect which he regarded with excessive optimism. On 12 February Churchill and the Defence Committee sent him with Dill on a new mission first to Cairo and then on 22 February to Athens. Eden promised to send reinforcements and thought he had the agreement of the Greek commander, General Papagos, to withdraw from Salonika to the so-called Aliakmon line. But when he returned on 2 March, having been to Cairo and Ankara, he found to his dismay that no troops had been withdrawn. Churchill, now thoroughly alarmed, gave him a free hand to call the whole thing off. Eden's military advisers, however, wanted to go ahead and so did Eden. The Greek expedition proved to be a major disaster for which Eden must bear his share of responsibility.

Hitler attacked Russia on 22 June 1941. Eden strongly supported Churchill's decision to announce, without Cabinet authority, an offer of full working partnership. He also agreed with Churchill's policy of doing nothing to improve the worsening relations between America and Japan. They hoped that it would lead to American involvement in Europe, as indeed it did, though the result was due to luck rather than good judgement—Hitler's unnecessary and still incomprehensible declaration of war on America immediately after Pearl Harbor. On 7 December, the very day of that calamity, Eden set out for Moscow to negotiate with Stalin. The Russian dictator sought recognition of his 1941 frontiers. Eden went dangerously near to promising this. There was a Cabinet revolt after he returned, and, if Molotov had not accepted a much more anodyne treaty under American pressure, Eden could have been in major trouble.

Eden's relationship with Churchill was not as harmonious as their memoirs, written in each other's lifetime, suggest. Eden remained optimistic about Russia far longer than Churchill and was much keener on opening a 'second front'. If Oliver Harvey (later Lord Harvey of Tasburgh), his Foreign Office private secretary, is correct he seriously contemplated as early as February 1942 taking steps to remove the prime minister, and began by pressing for a separate minister of defence. Churchill riposted by making Clement Attlee deputy prime minister and Sir Stafford Cripps leader of the House. Eden did not pursue the matter, and on 16 June Churchill on the verge of sailing to Washington left a letter with the King's private secretary advising that Eden should be his successor if anything happened to him. Eden took no part in the attacks launched against Churchill after the fall of Tobruk five days later, and Cripps, the other principal critic, found himself out on a limb. On 22 November Eden himself became leader of the House, retaining the Foreign Office—an almost impossible burden until eased in 1944 by the flying bombs which kept MPs out of London. Another source of dispute with Churchill was the question of 'recognizing' General de Gaulle's FCNL (French Committee of National Liberation). Eden correctly saw that this could be the only rallying point for Free France. Roosevelt, however, detested de Gaulle, and Churchill, indifferent on the merits of the case, was determined to support the president. Matters came to a head in July 1943 when Eden tried to persuade the Cabinet to make a unilateral announcement of recognition. Churchill forced Eden to climb down but in the end events obliged Roosevelt to give way.

Shortly before this episode Churchill had invited Eden to become viceroy of India. He was sorely tempted but he consulted Baldwin with whom he had always had friendly relations, and the old man advised him against it on the ground that 'if he went to India he would never come back to be PM'. Except for Casablanca from which foreign ministers were excluded he accompanied Churchill on all the major summit conferences with Roosevelt in 1943–4—the first Quebec conference in August, the first Cairo conference in November, Tehran (with Stalin as well) at the end of the month, the second Cairo conference in December, and the second Quebec conference in September 1944 where Eden violently objected to the 'Morgenthau plan' supported by Roosevelt for the 'pastoralization' of

Germany. He was entirely in the right and had a public row with Churchill. Luckily Roosevelt dropped the plan soon afterwards. Churchill and Eden then went to Moscow in October where the famous 'percentage agreement' was initialled by Churchill and Stalin, dividing the Balkan states into spheres of interest, Greece being ninety per cent British and American.

Earlier that year Eden was involved in decisions for which he has been fiercely attacked in books based on Foreign Office papers first made available in the 1970s. These concerned the problem of Russians wearing German uniforms who had fallen into British hands. The Soviet government insisted on repatriation. It was well known that this meant either execution or a slower death in Siberia. Since many of them had joined the German Army in order to escape murder or torture and others were not even Soviet citizens the propriety of agreeing seems highly questionable now. The principal reason for repatriation was a desire to meet Stalin's wishes in a matter to which Britain attached no great significance but which he evidently regarded as so important that refusal might have endangered the alliance and damaged the chances of a deal over the Balkans. Legally, moreover, Stalin was in the right. It was a fearful price to pay for averting a hypothetical threat, though Eden's biographer, David Carlton, may be correct in writing (*Anthony Eden*, 1981, p. 242): 'Yet, if as seems likely, the alternative was the loss of Greece into the Soviet orbit, the decision may possibly have constituted the lesser of two evils.' Whatever the truth of this, the policy was that of the War Cabinet. It was not a personal decision by Eden.

Greece was to be the only Balkan country salvaged from communism. The initiative came from Churchill who on this point was not going to give way to Roosevelt, but Eden was involved too, visiting Athens soon after the German withdrawal in the face of British occupation in October 1944, and again with Churchill that Christmas. He played an important part in persuading Churchill to agree to a regency rather than an immediate restoration of the monarchy—a decision which was undoubtedly correct in the circumstances.

Eden accompanied Churchill on that last great summit conference— Yalta in late January 1945. Proceedings were dominated by Stalin and Roosevelt. Neither Churchill nor Eden could make much difference to the new Russian empire taking shape in eastern Europe. Poland in particular, the *casus belli*, was abandoned to her fate. Eden felt bitterly about it but there was nothing he or any British statesman could do. The war was now drawing to an end. Eden was tired. On 12 April Roosevelt died. Eden represented Britain at the funeral and stayed on in America for the San Francisco conference which laid the foundations of the United Nations

Organization. He did not return till 17 May, thus missing the VE-day celebrations in London. Replying to his congratulatory telegram Churchill said: 'Throughout you have been my mainstay.' The coalition had broken up and on 23 May Churchill formed a caretaker government, Eden retaining the same post. An election was scheduled for 5 July.

At this juncture Eden became seriously ill with a duodenal ulcer. Apart from a broadcast at the end of June he played no part in the campaign. The result, owing to the delay necessitated by a postal vote for the forces, was not announced till 26 July. The month of June was made even more miserable for Eden by the news that his elder son and elder child, Simon, a pilot officer, was missing in Burma. With much courage Eden accompanied Churchill to the conference at Potsdam on 15 July. Two days later he wrote in his diary: 'Depressed, and cannot help an unworthy hope that we may lose, or rather have lost this election.' On 20 July Simon's death was confirmed—the last and most poignant of Eden's many wartime bereavements. On 26 July back in London Eden had his 'unworthy hope' fulfilled. The Conservatives, heavily defeated, were out for the next six years. After their last Cabinet meeting Churchill said to Eden: 'Thirty years of my life have been passed in this room. I shall never sit in it again.' The prophecy depended, however, on the prophet.

The end of the war left Eden physically and emotionally exhausted. His illness and bereavement go far to explain the inconspicuous part that he played at first on the opposition benches. Nor were these set-backs the only sources of his unhappiness. For some time past he and his wife had been drifting apart. When they made a visit to America late in 1946 she remained behind in New York and did not return with him. Divorce even for the 'innocent party' would have been a grave handicap before the war, but times had changed. Eden did not suffer politically: he was to be the first divorced person to become prime minister.

Eden adopted during most of his time in opposition a bipartisan approach to foreign policy. He admired Ernest Bevin and felt it his duty to support him against the vociferous Labour pro-Soviet lobby. This meant a certain caution about attacks on Russian policy, since they might be counter-productive. Eden did not welcome Churchill's celebrated 'Iron Curtain' speech at Fulton, Missouri, in March 1946, and maintained a studied silence. Much intrigue against Churchill's continuance as leader— he was over seventy—ensued. But Eden, however impatient he may have felt for the succession, did not participate, and it came to nothing. On the home front Eden was relatively quiescent. He made an important speech at the Conservative conference of 1946 about 'a nation-wide property-owning democracy'—a feature, as he saw it, of American society, which deserved attention in socialist Britain. He was to make it the keynote of his electoral appeal in 1955. But he did not take any great interest in the detailed domestic programmes designed to show that the Conservatives had a 'constructive' alternative. He warmly welcomed, as did Bevin, the Marshall Plan for economic aid to Europe. In the election of February 1950 Eden held his seat comfortably and the Conservatives were only defeated by the narrowest of margins.

Churchill showed no signs of retiring. Eden had to reconcile himself to a further period as second-in-command but there was now a prospect of returning to office. His attitude became less bipartisan. Although he strongly supported Bevin on the Korean war, he criticized Labour's hostility to the Schuman plan, a move towards the pooling of the French and German coal and steel industries. He disapproved too of Labour's policy towards Egypt. His divergence became more marked when Bevin was succeeded by Herbert Morrison (later Lord Morrison of Lambeth) whom he disliked and who had once described him as 'worth his weight in gold as a shop-walker in one of the West End stores'. When the Iranian oil crisis flared up in April 1951 he accused Morrison of feebleness in the face of Mussadeq's policy of nationalizing the British oil installations in Abadan. His speeches on most topics at this time were vigorous assertions of the greatness of Great Britain.

The election of October 1951 gave the Conservatives a parliamentary majority of seventeen. Eden became foreign secretary for the third time, Churchill at the age of seventy-seven still showing no sign of bowing out. Eden was fifty-four and the indisputable crown prince, but would the king ever abdicate? He was at first leader of the House as well as foreign secretary but in May 1952 the offices were separated. In foreign policy he possessed what the Earl of Kilmuir called 'a silencing authority' in the Cabinet room. He did not always get his way with the prime minister but their differences were settled in private. Outside Europe there were four problem areas—Korea, Iran, Egypt, and Indo-China. In Europe there was the minor but tiresome matter of Trieste and the much more important question of reconciling France to German rearmament. In all these matters Eden recognized that Britain had to take second place to America, eight times as rich and far better armed. If the American view was clear it prevailed, but there were questions on which American opinion was hesitant, and in these the Foreign Secretary could influence events.

To Eden Britain was a balancing force between the American continent, Europe, and the Commonwealth. The Americans regarded their continent as their monopoly, the Commonwealth as an anachronism, and Britain as just another European power. They feared a worldwide challenge from communism. Eden did not regard this as the only issue. He was concerned with traditional British interests. He wanted to leave the Far East to America and avoid trouble with China which might involve the loss of Hong Kong. The Middle East on the other hand he regarded as 'British'. Withdrawal from Egypt threatened the route through the Suez canal. Capitulation to Mussadeq would endanger British investments all over the world. In his memoirs Eden tends to personalize these differences in terms of his relations with Dulles whom he disliked. In reality they were as acute during the first fifteen months of his tenure when Acheson was secretary of state. They stemmed not from personalities but divergent national interests.

In fact the accession of Dulles was an advantage in Iran, for he agreed, as Acheson would not have, to the British proposal of a coup in conjunction with the CIA to overthrow Mussadeq. This came off successfully in August 1953 and solved the Iranian problem for the time being. In Egypt Eden had to deal with King Farouk's abrogation of the 1936 treaty in October 1951—an issue of which he had made much during the election. There was disorder in Cairo and Ismailia and several deaths after British punitive action. He refused Acheson's proposal to recognize Farouk as King of the Sudan. The King was deposed in July 1952 by a military coup and after a short interval Colonel Nasser became the effective ruler. The American government applied strong pressure for a deal. Eden agreed in 1954 to the evacuation of the Suez base with the right to return in an emergency. Some Conservative MPs led by Captain Waterhouse and known as the 'Suez Group' bitterly opposed the withdrawal. Privately Churchill was indignant too. Eden made a major contribution in negotiating an armistice and exchange of prisoners with North Korea in 1953, and in 1954 he was able to restrain Dulles from armed intervention in support of the tottering cause of France in her long-drawn-out war with the Vietminh in Indo-China.

Eden's most durable achievements were in Europe. In 1954 the French Assembly voted down the European Defence Community which involved unacceptably close integration of forces at too low a level. Eden's suggestion of an alternative form of alliance, together with his promise at just the right psychological moment to station British divisions in Europe, saved NATO from ruin, and the arrangement has lasted ever since. He was also prominent in healing two other sores, the Trieste question where Yugoslavia and Italy had been bickering for years, and the Austrian peace treaty which had been held up ever since 1945 by Soviet intransigence but was signed just after he became prime minister.

Meanwhile an important change took place in his private life. His marriage had been dissolved in 1950 and in August 1952 he married (Anne) Clarissa, daughter of Major John Strange Spencer-Churchill and the prime minister's niece. She was thirty-two and he was fifty-five, but, despite the gap in years, it was a most happy marriage which brought stability into his somewhat restless life. Within a year, however, he had a serious set-back. He had been suffering much pain and one attack of jaundice when gallstones were diagnosed. In April 1953 he had two operations in England which failed, and had to have a third in Boston in May which was relatively successful. But he was out of action till October, and at the end of June Churchill who had taken over the Foreign Office had a stroke. He made a remarkable recovery but he was never the same again. If Eden had been well he might have resigned, but he argued that it was his duty to remain. Otherwise R. A. Butler (later Lord Butler of Saffron Walden) would have become prime minister and Eden would be deprived of the succession. In the event he stayed on for another eighteen months.

Eden became prime minister on 6 April 1955. He made few changes in the Cabinet. Lord Swinton retired with an earldom. Macmillan went to the Foreign Office. Eden would have preferred Salisbury but considered it unwise to appoint a peer. His immediate problem was the timing of the next general election. He could have postponed it till October 1956, but the economy was booming, unemployment was negligible, and, largely thanks to Eden's own efforts, the international scene was tranquil. A tax-reducing budget was announced and he resolved to go to the country as soon as possible. His decision was vindicated. The election held on 26 May increased the Conservative majority over all other parties from seventeen to sixty. The result owed something to Eden's own conduct of the campaign. Repeating his theme of a 'property-owning democracy', he was the first prime minister to make effective use of television, addressing his audience alone, face to face and without a script.

The government, however, soon ran into trouble. There were strikes by London busmen and dockworkers during the weeks before the election. These may have damaged Labour, but a strike by ASLEF which was only ended by an inflationary settlement damaged the economy. The trade figures deteriorated and the 'give away' spring budget came to look like an electoral bribe. An autumn budget increasing purchase tax on various goods had to be introduced on 26 October. R. A. Butler, the chancellor of the Exchequer, was clearly an exhausted man and Eden decided to move him to the leadership of the House, replacing him at the Exchequer by Macmillan. The Foreign Office went to J. Selwyn B. Lloyd (later Lord Selwyn-Lloyd) who carried lighter political guns and was less likely to disagree with the prime minister. Shortly after this there was a reshuffle in the Labour Party. Attlee retired and Hugh Gaitskell was elected in his place. Eden did not welcome the change and his relations with the new leader were never as cordial as with the old. Gaitskell's accession seemed to give a mild boost to Labour who had a nine per cent swing in their favour at a by-election at Torquay. Personal criticism of the prime minister, already expressed with much malevolence by Churchill's son Randolph in the *Evening Standard*, began to spread to other Conservative organs. Eden, highly sensitive to an adverse press, took the unprecedented step of publicly denying that he intended to retire, and he referred in a speech in Bradford on 14 January 1956 to 'cantankerous' London newspapers. The impression was left that he was not quite as calm and cool as he had hitherto appeared.

Foreign affairs dominated Eden's premiership. There was a summit conference on the subject of Germany at Geneva in July 1955, but nothing came of it apart from a promise by the two Russian leaders, Khrushchev and Bulganin, to visit England in the spring of 1956. The major problem which faced Eden was the Middle East whose oil supplies were crucial for Europe. The Egyptian dictator had been in no way appeased by Britain's withdrawal and he continued to pour out pan-Arab propaganda against the pro-British regimes in the area, particularly Iraq and Jordan. Nasser was not pro-Soviet but he was ready to play the Russian card against Britain and America. The politics of the Middle East became more and more like a personal duel between Eden and Nasser. They only met once—at the Cairo embassy in February 1955 while Eden was still foreign secretary. Nasser claimed that Eden behaved 'like a prince dealing with vagabonds'. No doubt it was an exaggeration but Eden may have shown annoyance at Egyptian refusal to join the proposed Baghdad Pact between Iraq and Turkey, to which he intended to adhere and hoped to be supported by Pakistan, Iran, and the USA.

This was an error of judgement. Eden had not consulted Washington. What Dulles had been encouraging in a somewhat dilatory way was an Anglo-American alliance with the three non-Arab states on Russia's southern frontier. To include Iraq was quite another matter; it seemed an attempt to divide the Arab world and was bound to enrage both the Egyptians and the Saudis. Although Pakistan and Iraq did in the end join, Dulles would only send 'observers' to Baghdad. Eden felt he had been deceived. The episode contributed to their mutual mistrust.

In September 1955 Nasser announced a huge arms deal with Czechoslovakia which was obviously acting as a cat's paw for Russia. On paper it would change the whole balance of power in the Middle East, and the potential infiltration at once raised another question—that of the Aswan high dam. The purpose of this long-planned project was to improve the irrigation of the Nile and alleviate the poverty of the fellahin. Eden was anxious that it should be constructed by a western consortium rather than by Russian engineers. This meant some degree of western financial support. In December the American and British governments together with the International Bank made an offer of a loan of $400 million towards the cost. Nasser did not immediately accept, and the matter rested for several months.

Meanwhile Eden had been involved along with Macmillan in a vexatious problem of security. Guy Burgess and Donald Maclean, the two Soviet spies in the Foreign Office who had fled the country in 1951, were widely believed to be in Moscow, but no hard evidence emerged until 1955 when a Soviet defector published his memoirs. The government in September published a white paper on proposed ways of tightening up security. It was generally regarded as feeble, and Colonel Marcus Lipton, a Labour MP, took advantage of parliamentary privilege to name Harold ('Kim') Philby as the 'third man' who had enabled the spies to escape. He was right but there was no clear evidence, only strong suspicion. Eden and Macmillan, the latter with unnecessary emphasis, had to deny Philby's guilt. There was much press criticism of an alleged cover-up by 'the establishment', but Eden won general applause with a declaration in the debate on 7 November that he would never head a government which eroded the principle that a man is innocent until proved guilty.

Early in December Eden made an attempt to bring Jordan into the Baghdad Pact. It misfired. Riots inspired from Egypt brought down the government, and King Hussain's personal position was threatened. Jordanian refusal became inevitable; Eden ran into further trouble in the new year, this time at home. Macmillan was anxious to adopt deflationary measures, among others to abolish subsidies on bread and milk. Eden was reluctant in view of his election pledges. The chancellor threatened resignation. Eden agreed to a compromise which, Macmillan later claimed, 'gave me four-fifths of my demands'. On 1 March 1956 came another blow from the Middle East. King Hussain dismissed General (Sir) John Bagot Glubb, commander of the Arab Legion and the symbol of British influence in Amman. Eden's first instinct was to break off relations. On second thoughts he decided that Nasser was the culprit. His speech in the House dispirited a sour Conservative Party which scented appeasement. He was, however, able to dispel this impression to some extent soon afterwards by firm action in Cyprus. The movement for Enosis, i.e. union with Greece, had been gathering momentum under its leader Archbishop Makarios. There was a terrorist wing, EOKA, which did not hesitate to use violence. Britain could not acquiesce in Enosis if only because of the Turkish minority on the island, and efforts to produce an agreement between Greece and Turkey predictably failed. There seemed some evidence that Makarios was involved in EOKA's activities, and Eden decided to deport him to the Seychelles. This action rallied his supporters.

For the next few weeks Eden had slightly plainer sailing. The promised visit from the Soviet leaders took place. It did no particular good, but also no particular harm. One curious episode occurred. With the authority of MI6, but certainly without Eden's, a frogman, Commander ('Buster') Crabb, engaged in underwater examination of the naval vessels which had escorted the Russian leader to Portsmouth. He was spotted and was never seen alive again. The Russians made a strong protest. Eden was furious. The director of MI6, Sir John Sinclair, was on the verge of retirement; otherwise he would have been dismissed. In his place Eden appointed Sir Dick White, head of MI5. The two organizations detested each other. It was a crushing rebuff.

By now there was increasing concern, political and economic, about the still unaccepted loan for the Aswan dam. Dulles and Lloyd decided to 'let it wither on the vine.' Nasser, aware of their decision, resolved to press the matter in order to have a public excuse for something he had long planned anyway—the nationalization of the Suez Canal Company. On 19 July Dulles without consulting London called off the loan, after a series of importunate demands from Cairo. A week later in a flamboyant speech in Alexandria Nasser announced his take-over of the Canal Company. Eden received the news in 10 Downing Street while he was entertaining the young King of Iraq and his prime minister, Nasser's *bête noire* Nuri es-Said, to dinner. It could scarcely have come at a more painful moment.

Nasser's action was generally regarded as a breach of international law. Whether it justified the use of force was less clear, but from the outset Eden and Guy Mollet, the French prime minister, claimed that, if other methods failed, military action would be warranted in order to re-establish international control over a waterway so essential at that time to the interests of western Europe. The two prime ministers made no bones in private and in confidential communications with Washington that they hoped not only to 'internationalize' the canal but to 'topple' Nasser. Preparations were at once put in train for a joint Anglo-French amphibious operation based on Malta. It could not be ready till 8 September. Meanwhile the strongest pressure was to be applied. Eden's line received general support in Parliament and the country. Hugh Gaitskell spoke equally strongly against Nasser but, contrary to later legend, he made it clear, albeit in small rather than big print, that he could not endorse military action except with the agreement of the UN, and he repeated the point in several private letters of warning to Eden. This was broadly the American view too. For Washington the canal was not of vital importance. Eisenhower and Dulles had no use for Nasser, but they did not regard his action as sufficiently outrageous to produce the sympathy in the non-communist world needed by Britain and France for successful military intervention. If Nasser interfered with the operation of the canal it would be a different matter, but in fact shipping passed through without hindrance till the balloon went up on 29 October.

Apprehensive of a British resort to arms Dulles hastened to London on 31 July to argue for diplomatic pressure. He and Eden who for the time being had no choice announced on 2 August the summoning of a conference of the principal maritime powers. This met from 16 to 23 August. A five-man committee headed by the Australian prime minister, (Sir) Robert Menzies, was deputed to persuade Nasser to put the canal under an international board. It got nowhere. Eden now wished to refer the matter to the Security Council. Dulles was opposed, and came up with the idea of the Suez Canal Users' Association (SCUA). Eden agreed with much misgiving to announce this to Parliament on 12 September. It was most unpopular. The plan, which involved the user nations asserting their rights under the 1888 convention by hiring their own pilots and collecting their own dues, was deliberately ambiguous about force. The SCUA conference met from 19 to 22 September. Next day, contrary to Dulles's wishes, Eden and Mollet referred the dispute to the Security Council to be considered on 5 October. Meanwhile in a press conference on 2 October Dulles gave an interview on SCUA. This was claimed by some of Eden's intimates to have been the last straw. He observed that some people had said that the teeth had been pulled out of the plan, 'but I know of no teeth: there were no teeth in it as far as I am aware'. Eden was outraged. He knew that any UN resolution on this matter was sure to be vetoed by Russia, as indeed occurred on 13 October. The expedition could not be kept indefinitely on ice, and the end of the diplomatic road had been reached—at a very awkward moment, the week of the annual Conservative Party conference.

The fog of historical obscurity now begins to thicken. Of the British Cabinet ministers who have written their accounts only Selwyn Lloyd pierces the gloom to some degree; the full truth will probably never emerge. It is known that on 14 October two French emissaries, General Challe and Albert Gazier, put to Eden the idea perhaps not entirely new to him of making use of the Israelis who were contemplating a pre-emptive strike against the Jordanian and Egyptian frontier bases. If they could be persuaded to avoid Jordan, concentrate on Egypt, and threaten the Suez canal, Britain and France could intervene ostensibly to separate the combatants and ensure the free passage of shipping. With any luck Nasser would fall and the canal would be recovered in the process. On 16 October Eden and Lloyd conferred with Mollet and Pineau in Paris; no officials were allowed to attend. On 22 October Selwyn Lloyd and, two days later, (Sir) Patrick Dean of the Foreign Office had meetings of the utmost secrecy at a villa in Sèvres with French and Israeli representatives. A document was signed which has never been published, though the gist of it is known from Israeli sources. The attack would be launched on 29 October before the American presidential election. Although Israel had no need to threaten the canal, she would do so if Britain guaranteed to 'take out' the Egyptian air force, and she promised not to attack Jordan. Britain and France would launch an ultimatum calling for both sides to cease fire and withdraw ten miles from the canal and for Egypt to agree to temporary occupation of the canal by Anglo-French forces. On 25 October the Cabinet with varying degrees of knowledge and enthusiasm endorsed the plan. These arrangements were highly secret. Only a very few in the Foreign Office knew about them. No ambassadors were informed, and American enquiries were fobbed off with what can only be described as a series of lies.

On 27 October Israel mobilized and invaded Egypt two days later. On 30 October Eden announced the ultimatum which Egypt predictably refused to accept. The Anglo-French force had already set out from Malta, while on 31 October RAF planes based on Cyprus effectively eliminated the Egyptian air force. On 5 November a parachute descent at dawn was made on Port Said, and twenty-four hours later the main force landed. It met little resistance and the troops were soon twenty miles along the causeway of the canal. Meanwhile there was continuous uproar in Parliament. The pretence that the Israeli invasion had created an unexpected emergency deceived few people, but most Conservatives were all for a hit at Nasser anyway, though there were some dissidents. Two junior ministers, Anthony Nutting and Sir Edward Boyle (later Lord Boyle of Handsworth), resigned. Eden never forgave Nutting who had been minister of state at the Foreign Office. The Cabinet, though increasingly worried, remained united. Gaitskell, who had only been told of the ultimatum a quarter of an hour before its announcement, did all he could to persuade the Conservative doubters to bring down the government, but his appeal was probably counter-productive. Britain had little support in the Commonwealth or United Nations. At Lake Success the Americans did all they could to halt the action; Britain and France twice had to use their vetoes. On 6 November Egypt and Israel both accepted the call for a cease-fire. Eden ordered the troops on the canal to halt at midnight.

He has been as much criticized for stopping as starting the Suez operation. His reasons are still not clear. He could have ridden out the trouble in the UN and he did not take seriously vague Russian threats about rockets. His government was in no danger of falling. Public opinion polls were on his side. But Eisenhower who probably learned about 'collusion' at an early stage was very angry. He may have made threats that have not been revealed. There was a run on the pound and Macmillan, hitherto strong for action, went abruptly into reverse. Moreover what Selwyn Lloyd revealingly calls in his book the 'ostensible' purpose of the operation had been achieved; the combatants had been separated, hostilities had ceased. Eisenhower now took a very strong line against Britain and France. He refused Eden's requests for a personal interview. No Anglo-French troops were to participate in the Emergency Force (UNEF) set up by a UN resolution, nor were they allowed to take any part in clearing the canal which was now full of sunken block-ships.

Eden's health had been poor throughout the crisis. On 5 October he had collapsed with a temperature of 106 degrees—the first onset of the periodic fevers resulting from his bile duct troubles, which were to plague the rest of his life. He recovered in a few days but he was in constant need of drugs, and suffered sleepless nights because of the time gap between London and Washington. On 21 November he announced that on medical advice he was flying to Jamaica to recuperate, staying at the house of Ian Fleming. He left Butler in charge. He returned on 14 December and his speeches by no means rallied his demoralized party. On 9 January 1957 he resigned on medical advice, and was succeeded by Harold Macmillan. It is untrue, though often alleged, that the Queen did not consult him about his successor. He never revealed his choice, nor was it necessarily decisive, but there is good evidence that he did not recommend Butler.

It is unlucky that the Suez débâcle will always be the episode most clearly associated with Eden's name. The decision was, as Henry Kissinger said, 'misconceived', but in the same assessment Kissinger also pointed out that, if acts of international brigandage are not resisted the world becomes one of anarchy, and he is highly critical of the attitude of Washington. It might have been better to take military action as soon as the inevitable Russian veto was applied, thus avoiding any involvement with Israel. American pressure would probably have compelled withdrawal but the charges of duplicity and hypocrisy could not have been made. Eden's real error, however, was not 'collusion' nor an anachronistic overestimation of British strength. He was well aware that Britain and France were not superpowers. Where he erred was in failing to appreciate that Eisenhower and Dulles really meant what they said about their objection to force. They perhaps erred in not spelling out what America would do, if Britain and France decided to 'go it alone'. Perhaps they did not believe it would happen. What has been published of the exchanges between Washington and London reads like a dialogue of the deaf.

Eden lived, despite indifferent health, for another twenty years. He at first entertained some hope of a return to politics but realism broke through and he took his seat as the Earl of Avon on 26 July 1961. He spoke from time to time in the Lords and wrote occasional articles on foreign affairs, but he had little influence on events. In 1960 he published the first of three volumes of memoirs *Full Circle* which chronologically covers the last part of the period and leaves the key questions about Suez unanswered. Neither then nor later did he comment upon 'collusion'. It might have been better to write the volumes in the proper sequence but Eden was under strong pressure from *The Times* which had paid a large sum for the serial rights. *Facing the Dictators* (1962) and *The Reckoning* (1965) are, however, major contributions which every historian of the period is bound to consult. His last publication, *Another World 1897–1917*, appeared in 1976 shortly before his death. It is a beautifully written nostalgic memoir of his youth. He was taken seriously ill in the winter of 1976 while staying in Florida as a guest of Averell Harriman. Early in the new year it became clear that he could not live much longer. With the prime minister's assent he was flown back to England in an RAF plane. He died at his home, Alvediston in Wiltshire, 14 January 1977. His wife who had done so much to ease his life in retirement survived him. He was succeeded in the earldom by his son, Nicholas (born 1930), who died in 1985.

Eden was sworn of the Privy Council in 1934 and was made KG in 1954. He was awarded honorary degrees by thirteen universities (including Oxford and Cambridge), and elected honorary Student of Christ Church, Oxford, in 1941. He was chancellor of Birmingham University 1945–73. He was made an honorary bencher of the Middle Temple in 1952, and an honorary member of the Salters' Company in 1946 and of the Fishmongers' in 1955. He became an elder brother of Trinity House in 1953 and honorary FRIBA in 1955. He was a trustee of the National Gallery 1935–49. He was honorary colonel Queen's Westminsters KRRC 1952–60 and of the Queen's Royal Rifles 1960–2. He was honorary air commodore of No. 500 (County Kent) Squadron RAF 1943–57. He was president of the Royal Shakespeare Theatre 1958–66.

[Eden's own writings mentioned in the text; Winston Churchill, *The Second World War*, 6 volumes, 1948–54; Harold Macmillan, *Memoirs*, 6 volumes, 1966–73; Anthony Nutting, *No End of a Lesson*, 1967; Selwyn Lloyd, *Suez 1956*, 1978; David Carlton, *Anthony Eden, a Biography*, 1981—somewhat impersonal and unsympathetic but an essential work; private information; personal knowledge.]

ROBERT BLAKE

published 1986

King of Great Britain, Ireland, and the British Dominions beyond the seas, Emperor of India—the only British sovereign to relinquish the crown voluntarily—was born at White Lodge, Richmond Park, 23 June 1894, the eldest of the family of five sons and one daughter of the then Duke and Duchess of York. With the death of Queen Victoria in 1901 his parents became Prince and Princess of Wales, and in 1910, when Edward VII died, King George V and Queen Mary. As their eldest son Prince Edward was from birth in the direct line of succession, and of the seven names (Edward Albert Christian George Andrew Patrick David) given to him at his baptism four were those of British patron saints. In the family he was always known as David.

Though in most respects pampered by Fate, he was unlucky in the inability of his parents to communicate easily with their children, who consequently suffered from a lack of human warmth and encouragement in early life. Their father, though kind-hearted, was a martinet in his treatment of them, and their mother was deficient in the normal maternal instincts. Nor did the man chosen to be their principal tutor, Henry Peter Hansell, make up for what their parents failed to give, since he too was a rather aloof and limited character.

Edward was an intelligent child, endowed with curiosity and a powerful memory. Though it is unlikely that he would ever have developed as a scholar, his mental gifts deserved imaginative teaching. As it was, he grew up with a poor grounding of knowledge, no taste at all for any books worth the name, and unable even to spell properly. Only as a linguist were his attainments equal to his position, since he learnt French and German in childhood, and later acquired a fluent command of Spanish.

Other valuable qualities belonged to him naturally. Despite his small stature he had exceptional good looks, which never lost their boyish appeal. He had boundless energy and zest, and was full of courage. Above all, he had a spontaneous charm of manner which drew people to him and put them at their ease. His personality would have been remarkable even if he had not been royal; allied to his princely status it was irresistible.

In 1907 he was sent to Osborne, and two years later to Dartmouth. While he was there his father became King, and he himself heir apparent to the throne. On his sixteenth birthday he was created Prince of Wales, and on 13 July 1911 became the first English holder of the title to be formally invested at Caernarvon castle. The ceremony was stage-managed by the constable of the castle, David Lloyd George (later Earl Lloyd-

George of Dwyfor) who personally taught him a few words of Welsh to utter when he was presented to the crowd at Queen Eleanor's gate.

The following year he went into residence at Magdalen College, Oxford, but there was little to show for his brief university career. During vacations he paid two visits to Germany and one to Scandinavia. In 1914 he was anyway due to leave Oxford at the end of the academic year, to begin a period of service in the army; but in the event he did so as Britain was entering the most terrible war in her history.

Commissioned in the Grenadier Guards, he asked only to be allowed to fight alongside his contemporaries, but was told that this would not be possible, because of the danger that he might be captured and used as a hostage. Soon, however, he managed to get himself posted to the staff of the British Expeditionary Force's commander in France, and thereafter spent most of the war abroad, attached to various headquarters but essentially serving as a visitor of troops and general morale-raiser. He lived frugally and, though provided with a Daimler, preferred to travel around on a green army bicycle, covering hundreds of miles. His desire always was to be at the scene of action, and he had a narrow escape when visiting front-line positions before the battle of Loos.

Given his enforced role as a non-combatant he could hardly have done more to share the ordeal of other young men of his generation. Yet he was mortified that he could not share it more fully, and genuinely embarrassed when he was awarded the MC. The humility of his attitude enhanced the value of the work he did, which was never forgotten by the countless ordinary soldiers to whom he brought understanding and cheer.

His war service was a crucially formative episode in his own life, vastly broadening his range of human experience and showing how good he was at establishing contact with his fellow-men, whatever their backgrounds. As well as meeting people of all classes from the United Kingdom, he also got to know Allied troops, including Americans, and a variety of British subjects from overseas. While visiting the Middle East in the spring of 1916 he met Australians and New Zealanders evacuated from Gallipoli. At the time of the armistice in 1918 he was with the Canadian Corps in France, and after the armistice was attached to the Australian Corps in Belgium.

Thus he was unconsciously introduced to the next and most fruitful phase of his career, which began with his visits to Newfoundland, Canada, and the United States in the summer and autumn of 1919. Lloyd George, now prime minister, was convinced that 'the appearance of the popular Prince of Wales in far corners of the Empire might do more . . . than half a dozen solemn Imperial Conferences'. So it proved. The Canadian tour was a triumphal success, in Quebec no less than in the English-speaking provinces. Wherever he went the response was overwhelming. In Alberta he bought a ranch for himself—an admirable gesture, though a source of trouble to him later.

His first visit to the United States was equally successful, though briefer and far less extensive. In Washington, he called on the stricken President Wilson, and in New York was given a ticker-tape welcome as he drove to the City Hall to receive the freedom. Yet it was not such important occasions that lingered most persistently in his mind after his return to England, but rather the song 'A Pretty Girl is like a Melody', which he had heard at the Ziegfeld Follies. His endless whistling of this 'damned tune' caused annoyance to his father, and shows that American culture had made an immediate conquest.

In 1920 he visited New Zealand and Australia, travelling there in the battleship *Renown*, by way of the Panama canal, Hawaii, and Fiji. Again, he carried all before him. In 1921–2 he toured India, where nationalists had been disappointed by the modest scope of the Montagu–Chelmsford reforms, and where the Amritsar massacre was still a recent memory. Despite the unfavourable circumstances, he made an excellent impression on such Indians as he was allowed to meet, many of whom were quoted by a British observer as saying: 'If only all you Europeans were like him!' In many places large and friendly crowds turned out to greet him, defying the Congress boycott of his visit.

The same voyage took him to Nepal, Burma, Malaya, Hong Kong, Japan, the Philippines, Borneo, Ceylon, and Egypt. On his return to London after eight months' absence there was a banquet in his honour at Guildhall, at which his health was eloquently proposed by Lloyd George— the last official act of his premiership.

This intensive travelling during the early post-war years was not a flash in the pan, but set the pattern for his subsequent way of life as Prince of Wales. In all but three years until his accession he spent long periods outside Britain. Hardly any part of the Empire, however small or remote, failed to receive at least one visit from him, and he was also welcomed in many foreign countries. Particularly noteworthy were his South American tours in 1925 and 1931, which inspired the greatest enthusiasm in a region traditionally important to Britain, though much neglected by British public figures. (A by-product of the second tour was the Ibero–American Institute of Great Britain, founded under his auspices, which led in turn to the creation of the British Council in 1935.)

At home, too, he was very busy and mobile, giving special attention to ex-servicemen and young people. In a period of mass unemployment and widespread social deprivation there might be little he could do to help the victims, but at least he went out of his way to talk to them, and it was obvious that they had his sympathy.

For all his exertions in the public interest, his life was by no means all work. While touring overseas, no less than in Britain, he would always devote a lot of his time to games and sport, and at the end of the most arduous day he was usually eager to dance into the small hours. His daylight recreations could be dangerous—after repeated spills and fractures he was prevailed upon to give up steeplechasing, only to take to flying instead—but in the long run his late nights were more harmful to him. A tendency to unpunctuality and moodiness was certainly made worse by lack of sleep.

As he moved from youth to middle age the strain of his life began to tell upon a nature that was nervous as well as physically robust; and at the same time, inevitably, he was becoming rather spoilt by the universal adulation to which he was exposed. Above all he seemed increasingly solitary, and without any firm base to his existence.

From 1919 he had his own London establishment at York House, St. James's Palace, and in 1929 he obtained from his father the 'grace and favour' use of Fort Belvedere, a small architectural folly near Windsor (originally built for the Duke of Cumberland in the 1750s, but improved by Sir Jeffry Wyatville, in the reign of George IV). 'The Fort' became his favourite residence, where he could entertain a few friends at weekends, and in whose garden he invested much of his own—and his guests'—hard labour. But something vital was missing, as no one knew better than himself.

While his brothers were acquiring wives, the world's most eligible bachelor remained single. His natural craving for domesticity was satisfied only by a succession of affairs with married women. For many years he was very closely attached to Mrs (Freda) Dudley Ward, and his love for her was not fundamentally affected by passing affairs with Lady (Thelma) Furness and others. But through Lady Furness he became acquainted with her friend and fellow-American, Mrs Simpson (died 1986), and within a few years acquaintance had turned into the supreme passion of his life.

Wallis Simpson, daughter of Teakle Wallis Warfield who died when she was a few months old, came from Baltimore, Maryland, where she was brought up as a rather impoverished member of a family with pride of ancestry on both sides. When her first marriage (to Lieutenant Earl Winfield Spencer, of the US Navy, who became an alcoholic) ended in divorce, she married an Anglo-American, Ernest Simpson (who had a shipping business in England), with whom she lived comfortably in London. For a time they were together friends of the Prince, but when it became apparent that he wanted nothing less than to make Wallis his wife, Simpson resigned himself to divorce.

Her attraction, so far as it can be defined, owed much to her vivacity and wit, her sophisticated taste, and her ability to make a house feel like a home. She and the Prince shared a mid-Atlantic outlook—he being a child of Old-World privilege excited by American informality, she an east coast American with a hankering for the Old World and its gracious living. They met, as it were, half-way.

When George V died, on 20 January 1936, Edward came to the throne in the strong hope that he would be able to make Wallis Queen. This may, indeed, have been his principal motive for accepting a charge which he had often said, privately, he would rather be spared. Impatient of ritual and routine, he knew that his temperament would be less well suited to the role of King than to that of Prince of Wales.

There was, indeed, much that needed changing in the royal set-up, and it is possible that Edward VIII might have had some success as a reforming monarch if he had reigned for a fair number of years, with his mind on the job. No judgement can confidently be made either way on the strength of his brief reign, during which he was largely distracted by his anxiety about Wallis and their future. As it was, he merely gave offence to old courtiers and retainers by relatively trifling changes, and caused misgivings in official quarters by his casual attitude to state papers.

The public, however, neither knew nor cared about such matters, and he was a popular King. There was a shock when, in July, a loaded revolver was thrown in front of his horse on Constitution Hill, and relief that he had come to no harm. Later in the year he was cheered lustily in the Mall by the Jarrow hunger marchers at the end of their pilgrimage.

Meanwhile the so-called 'King's matter' was unfolding in a way destined to bring his reign to a swift close. It was only in Britain that his intimacy with Mrs. Simpson was a secret. When, during the summer, she accompanied him on a cruise in the Adriatic and eastern Mediterranean, in the private yacht *Nahlin*, full reports appeared in the foreign press, more especially in the United States, with the correct conclusions either stated or implied. The British press remained silent from a sense of loyalty, but it could not be long before the story would break at home. At the end of October the Simpsons' divorce suit was due to come up, and this might well arouse speculation even though it was to be heard in a provincial court.

On 20 October, therefore, the prime minister, Stanley Baldwin (later Earl Baldwin of Bewdley), saw the King by request and raised with him for the first time the question of his relations with Mrs. Simpson. At this meeting Baldwin tried to enlist the King's co-operation in persuading her to withdraw her divorce petition, but to no avail. The King would not co-operate, and at the end of the month a decree *nisi* was duly granted.

An interlude followed during which (on 3 November) the King opened Parliament—driving there in a closed car rather than in the traditional open carriage—and inspected the fleet at Portsmouth. But on 16 November there was another meeting with Baldwin, at which the King stated his determination to marry Mrs. Simpson, despite the prime minister's advice that the marriage would not receive the country's approval. On 18–19 November he visited the distressed areas of south Wales, where he made the much-quoted remark about the unemployed: 'Something must be done to find them work.' His hearers little knew how soon he would be unemployed himself.

On 25 November he saw Baldwin again, having meanwhile been persuaded by Esmond Harmsworth (later Viscount Rothermere) to suggest that he might marry Mrs. Simpson morganatically. This was a disastrous error, since it could be said to carry the admission that she was unfit to be Queen.

It is probable, though unprovable, that majority opinion in Britain and throughout the Empire would have been against the idea of Mrs. Simpson as Queen, though whether most people would have maintained their opposition, knowing that the price would be to lose Edward as King, is more doubtful. Ecclesiastical anathemas counted for much less, even then, than those who pronounced them liked to believe, and objections to Mrs. Simpson on social grounds were likely to be much stronger in privileged circles than among the people at large. But the idea of a morganatic marriage would almost certainly have been less generally acceptable.

In any case it would have required legislation, and this the government was not prepared to introduce. Moreover, the leader of the opposition, Clement (later Earl) Attlee, told Baldwin that Labour would not approve of Mrs. Simpson as Queen, or of a morganatic marriage; and similar, though rather less clear-cut, views were expressed by the dominion prime ministers. When, therefore, the facts were at last given to the British public on 3 December, the crisis was virtually over. If the King had no option but to renounce either Mrs. Simpson or the throne, the only possible outcome—granted the man he was—was abdication.

He would have liked to make a broadcast, taking his subjects into his confidence, before reaching a final decision; but when Baldwin told him that this would be unconstitutional and divisive, he at once abandoned the idea. Even (Sir) Winston Churchill's plea that he should stand and fight went unheeded. On 10 December he signed an instrument of abdication, and the following day ceased to be King when he gave his assent to the necessary Bill. That evening he delivered his farewell broadcast from Windsor Castle, containing the celebrated words: 'I have found it impossible to carry the heavy burden of responsibility, and to discharge my duties as King as I would wish to do, without the help and support of the woman I love.'

Later the same night he crossed to France, and the rest of his life was spent in almost permanent exile. It was some months before Mrs. Simpson's divorce became absolute, but in June 1937 she and Edward were married, at a chateau in Touraine, by a Church of England parson acting without authority from his bishop. No member of the royal family came to the wedding, which was attended only by a few old friends, including Walter Monckton (later Viscount Monckton of Brenchley), the attorney-general to the Duchy of Cornwall, and a busy go-between during the abdication crisis, and Major E. D. ('Fruity') Metcalfe, who was best man. There were no children of the marriage.

The new King, George VI (formerly Duke of York), had some of the qualities of his father, George V, but hardly any of his elder brother's—a fact of which he was painfully conscious. From the moment of his accession he seems to have been haunted by the fear that the ex-King would overshadow him, and this fear was undoubtedly shared by his wife and other members of his entourage. It was felt to be essential that the ex-King should be kept out of England, out of the limelight, out of popular favour; and self-righteousness came to the aid of self-interest, in the form of a myth that the Prince's abdication and marriage had brought disgrace upon the British monarchy.

Though it is unlikely that George VI was familiar with *The Apple Cart* by G. B. Shaw, he was nevertheless immediately alive to the theoretical danger that his brother might, unless made a royal duke, be tempted to stand for the House of Commons, in the manner of Shaw's King Magnus. The first act of his reign was, therefore, to confer upon Edward the title of Duke of Windsor. But under letters patent issued the following year the title Royal Highness was restricted to him, and expressly denied to his wife and descendants, if any. This studied insult to the Duchess cannot have been solely due to uncertainty about the duration of the marriage, since it was maintained by George VI and his successor throughout the thirty-five years that the Windsors were man and wife (and into the Duchess's widowhood).

As a result relations between the Duke and his family were poisoned, and further bitterness was caused by an indecent wrangle over money. No provision was made for the Duke in the Civil List, but the King eventually agreed that he should receive a net £21,000 a year, which was mainly interest of the sale of Sandringham and Balmoral to royal trustees, at a valuation which favoured the King rather than the Duke. An attempt to make the agreement conditional upon the Duke's willingness to stay abroad at the King's pleasure was only with difficulty resisted. (In addition to the income thus assured, the Duke had capital deriving from Duchy of Cornwall revenue unspent while he was Prince of Wales.)

Between their marriage and World War II the Windsors lived in France, but in October 1937 they paid an ill-advised visit to Germany as guests of the Nazi government. The Duke's declared reason for going was to see how unemployment had been tackled and to study labour relations, but of course the Nazis made the most of the visit for propaganda purposes, as he should have foreseen. At a meeting with Hitler the Duke gave no indication (according to the interpreter) of any sympathy with Nazi ideology, and there is, indeed, virtually no evidence that he had any such sympathy. But he had considerable affection for the German people, with whom he had many links, and above all he had the feeling—overwhelmingly prevalent at the time—that another war would be an unimaginable calamity.

When war came, however, he at once offered to return to Britain without conditions, and at first was offered a choice of two jobs, one of which, that of assistant regional commissioner in Wales, would have enabled him to stay in Britain. But when he accepted it, no doubt unexpectedly, it was promptly withdrawn, and he was then obliged to take the other job, that of liaison officer with the French army (which involved a drop in rank from field-marshal to major-general). He did it well, among other things sending home a remarkably prescient report of French weakness on the Ardennes front. But when France fell in the summer of 1940 he and the Duchess had to escape as best they might.

They made their own way to Madrid, whence the Duke was able to communicate with the British government, now headed by his old friend Winston Churchill. His requests for suitable employment at home, and the barest recognition for the Duchess (not that she should have royal status, but merely that his family should receive her) were turned down, even Churchill having in the circumstances neither time nor inclination to champion the Duke's cause against Buckingham Palace. He then reluctantly accepted the governorship of the Bahamas, and on 1 August sailed from Lisbon, as agreed, despite an elaborate plot engineered by Ribbentrop to keep him in Europe. Though at this time he undoubtedly believed that there would have to be a negotiated peace, he did not despair of his country and had no desire to be a German puppet.

In the Bahamas the Windsors were on the whole a conspicuous success, in a post which was both difficult and unpleasant. The Duke stood up to the 'Bay Street boys' (as the local white oligarchy was called), achieved some economic improvement in the neglected outer islands, and dealt effectively with a serious outbreak of rioting for which he was in no way to blame. In December 1940 he had the first of about a dozen wartime meetings with Franklin D. Roosevelt, at the president's invitation, and the two men got on particularly well. The authorities in London tried very hard to prevent the meeting, and in general did not at all favour visits by the Windsors to the United States, though a few were grudgingly permitted. The Duke's immense popularity there was regarded at home as invidious and embarrassing, rather than as a major potential asset to Britain.

In May 1945 the Windsors left the Bahamas and returned to Europe, no better alternative having been offered to the Duke than the governorship of Bermuda. The rest of his life was spent chiefly in France, where he was treated as an honoured guest. Partly to repair his finances—which had suffered from mismanagement, and more especially from a costly and futile attempt to strike oil on his Canadian ranch—he turned to authorship. With the help of 'ghosts' he wrote his memoirs, which were serialized in *Life* magazine and then published in book form as *A King's Story* (1951). This became a world bestseller, and was later turned into a film. He also published two much slighter books—*Family Album* (1960) and *The Crown and the People 1902–1953* (1953)—and two more were written, though unpublished at the time of his death.

Because of the continued ostracism of the Duchess, his post-war visits to Britain were brief and rare. On 28 May 1972 he died at his house in the Bois de Boulogne, from throat cancer. His body was then flown back to England and lay in state for three days in St. George's chapel, Windsor, while 57,000 people came—many over long distances—to pay their respects. On 5 June there was a funeral service in the chapel, and afterwards the Duke was buried in the royal mausoleum at Frogmore. The Duchess was present as the Queen's guest.

Though King for less than a year, Edward VIII will rank as an important figure in the history of the British monarchy. During the dangerous and volatile period which followed World War I, when republicanism was sweeping the world, he and his father succeeded, in their very different ways, in giving new strength to an old tradition. Neither could have succeeded so well without the other, and the contrast between them was of great value to the monarchy.

Edward will also be remembered as a character out of the ordinary. His faults were substantial, and aggravated by the circumstances of his life. His mind, inadequately trained, was incapable of deep reflection and prone to erratic judgement. He could on occasion be selfish, mean, inconsiderate, ungrateful, or even callous. Yet his virtues more than compensated for his faults. He was a brave man, morally as well as physically, and his nature was basically affectionate. He had a marvellous gift for conversing easily with people, and for making charming, unpompous speeches off the cuff. There was about him the indefinable aura known as star quality.

In a sense he was a harbinger of the Americanization of Europe. Superficially, his values were more those of the New World than of the Old. Playing the bagpipes wearing a white kilt or golfing in plus-eights, he seemed more like a Hollywood representation of a Scottish laird or English gentleman than like the genuine article. His anyway slightly Cockney accent became overlaid with American intonations (in his farewell broadcast he referred to the *Dook* of York), and he also acquired a number of American habits long before he was married to an American.

Yet at heart he was more a creature of the Old World than he appeared to be, or probably realized himself. What a Labour MP, Josiah (later Lord) Wedgwood, said at the time of the abdication—that he had given up his royalty to remain a man—was only a half-truth. Though he had, indeed, given up his kingship, he never ceased to be royal. Had it been otherwise, there would have been no problem about the duchess's status. All the same, he surely deserves honour for the chivalrousness of his decision to abdicate, no less than for the perfect constitutional propriety with which it was carried out; and above all for his pioneering work as Prince of Wales.

There are many portraits of Edward, representing almost every phase of his life. Only a selection can be mentioned here. A caricature appeared in *Vanity Fair* on 21 June 1911 (the original is in the National Portrait Gallery). The first full-length portrait in oil was painted by Sir A. S. Cope in 1912, the year after Edward's investiture as Prince of Wales. It is in the Royal Collection, which also contains, from the same period, a sketch (head only) by Sir John Lavery. A charcoal drawing by J. S. Sargent (*c* 1918) belonged to the Duchess of Windsor. In 1919 H. L. Oakley painted a full-length profile, and in *c* 1920 R. G. Eves a half-length portrait in uniform. Both of these are in the National Portrait Gallery. A full-length portrait in golfing dress (1928), by Sir William Orpen, hangs in the Royal and Ancient Golf Club, St. Andrews; and a full-length portrait in Welsh Guards uniform (1936) done by W. R. Sickert from photographs, in the Beaverbrook Art Gallery, Fredericton, NB, Canada. A full-length portrait in Garter robes by Sir James Gunn (*c* 1954) was in the Duchess of Windsor's possession, as were a number of portraits by the French artist A. Drian. Apart from paintings and drawings, there is a bronze statuette by Charles S. Jagger (1922) in the National Museum of Wales at Cardiff, and a marble bust by Charles Hartwell (*c* 1920–4) belonging to the Corporation of London.

[Hector Bolitho, *Edward VIII*, 1937; Compton Mackenzie, *The Windsor Tapestry*, 1938; Duke of Windsor, *A King's Story*, 1951; Duchess of Windsor, *The Heart Has*

Its Reasons, 1956; John W. Wheeler-Bennett, *King George VI*, 1958; Frances Donaldson, *Edward VIII*, 1974; Michael Bloch, *The Duke of Windsor's War*, 1982, and *Operation Willi*, 1984; private information.]

JOHN GRIGG

published 1986

FYFE D a v i d   P a t r i c k   M a x w e l l

(1900–1967)

Earl of Kilmuir

Lord chancellor, was born 29 May 1900 in Edinburgh, the only child by his second marriage of William Thomson Fyfe, an inspector of schools, to Isabella Campbell, a schoolteacher. After George Watson's College, Fyfe went up to Balliol College, Oxford, where he obtained a third class in *literae humaniores* (1921) and failed to become president of the Union, but made friends in the inner circle of English conservatism which it was his life's ambition to enter. Like John Buchan and Brendan Bracken he was fascinated by the romantic and aristocratic side of English political life, which had not yet been entirely submerged by the egalitarian tide of the twentieth century. There was nothing sordid in this. As Fyfe himself said of those who accused Buchan of snobbery, 'they never understood the living sense of history of the Scot'.

It was one of the paradoxes of politics that the Maxwell Fyfe report on the organization of the Conservative Party in 1949 proposed reforms, particularly in the selection of parliamentary candidates, which were of value to the party in the mid twentieth century, but which also produced, as Maxwell Fyfe was disconcerted to find, unromantic men of obscure interests and views. It was another paradox that his career was to be ended with savage abruptness by another Scot with an equally romantic attachment to English political traditions, Harold Macmillan.

Maxwell Fyfe had highly developed the barrister's power of getting up a complex subject quickly. He was called at Gray's Inn in 1922 and went into chambers at Liverpool with (Sir) George Lynskey. In 1934 he took silk and in 1936 he became recorder of Oldham. In the meantime he had been returned to Parliament in 1935 as member for the West Derby division of Liverpool. His appearance was unusual for a man seeking advancement on the Tory political ladder. His body was pear-shaped, and beneath a large square bald head there were dark heavy eyebrows and a face of middle-eastern pallor and swarthiness. Like many stocky men he had inexhaustible physical energy which he devoted to his legal and political careers. He recorded that 'during the Assizes I was constantly conferring from 9 a.m. until 10.30, in Court (with a short interval for lunch) until 5.15 p.m., then on the 5.25 from Liverpool or 5.45 from Manchester, reaching London at 9. Then in the House until after the 11 o'clock division, then back on the midnight train to the North ...' It was also appreciated that 'Under that forbidding shell, He does himself extremely well', and his personal popularity at the bar and at Westminster was great; his simple integrity was manifest.

In 1942 Maxwell Fyfe was appointed solicitor-general and knighted, the attorney-general being Sir Donald (later Lord) Somervell. When Somervell became home secretary in the caretaker Government of 1945 Maxwell Fyfe succeeded him as senior law officer, and was sworn of the Privy Council. Although the general election of July 1945 removed him from office after only a few months, his successor, Sir Hartley (later Lord) Shawcross, allowed him to continue as deputy chief prosecutor at Nuremberg. There he won international recognition for a brilliant forensic success. In particular he brought down a conceited tyrant by his use of a traditional English legal weapon. Goering ('the most formidable witness I have ever cross-examined') lost his dominant position in the court-room.

Maxwell Fyfe not only gave continuous support to his party in its intense struggle against the Labour Government, but also played a prominent part in the movement for European unity centred on Strasbourg. Unusually for a British lawyer, he was a strong advocate of the European Convention on Human Rights, to which the United Kingdom eventually acceded. He was proud of the fact 'that I have done something positive as well as negative in regard to tyranny, which so many of my generation in the twentieth century have accepted without a murmur', and never entirely forgave his seniors in the new Conservative Cabinet for their veto on Britain's entry into Europe. He saw further than many of his contemporaries, and was anxious that Britain should enter Europe on a tide of goodwill—and also on terms more favourable than were to be obtained twenty years later. 'Posterity, rightly, will deal harshly with those who quenched this flame and who did not see, until it was too late, that idealists are often the truest realists in mighty enterprises.'

Maxwell Fyfe had become home secretary in the Conservative Cabinet in October 1951, an office in which he was a firm upholder of the traditional principles of law and order. His was the controversial decision not to grant a reprieve to Bentley who, with Craig, had been convicted of the murder of a police officer. In 1953 Fyfe was appointed GCVO after successfully completing the official duties connected with the coronation, and in October of the following year he became lord chancellor with the title of Viscount Kilmuir. Had he not done so, his chances of succeeding Eden in January 1957 might have been very strong. As it was, Kilmuir took an active part in polling the Cabinet in order to inform the Queen that a clear majority favoured Macmillan. In the Suez episode Kilmuir had been an unrepentant and unwavering supporter of a policy of Thorough. The shock to the party and to the country was therefore all the greater when in July 1962 he was dismissed, together with six other Cabinet ministers, at seven hours' notice. Macmillan claimed that new blood was needed but Kilmuir's successor, Lord Dilhorne, was only five years younger, and patently more to the Right than Kilmuir himself. Kilmuir did not attempt to hide his anger at the way in which he (who had once said that 'loyalty was the Tories' secret weapon') had been treated. He accepted an earldom, but refused to take any further part in legal or political affairs, surrendered his pension, and went into the City. This sudden move, which did not escape criticism in legal circles, should not be ascribed entirely to pique. Kilmuir did not enjoy judicial work, and as this is almost the only activity open to an ex-lord chancellor, he seized the opportunity offered by an invitation from the Plessey Company to be its chairman. Life in the City more than satisfied Kilmuir's desire for constant activity, but it was more of a strain than he had expected. His health was no longer good, and he found it difficult to adjust himself to the interests, values, and conversation of industrialists.

Although he held the Great Seal for over seven years—with the exception of Halsbury, longer than anyone since Eldon—Kilmuir left little permanent mark on English law. He was not a great reformer like Jowitt or Gardiner, nor a great jurist like Simon or Simonds. Indeed, his judgement in *DPP* v. *Smith*, [1961] AC 290 on the mental element required for a conviction of murder, although concurred in by four law lords, attracted an exceptional amount of juristic criticism throughout the Commonwealth. Kilmuir held that it was unnecessary for the Crown to prove that the accused actually intended to kill or to cause grievous bodily harm if a reasonable man was entitled to conclude from the evidence as a whole that the accused must have had that intention: the test of criminal liability was to be objective and not subjective. The principle so laid down was reversed by the Criminal Justice Act, 1967. But, as always, Kilmuir was patient, courteous, and indefatigable—he personally examined the claims of every candidate proposed for the lay magistracy. His devotion to his work left him with little time for ordinary recreations, but he seldom refused an invitation to a dinner party if the hostess was notable for birth, beauty, or intelligence. He also achieved most of the honours which come to a lord chancellor—the honorary fellowship of his college, and honorary doc-torates of ten universities. He was rector of St. Andrews (1955–8) and visitor of St. Antony's College, Oxford, from 1953.

Fyfe married in 1925 Sylvia Margaret, daughter of William Reginald Harrison, civil engineer, of Liverpool, sister of Rex Harrison, the actor. They had three daughters, one of whom predeceased him. Kilmuir died at his house at Withyham in Sussex 27 January 1967. His widow married Earl De La Warr in 1968. Kilmuir's estate was sworn for probate at £22,202.

There are portraits of Kilmuir at Balliol (by Christopher Sanders), at St. Antony's (by A. C. Davidson-Houston), at Gray's Inn (by Simon Elwes), and one by Harold Knight in the possession of the family. A pastel by Dame Laura Knight is in the Imperial War Museum.

[The Earl of Kilmuir, *Political Adventure*, 1964; *The Times*, 28 January 1967; private information; personal knowledge.]

R. F. V. HEUSTON

published 1981

GAITSKELL Hugh Todd Naylor

(1906–1963)

Politician, was born in Kensington 9 April 1906, the younger son of Arthur Gaitskell, of the Indian Civil Service, and his wife, Adelaide Mary, daughter of George Jamieson, who had been consul-general in Shanghai. He was educated at Winchester and New College, Oxford, where he obtained a first class in philosophy, politics, and economics in 1927. His special subject for his final schools was 'Labour movements' for which G. D. H. Cole was his tutor. Gaitskell's rather simple and individual radicalism as an undergraduate led him naturally into the Labour Party. But he was in-capable of dilettantism. He threw himself into support of the general strike of 1926, doing practical and obscure work. When he left Oxford with a number of careers open to him he chose to spend a year as tutor in charge of extra-mural classes in Nottingham; then moved to London in 1928 as a lecturer in political economy at University College where he became head of the department of political economy and university reader in 1938. In the meantime he had stood unsuccessfully as Labour candidate for Chatham in 1935.

Gaitskell early formed the central and unshakeable conviction that socialism was about social justice—an ideal in his own words 'in no way inspired by class hatred'. He favoured a rather radical measure of nationalization, mainly to facilitate economic planning; but he utterly rejected the idea that socialism was synonymous with nationalization. The proper aim of a Labour government in his view ought to be a practical, relevant, and radical course of economic and social reforms which would permanently change and improve society, but would always leave more to be done. In the field of foreign affairs he was prepared to draw conclusions from which many of his colleagues and friends at first flinched. In 1934 he witnessed the crushing of the Austrian Labour movement and sprang into action with vigour and energy to raise funds in Britain and organize relief. He was not content with the conclusion that a socialist must oppose Fascism; he saw that democratic socialism also involved opposition to dictatorship from the Left. But Fascism was the imminent danger and in the thirties Gaitskell became convinced that war with Hitler was inevitable and that everything possible must be done to prepare for the onslaught. He tried but failed to shake the emotional bias of the Parliamentary Labour Party against conscription.

During the war Gaitskell served as a temporary civil servant, first in the Ministry of Economic Warfare, then went with Hugh (later Lord) Dalton to the Board of Trade. His great administrative ability attracted the attention of politicians and officials alike. In 1945 he was returned to Parliament as Labour member for South Leeds, a seat which he retained until his death. In 1946 he was made parliamentary secretary at the Ministry of Fuel and Power, taking over as minister in 1947, when he was sworn of the Privy Council. In February 1950 he joined the Treasury as minister of state for economic affairs.

The year before, Gaitskell had made a major impact, although behind the scenes, on national policy. He was given partial authority at the Treasury during the absence of Sir Stafford Cripps through illness. Concluding that devaluation was necessary he convinced Cripps and other leading ministers and prepared all the necessary measures with high efficiency and absolute secrecy.

In October 1950 on Cripps's resignation, Attlee made Gaitskell chancellor of the Exchequer at the age of forty-four. This opened out the prospect of ultimate leadership of the party. It was then that Gaitskell's combination of qualities led him to take a number of immense risks, each of which put his career at issue and each of which took him a step nearer his goal. Personal ambition of a kind this was: but Gaitskell was not after mere personal power and position—he wanted to stand for something in public life and to represent the modernized Labour Party of his vision. For this goal he fought with tenacious and challenging courage. His ambition was great but it was without stratagem or intrigue.

Aneurin Bevan was the chief obstacle in the way by reason of his high ability and passionate ambitions and his capacity to evoke devoted adherence to a concept of the Labour Party very different from Gaitskell's. This conflict of concepts was the true issue between Gaitskell and Bevan almost immediately after he became chancellor: not health service charges nor even the cost of rearmament. That was why Gaitskell stubbornly turned down the pleas of colleagues in Cabinet and party who saw the dispute as relatively trivial. At bottom lay the struggle between the idea of a party of government and a party of protest.

While the party was in opposition after 1951, strong controversy arose over German rearmament on which many in the centre of the party shared the views of the Left. Gaitskell saw that the American alliance, which he wholeheartedly welcomed, and steadfastness against the advance of Russian Communism was involved. Again he and Bevan took opposite sides. In 1954 the party narrowly approved German rearmament, and Gaitskell defeated Bevan for the treasurership; he did so again in 1955. On Attlee's resignation in December Gaitskell was elected leader of the Labour Party over Bevan and Herbert Morrison (later Lord Morrison of Lambeth) by the largest majority hitherto recorded. Bevan had been prepared to stand down if Gaitskell would do the same in order to allow Morrison to be elected unopposed; but Gaitskell considered that the party should have a choice. He showed his capacity to handle men by effecting a compromise with Bevan whom he made shadow foreign secretary in 1957; two years later they visited Russia together. The older rival had by now accepted the younger's supremacy.

It was not until the general election of 1959 that Gaitskell became a national figure. He fought the campaign with vigour, ease, and enthusiasm, confident of victory. Later he admitted to friends that his promise not to raise income tax was a misjudgement. He won national respect by his unprecedented gesture of appearing on television at 1 a.m. to concede defeat when many returns were yet to come in. Bitterly disappointed at his frustrated hopes of victory, he bore himself with dignified composure, encouraging his supporters to rally from the setback.

On the morrow of defeat he once again put his leadership in issue over clause iv of the party's constitution which amongst other things declared nationalization as an objective of the Labour Party. The lesson he drew from defeat was that the party was hopelessly handicapped so long as socialism seemed to be identified with nationalization. He put forward an alternative which stressed as the objectives of the party social justice, equality, planning. But he underrated the opposition to his proposals. Under great pressure he gave ground: the original clause iv and his new draft were both to be endorsed. The battle was lost but Gaitskell won the war for the concept of a party of power. Hardly was this conflict over than Gaitskell was involved in another—the toughest of his leadership. Against his strong advice to the annual conference at Scarborough in 1960 it carried a resolution in favour of unilateral disarmament. With unconcealed emotion Gaitskell called on his supporters to 'fight, fight, and fight again to save the party we love'.

At the beginning of the following twelve months Gaitskell frankly faced the probability that he would be defeated at the next conference and that this would almost certainly involve his retirement from the leadership, perhaps his withdrawal from public life. But he never for a moment considered compromise on a cardinal issue. In fact the party rallied to him and at Blackpool the previous resolution was overwhelmingly reversed. Gaitskell had at last, with immense courage, created the party he wanted. In 1962 he led it—against the advice of many close friends and with the support of his former critics—to oppose British entry into the EEC on the terms proposed. By then he was generally accepted as Britain's next prime minister. But he died suddenly in London 18 January 1963, and it was left to his successor to lead to victory a party with which it was possible to govern.

Gaitskell was often regarded as rational and unemotional. Bevan's gibe about a desiccated calculating machine seemed to many to have some of the truth in it. Certainly Gaitskell's forte was an appeal to reason: this he regarded as the mark of a good man and, in the end, as the most potent way of winning opinion. He developed an unusual mastery of logical argument in speech: with impeccable logic he would exhaustively set out the arguments for his case. Sometimes his supporters on the benches behind him in the House of Commons were in despair that there would not be a single fresh point for them to make after he had sat down.

But beneath these rational forms Gaitskell was driven by deeper emotions. Faith and conviction compelled him to bring certain issues— often prickly and dangerous ones—before the bar of rational public opinion. But for the emotion—the crusading spirit—that underlay his outward lack of emotion Gaitskell would never have made so deep an impression on public opinion. Of those who thought like himself he wrote: 'while accepting the ultimate emotional basis of moral valuation, they had great faith in the power of reason ... to persuade men to see the light' (Introduction to Evan Durbin's *Politics of Democratic Socialism*, 1964).

A further source of Gaitskell's political strength was that politics was not the whole of his life: he had other resources on which he could fall back. He enjoyed a lively social life, good food, and good living, and had a solid family relationship. He would never be led, in great matters, into the kind of compromise which men will make who must at all costs stay in public life. But had he lived to become prime minister his highest qualities would have come into play: his talents were creative and needed power to unfold. He had an intellectual framework into which specific reforms and policies would have fitted; nor would he have flinched from taking unpopular measures. He would have stood out as a man of principle who could look facts in the face and would, if necessary, risk all on an issue on which he felt a righteous cause to be at stake. He was appointed CBE in 1945 and received an honorary DCL from Oxford in 1958.

Gaitskell married in 1937 Anna Dora, divorced wife of David Frost, daughter of Leon Creditor. She was created life peeress within a year of her husband's death. They had two daughters. A portrait of Gaitskell by Judy Cassab is in the National Portrait Gallery where there is also a bronze head by L. C. Bevis. A drawing by Stephen Ward is in the possession of the family.

[*Hugh Gaitskell, 1906–1963*, ed. W. T. Rodgers, 1964; Hugh Gaitskell, 'At Oxford in the Twenties', in *Essays in Labour History*, ed. Asa Briggs and John Saville, 1960; Philip Williams, *Hugh Gaitskell*, 1979; personal knowledge.]

PATRICK GORDON WALKER

published 1981

GOSCHEN George Joachim

(1831–1907)

First Viscount Goschen

Statesman, born on 10 Aug. 1831 at his father's house in the parish of Stoke Newington, was eldest son and second child in the family of two sons and five daughters of William Henry Göschen, a leading merchant of the City of London, by his wife Henrietta, daughter of William Alexander Ohmann. His youngest brother, Sir William Edward Goschen, became British ambassador at Berlin in 1908. The father was son of Georg Joachim Göschen, an eminent publisher and man of letters at Leipzig, the intimate friend of Schiller, Goethe, Wieland and other 'heroes of the golden age of German literature' (see Lord Goschen, *Life and Times of Georg Joachim Göschen*, 1903). In 1814 young William Henry Göschen came to London, where, with his friend Henry Frühling from Bremen, he founded the financial firm of Frühling & Göschen. A man of strong character, great industry, and deep religious convictions, he found time throughout an exceedingly busy life to indulge his love of literature and his taste for music.

From nine to eleven (1840–2) Goschen attended daily the 'Proprietary School' at Blackheath. Thence his father sent him for three years to Dr. Bernhard's school at Saxe Meiningen. During this period he only once visited England, usually spending his holidays with his German relations. His father, who intended his son for a business career, now thought he perceived in him qualities which would ensure success in public life in England. For this end it was desirable that young George should mix more than he had yet done with English boys; and it was with the view of making an Englishman of him that he was sent in August 1845 to Rugby entering the house of Bonamy Price, afterwards professor of political economy at Oxford. After his first year, Goschen grew to like his surroundings and to be popular with his schoolfellows. He rose to be head of the school, and in that capacity he made his first reported speech, on the occasion of the resignation of the headmaster, A. C. Tait (afterwards archbishop of Canterbury). Amongst the boys he had been already recognised as the best debater in the school, especially in reply. Though his rise in the school had been rapid, it was not till June 1848 that he achieved positive distinction by winning the prize for the English essay; and shortly afterwards the English prize poem for the year. In 1849 he won the Queen's medal for the English historical essay; and in 1850, the prize for the Latin essay, 'Marcus Tullius Cicero'. In the autumn of 1850, after a couple of months of travel on the continent, Goschen entered Oxford as a commoner of Oriel. He failed to win scholarships at University and Trinity, but in 1852 his college awarded him an exhibition. Though in the technical Oxford sense his 'scholarship' was not considered pre-eminent, he obtained a double first in classical honours, with the general reputation in 1853 of having been 'the best first in'. At the Union he won great fame by his speeches on political and literary subjects; and in his last year was president of that society. In the previous year he had founded the 'Essay Club', of which the original members were Arthur Butler, first headmaster of Haileybury, Charles Stuart Parker of University, H. N. Oxenham, the Hon. George Brodrick, W. H. Fremantle of Balliol, and Charles Henry Pearson (cf. *Memorials of Charles Henry Pearson*, 1900). Having graduated B.A. in 1853, Goschen entered actively into the business of his father's firm, by whom in October 1854 he was sent to superintend affairs in New Granada, now part of the United States of Colombia. After two years in South America he returned home, and on 22 Sept. 1857 married Lucy, daughter of John Dalley, a marriage which greatly conduced to the happiness of his future life. He now energetically devoted himself to business in London, rapidly making a reputation with commercial men, amongst whom he was known as the 'Fortunate Youth'. When only twenty-seven he was made a director of the Bank of England. In 1861 he achieved wider fame by publishing his 'Theory of the Foreign Exchanges' (5th edit. 1864), a treatise which won the attention of financial authorities and business men all over the world, and which has been translated into the principal languages of Europe. In 1863, a vacancy having occurred in the representation of the City of London, Goschen was returned un-opposed as a supporter of Lord Palmerston's government. His views were those of a strong liberal, as liberalism was understood in those days; and he pledged himself to the ballot, abolition of church rates, and the removal of religious disabilities. On the latter subject, the abolition of tests in the universities, he took a leading position in the House of Commons, fiercely contending with Lord Robert Cecil (afterwards Lord Salisbury), who struggled hard to maintain the old close connection between the uni-versities and the Church of England. At the opening of the session of 1864 Goschen achieved a marked success in seconding the address to the speech from the throne. But the pains which he took to distinguish his position in the liberal party, especially as regards foreign policy, from that taken up by Richard Cobden and John Bright, called forth, not unnaturally, vigorous remonstrance from the former (*Life*, i. 71). Before parliament was dissolved (July 1865), Goschen's knowledge of commercial matters, his brilliant speech on the address, and his ability in fighting the battle against tests, had given him a good standing in the House of Commons; and when the new parliament met, Lord Russell, who had succeeded Lord Palmerston as prime minister, invited him to join his ministry as vice-president of the board of trade (November 1865); and two months later to enter his cabinet as chancellor of the Duchy of Lancaster (January 1866). On the same day Lord Hartington (afterwards Duke of Devonshire), with whom in after years Goschen was to be closely associated, entered the cabinet for the first time.

Goschen now retired finally from business and from the firm of Frühling & Göschen, and henceforward devoted himself wholly to a political career. In the short-lived ministry of Lord Russell, and on the front bench of opposition during the Derby-Disraeli government which suc-ceeded it, Goschen took an active part with Gladstone and other leading liberals in the reform struggles of the day. At the dissolution of 1868, standing as a strenuous advocate of Irish disestablishment, he was returned again for the City, this time at the head of the poll; and on Gladstone's forming his first administration, Goschen entered his cabinet as president of the poor law board. There he showed great zeal as a reformer of local government (see his remarkable *Report of the Select Committee of* 1870), and in substituting methodical administration for the chaotic system, or want of system, which had grown up. On the health of H. C. E. Childers breaking down, Goschen was appointed in March 1871 to succeed him as first lord of the admiralty, a department which at that time was subjected to much public censure. Here his administration proved extraordinarily successful in restoring the general confidence and in winning the enthusiastic admiration of the naval service. In 1874 the unwillingness of Goschen and Cardwell to reduce the estimates for 1874–5 below what they considered the needs of the country required was an important element in determining Gladstone's sudden dissolution (January 1874). This resulted in the advent to power for six years of Disraeli, and accordingly Goschen, who was again re-elected for the City, found himself for the first time in the House of Commons one of a minority, which on Gladstone's withdrawal was led by Lord Hartington. Until 1880 the interest of the public and parliament was mainly occupied with foreign affairs, and Goschen as a leading member of the liberal party was in continual consultation with Lord Hartington and Lord Granville on the serious condition of things in eastern Europe. His great position as a financier and a man of business, and his more than ordinary acquaintance with foreign politics, had led to his being chosen by the council of foreign bondholders, with the approval of the foreign office, and at the invitation of the viceroy of Egypt to proceed to that country, which was in a state bordering on bankruptcy, to investigate and report upon the financial position. With M. Joubert, representing the French bondholders, Goschen proceeded to Cairo, their joint efforts resulting in the promulgation of the Khedivial decree of 16 Nov. 1876, the Goschen decree, as it came to be called (Cromer, *Modern Egypt*, i. 13–15).

When Goschen returned to England, Gladstone's anti-Turkish agitation was at its height. In 1877, when Lord Hartington accepted on behalf of the liberal party the policy pressed upon parliament by Sir George Trevelyan, of equalising the county and borough franchise, Goschen's strong sense of duty compelled him to protest against what he believed must lead to the complete monopolising of political power by a single class of the community. This difference with his political friends as to a main 'plank' of the party 'platform' proved to be a turning-point in his career. At the general election in April 1880 Goschen, who had retired from the representation of the City of London, was returned for Ripon. The electorate repudiated Lord Beaconsfield, and Gladstone at the head of a large majority again became prime minister. Goschen felt it incumbent upon him to hold aloof from the new administration. Gladstone offered him the vice-royalty of India, which he declined. He consented, however, to go in May 1880 on a special and temporary mission to Constantinople as ambassador to the Sultan, without emolument; retaining, with the approval of his constituents, his seat in the House of Commons. The object of the British government was to compel the Turks, by means of the concert of Europe, to carry out the stipulations of the treaty of Berlin as regards Greece, Montenegro and Armenia, and to get established a strong defensive frontier between Turkey and Greece. Goschen has recounted at length the difficulties he encountered, and has described his interviews with Prince Bismarck at Berlin, and the negotiations at Constantinople with the representatives of the great powers (*Life of Lord Goschen*, vol. i. chap. vii.). His mission lasted for a year, and in June 1881 he was again back in London, receiving the congratulations of Gladstone and Granville upon the successful accomplishment of a most difficult task.

In the political situation at home he found much that he disliked. The fight over the Irish land bill was virtually at an end. A fierce struggle was raging between the government and the followers of Parnell, and Goschen felt it right at such a time to do what he could to strengthen the executive against the forces of disorder. In June 1882 he declined Gladstone's invitation to join his cabinet as secretary of state for war. In November 1883 Gladstone pressed him strongly to accept the speakership of the House of Commons, which he also declined, partly because he felt that his short sight would prove a disqualification for the successful performance of the duties of the chair. In truth Goschen was becoming more and more dissatisfied with the position of the liberal party, in which he feared the rapid growth of the influence of the advanced section led by Mr. Chamberlain and Sir Charles Dilke. He set himself to strengthen Gladstone against radical influences, and to secure for the present and future that due weight within the party should be given to moderate liberalism. But though disapproving much in Gladstone's conduct of affairs—foreign policy, Ireland, Egypt, South Africa—he was by no means disposed to place unlimited confidence in the conservative leader, Lord Salisbury. The ambition and influence of Lord Randolph Churchill in Goschen's eyes still further weakened the claims of party conservatism to the public confidence. He had, moreover, been disappointed that his own stand against a democratic franchise had found no conservative support. In January 1885 Goschen withdrew from the Reform and Devonshire Clubs; and his speeches to great meetings in the country gave further evidence of the independent standpoint he had now assumed. By moderate men of all parties those speeches were welcomed and admired.

The last session of the parliament elected in 1880 was momentous. In February 1885 came the news of the fall of Khartoum. A motion of censure on the Gladstone government was defeated only by fourteen votes, and Goschen voted in the minority. In June a combination between conservatives and Parnellites defeated the government on a clause of the budget.

Goschen voted with the government. Lord Salisbury at once became prime minister, and Lord Randolph Churchill leader of the House of Commons.

The city of Ripon, which Goschen represented, was to lose its separate representation under the Reform Act of 1885, and an influential committee in Edinburgh invited Goschen to become a candidate for one of the divisions of that city at the coming general election. During the following autumn Goschen's speeches in Scotland and elsewhere made a great impression on the public (*Goschen's Political Speeches*, Edinburgh, 1886). Their high tone, their clear reasoning, the independent and disinterested character of the speaker, and the absence of claptrap or appeal to unworthy motives, were a refreshing contrast to much of the platform oratory of the day. At the same time the late ministers were freely disclosing their individual views to the public. Mr. Chamberlain was the spokesman of extreme radicalism, and found in Goschen his chief antagonist. Lord Hartington, whose allegiance to the liberal party had never wavered, spoke out as essentially a leader of moderate liberals, whilst Gladstone by studied indefiniteness endeavoured to keep all sections of liberals united under his 'umbrella'. Parnell threw the whole voting power of Irish nationalists on to the side of the conservatives. And though little was said about it at the general election, Goschen clearly saw that Parnell's policy of home rule, and Gladstone's line with reference to it, were the questions of the future. In vain he sought (July 1885) from Gladstone some explanation of his views (*Life of Lord Goschen*, vol. i. chap. ix.).

In November 1885 Goschen, supported by moderate liberals and conservatives, won an easy triumph in East Edinburgh over an advanced radical candidate. The effect, however, of the general election as a whole was to make it impossible for either of the great parties to hold power without the assistance of the Irish nationalists. Hence a remarkable development of the party position occurred. The majority of the liberal party coalesced with Parnell and his followers; and Gladstone was placed in power to carry out the policy of home rule. Goschen threw himself into the struggle for the union with conspicuous ability and zeal. With Lord Hartington he formed and inspired the liberal unionist party, and brought about that alliance with Lord Salisbury which was essential if the union was to be saved. At the great meeting at the Opera House on 14 April 1886, the first outward sign of this new alliance, Goschen's speech was the one that most deeply stirred the enthusiasm of his audience. In the House of Commons and all over the country he did battle for his cause with a fiery impetuosity which hitherto had hardly been recognised as part of his character. His hope that Lord Hartington should be the centre and leader of a strong body of moderate opinion was now realised. But the division in the liberal party was not so much between those who were known as whigs and radicals, as between unionists and home rulers; and thus many of the strongest radicals, such as Mr. Chamberlain and John Bright, were amongst Lord Hartington's most vigorous supporters. The union triumphed in the House of Commons, where Gladstone's home rule bill was defeated on 7 June 1886, and when the unionists secured a majority at the general election in July, Lord Salisbury formed a conservative administration. In East Edinburgh, however, Goschen was defeated by the home rule candidate, Dr. Wallace; but he did not relax his efforts outside the House of Commons in the unionist cause. On Lord Randolph Churchill's sudden resignation (20 Dec. 1886) of the chancellorship of the exchequer in Lord Salisbury's government, and the lead of the House of Commons, Goschen, with the approval of Lord Hartington, accepted the offer made to him by Lord Salisbury to enter his cabinet as Lord Randolph's successor, W. H. Smith at the same time undertaking to lead the House of Commons.

Goschen's accession to the ministry at this crisis was of the greatest importance in keeping the unionist government on its feet. He met, nevertheless, one more personal reverse, in his failure to win back from the liberal home rulers the Exchange division of Liverpool (26 Jan. 1887). A fortnight later he was elected by a majority of 4000 for St. George's, Hanover Square, a seat which he retained till he went to the House of Lords. Henceforward, as a member of the Salisbury government, sharing the responsibility of his colleagues, Goschen necessarily played a less individual part than heretofore in the public eye, though he took a prominent share in the fierce conflicts inside and outside parliament against the powerful home rule alliance between liberals and Irish nationalists. For six years in succession he brought forward the budget, meeting with much skill the steadily growing expenditure of the country, whilst boasting with truth that at the same time he was gradually reducing its debt. His most memorable achievement whilst chancellor of the exchequer was his successful conversion of the national debt in March 1888 from a 3 per cent to a $2\frac{3}{4}$, and ultimately a $2\frac{1}{2}$ per cent stock. The great courage and ability required to carry through this operation received the recognition of political opponents, including Gladstone, not less than of his own friends. During the 'Baring crisis' in November 1890 his courage and firmness as finance minister were again demonstrated. The situation was saved; whilst he absolutely refused to yield to pressure to employ the funds or credit of the state to buttress up the solvency of a private institution (*Life*, vol. ii. chap. vii., and note in Appendix III. by Lord Welby). In the same year a good deal of unpopularity fell to Goschen's share, resulting from the 'licensing clauses' (ultimately abandoned) which it was proposed to introduce into the local taxation bill, for providing out of taxes on beer and spirits a compensation fund to facilitate the reduction in the number of public-houses.

At the end of 1891 Mr. Arthur Balfour succeeded to the leadership of the House of Commons (*Life*, ii. 186 seq.); but the days of the unionist ministry were already numbered, and the general election of the following June placed Gladstone once more in power. Over the home rule bill of 1893 the old controversy of 1886 was revived in all its bitterness, and Goschen was again in the front rank of the combatants. In opposition, he formally joined the conservative party, became a member of the Carlton Club, and repeated with undiminished power the efforts he had made nine years before to sustain the cause of the union. This time, however, Gladstone's policy was accepted by the House of Commons; but only to be rejected by the House of Lords, who were supported by the country at the general election of 1895.

Lord Salisbury's new administration was joined by Lord Hartington, Mr. Chamberlain, and other liberal unionists, whilst Goschen to his great satisfaction went to the admiralty (June 1895), where twenty years before he had won well-earned fame. His last period at the admiralty, which lasted till the autumn of 1900, was eventful; for though the country remained at peace with the great powers of the world, our foreign relations at times became severely strained. Difficulties connected with Venezuela, Crete, Nigeria, Port Arthur, Fashoda, and German sympathy with President Krüger, brought the possibility of rupture before the eyes of all men. Goschen felt that a very powerful British navy was the best security for the peace of the world, as well as for our own protection, and the vast increases of our naval establishments and the consequent growth of naval estimates were generally approved. The strain of these five years told upon his strength. The death of Mrs. Goschen in the spring of 1898 had been a heavy trial; and the weight of advancing years determined him to retire from office before the approaching general election. Accordingly on 12 Oct. 1900, to the regret of the public and the naval service, he resigned, and in December was raised to the House of Lords as Viscount Goschen of Hawkhurst, Kent.

The remainder of his life Lord Goschen hoped to spend mainly at Seacox Heath, his home in Kent, with more leisure than he had found in the past for seeing his family and friends, for indulging his strong taste for reading, and for attending to the interests of his estate. In 1903 he published the life and times of his grandfather, on which he had long been engaged; and in 1905 a volume of 'Essays and Addresses on Economic Questions'. This last consisted of contributions to the 'Edinburgh Review' and of addresses read to various bodies and institutions at different times, and of valuable comments by the author on the further light that the lapse of years had thrown upon the subjects treated. On the death of Lord Salisbury, Goschen was chosen chancellor of Oxford University (31 Oct. 1903), and devoted himself with energy to the interests of the university. He had been made hon. D.C.L. of Oxford in 1881, and hon. LL.D. of Aberdeen and Cambridge in 1888, and of Edinburgh in 1890.

Goschen's political life was by no means over. When in 1903 Mr. Chamberlain's fiscal policy was announced, causing rupture in the ministry and the unionist party, Goschen again came to the front as one of the foremost champions of free trade. He had, as he said, worked out these financial and commercial problems for himself; and accordingly he joined the Duke of Devonshire and other free-trade unionists in a vigorous effort to defeat a policy certain, in his opinion, to bring disaster on the nation. In the House of Lords and in the country, till the general election of January 1906 had made free trade safe, he threw himself into the conflict with much of his old energy and fire; and in the new parliament he once more solemnly warned conservative statesmen against the danger of identifying their party with the fiscal policy of Mr. Chamberlain. During the remainder of the session, he took part occasionally in the proceedings of the House of Lords, showing none of the infirmities of age excepting that his eyesight, never good, had deteriorated. On 7 Feb. 1907 he died suddenly in his home at Seacox, and was buried at Flimwell. Goschen left two sons and four daughters. His elder son, George Joachim, succeeded to the viscountcy.

Goschen showed throughout the whole of his career a remarkable consistency of character as a statesman, notwithstanding the fact that part of his official life was passed under Gladstone's, part under Lord Salisbury's leadership. Always moderate in his opinions, which were the outcome of honest and deep investigation, he disliked the exaggerations of party protagonists, and was as vehement in support of moderation as were the extremists on either side in fighting for victory. At the head of great departments, his industry, his grasp of principles, his mastery of details, and his determination to secure efficiency were conspicuous. But in the pressure of administrative work he remembered that his responsibilities as cabinet minister were not limited to his own department, and in all matters of general policy, especially as regards foreign affairs, of which he had exceptional knowledge, his counsels carried great weight. His courage and independence won him in a high degree the respect and confidence of his countrymen; and Queen Victoria placed much reliance on his judgment and his patriotism. Nature had not endowed him with the qualities that make an orator of the first rank. His voice was not good, nor his gestures and bearing graceful. Yet he proved again and again on public platforms that he possessed the power not only of interesting and leading men's minds but also of stirring their enthusiasm to a very high pitch. He never spoke down to his audience, or appealed to prejudice, but exerted himself to lead them to think and to feel as he himself thought and felt. His speeches very frequently contained some turn of expression or phrase which caught the public ear and for the time was in everyone's mouth. In 1885, 'He would not give a blank cheque to Lord Salisbury.' In his great fight against Irish nationalism, 'We would never surrender to crime or time.' In the fiscal controversy, 'He would be no party to a gamble with the food of the people.'

Goschen throughout his life did much useful public work outside the region of active politics. He had become an ecclesiastical commissioner in 1882. From its initiation in 1879 Goschen was a vigorous supporter of the movement for the extension of university teaching in London, and for many years he gave great assistance to the movement. With him the loss of office never meant the cessation of employment. In his private life his personal qualities and sympathetic nature won for him a large circle of real friends, whilst in society at large a strong sense of humour, his wide general knowledge of men and books, his power of conversation and of promoting good talk in others, made him highly valued. In his own house in the country and in London, where he delighted to gather round him friends and acquaintances, he carried the intenseness of interest characteristic of his working hours into the amusements of the day. It was not for the purposes of breadwinning alone that he set a high value on education. 'Livelihood is not a life', he said to the Liverpool Institute (29 Nov. 1877, on *Imagination*). 'Education must deal with your lives as well as qualify you for your livelihoods.' He knew from his own experience how much education had done for his life outside those regions of business and politics where his chief energies had been spent.

A portrait in oils by Rudolf Lehmann (1880) is in the possession of the present viscount and is now at Seacox Heath; a second, by Mr. Hugh A. T. Glazebrook, is at Plaxtol, Kent, in the possession of his daughters. A cartoon portrait of Goschen by 'Ape' appeared in 'Vanity Fair' in 1869.

[Arthur D. Elliot, *Life of Lord Goschen*, 2 vols. 1911, compiled from private papers and correspondence; see also Bernard Holland, *Life of the Eighth Duke of Devonshire*, 2 vols. 1911, and Morley's *Life of Gladstone*, 1903; Hansard's Debates; Annual Register; *Times* reports of speeches.]

A. R. D. ELLIOT

published 1912

GRIGG Edward William Macleay

(1879–1955)

First Baron Altrincham

Administrator and politician, was born 8 September 1879 in Madras, the only son of Henry Bidewell Grigg, of the Indian Civil Service, by his wife, Elizabeth Louisa, eldest daughter of Sir Edward Deas Thomson, colonial secretary of New South Wales (1837–56). A scholar of both Winchester and New College, Oxford, he obtained a second class in classical moderations (1900) and a third in *literae humaniores* (1902). In 1902 he won the Gaisford Greek verse prize.

Journalism was his first calling. In 1903 he joined the staff of *The Times* as secretary to G. E. Buckle, the editor; then moved to the *Outlook* as assistant editor (1905–6) to J. L. Garvin. In 1908, after two years of widespread and intensive travel, he returned to *The Times* as head of its colonial department. His family background, his personal knowledge of imperial affairs, and his reverence for Joseph Chamberlain and Lord Milner well fitted him for this post. At no time in its history, he was later proud to recall, did that newspaper exercise a more salutary and decisive influence upon national policy than in the years immediately before the war. He resigned in 1913 to become joint-editor of the *Round Table*.

Grigg was thirty-four at the outbreak of war in 1914. Scorning the posts of dignified safety which could have been his for the asking, he joined the Grenadier Guards as an ensign and was sent out to the 2nd battalion in France. 'The Scribe', as he was affectionately called in the Brigade, showed outstanding qualities of gallantry and leadership throughout the heavy fighting in which the Guards division was engaged. (Sir) Winston Churchill, then a major in the Oxfordshire Yeomanry, was for a short time attached to his company to gain experience of trench warfare. Early in 1916 Grigg was transferred to the staff. By the end of the war he had risen to be a lieutenant-colonel and G.S.O. 1 of the Guards division. He was awarded the M.C. in 1917, appointed to the D.S.O. in 1918, C.M.G. in 1919, and mentioned in dispatches.

It was during his years in the Grenadiers that Grigg first met the Prince of Wales, whom he accompanied on tours of Canada in 1919 and of Australia and New Zealand in 1920 as military secretary and special adviser. For these services, not always free from anxiety, he was appointed successively C.V.O. (1919) and K.C.V.O. (1920). On his return he joined the staff of the prime minister, Lloyd George, as a private secretary. To the traditional loyalties of the post he added an intense personal admiration for his mercurial chief which blinded him to all criticism, however well founded. He served his master with memorable fidelity throughout some difficult political situations. At Cannes in January 1922 he took part in the historic game of golf which caused the downfall of M. Briand. When the prime minister himself fell from power later that year Grigg was offered a choice of senior appointments in the Civil Service. He preferred instead to enter the House of Commons for Oldham (1922–5) as a Lloyd George Liberal. As secretary to the Rhodes Trust (1923–5) he was also able to maintain a close interest in imperial affairs.

In 1925 Grigg was appointed governor of Kenya. Two years before, he had married Joan Alice Katherine Dickson-Poynder, only child of Lord Islington (whose notice he was later to contribute to this Dictionary). Her instinctive sympathy for all races, expressed particularly in her patronage of nursing and maternity services, enhanced the distinction of her husband's administration. The task with which Grigg had been charged was to unite the three East African territories of Kenya, Uganda, and Tanganyika. Largely owing to the opposition of Sir Donald Cameron, governor of Tanganyika, and to lukewarm support from the home Government, this mission failed. But there was much else in his programme which brought lasting economic benefit to the colony and created stable conditions most likely to attract European capital. Agriculture and forestry, communications and schools, town planning and security of land tenure were all improved during his energetic and sometimes exacting rule. Believing that the civilization of an age is reflected in its buildings, he dignified Kenya with two splendid Government Houses, at Nairobi and Mombasa, designed by Sir Herbert Baker, but was unable to realize an ambitious project for central government offices. He was appointed K.C.M.G. in 1928.

Appreciation of his governorship has since been tempered by belittlement of his trust in tribal self-government and provincial autonomy. Grigg rejected the later fashion of thought that Kenya should progress through the multi-racial state towards a common citizenship. This, he believed, could lead only to the ultimate extinction of the white settler and to an overwhelming African ascendancy: a prospect he deplored, not because he felt that Africans as such were unfitted to govern themselves, but because he feared that they would be required to administer an alien system of western government without the necessary education and experience. To the end of his days he set his face against so abrupt an abdication of what he held to be Great Britain's imperial mission.

On returning to England in 1930 Grigg was offered a choice of Indian governorships. Neither he nor his wife, however, was in robust health and he refused them all. It was the fatal turning-point of his life. Whatever his opinion of African incapacity for self-rule, it did not extend to the peoples of India. As a boy he had seen his parents' house thronged with Indian visitors and developed a sympathetic understanding of their aspirations. He might have been one of the greatest of Indian administrators; instead he determined to remain at home and to plunge once more into the world of politics. Without the instincts of political manœuvre and self-advancement, and further handicapped by his known allegiance to Lloyd George, his venture was doomed to fail.

In the general election of 1931, although already adopted as Conservative candidate for Leeds Central, he stood down with characteristic unselfishness in favour of the former Labour member who proposed to stand as a 'national' candidate. Two years later, having in the meantime served as chairman of the milk reorganization commission, he returned to the House of Commons as member for Altrincham. It is to his credit that he recognized the menace of Nazi Germany before most of his colleagues. In two eloquent works, *The Faith of an Englishman* (1936) and *Britain Looks at Germany* (1938), he pleaded for a stern policy of defence. Yet he continued to believe that such a course of action was not incompatible with wholehearted support for the administrations of Stanley Baldwin and Neville Chamberlain. Too loyal to be a rebel, he would plead with his leaders in private but recoiled from criticizing them in public. His name is not to be found among those who voted against 'Munich'.

Denied office until the outbreak of war, he was appointed parliamentary secretary to the Ministry of Information in its opening days. In April 1940 he became financial secretary, and in May joint parliamentary under-secretary, at the War Office. He held the latter post until March 1942, having earlier refused Churchill's offer of promotion as first commissioner of works since it depended upon his acceptance of a peerage. Thereafter he was inadequately employed for a man of his talents, but in November 1944 returned to office as minister resident in the Middle East in succession to Lord Moyne and was sworn of the Privy Council. The defeat of the Churchill government in July 1945 put an end to both his political ambitions and his active political life, although he was to assume the editorship of the *National Review* in 1948. He was created Baron Altrincham in 1945 and died at Tormarton, his house in Gloucestershire, 1 December 1955, after a long illness. His last reserves of strength were drained in the completion of *Kenya's Opportunity* (1955), a final tribute to the land which was so much a part of his life. He had one daughter and two sons, the elder of whom, John Edward Poynder (born 1924), succeeded to the title, but disclaimed it in 1963.

'Ned' Grigg was a handsome man, well above middle height and with the complexion of a countryman. Yet his soldierly bearing concealed a nervous system ill suited to the hubbub of politics. Opposition to his impulsive enthusiasms evoked bursts of impatience, even of rage. Then the clouds would lift: in his family circle or when entertaining a few close friends drawn mostly from the Milner 'kindergarten' he would both show and inspire deep affection. He was half a poet. Few other colonial governors would have written: 'The very thought of Kenya is like sunlight to me, sunlight crisp as mountain air in the high places of the earth.' He found perennial solace in the plays of Shakespeare and in listening to music.

There is a pencil drawing of him by Ray Nestor at Tormarton.

[Grigg's own writings; *National and English Review*, January 1956; private information; personal knowledge.]

KENNETH ROSE

published 1971

HALL-PATCH Sir Edmund Leo

(1896–1975)

Civil servant, was born in Chelsea 4 March 1896, the youngest of the three sons (there were no daughters) of William Hall-Patch (earlier known as Hall) and his Irish wife, Honora Riley. His father, who became—with his children—a convert to Roman Catholicism, had started life in the Royal Navy and, after a period as major-domo at the legation in Brussels, was then a verger at the Brompton Oratory. Edmund never married and his family was important to him. When his second brother, an engineer rear-admiral, was killed in 1945, he assumed the guardianship of his children and, after his father's death, did much for his widowed stepmother.

As a child he was delicate and was sent to a religious house in the South of France. Both these experiences—France and a Roman Catholic education—strongly influenced his life. In France he became bilingual and he always felt quite as much at ease in France and in Europe as he did in England, while the only home he ever owned and to which, but for financial and legal difficulties, he would later in life have emigrated was in the South of France. And wherever in the world he worked he was always close to the Catholic hierarchy.

After a spell at school in England he returned at sixteen to Paris to train as a professional musician. He got a union card—later to be of great value to him—but soon decided he was not good enough. By 1914 he was studying French at the Sorbonne; he joined up, was commissioned in the Royal Artillery, won the croix de guerre with palms, was gassed, medically downgraded, and ended the war as a captain and railway transport officer near Paris.

In 1919 he was earning his living in the band of a Paris cabaret when he met (Sir) Frederick Leith-Ross of the Treasury who, with his family, became a lifelong friend and patron. Leith-Ross found him a job first with the Supreme Allied Economic Council and then in 1920 with the Reparations Commission. There he prospered and from 1925 to 1929 was head of its finance section. When this came to an end he went to Siam as financial adviser to the government. He greatly enjoyed it, learned the language, and steeped himself in the life of the country. But it was not an easy assignment for so scrupulous a man—and in 1932, unable to approve the Siamese government's financial policies and at loggerheads with the Bank of England whose expectations he regarded as unrealistic, he resigned.

There were few jobs in the depression. He tried America, living in a smart hotel and playing the saxophone at night. Back in London he was a successful if intrepid and often injured riding instructor. By 1933, however, he was back on course, as financial adviser to a British group in Turkey and in 1934 in Romania as British member of a League of Nations commission of economic experts. All this was prelude. In 1935 Leith-Ross invited him to join the Treasury as an assistant secretary, to accompany him on a mission to China, and then to stay on from June 1936 as financial adviser to the British embassy. He was a great success there and in Japan, which was soon added to his bailiwick. In 1938 he was appointed CMG and in 1940 became the government's financial commissioner throughout the Far East.

By 1941 war had closed in and he returned to the Treasury to keep an eye on the Far East and be involved in negotiations, on such matters as Lend-Lease, with the United States. In 1944 he was promoted to assistant under-secretary and transferred to the Foreign Office to direct and lay enduring foundations for its growing economic work. In 1946 he was promoted to deputy under-secretary and in the following year knighted as a KCMG. As the principal economic adviser to Ernest Bevin he played a central and demanding role in the British response to the Marshall Plan. In 1948 he was promoted again—this time to become ambassador and leader of the British delegation to the nascent Organization for European Economic Co-operation (OEEC). For the next four years he was chairman of its executive committee, working and travelling prodigiously, popular with his colleagues—American and European—and seen by them, and perhaps by himself, as the champion of closer British ties with Europe. In 1951 he was appointed GCMG. But by then the job was done; by 1952

Marshall aid was over and in Britain the initial attraction and impetus of the European ideal had faded. Hall-Patch handed over to his deputy, and went, a little sadly but still as ambassador, to be the British executive director of the International Monetary Fund and the International Bank for Reconstruction and Development in Washington. In 1954 he retired from the public service, and joined Leith-Ross on the board of the Standard Bank of South Africa, succeeding him as chairman from 1957 to 1962. The wind of change was blowing in Africa and under Hall-Patch the Bank prepared itself to ride the storm and made a start on the sweeping changes which were mainly carried through by his successor and friend, Sir F. Cyril Hawker. By 1962 his health was declining and he retired. In the years that followed he retained financial interests in Britain and the USA, wrote occasional articles, was on the board of Lambert International in New York, and travelled often to America and France.

His career was as surprising as it was successful. He had a brilliant, but rather tortuous and pessimistic mind, perhaps more French than English. He was a very private person and cultivated an air of myth and mystery; even to his family he tended to appear and disappear like a magician. Stories abounded—seldom confirmed, but few were finally denied; stories of sorrows and romances, of the anonymous authorship of a daring French novel, or of popular music for film or review, of unusual friends—Chou En Lai and Syngman Rhee, Yvonne Printemps and Sacha Guitry. His dress—slightly theatrical and antique, with stocks and stick-pins—an unscrutable air behind thick spectacles, and a tendency to break suddenly into French, all added to the enigma.

A cheerful and charming companion, his friends were many and various; he was always kind and ready to help—and a special delight to children. He enjoyed his material pleasures and everything French—food and wine, his music, and the rewards of his success. But he never felt quite at home in Whitehall and this diminished his influence and effectiveness. Perhaps exaggeratedly, he felt he had experienced life and taken its buffets at the grass roots and always saw himself as an outsider looking into the establishment, impelled by an austere conscience to warn his more sheltered and unwary colleagues against facile optimism or complacency. Bevin valued him and was amused by his Cassandra role. 'Morning 'all-Patch', he would say as he saw Hall-Patch lowering ominously in the corridor 'and what's the snags to-day?' When he had heard, he felt forearmed against the worst.

What, perhaps, was most surprising was that with his sceptical and traditional cast of mind, Hall-Patch often seemed a pioneer and even a rebel involved in great changes. His most lasting achievements were the pioneering and strengthening of the economic side of the Foreign Office and the handling of all the European developments arising from the Marshall Plan, with Britain very much in the lead. He was often a fervent, and some even thought an intemperate, advocate of attenuating Britain's diminished position in the world by closer involvement in Europe rather than by the more traditional and fashionable alternatives of closer Commonwealth ties and a special relationship with the USA. In this he was ahead of his time—and if he was disappointed that his views did not prevail, he accepted this loyally and played, with real distinction, a constructive and significant part in developments of great moment for the future of his country.

He died in a nursing home at Ascot 1 June 1975.

[Private information; personal knowledge.]

HENNIKER

published 1986

HARDIE James Keir

(1856–1915)

Socialist and labour leader, was born in a one-roomed cottage at Legbrannock, near Holytown, Lanarkshire, 15 August 1856. His father was a ship's carpenter and trade unionist, and his mother, Mary Keir, had been a domestic servant. His youth was passed in extreme poverty. At seven he became a messenger boy, then he worked for a time in a ship-yard, and afterwards as a baker's errand boy. His parents having moved back from Glasgow into the coal district, he went to work at ten years of age as trapper in a Lanarkshire mine, remaining for twelve years in the pits, and rising to be a skilled hewer. During these years he attended evening school, and became an active worker in the temperance movement, in which he met his wife, Lillie, daughter of Duncan Wilson, collier, whom he married in 1879. In the later 'seventies he began to agitate among the miners, then very badly paid and practically unorganized. His activity cost both him and his two younger brothers their jobs; and Hardie was black-listed by the coal-owners.

In 1878 Hardie opened a stationer's shop at Low Waters, and began journalistic work as local correspondent for the *Glasgow Weekly Mail*. He had now set to work in good earnest to get the miners organized, and for many years he acted as an unpaid official of various new miners' associations. Thus in 1879 the Hamilton miners made him their correspondence secretary, and he used this position to get into touch with the miners in other parts of the country, with a view to forming a national union. Later in that year he was appointed miners' county agent for Lanarkshire, and a conference of miners from the various Scottish coalfields gave him the title of national secretary, though no national organization yet existed. In 1880, still practically without organization, the Lanarkshire miners struck against a wage reduction, and, though they were defeated, the struggle prepared the way for a county union. After leading the men in this dispute, Hardie accepted an invitation from the Ayrshire miners to become their county secretary, and took up his quarters at Cumnock, where his home remained for the rest of his life. In 1881 the Ayrshire miners struck and were defeated; but Hardie continued the work of organization until, in 1886, the Ayrshire miners' union was at length formed on a stable basis, with himself as secretary. In the same year he was made secretary of the Scottish miners' federation, formed by the various county unions which he had helped to create. Hardie was paid either nothing at all or only small honoraria for his services with these bodies. He supported himself mainly by journalism, joining the staff of two local newspapers in 1882. During these years he was still a liberal; but in 1887 he was already mooting the idea of a distinct labour party, and proposing to stand for North Ayrshire as an independent labour candidate. In 1888 his rupture with the liberals was complete, and he stood as a labour candidate against both liberal and conservative at the Mid-Lanark by-election, sometimes described as the first independent labour contest. He polled only 617 votes out of 7,381. During the contest unsuccessful attempts were made by the liberals to buy him off. He was offered a safe liberal seat at the next general election and an income of £300 a year. This, as well as subsequent offers of money from several sources, he refused. The year of this election is also notable for the formation, under Hardie's chairmanship, of the Scottish labour party, the first independent labour political party in Great Britain, subsequently merged in the Independent Labour Party.

Before the Mid-Lanark election, at the beginning of 1887, Hardie started a paper of his own, *The Miner*, which was continued for two years. In 1889, the year of the great dock strike in London, generally regarded as the beginning of a new epoch in British labour history, this was succeeded by the *Labour Leader*, published monthly till 1894, and thereafter weekly. This paper, which became the principal mouthpiece of the new political socialist movement and the 'new unionism', greatly increased Hardie's influence; and in 1892 he was elected as independent labour member of parliament for South West Ham, the death of the liberal candidate shortly before the election giving him a straight fight with a unionist. At the same election John Burns was returned for Battersea. Hardie's election undoubtedly helped forward the movement for an independent working-class party, and early in 1893 the various local and sectional bodies united to form the Independent Labour Party, with Hardie as chairman. With this body and its work his name will always be principally connected. In parliament he rapidly made his name as 'the member for the unemployed', adopting from the first a militant attitude on this question. In 1895 he lost his seat owing to the withdrawal of support by the liberals. He then visited America and, on his return, fought an unsuccessful by-election at Bradford in 1896. He incurred much odium by taking up a strong attitude against the South African War; but in 1900, after being defeated at Preston, he was elected for Merthyr Burghs with D. A. Thomas (afterwards Viscount Rhondda). This seat he held continuously until his death. He took an active part in forming the labour representation committee in 1900. When this became the Labour Party, and a strong labour group was for the first time returned to parliament in 1906, Hardie became its first leader in the House of Commons; but he resigned the leadership, owing to illness, in the following year. In 1913 he again became chairman of the Independent Labour Party, a position which he had held from 1893 to 1900, and presided at its 'coming-of-age' conference in 1914. He was chairman of the British section of the International Socialist bureau at the outbreak of war in 1914, having taken from 1888 onwards an active part in international labour conferences and in stimulating international labour organization. The powerlessness of the working-class organizations to prevent war, to which he was strongly opposed, came to him as a severe shock, and from August 1914 his health broke down. After seeming for a while to regain his strength, he suffered a further breakdown. Pneumonia followed, and he died 2 September 1915. He left two sons and a daughter, a second daughter having died in childhood.

Hardie was, in his day, perhaps the best-hated and the best-loved man in Great Britain. To his opponents he was uncompromising and hard-hitting in his language, and he was commonly regarded as much more of an extremist than he really was. His speeches in parliament and still more, during his visit to India in 1907–1908, when his utterances were seriously misrepresented, roused furious anger. In the socialist movement, on the other hand, he was regarded with feelings almost of veneration, and his personal popularity was immense. He was an excellent speaker, relying on homely phrases and simple appeals, with some tendency to sentimentalism. Never an original thinker or theorist, he had a firm grip of practical affairs, which enabled him to carry out effectively his task of drawing the British trade union and labour movement into independent political action on semi-socialist lines. He wrote well, and his journalism had always that personal touch which is essential to popular political writing. At his best, he was not unlike William Cobbett in the manner of his appeal. Like Cobbett, too, he was an excellent companion, with an extraordinary faculty for making and keeping loyal friends. By his example and the force of his personal appeal, he certainly did far more than any other man to create the political labour movement in Great Britain, and to give to it the distinctive character of an alliance of socialist and trade union forces. His London home, in Nevill's Court, off Fleet Street, was the resort of all manner of British and foreign leaders of advanced thought and action. But, though Hardie's life was spent largely in London, he always retained both his home at Cumnock, where his wife and family remained, and his essential character as a Scottish miner. He was acutely class-conscious and clan-proud, obtruding in parliament and in private life his working-class origin and attitude. His cloth cap and tweed suit, which so scandalized parliament and the newspapers when he took his seat in 1892, were worn, partly at least, in order to help him in sustaining this character. In this he was perfectly sincere, and his egoism, like Cobbett's, arose rather from his sense of symbolizing his class than from any personal vanity. Time is already enabling even his opponents to take a more objective view of Hardie. His opportunist and even sentimental socialism exactly suited the mood of the more advanced groups of workers who, escaping from Victorian liberalism, sought a new gospel as the political expression of their economic condition.

[Apart from pamphlets, of which there are many, the only life of Hardie is William Stewart's *J. Keir Hardie: A Biography*, 1921, which contains a full account of the events of his life (with portraits). David Lowe's *From Pit to Parliament*, 1923, deals more fully with his early career. For his influence, see also volume ii of Max Beer's *History of British Socialism*, 1919–1920, and the somewhat malicious references in H. M. Hyndman's *Further Reminiscences*, 1912. Hardie's own works, in addition to a good many pamphlets and much journalism, include *From Serfdom to Socialism*, 1907, a simple piece of socialist propaganda, and *India: Impressions and Suggestions*, 1909.]

G. D. H. Cole

published 1927

(1893–1968)

Fourth Baronet, and first Baron Harvey of Tasburgh

Diplomatist, was born 26 November 1893 at Rainthorpe Hall, near Norwich, the only son of Sir Charles Harvey, second baronet, and landowner, by his second wife, Mary Anne Edith, daughter of G. F. Cooke, of Holmwood, Norwich. He was educated at Malvern College and at Trinity College, Cambridge, where he obtained a first in part i of the historical tripos in 1914. He served throughout the war in France, Egypt, and Palestine, and was mentioned in dispatches.

In 1919 Harvey entered the Diplomatic Service and after postings at home and to Rome and Athens became in 1931 head of Chancery at the embassy in Paris. From then on his career was an alternation between Paris and London where his service at the Foreign Office was closely related to that of Anthony Eden (later the Earl of Avon). In January 1936 Harvey was promoted counsellor and became private secretary to Eden whom he served with a dedication to which his *Diplomatic Diaries* bear eloquent witness. He was a convinced believer in Eden's policy of resistance to Fascist aggression and consequently, as his very outspoken diaries show, strongly hostile to Neville Chamberlain's appeasement policies. As private secretary to the foreign secretary Harvey interpreted his duties widely, often proffering advice on matters of internal policy in terms critical of the prime minister's policies and of his interferences in foreign affairs. After Eden's resignation in February 1938 Harvey continued to offer unofficial advice to his former chief. His personal relations with Lord Halifax were good, but he could not feel the same enthusiasm for his policies and he noted that the new foreign secretary was less inclined than his predecessor had been to rely on his private secretary for political counsel, and more in the habit of resorting to the conventional channel, via the permanent under-secretary, for the diplomatic advice he needed. Nevertheless, Harvey stayed on at his post, albeit with diminished influence, until he became minister in Paris in December 1939.

There his time was brief but eventful. France fell within a few months and he was involved in the embassy's odyssey from Paris, via a château in Touraine, to Bordeaux, and evacuation in a British warship. He worked briefly at the Ministry of Information in charge of propaganda to the occupied countries of Europe, but it was no surprise that Eden, who had returned to the Foreign Office in December 1940, took the first opportunity of reappointing Harvey as his private secretary, in June 1941, although he was by now well above the rank normal for the post. Thenceforward Harvey was closely involved in all the complicated issues which beset the Foreign Office during the war. He accompanied Eden on three trips to Moscow, the first at the dramatic moment when the Germans had just been stopped thirty kilometres away in December 1941, and once to the United States. He was closely involved too in the controversies over the employment of Darlan and Giraud, the struggle over the recognition of the National Committee of de Gaulle, the difficulties with the exiled Polish government, and the like. In all these questions his advice was forward-looking, realistic, and on the side of the new forces which he believed would emerge in the open at the end of the war. His *War Diaries* show him as very critical of Churchill and Roosevelt for their inability to recognize these new forces, and his admiration for Eden in this period was not unqualified, though he continued to hope for his succession as prime minister and discouraged him from accepting the vice-royalty of India. He continued as private secretary until 1943 when he became assistant undersecretary, and in 1946 he succeeded Sir Orme Sargent as deputy undersecretary (political), the second highest professional post in the Foreign Office, and one in which he worked closely with Ernest Bevin whom he much admired.

In 1948 Harvey was appointed ambassador in Paris in succession to Duff Cooper (later Viscount Norwich). He had served there twice before and he had accompanied King George VI and Queen Elizabeth on their state visit in July 1938 (when he received the grand cross of the Legion of Honour), and his intimate acquaintance with European and in particular French problems made his appointment natural, almost inevitable. His embassy was a very different one from the dazzling performance of the Coopers which he did not seek to emulate. He was strict in excluding from the embassy any Frenchman in any way tainted by collaboration with the Germans but filled the beautiful house in the Faubourg St. Honoré with small and well-selected parties of leading Frenchmen, mainly drawn from the political parties then ruling France. The food was delicious, the Harveys' distinguished collection of modern paintings ornamented the salon vert, and the discriminating style of their entertaining was exactly suited to the ethos of the Fourth Republic, whose leading statesmen were mostly men of intelligence and taste but without the pretentiousness which came later. Harvey's tenure of the British Embassy coincided with one of the least acrimonious periods of Anglo-French relations, and to this his personal contribution was far from negligible. His own style was entirely devoid of pretentiousness. His appearance was deceptively mild and owlish; in fact, as his diaries show, he was a man of strong convictions, even passions.

On his retirement from Paris in 1954 Harvey was created a baron and later in the same year he succeeded his half-brother as fourth baronet. He took little part in the debates in the House of Lords although he attended with some regularity, sitting on the cross-benches and normally voting on the Labour or Liberal side. His retirement, spent in London with winters in the south of France, was peaceful and uneventful. He enjoyed his trusteeship of the Wallace Collection, and was active in the Franco-British Society, of which he became chairman.

Harvey was appointed CMG (1937), CB (1944), KCMG (1946), GCMG (1948), and GCVO (1950). In 1920 he married Maud Anners (died 1970), daughter of Arthur Watkin Williams-Wynn, a landowner of Coed-y-Maen, Montgomeryshire. Lady Harvey was a woman of unusual charm and distinction of appearance who was a great help to Harvey in his career. They had two sons, the elder of whom, Peter Charles Oliver (born 1921), succeeded to the baronetcy and the barony when his father died at his London home 29 November 1968.

[*The Diplomatic Diaries of Oliver Harvey, 1937–1940*, ed. John Harvey, 1970; *The War Diaries of Oliver Harvey, 1941–1945*, ed. John Harvey, 1978; private information; personal knowledge.]

W. E. HAYTER

published 1981

HERBERT Aubrey Nigel Henry Molyneux

(1880–1923)

Politician, diplomat, traveller, and secret agent, was born 3 April 1880 at Highclere Castle, Hampshire, the son of Henry Howard Molyneux Herbert, fourth Earl of Carnarvon, secretary of state for the colonies under Lord Derby (1866–7) and Disraeli (1874–8), and lord-lieutenant of Ireland under Lord Salisbury (1885–6), and his second wife Elisabeth Catharine ('Elsie'), daughter of Henry Howard of Greystoke Castle, Cumberland, his first cousin. Aubrey was the elder son (there were no daughters) by the second marriage, Lord Carnarvon already having had a son and three daughters by his first. Although born into a family of great wealth and influence, Herbert suffered an affliction of the eyes from an early age which made him effectively blind for much of his life. He scraped through the Eton of Dr Edmond Warre, under the particular care of Arthur Benson, his housemaster, without distinction, but in 1902 gained a first class in modern history at Balliol College, Oxford, where he also made a reputation for himself as a roof-climber, despite his blindness.

On leaving Oxford, he was secured the position of honorary attaché at the embassy in Tokyo in 1902, but never allowed himself to become much interested in Far Eastern affairs. It was his next appointment in March 1904, to the embassy in Constantinople, which fired his enthusiasm for the Middle East and settled the subsequent course of his brief but eventful life. He was the model for the eponymous hero of *Greenmantle* (1916) by John Buchan, first Baron Tweedsmuir.

On his marriage in 1910 to Mary Gertrude, only child of John Robert William Vesey, fourth Viscount de Vesci, and his wife Lady Evelyn Charteris, daughter of the tenth Earl of Wemyss, his mother gave him Pixton Park, in Somerset, with 5,000 acres, and a substantial family property in Portofino, Italy. Lady de Vesci gave them her splendid London house at 28 Bruton Street, and it was thought he should have a seat in Parliament. After twice contesting South Somerset in the Conservative interest in 1910, he won in the 'coupon' election of 1918 and remained an MP for the rest of his life, for South Somerset until 1918, and then for Yeovil.

Membership of the House of Commons did not interrupt his extensive travelling in the Middle East. Throughout 1911 his attention was focused almost exclusively on the Balkans, to which he travelled frequently, having many friends among remote inland brigands as well as among the cream of Kemal Atatürk's reformist movement in Constantinople. His tireless work for the cause of Albanian nationalism was rewarded in 1913 with the first of two enquiries on the point of whether he would be prepared to accept the throne of Albania, if it was formally offered to him. On this occasion Herbert was quite keen to accept, but H. H. Asquith, later first Earl of Oxford and Asquith (a close family friend), was not encouraging and Sir Edward Grey (later Viscount Grey of Fallodon), the foreign secretary, was against any British involvement in the Balkan tangle. The prize this time went to Prince William of Wied, representing the Austrian faction. He did not last six months. Herbert was largely responsible for the creation of the modern, independent state of Albania after World War I, championing the rights of the Albanians against the other Balkan states.

On the outbreak of World War I Herbert joined the Irish Guards, despite his near-blindness, by the simple method of buying himself a second lieutenant's uniform and falling in as the regiment boarded ship for France in August 1914. After being wounded and briefly taken prisoner during the retreat from Mons, he joined the Intelligence Bureau in Cairo, later known as the Arab Bureau, in December 1914 with T. E. Lawrence, who became a close friend and ally. As liaison officer and interpreter, he took part in the Gallipoli campaign in 1915. He found that his ready command of French, Italian, German, Turkish, Arabic, Greek, and Albanian, and his personal friendship with many of the key figures in the area, made his presence invaluable to the commander-in-chief, although eyebrows were sometimes raised at his unremittingly pro-Turkish stance. He spent the rest of the war in intelligence work in Mesopotamia, Salonika, and Italy.

By 1920, although still receiving the Conservative whip in Parliament, Herbert regarded himself as an Independent, formally crossing the floor on the Irish vote on 20 November and thereafter sitting on whichever side he felt inclined. Effectively he was immersed in Albanian politics, although in February 1921, at the request of Sir Basil Thomson of Scotland Yard's Special Branch, he travelled to Germany for a secret meeting with Talaat, the Turk generally held responsible for the post-war Armenian massacres. Later that year, in Constantinople, he found himself put under surveillance by British military intelligence, the task being entrusted to his nephew, Henry Herbert, Lord Porchester (later sixth Earl of Carnarvon).

Herbert's eccentricity was to dress as a tramp, and his appearance was further affected by his blindness and by a piebald hair coloration, after an early attack of alopecia. Herbert and his wife had one son and three daughters, the youngest of whom, Laura, was the wife of Evelyn Waugh. In the last year of his life, Herbert was revisited by the total blindness which had afflicted his earlier years. In 1923, at a Balliol gaudy, he met his old tutor, A. L. Smith, now the master, who advised him that the best cure for blindness was to have the teeth extracted. Following this advice, Herbert developed blood poisoning and died 23 September 1923 at his London home in Bruton Street.

[Desmond MacCarthy, *A Memoir*, 1924; Aubrey Herbert, *Mons, Anzac, and Kut*, 1919 (reprinted 1930 with introduction by Desmond MacCarthy); Aubrey Herbert, *Ben Kendim, a Record of Eastern Travel*, 1924; Margaret FitzHerbert, *The Man who was Greenmantle*, 1983; personal knowledge.]

AUBERON WAUGH

published 1993

Sir Samuel John Gurney

(1880–1959)

Second Baronet, and Viscount Templewood

Statesman, was born in London 24 February 1880, the elder son of (Sir) Samuel Hoare, later first baronet, member of Parliament for Norwich (1886–1906), of Sidestrand Hall, Norfolk, by his wife, Katharin Louisa Hart, daughter of Richard Vaughan Davis, commissioner of audit. Educated at Harrow and New College, Oxford, he obtained first classes in classical honour moderations (1901) and modern history (1903) and represented the university at rackets and lawn tennis. A member of an old Norfolk banking family he unsuccessfully contested Ipswich in 1906 and first entered Parliament as Conservative member for Chelsea in January 1910, retaining the constituency until 1944. He was assistant private secretary to Alfred Lyttelton, colonial secretary, in 1905; served on the London County Council from 1907 to 1910; and succeeded to the baronetcy in 1915.

During the war of 1914–18 Hoare served as a general staff officer with the rank of lieutenant-colonel in the military mission to Russia, 1916–17, and later to Italy, 1917–18. He was mentioned in dispatches and appointed C.M.G. in 1917. In *The Fourth Seal* (1930) he gave an account of his experiences in Russia.

Hoare was prominent amongst the group of Conservative members who brought about the break-up of the Lloyd George coalition in October 1922 and he became secretary of state for air in Bonar Law's Conservative administration, a post he was to hold no fewer than four times in the course of his political career. He was sworn of the Privy Council in November 1922. It fell to him, therefore, between 1922 and 1929, with the exception of the Labour interlude of 1924, to build up a new Service department in Whitehall and to shape the pattern of the Royal Air Force in the post-war period. His close association in this task with that formidable protagonist of an independent air force, Sir Hugh (later Viscount) Trenchard, is fully told in Hoare's book *Empire of the Air* (1957). Hoare saw very clearly the immense possibilities of air communications within the Empire, for both civilian and military purposes. He did much to persuade the public to be air-minded and was the first secretary of state for air to use aircraft as a normal method of travel. His arrival by air at Gothenburg in 1923 to attend the first International Aero Exhibition was considered to be something of an innovation. On Boxing Day 1926 he and his wife set off in an Imperial Airways de Havilland aeroplane on the first civil air flight to India, arriving in Delhi on 8 January 1927. In February his wife was appointed D.B.E. and in June he was appointed G.B.E. He published a short account of the flight, *India by Air* (1927).

With the formation of the 'national' Government in 1931 Hoare, who had been a member of the first Round Table conference, became secretary of state for India. He made a real effort during the second Round Table conference to find common ground with M. K. Gandhi. This met with a degree of reciprocity on Gandhi's part but the result fell a good deal short of what was needed for agreement on policy. For the next four years Hoare was occupied in the immense task of preparing the new Indian constitution. In 1933 a joint select committee of both Houses was set up to consider the white paper published as a result of the Round Table conference's proposals. It sat from April 1933 to November 1934, holding 159 meetings during which over 120 witnesses were examined; Hoare himself, as one of the principal witnesses, answered more than 10,000 questions in the course of his evidence in cross-examination. Lord Halifax recalled in his *Fulness of Days* that this was done 'with a grasp of his subject that in comparable circumstances can never have been surpassed and seldom equalled by any previous minister of the Crown'. There was a dramatic interlude in April 1934 when Churchill alleged that Hoare as secretary of state had exercised undue influence in persuading the Manchester Chamber of Commerce to alter its original evidence tendered to the joint select committee in respect of the Indian tariff duty on Lancashire cotton goods, which was thought likely to be increased in the context of the proposed new constitution for India. Churchill further alleged that the incident, which gave rise to his accusation of breach of parliamentary privilege, occurred at a dinner given by Lord Derby, himself a member of the joint select committee, to members of the Manchester Chamber of Commerce, at which Hoare was present. The committee of privileges, however, arrived at the unanimous verdict that there had been no breach of privilege.

The government of India bill which eventually received the royal assent in August 1935 contained 478 clauses and 16 schedules and was piloted through the House of Commons by Hoare in the face of bitter opposition from Churchill and the right wing of the Conservative Party. Hoare himself made a substantial proportion of the speeches which were over 1,900 in number. In 1934 he was appointed G.C.S.I.

When Baldwin succeeded MacDonald as prime minister in June 1935 he was in two minds whether to make Hoare viceroy of India or foreign secretary. Hoare expressed his preference for the former, but Baldwin finally decided to send him to the Foreign Office where he succeeded Sir John (later Viscount) Simon at a difficult period. Britain's defence forces had been cut to the bone by successive chancellors of the Exchequer and disarmament discussions at Geneva dominated the League of Nations. Meantime Germany, Italy, and Japan were flouting the Covenant and beginning to form a hostile and threatening bloc. The Manchurian crisis of 1931 had demonstrated that there was no military help forthcoming from the United States. In Britain the pacifist movement was at its height. Collective security, the popular panacea, in practice depended upon collective action by Britain and France. Since Britain was clearly too weak to risk becoming involved simultaneously with Germany and Japan, Hoare's policy was based upon gaining time to build up Britain's military strength and on keeping Italy isolated from Germany. His first step was to sign the Anglo-German naval agreement, designed to limit the German fleet to a ratio of 35 per cent of Britain's. His next problem was the Abyssinian crisis. The French repeatedly made it clear that they would not contemplate military action against Italy over Abyssinia. In a speech at the League Assembly on 11 September 1935 Hoare attempted to rally the League by emphasizing that collective security to be effective must be comprehensive. 'If the burden is to be borne, it must be borne collectively. If risks for peace are to be run, they must be run by all.' He gave a pledge that Britain would be 'second to none to fulfil' her obligations and he repeated again that the League and Britain with it stood for 'the collective maintenance of the Covenant'.

Although similar phrases used previously both in the House of Commons and outside had made no particular impression, this speech stirred the audience at Geneva and achieved wide publicity on the Continent and elsewhere. The effect, however, was short-lived, for Britain alone had taken any military precautions and it became abundantly clear that any temporary enthusiasm for further 'collective action' by other members of the League was confined to words. Later in September 'the committee of five' appointed by the League to mediate put forward proposals which were rejected by Mussolini who in October finally embarked upon the invasion of Abyssinia. After limited sanctions had been imposed against Italy by the League, the British and French Governments were deputed to seek some basis of agreement acceptable to both Italy and Abyssinia. (Sir) Maurice Peterson was sent to Paris where officials from both Foreign Offices set to work upon a plan. It was clear that any such agreement would have to be negotiated, not dictated, unless the League, which for all practical purposes meant Great Britain and France, were prepared to go to war with Italy. The French Government again reaffirmed that they would not take military action and Laval himself expressed the view that an oil embargo, if imposed, might well drive Mussolini to an act of war. It was understood that the two Governments were acting on behalf of the League to which any plan produced would be referred for approval.

In December 1935 Hoare who had been ill, was persuaded to break his journey in Paris on his way to Switzerland for a short holiday, in order to put the finishing touches to proposals which had been worked out. The ill-fated Hoare–Laval plan, as it subsequently became known, provided—first an effective outlet to the sea, with full sovereign rights for Abyssinia; secondly, the concession to Italy of some, but not all, of the territory in Tigre occupied by Italian forces together with other minor frontier rectifications; thirdly, a large zone in the south and south-west in which Italy, acting under the League, would have the monopoly of economic development; fourthly, the maintenance of Abyssinian sovereignty over all but the districts actually ceded to Italy; fifthly, the reference of the plan to the League for approval, or otherwise.

These proposals were considerably less than Mussolini's earlier demands. Hoare recommended them to the Cabinet for submission to the League and began his Swiss holiday. The plan 'leaked' into the French press on the following morning and when the details became known the reactions of the British press and of the rank and file of the Conservative Party were very violent, since the plan was considered to be a complete *volte-face* from the Geneva speech. The British Cabinet, having first agreed to accept the proposals, had second thoughts when they doubted the capacity of the Government to ride the storm. Baldwin asked Hoare to withdraw his approval of the plan but Hoare refused to do so and resigned. He held strongly that unless Britain was prepared without French support to declare war on Italy unilaterally, nothing short of these proposals would prevent the Italian occupation of the whole of Abyssinia, or satisfy Mussolini.

This was the turning-point of Hoare's political career. His reputation was much damaged in the eyes of the British public, who expected their foreign secretary to stop Mussolini in Abyssinia without involving Britain in the slightest risk of war, although no other member of the League of Nations was prepared to lift a finger against Italy, least of all France which was far more concerned with the growing menace of Germany.

Baldwin took Hoare back into the Government as first lord of the Admiralty in June 1936 and in the following May Hoare succeeded Simon as home secretary under Neville Chamberlain. Penal reform had been a tradition in his family since Samuel Hoare, his great-grandfather, and Elizabeth Fry, his great-great-aunt, together formed the first committee for supporting it. He took immense pains in preparing the criminal justice bill which obtained its second reading in December 1938. The bill introduced two new types of prison sentence: corrective training and preventive detention; it dealt with alternative punishment for juvenile offenders; and abolished judicial flogging. Its final stages were almost completed when the outbreak of war in September 1939 intervened. Nine years were to elapse before another home secretary piloted an essentially similar bill through the House of Commons.

As one of Chamberlain's senior cabinet ministers and closest associates Hoare was invited by Chamberlain to join an inner group of four ministers in September 1938 during the events which led to the Munich agreement. Throughout all the contemporary and subsequent controversy, Hoare stoutly defended the agreement, holding that without support from the French or from the Commonwealth, and with the Labour Party and public opinion at home bitterly opposed to military action over the Sudetenland, Britain was not in a position to declare war on her own against Germany until further progress had been made with rearmament. At the Home Office in the meantime he was recruiting for the A.R.P. services and for the W.V.S., an organization which owed much to his inspiration.

On the outbreak of war in September 1939 Hoare left the Home Office to become lord privy seal and a member of the War Cabinet. He was appointed for the fourth time secretary of state for air in April 1940. It was his last ministerial post and when Chamberlain resigned in May 1940 it was the end of Hoare's parliamentary career as a minister of the Crown but not the end of his career of public service. In the same month he was appointed ambassador to Spain, a post which he filled until December 1944, in critical circumstances in which he showed considerable skill and subtlety in dealing with the Spanish Government. Madrid was a great centre of both allied and enemy activity and Hoare and his staff succeeded in establishing a good enough relationship with the authorities to secure the release from Spanish prisons of some 30,000 allied prisoners of war and refugees from across the frontier.

Some months before his retirement Hoare was created Viscount Templewood. His Spanish mission marked the end of an exceptionally varied career, during which he had held more high offices of state than any other contemporary minister, with the exception of Churchill. He retired altogether from public life and, apart from making a few speeches in the House of Lords, lived quietly on his Norfolk estate. He had sold Sidestrand Hall a few years before the outbreak of war but retained the rest of the property. He built Templewood, a small classical villa in the Palladian style, on a beautiful site surrounded by his woods, three miles inland from the coast, to the design of his architect nephew, Paul Paget, a temple in a wood. It was typical of his tidiness of mind that the avenues were laid out and flowering shrubs planted long before work on the house itself was begun. All his life he had been a first-class shot and he continued to shoot with astonishing accuracy until a year before his death. He was immensely proud of his woods and shrubs of which he had a great knowledge. He was no mean naturalist. In his retirement he was a prolific writer. *Ambassador on Special Mission* (1946) described his time in Spain. *The Unbroken Thread* (1949) told family history of his forebears against a setting of sport and the Norfolk countryside. In *The Shadow of the Gallows* (1951) he set out his objections to capital punishment. *Nine Troubled Years* (1954) comprised his political memoirs between 1931 and 1940.

Hoare was chairman of the council of the Magistrates' Association, 1947–52; president of the Howard League for Penal Reform from 1947 until his death; president of the Lawn Tennis Association, 1932–56; and an elder brother of Trinity House. He received honorary degrees from Oxford, Cambridge, Reading, and Nottingham, and was chancellor of Reading University from 1937 until his death. He received a number of foreign decorations, was deputy-lieutenant and J.P. for Norfolk; and was awarded the silver medal for skating. His precise manner of speech, his extreme neatness of appearance, and his meticulous care for detail sometimes conveyed the impression of a certain lack of warmth and humour to those who did not know him well. In fact they were no more than superficial trappings which covered a kindness and understanding born of deep religious convictions. Although of Quaker ancestry he was brought up and remained in the Anglo-Catholic tradition. Throughout fifty years of happy married life he was sustained and encouraged by his wife, Lady Maud Lygon (died 1962), fifth daughter of the sixth Earl Beauchamp, whom he married in 1909. There were no children and, his younger brother having predeceased him, both the viscountcy and the baronetcy became extinct when Templewood died in London 7 May 1959.

A portrait of him in the uniform of an elder brother of Trinity House by A. C. Davidson-Houston was presented to him in 1956 by the Lawn Tennis Association and hangs at Templewood.

[Lord Templewood's own writings; private information; personal knowledge.]

CHARLES MOTT-RADCLYFFE

published 1971

HOLLIS Sir Roger Henry

(1905–1973)

Head of MI5, was born at Wells, Somerset, 2 December 1905, the third of the four sons (there were no daughters) of George Arthur Hollis, vice-principal of Wells Theological College and later bishop suffragan of

Taunton, and his wife, Mary Margaret, the daughter of Charles Marcus Church, canon of Wells, a grand-niece of R. W. Church, dean of St. Paul's. His elder brother, M. Christopher Hollis, one-time Conservative MP for Devizes, has described the early years of his family life in his autobiography, *The Seven Ages* (1974, p. 4): 'I grew up not merely as a clergyman's son, but in a cleric-inhabited society—in a sort of Trollopean world.'

Roger Hollis was educated at Leeds Grammar School, Clifton College, and Worcester College, Oxford. At school he was a promising scholar who went up to Oxford with a classical exhibition. But at Oxford he read English and in the view of his contemporaries seemed to prefer a happy social life to an academic one. In the memoirs of Evelyn Waugh he appears as 'a good bottle man' and in Sir Harold Acton's as an agreeable friend. Because of this easy-going approach and for no more dramatic reason, he went down four terms before he was due to take his finals.

After barely a year's work in the DCO branch of Barclays Bank he left England to become a journalist on a Hong Kong newspaper. This too proved a brief assignment and in April 1928 he transferred to the British American Tobacco Co. in whose service he remained for the following eight years of his residence in China. His work enabled him to travel widely in a country torn by the almost continuous conflict of Chinese warlords and Japanese invaders. His family possess an unusually complete collection of his letters home—dry and witty accounts of life in China, free of the travel romanticism then so much in vogue. A further insight into his Chinese experiences comes from the lecture he gave to the Royal Central Asian Society in October 1937 (see the society's *Journal*, vol. xxv, January 1938). Entitled 'The Conflict in China', it shows a considerable grasp of a complex situation. The nine formative years in China were terminated by an attack of tuberculosis which led to him being invalided out of the BAT and returned to England in 1936, and a further brief spell with the Ardath Tobacco Co., an associate of the BAT. On 10 July of the following year he was married in Wells Cathedral to Evelyn Esmé, daughter of George Champeny Swayne, of Burnham-on-Sea, Somerset, solicitor in Glastonbury. Their one child, Adrian Swayne Hollis, became a fellow and tutor in classics at Keble College, Oxford, and a chess player of international reputation.

Hollis began his new career in the security service in 1938. It was to last twenty-seven years and to constitute his most absorbing interest. By qualities of mind and character he was in several ways well adapted to it. He was a hard and conscientious worker, level-headed, fair-minded, and always calm. He began as a student of international communism, a field in which he was to become an acknowledged authority in the service. During the war, when the bulk of the service's talents and resources were committed to German, Italian, and Japanese counter-intelligence, he managed with small resources to ensure that the dangers of Russian-directed communism were not neglected. Consequently when the war was over and the security service turned to face the problems of the cold war, he had already become one of its key figures. In 1953 he was appointed deputy director-general and three years later, when his predecessor was unexpectedly transferred to other work, he inherited the top position.

It was a post which he was to hold with quiet efficiency for the next nine turbulent years. For the whole of that time the cold war was at its height and especially manifest in the field of Soviet espionage. Spy case followed spy case at the Old Bailey: Anthony Wraight, W. J. Vassall, George Blake, Harry Houghton, Ethel Gee, Gordon Lonsdale, and the Krogers became notorious figures, while in a different context the case of John Profumo caused great political consternation. Parallel with these events new sources of information became available to the security service from Russian and satellite defectors arriving in the West. These depicted the KGB in vast and threatening terms but were difficult to assess and only rarely provided sure and certain guidance. In the light of these events and circumstances the governments of the day felt the need to allay public and parliamentary concern over national security standards, and during his nine-year tenure of office as director-general Hollis had to face on behalf of his service three major official inquiries which both he and the service survived with considerable credit. Lord Denning, in the course of his memoirs later serialized in *The Times*, commented on the confidence he felt in Hollis during the inquiry for which he was responsible.

By the time he retired in 1965 Hollis had become a respected figure in Whitehall. He was similarly respected inside his own service (and others within the intelligence community), though he did not enjoy easy personal relations with its ordinary members who tended to find him reserved and aloof. Outside these two fields he was hardly known at all, which was exactly how he would have wished things to be and how they would have remained but for the misfortune that clouded the last years of his life.

On his retirement he moved first to a house in Wells which he occupied only until 1967. In 1968 his first marriage was dissolved and he married, secondly, Edith Valentine Hammond, his former secretary, the daughter of Ernest Gower Hammond, of Stratford-upon-Avon. They moved to a new home in the village of Catcott in Somerset. Here Hollis was able to indulge his formidable skills as a golfer and to undertake some modest jobs in local government. He was then suddenly asked to visit his old service where he learned that, as a result of information tending to imply a high-level penetration of the service, he had among others become a subject of investigation. He was asked to submit himself to interrogation and agreed. Members of a service in the front line of attack by the KGB can appreciate the need for secret enquiries of this kind at whatever rank they may apply. Unfortunately some of the facts became public because of internal leaks and in 1981 *Their Trade is Treachery*, by Chapman Pincher, was published. This book's picture of the Hollis investigation implied that the former director-general of the security service had probably been a Russian spy throughout his career in the service. Not unnaturally it provoked such an outcry in press and Parliament that Margaret Thatcher, the prime minister, had to intervene. On 25 March 1981 she informed the House of Commons that the outcome of the last Hollis investigation (by Lord Trend, secretary of the Cabinet from 1963 to 1973) had been the clearance of his name and reputation. The great public interest in the matter was a severe ordeal for Hollis's family and a sad aftermath to the career of a man who had worked so hard and responsibly at his job. Hollis died at Catcott 26 October 1973.

He was appointed OBE (1946), CB (1956), was knighted (1960), and was created KBE (1966).

[Private information; personal knowledge.]

DICK WHITE

published 1986

HORE-BELISHA (Isaac) Leslie

(1893–1957)

Baron Hore-Belisha

Politician, was born in London 7 September 1893, the only son of Jacob Isaac Belisha, an insurance company manager, and his wife, Elizabeth Miriam, daughter of John Leslie Miers. His father's family were Sephardic Jews who were driven out of Spain under the Inquisition and eventually settled in Manchester where they built up a cotton import firm. His grandfather, David Belisha, was one of the leading backers of the Ship Canal project, using up most of his fortune before it was finally carried through.

His father died when Hore-Belisha was less than a year old, and in 1912 his mother married (Sir) (Charles Fraser) Adair Hore who later became permanent secretary to the Ministry of Pensions. At his mother's desire he coupled his stepfather's surname to his own. She had devoted her life to him (long refusing to remarry for that reason) and continued to have a profound influence on him throughout his career. She made sacrifices in order to send him to Clifton College, for short periods to the Sorbonne and Heidelberg, and then to St. John's College, Oxford. At Clifton he made a mark in school debates, wrote vivid essays and also political verse which gained acceptance by the London press, attended the law courts in the holidays, and dreamed of becoming another Disraeli. At Oxford he quickly distinguished himself in Union debates, speaking on the Liberal side and as a Radical supporter of Lloyd George's social reforms. At the end of his first year war broke out. Enlisting in the Public Schools battalion of the Royal Fusiliers he soon gained a commission, in the Army Service Corps, and went to France early in November 1914, being attached to an infantry brigade in the 5th division. The skill and energy which he showed in developing local sources of supply led a year later to his appointment to the staff of the Third Army for that purpose and subsequently, with the rank of major, to army headquarters in Salonika. Early in 1918 he was invalided home with malaria.

Returning to Oxford he became a prominent figure and the first post-war president of the Union. On going down he read law, gaining the means to do so by a brilliantly quick success in journalism. Besides being a leader-writer on the *Daily Express*, he became a social and political diarist on the *Sunday Express*, starting 'The Londoner's Log' and then, under the signature 'Cross-Bencher', the commentary on 'Politics and Politicians.' He also wrote for the *Evening Standard* and the *Weekly Review*. Having made enough money for his purpose, he gave up journalism for a while to concentrate on his law studies. He was called to the bar by the Inner Temple in 1923. In the meantime he had been adopted as Liberal candidate for the Devonport division of Plymouth and in the general election in the autumn of 1922 had made a promisingly strong challenge to the Conservative member. In 1923 he won the seat, which he held until 1945. To meet his expenses he found it necessary to return to journalism and also, with less successful results, to accept directorships in sundry companies. He had too little time to study their affairs and was only interested in money as a means to greater ends. Their failure was remembered against him later in his career.

In contrast, he made an intensive study of the many aspects of national life which came under discussion in Parliament, and frequently took a different line from the majority of his party. In particular he argued against cuts in social and defence expenditure. When the general election of 1924 swept away most of the Liberal Party, he was the only member in the south of England who survived, and in 1929 he was returned by a much increased margin. During these years he advocated bold measures of reform, particularly in the relief of unemployment. He criticized the second Labour Government for doing too little rather than too much and his own leaders for giving it continued support. At a party conference in the spring of 1931 he led an unsuccessful revolt and when the financial crisis came he quickly took the lead in organizing a new Liberal National Party to support the 'national' Government formed by Ramsay MacDonald and Baldwin. After the general election, in which he trebled his majority, Hore-Belisha was made parliamentary secretary to the Board of Trade; he succeeded so well that in 1932 he was appointed financial secretary to the Treasury at the special request of Neville Chamberlain who had found him of great help in working out tariff arrangements and now wanted his closer co-operation in steering the Ottawa agreements through the Commons. Hore-Belisha's grasp of the matter and his skill in debate and at subsequent international conferences rapidly increased his reputation for successfully tackling tough problems.

In 1934 when the road traffic bill had passed its third reading Hore-Belisha moved to the Ministry of Transport where he developed its provisions in fresh and impressive ways towards checking the rising toll of accidents. He extended the use of pedestrian crossings and introduced the illuminated amber globes mounted on black and white posts which were promptly christened 'Belisha beacons'. He put into force the provision for driving tests for new motorists; a revised highway code was brought out; and by these and other measures, and not least by the publicity which they received, he brought about a notable reduction in accidents. Looking to the future he sponsored extensive plans of new arterial road building, and as a preliminary transferred the care of the existing trunk roads from the county councils to the State. In 1935 he was sworn of the Privy Council and in 1936 raised to cabinet rank. In May 1937 Chamberlain, on becoming prime minister, transferred him to the War Office 'on the express ground', says his biographer, 'that he wished to see "drastic changes", writing "the obstinacy of some of the Army heads in sticking to obsolete methods is incredible"'.

Within a few months Hore-Belisha embarked on an extensive programme of reforms. He stimulated recruiting by increasing rates of pay and allowances, raising the standard of catering, modernizing barracks and building better ones, abolishing outworn restrictions upon the soldiers' freedom off duty, shortening the extent of service abroad, and providing more opportunity of training for a civilian trade. For officers up to the rank of major inclusive a time-scale was introduced which brought quicker promotion; the half-pay system was abolished; and the age limit of retirement for generals and colonels lowered. The cadet colleges were amalgamated, new tactical schools and courses provided, and facilities for staff training increased. Other reforms included the simplification of infantry drill, the introduction of battle-dress, and the fusion of the Cavalry and Royal Tank Corps in the Royal Armoured Corps. Much was done also to raise the status and standard of the Territorial Army.

At the same time Hore-Belisha sought to hasten the re-equipment and mechanization of the army and its tactical reorganization, and to develop its capacity for defence against air attack. The roles of the army were for the first time defined in order of priority, and the principle was adopted of regional strategic reserves in the Middle and Far East. Both the Middle East force and the larger strategic reserve maintained at home for the expeditionary force were intended to be primarily of a mobile armoured type likely to be more effective than infantry in a desert campaign and a more potent aid to European allies. These measures were not carried out as fast as Hore-Belisha desired or the situation demanded. After six months in office he sought, with Chamberlain's backing, to quicken the pace by appointing younger generals to the Army Council. The new men proved helpful in carrying out the lesser reforms which most soldiers had long desired; but they had been trained in the old school and when Hore-Belisha pressed measures of wider scope he soon found their hesitant acquiescence as frustrating as the direct resistance of their predecessors. Friction developed between him and his chosen official advisers who in their resentment at being pressed took little account of the frequent concessions to their point of view which he made, sometimes to the impairment of his plans. Nor were they mollified by his bigger change of course in April 1939 when he urged the Cabinet to introduce conscription in order to provide, as his official advisers and the French desired, a large army on the 1914–18 lines instead of the mechanized expeditionary force of high quality but smaller scale which had originally been envisaged.

Appreciation of his concessions was submerged by accumulated irritation over the way he prodded the generals, summoned them to meetings at short notice and inconvenient times, kept them waiting, expected them to be ready with detailed information and advice, and sometimes took quick decisions or made public announcements which committed them to steps for which they were not prepared. Such was the substance of their complaints, aggravated by dislike of forms of appeal to the public which they considered showmanship and self-advertisement. The habit of deference to superior authority prevented them from making their sentiments plain to Hore-Belisha, but their complaints were expressed very freely to influential circles outside the War Office and received a ready hearing among his political critics and rivals. Like most vivid personalities Hore-Belisha could arouse strong feelings.

By the time war came Lord Gort, Hore-Belisha's own choice as chief of the imperial general staff, had reached a state of acute irritation which was but temporarily allayed when he went to France as commander-in-chief of the Expeditionary Force. Even during the first month of war moves were being made for the ejection of the war minister, and the conflict was brought nearer the surface in November by Gort's explosive reaction to some critical remarks of Hore-Belisha's about the slow progress of the defences in France, following similar but sharper criticisms which the Cabinet had received from two war-experienced dominion ministers, R. G. (later Lord) Casey of Australia and Deneys Reitz of South Africa, who had visited the front. Gort's complaints were taken up with the prime minister by the King and other very influential persons at home, while the French commander-in-chief signified his solidarity with Gort over the defences. Chamberlain asked Hore-Belisha whether he wished to change the commander-in-chief or the chief of the imperial general staff. Hore-Belisha, however, did not wish to take advantage of this opportunity and hoped that relations would improve. The prime minister himself went to France in an attempt to allay friction; but the storm did not abate and eventually, in the interest of harmony, he reluctantly decided to transfer Hore-Belisha. On 4 January 1940, telling him that 'there existed a strong prejudice against him for which I could not hold him altogether blameless', Chamberlain offered him the Board of Trade. Hore-Belisha preferred to resign, and in a letter to Chamberlain that evening wrote: 'you have been categorically assured that there is no reason whatever for anxiety about a German break-through. Yet my visits to France have convinced me that unless we utilize the time that is still available to us with far more vision and energy, the Germans will attack us on our weak spot somewhere in the gap between the Maginot Line and the sea.' (Sir) Winston Churchill records in his memoirs that Hore-Belisha had on several occasions drawn the attention of the Cabinet to the weakness of the Ardennes sector south of the British line where the Germans in fact pierced the front four months later. Hore-Belisha ended '... if I explain, as is usual with retiring Ministers, the reason for my departure, I shall be giving to the enemy information about the weakness of our defences and, if I do not, I lay the reason open to conjecture and perhaps to misrepresentation ... this will be the real measure of the sacrifice which I am called on to make.'

The news of his resignation came as a shock to the nation and it became very evident that most of the press and many of the public were strongly in favour of Hore-Belisha who was considered to have been one of the ablest members of Chamberlain's administration; but by abstaining from explanation he gave them no grounds upon which to support him. He resigned in March from the chairmanship of the National Liberal parliamentary party which he had held since its inception, and it was not until 1945 that he returned to office, when Churchill included him in his 'caretaker' Government as minister of national insurance, in an effort to provide an alternative to the Labour Party's social policy. But Labour won the election and Hore-Belisha himself lost his seat. He was then persuaded to join the Conservative Party, but nothing was done to provide him with a likely seat, and although he fought Coventry South in 1950 he was not successful. The prolonged absence from the House was fatal to his political prospects. In 1954 he accepted a peerage, and began to exert a renewed influence by his speeches in the House of Lords and chairmanship of committees, but this was cut short by his sudden death at Reims, 16 February 1957, when leading a parliamentary delegation on a visit to France.

Hore-Belisha's career reached its peak when he was only forty-three and virtually ended when he was forty-six. Its untimely end was due more to 'natural causes' than to the faults attributed to him. Urgent action was essential in 1937 in view of the impending danger of war. But it was natural that each particular change was repugnant to some section of military opinion, even though welcome to most, and the cumulative effect tended to produce an atmosphere of hostility. It was increased by the pace at which the changes had to be pushed through. Chamberlain recorded that he sent him to the War Office because he had 'very exceptional qualities of courage, imagination, and drive ... he has done more for the Army than anyone since Haldane'. But he added: 'Unfortunately, he has the defects of his qualities—partly from his impatience and eagerness, partly from a self-centredness which makes him careless of other people's feelings.' Anyone who worked closely with Hore-Belisha often felt exasperation, but there were those who found that with deepening association it gave way to a growing blend of admiration and affection. The lack of patience and understanding shown by Gort and his fellows was the more regrettable since it is clear that more overdue and beneficial reforms were achieved in Hore-Belisha's years of office than in the previous twenty years.

Hore-Belisha married in 1944 Cynthia, daughter of the late Gilbert Elliot, of Hull Place, Sholden, Kent. There were no children and the peerage became extinct.

A portrait by Clarence White was exhibited at the Royal Academy in 1936.

[Keith Feiling, *The Life of Neville Chamberlain*, 1946; Sir Francis de Guingand, *Operation Victory*, 1947; Sir John Kennedy, *The Business of War*, ed. Bernard

Fergusson, 1957; John W. Wheeler-Bennett, *King George VI*, 1958; R. J. Minney, *The Private Papers of Hore-Belisha*, 1960; private information; personal knowledge.]

B. H. LIDDELL HART

published 1971

JENKINS John Edward

(1838–1910)

Politician and satirist, born at Bangalore, Mysore, Southern India, on 28 July 1838, was the eldest son of John Jenkins, D.D., Wesleyan missionary, by his wife Harriette, daughter of James Shepstone of Clifton. His father removed to Canada, where he became minister of St. Paul's Presbyterian church, Montreal, and moderator of the general assembly. The son, after having been educated at the High School, Montreal, and McGill University, and later at the University of Pennsylvania, came to London, and was called to the bar at Lincoln's Inn on 17 Nov. 1864. He secured some practice, and in 1870 he was retained by the Aborigines Protection and Anti-Slavery Society to watch the proceedings of the British Guiana coolie commission. He visited the colony and became the champion of the Indian indentured labourers there, publishing in 1871 'The Coolie: his Rights and Wrongs'. His zeal for social reform, however, turned him aside from his profession, and in 1870 he suddenly became famous as the anonymous author of 'Ginx's Baby, his Birth and other Misfortunes', a pathetic satire on the struggles of rival sectarians for the religious education of a derelict child, which attracted universal notice and had its influence on the religious compromise in the Education Act of 1870. An edition, the 36th, of 'Ginx's Baby' (1876) was illustrated by Frederick Barnard.

Jenkins was a strong imperialist and in 1871 he organised the 'Conference on Colonial Questions' which met at Westminster under his chairmanship. His inaugural address was entitled 'The Colonies and Imperial Unity: or the Barrel without the Hoops'. This originated the Imperial Federation movement as opposed to the policy of imperial disintegration advocated by Prof. Goldwin Smith and others, and led in 1874 to Jenkins's appointment as first agent-general in London for the dominion of Canada, an office which he held only two years. His imperialism did not, however, hinder him from protesting against the Act by which Queen Victoria became in 1876 empress of India, when he published anonymously 'The Blot on the Queen's Head' (1876). Notwithstanding his imperialism Jenkins was an ardent radical with political ambition. After unsuccessfully contesting in the radical interest Stafford and Truro, he was during his absence in Canada returned at the general election of 1874 as member of parliament for Dundee, and retained the seat until the dissolution of 1880. He then at a by-election in January 1881 contested Edinburgh as an independent liberal, but was defeated by Lord McLaren, then lord advocate. Subsequently, his dislike for Gladstone's views in imperial politics overcame his radicalism in home politics, and in 1885 he attempted to recover his seat for Dundee as a conservative, but he failed both then and in 1896. He was a fluent and popular speaker. He served on the royal commission on copyright in 1876–7.

Jenkins, who wrote articles on 'Imperial Federation' in the 'Contemporary Review' for 1871, made some unsuccessful attempts to repeat the popular success of 'Ginx's Baby', publishing 'Lord Bantam', a satire on a young aristocrat in democratic politics (2 vols. 1871); 'Barney Geoghegan, M.P., and Home Rule at St. Stephen's', reprinted with additions from 'Saint Paul's Magazine' (1872); 'Little Hodge', supporting the agitation led by Joseph Arch on behalf of the agricultural labourer (1872); 'Glances at Inner England', a lecture (1874); 'The Devil's Chain', a tale (1876); 'Lutchmee and Dilloo', a tale (3 vols. 1877); 'The Captain's Cabin, a Christmas Yarn' (1877); 'A Paladin of Finance', a novel (1882); 'A Week of Passion: or, The Dilemma of Mr. George Barton the Younger', a novel (3 vols. 1884); 'A Secret of Two Lives', a novel (1886), and 'Pantalas and what they did with him', a tale (1897). He was from 1886 editor of the 'Overland Mail' and the 'Homeward Mail', newspapers of which his brother-in-law, Sir Henry Seymour King, is the proprietor. From the beginning of Sir Henry King's political career he acted as his parliamentary secretary.

Jenkins died in London on 4 June 1910, after some years' suffering from paralysis. He married in 1867 Hannah Matilda, daughter of Philip Johnstone of Belfast, and left a family of five sons and two daughters.

[*The Times*, and *Morning Post*, 6 June 1910; *Overland Mail*, 10 June 1910; *Dod's Parliamentary Companion*; Brit. Mus. Cat.; Sir Leslie Stephen, *Life of Sir James Fitzjames Stephen*.]

R. E. GRAVES

published 1912

(1870–1955)

Civil servant, administrator, and author, was born 27 September 1870 at Rhymney, a border mining village in Monmouthshire, the eldest of the nine children of David Benjamin Jones, who worked in the truck shop of the Rhymney Iron Company, and his wife, Mary Ann, daughter of Enoch Jones, a Rhymney storekeeper. His father was a Cardiganshire man, his mother was half Cardiganshire and half Somersetshire. After his early education at Rhymney board-school and the Lewis School, Pengam, Jones began work as a timekeeper-clerk with the Rhymney Iron Company. His passion for reading had been roused by one of his teachers and it was nurtured by Rhymney's active Welsh literary life. This was centred in its churches and chapels, in his case Brynhyfryd Welsh Calvinistic Methodist chapel. He was Scripture gold-medallist and a promising preacher when in 1890 he entered the University College of Wales, Aberystwyth, where he became outstanding in its cultural and social life. He achieved London matriculation with difficulty but repeatedly failed in mathematics at the Intermediate level. In 1895 he migrated to Glasgow University, where the professor of moral philosophy, (Sir) Henry Jones, rated him 'the best student I have ever had amongst my pupils'. In 1900 'Tom' Jones graduated, was elected Clark scholar, awarded a Bertrand Russell studentship at the London School of Economics and Political Science, and began examining in economics at the university of St. Andrews. He was placed in the first class in the honour school of economic science at Glasgow in 1901.

By this time Jones had given up preaching, partly under the influence of Henry Jones, but mainly because evangelicalism had lost its appeal and the prospects of an exclusively ecclesiastical career repelled him. In 1895 he joined the Independent Labour Party and the Fabian Society and became a close student of the problems of poverty. For some time he lived and worked in social settlements in Glasgow and Cardiff. This interest in social work became lifelong, but his family and not a few Nonconformists regretted the loss of an outstanding preacher.

In 1899 William Smart, the professor of political economy at Glasgow, made Jones a part-time assistant. In the following year he became a university assistant in political economy and so remained until 1909. He was Barrington visiting lecturer in Ireland (1904–5) and a special investigator for the royal commission on the Poor Law (1906–9). He became professor of economics in the Queen's University, Belfast, in 1909, but on the invitation of David (later Lord) Davies he returned to Wales in 1910 to become the secretary of the Welsh campaign against tuberculosis later known as the King Edward VII Welsh National Memorial Association. Two years later he became the first secretary of the National Health Insurance Commission (Wales).

Davies and his sisters, Gwendoline and Margaret, had great wealth, which they used with a high sense of social responsibility. They found in their fellow Calvinist a trusted adviser. In the case of the two sisters this developed into a close friendship which was immensely profitable to the cultural life of Wales. Jones helped to start the *Welsh Outlook* and edited it from its beginning in 1914 until 1916. During these years he was a treasurer of the Welsh district of the Workers' Educational Association and a governor of the University College of Wales, Aberystwyth, the National Library of Wales, and the National Museum of Wales.

His work in the National Health Insurance Commission brought him to the notice of Lloyd George who, when he became prime minister in December 1916, made Jones first assistant secretary (later deputy secretary) of the Cabinet. He held this office until 1930. He was a member of the cabinet reconstruction committee in 1917. In the Irish troubles his services as an official negotiator were acceptable to both sides, and with Lionel Curtis he was secretary to the British delegation at the conference on Ireland, 11 October–6 December 1921. Throughout the industrial unrest and economic depression of the twenties, and during the general strike, he exercised great influence behind the scenes. His experience, academic training, and wide range of personal acquaintances made him one of the best-informed civil servants of his day. His integrity, insight, and judgement made him the trusted counsellor of three of the four prime ministers whom he served—Lloyd George, Bonar Law, and Stanley Baldwin; his relations with Ramsay MacDonald were less happy.

Jones refreshed himself from the burdens of a busy official life with a round of good works spontaneously undertaken. His friendship with Lord Astor and Lady Astor introduced him to the company of eminent and distinguished leaders in many walks of life; some accepted him as a guide to philanthropy who was ready to ease opulent consciences. In the days of post-war reconstruction he was alert to the interests of the university of Wales and other cultural institutions in the principality. He helped to establish the Gregynog Press which between 1923 and 1940 published 42 limited editions of finely printed books. He was the principal founder (1927), chairman, and later president of Coleg Harlech (the residential college for adult education at Harlech). From 1921 to 1955 he was a commissioner for the Royal Commission for the Exhibition of 1851.

In 1930 Jones became the first secretary of the Pilgrim Trust, serving until 1945, and thereafter until 1952 was a trustee, and (1952–4) chairman. He was chairman of the South Wales coalfield distress committee, and a member (1934–40) of the Unemployment Assistance Board. In 1933 he was a member of the unemployment committee of the National Council of Social Service which was largely subsidized from public funds to undertake recreational and rehabilitation work in the depressed areas. Hundreds of clubs were organized in these areas and several social settlements, which usefully survived into happier days, were founded. His leadership of various voluntary movements in the attack upon the demoralizing effects of unemployment was positive, humane, and for a host of people redeeming. He was chairman of the York Trust (1934–40) and of the Elphin Lloyd Jones Trust (1933–45).

In May 1936 Jones was invited to pay a visit to Germany where he had an interview with Hitler. He tried to bring about a meeting between Baldwin and Hitler, and accompanied Lloyd George on his visit in September. In 1939 he was the prime mover in the establishment of the Council for the Encouragement of Music and the Arts (which became the Arts Council of Great Britain) and was its first deputy chairman (1939–42). He was chairman of the Royal Commission on Ancient Monuments in Wales (1944–8). When the *Observer* Trust was founded in 1946 he became a founder-trustee.

In October 1944 Jones was elected president of the University College of Wales, Aberystwyth, and from 1945 to 1954 he lived in Aberystwyth. He strove to develop the college as a centre of advanced learning and of Celtic studies. After resigning from the presidency he moved to Manor End, St. Nicholas-at-Wade, near Birchington, Kent, a place dear to him because he had built a cottage there in the early twenties. He continued to correspond with a wide circle of friends and busied himself with his literary reliquiae. His literary output was considerable: some of his occasional addresses appeared in pamphlet form; and he edited a volume of Mazzini's essays for the Everyman's Library (1907), William Smart's *Second Thoughts of an Economist* (1916), and Sir Henry Jones's *Old Memories* (1922). His other works included *A Theme with Variations* (1933), the mainly autobiographical *Rhymney Memories* (1938), *Cerrig Milltir* (1942), *Leeks and Daffodils* (1942), *Welsh Broth* (1951), and *A Diary with Letters, 1931–1950* (1954). In 1951 he published his biography of Lloyd George, the notice of whom he also wrote for this Dictionary as well as those of Bonar Law and Baldwin. His political diaries (1916–30) were edited by Keith Middlemas and published in two volumes under the title *Whitehall Diary* in 1969, to be followed by a third volume dealing with Irish affairs.

Jones was appointed C.H. in 1929 and was elected a member of the Athenaeum in 1931. His native village of Rhymney honoured him with a public testimonial (1939) and he received honorary degrees from the universities of Glasgow (1922), Wales (1928), St. Andrews (1947), and Birmingham (1955). He was awarded the medal of the Honourable Society of Cymmrodorion in 1945, and in 1950, on the occasion of his eightieth birthday, an impressive company gathered in the dining-room of the House of Lords to do him honour.

In appearance Jones was firmly built, of medium height, with a quick, alert gait. In youth his hair was brown but it turned white somewhat prematurely. His eyes were large, lively, and grey-blue in colour. He was awkward with his hands and played no games. He was careless about his appearance but fastidious in his personal habits. He had a musical, light baritone voice which was pleasant to the ear. In his later years he avoided much public speaking. His style was conversational, crisp, and whimsical; his addresses were prepared with nervous care. His industry was immense, his use of time remorseless. His reading was serious and consistent—it ranged widely and was garnered into notebooks for ready reference. His Welsh upbringing never left him. His early Calvinism rooted him in Christian morality; his philosophy made the pursuit of the good, the beautiful, and the true the accepted ends of life; his knowledge of economics gave them a context in his day and generation. He was always on the lookout for promising persons and he helped them regardless of social distinctions. No conversation or person was safe from his disinterested exploitation. He turned many friendly gatherings into committees of ways and means. He acted swiftly and took short cuts. Occasionally he opened his ears to the wrong people; he consistently cultivated the right ones. His range of friends and acquaintances was exceptionally wide—to them he was known as 'T.J.' Throughout his life he was a diligent letter-writer. To his friends everywhere, notably in Rhymney and in the United States which he visited several times, he sent innumerable messages. Their quality may be seen in *A Diary with Letters* in which he candidly admitted that he had enjoyed 'the plutocratic embrace'.

In 1902 Jones married Eirene Theodora (died 1935), daughter of Richard John Lloyd, D.Lit., reader in phonetics at Liverpool. There were three children: a daughter and two sons. The daughter, Mrs. Eirene Lloyd White, became Labour M.P. for East Flint in 1950, minister of state for foreign affairs (1966), for the Welsh Office (1967). The elder son, Tristan Lloyd Jones, became manager of the *Observer*. The younger son, Elphin Lloyd Jones, was killed in a motoring accident in 1928. In June 1955 Jones himself fell indoors at his home and was seriously injured. He died in London 15 October 1955; his remains were cremated.

The National Museum of Wales has drawings of Jones by Paul Artot (1914) and S. Morse Brown (1938), and a portrait by Ivor Williams (1939). The National Library of Wales has a bust by L. S. Merrifield (1929) and the Newport (Mon.) Museum and Art Gallery has one by Siegfried Charoux (1939). The University College of Wales, Aberystwyth, has a portrait by E. Perry (1951); Coleg Harlech has one by Murray Urquhart (1944). Mrs. Eirene White has a drawing by (Sir) William Rothenstein (1923) and a portrait by R. O. Dunlop (1929). Mr. Tristan Lloyd Jones has a portrait by John Merton (1937).

[Thomas Jones's own writings; private information; personal knowledge.]

B. B. THOMAS

published 1971

KENYATTA Jomo

(1890s–1978)

African nationalist and first president of Kenya, was born at the advent of British colonial rule in East Africa in the 1890s (the exact date of birth is unknown) to Muigai, a Kikuyu farmer, and his wife Wambiu, at Ngenda, in the north-eastern part of the Kiambu district. He spent his early childhood in traditional Kikuyu peasant homesteads. Early an orphan, he was called Kamau wa Ngengi; he lived with his father's brother, Ngengi, and then his grandfather, Kongo wa Magana, a tribal medicine-man.

In November 1909 Kenyatta became one of the earliest boarders at the newly founded Scottish mission at Thogota (near Nairobi). At the end of his formative years he was baptized Johnstone Kamau in 1914, but he had retained his traditional ties to his people by being initiated into his tribal age-grade (Mubengi) in 1913. After completing his primary education, the young Kenyatta held a number of jobs in Nairobi and the surrounding area during the next fourteen years, of which the most important was with the Nairobi Water Department in the 1920s. He married his first wife, Grace Wahu, in 1919; this union produced a son and a daughter. (His daughter, Margaret Wambui, was mayor of Nairobi from 1969 to 1976.)

Now known as Johnstone Kenyatta, he embarked in 1928 on his political career as general secretary of the aspiring Kikuyu Central Association (KCA) as well as the first editor of the Kikuyu vernacular monthly, *Muigwithania*, 'The Unifier.' In 1929–30 he spent some eighteen months primarily in Britain, representing the KCA, presenting its grievances and promoting its aims. During this period he made his first trip to the Soviet Union; he also visited Germany, France, and Holland.

In 1931 Kenyatta returned to Britain with Parmenas Mockerie on behalf of the KCA to give evidence before the joint parliamentary commission on closer union in East Africa, but they were not asked to testify. This time Kenyatta remained for fifteen years, during which he matured into a confident and commanding leader. He wrote articles and letters to the press, attended the Quaker College of Woodbrook, Selly Oak (1932), and gave evidence to the Carter land commission prior to its departure for Kenya. In 1932–3 he made a second visit to the Soviet Union and then later travelled to various European countries.

In London Kenyatta associated with a number of Pan-Africanists, including George Padmore, T. R. Makonnen, and C. L. R. James, who championed Ethiopia's plight in its struggle against conquest by Italy, and in 1937 founded the International Africa Service Bureau to advance the ideas of Pan-Africanism and self-determination. A student of Malinowski's at the London School of Economics, Kenyatta published a study of Kikuyu customs and practices in 1938. Entitled *Facing Mount Kenya*, it remains an important anthropological document of the Kikuyu people. By now he had dropped 'Johnstone' in favour of 'Jomo'. The banning of the KCA in 1940 and the exile of its main leaders to the northern part of the country cut Kenyatta's channels of communication with Kenya. He spent part of World War II in Sussex farming and lecturing to British troops about Africa. He was married in 1942 to Edna Grace Clarke—his second wife—and in 1943 their son, Peter Magana, was born. Before answering a call to return to Kenya, he took part in the sixth Pan-African Congress (1946) in Manchester.

In 1946 Kenyatta returned to Kenya, leaving his wife behind (she only visited Kenya at independence), and he became president of the Kenya African Union (KAU) in 1947, articulating a concept of Kenyan nationalism, although the organizational base of the movement was largely among the Kikuyu. The immediate post-war period was one of an expanding conflict between Africans, especially Kikuyu, and Europeans. The KAU sought increased and elected representation in the Legislative Council and a resolution of major African land grievances. As the politics of moderation gave way increasingly to violence in the early 1950s, Kenyatta was accused of leading a secret movement known as 'Mau Mau'. A state of emergency was declared on 20 October 1952, and Kenyatta, along with several colleagues in the Kenya African Union, was arrested and charged with heading 'Mau Mau'. He was unjustly convicted of this charge on 8 April 1953. The evidence on which he was convicted was later proven to be false, and he spent the next seven years in prison and two additional years under restriction in the northern desert part of Kenya.

While Kenyatta was detained there developed a new nationalism, far more national in character and organization, which embraced leaders and followers from many ethnic groups. However, the colonial government refused to permit a national African organization to exist, and by 1958 Kenyatta again had become the symbol of Kenyan nationalism and unity. In early 1960 Britain made a critical decision to allow Kenya to become an African-governed state, and the first general election took place in February 1961 with Kenyatta as the *de facto* leader of the dominant Kenya African National Union (KANU).

The British colonial government continued to regard Kenyatta as a 'leader into darkness and death', but it finally had to release him from restriction in August 1961. He assumed the presidency of KANU in October 1961, entered Parliament in January 1962 as leader of the opposition, and led KANU to the London constitutional conference, February–March 1962. In April 1962 he joined the transitional coalition government as minister of state for constitutional affairs and economic planning, and in June 1963 KANU won the internal self-government election with Kenyatta becoming prime minister. On 12 December 1963 Kenya became independent with Kenyatta as prime minister, and a year later the Republic of Kenya was established and Kenyatta became president.

Kenyatta ruled Kenya for fourteen years, during which he faced no serious challenges. He was a moderately conservative 'presidential monarch' who elevated the presidency to a far more powerful institution than anticipated in the independence constitution of 1963. Though parliament was clearly not supreme, it none the less remained a vital forum for political debate and the expression of public attitudes. An Africanized provincial administration 'modelled' on that of the colonial period became the president's direct personal link with the people and the critical channel of rule. The spirit of his administration from the beginning was one of conciliation and unity which did much to heal the inter-racial wounds of the 'Mau Mau' emergency of the 1950s. A grass-roots democracy persisted within the framework of a *de facto* one-party state. There was genuine competition in the elections of representatives to the national parliament, and many members and ministers suffered electoral defeats. But Kenyatta himself was above the electoral struggle.

Kenyatta did not radically alter Kenya's economy after independence, although major efforts were made to expand and Africanize important sectors. To some, Kenyatta's favouring of private enterprise and foreign investment resulted in a neo-colonial economy of marked inequalities in wealth and opportunity; to others that strategy accelerated the comparatively high rate of economic growth Kenya enjoyed during his presidency. His greatest contribution was building the foundations for a Kenyan state and establishing the authority of the national government.

Pan-Africanism to Kenyatta was primarily the ending of colonial rule. He was a founding member of the Organization of African Unity (OAU), but he did not play a prominent role in continental politics. In 1964 he sought to bring about a reconciliation between rival Congolese leaders, and again in 1975 he endeavoured to negotiate a compact between Angola's competing leaders and groups. Both efforts, however, ended in failure. The East African Community also collapsed during his regime (1977) but it is doubtful that Kenyatta was seriously concerned. A strong and orderly Kenya was his major goal, not regional unification.

As a political leader Kenyatta was a commanding figure, able to capture the loyalty of the African masses while dominating would-be rivals. He refused to pick a successor, but his passing led to a succession in which the constitution's provisions were observed, rather than the struggle for power which was widely expected. His death at Mombasa, 22 August 1978, was noted throughout the world, attesting to his stature as a leading African nationalist and statesman.

Kenyatta married Grace, daughter of Senior Chief Koinange, soon after returning to Kenya in 1946. She died in childbirth. In 1951, he married for the final time the daughter of Chief Muhoho, Ngina. They had two sons and three daughters.

In July 1974 Kenyatta became life president of KANU. His other honours included an honorary fellowship of the London School of Economics; a knighthood of St. John, 1972; the Order of the Golden Ark of the World Wildlife Fund, 1974; and honorary LL Ds of the University of East Africa (1965) and Manchester University (1966).

[Jeremy Murray-Brown, *Kenyatta*, New York, 1973; Jomo Kenyatta, *Suffering Without Bitterness: The Founding of the Kenya Nation*, Nairobi, 1968; Carl G. Rosberg and John Nottingham, *The Myth of 'Mau Mau': Nationalism in Kenya*, 1966; F. D. Corfield, *Historical Survey of the Origins and Growth of Mau Mau* (Cmnd. 1030), 1960; personal knowledge.]

CARL G. ROSBERG

published 1986

Sir Ivone Augustine

(1897–1964)

Diplomatist, was born in Wellington, India, 3 February 1897, the elder son of Colonel Ivone Kirkpatrick of the South Staffordshire Regiment, a descendant of a branch of a Scottish family which had settled in Ireland in the eighteenth century. But his talents for public service may have come more from his mother, the daughter of (General Sir) Arthur Edward Hardinge, later commander-in-chief, Bombay Army, and governor of Gibraltar. She was a former maid of honour to Queen Victoria. Her grandfather, Viscount Henry Hardinge, served in the Cabinets of Wellington and Peel, and was later governor-general of India, 1844–8. Her first cousin, Charles Hardinge, Baron Hardinge of Penshurst, was permanent under-secretary of the Foreign Office, 1906–10 and 1916–20, and viceroy of India, 1910–16. Ivone Kirkpatrick spent much time with his mother between the ages of seven and ten in Switzerland, Belgium, and Germany, learning French and German.

Kirkpatrick, a Roman Catholic through his mother, went to Downside in 1907. He was commissioned in the Royal Inniskilling Fusiliers in November 1914, when he was still only seventeen years old. He was severely wounded in action against the Turks in August 1915. Fit for duty six months later, he spent the rest of the war on intelligence and propaganda work, the last year of it in neutral Holland in charge of a network of British agents operating in German-occupied territory. In February 1919 he passed the Foreign Office examination.

After a year in Brazil Kirkpatrick spent the unprecedentedly long period of ten years in the Western Department of the Foreign Office. In these years he made his reputation as a rapid, reliable, and incisive worker, eager for responsibility. He gained experience of international negotiations, and became well known to senior officials and ministers.

After three years in Rome (1930–3), Kirkpatrick went in August 1933 as head of Chancery (first secretary) to Berlin. There he remained for over five years, as chief of staff to two very different ambassadors, Sir Eric Phipps and (from April 1937) Sir Nevile Henderson. By his personality, his energy, his wide range of German acquaintance, he acquired in Berlin a position of real authority and influence. His long service there culminated in the Czechoslovakian crisis and the Munich settlement. In his memoirs (*The Inner Circle*, 1959), Kirkpatrick made clear his detestation of the Nazis and his conviction that they must be resisted, while leaving open the question whether they should have been opposed at the time of Munich.

However, his views seem to have made little impression on those of Sir Nevile Henderson. Kirkpatrick was loyal to his service and political chiefs, and accepted his duty to authority. He wrote of Henderson: 'He was a human chief for whom it was a pleasure to work . . . except for a few angry outbursts when I tried to prove that war was inevitable.'

Kirkpatrick returned to London in December 1938. After a variety of posts he found what suited him when in February 1941 he became foreign adviser to the BBC, and six months later controller of its European services. He was back in the sphere of wartime propaganda, where he had operated with such zest twenty-five years before, and here for three years he made a major contribution. One interlude, in May 1941, found Kirkpatrick employed to identify and interview Hitler's deputy, Hess, after his flight to Scotland.

From August 1944 until the end of the war Kirkpatrick was in charge of organizing the British element of the German Control Commission. He then went for a few months as British political adviser to General Eisenhower at Supreme Allied Headquarters, until its disbandment. After two years as assistant under-secretary in charge of Foreign Office information work, he served from 1947 to 1949 as deputy under-secretary for Western Europe, and then for a year as permanent under-secretary of the German Section of the Foreign Office—the former 'Control Office for Germany and Austria'. In these last two posts he worked closely with Ernest Bevin, for whom he came to feel deep respect and affection. In 1950 he went as high commissioner to Germany. His three years of office included, most notably, the negotiation and signature (May 1952) of the immensely important and complex series of Bonn Conventions, which eventually restored sovereignty to the Federal Republic; and, in parallel, the first steps towards German rearmament. As high commissioner—one of the three joint sovereigns of Western Germany—Kirkpatrick carried immense responsibility; and in his brisk, authoritative, relaxed way he shouldered it easily enough. He established good relations with Chancellor Adenauer, but not so close and cordial as those of his predecessor, General Sir Brian Robertson (later Lord Robertson of Oakridge).

In November 1953 Kirkpatrick succeeded Sir William (later Lord) Strang as permanent under-secretary in the Foreign Office. His three years in office—under three foreign secretaries, Eden, Macmillan, and Selwyn Lloyd—presented the usual infinite variety of problems; but they culminated, only three months before his retirement, in the Suez crisis. His part in this has certainly, whether deservedly or not, scarred Kirkpatrick's reputation. He has been severely criticized in several books, but they are not based on full information. In his own memoirs he was reticent, writing that these events were so recent and controversial that he did not propose to comment on them. Yet he wrote enough to show how strongly he had felt, and to suggest that he may have been over-influenced by the lessons he drew from his German experience of the thirties—the need to stand up at all costs against outrageous conduct. Many members of the Foreign Service were indignant at the intensely secretive handling of the crisis, and blamed Kirkpatrick for it. But the secrecy may have been imposed on him. Kirkpatrick may have been guilty of no more than fulfilling a civil servant's duty of loyalty to his political chiefs.

Yet it may be doubted whether Kirkpatrick was well fitted, by temperament, training, and experience, to fill this post at what was—as it is easy, in retrospect, to see—a period of rapid decline in British power. In appearance and manner, Kirkpatrick was small, slight, brisk, dapper, decisive, self-confident; and his mind matched. Superficially outgoing, he was not an easy man to know well. He took pride in thinking, working, and deciding fast—perhaps too fast. He had little use for research or analysis or for prolonged discussion. It may be significant that he was probably the only man in the senior branch of his service with no university education, or indeed any formal education after the age of seventeen, although he had been accepted by Balliol in October 1915. He was combative, even aggressive. He had no great respect for foreigners. He had great courage, and great appetite for responsibility. He had carried great responsibilities through a period of great apparent British power. By 1956, he may have over-estimated what remained of it. Few people did not. But if anyone should not, it is the head of the Foreign Office.

Kirkpatrick was appointed CMG (1939), KCMG (1948), GCMG (1953), KCB (1951), and GCB (1956).

Kirkpatrick served as chairman of the Independent Television Authority from 1957 to 1962. In addition to his memoirs he wrote *Mussolini, Study of a Demagogue* (published posthumously in 1964). In 1929 he had married Violet Caulfield, daughter of Colonel Reginald C. Cottell. They had a son, who went up to Balliol in place of his father in 1950, and a daughter. Kirkpatrick died at Celbridge, county Kildare, 25 May 1964.

[Ivone Kirkpatrick, *The Inner Circle*, 1959; personal knowledge.]

CON O'NEILL

published 1981

Harold Joseph

(1893–1950)

Political theorist and university teacher, was born at Cheetham Hill, Manchester, 30 June 1893, the second son of Nathan Laski, a cotton shipping merchant, a Liberal and a leader of Manchester Jewry, by his wife, Sarah Frankenstein. Laski, who was extremely precocious, was educated at Manchester Grammar School in the days of the great J. L. Paton and studied eugenics under Karl Pearson at University College, London, in the first half of 1911. In the same year the aged Sir Francis Galton wrote congratulating him upon an article on heredity in the *Westminster Review*. Laski entered New College, Oxford (1911), with a history exhibition, and in 1914 he was placed in the first class of the honours list in modern history and was awarded the Beit memorial prize.

After working for a few months with George Lansbury on the then struggling *Daily Herald*, and having been rejected from the army on medical grounds, Laski in the autumn of 1914 accepted a lectureship at McGill University, Montreal, where he remained until 1916. He then joined the staff of Harvard University where he was associated with a distinguished group of Harvard lawyers, and formed specially close friendships with two famous justices of the Supreme Court, Oliver Wendell Holmes (a volume of whose legal papers he edited in 1920) and Louis Dembitz Brandeis, and with Professor Felix Frankfurter who was later also to be appointed to the Supreme Court. In 1919 Laski was bitterly attacked for his sympathetic attitude to the Boston police strikers, and although supported on grounds of academic freedom by the president of Harvard, Abbott Lawrence Lowell, he was warned not to expect further promotion. In 1920 he was appointed to a lectureship at the London School of Economics and Political Science where he became professor of political science in 1926, a post which he retained until his death. His early experience of America had an important effect on his career and the development of his ideas. He visited America frequently, and was a friend of President Franklin Delano Roosevelt. His two principal books on America were *The American Presidency* (1940) and *The American Democracy* (1948). The latter, which was his last large work, aroused much controversy in the United States, mainly on account of its Marxist approach to American history and institutions.

Laski's work during thirty years at the London School of Economics may be classified under three headings. He was a teacher, a political philosopher, and a Labour Party leader. As to his success and influence as a teacher, there is no dispute. His lectures, brilliantly delivered and based on great erudition and a memory of extraordinary power, were always crowded, and his personal popularity with students from Britain, the Empire and Commonwealth countries, from Asia, and from Europe was unparalleled. After his death hundreds of letters from ex-students in various parts of the world testified to his influence and also to his generosity; some later revealed that they owed their chance of education to his personal and secret payment of their fees.

As a political theorist, Laski's numerous books, both historical and topical, were mainly concerned with sovereignty, the nature of the State, and the problem of social change. In his early books, for instance *Studies in the Problem of Sovereignty* (1917), *Authority in the Modern State* (1919), and in his articles in the *Harvard Law Review*, he expounded the pluralist doctrine that the State should be no more than the most powerful of many voluntary associations within a given society. This he argued on the basis of church history, acknowledging his debt to F. W. Maitland and J. N. Figgis, and in *A Grammar of Politics* (1925) he applied a modified pluralism to the entire range of political institutions. In a long preface which he contributed to the 1938 edition, he gave his reasons for jettisoning the pluralist theory of the State. In 1927 he had explained the objections to the Marxist creed in a small volume on *Communism*; these objections, based on his passion for individual liberty and his belief that revolution on the Russian model was not inevitable or desirable in a Western democracy, he maintained until the end of his life. But experience undermined his optimism, and after the downfall of the second Labour Government in 1931 and the slump in Britain and America, he accepted in general the Marxist interpretation of history, and, in innumerable letters, lectures, articles, and books which had wide influence in many countries, he argued that a social revolution in some form was inevitable, but that whether it came peacefully or violently depended on the readiness of the ruling class to yield its power and privilege. In *The Crisis and the Constitution, 1931 and After* (1932), *Democracy in Crisis* (1933), *Parliamentary Government in England* (1938), and other works, he discussed the position of the monarchy and the House of Lords as bulwarks of property, and analysed the functions of British institutions to discover whether they would serve the purposes of the working-class democracy which he believed to be inevitable and what reforms would make them more serviceable. Shortly before his death he delivered the more optimistic Simon lectures in Manchester University which were posthumously published in 1951 under the title *Reflections on the Constitution*.

As a practical politician Laski was on the executive committee of the Fabian Society from 1921 to 1936, and of the Labour Party from 1936 to

1949. His object was to adapt Marxism to British conditions, and thereby to create a political philosophy for the Labour Party. A close friend of Léon Blum, he was an ardent advocate of the Popular Front, and associated with Mr. Victor Gollancz and Mr. John Strachey in the Left Book Club. In 1939 he denounced the Soviet-German Pact and the Communist change of front (see his pamphlet *Is This an Imperialist War?*, 1940, and his preface to *The Betrayal of the Left*, 1941). During the war the central theme of his books, articles, and speeches was that out of the war should come working-class unity and a unique opportunity for revolution by consent (*Where Do We Go From Here?*, 1940, and *Reflections on the Revolution of Our Time*, 1943). In 1945 he was chairman of the Labour Party and during the election was chosen by his opponents as a figure on which to hang the thesis that victory for Labour would mean violent revolution in England. He himself commented on this campaign, which made his name headline news throughout the world's press, in a characteristic article 'On Being Suddenly Infamous' (*New Statesman and Nation*, 14 July 1945). After the election he toured Europe advocating the thesis that social democrats should as far as possible co-operate with Communists, but on no account accept fusion with them, a view he later developed, with much criticism of Communist tactics, in a pamphlet, *The Secret Battalion* (1946).

Laski was a brilliant talker and raconteur, and was known throughout the Labour movement for his platform oratory. Those who most detested his political views and public activities appreciated his lack of personal ambition, his disinterestedness, and his really extraordinary generosity. His personal friendships were numerous and lifelong. Probably the most remarkable was his deeply affectionate, almost filial relationship with Oliver Wendell Holmes, who was fifty-two years his senior. Their voluminous correspondence covered a period of almost twenty years and deals with an immense range of literary and political topics. Its publication, after Laski's death, had the incidental result of confirming before the world—a fact which was already well known to Laski's intimates—that his innumerable anecdotes, though usually founded on fact, were not to be relied upon as historical evidence. Laski received the honorary degree of LL.D. from the university of Athens in 1937; he was a member of the Industrial Court from 1926, a member of the lord chancellor's committee on ministers' powers (1929–32), the departmental committee on local government officers (1930–34), and the lord chancellor's committee on legal education (1932–4). His single hobby was the collection of a remarkable library, mainly of books on political theory of all periods.

In 1911 Laski married Frida, daughter of Francis John Kerry, farmer and landowner, of Acton Hall, Suffolk, by whom he had one daughter. This early marriage, which was without the consent of his parents, led to a breach of relations with his family which was not healed until 1920. He died in London 24 March 1950.

[Kingsley Martin, *Harold Laski*, 1953; *Holmes–Laski Letters*, edited by Mark De Wolfe Howe; 2 vols., 1953; private information; personal knowledge.]

KINGSLEY MARTIN

published 1959

LAW A n d r e w   B o n a r

(1858–1923)

Statesman, born 16 September 1858 at Kingston, near Richibucto, New Brunswick, Canada, was the first man of colonial birth to become prime minister of Great Britain. His father, the Rev. James Law, a Presbyterian minister, was an Ulsterman who came of farming stock from the neighbourhood of Portrush. His mother, a native of Halifax, Nova Scotia, was Elizabeth, daughter of William Kidston, a Glasgow iron-merchant. They had four sons, of whom Bonar was the youngest, and one daughter. The manse was a lonely wooden farmhouse, four or five miles above the mouth of the Richibucto river. The Sunday congregation consisted of settlers drawn largely from Dumfries and Galloway. The pastor was a man of intellectual gifts and an eloquent preacher. But he was the victim of a brooding melancholy which increased as the years advanced, and the memory of this affliction sometimes depressed his youngest son and made him fear a similar fate. Bonar Law's mother died when he was two years old, and in his twelfth year he was brought by an aunt from Canada to Scotland. He now found himself in affluent surroundings, but the lessons of his simple home, where the tasks of the kitchen and the farm were shared by all, were not lost upon him. After a short period at Gilbertfield School, Hamilton, he was sent to Glasgow high school, where James Bryce and Henry Campbell-Bannerman had been educated a few years earlier. He had a quick and energetic mind, but neither there nor at lectures which he attended later at the university, did he show unusual promise. He was an omnivorous reader, and delighted in recalling the fact that before he was twenty-one he had read Gibbon's *Decline and Fall of the Roman Empire* three times. But undoubtedly the author who gripped him at this period was Thomas Carlyle, from whose pages he later drew the literary quotations with which he occasionally graced his political speeches: his favourite quotations were figures from blue books.

Bonar Law's relatives, William, Richard, and Charles Kidston, were partners in a Glasgow firm of merchant bankers. Their business had been mainly concerned with financing trade in iron and steel, but at this time they were in the autumn of their commercial careers, nursing their investments rather than actively trading with them. From these conservative cousins he imbibed his earliest political impressions, including dislike of Mr. Gladstone and admiration of Mr. Disraeli. At the age of sixteen he entered the family business and had leisure and means to visit France, Germany, and Italy, to learn to read French and German, and to speak French. His speech in French, as in English, betrayed his ancestry and upbringing. In 1885, at the age of twenty-eight, he joined the Glasgow firm of William Jacks & Co., iron-merchants, as a junior partner. The business of the Kidstons was merged in the Clydesdale Bank, of which, later, Bonar Law became a director. Other directorships and the chairmanship of the Glasgow Iron Trade Association followed. He lived with the Kidstons at Helensburgh and there met Annie Pitcairn, daughter of Harrington Robley, of Glasgow, whom he married in 1891, and by whom he had four sons and two daughters. He continued after his marriage to travel daily between Helensburgh and Glasgow.

When about twenty years of age Bonar Law had joined the Glasgow Parliamentary Debating Association, the procedure of which was closely modelled on that of the House of Commons. As member for 'North Staffordshire' of this local 'parliament' for many years, he rehearsed his later triumphs as a debater and made himself thoroughly familiar with parliamentary procedure. It is probable that during these debates was born the ambition to exchange the local for the national forum, and the way was made possible not only by such means as he acquired in business, but also by the receipt of two legacies of £30,000 each, from Miss Catherine Kidston and Mrs. Janet Kidston, the childless widow of Charles Kidston. The abilities which he displayed at the Debating Association impressed officials of the Conservative and Liberal Unionist Associations, and in 1898 he was adopted as their candidate for the Blackfriars and Hutchesontown division of Glasgow. It was and had long been a radical seat, but in the general election of 1900 the liberal candidate deserted his party on the question of Home Rule. The Irish voters preferred to support the unionist, and with their help Bonar Law was returned by a majority of 1,000 and entered parliament at the age of forty-two.

In February 1901, in a debate on the Address, Bonar Law delivered his maiden speech—a defence of Joseph Chamberlain and Cecil Rhodes, who had been attacked on the previous day by Mr. Lloyd George. It was ignored by the press, which was more interested in the maiden speech made during the same sitting by Mr. Winston Churchill. The speech which singled out Bonar Law for special notice by the government was made on 22 April 1902 in favour of the corn duty proposed by the chancellor of the Exchequer (Sir Michael Hicks Beach). This speech was widely praised, and led to Bonar Law's appointment as parliamentary secretary to the Board of Trade, after a parliamentary apprenticeship of barely eighteen months. He soon distinguished himself in a twenty-minutes' speech on the Sugar Bounty Convention, the colonial secretary (Mr. Chamberlain) describing it as 'one of the most admirable short speeches he had ever listened to in the House of Commons'. These early speeches were closely reasoned and delivered without notes, but they were marred by a too rapid delivery. Their strength lay in the speaker's familiarity with the intricacies of imperial and foreign trade, and it was these matters which were to become in the immediate future the warp and woof of party warfare. In May 1903 Chamberlain launched his scheme of colonial preference and tariff reform. Nothing could have better suited the retired Glasgow iron-merchant, and he advanced steadily to the front rank of the exponents of the new policy. On 16 September 1903 Chamberlain resigned from Mr. Balfour's administration in order to be free to carry on his campaign in the country. This and the simultaneous resignation of free-trade ministers weakened the government, and in the general election of January 1906 it suffered overwhelming defeat. The conservative party was reduced to 157 members, who were divided into Balfourites, Chamberlainites, and unionist 'free-fooders'. At Blackfriars (Glasgow) Bonar Law was defeated by Mr. G. N. Barnes, a labour candidate, but on 15 May 1906 he was returned for Dulwich at a by-election. In the summer of 1906 Chamberlain's health broke down. Balfour's attitude to tariff reform, however clear to himself, was incomprehensible to the multitude. Bonar Law, on the other hand, was sure of himself and his utterances bore no trace of philosophic doubt. He was a merchant. He and Mr. Austen Chamberlain were now recognized as the most effective advocates of fiscal change in the unionist party. Bonar Law delivered innumerable speeches on the one subject, buttressed by an array of statistics which impressed those less skilful in their use.

The mantle of Joseph Chamberlain, now aged seventy, passed quietly to Bonar Law. Their careers were similar. Both were metal merchants, who entered parliament in middle age after succeeding in business; both found office at the Board of Trade; both were fighting men and effective speakers in and outside the House of Commons; both were ardent advocates of imperial preference. In origin and outlook they were both middle class. Neither belonged to the Church of England.

On 29 April 1909 Mr. Lloyd George, as chancellor of the Exchequer, made his first budget statement. Bonar Law denounced it as socialism 'pure and unadulterated.' Nor was he enamoured of the chancellor's schemes for health and unemployment insurance. 'It was the success of tariff reform', he argued, 'which had made the German insurance system possible.' Also he would have made the scheme for old age pensions contributory. The struggle over the budget had been preceded by a demand on the part of the conservatives for the construction of battleships of the *Dreadnought* class in reply to the German naval programme. Throughout this and the following year party feeling ran high. Joseph Chamberlain, from his retirement, declared that the fate of the budget involved the fate of tariff reform, and called upon the House of Lords to reject the measure. The Lords did so, and on 1 December Mr. Asquith moved that the action of the House of Lords was a usurpation of the rights of the Commons.

At the general election which followed, in January 1910, Bonar Law was again returned for Dulwich, but at that of December 1910, at the bidding of his party, he gave up a safe seat and essayed to win North-West Manchester. This fight aroused intense interest, as the seat had been wrested from Mr. Winston Churchill in 1908 by Mr. William Joynson-Hicks (afterwards Viscount Brentford), and had been lost again to the liberals in January 1910. Bonar Law failed to capture it, but he reduced the liberal majority from 783 to 445. In March 1911, however, he was returned for the Bootle division of Lancashire at a by-election. Throughout these contests his main themes were: 'naval supremacy and not merely naval superiority over Germany'; 'the defence of the loyal minority in Ireland against the imposition of a tyranny'; and tariff reform as 'the greatest of all social reforms'. 'We propose two things: to raise part of our revenue by the imposition of a duty on foreign manufactured goods that compete with those made in this country, and we propose also so to readjust our taxation as to obtain the largest possible amount of preference for the work of our own people in the overseas markets of the Empire' (Manchester, December 1910).

Disaffection in the conservative party over the questions of tariff reform and the Parliament Bill had undermined Mr. Balfour's prestige as leader. Bonar Law supported Lord Lansdowne and Mr. Balfour in their decision to accept the Parliament Bill rather than proceed to extreme courses with Lord Halsbury and the 'diehards'. On 8 November 1911 Balfour resigned, and on 13 November Bonar Law was elected leader in the Commons. The party was pretty evenly divided between supporters of Mr. Walter (afterwards Viscount) Long and (Sir) Austen Chamberlain. These two respectively proposed and seconded, as a compromise, the election of a man much their junior in parliamentary experience and public recognition, who had never held Cabinet office. 'The fools have stumbled on their best man by accident' was Mr. Lloyd George's comment at the time.

When his wife died in 1909 Bonar Law was desolate; old associations were ended and never renewed. Into the void came Mr. William Maxwell Aitken, a young Canadian man of business, full of energy and confidence. A strong and lasting friendship sprang up between the two men. In Lord Beaverbrook, as Aitken became in 1916, Bonar Law found the kind of assistance which is given to a minister by a first-rate parliamentary secretary in whose judgement the minister has confidence and who can be used as a sounding-board for ventilation of ideas and criticism of persons, and for the expansion of the minister's influence.

On 23 November 1911 the new leader of the opposition addressed a conference of the National Union of Conservatives at Leeds, where he denounced Home Rule, the disestablishment of the Welsh Church, and free trade with a stinging directness which contrasted sharply with Balfourian subtleties. 'The waters of Marah were not more bitter than his speeches' wrote a contemporary. This bitterness found its most tart expression in his handling of the Irish question which, with tariff reform, almost monopolized the attention of politicians in the years preceding the European War. With Sir Edward Carson he shared the leadership of the section which repeatedly postponed and paralysed a succession of Home Rule Bills, carrying their opposition to the brink of civil war. At vast demonstrations in 1912 at Belfast (Easter) and at Blenheim (27 July) and in the House of Commons itself Bonar Law imported into his speeches a deliberate note of defiance of authority. To the organizers of the Orange celebrations (12 July 1913) he sent a message declaring that 'whatever steps they might feel compelled to take, whether they were constitutional, or whether in the long run they were unconstitutional, they had the whole of the Unionist Party under his leadership behind them'. At Wallsend (29 October) he indicated the various courses which were open to the government. Either it must go on as it was doing and provoke unionists to resist—that was madness; or it could consult the electorate, whose decisions would be accepted by the unionist party as a whole; or thirdly, it could try to arrange a settlement which would at least avert civil war. When parliament met in February 1914, the prime minister, Mr. Asquith, struck a conciliatory note and promised to introduce a proposal which would 'consult . . . the susceptibilities of all concerned'. This proved to be county option with a time limit of six years. In an Amending Bill to the Home Rule Bill which the Commons had passed (25 May) the Lords substituted the permanent exclusion of the whole province of Ulster for the proposed county option with a time limit (8 July). But instead of introducing the Amending Bill in the altered form in which it had left the Upper House, Asquith announced the meeting of a conference at Buckingham Palace to discuss the Irish situation. Lord Lansdowne and

Bonar Law represented the unionist party. The conference failed to reach agreement on the portion of Ulster which should be excluded from the jurisdiction of the Dublin parliament. On 30 July the prime minister, prompted by Bonar Law and Carson, said that the Amending Bill would be indefinitely postponed in order that the country might present a united front to the threatened outbreak of war in Europe.

The rest of the Irish story may be outlined here before Bonar Law's services during the War are described. On 18 September the Home Rule Bill received the royal assent, and a Suspensory Bill simultaneously provided that it should remain in abeyance until after the end of the War. Bonar Law denounced this as a breach of faith, left the House with his followers in protest, and crossed to Belfast in order to renew and even to extend the pledges of the unionist party to Ulster (28 September). Abortive negotiations for a settlement proceeded intermittently throughout 1915 and 1916, and in 1917 (16 May), when Bonar Law was chancellor of the Exchequer, Mr. Lloyd George offered Ireland the alternative of a bill for the immediate application of the Home Rule Act to Ireland, excluding the six counties of North-East Ulster, or the summoning of a convention of Irishmen of all shades of opinion for the purpose of drafting a constitution. The latter was accepted, but its report (8 April 1918) showed that the 'substantial agreement' laid down by the prime minister as the condition precedent to legislation had not been reached. Ten days later the Military Service (No. 2) Act, 1918, extended conscription to Ireland, and in announcing that the government intended to enforce it, Bonar Law announced also the introduction of a further Home Rule Bill. This was never produced owing to the discovery in May of a widespread mutinous intrigue in Ireland and the arrest of Arthur Griffith and Mr. Eamon de Valera. Conscription remained a dead letter. On the eve of the general election of December 1918, Mr. Lloyd George and Bonar Law issued a joint letter which declared: 'Two paths are closed: the one leading to a complete severance of Ireland from the British Empire, and the other to the forcible submission of the six counties of Ulster to a Home Rule Parliament against their will.' The policy of alternating repression with conciliation continued. At the end of 1919 the government introduced the last Home Rule Bill, providing a parliament for Northern Ireland (the six counties), a parliament for the rest of Ireland, and a federal council for all Ireland. Bonar Law supported the Bill in a speech in which he condemned Dominion Home Rule as tantamount to giving the right to set up an Irish republic. On 17 March 1921, his health undermined, Bonar Law resigned the leadership of the House of Commons and of the unionist party after filling the one post for over four years and the other for nearly ten. He was thus not a member of the Coalition ministry which concluded the Irish

Treaty (6 December 1921). But he was frequently consulted by the government and by Sir James Craig (afterwards Lord Craigavon), who spoke for Ulster, and he emerged unexpectedly from his temporary retirement in order to recommend the treaty to the House of Commons. Had he opposed the negotiations there would have been no treaty.

On the outbreak of the European War Bonar Law tendered the liberal prime minister (Mr. Asquith) the support of the unionist party in resisting German aggression (2 August 1914). During the opening months of the War this support was loyally given, but with growing impatience on the part of the opposition. Traces of the conflict over Ireland still remained and made co-operation difficult. Finally, on the resignation of Lord Fisher from the Admiralty, Bonar Law informed the prime minister (17 May 1915) that a change in the composition of the government had become inevitable. Two days later the formation of the first Coalition ministry was announced, and the leader of the unionist party found himself relegated to the insignificant position of secretary for the Colonies, an appointment which not only reflected Bonar Law's self-abnegation but also Asquith's preference for Balliol men to business men as close colleagues. In the autumn of 1915 Bonar Law led the group in the Cabinet which pressed for the evacuation of the Dardanelles, carrying his own opposition to the verge of resignation, at which point Asquith surrendered. In January 1916 he took charge of the Compulsory Military Service Bill. He resisted its application to Ireland as, on balance, unprofitable, and skilfully surmounted amendments dealing with conscientious objection. The third reading was carried by 383 votes to 36. In June 1916 he attended an economic conference in Paris and agreed to the policy of joint economic action by the Allies during the War and permanent defensive collaboration thereafter. It was not until April 1917 that he had the satisfaction of announcing that the Imperial War Cabinet had accepted the principle of imperial preference for the British Empire.

As early as March 1916 Bonar Law had expressed the view to John Redmond that while Asquith was then the best possible prime minister, he would probably eventually be replaced by Mr. Lloyd George. This actually happened in December 1916. The devious operations by which Bonar Law's mistrust of Mr. Lloyd George was changed into active co-operation have been described by Lord Beaverbrook, who largely engineered them, by the biographers of Mr. Asquith, and by Mr. Lloyd George in his *War Memoirs*. They cannot be disentangled here. On 3 December, after a meeting of conservative ministers, Bonar Law saw the prime minister at Downing Street and demanded the resignation of Asquith's government. Mr. Lloyd George resigned on 5 December and Asquith a few hours later on the same day. On the same evening King George V invited Bonar Law to form an administration. He first sought the co-operation of Mr. Lloyd George and then that of Asquith, and when this was not forthcoming he advised the king to call on Mr. Lloyd George. On 7 December Mr. Lloyd George became prime minister. In the new government Bonar Law became chancellor of the Exchequer and leader of the House of Commons. He was also a member of the War Cabinet, but he was not expected to take the same active part in it as the other four members. At the Treasury and in the House Bonar Law quickly revealed abilities which had been fatally underestimated by Asquith. He reversed the prevailing policy of high money rates and short-term indebtedness and issued a series of War Loans, on a lower interest basis for long terms, which rank among the greatest achievements in the history of British finance. In October 1917 he launched a campaign for national war bonds to an unlimited amount on terms which ingeniously combined the advantages of short- and long-dated securities. This was remarkably successful and provided the state with a continuous flow of money until the end of the War.

The fifth war budget was introduced by Bonar Law on 2 May 1917. He recounted with pride the great success of the war loan which he had floated in a memorable appeal at the Guildhall on 11 January. By 31 March the total yield, including conversions, amounted to £2,067 millions. In fixing the low terms of this loan he had defied the advice of the City and of his own officials, and the public response amply supported his judgement. He now added no new taxes, but increased the excess profits duty from 60 to 80 per cent. and the tobacco duties and entertainments tax were also increased. Critics denounced the budget for 'its miserably small addition to taxation' and the needless burden which would cripple industry in the post-War years. The chancellor argued that no belligerent country had provided, as Great Britain had done, 26 per cent out of revenue to meet expenditure during the War. Replying to those who desired conscription of wealth as of men, he said: 'If we can get the money we need by voluntary methods, by unsettling as little as possible the existing machinery, then I am certain you will get more of it and for a longer time than by an attempt at conscription.'

On 22 April 1918 Bonar Law submitted the sixth war budget, 'a financial statement on a scale far exceeding any that had ever been known at any time or in any country.' The revenue for 1918–1919 he estimated at £842 millions, expenditure at £2,972 millions. New taxes were expected to produce £114 millions in a full year. Income tax was placed at 6s. in the £ at £2,500 a year, and super-tax at 4s. 6d. in the £ on excess over £10,000 a year. Farmers' tax was doubled. A proposal to tax luxuries, a French fiscal device, was later withdrawn as impracticable. The balance to be borrowed, roughly £2,000 millions, was more than three times the pre-War national debt. The chancellor declared himself to be guided by the rule of his predecessor, Mr. Reginald McKenna, that 'on the assumption that the War came to an end at the close of the year for which the financial statement was made, there would be a sufficient revenue without new borrowing or new taxation to make sure that not only the expenditure left after the War, but the debt charge could be met'. This unparalleled budget coincided with some of the most desperate struggles of the War, and it passed very easily and with so little change that the chancellor's revenue proposals were modified only in respect of two million pounds.

Throughout these years of vast and anxious responsibility the chancellor, while confident of the ultimate victory of the Allies, deprecated optimism and pessimism alike, and couched his appeals for sacrifice in speeches of marked sobriety. These were in sharp contrast to the flamboyant manifesto issued by Mr. Lloyd George and himself on the eve of the general election of December 1918, which followed the Armistice (11 November). Bonar Law justified the continuance of the Coalition as the one condition of ensuring peace abroad, and preventing revolution at home. The 'orgy of chauvinism' which characterized the election was not his doing, and he discouraged extravagant hopes of the financial terms to be imposed upon Germany. But he was a consenting party to the device of issuing 'coupons' to approved unionist and coalition liberal candidates, whereby the sacrifice of seats to labour candidates and independent liberals was avoided. The result was a coalition majority of nearly 250, and a large accession of unionist members. Bonar Law himself was returned for Central Glasgow, the division in which his business life had been spent. He took the office of lord privy seal and leader of the House of Commons, and during the prolonged absences of Mr. Lloyd George while attending conferences abroad he acted as prime minister. Only when his presence was absolutely necessary did he attend the Peace Conference at Paris, travelling by air whenever possible. He was one of the signatories to the Treaty of Versailles. At home, during the years 1919 and 1920, he was absorbed in the problems of demobilization and resettlement, the removal of war-time restrictions, and the transfer of industries from a war-time to a peace basis. And there was always the Irish question. When delivering his address as lord rector of Glasgow University on 11 March 1921, he betrayed signs of momentary collapse, and on 17 March, broken down by years of incessant labour and by personal sorrows, he resigned office and sought rest in the south of France. His health improved and he returned home in the autumn, emerging from his retirement to recommend the Irish Treaty.

Meanwhile a growing section of conservatives was chafing under the dominance of Mr. Lloyd George and the Coalition. Matters came to a head

415

over 'the Chanak crisis'—the fear that the prime minister and certain of his colleagues were bent on resuming war against Mustapha Kemal, who was threatening the neutral zones by which Constantinople, the Bosphorus, and the Dardanelles were then protected. This policy aroused widespread opposition in the country among all parties, but conflict was avoided by the tactful attitude of Sir Charles Harington, the Allied commander-in-chief at Constantinople. At the Carlton Club on 19 October 1922 a speech by Mr. Stanley Baldwin, and the declaration of Bonar Law that the unity of his party could only be saved by withdrawing from the Coalition, combined to bring about the fall of the government. Mr. Lloyd George resigned, and on 23 October Bonar Law became prime minister with a purely conservative Cabinet. On the same day he was unanimously elected to the leadership of the party in place of Mr. Austen Chamberlain. The new prime minister at once struck the note of his policy: tranquillity and stability, 'leaving the recovery to come, not so much by action from above, as by the free play and energy of our own people. . . . There are times when it is good to sit still and go slowly.' This programme of negation secured him an independent majority of 75 at the general election in November. Nevertheless, unemployment, housing, and foreign affairs gave the prime minister little of the 'freedom from disturbance at home and abroad' for which he yearned.

During 1922 British and French 'reparations' policies, which had hitherto been in general accord, showed signs of increasing divergence. At the conference held at Cannes in January, and indeed throughout that year, British influence was being used to mitigate and postpone payment of reparations by Germany in face of the vigorous and literal demands of M. Poincaré, and to question the right of independent action by France in the event of default. The German mark fell in the course of the year from about 800 to 34,000 to the £. Inter-allied debts, reparations, the co-operation of the United States of America in the affairs of Europe, and the mounting figures of unemployment had been treated by the Coalition Cabinet as interlocked problems, and the solution of none of them was in sight when Bonar Law took office. He presided over a conference of Allied prime ministers in London, 9–11 December, which was adjourned to Paris until January 1923. Between the two sessions Bonar Law announced that on certain conditions Great Britain 'would be willing to run the risk in the end of paying more to the United States than she would receive from the Allies and Germany', and the Reparations Commission, the British member dissenting, declared that Germany's failure to deliver timber to France during 1922 constituted a default and that this paved the way for the imposition of sanctions. In Paris (2 January 1923) Poincaré and Bonar Law tabled proposals too complicated for summary here; in essence their differences were accentuated. Great Britain wished to fix figures within the reasonable capacity of Germany to pay, on condition that she should stabilize the mark and balance her budget under supervision. France would agree to no policy which did not involve strict control of Germany's finances, together with the taking of extensive 'productive pledges' of material assets guaranteeing future payments. At the close of the first session of the conference Bonar Law was convinced that compromise was impossible, and but for the demands of courtesy and the pressure of advisers he would have returned to London at once. On 4 January he declared that 'the ditch was one which no bridge could span', and the conference broke down. Within a week the French and Belgian governments announced their intention of occupying the Ruhr, the policy against which Bonar Law had protested in vain. It is difficult to imagine him conducting international conferences extending over many weeks, like Lord Curzon at Lausanne, or Mr. Lloyd George on several occasions. He was quick to understand a situation, deliberate and dexterous in handling it, lucid and accurate in his statement of it, but his patience and resource were very limited. He never practised self-deception, and of two views he chose the one less favourable to himself. He did not preen himself, delivering elaborate pronouncements after the manner of Lord Curzon, nor revel in a battle of bargaining wits like Mr. Lloyd George. He was free of the vanity which clothes failure in a formula, and, like Mr. Asquith, he 'disdained the minor arts of popularity'.

One of the major questions which called for immediate action by the new conservative administration was that of the funding of the American debt. The parts played respectively by the prime minister and the chancellor of the Exchequer (Mr. Baldwin) in the settlement ultimately concluded have been the subject of much debate, and until contemporary state documents are available in Great Britain and in the United States no final judgement is possible. Reluctance to surrender office and disperse colleagues newly assembled in a purely conservative Cabinet after seventeen years in opposition or coalition, must have weighed heavily with the prime minister. Mr. Richard Law, member of parliament for South-West Hull, in a speech delivered in the House of Commons on 13 June 1933, stated it as his view that, but for the fact that his father was at the time a very sick man, he would not have accepted the settlement, and would sooner have broken up his own government, fresh as it then was.

As early as November 1918, Bonar Law, then chancellor of the Exchequer, had considered the possibility of the entire cancellation of inter-Allied debts, and throughout the years of negotiation which followed, this idea persisted in the minds of some British ministers, despite recurrent and emphatic discouragement from Washington. Another body of opinion, considering the economic restoration of Europe to be the matter of chief urgency, favoured the funding of the debt without delay and on such terms as were then obtainable. There were also those who, while willing to forgo Great Britain's reparation claims as part of a general settlement, were unwilling that the United States should play off debtors against each other, and insisted on a most-favoured-nation clause as a condition of agreement. After protracted debate and delay the Cabinet succeeded in harmonizing its views in the Balfour Note (1 August 1922). It had already agreed to dispatch a delegation to Washington. Certain other antecedent facts must be borne in mind in judging the position as it stood when Bonar Law became premier. On 31 January 1922 the American senate had passed an Act establishing a World War Debt Funding Commission, closely defining its powers, fixing the minimum rate of interest at 4¼ per cent and the period of debt repayment at twenty-five years. On 20 February 1922 the financial secretary to the British Treasury had announced that £25,000,000 would be provided in the budget estimates for 1922–1923 to cover one half-year's interest, and on 21 March the chancellor of the Exchequer (Sir Robert Horne) told the House of Commons that he did not propose 'to make any conditions to the United States for the payment of our due obligations.' The absence of hostile criticism of this announcement suggests that the prevailing opinion was that, whatever other nations might do, Great Britain meant to pay. Speaking in New York (4 October 1922) Mr. Reginald McKenna, a leading banker and former chancellor of the Exchequer, declared that Great Britain had both means and determination to pay the debt in full. The effect of the Balfour Note on American opinion was bad, and would have been worse but for the good will engendered by the signature of the agreement constituting the Irish Free State (6 December 1921) and of the Washington Naval Treaty (13 December 1921 and 6 February 1922).

The British delegates, the chancellor of the Exchequer (Mr. Baldwin) and the governor of the Bank of England (Mr. Montagu Norman), arrived in Washington on 4 January 1923. They had been given no written instructions, but they knew that the annuity envisaged by the prime minister was in the neighbourhood of £25,000,000 and a rate of interest of 2½ per cent. Even lower figures than these had been hinted at by the American ambassador to Great Britain (Mr. George Harvey) as likely to satisfy Congress, and this had coloured Bonar Law's views. This optimism had no basis in fact. Negotiations between the British and American commissions proceeded and were reported to the prime minister, who grew increasingly despondent. On 14 January the American commission offered a settlement on the basis of 3 per cent interest for the first ten years and 3½ per cent thereafter; a sinking fund at ½ per cent throughout, and back interest to be calculated at 4¼ per cent. This offer was equivalent to annual payments of $161,000,000 for ten years, and of $184,000,000 for fifty-two years, and was in reply to Mr. Baldwin's provisional suggestion of 3 per cent throughout. Its acceptance was strongly pressed upon the Cabinet by the delegation and by the British ambassador to the United States (Sir Auckland Geddes) as the best obtainable, and on 21 January Sir Robert Horne, then in New York and in consultation with interests friendly to England, cabled the same advice. Bonar Law denounced the terms as exceedingly harsh and unfair; they would inflict a crippling burden of taxation on the British people for two generations and would severely strain their relations with the people of the United States. The French were in occupation of the Ruhr, and he saw little hope of payments being made to England from Europe. Mr. McKenna and Lord Beaverbrook, two of his closest friends, and also Mr. J. M. Keynes, the economist, confirmed the prime minister in his opposition. A meeting to adjourn the Washington negotiations and to permit consultations in London was fixed for 18 January, but on 16 January the respective offers of the two commissions appeared in the American press and the result was to stabilize the American offer. Some observations made by Mr. Baldwin to pressmen on his arrival at Southampton on 27 January stiffened opinion in the United States against any further concession. The British Cabinet met on 30 January, and Bonar Law made it clear that he would resign rather than be a party to the proposed terms. He refused to believe that a day would not come when the rank and file of Americans would share what he knew to be the mind of their more enlightened compatriots. The discussion was inconclusive and was adjourned to the following afternoon. In the interval certain ministers indicated that they were not prepared even to appear to repudiate acknowledged obligations. This became the dominant view of the large majority of ministers. On the morning of 31 January Mr. McKenna, convinced that the City favoured acceptance, advised Bonar Law to yield. In the afternoon the Cabinet decided to accept the American terms and the crisis ended. Whether Bonar Law yielded because he was at the time a very sick man, or whether, but for his sickness, he would have shared the views of his colleagues, no one can say.

When Bonar Law had left office in March 1921 he had told the prime minister that he was 'quite worn out'. Before returning to office on 23 October 1922 he had 'hesitated up to the last moment'. He was prime minister for 209 days only, resigning on Whitsunday, 20 May 1923. When, on 30 October following, he died, there could be no doubt that, in the words of his successor, Mr. Baldwin, Bonar Law had given his life for his country, just as much as if he had fallen in the European War. He died at 24 Onslow Gardens, London, and was buried in Westminster Abbey on 5

November. Two of his sons were killed in the War, Charles in Palestine, and James in France. He was survived by two sons and two daughters.

No one will claim for Bonar Law a place among the greatest of England's prime ministers. Posterity indeed may give him a lower rank than is his due, not only because of his own indifference to fame but also because his solid qualities made no popular appeal. When he reached the top he was a tired man. He had filled the highest offices in the state with great ability and sagacity in years of unparalleled strain and anxiety. His mind worked rapidly; he grasped clearly the most technical memoranda submitted to him; his criticism was swift, acute, and extremely practical; his memory was abnormally retentive and accurate. His industry was concentrated and his curiosity severely restricted. He had none of Lord Curzon's insatiable appetite for information. Literature and art had no interest for him; to music he was deaf and to scenery blind. His sceptical outlook was tinged with melancholy. He lived simply, smoked excessively, and shunned society. He rarely left London and made no use of Chequers Court in Buckinghamshire, the official country residence of the prime minister. All this is true, but it gives a completely misleading picture of the man. Bonar Law united a character 'honest to the verge of simplicity' with a disposition 'sweet and kind' and a manner so gentle and charming as to prove irresistible to his associates. Diffident about his own powers, he could, when roused, show a stubborn firmness and decision. But his normal attitude was one of repose and quiet friendliness, which kindled a loving loyalty in all who became intimate with him. In human affection and hard work, he told the Glasgow students, he had found the best that life could offer. He played chess and bridge, lawn-tennis and golf, and was proficient in all, but parliament absorbed his energies. He was supreme as leader of the House of Commons, and his ascendancy has been compared with that of Walpole in the eighteenth century and of Peel in the nineteenth. He conducted its business with easy mastery from day to day, judging bills primarily by the smoothness of their passage, and untroubled by dreams of millennial achievement. For him, as for his hero, Joseph Chamberlain, a fortnight's future sufficed in politics. By Ulster alone was he stirred to the depths as by some primitive passion. Tariff reform was a paying business proposition. For the rest, he was open to argument, and it was parliamentary expediency which was apt to turn the scale. In the election of November 1922, where his was the determining voice, he envisaged 'as little legislation as possible'. This was doubtless in part reaction from the methods of December 1918, but it was also in harmony with the speaker's native caution and distrust of glittering promises.

Bonar Law's speeches are no longer read, but if judged by their fitness for their immediate purpose they must be given high rank. Speaking with engaging candour, his lucidity, moderation, and plain sense were perfectly adapted to convince and unite those who listened to him and to dissolve opposition. During the years of the War his fairness in debate, his modesty in demeanour, his freedom from envy and all uncharitableness, no less than the purity of his patriotism, made him beloved of all parties in the House of Commons. A passage from Macaulay's description of William Pitt the younger as a speaker can be applied to Bonar Law:

'He could with ease present to his audience, not perhaps an exact or profound, but a clear, popular, and plausible view of the most extensive and complicated subject. Nothing was out of place; nothing was forgotten; minute details, dates, sums of money were all faithfully preserved in his memory. Even intricate questions of finance, when explained by him, seemed clear to the plainest man among his hearers. . . . He was the only man who could open a Budget without notes.'

In December 1916 it was Bonar Law's action which made possible the second Coalition government and which brought Mr. Lloyd George to the premiership. The partnership of the two men—'the most perfect partnership in political history'—with their humble origin and austere upbringing, with their complementary gifts and divergent temperaments, profoundly affected the fortunes of the War. For over four years the one never took an important step without conferring with the other, and to compute the contribution of Bonar Law to the partnership it would be necessary to know not only the policies and projects of his sanguine colleague which he approved, but also those which he resisted, modified, or defeated. That colleague has placed on record his sense of the value of Bonar Law's searching criticism and his real courage when together they were responsible for the momentous decisions of the European War.

There is a portrait of Bonar Law by Sir James Guthrie in the National Portrait Gallery; a second by René de l'Hôpital at the Carlton Club; a third, outlined by Sir James Guthrie and painted by J. B. Anderson, at the Constitutional Club; a fourth by J. B. Anderson at the Conservative Club, Glasgow; a cartoon by 'Spy' appeared in *Vanity Fair* 2 March 1905, and an anonymous one 10 April 1912.

[Lord Beaverbrook, *Politicians and the War 1914–1916*, 2 vols., 1928 and 1932; J. A. Spender and Cyril Asquith, *Life of Lord Oxford and Asquith*, 1932; *War Memoirs of David Lloyd George*, vol. ii, 1933; H. A. Taylor, *The Strange Case of Andrew Bonar Law*, 1932; Sir Austen Chamberlain, *Down the Years*, 1935; private information; personal knowledge.]

THOMAS JONES

published 1937

LEE Sir Frank Godbould

(1903–1971)

Civil servant and master of Corpus Christi College, Cambridge, was born at Colchester, Essex, 26 August 1903, the eldest of three children and the only son of Joseph Godbould Lee and his wife, Florence Brown. Both parents were schoolteachers, and they soon moved to Brentwood where Frank won a scholarship to Brentwood School and from there in 1921 another to Downing College, Cambridge. He read English in part i of the tripos (1923) and history in part ii (1924) and took a first class in both. He then passed into the Indian Civil Service, but, under parental pressure, returned to teach at Brentwood for a year. In 1926 he took the Civil Service examination again and entered the Colonial Office. He spent two years as district officer in Nyasaland and visited Cyprus and Bechuanaland. He became a principal in 1934. On 25 September 1937 he married Kathleen Mary, the daughter of Walter Harris, a chartered accountant in Hull, and in the following year he went to the Imperial Defence College.

In January 1940 he moved to the Supply side of the Treasury, where he dealt with the Service departments and the Ministry of Supply. He became head of the division in 1943, but in 1944 he went to Washington as deputy head of the Treasury delegation under R. H. (later Lord) Brand. There he became closely associated with Lord Keynes in negotiations over the end of Lend-Lease and the British loan agreement. He got on well with Keynes and was able to deal with him on equal terms. A racy account by him of the Lend-Lease negotiations appears in chapter 19 of the *Essays on John Maynard Keynes*, edited by Milo Keynes (1975). In 1946 he returned to London as deputy secretary of the Ministry of Supply but in 1948 he went back to Washington as a minister at the embassy. He returned to London in 1949 as permanent secretary of the Ministry of Food. In 1951 he became secretary to the Board of Trade, and in 1960 he returned to the Treasury as joint permanent secretary in charge of financial and economic policy. In 1962 he had a heart attack, and left the service. He was appointed CMG in 1946, KCB in 1950, GCMG in 1959, and a privy councillor in 1962.

Frank Lee was an outstanding civil servant. Apart from an insatiable capacity for work, he was lucid and persuasive in argument, and had good personal relations with his staff, his colleagues in other departments, and his ministers, who were generally disposed to take his advice. His understanding of Americans and their ways was profound; in return Americans admired and liked him, as did his Commonwealth colleagues, and this was a great help in his negotiations. His weakness as an administrator was a temperamental inability to delegate; he often drove himself too hard and his staff too lightly. Nevertheless he was a success at the Board of Trade, and perhaps this was the apogee of his official career. He showed great promise at the Treasury but his reign there was short. As a committed advocate of European integration he did, however, play an influential part in the reappraisal of British policy towards Europe in 1960–2.

In 1962 he was elected master of Corpus Christi College, Cambridge, and threw himself into the life of the college and the university. He became chairman of the Press Syndicate, of the faculty board of engineering, and, as deputy to the vice-chancellor, of the University Appointments Board. He was also a member of the financial board of the university, and treasurer of the University Rugby Club. He was a governor of the Leys School, and vice-chairman of the board of Addenbrooke's Hospital, where he initiated a project for a sports and social centre for young doctors and nurses from the hospital which was completed after his death and named the Frank Lee Recreation Centre.

Outside Cambridge he was a member of the council of the University of East Anglia, a governor of the London School of Economics, and a director of Bowaters. He was an honorary fellow of Downing and received an honorary LL D of London University. He carried on all these varied activities with undiminished zest in spite of three further heart attacks and three strokes. He died in Cambridge 18 April 1971.

He was a short, stocky man with a florid face, sharp pointed nose, and black, often crew-cut, hair. Energetic and forceful, he attacked the business in hand like a keen terrier attacking a large rat. He found enjoyment in work of all kinds and it was never a burden to him. He was full of humour, gregarious, and a lover of good food, good wine, and good company. He had a well-stocked and retentive mind and a fund of quotations and good stories. He was an avid reader of poetry, especially contemporary work. A good footballer in his youth, he played cricket whenever he could, and became a baseball fan. He wrote very little, and did not approve of public servants publishing their memoirs. But his Stamp memorial lecture of 1958, *The Board of Trade* (University of London, Athlone Press), reveals much of his quality of mind and his approach to life. It was characteristic of him to decline a peerage, and to prefer appointment as a privy councillor. Before moving to Cambridge, the Lees lived a happy family and social life for twenty years at Much Hadham with their three daughters, all of whom followed their grandparents into the teaching profession.

[*The Times*, 29 April 1971; private information; personal knowledge.]

SHERFIELD

published 1986

(1904–1988)

Baroness Lee of Asheridge

Politician, was born 3 November 1904 in Lochgelly, Fifeshire, the third of four children, two of whom died young, and only daughter of James Lee, miner and active member of the Independent Labour party, and his wife, Euphemia Greig. She was educated at Beath Secondary School from which she won her way to Edinburgh University and learned from the great English literature teacher, (Sir) Herbert Grierson, how to read and how to write. She described her Scottish childhood in *To-morrow Is a New Day* (1939), a socialist classic suffused with her vibrant compassion.

Taking the finals of her Edinburgh MA in June 1926 (she also gained an LL.B., a teacher's certificate, and a diploma in education), she longed to return home, where the miners' struggle was reaching a fresh climax as their communities were ruthlessly destroyed by the coal-owners and the state. She began to earn her living as a schoolteacher, involved herself in politics, and, at a by-election in North Lanark in February 1929, she turned a Tory majority of 2,028 into a Labour majority of 6,578, and became the youngest woman ever elected to Westminster. Introduced into the House of Commons by Robert Smillie, the miners' leader she most admired, and James Maxton, she made many new friends, all on the left of the party: Ellen Wilkinson, Sir Charles Trevelyan, Aneurin Bevan, and, most especially, Frank Wise, with whom she fell in love (he died suddenly in 1933). All were outraged by the failure of their own government to tackle the scourge of mass unemployment.

After her defeat in the general Labour rout of 1931, she became involved in a classic battle with the Labour leaders about party discipline; she believed the rules binding MPs not to vote against party decisions to be an infringement of their duties and rights and said so forcibly. This involved her in arguments with many of her closest associates, notably Aneurin Bevan. She recorded in her book one famous argument with him: 'as for you, I tell you what the epitaph of you Scottish dissenters is going to be— pure, but impotent . . .Why don't you get you into a nunnery and be done with it? Lock yourself up in a separate cell away from the world and its wickedness. My Salvation Army lassie.'

Bevan's brilliant remonstrance may have been part of his wooing. On 24 October 1934 they were married at Holborn Registry Office. Bevan, the Labour MP for Ebbw Vale, was the son of David Bevan, a Welsh miner. Jennie Lee's ego, like his, could take a collective form. She wanted her beloved working class to acquire a touch of arrogance. She created a series of homes for Bevan, with the aid of her own mother and father, and, to the surprise of her parliamentary colleagues, put herself second. The first of those blazing, comradely firesides was established at Lane End Cottage at Brimpton Common in Berkshire in 1939; in 1944 they moved to Cliveden Place in Chelsea; and finally to Asheridge Farm in Chesham, Buckinghamshire. For their closest friends, these homes were political havens, heavens on earth. The Bevans had no children.

Outside Parliament Jennie Lee played a big part in the politics of the 1930s, always insisting on the international allegiance of her socialism. She undertook annual lecture tours in America and some journalism. She went to Vienna in 1934, soon after the fascist attack on the socialists there. She was stirred from the start by the fascist attack on the democratic government in Spain, yet shamed by the feebleness of the British government's response and, worse, by the initial Labour party response. When full-scale war did come, she, like Bevan, had no doubts that the contest must be fought on two fronts: to defeat the fascist enemy and to prepare for democratic socialist victory afterwards. She accepted a job with the Ministry of Aircraft Production touring the aircraft factories and in 1941 went on a propaganda tour to the United States: 'Don't come back', said Bevan, 'until you've brought them into the war.' When Hitler attacked the Soviet Union, she wrote a speedy good seller, *Our Ally Russia* (1941).

In 1943, at a by-election in Bristol Central, she stood as an independent in support of the two-front war, but lost. As peace came, she in turn sought her peace with the Labour party. In 1945 she won the mining constituency of Cannock for Labour with a 19,634 majority. Soon after the formation of the Labour government in 1945, Aneurin Bevan became one of its foremost and controversial figures. He was the chief architect of the National Health Service and Jennie Lee could see more closely than anyone what difficulties he had to encounter. She too wanted to see these principles established over wider fields. In the process she made friends with many of his friends: Jawaharlal Nehru and Indira Gandhi in India, Yigal Allon in Israel, and Milovan Djilas in Yugoslavia. She could share his victories and his bitter defeats. She felt the attacks upon him more closely than anyone. When he died of cancer in 1960, she felt that he had been murdered.

However, even before the wounds were healed, she resumed her own political activity—notably in the Labour government formed by Harold Wilson (later Baron Wilson of Rievaulx) in 1964. The titles of her offices—parliamentary secretary at the Ministry of Public Buildings and Works (1964–5), parliamentary under-secretary of state, Department of Education and Science (1965–7), minister of state (1967–70)—give no proper indication of how she became one of the administration's most successful ministers. She was sworn of the Privy Council in 1966 and elected chairman of the Labour party the following year. She was, in effect, Britain's first 'minister for the arts', and thereafter no government could abandon the idea. She became an honorary fellow of the Royal Academy in 1981. Cambridge gave her an honorary LL.D. in 1974. Above all, she played the leading part in the establishment of the Open University. A commitment to experiment with a University of the Air had been included in Labour's manifesto and Wilson had always been an enthusiastic supporter. But, without Jennie Lee, the project would have been a pale imitation of a real university. She insisted that the highest academic standards must apply from the start. The new university received its first students in 1971, and by 1984 it was Britain's largest university, with 100,000 students.

Jennie lost her Cannock seat in the 1970 election and accepted a life peerage, as Baroness Lee of Asheridge. She lived happily at her Chester Row house in London for the next eighteen years, giving delight and good instruction to her family and friends. She never lost her zest for the causes of her youth, most of them celebrated in her last book of memoirs published in 1980, *My Life with Nye*. Dark, and strikingly beautiful in her youth, she had the physical, tough vivacity of many girls of mining families. She died 16 November 1988 at her London home, 67 Chester Row, Westminster.

[Jennie Lee, *To-morrow Is a New Day*, 1939, *This Great Journey*, 1963, and *My Life with Nye*, 1980; Michael Foot, *Aneurin Bevan*, 2 vols., 1962, 1973; personal knowledge.]

MICHAEL FOOT

published 1996

LENNOX-BOYD Alan Tindal

(1904–1983)

First Viscount Boyd of Merton

Politician, was born 18 November 1904 at Loddington, Boscombe, Bournemouth, the second of four sons (there were no daughters) of Alan Walter Boyd, a barrister, of Bournemouth, and his second wife, Florence Anne, daughter of James Warburton Begbie, MD, of Edinburgh. He had a half-sister born of his father's first marriage. His eldest and youngest brothers were killed on active service in World War II and his second brother died in mysterious circumstances on secret service in Germany in 1939. Alan Walter Boyd assumed the additional surname of Lennox by deed poll in 1925.

Lennox-Boyd was educated at Sherborne School and Christ Church, Oxford. He won the Beit prize in colonial history, was elected chairman of the Oxford University Conservative Association, and in 1926 became president of the Oxford Union. He obtained a second class honours degree in modern history (1927).

In 1929 Lennox-Boyd stood unsuccessfully for the Gower division of Glamorgan but in 1931 was elected Conservative MP for mid-Bedfordshire, a constituency he held until his retirement from politics in 1960. In December 1938 he married Patricia Florence Susan, daughter of Sir Rupert Edward Cecil Lee Guinness, second Earl of Iveagh, chairman of Arthur Guinness, Son, & Company Ltd. They had three sons. She brought him a substantial fortune which spared him the anxieties that can beset a public man and enabled him to indulge his own generous sense of hospitality.

In the House of Commons Lennox-Boyd was a strong supporter of Neville Chamberlain's efforts to reach an accommodation with the Axis powers and was closely associated with R. A. Butler (later Lord Butler of Saffron Walden), Sir Henry ('Chips') Channon, and Harold Balfour (later Lord Balfour of Inchrye). Foreign and colonial affairs were always his main interest but he gained his early ministerial experience between 1938 and 1940 as a junior minister in the Ministry of Labour, Ministry of Home Security, and Ministry of Food.

In May 1940 Lennox-Boyd left active politics to serve in the RNVR as a lieutenant commanding a motor-torpedo-boat on the east coast and in the Dover patrol. He was called to the bar (Inner Temple) in 1941. He was recalled to office by (Sir) Winston Churchill in 1943 as a junior minister at the Ministry of Aircraft Production where he served until the general election of 1945. For the next six years the Conservative Party was in opposition. In this period Lennox-Boyd established his reputation as an authority on colonial affairs. He travelled widely to the colonies and was often called upon to intervene in colonial debates from the front bench.

When the Conservatives returned to power in 1951 he was appointed minister of state at the Colonial Office, under Oliver Lyttelton (later Viscount Chandos), and was admitted to the Privy Council. After only six months, however, he was promoted to become minister of transport, a post he held for two years. It was not until the summer of 1954 that he at last achieved his abiding ambition to be secretary of state for the colonies. He held this post until 1959 and was thus the longest serving secretary of state since Joseph Chamberlain. He never aspired to any other office.

Lennox-Boyd had a commanding presence (he was six feet five inches tall), a very quick mind, and an unusual capacity for work. As colonial secretary he would start work early, between five and six in the morning, arriving in the office having already mastered his briefs. Thereafter he would seldom read or write in the office but spend the day listening to advice or giving it. He was persuasive in council and dominated the House of Commons on colonial affairs, not so much by his oratory as by his knowledge of the facts and his grasp of the arguments involved.

He saw his task as colonial secretary as one of preparing the colonies for self-government within the Commonwealth. But he knew that political progress would be meaningless or worse unless underpinned by economic development. To this end he devised a series of federal systems for South East Asia, Aden and its associated protectorates, East Africa, Central Africa, and the West Indies. The essential feature of each of these was that it contained a substantial source of wealth and so could carry the less favoured territories involved. It was a grand and practical concept but could only be brought to fruition gradually and with British administrative and if necessary military support. But here Lennox-Boyd's classical concept of colonial evolution clashed with events outside Britain's control. The defeat suffered by Britain and France at Suez in 1956 undermined the French position in Algeria. With Algeria lost, General de Gaulle decided to decolonize the whole of French black Africa as soon as possible. Could Britain have continued with the gradual progress to which Lennox-Boyd aspired? This would not have been impossible but it might have involved a growing military commitment and would have clashed with the efforts of Harold Macmillan (later the Earl of Stockton) to convince de Gaulle that Britain was more interested in Europe than with hanging on to the colonial empire. Lennox-Boyd appreciated Macmillan's problem and could not resist his conclusions. But he knew that premature independence must mean the betrayal of friends, the installation of oppressive regimes, and the impoverishment of the mass of people—to say nothing of the sacrifice of British interests. As the last imperial statesman in a long and distinguished line he was not prepared to become the undertaker of imperial responsibility. He offered to resign but was persuaded, with some difficulty, to remain as colonial secretary until the 1959 election.

After the election Lennox-Boyd left the House of Commons and accepted a viscountcy (1960). He was also made a Companion of Honour (1960). He held certain directorships and found time for a wide range of charitable and social concerns. In particular he was a trustee of the British Museum and the Natural History Museum.

Lennox-Boyd returned briefly to colonial affairs in 1979 when Margaret Thatcher, then leader of the opposition, asked him to lead a mission sent by the Conservative Party to Rhodesia to observe the general election which was won by Bishop Muzorewa. The delegation found that the election was a valid test of opinion and recommended that a future Conservative government should recognize the Muzorewa-Smith government.

In private Lennox-Boyd had a wide circle of friends of every race, colour, and social origin. He also had a talent for taking trouble over seemingly unimportant things. Few colonial visitors came to London without being invited to his house in Chapel Street. Their particular interests or foibles were invariably carefully attended to. He always carried a small notebook in his pocket and would jot down any thought or suggestion as to how he might please visitors. On leaving politics he gave up his house in Chapel Street and retired to Ince Castle, a lovely seventeenth-century house in Cornwall overlooking the river Tamar. There at last he was able to enjoy his family, sail his yacht, and indulge his hobbies. He died on the evening of 8 March 1983 in Fulham Road, Chelsea, London, when run down by a car driven by an unaccompanied learner driver. He was succeeded in the viscountcy by his eldest son, Simon Donald Rupert (born 1939).

[Personal knowledge.]

JULIAN AMERY

published 1990

LLOYD John Selwyn Brooke

(1904–1978)

Baron Selwyn-Lloyd

Speaker of the House of Commons and politician, was born 28 July 1904 in West Kirby, Wirral, the third of four children and only son of John Wesley Lloyd MRCS, LRCP, a dentist in Hoylake and a leading member of the local Methodist church, and his wife, Mary Rachel Warhurst. He was educated at Fettes College, Edinburgh, and Magdalene College, Cambridge, where he was president of the Union in 1927. He obtained a second class in both classics part i (1925) and history part ii (1926) and a third class in law part ii (1927). His Nonconformist background and a family connection with the Lloyd Georges of Criccieth at first drew him towards the Liberal Party and in the 1929 election he stood unsuccessfully as the Liberal parliamentary candidate for Macclesfield. Some months later the economic crisis persuaded him of the need for a protective tariff and he became a Conservative for the rest of his political career.

Selwyn Lloyd was called to the bar, as a member of Gray's Inn, in 1930 and steadily built up a general common law practice on the Northern circuit. He took an active part in local government affairs in Cheshire, serving on the Hoylake Urban District Council for ten years. His diligence and competence were rewarded when he became chairman of the council at the early age of thirty-two.

In 1939 Selwyn Lloyd enlisted in the Royal Horse Artillery as a private and was commissioned as a second lieutenant at the outbreak of war. By 1942 he had been promoted to lieutenant-colonel on the general staff. He was posted to the headquarters of the Second Army on its formation in May 1943 to head the assault on Europe.

His industrious dispatch of military paperwork, combined with intense loyalty to sometimes difficult commanders, made him a successful staff officer. He was promoted to brigadier in 1944. In 1943 he was appointed OBE, in 1945 CBE, and he was twice mentioned in dispatches.

In the 1945 general election Selwyn Lloyd's good war record helped him to win a comfortable majority when he was elected MP for Wirral, where he had been adopted as Conservative candidate in 1939. In his maiden speech, and throughout his thirty-five years of service as an MP, he often spoke of his pride at representing the area in which he was born and bred.

During his first years in Parliament, Selwyn Lloyd concentrated more on his legal practice than his political career. He remained busy in the Northern circuit, taking silk in 1947. He was recorder of Wigan from 1948 to 1951. But as the Conservative Party sharpened its attacks in Parliament on the record of the Labour government, Selwyn Lloyd emerged as one of the most promising and hard-working of the 1945 intake of opposition back-benchers. In 1949 he was selected as one of the three parliamentary members of the Beveridge committee set up to inquire into the organization of the BBC. When the committee's findings were published in January 1951, Selwyn Lloyd submitted a minority report of his own opposing the retention of a BBC monopoly of broadcasting and advocating a competitive television system with power to draw revenue from advertising. His view was later put into practice by the Conservative government.

In 1951 Selwyn Lloyd married his secretary Elizabeth ('Bay'), daughter of Roland Marshall, solicitor, of West Kirby, Cheshire. They had one daughter. The marriage was dissolved in 1957.

In 1951, when the Conservative government returned to power, Selwyn Lloyd became minister of state at the Foreign Office. Under the tutelage of the foreign secretary, Anthony Eden (later the Earl of Avon), Selwyn Lloyd overcame his own doubts about his inexperience and enjoyed considerable success. He led the United Kingdom delegation to the sixth, seventh, eighth, and ninth sessions of the General Assembly of the United Nations, and made several notable speeches there. In the Middle East he was instrumental in guiding the Sudan to independence, and in negotiating the terms of the agreement for the withdrawal of British troops from Egypt. During 1954, when Eden was away for long periods on overseas visits and with bouts of ill health, much of the day-to-day conduct of foreign policy was in Selwyn Lloyd's hands. This brought him into close contact with Sir Winston Churchill, who gave him praise and eventual promotion to the post of minister of supply in October 1954. Six months later, when Eden became prime minister, Selwyn Lloyd entered the Cabinet as minister of defence and in December 1955 he was made foreign secretary. Although this last appointment was partly due to the friction that had developed between Eden and the outgoing foreign secretary, Harold Macmillan (later the Earl of Stockton), nevertheless Selwyn Lloyd's rise owed much to his own impressive performances in Cabinet committees as a strong departmental minister as well as to his good, if somewhat subservient, relationship with the prime minister.

As foreign secretary, Selwyn Lloyd's immediate priority was to mobilize international public opinion against the Egyptian leader, Colonel Nasser, and to seek support for international control of the Suez canal. Nasser, whom Selwyn Lloyd regarded as 'a potential Hitler who must somehow be checked if British influence is not to be eliminated from the Middle East and all our friends destroyed', had nationalized the Suez Canal Company on 26 July 1956. In August Selwyn Lloyd organized and chaired a conference in London attended by twenty-two countries who were the principal users of the canal. Eighteen of them agreed on a resolution asserting six principles for international control, recognizing Egypt's sovereign rights, guaranteeing her a fair return for the use of the canal, and proposing the negotiation of a new convention for canal usage. Unfortunately the high hopes encouraged by the almost unanimous support for the conference resolutions were short lived for it emerged that Selwyn Lloyd and the entire British Cabinet had seriously misjudged the degree of American support for their policy. The conference had dispatched a mission, led by Sir Robert Menzies, to Cairo, which was undermined by President Eisenhower unexpectedly saying at a press conference that the United States would only support a peaceful solution. As the threat of force was one of the few good cards which Menzies held, Eisenhower's statement made the mission futile and Nasser promptly rejected the proposals of the eighteen nations.

Selwyn Lloyd regarded the collapse of the Menzies mission as the initial major tragedy in what proved to be an uncoordinated and divided response by the West to the seizure of the canal. Further strains in the alliance occurred when John Foster Dulles, the US secretary of state, thwarted the initial British attempt to refer the crisis to the UN Security Council by insisting that his own plan for a Suez Canal Users Association (SCUA) was tried first. After this plan proved abortive, a series of subsequent American statements and actions showed only too clearly to Nasser that the allies were in disarray.

During this period of the crisis, Selwyn Lloyd had profound political and personal misgivings about the search for the next steps in policy-making. He had doubts about toppling Nasser and feared having to prop up a prowestern regime in Cairo. He privately believed that the judgements and temperaments of both Eden and Dulles were being affected by the onset of their respective illnesses, while he saw Eisenhower as being excessively preoccupied with the domestic considerations of the November 1956 presidential election. Although on at least one occasion he offered his resignation to the prime minister and Cabinet, when it was refused he continued to work in vain at the United Nations towards greater agreement for an international policy on the operation of the canal.

Meanwhile the lack of American support had prompted the French government to move towards a secret plan for military collusion with Israel. Selwyn Lloyd, who was at the United Nations in New York until 15 October still struggling to obtain a Security Council resolution on the canal, was entirely ignorant of this Franco–Israeli plan. On 16 October he and Eden went to Paris for talks with the French ministers Pineau and Mollet. Their discussions resulted in Britain's acceptance of Operation Musketeer, which envisaged Anglo–French intervention to halt an Israeli thrust if this occurred. However this conditional acceptance was apparently inadequate in the view of Pineau, so on 22 October Selwyn Lloyd again flew to France for secret talks with French and Israeli leaders at Sevres. This has subsequently led to the allegation that he was implicated in the Franco–Israeli agreement for military collusion which had been made some weeks earlier. The charge is unfair. Selwyn Lloyd neither knew of the collusion before Sevres, nor approved of it at the meeting. Indeed throughout the talks at Sevres he made it clear that a prearranged Israeli–French–British agreement to attack Egypt was impossible because of the risks to the lives and property of British subjects in Arab countries.

The Israeli invasion began on 26 October 1956. During the ten days following Selwyn Lloyd was stretched to the limits of his physical and political endurance by the hectic pace of the crisis. In Parliament he made statements, answered questions, and spoke in debates almost every day including Saturday. He was in constant touch, often throughout the night, with Britain's delegation to the United Nations and other diplomatic missions overseas. He was intensively involved in the planning of the military operation and attended all Cabinet meetings. He was required to make platform speeches in the country and to give a ministerial broadcast. An additional burden which he had to bear was the fundamental policy disagreement of his minister of state at the Foreign Office, (Sir) H. Anthony Nutting, who resigned on 2 November. Selwyn Lloyd, who regarded Nutting as a friend and protégé, was shaken by this resignation which he felt to be a personal and political stab in the back.

By the time British troops parachuted into the canal zone on Monday 5 November Selwyn Lloyd was a tired and disappointed minister. His disappointment deepened when, despite a successful military operation which secured the first twenty-three miles of the canal in as many hours, the Cabinet felt it had to order a cease-fire on 6 November.

With hindsight Selwyn Lloyd came to believe that he should have argued more forcefully in Cabinet for delaying the cease-fire until Britain had taken the whole canal. But at the time he bowed to the chancellor of the Exchequer's advice that an American-induced sterling crisis would be the consequence of continuing the fighting.

Although the aftermath of Suez brought about the resignation of Eden, it had no adverse effect on the career of Selwyn Lloyd. Credited with having carried out the Cabinet's policy loyally and conscientiously, he retained the post of foreign secretary for the next three-and-a-half years in Macmillan's government. As the new prime minister enjoyed playing a dominant role in foreign affairs, Selwyn Lloyd was at times somewhat overshadowed at the Foreign Office. Nevertheless he soon built up a good working partnership with Macmillan. Their immediate priority in the post-Suez period was the reaffirmation of Anglo-American relations and this was largely achieved in March 1957 at the Bermuda conference where they had long discussions with Eisenhower and Dulles. In 1959 Selwyn Lloyd and Macmillan made a ten-day visit to the Soviet Union where they had talks with Khrushchev and other Soviet leaders which improved Anglo-Soviet relations. Later that year Selwyn Lloyd opened the first set of negotiations for Britain's entry into the European Economic Community.

In July 1960 Selwyn Lloyd became chancellor of the Exchequer. His economic policy was cautious and orthodox, dedicated to curbing the now familiar inflationary pressures of rising wage demands and soaring government expenditure. To achieve these objectives he introduced an unpopular but effective freeze on wages known as the 'pay pause' which he followed with a more flexible incomes policy that allowed increases of up to 2.5 per cent. This became known as 'the guiding light' and was partially successful, although it led to further political unpopularity because of its allegedly unfair effects on some public sector employees, notably nurses and teachers. Selwyn Lloyd's major innovation at the Treasury was the setting up of the National Economic Development Council, nicknamed 'Neddy', a discussion forum for representatives of the employers, the trade unions, and the government.

By the spring of 1962 Selwyn Lloyd's strategy of restraint was causing the Conservative party some public relations difficulties, particularly in local and by-elections. On Friday 13 July he was abruptly dismissed from the government, the senior casualty of a surprise ministerial reshuffle, known as 'the night of the long knives', in which a third of the Cabinet was removed. Although remaining characteristically loyal in public to the prime minister throughout the controversy that followed this upheaval, Selwyn Lloyd was deeply hurt by the manner and timing of his departure. He felt that Macmillan had betrayed both a personal friendship and a political alliance by sacrificing his chancellor just as their jointly planned economic policy of counter-inflationary wage restraint was ready to be relaxed. He believed that his career was over and in the twilight of approaching retirement he began writing memoirs and accepting honours. In July 1962 he was created CH. In 1963 he became deputy lord lieutenant of Chester and an honorary fellow of Magdalene College. He also had honorary degrees from Sheffield, Liverpool, Oxford, and Cambridge.

After his dismissal Selwyn Lloyd carried out a nationwide inquiry into Conservative Party organization and published a report in June 1963 which contained a number of important recommendations on matters such as candidate selection, subscriptions, and the role of agents. It was to influence party administration for the next two decades.

In October 1963 a combination of political misfortune and personal ill health caused Macmillan's resignation as prime minister. To the surprise of many, though not of Selwyn Lloyd who played an influential role in guiding the succession, the new Conservative leader was his close friend the Earl of Home (afterwards Sir Alec Douglas Home and later Lord Home of the Hirsel). Amidst widespread approval from party loyalists, Selwyn Lloyd was brought back into the government as leader of the House of Commons. His tenure of this office for the next eleven months was perhaps the happiest period of his entire political career. His natural gift for conciliation and his readiness (not easy in an election year) to eschew political partisanship in the wider interests of the House of Commons as a whole, gave him a degree of parliamentary popularity he had never previously enjoyed. The good personal relationships he built up at this time among MPs of all parties were the foundation of his successful Speakership in later years.

After the Conservative government was defeated in the general election of 1964, Selwyn Lloyd remained a member of the shadow cabinet. When Edward Heath became leader of the opposition in 1965 Selwyn Lloyd was appointed the Conservative Party's principal front bench spokesman on Commonwealth affairs. In this capacity he visited New Zealand and Australia in 1965 and Rhodesia in 1966 shortly after Ian Smith's unilateral declaration of independence. He remained on the front bench for three months after the 1966 general election, until resigning from the shadow cabinet at his own request.

During the next five years Selwyn Lloyd was active in the world of business and accepted several company directorships. But he did not neglect politics, remaining an indefatigable speaker and fund raiser for the Conservative Party, particularly in the north-west of England. Although rarely participating in parliamentary debates, he was always a diligent House of Commons man, happily serving on the estimates, privileges, procedure, and services committees.

In 1971 Selwyn Lloyd was elected Speaker of the House of Commons. His election was vigorously opposed by some fifty MPs who held the view that a Speaker who had served for so long as a Cabinet minister might not be sufficiently zealous in protecting the rights of back-benchers. Once installed as Speaker, Selwyn Lloyd soon calmed these fears. He amended the practice of giving automatic priority to privy councillors in catching the Speaker's eye and took great pains to ensure that minority parties and viewpoints were heard. However, he faced some criticism from those who believed he was too lenient with vociferous and at times badly behaved parliamentary exhibitionists.

After skilfully guiding the House through twenty-one difficult months of minority government, Selwyn Lloyd retired as Speaker in 1976, and was created a life peer. Gardening, charitable fund raising, and authorship were the main activities of his retirement. In 1976 he published *Mr. Speaker Sir*, a personal account of that office, and followed this with *Suez 1956*, a memoir of the crisis which was posthumously published in 1978. He died at Preston Crowmarsh, Oxfordshire, 17 May 1978.

Selwyn Lloyd's career surprised some of his contemporaries. Shy to the point of awkwardness in manner, and reticent in conversation, he lacked many of the extrovert gifts of the natural politician. Although a good Whitehall administrator and an effective platform speaker when using a prepared text, his parliamentary debating skills were limited, and his public persona was stamped with caution rather than charisma. Yet he was the embodiment of the dictum of the fifth Earl of Rosebery that in political life it is the 'character breathing through the sentences that counts'. He was the confidant whose discretion could always be trusted; the lieutenant whose loyalty was unshakeable; the political ally whose reliability never faltered. This inherent goodness of character was supported by an ability to make shrewd political judgements and by an immense capacity for application which he developed as a compensation for his lonely personal life.

[J. S. B. Selwyn Lloyd, *Mr. Speaker Sir*, 1976, and *Suez 1956*, 1978; Nigel Fisher, *Harold Macmillan*, 1982; Earl of Kilmuir, *Political Adventure*, 1964; personal knowledge.]

JONATHAN AITKEN

published 1986

LLOYD GEORGE David

(1863–1945)

First Earl Lloyd-George of Dwyfor

Statesman, was born in Manchester 17 January 1863, the second child and elder son of William George, a schoolmaster, by his wife, Elizabeth, daughter of David Lloyd, of Llanystumdwy, Caernarvonshire. Failing health led the father to return to his hereditary occupation of farming in Pembrokeshire; here he died in 1864. His widow's brother, Richard Lloyd, like his father a master-shoemaker, immediately welcomed her with her infant daughter and son back into the old home where a third child (William) was born posthumously. Richard Lloyd was a dissenter in whose heart still burned the evangelical and puritanical fervour of the religious revival which had transformed the life of Wales in the eighteenth century; who was versed in the thousand-year-old Welsh literary tradition, and was openly Radical in politics even before the secrecy of the ballot shielded Liberal voters from persecution by the anglicized Tory landowners.

From the daily example of this remarkable man Lloyd George absorbed the Welsh social ideal of the time. He attended the church school, the only one available in his predominantly nonconformist village, where the pupils had to recite the formulas of the established Church of England. Hostility to privilege and to English domination was early sown in his arrogant and sensitive nature alongside an intense pride in a national heritage ignored by the local ruling caste. Thus was nurtured the champion of the underdog and of small nations. Lloyd George was, and remained, a countryman, the child of the village spanning the river Dwyfor near the sea, set in the midst of trees and farmlands, with the heights of Snowdonia in the background.

Poverty was not allowed to interfere with the career of the two boys: both became lawyers. Lloyd George passed the final examination of the Law Society with honours in 1884. By this time the family had moved to Criccieth, which was more convenient for Portmadoc, where the boy had been articled to Breese, Jones, and Casson, solicitors. After qualifying, Lloyd George set up for himself and soon established a high reputation as a wise counsellor and fearless advocate, especially when the interests of landowners or the established Church clashed with those of Welsh peasants and nonconformists.

Endowed with unusual gifts and inspired by the superb eloquence of the preachers of that time, Lloyd George early made his mark as a speaker. Although his personal creed may not have been orthodox, he was always a staunch supporter of organized Christianity and, as one of the Disciples of Christ, a sect of Baptist origin, he delighted his uncle, one of its unpaid ministers, by his addresses. He also spoke in the district on temperance and foreign missions and his political speaking attracted attention by its incisive, graphic quality. He took an active part in parliamentary elections and in the first county council elections of 1889 which resulted in a sweeping victory for Liberals throughout Wales. It was then imagined that the county councils would, by acting together, achieve self-government for Wales. Lloyd George also in his own area organized a farmers' union and as secretary of the Anti-Tithe League for South Caernarvonshire encouraged farmers to defy the law by refusing to pay tithes. His political ambition was early kindled and these activities advanced his prospects. In January of 1889 he was chosen Liberal candidate for Caernarvon Boroughs and, in 1890, he was returned at a by-election, by eighteen votes on a recount, against Ellis Nanney, the squire of Llanystumdwy. He took his seat on 17 April as a member of the Liberal Opposition under Gladstone and on 13 June delivered his maiden speech on a temperance issue. In the House, among the supporters of Lord Salisbury's administration, he found Joseph Chamberlain, once in his eyes a hero, but now a renegade, whom he never forgave or missed an opportunity to attack. He soon impressed the wider audiences provided by London and the provinces, but it was the cause of Wales which was nearest to his heart. Nor was his enthusiasm at all abated by the supercilious denial of nationhood to Wales shown by certain members of the House, and he studied parliamentary procedure and the tactics of the Irish party until he became as adept in advancing, and hindering, business in the House. Among the Welsh members was Thomas Edward Ellis, a pioneer of the Cymru Fydd (Wales of the future) movement with which Lloyd George later sought (in vain as it proved) to identify the North and South Wales Liberal Federations in order to strengthen the advance of Welsh home rule. At the end of 1890 he became the political correspondent of *Y Genedl Cymreig* (The Welsh Nation), and a little later he promoted a company for the purchase of a group of North Wales newspapers.

In the general election of 1892 Lloyd George defeated Sir John Puleston in the same constituency. Under the premierships of Gladstone (1892) and Rosebery (1894), when the Government was in difficulties owing to the rejection of the second Home Rule bill by the Lords and the drastic amendments made by them to two other government measures, Lloyd George himself contributed to those difficulties not a little. Together with (Sir) Francis Edwards, D. A. Thomas (later Viscount Rhondda), and (Sir) Herbert Lewis, he led a revolt after Gladstone's resignation of the premiership to obtain precedence for the Welsh disestablishment bill. Although this bill passed its second reading in the Commons in 1895, it made no further progress owing to Rosebery's resignation. In the Conservative victory in 1895, Lloyd George retained his seat against his squire, Ellis Nanney.

Soon after entering Parliament Lloyd George had settled with his family in London and started practice as a solicitor. His attendance at the House was constant and now, during this eclipse of Liberalism, the persistence, energy, and skill with which he and his Welsh colleagues assailed the Government reanimated the dejected Opposition. His chief attacks were made on measures designed in his view to entrench privilege, such as the agricultural rates bill (1896) and the voluntary schools bill (1897) with its proposals to aid Anglican schools. During a debate on the former bill he and four others were suspended by the Speaker.

In April 1899 occurred the untimely death of the young Welsh leader, Tom Ellis, and in the autumn the South African war broke out. The one tragedy elevated Lloyd George to the chief place in the political life of Wales, the other brought him notoriety and fame throughout the British Isles. Fully realizing the consequences, he plunged into a course of bitter opposition to the war which to him was a crime against a small nation and unworthy of the British Empire. This nearly cost him both life and livelihood and might have ended his parliamentary career. At a meeting in Birmingham in 1901 he only escaped from the mob by disguising himself as a policeman. Nevertheless, although his life had been threatened in his own constituency, he had been returned at the 'khaki' election of 1900. The peace of Vereeniging of 31 May 1902 found him, therefore, still in the House and ready to attack the Government from a new angle.

A. J. Balfour on 24 March had introduced an education bill which received the royal assent in December 1902. Lloyd George, ever zealous in the cause of popular education, did not quarrel with the admirable systematization now applied to it. But the proposal to grant rate-aid to voluntary schools not under complete public control he fought fiercely in and out of Parliament, but without success. In Wales his plan for the closure of church schools by the county councils was checkmated by the ingenuity of the Government's one-clause Act of 1904 permitting the Treasury to aid these schools directly and repay itself from moneys due to the local authority. Lloyd George countered this by urging the county councils, where the so-called Welsh Coercion Act was applied, to refuse to concern themselves with elementary education; this would be provided by revolt schools to which nonconformists would send their children. Funds were collected and a few schools were actually started but the movement ended with the advent to power of the Liberals in 1905. The agitation had greatly strengthened Lloyd George's position. The campaign had also reconciled the Liberals, divided on the issue of the South African war, and their new unity was cemented by opposition to Joseph Chamberlain's advocacy of protection, which had brought about the collapse of Balfour's Government.

Lloyd George's popularity among his fellow countrymen on the eve of his elevation to Cabinet office led a friend to comment: 'Wales is indeed a one-man show at the present time.' Never again could this be said: his devotion to Welsh causes became suspect as they took their place with other matters in the hierarchy of the new minister's preoccupations. He had in his early days at Westminster complained that Welsh members lacked the single-mindedness of the Irish; he himself proved to be no Parnell but a Welsh leader who took office. On his side it may be urged that Welsh failure to combine through the county councils or under the banner of Cymru Fydd discouraged him from further attempts to unite Wales, except within a scheme of federal home rule in which he always believed. He never wanted Wales to be separated from and independent of the United Kingdom and in his later considered utterances, while expressing his joy in the revival of the Welsh language, he dissociated himself from the view that a nation dies with its ancient tongue, and appeared as a cultural rather than a political nationalist.

Liberal efforts at removing the obnoxious clauses of the Education Act failed for reasons understood in Wales—the might of the Church of England fortified by the veto of the Lords. Moreover, although the Lords had in November 1906 rejected a clause in the education bill setting up a Welsh National Council, Lloyd George had secured a separate Welsh department, with its own permanent secretary, in the Board of Education. The postponement of disestablishment of the Church in Wales was not so well received, and the appointment and conduct of a Royal Commission to look into an issue long since decided proved a further irritant. Welsh nonconformist attempts to embarrass the Government incensed Lloyd George, who faced and won over the trouble-makers at a convention at Cardiff in October 1907. A Welsh Church bill was introduced in April 1909, but the controversies over the budget and the House of Lords put it into cold storage until April 1912. It was bitterly opposed and some of Lloyd George's most vituperative speeches were made in reply to the contention of its opponents, expressed with equal virulence, that the disendowment clauses entailed downright robbery of the Church. In Wales the fight waxed fast and furious, with Lloyd George in the thick of it. The bill, by the operation of the Parliament Act, became law on 18 September 1914. But war had begun and its operation was postponed 'for a year or until the end of the war.' Within a few months Lloyd George, entirely absorbed in the struggle, again vexed his Welsh friends by condoning an attempt at further postponement which, however, was checkmated by the firm stand of the Welsh members. After the election of 1918 had supplied him with an overwhelming majority of Conservative supporters he stood firm against those Church interests which would have sought a repeal or a drastic revision of the Act, but he readily met by a Treasury grant unforeseen financial difficulties created by the war, and on 1 June 1920 Lloyd George, as prime minister, attended the installation of A. G. Edwards, bishop of St. Asaph, as first archbishop of Wales.

In Campbell-Bannerman's Liberal ministry of December 1905 Lloyd George was appointed president of the Board of Trade and sworn of the Privy Council, and he and his colleagues initiated a series of measures which were destined during the next forty years profoundly to affect the structure of British industrial society and the distribution of the national income. The period was one when public opinion had been stirred by the London dock strike, the Taff Vale decision, the investigations of Charles Booth, and Joseph Chamberlain's tariff reform campaign. Lloyd George promoted the Merchant Shipping Act, 1906, the Patents and Designs Act, 1907, the Port of London Act, 1908, and in the process he added to his fame as an adroit debater the reputation of a patient negotiator in settling strikes. In 1908 Asquith became prime minister and was succeeded as chancellor of the Exchequer by Lloyd George. This intensified the struggle with the House of Lords which during 1906–8 had blocked Liberal measures of education, land reform, and temperance.

In his first ('the People's') budget (1909) Lloyd George declared war on poverty and unfolded new methods of taxation which provided an expanding mechanism for the future provision of funds for social services. He set up a Road Fund, and a Development Fund for the improvement of transport and agriculture and for the endowment of research, and levied taxes on unearned increment in land values which were the chief bone of contention, but eventually proved unremunerative and were abolished in 1920. In provocative speeches in Limehouse and elsewhere he roused the passions of the electorate against 'the Dukes', and in the House of Commons the bitter fight over the 'revolutionary' finance bill went on for many months. The rejection of the budget by the Lords led to the general election of January 1910. Opinion was evenly divided, so that Asquith had to rely for a working majority on the Irish nationalists and the Labour members. The budget of the previous April now passed both Houses materially unchanged. Asquith in the meantime tabled the resolutions defining the powers of the Lords which subsequently formed the basis of the Parliament Act of 1911, passed after a second appeal to the country in December 1910.

King Edward VII had died on 6 May 1910. At a conference which met in June to resolve the conflict between Lords and Commons, Lloyd George sought to reach agreement with the Opposition leaders on other controversial measures also—Home Rule, tariffs, conscription—but without success. In 1911 on the appearance of the German gunboat, the *Panther*, at Agadir, he surprised all Europe by warning Germany that Britain would actively resist interference with her international interests and obligations. But his main preoccupation at this time was his first, and epoch-making, contributory scheme of insurance covering health and unemployment. It made his name a household word long before the war. In spite of bitter opposition from all classes it passed after many compromises and was followed by further measures dealing with health, education, wages, and employment. These fell short of theoretical Socialism but involved considerable central organization.

Lloyd George was engaged in launching a campaign for the reform of the land system when he was halted by the results of an ill-judged investment suggested to him by his friend Sir Rufus Isaacs (later the Marquess of Reading) then attorney-general. In April 1912 he had bought a thousand shares in the American Marconi Company at a moment when the postmaster-general, (Sir) Herbert (subsequently Viscount) Samuel, was concluding a contract with the British Marconi Company. This transaction led to much public criticism and to an investigation by a select committee of the House of Commons. Ultimately in June 1913 a vote of censure on the ministers concerned was defeated, and a motion was adopted accepting the expression of regret on their purchase of the shares and their failure to disclose it earlier, but clearing their honour.

At the end of July 1914 war with Germany was imminent and the crisis found the Cabinet divided. Lloyd George stood with the non-intervention group until it was clear that the Germans had violated the Belgian frontier.

Lloyd George

At this attack by a powerful state on a small nation his vacillation ceased and with his mind made up he waged war with a will to achieve victory which was not equalled by any of his colleagues.

As chancellor of the Exchequer he sought the advice of experts and handled the immediate crisis with courage and skill. Public credit was put at the disposal of the banks, suspension of specie payments was avoided, new one-pound and ten-shilling notes were issued by the Treasury as legal tender, banks were guaranteed against bad debts made on pre-war bills of exchange, and a moratorium was proclaimed on 3 August which lasted until November.

On 17 November Lloyd George introduced his first war budget, in which he partially suspended the sinking fund, doubled the income-tax, and increased the tea and beer duties. He made repeated attempts, now and later, to check the loss of output due to excessive drinking by reducing hours of sale, by diluting the strength of beer and spirits, and by steep taxation. He very nearly brought off nationalization of 'the trade' but was overborne by the united opposition of temperance extremists and Conservative diehards.

Months passed before the public grasped the vast scale of preparations in men and material and money which would be required to defeat the enemy. 'Absolute war', as waged by Germany, was outside the experience of British soldiers and, indeed, outside their vision. By January 1915 Lloyd George had convinced himself that the higher conduct of the war by the Allies was seriously at fault, and in the first of his many memoranda he advocated the policy of 'side-shows'. The British general staff, on the other hand, favoured concentration in the West so as to give France the maximum support while protecting the Channel ports and the home front. This division of opinion between Easterners and Westerners persisted to the end of the war and was exemplified in the conflict between Lloyd George on the one hand and Sir Douglas (later Earl) Haig and Sir William Robertson on the other. Some operations in the East could not be avoided once Turkey had thrown in her lot with the Central powers, but it was agreed to regard France and Flanders as the main and decisive theatre of war for the British Empire, a view with which Lloyd George was never really content.

In this area, stretching from the English Channel to the Swiss border, the enemies were locked in almost static trench warfare for nearly four years. Lloyd George was soon obsessed with the costly expenditure of guns and munitions involved and he was also very conscious of the needs of the Allies. When therefore the coalition Government was formed in May 1915, Asquith set up a Ministry of Munitions, with Lloyd George at its head. Here he put forth inexhaustible and ubiquitous energy, issuing orders to existing factories, erecting scores of new ones, mobilizing the engineering and chemical industries of the entire kingdom with the help of big business men of 'push and go'. It was a gigantic task. He early encountered serious difficulties with labour, but succeeded, while still at the Treasury, in concluding an agreement with the trade unions which permitted the relaxation of restrictions on output in return for the limitation of profits. A further result was the extension of the employment of women and of welfare agencies in war industries. Widespread suspicion among the rank and file hindered the enforcement of the Treasury agreement, and compulsory legislation followed. By eloquent speeches Lloyd George sought to rouse the workers to a sense of the gravity of the struggle. In Glasgow on Christmas Day 1915 he was refused a hearing for three-quarters of an hour, but he was undaunted: production was pressed to such a pitch that for the battle of the Somme supplies proved reasonably adequate, and when, on 6 July 1916, he left the ministry to become secretary of state for war, what had taken a year to produce in 1914–15 could be obtained in two or three weeks. Good judges have claimed that by its boldness, its vastness, and its speed his work as minister of munitions was the supreme contribution made by Lloyd George to the winning of the war.

During these months Lloyd George drew nearer to his Tory colleagues; and on the conscription issue he was closer to Curzon and Carson than to the Liberals, Runciman and McKenna. The first military service bill received the royal assent on 27 January 1916. On 5 June Kitchener was lost in the *Hampshire*. Lloyd George was to have travelled with him to Russia but had been detained to deal with the troubles arising out of the Easter rebellion in Ireland. He apparently reached agreement with Carson and with John Redmond on the question of the six counties, but misunderstandings which followed and opposition from some Cabinet colleagues destroyed all hope of a settlement.

Lloyd George spent five months at the War Office, where Robertson, as chief of the imperial general staff, wielded great power and where the secretary of state chafed and fretted at his inability to change the major strategy of the war. In two directions, however, he left his mark: he persuaded Haig to invite Sir Eric Geddes to report upon and then to reorganize the transport services of the armies in France, and secondly he chose Sir John Cowans, quarter-master-general throughout the war, to reorganize the transport system in Mesopotamia which had been mishandled by the Indian Army authorities.

The summer and autumn of 1916 saw a series of offensives: by the Russians in Poland, the British on the Somme, and by the Italians. In August Romania declared war on Austria-Hungary and Italy on Germany.

Lloyd George

The results were disappointing. On the Somme casualties were terribly heavy, Romania was quickly overrun and her oilfields secured by Germany. At sea, sinkings increased rapidly. In September Lloyd George told an American journalist, in what was known as the 'knock-out blow' interview, that the British would fight to a finish; but, behind the scenes, there was much uneasiness and departmental friction. He had appealed in vain for some effort to save Romania. The urgent need of equipping the Russian armies weighed so much upon him at this time that he proposed to visit them and examine the position for himself, but he was again prevented.

In November Lord Lansdowne submitted a secret memorandum to the Cabinet in which, in a spirit of pessimism, he examined proposals for a negotiated peace. Throughout these autumn months Lloyd George was deeply agitated by the general situation and by his own impotence to improve it. He talked of exchanging the War Office for a minor post, of resigning from the Government and 'telling the country the truth'; in the press he was being both flattered as the man of destiny and attacked as disloyal. His capricious moods and unguarded rebellious conversations did not prevent his Conservative friends, Bonar Law, Sir William Maxwell Aitken (subsequently Lord Beaverbrook), and Carson, from helping him to reach the summit of power, although he avowed that he had no wish to supplant Asquith. He had a sincere admiration for his great qualities of mind and speech and temper, but believed that Asquith was losing the war and that he himself could do better if given executive control as chairman of a small War Cabinet with Asquith occupying a presidential position in the background but free, at his own discretion, to attend its meetings. This was the proposal which in substance Asquith first accepted, then rejected. The change was mainly wrought by a leading article in *The Times*, 4 December 1916, written by Geoffrey Dawson, which the prime minister wrongly thought to have been inspired by Lloyd George. Lloyd George resigned on 5 December and precipitated a crisis, the outcome of which was that Asquith resigned on the same day and was succeeded by Lloyd George on 7 December. The new prime minister secured the support of Conservatives, Labour, and about one-half of the Liberal members of the House of Commons. To Asquith's surprise, Bonar Law and Balfour agreed to serve under Lloyd George.

Lloyd George was now fifty-four years old and had spent half his life in Parliament. He was at once the most widely known, the most dynamic, and the most eloquent figure in British politics. His primacy in 10 Downing Street was immediately felt. The Cabinet of twenty-three was replaced by a War Cabinet of five provided, for the first time, with a secretary, Sir Maurice (subsequently Lord) Hankey, and numerous assistant secretaries who attended meetings and recorded minutes and conclusions. It met daily and only one of its members was occupied with a department. This was Bonar Law, who became chancellor of the Exchequer, the next-door-neighbour and the closest counsellor of the prime minister. Curzon was lord president of the Council, Milner and Arthur Henderson were ministers without portfolio. The new foreign secretary was Balfour, who usually attended the War Cabinet. Ministries of Labour, Food, and Shipping were at once set up.

Throughout his first year as prime minister Lloyd George displayed the extraordinary energy, application, and (except at the time of Passchendaele) buoyancy which were characteristic of him. The first four months saw the opening of the unrestricted German submarine campaign on 1 February which entailed the entry of the United States into the war on 6 April, whereas the Russian revolution of 12 March heralded the collapse of that power in the East. The most intractable problem (and one never yet solved) was that of submarine attacks on shipping. In April the losses amounted to an average of ten merchantmen a day. The Board of Admiralty had shown itself resolutely opposed to the convoy system, but shortly before Lloyd George became prime minister Sir John (later Earl) Jellicoe became first sea lord, and with his trained staff had begun to tackle the problem of the protection of shipping. However, he approached its solution by convoys with a caution which exasperated the anxious and impatient prime minister who persisted in urging them. With their adoption, the accession of the American navy, and Lloyd George himself acting as a constant spur to the Admiralty, the losses began slowly to fall after April 1917, and the most grievous danger passed. This was the chief consolation of a year full of military disappointments abroad.

In the land campaign the three ruling strategical ideas of Lloyd George were that allied resources should be pooled, that the allied front from Flanders to Mesopotamia should be regarded as one, the enemy being attacked at their weakest points in the line, and that unity of command on the western front was essential. He succeeded but slowly and very partially in applying these ideas, not only because he was opposed by British and French generals, but also because the heavy responsibilities borne by the British navy and the shortage of shipping made the full execution of the 'side-show' policy impracticable.

In accordance with these ideas, at a conference of the Allies held in Rome 5–7 January 1917, Lloyd George proposed a Franco-British-Italian offensive through the Julian Alps to Laibach and Vienna, but at a conference in London on 15 and 16 January final agreement was reached instead on what came to be known as the Nivelle offensive. Delayed until April, it caused the Germans no surprise, and failed. Simultaneously Haig fought the battle of Arras with some success until it declined into a stalemate in the middle of May. Nivelle's failure spread dejection and mutiny in the French armies, and in May he was superseded by General Pétain, who informed Haig of the situation under pledge of secrecy. From 7 to 14 June Haig fought the battle of Messines, and on 20 July, with grave misgivings, Lloyd George, in the War Cabinet, gave his consent to a heavy offensive with a view to clearing the Germans from their submarine bases on the coast, as was being advocated by Jellicoe. His misgivings arose from lack of confidence in Jellicoe's opinion, and from his preference for Pétain's policy of limited objectives which were constantly to surprise the enemy, as against the long-prepared and elaborately staged offensives favoured by Haig. Accordingly Haig launched his attack on 31 July on the under-standing that if progress were not satisfactory the offensive should be called off. It developed into the third battle of Ypres which ended in November at Passchendaele, having entailed terrible casualties, having gained no strategic advantage, yet having provided Pétain with the respite needed to restore the morale of the French Army. On 20 November, ten days after the close of Passchendaele, Haig renewed the attack at Cambrai. The surprise use of tanks without any artillery preparation made such progress that the claim has been made that had not five British divisions been taken away by Lloyd George to relieve the Italians after Caporetto, Haig might have 'consummated a great victory'. However that may be, Lloyd George was profoundly depressed by Passchendaele and would have removed Haig could he have found an acceptable successor.

The military events of 1917 increased Lloyd George's dislike of offensives in the West. His mind was turning towards a policy of delay on that front pending the arrival of American reinforcements. Since Austria was showing signs of exhaustion, and was rumoured to be seeking for peace, he renewed his advocacy of 'knocking away the props' in the East: Austria, Bulgaria, Turkey. The idea was encouraged by the capture of Jerusalem in December. But still more was his desire accentuated for his third principle, unity of command. Some temporary progress had been made in this direction when, much impressed by Nivelle, Lloyd George had given him wholehearted support, even to the extent of temporarily subordinating Haig to Nivelle at the time of his offensive.

One of the first acts of Lloyd George's Government was to summon Dominion ministers to an Imperial War Conference and War Cabinet, and these bodies did much to co-ordinate the war effort of the Empire. Lloyd George found J. C. Smuts so valuable that he offered him a seat in the War Cabinet and Smuts remained a member until December 1918. Peace overtures from Germany and Austria were repelled after consultations with France. A mission under Milner was sent to Petrograd to arrange about munitions and supplies and returned to this country on the eve of the revolution, which the mission did not foresee. In October 1917 Lloyd George propounded his views on a central co-ordinating council to Lord French (later the Earl of Ypres) and Sir Henry Wilson, and also to the French. The proposals were then submitted to Italy and the United States. On 2 November Lloyd George obtained Cabinet approval for an inter-allied council consisting of prime ministers and a member of the Government of each of the great powers fighting on the western front. Each power was to appoint a military representative to serve as a technical adviser to the council. The British representative was Sir Henry Wilson. At a conference at Rapallo Lloyd George used (7 November) the Caporetto disaster to advance the cause of unity of command, and he defended his action when challenged in the House of Commons, a challenge which he had deliberately provoked on his way home by a sensational speech in Paris, deploring lack of allied unity (12 November). The lesson was illustrated by what followed from the overthrow of Kerensky by Lenin, and enforced by military disaster in March 1918.

On the home front the prime minister comprehensively directed the national effort and dealt specially with shipbuilding, food rationing, wages and prices, recruiting, women's suffrage, and post-war reconstruction. The future of Ireland was handed over to a convention of Irishmen who failed to agree. A Cabinet pronouncement in August forecast 'the progressive realization of responsible government in India as an integral part of the British Empire'. A committee under Milner was appointed to study terms of peace, and the publication in the *Daily Telegraph* in November of a letter from Lansdowne, advocating a negotiated peace, led to a demand for a restatement of the Government's war aims. Lloyd George complied on 5 January 1918 in a speech to trade-union delegates in which he placed the restoration of the independence of Belgium in the forefront of a series of conditions which were later to be embodied in the peace treaties. The publication of President Wilson's Fourteen Points three days later showed the two statesmen to be substantially agreed. The Balfour declaration on a national home for the Jews, issued in November 1917, had Lloyd George's enthusiastic support.

The Supreme War Council, born at Rapallo, met at Versailles in December and again at the end of January. In framing plans for 1918 it had to reckon with the transfer of German divisions from Russia, with the slow arrival of reinforcements from America, with war-weariness in France, and with the terrific strain on the limited productive manpower of Great Britain. All these pointed to a defensive policy on the western front to which at this stage Haig and Robertson did not object. But several major and minor disputes agitated the Council in the opening weeks of this fateful year. Lloyd George still hankered after bigger efforts against Turkey, and the technical advisers of the Council, to whom the problem was referred, went so far as to agree (21 January) that it would 'be worth any effort that can be made compatibly with the security of our defence in the Western theatres'—a vital qualification. The comparative length of line assigned to the French and British armies caused much soreness in French circles. Haig attributed his failure to extend the British line, as he had promised to do, to the aforementioned dispatch of five divisions to Italy at the bidding of Lloyd George. But Haig had in fact taken over the French line as far as Barisis and Lloyd George (2 February) strongly supported his refusal to yield to further French pressure. When a compromise was reached it was left to Haig and Pétain to arrange when and how a change should be effected.

A third main question before the Council was the formation of a mobile general reserve. This task was placed under an executive War Board of which Lloyd George proposed that Foch should be president, thus paving the way for his appointment (14 April) as général-en-chef des armées alliées en France. Robertson objected to this device and on 18 February he was transferred to a home command and replaced as C.I.G.S. by Wilson.

On 21 March 1918 the Germans launched their great offensive, the blow falling mainly on the British Fifth Army, which covered Amiens. Within less than a week the situation became extremely critical. Pétain, anxious for the safety of Paris, seemed prepared to risk the separation of the French Army from the British. A telegram from Haig brought Milner and Wilson post-haste to a conference with Clemenceau and the British and French generals at Doullens (26 March) where, with Haig's full support, Foch was given powers to co-ordinate the efforts of the British and French armies on the western front, a decision of crucial importance. On 3 April at a similar conference at Beauvais, but with Lloyd George and the American generals, Pershing and Bliss, present, Foch was 'entrusted with' the 'strategic direction of military operations'. Thus, at last, the plan for which Lloyd George, more than any other statesman or general, had so long laboured in public and in private was adopted: only just in time to make its supreme contribution to victory.

(Sir) Winston Churchill, who saw Lloyd George during the anxious opening days of the German offensive, records: 'The resolution of the prime minister was unshaken under his truly awful responsibilities.' Lloyd George took extreme measures. Men were combed out of essential industries and partly trained lads were sent to France. Reinforcements were summoned from Italy, Egypt, and Salonika. Appeal for help was sent to President Wilson. There were hot debates on the training and use of American troops in response, Lloyd George supporting Foch's plea that they should be shipped as infantry units and merged with allied divisions in France.

On 7 May Major-General Sir Frederick Maurice in a letter to *The Times* charged Lloyd George and Bonar Law with making inaccurate and misleading statements in Parliament on military matters. Public opinion at the moment was extremely sensitive owing to losses in France and to the tightening pressure of conscription at home. Asquith proposed an inquiry by select committee but Lloyd George forced an immediate debate in the Commons, persuaded the House at the time that the charges were unfounded, and scored a parliamentary triumph. The importance of the incident was seen later at the general election when those who voted against the Government in this division were refused the coalition 'coupon' and only thirty-three independent Liberals were returned to Westminster.

During the anxious months of this summer and autumn Lloyd George resided at a country house, Danny Park, in Sussex, but was frequently called away to conferences in London and in France. In July he was still contending for an autumn offensive in Palestine and considering the supersession of Haig as British commander-in-chief. But his own disquiet was not allowed to interfere with the task of sustaining the war-will of the people. His incomparable gifts of popular appeal were used to brace the public to hold fast and endure the military casualties, the sinking of naval and merchant crews on the seas, the air raids and food queues at home. To mark the fourth anniversary of the outbreak of war a rousing message from him was read in every theatre and cinema in the country and on 7 August he spoke to a crowded House of Commons in the same confident and resolute spirit. According to his annual custom in Bank Holiday week he attended the national Eisteddfod in Wales, and it was there he heard of the opening of the battle of Amiens (8 August), in which Haig commanded and with the aid of Canadian and Anzac troops began a movement which was to force back the whole German line. This victorious operation ended all thought of removing Haig, who now, at the request of Foch and with the Cabinet's hesitating approval, proceeded to attack and to pierce the 'impregnable' Hindenburg line. The next few weeks saw the collapse of German resistance at an astonishing rate and the falling of 'the props' which had been held up by Germany. In September Lloyd George supported the attack of Franchet d'Esperey on Bulgaria and of Allenby in Palestine, and he was at Versailles urging on Orlando the importance of an Italian offensive when he learnt (5 October) that the German chancellor, Prince Max of Baden, had requested President Wilson 'to take steps for the restoration of peace'. On 3 November at the residence of Colonel House in Paris he had the satisfaction of hearing that Austria had signed an armistice; but it was hard to realize that fighting was over, and there was a natural suspicion that the German generals might use the armistice to strengthen their position.

On 11 November Lloyd George announced from 10 Downing Street: 'The Armistice was signed at 5 a.m. this morning, and hostilities are to cease on all fronts at 11 a.m. to-day.' That afternoon the greatest war minister this country had known since the elder Pitt received a great ovation in the House of Commons, and after he had moved its adjournment, with Asquith beside him, he led the House, behind the Speaker, to St. Margaret's, Westminster, to render thanks for the world's deliverance from its great peril. Honours flowed upon him with the same profusion which had 'rained gold boxes' on Pitt. The King in 1919 appointed him to the Order of Merit; from France came the grand cordon of the Legion of Honour, from other countries the highest orders which it was in their power to bestow; universities showered upon him their honorary degrees, and municipalities their freedoms.

The peace terms presented to the Germans by President Wilson had been debated in Paris in the week before the armistice. Two modifications in the Fourteen Points were made at the instance of Lloyd George: the one was concerned with 'the freedom of the seas', the other with the restoration of the invaded territories and compensation for damage done. Colonel House, acting as Wilson's intermediary, objected to the former modification and went so far as to hint at a separate American peace if this were not agreed. But Lloyd George was adamant and had Clemenceau's support when he declared that Britain and France would go on fighting. The changes were accepted and transmitted by Wilson to the German Government on 5 November.

Since the return of the Liberals in December 1910 there had been no general election. In the meantime there had been profound changes in the size and composition of the electorate, notably the extension of the suffrage to women. Lloyd George and Bonar Law decided to appeal to the country as a coalition and obtain a mandate to negotiate the peace and carry out a post-war policy of reconstruction. The Labour Party and the Asquith Liberals decided to go their own way. The coalition programme included 'trial of the Kaiser', payment of indemnities by the Central powers up to the limit of their capacity, and domestic reforms in all spheres.

Lloyd George was justified in consulting the country, but his demagogic conduct of the election did his reputation permanent harm. The Government obtained 526 seats out of 707, an immense majority, but one in which, as Lloyd George found to his cost, Unionists largely predominated, his Liberal supporters numbering only 133.

The country was impatient to bring the soldiers home and to resume 'business as usual', but the peacemakers had been caught unprepared and two months passed before the conference opened in Paris (18 January 1919) and two more months before it brought matters to a head with the reduction of its unwieldy executive, the Council of Ten, to a Council of Four, largely on the initiative of Lloyd George who was used to a small inner Cabinet. The German treaty was signed on 28 June. For most of these five months Lloyd George was in Paris, with Balfour as his colleague, and Sir Maurice Hankey and P. H. Kerr (later the Marquess of Lothian) as his secretaries. He at once secured the effective participation of the Dominions and India in the proceedings.

Wilson, idealist as he was, was preoccupied with promoting self-determination and the creation of a League of Nations; Clemenceau, the realist, sought ways of keeping Germany weak and preventing a recurrence of her attack on France; Lloyd George, a blend of idealist and realist, moving between the two, was firm on a few and flexible on many matters but mainly desirous that the wheels of European industry and trade should be made to revolve again. On the day of the armistice he had asked the British food controller 'to pour food into Germany' and in Paris at the Council of Ten he repeatedly urged that Germany should be revictualled, if only to prevent the spread of Bolshevism in Europe. In a memorandum, dated 25 March and written at Fontainebleau, he considered, belatedly, the treaty as a whole and outlined the principles of a settlement with a moderation which infuriated the French and alarmed the 'hard-faced' members of the House of Commons, who telegraphed their protest to Paris. He returned to Westminster and defended his policy with brilliant debating power and audacity.

Back in Paris he fought to place Danzig under the League of Nations and for plebiscites in Upper Silesia and in the Saar basin. In dealing with Italy he and Clemenceau were bound by the Treaty of London of 1915. Wrangling over Italian claims, over Fiume in particular, went on for months and was only ended by the Treaty of Rapallo on 12 November 1920. To meet Clemenceau's demand for occupation of the left bank of the Rhine and the bridgeheads on the right bank, Lloyd George and Wilson offered France a guarantee of military aid against unprovoked aggression, an offer which Wilson was unable to confirm and which therefore lapsed. A similar fate befell the Reparation Commission, which was Lloyd George's device for fixing the amounts and methods of Germany's payments. The decision of the United States not to ratify the treaty involved their withdrawal from the Reparation Commission. In future conferences Lloyd George had to struggle with the French for the reduction of Germany's payments to realistic proportions, and in March 1932 he published *The Truth about Reparations and War-Debts* in which he pleaded for their total abolition.

When Lloyd George left Paris on 29 June 1919 a council of heads of delegations was charged with unfinished business which included treaties with Austria, Bulgaria, and other states. On 25 June Lloyd George had tried in vain to arrange 'a short sharp peace' which would 'put Turkey out of her misery', a failure which was later to have calamitous results.

The Treaty of Versailles was ratified on 10 January 1920, and at this period Lloyd George was at the summit of his authority and fame. Henceforward he was to be much occupied in a series of conferences aiming at the pacification and economic revival of Europe. 'Diplomacy by conference' provided him with opportunities for the exercise of his gifts of persuasion, and the publicity inseparable from his perambulations introduced the newly enfranchised millions to the discussion of foreign affairs. The climax of the series was the Genoa conference (April, May 1922), his supreme effort to unite the nations of Europe. It was handicapped by Poincaré's refusal to attend and maimed in the first week by Germany and Russia agreeing to resume diplomatic relations and to cancel their mutual claims to compensation. A face-saving adjournment to The Hague for a conference of experts brought no settlement of the Russian debts owed under the Tsarist régime but repudiated by the Soviet Government. From the revolution onwards Lloyd George had sought to maintain friendly relations with the new rulers of Russia; he had been in favour of meeting them in Paris or Prinkipo in 1919 and in March 1921 he welcomed the conclusion in London of a trade agreement with their delegate, Krassin.

During these attempts at peacemaking abroad Lloyd George was haunted by the spectre of a mutinous Ireland. He himself had been a consistent devolutionist and a supporter of all home-rule measures from the day he entered Parliament. Now, repudiating Westminster, the Sinn Fein members were setting up their own Government. In the fighting which followed Lloyd George defended the use of British forces nick-named 'Black and Tans', who replied in kind to the outrages of Irish republicans. These reprisals shocked British public opinion, which would not support a policy of 'Thorough'. An appeal by King George V for all Irishmen 'to forgive and forget' led to negotiations in London. The Irish 'treaty' which finally resulted was signed on 6 December 1921 and was achieved mainly by Lloyd George's patience and negotiating skill.

The demobilization of four million men and their absorption into industry was bound to create grave social and political difficulties. The lop-sided expansion of war industries had to be adjusted and the housing industry expanded to 'provide homes for heroes'. Lloyd George devised measures to meet this situation and set up new ministries of Health and Transport, an Electricity Commission, and a commission under the chairmanship of Sir John (later Viscount) Sankey to examine the coal-mining industry. All these matters Lloyd George handled very much as a constitutional dictator. The majority of his supporters were Tories; the Liberals were split into coalitionists, Asquithians, and those partial to the Labour Party. There were moments when Lloyd George seemed about to form a centre party, his rooted Liberalism making desertion to the Unionists unthinkable. On 27 February 1922 he wrote to (Sir) Austen Chamberlain offering to give up the premiership and to support a homogeneous Government which undertook 'to carry through the Treaty with Ireland' and would devote itself 'to the work of the pacification of the world'. Chamberlain declined the invitation but in the autumn Lloyd George's resignation was precipitated from another and unexpected quarter.

The fate of Turkey had not been settled at Versailles. The delay was mainly due to uncertainty whether President Wilson could induce America to accept the proposed mandate for Constantinople and Armenia. The Treaty of Sèvres which was signed in August 1920 reserved Constantinople to the Turks but gave to the Greeks, *inter alia*, Smyrna and a large slice of Asia Minor. This was the policy of Venizelos, who had Lloyd George's enthusiastic support. It was successfully resisted by Mustapha Kemal who had gradually gained control of Turkey. He had been no party to the Treaty of Sèvres and he now had the backing of France and Italy. In the dangerous situation created by Kemal's attempt to invade the neutral zone at Chanak, war was finally averted by the firmness of Lloyd George and the tact of Sir Charles Harington, but the fear that Lloyd George was about to plunge the country into a new war rallied his opponents and provided a pretext for ending his dominion. Most of the Tory ministers stood by him, but at a Carlton Club meeting (19 October 1922) a majority of the Conservatives were against continuing the coalition. Lloyd George resigned, Bonar Law became prime minister on 23 October, and at the subsequent appeal to the country the Conservatives headed the poll.

Lloyd George was returned at the head of fifty-five National Liberals. They were buttressed by a strong party fund believed to have been acquired largely by traffic in honours. This was later swollen to considerable dimensions by highly remunerated journalism at home and abroad, judicious investment in the *Daily Chronicle* and other periodicals, and their successful management by Lloyd George himself. His personal possession and control of the fund was a matter of much controversy and some scandal for many years. Much of it was put to admirable use in promoting expert investigations into social problems—coal, land, roads, unemployment—into which Lloyd George now threw his reforming energies. A series of able reports followed, the recommendations of which anticipated the planning programmes of later years. He was neither a Socialist nor a rigid doctrinaire Liberal; in the main a free trader and friendly to big business, he encouraged the creating of buffer bodies between the State and the consumer for the provision of public utilities and social services.

In September 1923 Lloyd George left for New York, returning in November. He addressed many meetings in Canada and the United States and was everywhere given a tumultuous welcome. He sought the co-operation of America in the settlement of a desperate Europe and pleaded in the words of his hero Lincoln for 'clemency in the hour of triumph'.

In November the two wings of the Liberal Party were reunited when Stanley Baldwin, seeking to cure unemployment by means of protection, launched a general election. The Conservatives were returned in December with only 258 seats and were defeated in January. Labour with 191 held office for nine months by arrangement with the Liberals who had 159 seats, until after the 'Zinoviev election'. Differences between Asquith and Lloyd George, partly over the personal fund and partly over the line taken by Lloyd George in the general strike of 1926, finally separated them. Lloyd George was in favour of negotiating with the strikers while the strike was on and ridiculed the notion that they had revolutionary aims. In October 1926 Asquith, now Lord Oxford, resigned the leadership of the party. Lloyd George who was chairman of the parliamentary party worked hard for the next two years to restore the strength and influence of Liberalism.

The dominant domestic problem continued to be unemployment, which reflected a world-wide fall in trade. Lloyd George denounced (Sir) Winston Churchill's return to the gold standard in 1925, and more and more insistently in the next decade he turned to expansionist remedies, then, and for some years to come, considered heterodox. In September 1925 he proclaimed a scheme whereby the State should buy out all landlords and thus give security to the tenants, and in February 1926 his proposals were generally endorsed at a Liberal convention in London.

The fullest exposition of his ideas of reconstruction appeared in January 1928 in *Britain's Industrial Future*, the fruit of the labours of a group of progressive economists. It provided a Liberal policy for the general election of May 1929, and was popularized in a booklet *We Can Conquer Unemployment* (March 1929) which had a large circulation. Money was lavishly spent on helping Liberal candidates and Lloyd George expounded his policies to crowded meetings everywhere. He had discussed privately with (Sir) Winston Churchill (February 1929) the situation which might arise if no party obtained a clear majority. He would have preferred in that event that Liberals should support Conservatives rather than Socialists. Labour led with 288 members, Tories took second place with 260, and after his superhuman efforts Lloyd George's followers numbered only 59. Baldwin did not invite Liberal co-operation, but resigned and made way for a Labour Government. It soon found itself in difficulties, which were accentuated by the slump in the United States. Unemployment continued to increase. In the spring of 1931 Ramsay MacDonald was privately exploring some possible coalition with Lloyd George and his followers. In July Lloyd George had to undergo a major operation which removed him from the arena during the financial crisis which overtook the Labour Cabinet and led to the formation of a 'national' Government with Ramsay MacDonald as prime minister. Lloyd George strongly opposed the general election, upon which the Tories insisted, in October and from which emerged a House of Commons composed of 471 Conservatives, 52 Labour members, and 72 Liberals, divided between 'Simonites' and 'Samuelites' and a family party of four: Lloyd George, his son Gwilym, his daughter Megan, and his son's brother-in-law Goronwy Owen. On 3 November he wrote to Sir Herbert (subsequently Viscount) Samuel declining to stand again for the party leadership and on 19 November he set out for a holiday voyage to Ceylon.

In the field of foreign affairs in this period (1923–31) the Locarno treaties and the Kellogg Pact were signed; but Lloyd George was more concerned that the allied policy of disarmament to which he had pledged himself at Versailles should be carried out. The failure of the British-American guarantee had renewed the determination of France to put security before disarmament. Lloyd George had collaborated with Wilson in Paris in setting up the League but he had never given it his wholehearted support and later was very critical of its delays when dealing with disarmament.

The attempt to disarm Germany in accordance with the treaty had been foiled by many deliberate evasions. As the years passed, open and secret breaches became common and were discounted or justified by Lloyd George, who had misgivings about the treatment meted out to Germany in the peace settlement. In September 1933 he summed up his views plainly on one of its aspects, saying that all the trouble that had arisen in Europe and in Germany in particular had come from a flagrant breach of the undertaking to disarm by all the victor nations except one (Britain), and that the failure of the League of Nations to enforce that pledge had destroyed its moral influence. His hostility to France and partiality to Germany became increasingly marked and in the autumn of 1936 he visited Hitler at Berchtesgaden. He was much impressed by the Führer, who had abolished unemployment in Germany partly by measures similar to those which he himself had vainly advocated at home. It was only slowly that he was brought to recognize that full employment in Germany was mainly due to rearmament and that by treacherous diplomacy Hitler was bent on becoming the master of Europe.

Shortly before leaving office Lloyd George built himself a house at Churt in Surrey, and here, with further purchases of land, he developed an agricultural estate of some 600 acres and learnt farming and fruit-growing. Here also he accumulated his books and papers, and in the summer of 1932 he settled down to the more onerous task of writing his *War Memoirs* (1933–6) and *The Truth about the Peace Treaties* (1938). Every page of these volumes displays the forensic skill with which the combative author marshals the vast documentary evidence to confound his critics and to justify his own actions and policies. Portraits of the great figures of the war and the peace are drawn with a broad brush, not seldom dipped in venom. He concedes nothing to those who believed that the decisive theatre of war would be in the West and rarely pleads guilty to any mistake of his own.

On 17 January 1935, his seventy-second birthday, at Bangor, amidst a blaze of press publicity, Lloyd George launched a programme for a 'new deal', a revival in essentials of the bold economic remedies he had pre-scribed in 1929. The Cabinet was compelled to take notice, since not a few young Conservatives were attracted by the 'wizard', and Baldwin even went so far as to consider an invitation to him to join the Government. The ex-prime minister agreed to submit himself to cross-examination. But Ramsay MacDonald was hostile to co-operation with him and the chancellor of the Exchequer (Neville Chamberlain) had not only his own programme (cheap money, tariffs), but had also the strongest personal antipathy to the 'new dealer'. The only result of ten meetings was *A Better Way to Better Times*, issued by the Government by way of reply to Lloyd George's *Organizing Prosperity*.

Rebuffed but undaunted, Lloyd George now attempted to associate his domestic programme with that of the League of Nations in a non-party 'Council of Action for Peace and Reconstruction' at a time when the peace ballot revealed wide support for a policy of disarmament and collective security. The council exercised little influence on the general election which followed, but it continued for a year or two to maintain a staff which assisted candidates pledged to its views to fight by-elections. Lloyd George returned to his farm in Surrey to experiment with stock poultry and fruit and to the task of completing his war memoirs.

Little remains to be said of the last ten years of his life when again war clouds gathered and broke over Europe. At the time of the proposed marriage of King Edward VIII to Mrs. Wallis Simpson Lloyd George was in the West Indies, and he may not have realized the difficulties attendant on the policy which he favoured of a 'morganatic' marriage.

As it became plain that Hitler would not stop short of war to gain his ends Lloyd George advocated closer co-operation with Russia. He seldom spoke in the House of Commons but when he did it was to denounce the cowardice of the 'national' Government in face of Mussolini's Fascist activities in Spain and his rape of Abyssinia, and to chastise Neville Chamberlain in merciless terms for his appeasement policy and demand his resignation. He had no electoral power with which to enforce his appeal but his voice was not without influence in shaping opinion.

Britain declared war on Germany on 3 September 1939 and Churchill became prime minister in May 1940. He formed a coalition of the three parties and in June 1940 he invited Lloyd George to join it. Lloyd George refused the offer: he would have had Chamberlain as one of his colleagues and probably differences with the prime minister in the conduct of the war; besides, he was no longer equal to the strain of a Cabinet post. The same lack of physical resilience prevented his acceptance of the ambassadorship at Washington rendered vacant by the death of Lord Lothian in December.

Five weeks later (20 January 1941) Dame Margaret Lloyd George died at Criccieth. She was the daughter of Richard Owen, a substantial farmer of Mynydd Ednyfed, Criccieth, and Lloyd George had married her in 1888. Delayed on his way to her from Churt by a blizzard in the Welsh mountains he did not reach Criccieth in time to see her. For fifty-three years she had been his loyal comrade, his meteoric career and world fame only serving to bring into relief her serenity, natural dignity, and steadfastness. She was appointed G.B.E. in 1920. There were born to them two sons and three daughters: Richard (born 1889), who succeeded his father as second earl; Mair Eiluned who died in 1907 aged seventeen; Olwen Elizabeth, now Lady Olwen Carey Evans; Gwilym, home secretary from 1954 until 1957, when he became Viscount Tenby; and Megan, from 1929 to 1951 Liberal member of Parliament for Anglesey and from 1957 Labour member for Carmarthen. On 23 October 1943 Lloyd George married Frances Louise, daughter of John Stevenson, of Wallington, Surrey. She had been for thirty years his personal secretary. In September 1944 he left Churt with her for Ty Newydd, a small farming property he had bought in 1939 near his early home at Llanystumdwy and had transformed into an attractive residence. His powers were now failing and the question of the future representation of the Boroughs had to be faced. The party associations were not agreed on his unopposed return and he was not equal to a contest. In these circumstances the prime minister's offer to submit his name to the King for an earldom was accepted and on New Year's Day

1945 his elevation to the peerage was announced. He took the titles of Earl Lloyd-George of Dwyfor and Viscount Gwynedd of Dwyfor, in the county of Caernarvon. On 26 March he died and on the 30th he was buried in a solitary spot chosen by himself on the bank of the river by which he had played as a boy and from which he had taken his title. It was a strange exit: the deliberate choice of a grave among but not alongside the rude forefathers, the boast of heraldry for the village Hampden but not the Abbey. This assertion of complete separateness was in character.

Lloyd George was not hewn out of one solid block: he was built not of one but of many pieces. His outstanding and varied gifts launched him on a brilliant political career and kept him on a triumphant course for twenty years. By then he had split his own party, and he was now discarded by the Tories. The emergence of the Labour Party and the distrust and hostility of the two older parties combined to exclude him from office for the rest of his life. Possessed of great ability, shrewdness, and nimbleness, neither an echo nor a borrower, he always displayed innate independence and immense courage. He had abounding energy, lived intensely and positively, and was more resourceful and subtle than any of his ministerial colleagues. Neither metaphysician nor mystic, he was artist and actor with nothing prosaic or pedestrian about him; in the daily traffic of life his charm was irresistible and his good temper unfailing. His instinctive adaptability to every sort of audience was uncanny and on high occasions his eloquence was overpowering. He secured innumerable successes in parliamentary debate by his harmonious command of voice and gesture, imagery and humour. Endowed with an exceptional sense of the realities of political power, he did not disdain the popular arts of the demagogue, and there were moments when he stooped to low artifice. Although without the magnanimity of the finest characters, he commanded the allegiance of statesmen as distinguished and diverse as Balfour and Smuts, Milner and Austen Chamberlain. His hatred of oppression and his genuine human sympathy were revealed most persistently in his radical measures of social reform and in the programmes he provided for his successors of all parties. His genius for leadership found its supreme expression in war, when his indomitable will and buoyant spirit steered the nation to victory in 1918. At Versailles and indeed for the rest of his life he laboured consistently to raise the living conditions of the peoples, to restore Germany, to pacify Europe, and so avert what he desperately feared, and lived to endure, a second world war.

There are portraits of Lloyd George by Sir William Orpen (oils, 1927), Sir Max Beerbohm (pencil and wash), and R. Guthrie (chalk) in the National Portrait Gallery; by Sir John Lavery (1935) and by Christopher D. Williams (1917) in the National Museum of Wales; by Christopher D.

Williams in the National Liberal Club; by Sir Luke Fildes, presented to the Incorporated Law Society in 1909; by Augustus John in the Aberdeen Art Gallery. In sculpture, there is a statue in the square in Caernarvon, also a bronze bust (1921) in the National Museum of Wales, a bust and bas-relief in the Ceiriog Memorial Institute, by Sir W. Goscombe John; busts by Lady Kennet in the Imperial War Museum and the National Museum of Wales; a bas-relief by Dora Ohlfsen in the National Library of Wales, Aberystwyth. A cartoon by 'Spy' appeared in *Vanity Fair* in 1907 entitled 'A Nonconformist Genius'. Decorations, caskets, deeds of freedom, and other personal mementoes are preserved in the Lloyd George Museum, Llanystumdwy, North Wales.

[*The Times*, 27 March 1945; W. Watkin Davies, *Lloyd George 1863–1914*, 1939; Herbert du Parcq, *Life of David Lloyd George*, 4 vols., 1912; E. T. Raymond, *Mr. Lloyd George*, 1922; A. J. Sylvester, *The Real Lloyd George*, 1947; Malcolm Thomson, with the collaboration of Frances, Countess Lloyd-George of Dwyfor, *David Lloyd George, the Official Biography*, 1948; Thomas Jones, *Lloyd George*, 1951; David Lloyd George, *The Great Crusade*, 1918; *The Truth about Reparations and War-Debts*, 1932, *Some Considerations for the Peace Conference before they finally draft their Terms*, 25 March 1919 (Cmd. 1614, 1922), *Is it Peace*, 1923, *Slings and Arrows* (extracts edited by Philip Guedalla), 1929, *War Memoirs*, 6 vols., 1933–6, and *The Truth about the Peace Treaties*, 2 vols., 1938; personal knowledge.]

THOMAS JONES

[Frank Owen, *Tempestuous Journey*, 1954; Robert Blake, *The Unknown Prime Minister, The Life and Times of Andrew Bonar Law*, 1955; Lord Beaverbrook, *Men and Power, 1917–1918*, 1956; William George, *My Brother and I*, 1958.]

published 1959

MACDONALD James Ramsay

(1866–1937)

Labour leader and statesman, was born in a two-roomed 'but and ben' at Lossiemouth, Morayshire, a grey, lowland village of fishermen and farmworkers in the parish of Drainie, within a few hours' walk of the Highlands, 12 October 1866. Isabella Ramsay, his grandmother, a woman of exceptional courage and character, had successfully reared her four young children after being left penniless by an absconding husband. Of these, the youngest, Anne, said to have been the most intelligent of the family, when working at a farm in the parish of Alves, near Elgin, became with child by the head ploughman, John MacDonald, a Highlander from the Black Isle of Ross. She did not marry, and her son was born in her mother's cottage. The peculiar circumstances of MacDonald's childhood may well have accounted for the unusual later combination of mental toughness, physical courage, and extreme sensitiveness in his character.

At Drainie school, where the fees were eightpence a month, the boy studied Euclid and the ancient tongues, and devoured such books as were available in his grandmother's cottage or were lent him by a consumptive watchmaker, who introduced him to the works of Dickens. Before he was fifteen he was head of the school. For a short while, after leaving, he worked on a farm, but when he was about sixteen the 'dominie' of Drainie invited him to become a pupil teacher, at seven pounds ten shillings a year. With the free run of the 'dominie's' shelves he made the acquaintance of Shakespeare, of Carlyle's tory socialism, Ruskin's socialist aesthetics, and Henry George's then extremely influential *Progress and Poverty*. Although he was fundamentally of a religious turn of mind, with an unfailing reverence for what he called 'the grand, crowned authority of life', an obstinate streak of rationalism combined with that instinct of the insurgent, which sprang perhaps from his fatherless childhood, to prevent any of the rival Scottish orthodoxies from gaining his allegiance.

In 1885, at the age of eighteen, MacDonald obtained employment in Bristol from a clergyman who was inaugurating a boys' and young men's guild there. Chance thus brought him to what was at that time almost the only English city in which there was some nucleus of socialist activity. This was a branch of the Social Democratic Federation, founded in 1881 as the Democratic Federation by H. M. Hyndman, which professed those Marxian doctrines which MacDonald was to spend so much of his later life in combating. He joined the branch, and took his share in its members' persistent but unsuccessful efforts at outdoor evangelism. Meanwhile he became an enthusiastic geologist, and spent on books money which should have gone on food and clothes. Before the end of the year, however, he had returned to Lossiemouth with the few pounds which he had contrived to save, and the resolve that, when he next left home, he would return successful, or not return at all.

A few months later MacDonald went south again, this time to London. The post which he had hoped to obtain was filled a day before his arrival, and for a while he nearly starved, tramping the city in search of work and living mainly on oatmeal sent from home—for which he scrupulously paid—and hot water. He is said to have found employment on the very day on which his last shilling was spent—the addressing of envelopes, at ten shillings a week, for the newly formed Cyclists' Touring Club. A little later, as an invoice clerk in a warehouse at fifteen shillings, he 'lived like a fighting-cock', helped his mother, paid fees at the Birkbeck Institute and other places of education, and saved money into the bargain. In later life he seldom spoke of these early struggles, but they certainly coloured his political creed and reinforced the belief, which he sometimes afterwards expressed, in the power of extreme poverty to breed 'the aristocratic virtues'. Before long, however, thanks to underfeeding and overwork—he was spending every spare moment on reading science—his health broke down completely and he was compelled to return home.

By 1888 MacDonald was back in London, and, after another period of unemployment, was fortunate enough to be chosen as private secretary to Thomas Lough, Gladstonian parliamentary candidate for West Islington, with whom he remained until 1891. Thus for the first time he came into contact with the politically minded middle class. He was still speaking at open-air meetings for the Social Democratic Federation, and in 1887 he was present in Trafalgar Square on the celebrated 'Bloody Sunday' (13 November). But, what was far more significant, in 1886 he joined the Fabian Society. Conscious that by now 'almost all organisations contain elements making for Socialism' this body had set its face, almost from the first, against 'revolutionary heroics', and concentrated upon conciliating and harnessing, instead of antagonizing, the latent forces of the age as did the social democrats, MacDonald found its middle class and eminently practical environment a novel and congenial atmosphere. In particular the Fabians had wisely resolved to eschew all the distracting shibboleths of those vague idealists, so prominent in the 'eighties and 'nineties, who were ready to embrace any cult, from vegetarianism to bimetallism, provided that it was labelled 'progressive'. MacDonald was never a crank.

Nevertheless, the Fabians were scarcely more qualified than the Social Democratic Federation to convert the man in the street, and it was not until 1893, with the foundation of the independent labour party, that there appeared a body capable both of fusing the working class, skilled and unskilled, into political unity, and of popularizing socialist doctrines. It stood both for independent labour representation as against alliance with one or other of the traditional parties, and for socialism. Of both aims MacDonald wholly approved and in 1894 he applied for membership in a personal letter to Keir Hardie. At the general election of 1895 he stood as independent labour party candidate for Southampton, polling only 886 votes. At this time he was earning a slender income by journalism, and it is remarkable evidence of the resolute process of self-education upon which he had embarked that he should have been invited to contribute a considerable number of articles to the Dictionary of National Biography.

In the following year MacDonald married Margaret Ethel, daughter of John Hall Gladstone, F.R.S., of Pembridge Square, London, and a great-niece of Lord Kelvin. Her father was both a distinguished scientist and an active social and religious worker—he was one of the founders of the Young Men's Christian Association—and Margaret Gladstone had been attracted to socialism through her own social work in Hoxton and elsewhere. The marriage opened a new life for MacDonald. Not only did it mean financial independence, but the influence of his wife began insensibly to colour his own views. 'She saw spirit in everything', he wrote of her after her death; and thenceforth the faint streak of rationalism seems to fade out of him, and he was carried yet farther from the bleak materialism of Marx. Margaret MacDonald also possessed a genius for friendship which MacDonald himself had always lacked, and she made their new home at 3 Lincoln's Inn Fields the centre of a wide circle of friends. Here their six children were born, and despite the unceasing public activities of both parents their family life was exceptionally happy and united. The next few years were filled with expanding activities. There was foreign travel, which marriage had made possible, and for which Mac-Donald retained a passion to the end of his life. There were the regular gatherings in his home of labour and socialist protagonists, and friends and well-wishers from overseas. Moreover, in 1900 MacDonald had become secretary of the labour representation committee, the germ of the labour party: he held the post until 1912, and was treasurer from 1912 to 1924. Since 1896 he had been a member of the national administrative council of the independent labour party (where he was regarded as markedly cautious), and from 1894 to 1900 he served on the executive committee of the Fabian Society (which considered him a dangerous intransigent). From 1901 to 1904 he represented Central Finsbury on the London County Council. The acquisition through his marriage of an upper-middle-class social background undoubtedly accelerated MacDonald's rise to prominence in the labour movement. It was, for example, a strong recommendation for his secretaryship of the labour representation committee that he was not dependent upon the trade unions for an income.

With Hardie, MacDonald drafted the resolution by which in 1899 the Trades Union Congress convened a special congress to devise plans for returning more labour members to the next parliament. He was largely responsible for next year's decision representing a compromise between the traditional liberal-labourism of the Trades Union Congress and the class-war socialism of the Social Democratic Federation—to set up the labour representation committee, which in 1906 became the labour party. He had taken an active part in the resistance to the South African war, and his *What I Saw in South Africa* (1903) was based upon a journey undertaken with his wife on the morrow of the peace. More significant was *Socialism and Society* (1905), the whole argument of which is characteristically based upon the analogy between politics and biology. Not unnaturally this book rejects, as antiquated, Marxism and the doctrine of the class war, 'on the threshold of scientific sociology, but hardly across it'. At the general election of 1906 he was returned for Leicester, which he had unsuccessfully contested in 1900. All but five of the twenty-nine successful labour representation committee candidates, and MacDonald among them, owed their success to an electoral arrangement made with the liberals, a fact which goes far to explain labour political strategy during the next few years. The new party was bound to support the liberals because the liberals were now about to establish the new system of social insurance, which was sound collectivist doctrine, but it was also bound to support them because it owed most of its own seats to liberal complaisance.

From the first MacDonald attended regularly, and spoke frequently, in the House of Commons, and at once established his reputation; 'a born parliamentarian' was Lord Balfour's subsequent verdict. In public as in private life there was an impenetrable hinterland in MacDonald; it would often be his strength, and sometimes his weakness, that in a sense he was always a man of mystery. His writings—*Socialism* appeared in 1907 and *The Awakening of India*, which has been described as the best short book on India ever written by a tourist, in 1910—helped to mark him out as not only the most distinguished spokesman but the most distinguished thinker of the labour group in parliament. But perhaps it was his dominating influence in the independent labour party, at this time the 'praetorian guard' of the labour movement, which was most significant for the fortunes of the country, and which eventually most affected his own career. As chairman from 1906 to 1909, and as a leading figure for many years, he did more than anyone else to implant in a society abounding with visionaries and extremists his own practical instinct for moderation. The triumph of moderation is never inevitable, unless moderates of sufficient stature are forthcoming, and but for the influence of MacDonald during this seminal phase the labour party between the two wars might have preferred revolution to evolution. Meanwhile the world-wide journeyings, which did much to give him his grasp of foreign affairs, were continuing. Each summer from 1907 to 1916 he was on the continent on a political mission; in 1906, with his wife, he embarked upon a world tour, and in 1909 they visited India.

MacDonald retained his seat at the two general elections of 1910, and in 1911 he became chairman of the parliamentary labour group. It was in this year that he suffered a crushing blow in the loss of his wife, which followed that of his youngest son eighteen months previously. With his wife's death MacDonald's social circle contracted; his natural sensitiveness and aloofness revived; thenceforth he was always in a sense a lonely man. The short memoir of his wife which he wrote for private circulation that year was expanded and published in 1912 as *Margaret Ethel MacDonald*. It is a most moving tribute and an unconscious portrait of the author as well as of his wife.

1911–1914 were years of international tension, and industrial strife. MacDonald was closely involved in negotiation over the great railway strike of August 1911, which was the climax of a series of savage industrial disputes. In parliament on 16 August he deplored the strikes but argued that the business of the House was not merely to talk law and order but to listen to the men's case, and to realize that behind it there was a long history of social injustice. Industrial unrest persisted into 1912 and Mac-Donald continued to put the case of the strikers to parliament, to exhort them to patience and discipline, and to advise on parliamentary tactics. Throughout these years, in which support in parliament for the liberal government had to be combined with socialist propaganda in the country, there were recurrent complaints of the moderation and 'subservience' of the parliamentary labour group, and in particular of MacDonald, its leader; but in spite of all he contrived to retain the confidence of the party, and even of the independent labour party. The successful struggle for moderation within his own party lent all the more force to his denunciation in 1914 of Sir Edward Carson and those conservatives who planned violent resistance in Ulster to the government's policy of home rule: 'let them start that sort of appeal to lawlessness and anarchy . . . and he would not like to prophesy as to who was going to write the last sentence.' In December 1912 he paid a second visit to India, as a member of the royal commission on the public services in India. He signed the subsequent Report with some reservations, but embodied what he had learnt at greater length in his *The Government of India* (1919).

On 5 August 1914, the day after the declaration of war on Germany, MacDonald resigned his chairmanship of the party, which declined to support his proposal that labour members should oppose the government's demand for a war credit of £100 millions. On the same day the executive and the parliamentary group had resolved '. . . that it has opposed the policy which has produced the war, and that its duty now is to secure peace at the earliest possible moment on such conditions as will provide the best opportunities for the re-establishment of amicable feelings between the workers of Europe'. Both MacDonald and the majority of his colleagues could claim that throughout the years of war which followed he and they alike were faithfully discharging the duty thus defined; yet while they were to become loyal supporters of the wartime coalition, recruiting orators, and Cabinet ministers, he was soon to be the best-hated man in Great Britain, widely, although quite erroneously, regarded as a pro-German and a pacificist. Yet the views which, despite violence and misrepresentation, MacDonald continued to expound throughout the war accurately, if not always altogether lucidly, embodied the substance of the original resolution. Great Britain was wrong to enter the war; having entered it she must win it; yet even in wartime the rational temper of the moderate must somehow be preserved, lest the eventual peace be of that vindictive kind which must ensure further wars. That the war must be won he had no doubt; and although he would not join in the highly coloured oratory of the recruiting platform, he told his audiences that 'those who can enlist, ought to enlist, those who are working in munition factories should do so whole-heartedly'. Early in December 1914 he went to Belgium as a volunteer member of a British ambulance attached to the Belgian army—only to be promptly sent back to England on instructions from home. A fortnight later he returned, with a pass from Lord Kitchener, as an official visitor and showed much coolness under fire during an adventurous journey with Colonel John Edward Bernard Seely (later Lord Mottistone). But although he was always for winning the war, he did not cease to believe, and to say, that Great Britain had been wrong to embark upon it. Indeed the use to which German propagandists were able to put some of his strictures on British foreign policy did much to make him appear as an enemy of his country. But his main theme was the necessity for keeping alive, even in wartime, the generous and unimpassioned temper of peace. He was never a pacifist, yet, excluded from the platform of the official labour party, he necessarily worked closely with the independent labour party, the membership of which was overwhelmingly pacificist. Temperamentally a moderate, and now more than ever standing for a middle course, he was never wholly at ease with the violence and illogicality of much of the independent labour party propaganda. Partly no doubt for this reason he had been largely instrumental in founding, in September 1914, an *ad hoc* organization, the Union of Democratic Control, which included many liberals as well as socialists, and the object of which was to secure a democratic foreign policy. Another wartime organization on the platforms of which he was able to speak, the National Council for Civil Liberties, also included liberals as well as socialists in its membership. Whatever his platform, however, every meeting at which MacDonald spoke was a potential riot, and the popular press did much to provoke violence, by attributing to him provocative sayings invented by itself, and encouraging the public to break up his meetings. In comparison with MacDonald the other spokesmen of the opposition, including the pacificists, were ignored, and he became the personification of all that the average patriotic citizen disliked and mistrusted. The courage with which MacDonald sustained this concentration of venom did much to deepen the devotion of his followers, and earned him a new affection even among the orthodox labour majority. Indeed it was to his new hold over both wings of the party, and particularly over the independent labour party, that he was to owe his return to the leadership in 1922, and therefore the premiership in 1924.

The welcome extended by MacDonald and his friends to the first Russian revolution, that of Kerensky and the moderates, of March 1917 was long quoted against him as if it had been accorded to the later revolution of Lenin and the Bolsheviks. But the first revolution had appeared to herald the establishment of democracy, the disavowal of imperialism, and an early negotiated peace. When, however, a delegation from the labour party and the independent labour party, which included MacDonald, was about to sail from Aberdeen to visit the provisional government at Petrograd, with the permission of the British Cabinet, the crew of its ship refused to sail if MacDonald and two other members were to be allowed to travel. This incident, which was widely reported, served to discredit MacDonald yet further. It is just possible that if the delegation had been permitted to sail its visit might have assisted the Kerensky government to resist the subsequent onslaught of the Bolsheviks. The two wings of the labour party, however, in which there had been no formal split, were brought closer together by the resignation that August of Arthur Henderson from the coalition War Cabinet, over the question of the socialist conference to be held in Stockholm. Thenceforth, until the end of the war, MacDonald and Henderson spoke very much the same language, and each helped the other to gain the ear of that wing of the party to which he had hitherto been suspect. MacDonald warmly welcomed President Wilson's Fourteen Points but was doubtful whether at this late hour the declaration would avail to stave off a 'military' peace. As the war ended he was respected by the bulk of his party, and was the object of the passionate devotion of an influential minority in it, but for the general public he was still the most unpopular and mistrusted man in Britain, and at the general election in December 1918 he was defeated at West Leicester by just over 14,000 votes.

In February of the following year MacDonald was active as a delegate to the International Socialist Conference at Berne, which he hoped to see paving the way to a conciliatory peace, but which was soon rent by that conflict between revolutionary communism and parliamentary socialism with which MacDonald was chiefly occupied during the next few years. In 1920 he succeeded in persuading the annual conferences of both the independent labour party and the labour party to reject communism. Thereafter the extremists seceded, and the subsequent concentration of their hostility upon MacDonald did much to restore his reputation with the general public. In March 1921 he was defeated by a narrow majority at a by-election at East Woolwich, in which his opponents made much play with his war record, but at the general election of 1922, with the rising tide of reaction against Lloyd George's coalition, he was returned with a comfortable majority for the Aberavon division of Glamorganshire. He was at once elected chairman of the parliamentary labour party, after a close contest with Mr. John Robert Clynes, thanks primarily to the enthusiastic support of the so-called Clydeside group of left-wing socialists, with whose extreme views MacDonald was to be constantly in conflict throughout the rest of his career. Since the labour members now outnumbered the liberals he at once became official leader of the opposition, and it was probably now that his gifts as a House of Commons man were most conspicuous.

At the general election of 1923 the labour party, with 191 seats, was again more powerful than the liberals, and the two together were strong enough to defeat the conservative government. A vote of no confidence having been carried on 17 January 1924, MacDonald did not hesitate to form the first labour government, although it could only exist upon sufferance. He was then sworn of the Privy Council. He made what was thought by many to be the mistake of himself filling the office not only of prime minister but of foreign secretary. Inevitably his preoccupation with foreign affairs made it difficult for him to do himself full justice as leader of the House, and it probably diminished his interest in the domestic programme of his government. Moreover, the twofold responsibility involved a severe physical strain: for MacDonald was conscientious almost to a fault, and he never acquired the art of delegating responsibility; it was said of him that he had been known, when prime minister, to look up trains for one of his secretaries. His diplomacy was on the whole successful. He found France and Germany disposed for conciliation, came to an understanding with the French prime minister, M. Herriot, whose outlook was much the same as his own, and accepted, on behalf of this country, the Experts' Report on German Reparations. The Allied Conference of July in London was summoned to translate this Report into action, and led to the settlement of the following month. In September, at Geneva, MacDonald and Herriot together proposed a protocol for security, arbitration, and disarmament, which was subsequently drafted, though never ratified.

In domestic affairs, however, MacDonald's touch appeared to be less certain. He made little attempt to conciliate the liberals, on whose support his government depended, and although he was in fact by no means comfortable with his Clydeside supporters, the impression got abroad that he was unduly subservient to them. The abrupt reversal in August of the government's previous intention not to guarantee a loan to the Russian government was ascribed to the intervention of backbench Russophils, and about the same time the abandonment of the prosecution of a journalist charged with inciting the armed forces to mutiny was also denounced by the opposition as a concession to forces outside the Cabinet, and brought about the defeat and resignation of the government. MacDonald's premiership had substantially increased his own reputation; and it was gratefully recognized, even by opponents, that in parliamentary tradition, in public ceremonial, and in the relations of Cabinet and Crown there had been no breach with tradition; but in the election which followed in October 1924 the public was prevented from pronouncing a clear-cut verdict on the record of his government by the publication a few days before polling-day of the so-called Zinoviev letter. The precise significance of this document was not understood by the public, even after Mac-Donald's explanation, delayed by the exigencies of a strenuous election tour, had reached it; but the letter, as presented by his opponents, served to strengthen the vague general impression that the labour government had been discreditably subservient to extremist influences. This was the charge of which MacDonald's whole career had been an emphatic repudiation, and after the election, in which his party lost forty-one seats, it was again his influence which secured the emphatic repudiation of communism by the labour party conference of 1925.

Extremist influences, however, were in the ascendant in the industrial wing of the movement, and the following year saw the abortive General Strike. MacDonald had always disapproved of 'direct action', and behind the scenes, although the extremists had not sought his advice, he did his best to avert the explosion. Having failed he felt bound, as leader of a party so closely allied to the Trades Union Congress, to acquiesce in what followed. In 1927 he just survived a severe illness contracted during a visit to the United States of America, but recovered rapidly enough to play a principal part in drafting the party manifesto *Labour and the Nation* (1928), a lengthy document which characteristically combined a comprehensive programme of reform with a restatement of theory and a renewed repudiation of communism. Before the general election in May 1929 he undertook an exacting nation-wide speaking campaign which contributed markedly to the victory of his party: he himself was returned for the Seaham division of county Durham. With 287 seats labour was for the first time the strongest party.

For the administration which he now formed MacDonald was mainly concerned to select colleagues whose outlook was akin to his own; trade unionism was not so strongly represented as in 1924, and the extremists were almost wholly excluded. This time he did not attempt to combine the office of foreign secretary with the premiership, but he continued to devote his attention chiefly to foreign affairs, on which, he believed, all else depended. After conversations with General Dawes, the American ambassador, and a visit to President Hoover in the United States—the first to be made by a prime minister of Great Britain—he succeeded in bringing about a revival of the Naval Conference, which was held in London in January 1930. Agreement was reached between Great Britain, the United States, and Japan and it seemed that a genuine advance towards naval disarmament had been made. Meanwhile the Hague Conference, at which Philip Snowden effectively represented Great Britain, had removed the obstacles to the application of the Young Plan for the payment of reparations. Once again, however, the government's domestic record was less satisfactory, at any rate to socialists. Its difficulties were due partly to the breach between MacDonald and the independent labour party, partly to the steady darkening of the general economic horizon. An informal understanding with the liberals meant that for the first time labour was not merely in office but in power. It was all the easier, therefore, for the government to disregard its left-wing critics, and, except that they persuaded it to relax the regulations governing unemployment insurance, they exercised scarcely any influence on domestic policy. At the annual conference of the party a vote of censure by the rebels was early defeated, thanks to a fighting speech by MacDonald. At the first Indian Round Table Conference, held towards the end of 1930, his skilful chairmanship was generally admired, although the gulf between Hindus and Moslems was not bridged. But throughout the year, with the deepening of the universal economic depression, unemployment rose, and its cost had been greatly increased by the more generous conditions of benefit. The Report of the economy committee set up under the chairmanship of Sir George (later Lord) May, published on 31 July 1931, estimated a deficit of £120,000,000 by April 1932. The Report, which made the financial position of the country appear even more precarious than it actually was, was followed by a flight of foreign investors from the pound, and a serious drain on British gold reserves. Throughout the subsequent meetings of the special economy committee of the Cabinet, and of the Cabinet itself, MacDonald pressed for economies sufficient to balance the budget. Some of his colleagues, however, although ready to accept reductions of expenditure totalling more than £56,000,000 were not prepared to face a further saving of £22,000,000 on unemployment insurance, to which the general council of the Trades Union Congress, which was consulted on 20 August, had shown itself resolutely opposed. After prolonged discussions within the Cabinet, and negotiations which it had sanctioned with the leaders of the other parties, MacDonald had to report to the King on the morning of 23

August that his colleagues could not agree. Later that Sunday the King saw Sir Herbert Samuel and Baldwin separately, and at night again received MacDonald, who tendered the resignation of the labour government. The King urged MacDonald to reconsider his own position, and next morning, at MacDonald's request, the King held a conference of the three party leaders at Buckingham Palace, and within a few hours MacDonald had formed an all-party government in conjunction with the leaders of the conservative and liberal parties. Although Snowden, J. H. Thomas, and Lord Sankey followed him into the 'national' government, MacDonald had made no attempt to carry the bulk of his party with him, and he was at once succeeded in its leadership by Henderson. Yet at first he regarded the coalition as no more than a temporary expedient for overcoming the financial crisis, after which parties were to revert to their normal alignment. Inevitably, however, subsequent controversy, let alone the bitterness with which many of his former colleagues and followers now assailed him, made the breach permanent. Some of his critics, indeed, maintained that in forming the new government he had yielded to the temptations of what Lord Passfield called 'the aristocratic embrace', and even that he had himself long plotted to bring about the fall of his own government. There can be no doubt, however, that at the outset of the crisis he had expected to fall permanently from power, or that he did not at first desire the coalition to outlast the immediate crisis.

The exodus of short-term capital compelled the new government to abandon the gold standard which it had been formed to defend, but it was not long before confidence was restored and foreign capital was pouring in again. In the election which followed in October the government, appealing for a virtually free hand or 'doctor's mandate', secured all but fifty-nine seats. MacDonald himself won a remarkable personal triumph at Seaham, which had been hitherto as impregnable a labour stronghold as any in the country.

MacDonald now formed his fourth administration, with an unchallengeable majority composed of the conservative and liberal parties and a small 'national' labour group, which at first exercised an influence disproportionate to its size. MacDonald found himself at ease with his new colleagues, and is said to have done much to preserve harmony between them. Snowden and the free-trade liberals, although retained for a while by the 'agreement to differ' on tariffs announced on 22 January 1932, left the coalition after the preferential tariff agreements reached at Ottawa that summer. The government, however, pressed on with a programme of domestic retrenchment and reform, which included a number of socialist measures, notably in agriculture. MacDonald continued to regard the European situation as the key to domestic recovery, and despite operations for glaucoma in each eye in February and May of 1932 he presided at a Four Power Conference in London in April and was present at the Disarmament Conference in Geneva in the same month. He was mainly responsible for the summoning of the abortive World Economic Conference of 1933 in London, which was doomed by the refusal of President Roosevelt's government to agree to the stabilization of currency. MacDonald was also the author of the draft convention which saved the Disarmament Conference from collapse. He was always a believer in personal diplomacy, and his visits to Paris and Rome did much to bring about a consultative pact between Great Britain, France, Italy, and Germany. By now, however, the shadow of Hitler was beginning to fall across the European scene, and MacDonald, with his colleagues, was convinced that appeasement must thenceforth be pursued simultaneously with a restoration of Great Britain's dangerously impaired defences. The White Paper on National Defence of March 1935, which heralded a programme of rearmament, bore not only his initials but clear evidence of his drafting. Three months later (7 June) he resigned the premiership, and assumed the sinecure office of lord president of the Council.

MacDonald's powers were clearly impaired by prolonged overstrain: he had probably worked longer hours than any previous prime minister. The remorseless vendetta waged against him by a few of his former associates had also had its effect. He had not played a prominent part in the House of Commons of late, partly because the government's huge majority rendered personal intervention seldom necessary and partly owing to his preoccupation with foreign affairs, but partly also because he was conscious that failing health had begun to make his speaking involved and obscure. At the general election in November 1935 his courageous decision to contest Seaham undoubtedly contributed to the victory of the 'national' coalition, and to the survival of the small 'national' labour group, but his own defeat was inevitable. He was returned, however, at a by-election in January 1936 for the Scottish Universities. He died suddenly 9 November 1937, on a holiday voyage to South America, and after his body had lain in state in the cathedral of Bermuda and after a funeral service in Westminster Abbey, he was buried beside his wife in Spynie churchyard, near Lossiemouth. He left two sons, of whom the younger, Malcolm, was at the time secretary of state for Dominion affairs, and three daughters.

MacDonald was somewhat above middle height. His face, with its sensitively chiselled features and large and luminous eyes, was that of an artist rather than a statesman. He had always been a handsome man, but in later life, when his dark waving hair had turned white, and there was a marked suggestion of strain and self-restraint about eyes and mouth, his appearance was particularly striking. He had a taste for physical hardship and danger and was a great walker. His two collections, *Wanderings and Excursions* (1925) and *At Home and Abroad* (1936), contain many of his travel experiences. He received honorary degrees from the universities of Glasgow (1924), Edinburgh (1925), Wales (1926), Oxford (1931), and McGill (1929). In the year of the General Strike it was proposed at Cambridge that an honorary degree should be conferred upon him, but he refused to accept one which at that time would certainly have been passed only by a majority.

Portraits of MacDonald by Solomon J. Solomon (presented to him in 1912 by the labour party) and by Ambrose McEvoy are in the possession of his family, who also own portraits by Augustus John and Sir John Lavery (unfinished), as well as two bronze busts by Jacob Epstein (1926 and 1931) and one by Felix Joubert (c 1936). Another portrait by Lavery (1931), and a bronze bust by Epstein (1934), a copy of one of those mentioned above, are in the National Portrait Gallery.

[*The Times* and *Manchester Guardian*, 10 November 1937; Lord Elton, *Life of James Ramsay MacDonald* (1866–1919), 1939; Lord Snowden, *An Autobiography*, 2 vols., 1934; *Reports* of the annual conference of the labour party and independent labour party; private information; personal knowledge.]

ELTON

published 1949

MACKINTOSH John Pitcairn

(1929–1978)

Politician and professor of politics, was born in Simla 24 August 1929, the elder of two brothers. He spent his first eleven years in British India where his mother, Mary Victoria Pitcairn, taught at a Teacher Training College. Her husband, Colin M. Mackintosh, had gone to India to sell cotton piece goods; then he represented McCallum's Perfection Whiskey, finally transferring to insurance work. Later, John Mackintosh used to recall how one of his earliest childhood memories was the image of demonstrators lying round the lorries carrying Lancashire piece goods, so that they could not move. The campaign of M. K. Gandhi to protect Indian home industry was, perhaps, Mackintosh's introduction to his lifelong concern with overseas issues, and the problems of the third world.

At the beginning of World War II the Mackintosh family returned to Edinburgh, sending the boys to Melville College. Mackintosh was to speak with affection of individual teachers, and of unhappy times at the school. He progressed to Edinburgh University, where he achieved a first class honours degree in history (1950), and then to Balliol College, Oxford, to read PPE, in which he achieved a second class in 1952.

At Oxford certain lifelong scars were inflicted. Whereas Scottish undergraduates, straight from school or National Service, tended to enjoy Oxbridge, those already having a degree from a Scottish university often returned disenchanted. Mackintosh held that Balliol men were very arrogant: 'I resented them very much. They said that a first class honours degree at a Scottish University meant that one was probably fit to come up to Oxford as an undergraduate.' This early encounter with the English establishment possibly sowed the seed of lifelong scepticism about mandarin-level civil servants, and caused his concern with Scottish devolution and an assembly in Edinburgh. The Oxford experience might also partially account for Mackintosh giving vent to witty irreverence towards so many of the products of Oxbridge, something that was to disadvantage him in later life when his political preferment was being contemplated. His malicious tongue was more wounding than perhaps he realized, and therefore sour jokes at his expense were well received both among his university colleagues and MPs. For example, the story went the rounds that Harold Wilson (later Lord Wilson of Rievaulx), in 1967, commented to the long-serving secretary of state for Scotland: 'You had better keep an eye on that man Mackintosh, Willie. He wants your job.' 'No, Harold', came Ross's reply, 'He wants yours!'

This rather-too-obvious and impatient ambition, dangerously allied with an incapacity to suffer fools gladly, may have been developed by an American influence, fostered during postgraduate work at Princeton, where he was Sir John Dill memorial fellow in 1952–3. Brash, Mackintosh was not. Insensitive, as to how he could grate on other less gifted men, he certainly was.

His first job was that of a junior lecturer in history at Glasgow University (1953–4), followed by seven years as lecturer at Edinburgh University between 1954 and 1961. His many pupils testify to the brilliance of his lecturing and his capacity to inspire undergraduates. He was entertaining and articulate to the point of being envied by his colleagues, and he displayed a genuine concern for his students. In 1957 he married one of his history students, Janette, daughter of J. D. Robertson; they had a daughter and a son. Having unsuccessfully contested the Pentlands division of Edinburgh as Labour candidate in the 1959 general election, in 1960 a parliamentary career seemed open to Mackintosh when he had the all-powerful backing of the general secretary of the Scottish Trades Union Congress, George Middleton, in a by-election for the Paisley seat. At the last moment, Mackintosh declined to go forward and departed to take up a professorial post at the University of Ibadan in Nigeria. It was in this period that he was to publish his book *The British Cabinet* (1962), which, in the eyes of Richard Crossman, who reviewed the volume of this still obscure academic, initiated the concept of prime ministerial government and placed Mackintosh in the same league as Walter Bagehot. It was indeed a seminal thesis. The irony is that, had Mackintosh gone to Parliament as MP for Paisley in 1960, he could hardly have been denied a post in the 1964 Labour government, leading to a Cabinet position before the end of the first Wilson administration in 1970. He would then doubtless have written about the myth and the reality of Cabinet government, in the light of experience.

In 1963 he returned to be senior lecturer in politics at Glasgow University, and, to the dismay of his friends, his marriage to Janette Robertson, willing hostess to a generation of undergraduates, was dissolved. In that year he married Catherine Margaret Una Maclean, a lecturer in social medicine, the daughter of the Revd C. Maclean, of Scarp, Harris; they had a son and a daughter.

In 1965–6 he was professor of politics at the University of Strathclyde, working on *The Devolution of Power: Local Democracy, Regionalism and Nationalism*, which was to be published in 1968. This was the intellectual furniture of much of the Scottish devolution campaigns of the 1970s—though Mackintosh himself, shortly before his death, was scathing about the opportunism and unworkability of the proposals embodied in the Labour government's Scotland Bill. With some justice, he supposed that any prime minister, really concerned to allow devolution, other than for reasons of sheer short-term political expediency, would have given him the post of minister of state in the Cabinet Office, responsible for the devolution proposals.

Mackintosh was elected Labour MP for Berwick and East Lothian in 1966. The fact that so talented a man, who was arguably, alongside Brian Walden, the most compellingly persuasive parliamentary orator of his generation, never achieved ministerial office, requires some explanation. One clue is to be found in his maiden speech, a dazzling performance, which lingers in the memory of all who heard it. His tribute to his defeated opponent, Sir William Anstruther-Gray, former deputy chairman of ways and means and chairman of the 1922 Committee, was one of the handsomest ever heard: 'It is perhaps not well known to hon. Members that Sir William was one of the men who returned from the Front in May, 1940, and persuaded 32 of his backbench colleagues to go into the Lobby against their own Government—against the leadership of Neville Chamberlain— thus helping to bring down that Government. On that occasion he was a true patriot. Like my predecessor, I hope to represent efficiently the constituency which has elected me. I shall work hard on its behalf' (*Hansard*, 9 May 1966, col. 77).

This he did, prodigiously, with a six-month interregnum in 1974, when he was defeated in February and returned the same October. At the memorial meeting in the House of Commons, Gerald O'Brien, the full-time agent of the Berwick and East Lothian Constituency Labour Party, moved an ultra-sophisticated audience by claiming that the Lammermuir hills wept when Mackintosh died; and, on the way to his funeral, little groups of constituents from the farming areas could be observed all along the route of the cortege paying their last respects to a politician who had come to be loved by those for whom he worked. In dealing with constituents' problems Mackintosh was patient, caring, and charming, a different person from he who, in London, chastised the Wilsons and the Callaghans with his acerbic wit. Moreover, the very point which Mackintosh selected in Anstruther-Gray's career for favourable mention was, with hindsight, to be a trailer for his own rebellions, too numerous to chronicle. Among the more remembered must be that hectic night in November 1976, when Mackintosh and Walden abstained on the Docks Bill, which was consequently lost, to the consternation of the hierarchy of Labour ministers.

Mackintosh's interest in constitutional and procedural questions was put to immediate use when he entered Parliament by his appointment to the select committees for the oversight of government, and he served on experimental committees on agriculture (1967–8) and Scottish affairs (1968–70), forerunners of the departmentally related committee system introduced in 1979. Never was there a more spectacular, intellectual, verbal clash of arms, than when Mackintosh bearded Richard Crossman, then leader of the House, on the proposal to terminate the activities of the embryo agriculture committee. After a Wagnerian battle Mackintosh lost, but won the war of select committees. He delighted in arguing questions of parliamentary reform with his colleagues and the clerks of the House, and was generous with his time in exposition of the practicalities of parliamentary government to those outside. He gave valuable help to the Commonwealth Parliamentary Association, and to the Hansard Society, of which he was chairman from 1974 until his death. To this Dictionary he contributed the notice of Lord Morrison of Lambeth.

No picture of Mackintosh can be complete without an attempt to convey his demonic energy—apparent whether playing with his children, step-children, or the children of others, or pouring out polished, provocative articles for *The Times*, the *Scotsman*, the *Political Quarterly*, and a host of other newspapers and journals, or fascinating Königswinter conferences, or electrifying the special conference of the Labour Party, a largely hostile audience, when speaking in the Central Hall, Westminster, on EEC entry, from an unusual and even physically hazardous position, in the front row of the gallery, leaning over a balcony. There was also the extraordinary courage and self-discipline which he exercised during the last year of his life, when he knew he was fatally ill, but kept the knowledge to himself, seeking no pity, and working with frenetic effort. He died in the Western General Hospital, Edinburgh, 30 July 1978.

[Personal knowledge.]

TAM DALYELL

published 1986

MACLEOD Iain Norman

(1913–1970)

Politician, was born at Skipton, Yorkshire, 11 November 1913, the second child and eldest of three sons of Norman Macleod and his wife and second cousin Annabel, daughter of Rhoderick Ross, a doctor on the isle of Lewis. His father, the son of a crofter on the island, was a popular and respected doctor in Skipton for nearly thirty years. Of wholly Scottish ancestry Macleod was brought up in Yorkshire, although in 1920 his father bought for a small sum a property, Scaliscro, on Lewis, where the family often spent the holidays and where Macleod was taught to shoot and to play bridge. His roots were at least as much in the Highlands as in Yorkshire.

As a child Macleod conceived an enduring love of poetry, for which he had a Macaulayan memory, and which he himself wrote. Neither at Fettes College, however, nor at Gonville and Caius College, Cambridge, where he got a second in history in 1935, were his intellectual gifts revealed. He was fond of rugby and cricket, although only a moderate player, and he always remained a keen follower and spectator of most sports. Apart from poetry and a little acting, Macleod's chief interests at Cambridge were bridge and gambling. He spoke only once at the Union and joined none of the political clubs, but he formed the Cambridge Bridge Club and made himself president. He was a top-class player.

After Cambridge Macleod was given a place in Thomas de la Rue, whose chairman he had met at the bridge table, but he had no interest in his job, which he was in any case often too tired to do, having spent most of the night playing bridge. De la Rue's forbearance lasted two years, whereupon Macleod claimed to be reading for the bar, perhaps to please his father. His manner of life at Cambridge and in London, although not in accord with the Protestant ethic, had its reasons. His earnings from bridge were on average more than ten times the £3 a week he gained from de la Rue, and his intellect was well trained.

In September 1939 Macleod joined the Royal Fusiliers as a private, and after being commissioned in the Duke of Wellington's Regiment in April 1940 he was sent to the BEF which was already in retreat. Near Neufchâtel he was badly wounded in the thigh and returned to hospital in England. In 1941 Macleod married Evelyn Hester, daughter of the Revd Gervase Vanneck Blois, rector of Hanbury, Worcestershire, whose first husband, Mervyn Charles Mason, had been killed at sea in 1940. A boy and a girl were born in 1942 and 1944. Macleod's early soldiering extended him no more than had university or commerce. It was only at Staff College in autumn 1943 under the stimulus of high-class competition that he realized the extent of his abilities and determined to use them. He landed on D-Day as DAQMG of the 50th Northumbrian division, and served in France until his division returned to Yorkshire in November 1944.

He was on leave at Scaliscro when the general election of 1945 was announced. There being no Conservative organization in the Outer Hebrides, Macleod supplied it. His father, who supported Churchill although a Liberal, was elected chairman and Macleod the candidate. Since there was no one else present, this was not a difficult meeting. Defeat in the election was, however, certain, and Macleod's creditable 2,756 votes out of nearly 13,000 cast left him at the bottom of the poll.

Macleod was demobilized as a major in January 1946 and shortly afterwards joined the Conservative Parliamentary Secretariat. On the amalgamation of the new Secretariat with the Research Department in 1948 Macleod, now one of the party's few experts on the social services, was put in charge of home affairs. In 1946 he had been adopted as Conservative candidate for Enfield, then a safe Labour seat; only after it divided into two in 1948 did he seem likely to be successful. At no time in his life was Macleod well off. Until 1952, when he virtually gave it up, bridge remained necessary for paying the mortgage on his home in Enfield and other expenses. He wrote a weekly bridge column for the *Sunday Times* and in 1952 published the lively and authoritative *Bridge is an Easy Game*.

Elected in 1950 for Enfield West with a majority over 9,000, Macleod wisely concentrated on the subjects he knew best: health and social services. An original member of the One Nation Group he edited with Angus Maude the group's pamphlet *One Nation* (1950). He was not given office when the Conservatives regained power in 1951 but became chairman of the Conservative parliamentary health and social services committee. As such, on the second reading debate on the National Health Service Bill on 27 March 1952 he was likely to be the third speaker after the minister and Dr (later Baroness) Summerskill, the shadow minister, a good position when the House would be well filled. However, a maiden speaker was given precedence. Bitterly disappointed, Macleod decided not to speak and threw away his notes. But when Aneurin Bevan followed the maiden speaker, Macleod changed his mind again and also his speech. Bevan was a much better target than Dr Summerskill, and by now Churchill was in the House. Macleod's opening sentence, 'I want to deal closely and with relish with the vulgar, crude and intemperate speech to which the House of Commons has just listened', followed shortly afterwards by the remark that to have a debate on the National Health Service without Aneurin Bevan 'would be like putting on Hamlet with no one in the part of the First Gravedigger', established his hold over the House. Complete master of his subject in all its details, Macleod dealt effectively with several interruptions from Bevan, and his victory over the most formidable debater in the Opposition was not in doubt. Six weeks later Churchill appointed him minister of health. At that time the Ministry, which had lost its responsibilities for housing and for planning, was a declining department, and its minister was not in the Cabinet. Nevertheless, to achieve the post in one jump from the backbenches and to become a privy councillor at the age of thirty-eight was remarkable.

Two months later Eve Macleod was struck by meningitis and polio; eventually she was able to walk again with the aid of sticks. Despite her disability she continued to work tirelessly in the constituency and to help Macleod in every way she could. Macleod's own health was already bad. He suffered from ankylosing spondylitis, a form of rheumatoid arthritis which attacks the spine and which made it progressively more difficult for Macleod to move his back, neck, or head. Its effect was no doubt aggravated by his wartime injury which made walking difficult and led to a slanting of the pelvis. Social occasions when he had to stand or look up were an increasing trial. The pain was virtually permanent for the last twenty years of his life. It was unflinchingly borne.

Macleod's ill health and that of his wife naturally sharpened his sympathy for the suffering of others, which was demonstrated during his visits to hospitals and by his successful efforts to humanize their administration and to encourage help from voluntary organizations. Although the last man to parade his concern, he was both in private and in public life notably and genuinely compassionate. Otherwise, as minister of health Macleod was sound but not spectacular: money was scarce, and housing had much higher priority; consolidation was the only possible course.

Macleod showed himself a quick and competent administrator, and as always was good in the House. His reputation steadily grew, but promotion did not come until Eden's reshuffle in December 1955 when Macleod entered the Cabinet as minister of labour.

Macleod's predecessor, Sir Walter Monckton (later Viscount Monckton of Brenchley), had been given by Churchill the task of maintaining good relations with the trade-union leaders. But conciliation had bred inflation, and by 1955 greater heed had to be paid to the economic effects of conceding wage claims. If Macleod could not be as open-handed with the unions as Monckton had been, his employment policies followed the ideal of 'One Nation'. He tried to improve relations in industry by persuading employers to treat their employees as responsible individuals, and he favoured the introduction of a code of practice setting out the rights of workers, contracts of service, and redundancy payments: all later achieved. In 1957 he was glad to be able to announce the beginning of the end of national service. But it was his defeat of Frank Cousins in the bus strike in 1958 which first made Macleod a national figure. He himself was unhappy about some aspects of the lengthy struggle, in particular the forced departure from his department's traditional role of mediator; but in public his handling was firm and sure, and he accompanied it with a biting attack on Hugh Gaitskell, one of several notable parliamentary performances at this period. Sometimes speaking without notes, Macleod always presented a clear argument heavily buttressed by detailed facts, which his photographic memory had no difficulty in retaining. His phraseology was colourful and often witty: 'I cannot help it if every time the Opposition are asked to name their weapons they pick boomerangs.'

Macleod had his misgivings over Suez but he was not sufficiently involved to consider resignation. Although he got on well enough with Eden, his relations with Macmillan were far closer. With the planning for the 1959 election Macleod was closely concerned. Immediately afterwards he was made secretary of state for the colonies, the social and political demands of the appointment necessitating a move from Enfield to a flat in London. With Macmillan's support Macleod deliberately speeded up the movement towards independence in Africa. Conferences on Kenya, Tanganyika, Nyasaland, and Uganda quickly succeeded each other; Hastings Banda and Kenyatta were released from jail. Within a few years Macleod's policy had the appearance of inevitable rightness, but at the time it was strongly opposed by the Conservative right wing. In the Lords, Salisbury delivered a strong personal attack on the colonial secretary (7 March 1961) for adopting, especially 'to the white communities of Africa, a most unhappy and an entirely wrong approach. He had been too clever by half.' Salisbury went on to accuse Macleod of bringing into the sphere of politics the bridge technique of seeking to outwit his opponents—the white settlers. Highly sensitive, Macleod seemed unduly put out by this onslaught, but his assessment turned out to be correct. 'Too clever by half' stuck, and almost to the end it distorted many people's picture of Macleod.

It was not true of his African policy, let alone of the man. A calculating man would never have set about dismantling the British Empire so openly and with something approaching enthusiasm; he would have feigned reluctance. Macleod was fully aware that he was going against the grain of his party and damaging his own prospects. In early 1961 he thought he might well be forced out of office by the end of the year. Yet he stuck to his policy, convinced that speedy de-colonization in Africa was vital. Elsewhere he was less successful: both the South Arabian and the West Indian federations were short-lived. But Britain's withdrawal from Africa in peace instead of with ill grace and in bloodshed was Macleod's greatest political achievement and put him perhaps second only to Joseph Chamberlain among reforming colonial secretaries.

In October 1961 Macleod was moved. Over Northern Rhodesia he had become over-exposed both in the Cabinet and in the party. Sure of the correctness of his policy and aware of the dangers of going too slowly, he had sometimes been inflexible over details. He became chancellor of the Duchy of Lancaster, leader of the House of Commons, and chairman of the Conservative Party organization. The first job was a sinecure; the other two doubtfully compatible; nor did Macleod's occasional abruptness of manner and impatience with the slower-witted make him an ideal choice. Yet, he was well fitted to be party chairman. If his African policies had done him harm in the party, they had done the party itself a lot of good and had given Macleod a broad cross-party appeal. His attitude at home was similarly attractive, especially to the young. He always called himself a Tory, regarding 'Conservative' as stodgy and uninspiring. (Not surprisingly, Macleod's book on *Neville Chamberlain* (1961), amongst the dullest of Conservatives, was disappointing; he wrote it because he admired Chamberlain's work for social reform.)

It was the element of romanticism or poetry in Macleod which, as much as the liberalism of his political views, helped to attract the young and uncommitted. Macleod's faith in democracy was unusually strong for a democratic politician. He knew that a party's policy had to be much more than an invocation of past dogmas; it had to learn from the voters as well as try to lead them: width of appeal was vital. For Macleod winning elections by being a national party was only part of the Tory task. If the country was one nation, this was not inevitable: the one nation had to be preserved and constantly re-created.

Unfortunately Macleod had become chairman of the party when the Government's fortunes were beginning to decline. Its economic policy was unpopular, and a series of by-election disasters followed. Macleod never shirked the battle, and in private was full of suggestions and expedients for lessening the party's unpopularity. He was, too, always resourceful in the Government's defence in the House of Commons. But a modern party chairman, like a modern football manager, is judged by results. For that reason, as well as his unpopularity with the Right over Africa, Macleod in the leadership crisis in 1963 was not seriously in the running to succeed Macmillan.

Whether or not he occasionally nursed hopes that in a deadlock the party might turn to him, Macleod's usually sure-footed political judgement failed him during the leadership controversy. His subsequent refusal to join Douglas-Home's Government was due in part to his belief that Macmillan's successor should have been chosen from the House of Commons and that Douglas-Home, too exclusively associated with foreign affairs, could not win an election; and in part to the view that having said, in his support for R. A. Butler (later Lord Butler of Saffron Walden), that he would not serve under Douglas-Home, it would be dishonourable to change his mind. Others might retract or waver but not he. 'One does not expect', he said, 'to have many people with one in the last ditch.'

Having imprudently jeopardized his political career, Macleod shortly afterwards became editor of the *Spectator*, a post which he held until the end of 1965, and a director of Lombards Bank. As an editor he was unstuffy and approachable, and always gave full freedom to his writers, even though a good deal of the political writing in the paper was to say the least inconvenient to him. While not devoid of the politician's egotism, he was far more egotistical in print than in life. This made his journalism unrepresentative of the man, but it made his weekly column enormously readable. Macleod considerably added to his unpopularity in his party by publishing an article in the *Spectator* (17 January 1964) on the leadership row. Although under some pressure in his constituency to explain himself, the prudent course was unquestionably silence.

After the 1964 election, Douglas-Home invited Macleod to join the shadow Cabinet, which he did, with steel as his subject; an unfortunate choice since, with a tiny majority, the Labour Government was not anxious to hurry on its plans for nationalization. Nevertheless Macleod made many effective speeches in the country in order to rehabilitate himself. He felt his abilities fitted him to be party leader and prime minister, but knew he had too much to live down and too much distrust to dispel. Well before Douglas-Home resigned in 1965, Macleod had decided not to stand for the succession. Appointed shadow chancellor of the

Exchequer by Edward Heath, for whom he had voted, his eyes were henceforth firmly fixed on No. 11.

Macleod was not an economist and had no inclination to become one. Experience had engendered doubts about the possibilities of detailed management of the economy by the Treasury, and he always believed that an Opposition should not over-burden itself with policy. For these reasons Macleod avoided large theoretical pronouncements as shadow chancellor, but at a time of almost continuous economic trouble for the Government his natural ability and his eye for essentials as well as his loathing of unemployment made him an outstandingly effective Opposition spokesman. Before the 1970 election Macleod was aware that he had been pushed too far in the non-interventionist direction and that this would have to be redressed in office.

A belief in opportunity, although with proper safeguards for the less fortunate, was a consistent theme throughout Macleod's career. Accordingly he embraced the idea of a radical reform of the system of taxation with enthusiasm and intense industry. The package of tax reform enacted in the early years of the Heath Government had been closely prepared by Macleod and his team in opposition.

Macleod was a superb orator in Parliament and on the platform. He was probably the best conference speaker in any party since the war. Small in height, and bald on the top of his head since his Cambridge days, his large forehead seemed to have difficulty in encasing his brains. Added to this arresting appearance, his unusually resonant voice had a dramatic intensity which excited his audience, and easily moved it to laughter or enthusiasm. Macleod was a brilliant communicator not only in the sense that he spoke and wrote exceptionally well, and was a master of television, but in the more important sense that he had something to say. Never trendy—he had a profound contempt for the BBC and for a period near the end refused to appear on its programmes—he was totally unpompous, and his opinions reflected both freshness of mind and stability of attitude.

He regarded the Commonwealth Immigrants Bill of 1968 as a betrayal of the Kenyan Asians, and although the shadow Cabinet supported the Government, Macleod together with fourteen other Conservatives voted against it. When his friend, Nigel Fisher, was in trouble with the far Right in his constituency, Surbiton, in 1969, Macleod made it clear that if Fisher was pushed out he would leave too. He had strikingly shown his loyalty to other friends in trouble before. Although his ill health seemed to get even worse in the last two years of his life, he remained good and amusing company.

When his mother died during the 1970 election, Macleod suspended his electioneering for a week. He returned to make two extremely telling television appearances. On 20 June he was made chancellor of the Exchequer, but had no chance to make his mark before being taken ill on 7 July. He was operated upon for appendicitis and returned to 11 Downing Street. But the years of ill health and pain had taken their toll, and he died there after a heart attack 20 July 1970. He was buried at Gargrave, Yorkshire, near his parents and his sister.

A posthumous portrait by Alfred Janes hangs in the Constitutional Club.

[Nigel Fisher, *Iain Macleod*, 1973; private information; personal knowledge.]

IAN GILMOUR

published 1981

MACMILLAN (Maurice) Harold

(1894–1986)

First Earl of Stockton

Prime minister, was born 10 February 1894 at Cadogan Place, London, the youngest of three sons (there were no daughters) of Maurice Crawford Macmillan, publisher, and his wife, Helen ('Nellie') Artie, only surviving daughter of Joshua Tarleton Belles, surgeon, of Indianapolis, and his wife, Julia Reid. Nellie Belles's first husband, a young painter, died in November 1874, five months after their marriage. Ten years later she married Maurice Macmillan, a taciturn, austere workaholic, who left domestic matters exclusively to her. It has been often said, not least by Macmillan himself, that he was the grandson of a crofter. In fact he was the great-grandson; his grandfather Daniel left the croft at the age of eleven to become a bookseller's apprentice and to lay the foundations of the publishing firm which became one of the most prosperous and famous in Britain.

Nellie Macmillan was intensely and at times embarrassingly ambitious for her children. Neither Daniel ('Dan'), the brilliant donnish eldest son, nor Arthur, the gentle self-effacing second, were suitable instruments for her purpose. She concentrated on Harold, who later wrote: 'I can truthfully say that I owe everything all through my life to my mother's devotion and support.' But a price can be paid for matriarchal bossiness. Her constant vigilance and perpetual interference made her in the eyes of some members of the family 'a fiend'. Macmillan himself told a friend many years later when he was prime minister: 'I admired her but never really liked her. . . . She dominated me and she still dominates me.' One asset she gave him was the ability to speak French. She had spent time in Paris before her marriage, and in London she employed French maids and insisted on her sons speaking French at meals 'downstairs'. Macmillan claimed that it was to be a help in dealing with General Charles de Gaulle. The combination of a reclusive father and an obsessive mother, together with two much older and not very sympathetic brothers, resulted in a solitary life for a small boy. He found solace to some extent, like Sir Winston Churchill, in the affection of a devoted nanny, but he remained all his life a bit of a loner who found it hard, as did his brothers, to relate at all easily to his contemporaries, to his children, and to women. He was a shy and anxious child who hated to be conspicuous—curious characteristics in a future prime minister. To the end of his days he remained intensely nervous before making a speech. Of his famous 'unflappability' he said that people little knew how much his stomach flapped on those occasions. He suffered all his life from sporadic moods of deep depression. He was also a hypochondriac, although, since he lived to ninety-two, his health cannot have been too bad.

He was educated at Summer Fields, Oxford, in those days a rather bleak factory programmed to produce scholars for the leading public schools. Although unhappy there, he gained a scholarship for Eton, where he was equally unhappy and from which in 1909 he was withdrawn early by his parents on grounds of health. Rumours of sexual impropriety have no foundation. Although he habitually wore an Old Etonian tie (that and the Guards' tie seemed in later life to be the only ones he possessed) he had little affection for the place. He never became a fellow and seldom revisited it.

To bridge the gap between leaving school early and the goal of Oxford set by his parents, a private tutor was needed. Their first choice was Dilwyn Knox, son of the Anglican bishop of Manchester, who proved cold and unsympathetic; their second choice was his brother 'Ronnie' Knox, an Eton and Balliol contemporary of Dan Macmillan and widely acclaimed at twenty-two as one of the intellectual stars of his time. He struck up a close friendship with his sixteen-year-old pupil. It was abruptly terminated in November 1910 by Nellie Macmillan, who may have suspected 'inordinate affection' and who certainly from her low-church angle disliked Knox's Anglo-Catholicism, which she saw, rightly in this case, as a stepping-stone to that arch-bugbear, 'Rome'. Their friendship was, however, renewed in 1912 at Oxford, where Macmillan was an exhibitioner at Balliol and Knox, also a Balliol man, had just become chaplain of Trinity College. Knox had loved Eton but was not keen on Balliol. Macmillan was exactly the opposite. He blossomed as never before at that supremely élitist college. He was secretary and then treasurer of the Oxford Union, and might well have become president but for World War I. He obtained a first class in classical honour moderations (1914). He made a host of friends, and many years later, when chancellor of the university, would dwell with nostalgia on the 'golden summer' of 1914—the last summer that so many of his Balliol companions were to see. Long after 1918, Oxford was to him a 'city of ghosts' and he could not bear to go back in the interwar years. Pictures show him at Oxford as a good-looking, dark-haired young man. He was tall and broad-shouldered. It was not till the war that he grew a bushy moustache which did not improve his appearance but which he kept for the rest of his life. Although he had the looks often associated with the Highlanders he had no trace of a Scottish accent but spoke the orthodox English of Eton and Oxford.

On the eve of war Macmillan, along with Knox and another Oxford friend, Guy Lawrence, seriously considered whether to 'Pope', in the jargon of their set. Lawrence did and Knox followed rather later, but Macmillan, to Knox's bitter disappointment, wrote in July 1915 to say that he intended to postpone a decision till after the war 'if I am alive'. In the end he resolved to remain an Anglican. He took his religion very seriously and continued to be a devout high churchman to the end of his life. In 1914 he was commissioned into the King's Royal Rifle Corps, but was soon transferred, thanks to wire-pulling by his mother, to the socially grander Grenadier Guards. He sailed to France in August 1915 and was wounded three times, a bullet permanently damaging his right hand on one occasion. The war left him with a limp handshake, a dragging gait, and sporadic pain. Mentally it gave him a deep sympathy with the largely working-class 'other ranks' and strong antipathy to the 'embusqués', who held office jobs far away from the front.

Yet, unlike so many 'demobbed' officers, he was financially secure, with a junior partnership in the publishing firm. Before taking it up he wanted to travel. His mother pulled wires again and in 1919 got him the job of aide-de-camp to Victor Christian William Cavendish, ninth Duke of Devonshire, governor-general of Canada. There he fell in love with one of the duke's daughters, Lady Dorothy Evelyn Cavendish, to the consternation of the formidable duchess ('Evie'), who had intended her for the heir of the Duke of Buccleuch. On 21 April 1920 they were married, amid suitable pomp and circumstance, at St Margaret's, Westminster. The bride's side was lined with royals and peers, the bridegroom's with Macmillan authors, including six OMs. It seems to have been a genuine case of love at first sight although, as Alistair Horne says in the official biography, it is not clear 'what exactly it was that drew Dorothy to the earnest crofter's great-grandson, the ambitious middle-class publisher's son, with his shy, somewhat stilted manners, his Groucho moustache, and the shuffling walk that was a legacy of his war wounds'.

Macmillan's life was not entirely easy. The publishing firm was dominated by his father and his two uncles. He lived during working days at his parents' home in Chester Square and on weekends at Birch Grove, the family house in Sussex, which his father intended to leave to him, although he was the youngest son. A set of rooms on the top floor was kept for him and for his wife and children, who lived there most of the while, apparently not disconcerted by the presence of the formidable American matriarch, though it was hardly an ideal arrangement. Nor was he at ease with the Cavendish clan and their closely related Cecil cousins. They called him 'the publisher' behind his back and regarded him as something of a snob. He certainly in those early days liked being a duke's son-in-law. But he was bored by the Cavendish passion for horse-racing, and they were bored by his prolixity. He cut a slightly uncomfortable figure at the vast Chatsworth house parties which, as Maurice Macmillan told Alistair Horne, must have been 'absolute hell' for his father. But he did genuinely enjoy shooting and made himself into a proficient, if slightly over-dressed, performer.

Macmillan, strongly encouraged by his mother, had for some time had parliamentary ambitions. Like more than one such aspirant he was not quite sure which side to join. He admired David Lloyd George (later first Earl Lloyd-George of Dwyfor) but he sensed that the Liberal party was on its way out. He stood as a Conservative for Stockton-on-Tees in the election of 1923 and lost, but he won a few months later in the election of 1924, which was a Conservative triumph. His diffident electioneering was compensated for by his wife's outgoing energy. But he made little impression on the House of Commons, and was regarded as an earnest bore, destined at best for some minor office.

In 1926 Birch Grove was rebuilt by Nellie and converted into a vast neo-Georgian mansion. The result was a house that could not be divided and the young couple had no refuge. This may have been a contributory cause of marital disaster. No one can say how far his mother's dominating presence affected Harold's relations with Dorothy, but in 1929—a year of calamity for Harold in every respect—she fell in love with Robert (later Baron) Boothby, a reckless, good-looking, 'bounderish' Conservative MP. The affair lasted in various ways till she died in 1966. She craved a divorce, but Macmillan, after some hesitation, decided against it and that, as the law then stood, settled the matter. They never separated. She continued to act as his hostess and canvass at his elections. But it was an empty shell of a marriage. They had three daughters and a son, Maurice, who died in 1984. Lady Dorothy claimed that their fourth child, Sarah, born in 1930, was Boothby's. But, although Boothby accepted responsibility, he did so with considerable doubt and it is by no means certain that she really was his daughter. Lady Dorothy's claim may have been a move to persuade Macmillan to divorce her. If so, it did not succeed. Sarah died in 1970.

The year 1929 brought another disaster. Macmillan lost his seat at Stockton and with it what slight chance he might have had of promotion when the Conservatives next regained office. After a brief flirtation with the 'New Party' run by Sir Oswald Mosley, he was returned for Stockton in the landslide election of 1931. Shortly before that he had a serious nervous breakdown, which lasted for several months. He embarked upon the uneasy currents of the 1931 Parliament in a state of doubt and anxiety, which he sought to alleviate by writing some dull quasi-Keynesian pamphlets and a book, *The Middle Way* (1938). Their *dirigiste*, corporatist, and collectivist tone seemed very un-Conservative even then.

He was again returned for Stockton in 1935. He supported Winston Churchill's criticisms of defence policy and appeasement and signalled his dislike of the government's foreign policy by resigning the party whip when sanctions against Mussolini were lifted in 1936, the only back-bencher to do so. He was a rather solitary figure. His father and his two uncles died in 1936 and his mother in 1937. He now had far more re-sponsibility as a publisher and found himself to be a good man of business. In politics and private life he ploughed a lonely furrow. In 1937 he applied successfully for the Conservative party whip, in the hope that the new prime minister, Neville Chamberlain, would impart drive instead of drift to national policy. Chamberlain did, but, from Macmillan's point of view, the drive was in the wrong direction. He was dismayed at the resignation of Anthony Eden (later the first Earl of Avon)—a heavy blow to the anti-appeasers. There were two groups, one centred on Churchill and called the 'Old Guard', the other on Eden and described by the whips as the 'Glamour Boys'. Macmillan joined the latter. On terms of outward friendship with Churchill, he was never a member of his 'court'. The presence of Boothby there was one reason. Moreover, Macmillan had disapproved of Churchill's attitude to India, and with his strong high-church views, disapproved even more strongly of Churchill's attitude to the abdication crisis. Churchill never personally liked him.

The Munich agreement had an ambivalent effect on Macmillan. He cheered in the House of Commons when Chamberlain announced his third visit to Hitler, but later took the view that Britain should have fought rather than accept Hitler's terms. He campaigned unsuccessfully in the Oxford City by-election against Quintin Hogg (later Baron Hailsham of St Marylebone), and in favour of the anti-Munich candidate A. D. Lindsay (later first Baron Lindsay of Birker), the master of Balliol. For this rebellion he narrowly missed 'deselection' and expulsion from the Carlton Club.

When war came, Chamberlain had to give office to Churchill and Eden, but their followers were excluded. Macmillan was briefly involved in a fact-finding mission to Helsinki in January 1940, the idea being a possible Anglo-French expedition to help the Finns in their war with the USSR. Fortunately—though not thanks to Macmillan—this insane project came to nothing; the Finns had to sue for peace before any troops could be sent. The fall of Chamberlain in May 1940 at last brought Macmillan some recognition. He became parliamentary under-secretary to the Ministry of Supply (1940–2). His Civil Service private secretary was John Wyndham (later first Baron Egremont), who was to be closely associated with him as aide and personal friend till he died in 1972. In June 1941 the first Baron Beaverbrook became minister of supply, with quasi-dictatorial powers. As spokesman in the Commons Macmillan moved up a rung in the ladder. He coped with his strange and formidable chief both warily and successfully, laying on flattery, but keeping his distance, for he knew that Beaverbrook could morally seduce men as easily as he physically seduced women. To the end of Beaverbrook's life they remained on excellent terms. In February 1942 a reconstruction of the ministry suggested by Macmillan himself meant that Beaverbrook would cease to be represented by a parliamentary under-secretary in the Commons. Macmillan was shunted into the Colonial Office to represent the first Baron Moyne and then Viscount Cranborne (later fifth Marquess of Salisbury). It was, he said, 'like leaving a madhouse in order to enter a museum'. But he had the consolation of being made a privy councillor (1942), in those days a rare honour for a junior minister.

In the autumn of 1942 came the turning-point of his career. Churchill appointed him—his second choice—minister resident with cabinet rank at Allied Forces Headquarters in Algiers (1942–5). It was a make or break situation. It made Macmillan. He displayed remarkable diplomatic skill in dealing with such disparate characters as generals Eisenhower, Giraud, and de Gaulle, and with Robert Murphy, his American opposite number. He was helped by his American ancestry and his fluency in French. At the Casablanca conference shortly after his arrival he acquitted himself with notable success and was warmly congratulated by Eden. This warmth was not destined to last. Despite being badly burned and nearly killed in a plane accident soon afterwards, Macmillan was able to continue in his important office, much appreciated by Churchill, till the end of the war. He was head of the Allied Control Commission in Italy and thus in effect, as John Wyndham described him, 'viceroy of the Mediterranean'—a situation far from palatable to Eden.

His next major problem was Greece, where German withdrawal in October 1944 had left a situation of civil war between the Greek communists and the forces of the centre and the right. Macmillan spent some uncomfortable weeks during the bitter winter of 1944–5 in Athens, where the British army of occupation was very thin on the ground and the embassy was a beleaguered garrison under constant sniper fire. In the end Churchill and Eden made a personal foray; despite the hostility of the Americans and the *bien pensant* left–liberal media in England, the communists were ousted.

Then came the highly controversial question of the 'repatriation' of Soviet citizens who had been captured by the Germans. To be a prisoner at all was unforgivable by Stalin, and some of them had fought on the German side. Repatriation had been agreed at the Yalta conference (1945), but it did not apply to White Russians, who were also involved but had never been Soviet citizens. When the war ended large numbers of both categories were in British hands in northern Yugoslavia and Austria. Macmillan discussed the matter on 13 May with General Sir Charles Keightley, who commanded V Corps at Klagenfurt. It is clear that repatriation (which also involved handing Chetniks and Ustasi over to Tito's partisan forces in Yugoslavia) was effected in deplorable circumstances of force and fraud, but there is no evidence of a conspiracy on the part of Macmillan, who had no executive authority nor any part in decisions taken at Yalta or the orders for their implementation made in Whitehall. The charge of being a war criminal, made many years later, haunted Macmillan in his old age, but it was baseless.

On 26 May 1945 Macmillan returned to Britain. By now he had made his mark. Churchill appointed him air minister in the caretaker government, pending the verdict of the general election to be announced on 26 July. The result was a disaster for the Conservatives and for Macmillan personally. The party was defeated by a huge majority and he lost Stockton. He might have been out of the house for two or three years and become a forgotten man but for a lucky chance. The sitting member for Bromley, a safe Conservative seat, died just before the election figures were announced. Macmillan was promptly adopted as candidate and was back in November with a majority of over 5,000.

For the next six years he devoted himself to the postwar problems of publishing and the opposition front bench. He had no difficulty in holding his seat in 1950 and 1951. On the personal side he had come to a bleak but balanced *modus vivendi* with his wife. She continued to support him socially and politically but her obsession with Boothby never waned. Politically Macmillan was active in trying to adapt the Conservative party to the challenge of its defeat. His theme was the occupation of the 'middle ground'—a Conservative heresy thirty years later but reasonable at the time, though it gave him a reputation among the right of being a 'neo-socialist', as Brendan (later Viscount) Bracken described him. He hoped for an alliance with the Liberals and even toyed with proportional representation.

In foreign policy he was a 'European' up to a point. He regarded Clement (later first Earl) Attlee's refusal in June 1950 to join the discussions of the six European nations about the Schuman plan as a disastrous error. But, like Churchill and other prominent Conservatives, he blew hot and cold. Although he served for three years on the Council of Europe at Strasburg, he wrote in 1949 'the Empire must always have first preference for us.'

When Churchill returned to office with a precarious majority in October 1951 he offered Macmillan the ministry of housing and local government. Macmillan nearly refused and only accepted with reluctance. The Conservative party conference, in a rush of blood to its collective head, had insisted on a mandate to build 300,000 houses a year compared with the 200,000 or so achieved by Labour. The target was widely regarded as unattainable—or only attainable at the unacceptable expense of industrial investment and infrastructure. Injecting into the ministry something of the hustle and bustle he had experienced under Beaverbrook, Macmillan reached the figure in 1953. He was helped inside the ministry by Dame Evelyn (later Baroness) Sharp, the first woman to become a permanent under-secretary, outside it by Sir Percy Mills, a Birmingham businessman. Equally valuable was his junior minister Ernest (later Baron) Marples, who had also made his fortune from humble origins, as an engineer and road-builder. He introduced American principles into the torpid British building industry, with notable success. Macmillan told Alistair Horne: 'Marples made me PM: I was never heard of before housing.' The critics were probably right about the damage done to the balance of the economy, but politically the achievement was a notable feather in the caps of both the party and the minister.

In October 1954 there was a cabinet reshuffle and Macmillan became minister of defence for five unhappy months. At housing Churchill backed him and left him to get on with it. At defence he did neither and Macmillan became irritated at the ceaseless flow of memoranda on the most detailed topics from the aged prime minister. Perhaps this experience prompted him to take the lead in persuading Churchill to retire in favour of Eden. It was high time, but he was never forgiven by Clementine, Lady Churchill, who had always mistrusted him. Eden succeeded on 5 April 1955, and the ensuing general election in May resulted in a Conservative majority of fifty-nine. Macmillan became secretary of state for foreign affairs, the post which he most wanted and believed would be the culmination of his political career. He was very much Eden's second choice.

The prime minister would have preferred the fifth Marquess of Salisbury (the former Viscount—'Bobbety'—Cranborne), but feared a row about a peer in this position—unnecessarily, in view of the later appointments of lords Home and Carrington.

Like Churchill over defence, Eden could not keep his hands off foreign policy. At the end of the year he used the ill health of R. A. Butler (later Baron Butler of Saffron Walden) to move him to the leadership of the Commons and replace him as chancellor of the Exchequer by Macmillan, who was replaced by Selwyn Lloyd (later Baron Selwyn-Lloyd). Macmillan resented the change. He had never liked Eden, nor Eden him. He only introduced one budget. His more radical proposals were vetoed by the prime minister. The budget is mainly remembered for the introduction of premium bonds. The second half of 1956 was dominated by the Suez crisis. Macmillan does not come well out of it. He was a leading 'hawk', and he totally misjudged the American reaction. On 25 September he had a conversation with Eisenhower at the White House, from which he inferred that the American president would support British military action against Gamal Abdel Nasser, the Egyptian leader. Sir Roger Makins (later first Baron Sherfield), the British ambassador, was present and took notes. He was astonished to learn later that Macmillan had sent a dispatch to this effect to Eden, for the discussion in no way warranted such a version of the president's attitude. But the report inevitably reinforced Eden's already erroneous view of the American reaction.

Macmillan's second major error was one of omission. The Suez operation constituted an obvious risk to sterling. He took no precautions and failed to do what the French did, draw out a tranche of funds from the International Monetary Fund well in advance of the invasion. The ensuing run on the pound was exactly what a chancellor of the Exchequer might have anticipated and avoided. Instead he panicked and with all his power pressed the case for withdrawal. 'First in, first out', was the justified jibe from Harold Wilson (later Baron Wilson of Rievaulx). Macmillan was unhappy about his role for ever afterwards. It was, he said, 'a very bad episode in my life'.

Credulous adherents of the conspiracy theory of history have seen in Macmillan's conduct a plot to oust and replace Eden. There is no evidence at all for this implausible theory. Eden resigned on 9 January 1957 on genuine grounds of health. He made no recommendation to the queen about his successor, merely advising her private secretary to consult Lord Salisbury as a senior peer who could not be a runner himself. He and the lord chancellor interviewed each member of the cabinet separately and took slightly perfunctory soundings in the parliamentary party and the National Union. The result was a strong preference for Macmillan rather than Butler, whose attitude over Suez had been ambivalent, indecisive, and obscure. Macmillan was appointed by the queen at 2 p.m. next day.

The outlook for the Conservative party could hardly have been bleaker. Suez had been a fiasco and it looked as if Labour would have a walkover at the next general election. Macmillan transformed the situation. He soon dominated the House of Commons and his apparent confidence radiated out to the electorate. He also dominated his party, taking in his stride the resignation of Lord Salisbury over the release of Archbishop Makarios in March 1957, and the resignations of Peter (later Baron) Thorneycroft, Enoch Powell, and Nigel Birch (later Baron Rhyl)—the whole Treasury 'team'—nine months later in protest against his refusal to accept expenditure cuts of £50 million in the next budget. On the eve of his departure on a Commonwealth tour he dismissed the resignations as 'little local difficulties'. Meanwhile he had mended fences with Eisenhower and, in the 1958 crisis involving Iraq, Jordan, and Lebanon, the USA and Britain acted in harmony. Despite some awkward negotiations with the trade unions, he approached the election of 1959 at the head of a party in far better shape than in 1957. His ebullient behaviour caused the cartoonist 'Vicky' to depict him ironically as 'Supermac'. The joke backfired and made him in Horne's words 'something of a folk hero'. He was accused by many moralists of excessive 'materialism'. A famous phrase which he used—'most of our people have never had it so good'—was wrenched out of its context, which was a warning against rising prices and contained a forgotten qualification: 'Is it too good to be true?' On the foreign and colonial front there were difficulties—Cyprus, the Hola incident in Kenya, and other episodes. But Macmillan kept calm, plumped for autumn 1959 rather than spring for the election, and won easily, almost doubling the majority he had inherited from Eden.

His premiership lasted for another four years. But after the major triumph of the general election and the minor one of defeating Sir Oliver (later Baron) Franks in 1960 for the chancellorship of Oxford University, the tale is anything but a success story. It is clear now—and many people thought so then—that he spent too much time on foreign and post-colonial affairs, and too little on matters at home. These years were the period when France and Germany caught up and surpassed Britain in terms of economic success. The major British problems—trade-union power and chronic inflation—were never recognized by Macmillan, who was not helped by two singularly mediocre chancellors of the Exchequer, nor by the expansionist advice of his economic guru, Sir Roy Harrod. When unemployment rose from 500,000 to 800,000 Macmillan, obsessed by his memories of Stockton-on-Tees in the 1930s, was horrified. Attempts at an 'incomes policy' flopped as they always have. No serious effort was made to amend trade-union legislation. In July 1962 Macmillan got rid of his second chancellor of the Exchequer, Selwyn Lloyd, but made the major error of combining his dismissal with a reconstruction of the government, which involved sacking a third of the cabinet. It looked like panic and probably was. His prestige never recovered. He was not helped by the general anti-establishment sentiment that dominated the early 1960s. It was not exactly pro-Labour, but it was certainly anti-Conservative.

In external affairs Macmillan achieved a certain *réclame* in 'liberal' circles by his speech at Cape Town in 1960, on Monday 3 February, warning of the 'wind of change' which was blowing through Africa. To the Tory right it was anathema—'Black Monday'—and led to the formation of the Monday Club. Macmillan was of course correct about the strength of African nationalism, which was affecting the Central African Federation of the two Rhodesias and Nyasaland (later Zimbabwe, Zambia, and Malawi). The Federation had to be dissolved but the labyrinthine and disingenuous process won few friends even among the Africans and bitterly alienated its prime minister, Sir Roy Welensky, and his white supporters. They felt they had been double-crossed.

Macmillan was determined to keep in with America. He played the card of his American ancestry for all it was worth. The Cavendishes were related by marriage to the Kennedys, and the president genuinely admired the wit and wisdom of the older man. During the Cuban crisis of 1962 he kept in touch with Macmillan more closely than with any other European leader, but there is no evidence to suggest that the prime minister gave any advice which affected the course of events. He did, however, extract from Kennedy some concessions about the British independent nuclear deterrent, and the president paid full tribute to Macmillan for his part in negotiating the Atmospheric Test Ban treaty with the USSR on 5 August 1963. Macmillan came to regard this as one of the principal achievements of his premiership.

But long before that he had been in major trouble. Britain had applied in July 1961 to accede to the Treaty of Rome. From the start it was clear that President de Gaulle was hostile, but it was not clear that he could carry France with him till the referendum on the presidency in October 1962, followed by a sweeping electoral victory for his party a month later. Despite his earlier policy—he had tried to wreck the European Economic Community by setting up the European Free Trade Association in May 1960—Macmillan now put much political capital into accession to the EEC. But Britain was doomed. On 29 January 1963 de Gaulle delivered his formal veto. 'All our policies at home and abroad are ruined', Macmillan wrote in his diary.

If that was not enough, a series of scandals, connected with espionage, security, and sex, erupted, culminating with the famous John Profumo affair when the secretary of state for war denied in Parliament in March 1963 a charge that he had slept with a woman who shared his favours with those of the Russian military attaché. A few weeks later Profumo had to retract and resign from public life. Macmillan was unfairly criticized as gullible and out of touch. Nigel Birch made a long-remembered attack, quoting Robert Browning's *The Lost Leader*, 'Never glad, confident morning again'. The government tottered but survived.

An election was due at the latest by autumn 1964. Macmillan, now nearly seventy and feeling none too well, had to decide whether to fight it himself or pass the lead to someone else. But whom? He resolved to go ahead. On the eve of the Conservative conference at Blackpool he was taken ill with an inflamed prostate gland, which necessitated an immediate operation. A prostate operation was a relatively minor matter but Macmillan, hypochondriac as ever, convinced himself that the malady was malignant and decided to resign at once. In fact it was not, and there was no need to retire at this singularly awkward political moment. He was to regret his decision for ever after.

When the operation was over, it was indicated that the queen would welcome his advice about the succession. He did not have to give it. Perhaps it would have been better if he had politely declined, like Bonar Law in 1923 and Eden in 1957. But he was determined, despite later disclaimers, to block the obvious heir presumptive, R. A. Butler, whom he regarded as a ditherer. After complicated indirect consultations with the cabinet and other elements of the party—which have been the subject of controversy ever since—he plumped for the fourteenth Earl of Home (later Baron Home of the Hirsel) in preference to his first choice, Quintin Hogg, who was then second Viscount Hailsham. Both of them had taken advantage of a recent Act to disclaim their peerages. It was the last occasion when this informal and secretive system of consultation was employed.

Macmillan left the House of Commons at the election of October 1964. He declined for the time being the traditional earldom offered to ex-prime ministers. He recommended a barony for John Wyndham but took nothing for himself. He did not wish to damage the prospects of his only son Maurice, now at last a minister. He may also have dreamed of being recalled to office himself in a crisis as head of an all-party coalition. In 1966 his wife died. He missed her despite their latterly loveless marriage, but the Chatsworth connection remained and the reigning duke and duchess of Devonshire made ample hospitable amends for any snubs by an earlier Cavendish generation. Another consolation for his rather lonely life in the chilly emptiness of Birch Grove was Garsington Manor near Oxford, where he often stayed with Sir John Wheeler-Bennett. Then there was clubland, which he regularly frequented.

In the long twilight—or perhaps Indian summer—of his career his chancellorship of Oxford University (from 1960) meant much to him. It also meant much to Oxford. He attended the various occasions—dinners, centenaries, laying of foundation stones, and the like—more assiduously than any previous chancellor. Dons and undergraduates alike were fascinated by his speeches and his conversation—an inimitable combination of wit, emotion, and nostalgia, which made it almost incredible that he had once been regarded as a parliamentary bore. He travelled a good deal, especially in America, where he raised money for Oxford. He even paid a visit to China, where he was fêted. He spent much time on his memoirs in six volumes (1966–73), published profitably by his firm, in which he took a renewed interest. They are in places somewhat heavy going but essential for historians. Much more 'fun', to use a favourite word of his, are his *The Past Masters* (1974), a series of political sketches and reminiscences from 1906 to 1939, and his diary of his time as minister resident in the Middle East, *War Diaries: Politics and War in the Mediterranean 1943–1945* (1984). He frequently appeared on television, almost always with great success. In the last ten years of his life he gave many long interviews at Birch Grove to Alistair Horne, his chosen official biographer. His relations with Margaret (later Baroness) Thatcher, who always treated him with respect, were ambivalent. She sought and followed his advice about the Falklands war in 1982. But he had led his party from left of centre whereas she did so from the right. Towards the end his coded criticism of her economic policy was abundantly clear.

He changed his mind about the peerage and, on his ninetieth birthday in 1984, his acceptance of an earldom was announced. Maurice was very ill (he died on 10 March) and the main reason for refusal had gone. Macmillan took the title of Earl of Stockton, after his old constituency. By now he was almost blind—a great blow to such a voracious reader though relieved by his discovery of 'talking books'—and he made his thirty-two-minute maiden speech in November without a single note. It was a wonderful performance, which those who heard it will never forget.

Macmillan's political hero was Benjamin Disraeli (first Earl of Beaconsfield), who had something of the same mixture of wit, irony, cynicism, romance, and sheer play-acting. To the end of his days Macmillan loved to put on a show. His last performance was a speech to the Tory Reform Group in November 1986. By now well distanced from Margaret Thatcher he compared privatization to 'selling the family silver'—a specious simile since the silver was, after all, being sold to the family. It is arguable whether Disraeli was a great prime minister, but he was certainly a great character. The same can be said of Harold Macmillan.

Macmillan was sworn of the Privy Council in 1942 and admitted to the Order of Merit in 1976. He became an honorary fellow of Balliol (1957), honorary DCL of Oxford (1958), and honorary LL.D. of Cambridge (1961). He died 29 December 1986 at Birch Grove, Hayward's Heath, East Sussex. He was succeeded in the earldom by his grandson, Alexander Daniel Alan Macmillan (born 1943).

> [Macmillan's own writings mentioned in the text; Alistair Horne, *Macmillan, the Official Biography*, 2 vols., 1988, 1989; George Hutchinson, *The Last Edwardian at No 10*, 1980; Nigel Fisher, *Harold Macmillan, a Biography*, 1982; private information; personal knowledge.]

ROBERT BLAKE

published 1996

MANNINGHAM-BULLER Reginald Edward

(1905–1980)

Fourth Baronet, and first
Viscount Dilhorne

Lord chancellor, was born at Amersham 1 August 1905, the eldest of the five children and only son of (Lieutenant-Colonel) Mervyn Edward Manningham-Buller, later third baronet, a former MP for Kettering and Northampton, and his wife, Lilah Constance, daughter of Charles Compton William Cavendish, third Baron Chesham. Sir Mervyn was tenth in descent from Sir Edward Coke (1552–1634), lord chief justice, and fifth in descent from Sir Francis Buller (1746–1800), the youngest man ever to be made a judge in England. After Eton, Manningham-Buller went up to Magdalen College, Oxford. He was placed in the third class of the honour school of jurisprudence in 1926, and just missed his blue for rowing.

Manningham-Buller was called to the bar (Inner Temple) in 1927, and practised on the common law side with chambers at 2 Harcourt Buildings. His practice as a junior was steady rather than sensational, but in 1946, after war service in the judge advocate-general's department, he was able to take silk. Meanwhile he had been returned unopposed in 1943 as Conservative MP for Daventry. In 1950 the constituency was reorganized as the southern division of Northamptonshire, and Manningham-Buller held it until 1962, increasing his majority at each election.

In 1951 (Sir) Winston Churchill, in whose brief caretaker government in 1945 he had been parliamentary secretary to the minister of works, appointed him solicitor-general. In 1954 he was sworn of the Privy Council in June and succeeded Sir Lionel Heald as attorney-general in October. As he held this post until 1962, he was a law officer of the Crown continuously for ten years and nine months—a period five months longer than that achieved by the first Viscount Finlay but four years shorter than that of the first Earl of Mansfield.

He took some time to obtain the respect of the bar, whose members found it hard to believe that someone from such a background could have the industry and ability necessary to discharge the responsibilities of his position. The government departments, in particular the Inland Revenue, and the judges were quicker to discern the massive talents hidden under that formidable exterior. 'During his term of office first as Solicitor-General and then as Attorney-General it was not unusual to find him, when all had gone home, working in the small hours in his room just off the central lobby, a pipe firmly in his mouth, alone, and unmoved by the hour of the night or the fatigues of the day, in court and in the House, that would have exhausted a less robust man' (*The Times*, 10 September 1980). Parliamentary criticism of his handling of the prosecution for murder of an alleged poisoner, Dr Bodkin Adams, was decisively beaten off, but may have had some effect on the decision to ignore his claims to succeed Lord Goddard as lord chief justice in 1958.

In July 1962 Manningham-Buller was appointed lord chancellor in place of the Earl of Kilmuir in the drastic Cabinet reconstruction undertaken by Harold Macmillan (later the Earl of Stockton). Of the sixteen attorneys-general since 1901 who have reached the woolsack, only three have been promoted direct from the position of first law officer—Westbury, Birkenhead, and Dilhorne, as Manningham-Buller now became, taking the title of his barony from a Buller property on the Cheadle side of Stoke-on-Trent. (The inhabitants of the area now call it Dill-horne: but the lord chancellor insisted on the traditional pronunciation Dil-urne.) He was a few weeks short of his fifty-seventh birthday in a Cabinet of which the average age was fifty-one. So Dilhorne was amongst the seniors to whom the prime minister turned for help in a succession of government crises in 1963—Nyasaland, William Vassall, and John Profumo. When strain and ill health drove Macmillan into retirement in the autumn of that eventful year, Dilhorne was asked to sound the Cabinet as to the succession. This he did, in the words of R. A. Butler (later Lord Butler of Saffron Walden), 'like a large Clumber spaniel sniffing the bottoms of the hedgerows', and duly reported a clear majority for the Earl of Home (later Lord Home of the Hirsel), who continued Dilhorne in his position until he was replaced by Lord Gardiner in October 1964. In the dissolution and resignation honours list of that year he was promoted viscount. (But the fellows of Magdalen did not then feel able to elect either him or Lord Gardiner to an honorary fellowship.) In 1967 he became a deputy lieutenant of Northamptonshire, a distinction which in that county of squires and spires he valued as much as any which he had achieved. (He had succeeded his father as fourth baronet in 1956.)

His time on the woolsack was too short for Dilhorne to make any permanent mark on the statute book or the law reports. But as an ex-lord chancellor he threw himself with such vigour into the judicial and parliamentary work available to him, in particular sitting constantly on the Privy Council, that there was general welcome in 1969 for the unusual step of appointing him a lord of appeal in ordinary. (The rules of precedence had previously been altered so as to deprive an ex-lord chancellor of his automatic right to preside.) Over the next decade a series of weighty judgements fully justified the appointment. He was especially good in the areas of constitutional and revenue law.

Dilhorne disdained the arts by which a lawyer–politician often seeks popularity. He evoked respect rather than affection: even some of his Cabinet colleagues were a little frightened of him. But the respect was given to qualities which were once thought to be characteristic of his class and his profession—integrity, loyalty, and a desire to do the state some service. In an age when the characters and capacities of public men were probed more mercilessly than at any time since the late seventeenth century, this was an important achievement.

During a lecture tour in Canada and the United States in 1956 honorary degrees were conferred on him at McGill University, Montreal, and the Southern Methodist University, Dallas, Texas.

In 1930 he married Lady Mary Lilian Lindsay, fourth of the six daughters of David Alexander Edward Lindsay, the twenty-seventh Earl of Crawford and Balcarres, and sister of the twenty-eighth Earl. They had one son and three daughters. Dilhorne died suddenly at Knoydart in Inverness-shire 7 September 1980, and it was characteristic of him that he had prepared for delivery in October a judgement in a major appeal. He was buried at Deene in Northamptonshire, his estate being sworn for probate at £111,754. He was succeeded in the viscountcy by his son, John Mervyn (born 1932).

There is a portrait of Dilhorne in the hall of the Inner Temple.

[*The Times*, 10 September 1980; private information; personal knowledge.]

R. F. V. Heuston

published 1986

Frederick James

(1883–1964)

First Earl of Woolton

Politician and business man, was born in Salford 23 August 1883, the only child of Thomas Robert Marquis, saddler, and his wife, Margaret Ormerod. From Ardwick higher-grade school he went to Manchester Grammar School and thence to the university where he read mathematics, chemistry, physics, and psychology and obtained his B.Sc. in 1906. He could not afford to accept the offer from London of a research fellowship in sociology but became senior mathematical master at Burnley Grammar School and part-time mathematics and science lecturer in the evening technical school. Increasingly concerned as a young man with problems of poverty, he deliberately acquired first-hand experience of them, first from the Manchester University settlement at Ancoats Hall (where he first met J. J. Mallon, later one of his close friends, who was then starting his campaign against sweated labour), and later from bachelor life in Burnley. He was a research fellow in economics at Manchester in 1910 and obtained his MA in 1912.

Led away from schoolmastering by his social concern, Marquis became assistant to an enthusiastic Congregational minister, T. Arthur Leonard, founder of a co-operative association in nearby Colne for organizing family holidays with the help of undergraduates during their long vacations. This was the one decision of all those mentioned in his memoirs which he says that he was wrong to take. Six months later the misdirection was corrected. Fred Marquis took a step which led decisively to all the subsequent stages of his life. He became the warden of a unique social settlement, oddly named the David Lewis Hotel and Club Association, in the Liverpool dockland. Amply provided with funds, it consisted of a 'sleep-shop' (where for sixpence a night a man could get a clean bed), a 'people's palace' (club, meeting-rooms, library, temperance bar), and a theatre seating 800. The warden was under obligation, besides organizing social activities, to undertake research into the social problems of the neighbourhood, and not to allow in the club any party politics or religious teaching.

Soon Marquis was asked by the vice-chancellor of the university of Liverpool to become warden of the university settlement as well: this widened the scope of the club work and enabled the warden to get new premises built which could serve as a centre in dockland both of research and of collegiate life for the residents. There Marquis himself lived and in

1912 brought with him as his bride an old Lancashire friend, Maud Smith, by temperament and training the ideal wife for any warden, who was to prove no less invaluable a partner in each of her husband's later posts. Their joint efforts had many kinds of success. A school dental clinic was established, about which such good propaganda was made at the next municipal elections that Liverpool was induced to start dental clinics throughout the city. Similar results followed the establishment of a pioneer maternity clinic, and the warden's name was rightly linked with the movement to decasualize dock labour. On occasion his timely appearance would save the situation when Protestants and Catholics were nearly at each other's throats.

Rejected on health grounds for military service when war broke out in 1914, Marquis was already well enough known in Whitehall to be given some urgent work by one of the shrewdest officers in the Local Government Board. But as this did not satisfy him, he got himself appointed by the War Office as an economist and was told to find, first, blankets for the armies of France, Belgium, and Italy, and then equipment for Romania and Russia. He became secretary of the Leather Control Board and then civilian boot controller, securing the goodwill of manufacturers and distributors with such success that the whole scheme could soon be left to the boot industry's own federation, with only a small headquarters staff of temporary civil servants, (Sir) Adrian Boult among them. This proved to be the prototype for control of standard articles during the war of 1939–45.

Success in large-scale public administration had significant effects on Marquis. It confirmed his conviction that normally the public could best be served by business men competing for the public's favour without control by Government: only in times of scarcity, such as a war, should use be made of regulations or the Civil Service. As soon, therefore, as he thought that leather supplies were adequate he sent in his resignation as controller and at the same time resigned from the Fabian Society. While his war work had impressed Marquis with the competence and patriotism of the great majority of business men, many of them had been equally impressed by Marquis. For the rest of his life he was to be subject to frequent offers of highly profitable employment.

From several possibilities he now chose to accept the secretaryship of a new post-war federation of the boot industry. This body was to have 'high public purpose': to maintain the reputation made by British boot manufacturers in war, extend their trade, and work in such harmony with the trade union that there should never be a strike—in short, to prove the Marquis theory that welfare and profits are inseparable partners in a well-organized industry. He proved a highly successful secretary, while substantially increasing his income by freelance journalism and learning to put his theory into words. Soon there came the opportunity to put his theory into practice.

Boot business took Marquis to the United States and with him went Rex Cohen, one of a family which had established in Liverpool, Manchester, and Birmingham the highly successful department store of Lewis's and, as a philanthropic by-product, the David Lewis Club. Marquis drafted for Cohen the report to Lewis's on the American stores they visited and on their return he received a surprising invitation. Although since its foundation more than sixty years before Lewis's had been an exclusively Jewish family firm they now asked Marquis (who had no Jewish blood) to join their board. After a characteristic pause he accepted the invitation, on his own terms: a salary not much higher than his present one, and at the end of two years either side to be free to cancel the arrangement without ill feeling. Before the two years were up he did offer his resignation, but neither then nor at any time was there danger of its acceptance. He became joint managing director in 1928 and chairman in 1936. The firm went from strength to strength, the gentile quickly and happily became its moving spirit and remained, except during war, its tutelary genius until 1951, in due course arranging a marriage of convenience between Lewis's and the London firm of Selfridges; with the London John Lewis partnership there was no connection.

Although Marquis wanted to make money, he wanted still more to prove by his own practice that that was compatible with public service. So, literally, he walked the shop, studied the customer, questioned the firm's buyers, exploited American experience, took major risks—and constantly increased the turnover and profits of the business. But he was soon finding time for much besides the firm: not for local or national party politics but for meetings of a private luncheon club in Liverpool and dinner parties where leading business men and city fathers met. Among the results were the municipal airport at Speke and a major public relations effort to attract industry to Merseyside.

Whitehall meanwhile had not forgotten him. It was Sir Horace Wilson who from his personal knowledge of Marquis was chiefly responsible for first bringing him into national affairs and later for securing his appointment by Neville Chamberlain in 1940 as minister of food. During the pre-war period Marquis was one of three commissioners for areas of special distress through unemployment—in his case Lancashire and the north-east coast; and he was a member of advisory councils to the Overseas Development Committee (1928–31), the Board of Trade (1930–4), and the Post Office (1933–47). A committee under Frank Pick, studying relations between art and industry, appointed a special group, under Marquis's chairmanship, on women's fashion trade. Years later the value of this work was recognized when a rejuvenated Royal College of Art made him one of its honorary fellows. Other recognition came more swiftly. Besides his public service Marquis had turned the Retail Distributors Association of which he was president (1930–3) and chairman (1934) into a national body of some influence. In 1935 he was knighted and in 1939 created a baron as Lord Woolton.

Meanwhile he had deliberately widened his experience by joining the boards of the Royal Insurance Company and Martins Bank and becoming a council member of Liverpool and Manchester universities. But from 1936 onwards Marquis was more involved, behind the scenes, in war preparation than any private business. In 1937 he was one of a four-man government committee, nominally concerned with fire brigades but secretly charged with the general problem of defending civilians under conditions of heavy bombing. Later that year he was one of a small high-powered group under Lord Cadman on the aircraft industry which greatly influenced the future of British aviation and the course of the coming war. Before long Marquis was absorbed in another crucial inquiry, under Lord Hailey, which decided that deep shelters should not be built for civilian protection. Within hours of completing this work, in April 1939, he was called to undertake the clothing of the army.

Before agreeing to serve he made a characteristic reconnaissance. Although the country was within four months of war he found chaos in Whitehall: politicians without organization or sense of urgency, administrators overworked and leaderless. He decided how much authority he needed; went personally and got it, from the head of the Treasury, Sir Warren Fisher, and (through Horace Wilson) from the prime minister; and only then accepted the job. On 30 August he reported its completion— and for the rest of his life regarded this as the most difficult and anxious work he ever did. He had contrived to cover this wide field of public and private activity because he never stopped working, had no inclination to spend time on games or cultural enjoyment, and knew how to delegate.

When war broke out Woolton was asked to become director-general of the Ministry of Supply. This he accepted with uncharacteristic speed, because he thought non-political war service preferable to ministerial office and was well aware that in sending him to the House of Lords Chamberlain had him in mind for a Cabinet post.

Woolton did not have his way for long. Parliamentary and press critics of the Government had quickly found a 'sitting rabbit' in the Ministry of Food; a new minister was needed; the choice of Woolton in April 1940 was obvious enough to those who knew his work and in the eyes of the press and public it was a positive gain that he was politically unknown. Feeding an island population of fifty million, previously accustomed to import two-thirds of its food supplies from cheap world markets, throughout an indefinite period of air and sea attack was a tougher problem than clothing the British Army in four months. Woolton was responsible for solving it. On taking office he found none of the chaos of unpreparedness with which he had had to cope when called on to clothe the army. Much had been done before war broke out to accumulate supplies, print ration books, and arrange for leading members of the food industry to join the staff. By 1940 a large department had been working for some months. The chief civil servant, Sir Henry French, who had himself been in charge of preparations from the start, differed greatly from Woolton in temperament as well as training, and at first it seemed unlikely that they could work happily together: the eventual closeness of their collaboration was the real secret of the Ministry's success. Woolton's most obvious contribution was in his dealings with the public. Through broadcasts lengthily rehearsed under the expert guidance of Howard Marshall, public meetings, weekly press conferences and private meals with newspaper proprietors, and by personally dealing with a great volume of daily correspondence, he became the popular 'uncle Fred' who gave people, especially housewives, the impression of personal concern for them—taking them into his confidence, warning them in advance of shortages, admitting and correcting occasional errors of judgement. Many a child who was wayward with his food was threatened with the displeasure of Lord Woolton.

But he was much more than a superb presenter of his case. Inside the Ministry he gradually built up morale, from the depths in which he found it to an increasingly high level, despite the appalling loss of essential foods throughout the summer of 1940 as one source after another was cut off, air raids destroyed stocks and essential food services in Britain, and submarine attacks on shipping were intensified. In particular, he brought the squabbling business men and civil servants into partnership, paying them personal visits in their offices, goading them with occasional rude memoranda (channelled correctly through French), and putting new ideas at a premium. Nor did he hesitate to cut bureaucratic corners or exploit personal friendships in the Treasury and elsewhere in Whitehall.

As minister of reconstruction from November 1943 to May 1945 and a member of the War Cabinet, Woolton had no relations with the public, no power base in a major Whitehall department, no political party behind him; and the eighteen months of this appointment did not enhance his reputation. His work had chiefly to be done through the reconstruction committee of the Cabinet, and as chairman of this committee he was not in his element. All other members were long-term party politicians. In determination to avoid mass unemployment after the war they were united, and Woolton easily obtained unanimous approval for the famous white paper pledging all parties to maintain 'a high and stable level of employment'. Agreement was also reached on housing policy, and commissioners were appointed to review local government boundaries. But as the end of the war came into sight, with the prospect of a general election, the party leaders looked to their business, compromise became impossible, and no reconstruction minister could expect his colleagues to agree on future policy for land, national health, social insurance, or electricity.

In the caretaker Government Woolton was lord president of the Council. The Labour election victory which followed faced Tories with as grave a party prospect as that of a hundred years before. That the election five years later reduced the Labour majority to single figures, and that of 1951 brought Churchill back as prime minister, with a Tory majority which was to increase its size in 1955 and again in 1959, was an astonishing achievement. Much of the credit was due to R. A. Butler (later Lord Butler of Saffron Walden), the moving spirit in the process of rethinking Tory policy to match post-war British circumstances. But for electoral victory the party had to be galvanized into new energy, reorganized from top to bottom, refinanced, its social base extended, and a new army of constituency workers mobilized. Of this complete restructuring Woolton was, quite unexpectedly, the architect. He had joined the Conservative Party as the 1945 election results were coming in and next year, after a brief show of reluctance, he accepted Churchill's invitation to become party chairman. By 1955, when he gave way to Oliver (later Lord) Poole, the work was done. Woolton himself served as lord president of the Council (1951–2), chancellor of the Duchy of Lancaster (1952–5), and as minister of materials, to wind up the Ministry (1953–4).

Tall, fastidiously dressed, and consciously squaring his shoulders, Woolton was a formidable figure both in private and on the platform. He never enjoyed good health but his courage and ruthless determination to succeed proved irresistible—even in 1952 when he was thought to be dying. His first wife (who died in 1961) was a major element in his success, invariably telling him what she thought, in a downright north-country idiom which he loved even when his vanity or tendency to be pompous was under fire. Despite his wide business experience he was no economist or intellectual, and he became a successful speaker only because he took great pains to learn the art. His critics, particularly in the Labour Party, consistently underrated his powers, questioning the sincerity behind his bland manner and envying the undoubted reach of his popular appeal. He was frankly scared of Churchill and never became intimate either with him or, through lack of social self-confidence, with other leading Tory politicians. But he won their affectionate respect, nor did he lose as party politician the trust which he had won from housewives as minister of food. For he was an endearing man of strong principle who thought hard, cared fiercely both for individuals (especially the young) and for his country, and was humble enough never to stop learning.

He was chairman of the executive committee of the British Red Cross Society (1943–63), a governor of Manchester Grammar School, chancellor of Manchester University from 1944, and received honorary degrees from Manchester, Liverpool, Cambridge, McGill, and Hamilton College. He was sworn of the Privy Council in 1940, made a CH in 1942, and created a viscount in 1953 and an earl in 1956. In 1962 he married Dr Margaret Eluned Thomas. By his first marriage he had a daughter and a son, Roger David (1922–69), who succeeded him when he died at his home at Walberton 14 December 1964.

A bronze portrait bust by Lady Kennet remained the property of her family. A portrait by Sir James Gunn hangs in the Whitworth Hall of Manchester University.

[*The Memoirs of the Rt. Hon. the Earl of Woolton*, 1959; personal knowledge.]

REDCLIFFE-MAUD

published 1981

MAUDLING Reginald

(1917–1979)

Politician, was born in North Finchley 7 March 1917, the only child of Reginald George Maudling, actuary, of Hastings Court, Worthing, and his wife, Elizabeth Emilie Pearson. Educated at Merchant Taylors' School, he gained a scholarship to Merton College, Oxford, where he obtained a first in *literae humaniores* in 1938, and was *proxime accessit* for the John Locke scholarship in philosophy. G. R. G. Mure (later warden), a lifelong friend, regarded Maudling as among the three ablest pupils he ever taught. As an undergraduate Maudling developed a lifelong habit of travelling widely.

Maudling was called to the bar, Middle Temple, in 1940. The previous year he had married Beryl, daughter of Eli Laverick, naval architect. They had three sons and one daughter. At the outbreak of World War II he volunteered for active service but, owing to defective eyesight, was commissioned in RAF intelligence and subsequently became private secretary to Sir Archibald Sinclair (later Viscount Thurso), secretary of state for air. The belief that relations between government and industry would present the most urgent post-war problems caused Maudling to take the decision to enter politics he had first contemplated in 1939. By temperament a Conservative, he had been convinced by Mure that political progress depended more on the clarification of relevant questions than on strongly partisan commitment to conflicting answers.

Maudling unsuccessfully contested Heston and Isleworth at the 1945 general election, after which he became the first recruit to the Conservative Parliamentary Secretariat (amalgamated with the Research Department in 1948). Maudling not only serviced the party finance committee, but also gave assistance to (Sir) Winston Churchill and Anthony Eden (later the Earl of Avon), both on economic and broader issues. He was an assistant secretary to the group headed by R. A. Butler (later Lord Butler of Saffron Walden) which produced the industrial charter, and successfully moved an amendment committing the 1947 Conservative Party conference to its acceptance.

In February 1950 Maudling won the constituency of Barnet, which he represented until his death. He became parliamentary secretary to the Ministry of Civil Aviation in April 1952, and economic secretary to the Treasury the following November. In his *Memoirs* (1978) he has described this post, which he held until April 1955, as 'on the whole the most exciting and most satisfying time of my political career'. This was the most successful period of post-war Conservative economic policy, and Maudling's personal relations both with the chancellor of the Exchequer, R. A. Butler, and with leading Treasury civil servants, were excellent. He deputized for Butler at the annual meeting of the World Bank and International Monetary Fund in 1953, at a time when Britain was still the second world power in monetary terms. The quality of Maudling's mind, together with his ease and speed of working, already impressed those who were closest to him. Once policy was agreed he did not require detailed briefing, nor full drafts for speeches which he practically extemporized. His style in debate, sometimes slipshod, lacked the lucid force of his letters to the press.

When Eden succeeded Churchill in 1955 he appointed Maudling minister of supply, his first full ministerial post, and a member of the Privy Council. Maudling was never convinced by the argument for a Ministry which interposed a third party between customer and supplier, and he recommended its abolition. He had a realistic appreciation of the problem caused by the competition of the American air industry, and was possibly the first minister explicitly to recognize, in a memorandum written in January 1956, that Britain must henceforward regard herself as 'at the top of the second league' of world powers. Nevertheless Maudling strongly defended the Suez episode as 'a morally correct action'.

In the government of Harold Macmillan (later the Earl of Stockton) of January 1957, Maudling became paymaster-general, deputizing in the Commons for Lord Mills, minister of fuel and power, and within three months displayed a typically rapid mastery of British energy policy. In August Maudling was invited to lead the British delegation at the discussions designed to negotiate a European free trade area, with the members of the common market who had recently signed the treaty of Rome. Maudling was promoted to the Cabinet in September, and a successful Commons speech in November caused him to be described as 'the best chancellor of the Exchequer we could have'. The period 1957 to 1965 can be regarded as the most significant of his career.

It is doubtful whether, due to French opposition, the negotiations for a free trade area, which finally broke down in November 1958, could ever have succeeded. But Maudling's own position was handicapped by the reiterated pledge to British farmers that agriculture would be excluded, and by doubts as to the wholeheartedness, as yet, of Britain's desire to enter Europe. In a debate in February 1959 Maudling forcefully argued the case against common market membership in a speech which was to be remembered (and quoted against him) by 'anti-marketeers' in later years. Maudling believed that freedom of trade in industrial products should at least be expanded as widely as possible, and the personal reputation he had built up in the Paris negotiations played a notable part in bringing about a European Free Trade Association in November 1959 between Britain, the Scandinavian countries, Portugal, and Switzerland. When in 1961 the Macmillan government made formal application to see if a satisfactory basis existed for joining the EEC, Maudling changed his mind, mainly on the grounds of the advantage for Britain in participating in a large single market. He never became a European 'supra-nationalist', and in one of his last speeches in the Commons (1978) opposed Britain's joining the European monetary system, arguing that the achievement of a common currency should constitute the last stage of the natural development of economic unity rather than be a means of achieving it.

After the election of 1959, Maudling went to the Board of Trade where he administered effectively the Local Employment Act which improved distribution of industry policy and, against some departmental advice, he insisted that the new Rootes factory should be located at Linwood. He also took much interest in export promotion, recognizing the centrality of rising exports to the future of the British economy. There followed the economic crisis of 1961, and Maudling now had his gaze fixed firmly on his own prospects for a spell at the Treasury. But before he could fulfil this ambition, he spent nine months (October 1961 to July 1962), among the most fruitful of his career, as colonial secretary. He pushed through, against strong right-wing resistance within his own Cabinet (and a threat of resignation), the independence constitution for Zambia; and he devised an African land settlement scheme for Kenya, which by its provision for fair compensation for European farmers virtually ended their monopoly of the White Highlands and thereby contributed to lasting stability.

The appointment of Butler in March 1962, with overall responsibility for Central African affairs, helped to bring Maudling's promotion closer. The 'pay pause' of J. S. B. Lloyd (later Lord Selwyn-Lloyd) had raised a number of unprecedented problems and Maudling, while not a member of the Cabinet economic policy committee, was invited to attend ministerial meetings on this subject. In June Maudling published an 'open letter' to his constituents, stressing that 'freedom ... does not include the right to undermine the economy', which was widely admired. His choice as Lloyd's successor as chancellor of the Exchequer in July was generally welcomed and had the leadership of the party fallen vacant at this time, Maudling would have been better placed to 'emerge', under the old system, than any rival.

Maudling's period as chancellor remains controversial. The approval in February 1963 by the recently established National Economic Development Council of a 4 per cent growth target not only committed Maudling (himself chairman of NEDC) to endorsing this figure, but also influenced the shape of his 1963 budget which distributed £250 million so as to maximize union support for the incomes policy he regarded as indispensable to the achievement of sustained growth. Maudling's 1963 budget speech did, however, acknowledge the need for adequate borrowing facilities within the International Monetary Fund, at whose meetings he consistently advocated measures to increase international liquidity during a period of industrial recovery. In October 1963 the enforced resignation of Macmillan left Maudling a potential successor, though it is doubtful whether he now stood so high with the parliamentary party as in 1962, and a disappointing performance at the party conference (an audience with whom he was never at his best) further damaged his chances.

Those who had regarded Maudling's 1963 budget as overcautious made the opposite criticism of his 1964 budget which increased indirect taxation by £100 million. But the boom in manufacturing output, down to mid-summer, appeared to be moderating. Maudling was much hampered by the decision to postpone the impending general election to October which made it impossible to achieve agreement on incomes policy with the Trades Union Congress. As the election approached it became clear that the balance of payments constituted the most urgent problem, mainly because exports were still holding back. But there was as yet no sign of lack of confidence in sterling, and as Maudling told the Commons after the

Conservative defeat 'no figure (of the prospective 1964 deficit) larger than £600 million was ever given to the previous government'. Whatever the outcome of the 1964 election, some immediate action would no doubt have become imperative. But Labour's repeated claim that they had inherited an '£800 million deficit' damaged confidence unnecessarily, and the prospects for consistent growth might have remained brighter had Maudling remained chancellor; certainly he would have avoided the series of often contradictory decisions taken during the years that immediately followed.

Nevertheless Maudling's reputation had become tarnished by the charge that he had misled the electorate, nor did he retrieve his position as his friends had hoped, and in February 1965 he permanently lost his position as principal party spokesman on economic affairs. When Sir A. Douglas-Home (later Lord Home of the Hirsel) resigned in July, the feeling that Edward Heath would provide a new style of opposition may have accounted for his (albeit narrow) victory over Maudling in the first leadership election in the party's history. Maudling felt this rejection intensely (as those who saw him in the Commons that afternoon will vividly remember) and his political determination became permanently weakened. He became Heath's deputy, but played little part in the rethinking of policy, finding himself out of sympathy with the growing party support for an economic policy based solely on market forces and monetary controls.

When in 1970 Maudling became home secretary, his innate reasonableness and liberal instincts enabled him to bring an exceptional range of qualities to the exercise of his powers. For instance his handling of the Immigration Bill meant that never again could it be claimed that repatriation was a significant part of Conservative immigration policy. It was Maudling's misfortune that so much of his period at the Home Office was dominated by Northern Ireland, and by passions and irrationality of a kind particularly abhorrent to him. Maudling began by believing that the co-operation of Stormont was essential, and for this reason, and with many misgivings, he was prepared to concede the policy of internment; but eventually he became convinced that the slide towards civil war in Northern Ireland could only be averted by a complete political break with the past including a secretary of state who would take over from the home secretary responsibility for the province.

In July 1972 Maudling felt compelled to resign when it was decided that there were issues arising out of the bankruptcy case of John Poulson, with whose export business Maudling had been associated in the later 1960s, which required criminal investigation by the Metropolitan Police for whom Maudling bore ministerial responsibility. Maudling's business judgement had never been good and even fifteen years earlier civil servants had been concerned at his tendency to be careless about protecting himself from possible criticism. Indeed, a more serious error on Maudling's part had been his brief acceptance of the presidency of the Real Estate Fund of America, a Bermuda-based investment company run by an American whose activities eventually landed him in prison for fraud. But the Poulson affair pursued Maudling unrelentingly. One of Poulson's companies which Maudling had joined had obtained the contract for a hospital on the island of Gozo which resulted in a heavy loss for the taxpayer; and in July 1977 a select committee of the Commons reported that Maudling should have declared his interest to the House when aid to Malta had been debated ten years earlier since, while Maudling himself received no salary, Poulson had contributed generously to a trust to which Maudling's wife was devoted. A motion to approve the report of the select committee was defeated, but innuendoes persisted, and during his last illness he was unwilling to undergo treatment that might have interfered with his plans for a costly libel action in which he would be the principal witness and which, he firmly believed, would finally clear his own name and that of his family. Maudling, at Heath's advice, had not left public life when he resigned in 1972. He returned to the shadow cabinet when Margaret Thatcher succeeded Heath in 1975, but was dropped in November of the following year. He now had little political following in the Commons but his Conservative colleagues, practically without exception, rallied to him when the crisis came.

Maudling had one of the quickest and best analytic brains in recent British politics. Frequently accused of laziness he could certainly appear casual, yet he had also a capacity for intense concentration when he chose. Nor was it true that he lacked convictions; in his later years he cared a great deal about what he regarded as the growth of ugliness in our society. But there was perhaps more justice in the suggestion that his political outlook was not founded in an ultimate sense of purpose. While eager to be chancellor he was never sure he would succeed, and he knew very well the limitations of economic forecasts. The events of 1964 left him jaded, and his crucial rejection in the following year not only sapped his determination but left him more vulnerable than ever to his inherent weakness of business judgement. Yet whether the consequences of victory in 1965 would have made him happier may be doubted. He would surely have been most suited as prime minister to that era of 'Butskellism' and 'consensus' to which he seems so clearly in retrospect to belong. What can be claimed with confidence is that his easy-going and affable temperament, with its dispassionate rationality, more interested in solving problems than in the rhetoric that moves party conferences, represents one aspect both of politics and of Conservatism that can too easily be underrated in harassing times. Maudling died at the Royal Free Hospital, London, 14 February 1979.

[Reginald Maudling, *Memoirs*, 1978; personal knowledge.]

EDWARD BOYLE

published 1986

MAXTON James
(1885–1946)

Politician, was born in the small burgh of Pollokshaws near Glasgow 22 June 1885, the son of James Maxton, schoolteacher, by his wife, Melvina Purdon, who had also been a schoolteacher before her marriage. Maxton himself started life in the same profession, as did his three sisters; he also married a schoolteacher, so that teaching might be said to have been in his blood. His younger brother, John Purdon Maxton, was director of the Institute of Agrarian Affairs at Oxford from 1941 until his death ten years later.

When Maxton was five years old the family, upon the appointment of his father as headmaster in a Barrhead school, removed there. After some years under his father's tuition, Maxton went with a county bursary to Hutcheson's Grammar School in Glasgow, then trained as a teacher, and leaving the university before taking his degree taught in elementary schools at Pollokshaws and then in Bridgeton, Glasgow. While so engaged he completed his degree course at the university and graduated M.A. in 1909. His university career was not of any exceptional note, but it is interesting to record that the future leader of the Independent Labour Party gave his first political vote to George Wyndham as Conservative candidate for the lord-rectorship; that he joined the Conservative Club and the 1st Lanarkshire Rifle Volunteers, and is remembered at Gilmorehill as an athlete and for his performances in running the half-mile. In 1904, however, after attending a meeting addressed by Philip (later Viscount) Snowden, he joined the Independent Labour Party at Barrhead, became an omnivorous student of Socialist literature, and devoted all his spare time to public expositions of Socialism. He rapidly acquired an all-Scottish reputation as an orator, witty and sentimental, and, eschewing altogether the heavy Marxian dogmas and phrasemongering then so much in vogue, he attracted large audiences of the common folk.

When war broke out in 1914 he was soon in conflict with the authorities and in 1916, after a speech at Glasgow denouncing the deportation of some engineers who had opposed dilution of labour schemes, and calling for a general strike on the Clyde as a protest, he was arrested and sentenced to twelve months' imprisonment for sedition. Upon his release from prison Maxton obtained work as a labourer in a shipyard not engaged upon war work. His dog was stoned to death for his master's anti-war opinions. At the general election of 1918 he stood for the Bridgeton division of Glasgow, and although beaten by 3,027 he polled 7,860 votes and succeeded later in persuading his successful opponent, Alexander MacCallum Scott, to join the Independent Labour Party. He himself became an organizer for the party, and in 1919 was elected to the Glasgow education authority. In that year he married Sarah Whitehead, daughter of John McCallum, master wright, and the next three years of his life, he said, were his happiest. When his wife died in 1922, having exhausted herself in nursing their infant son, the shock nearly broke Maxton and it took him years to recover.

At the general election in 1922 he was elected member for Bridgeton by a majority of 7,692. During the debate in the House of Commons upon the Scottish estimates in 1923 he severely criticized cuts in public health expenditure, and was suspended for describing some members as murderers. He succeeded Reginald Clifford Allen (later Lord Allen of Hurtwood) as chairman of the Independent Labour Party in 1926, a post he held until 1931 (and again 1934–9), but administrative responsibility rather irked him; the party drifted into antagonism to the official Labour Party from which it disaffiliated in 1932; and in a few years it sank out of sight as an effective propaganda instrument.

Maxton's personal charm was irresistible; his hold upon the Bridgeton constituency in every general election between 1922 and 1945 unshakeable: his political opponents, both inside and outside the House of Commons, classed him not only as a persuasive propagandist but as a great gentleman, and his wit, his humour, and his burning eloquence contributed greatly from a thousand platforms to the upsurge of the Labour and Socialist movement in Great Britain. He did not enjoy good health, and, taking little exercise, was spendthrift in what he had of it. In 1935 he married again, this time his secretary, Madeline Grace, daughter of the late George Henry Brougham Glasier, estate agent. After a lingering illness, he died at Largs, Ayrshire, 23 July 1946. In 1932 he published *Lenin* and in 1935 *If I were Dictator*. He was, however, happiest on the platform; there he was master. A portrait by Sir John Lavery is in the Scottish National Portrait Gallery, and a portrait head sculpture by Lady Kennet is in the Glasgow City Art Gallery.

[Gilbert McAllister, *James Maxton, the Portrait of a Rebel*, 1935; John McNair, *James Maxton, the Beloved Rebel*, 1955; *Daily Express*, Scottish edition, 23 April 1935 et seq.; private information; personal knowledge.]

THOMAS JOHNSTON

published 1959

MENZIES Sir Stewart Graham

(1890–1968)

Head of the Secret Intelligence Service, was born in London 30 January 1890, the second son of John Graham Menzies, of independent means, and his wife, Susannah West, daughter of Arthur Wilson, of Tranby Croft. After the death of John Menzies his widow married in 1912 Lieutenant-Colonel Sir George Holford, an officer in the Life Guards and equerry-in-waiting to Queen Alexandra and extra equerry to King George V.

Stewart Menzies was educated at Eton where he won no academic distinctions but was a popular boy and a fine athlete who was master of the beagles, and president of the Eton Society ('Pop') in 1908 and 1909. Immediately on leaving school he joined the Grenadier Guards in 1909 but was transferred to the Life Guards in the following year. While in the army he acquired a love of horses and of hunting which remained with him for the rest of his life and to which he returned with special zest after his retirement. His country home was in Wiltshire and he hunted mainly with the Duke of Beaufort's hounds. He was well into his seventies when a fall in the hunting field started a decline in his health. While resident in London, Menzies enjoyed an active social life. He was a great frequenter of White's Club and also belonged to St. James's and the Turf.

Menzies first came into contact with the intelligence world during the war of 1914–18. He was sent to France in 1914 with the British Expeditionary Force and in 1915, after recovering from a gas attack, was assigned an intelligence appointment at GHQ. The work appealed to him and he showed a flair for it, which was aided by his knowledge of European languages. He ended the war with the DSO and MC and the rank of brevet major and in 1919 was again selected for an intelligence appointment: military liaison officer with the Secret Intelligence Service, also known as MI6. He thus began a career in professional intelligence which was to continue for thirty-two years. He was promoted colonel in 1932 and retired from the Life Guards in 1939.

Menzies became 'C' in full command of the Secret Intelligence Service only three months after the outbreak of war in 1939. It was a crucial moment in the history of his service. Between the wars it had been starved of funds by successive Governments and consequently entered the war ill-prepared for the tasks demanded by total warfare. Expansion and re-construction had to take place simultaneously, and these tasks were further complicated by set-backs such as that at Venlo, when Gestapo men crossed the German-Dutch border to capture two SIS officers who had gone there to contact agents of the underground opposition in Germany. The whole character of the service gradually changed. Hitherto the staff had been recruited mainly from retired Service officers; now that it could attract men and women of talent from all walks of life the management problems were new and intricate. Added to these Menzies had to steer his service through a complicated maze of inter-Service relations, created by the existence of a new British secret service—SOE—and a new American service—OSS—operating in parallel with his own in neutral and enemy territories. In these circumstances it was to take some time before SIS could develop a momentum of its own and forge those links with Allied intelligence and resistance organizations which were to prove valuable in the later stages of the war.

Besides commanding SIS, Menzies was responsible for the overall supervision of the Government Code and Cipher School (GC & CS), whose greatest achievement in the war of 1939–45 was the breaking of the German 'Enigma'. This was an electro-magnet enciphering machine, which generated a wide range of separate ciphers in use by the German army, navy, and air force. German experts had rendered their machine so sophisticated that by the outbreak of the war they considered it safe even if captured. It was therefore used to communicate vital German war secrets. These began to be made available by GC & CS by the end of 1940 and by the end of 1943 they were decrypting as many as 40,000 naval and 50,000 army and air force messages a month. It is therefore not difficult to imagine the crucial importance of this source of intelligence to the Allied war effort. But it was also a highly vulnerable source for the security of which Menzies was finally responsible. This could mean refusing some forceful operational commander the right to act on one of its intelligence leads if by so doing he might endanger the source. In retrospect this responsibility was admirably discharged and the secret of the GC & CS's remarkable cryptographic successes was preserved until the end of the war. Not surprisingly, with such excellent information at his disposal, Menzies's influence with the prime minister, War Cabinet, and chiefs of staff was considerable.

The stamina and toughness Menzies displayed during the war years came as something of a surprise to those acquainted with his easy and affluent way of life between the wars. Running his service and supervising GC & CS meant exceptionally long hours of office work, besides which he became in time a member of Churchill's intimate circle of war advisers. This meant being on call to brief the prime minister at any hour of the day or night. On such occasions he had to answer for more than his own responsibilities for he was the only intelligence director to enjoy this privileged position. As an intelligence man his strength lay in a quick grasp and understanding of operational issues and in his shrewd management of a network of powerful contacts. Organization and long-term planning were not his strong points. He preferred the getting of intelligence to the mosaic work of the assessors and in this respect he resembled one of his American opposite numbers, Allen Dulles, another man to enter intelligence from a patrician background.

To many foreigners Menzies came to seem the personal embodiment of an intelligence mystique they believed characteristically and historically British. Whatever the truth of this, it contributed to his international influence and was a potent factor in establishing the Anglo-American and other Allied intelligence alliances. During the war years his service had a greater role to play than ever before. By the time he retired in 1951 the pressures of the cold war had caused the intelligence world to develop in major ways, and to acquire potent technological resources: a very different world from the one he had entered in 1919.

Menzies was appointed CB in 1942, KCMG in 1943, KCB in 1951, and received a number of foreign decorations.

In 1918 he married Lady Avice Ela Muriel Sackville, daughter of the eighth Earl De La Warr. He obtained a divorce from her in 1931 and in 1932 married Pamela Thetis (died 1951), daughter of Rupert Evelyn Beckett, nephew of the first Baron Grimthorpe, and divorced wife of James Roy Notter Garton. He married thirdly in 1952 as her fourth husband, Audrey Clara Lilian, daughter of Sir Thomas Paul Latham, first baronet. Menzies had one daughter by his second wife. He died in London 29 May 1968.

[*The Times*, 31 May and 6 June 1968; private information; personal knowledge.]

ANON

published 1981

Sir (Edward) Penderel

(1905–1987)

Indian civil servant and writer, was born 13 November 1905 in Green Street, Mayfair, London, the only son and second of five children of Robert Oswald Moon, consultant cardiologist, and his wife, Ethel Rose Grant Waddington. Dr Moon wrote about philosophy and Greek medicine as well as diseases of the heart; he stood several times as a Liberal candidate for Parliament.

Penderel Moon followed his father to Winchester and New College, Oxford, was placed in the first class in *literae humaniores* (1927), and in the same year was elected to a fellowship at All Souls College, Oxford, which he held until 1935. In 1929 he was appointed to the Indian Civil Service, arriving in India on 29 November. He was posted to the Punjab and attached for instruction to Gurdaspur district under (Sir) Evan Jenkins, later private secretary to the viceroy and governor of the Punjab, who formed very early a high opinion of his administrative ability. By the time he had charge of the difficult district of Multan, it was known that Moon decided quickly and acted firmly but was not notably tolerant of the opinions of others, even his elders. None the less, he was appointed in 1938 private secretary to the governor of the Punjab, Sir Henry Craik; he was young for this key position and was also unusual in winning races on the governor's horses.

After his spell as private secretary, Moon was posted in 1941 as deputy commissioner to Amritsar, the focal point of the Sikh religion and of special importance in war in view of the Sikh contribution to the Indian army. Like many young British officers in the ICS, Moon considered that the government of the second Marquess of Linlithgow was dragging its feet about Indian advance towards self-government. In November 1942 he addressed to the Punjab government a letter arguing that those imprisoned for preaching civil disobedience should receive better treatment; this was in order, but when he received an unsympathetic reply, explaining the critical war situation, Moon's reaction was not. He sent a copy of the government's letter, with his own acid comments, to a brother of Rajkumari Amrit Kaur, secretary to M. K. Gandhi. She was at the time in gaol. This letter was intercepted and Moon was in serious trouble. Eventually the new governor, Sir Bertrand Glancy, persuaded him not to insist on dismissal, but to resign; he refused the suggestion of a proportionate pension.

Moon returned to England in April 1943, on six months' leave pending retirement, but in 1946 Viscount (later first Earl) Wavell, now viceroy, on the advice of his private secretary, Sir Evan Jenkins, invited him to return, on contract, as secretary to the boards of development and planning. In April 1947 he became revenue minister of the state of Bahawalpur and stayed on after India's independence, serving as chief commissioner of Himachal Pradesh, as chief commissioner of Manipur state, and as adviser to the planning commission. The tone of an address to the Indian Administrative Staff College suggests that he was sometimes as critical of the new rulers of India as of the old.

During the war Moon had published *Strangers in India* (1944), in which he argued that the ills of India could not be solved by a foreign government; it was followed by *Warren Hastings* (1947), brilliantly written in a simple, lucid style and notable for its sympathy with Hastings.

His last appointment in India ended in 1961. He was knighted in 1962 for services to good relations between Britain and India, to which indeed he had notably contributed. After his return to England he held brief appointments with the World Bank and as adviser to the government of Thailand but soon put the main thrust of his life into scholarly work on India. In 1961 he published *Divide and Quit*, which he later believed the most likely to survive of any of his books. It contains a lucid account of the events leading up to the partition of India and Pakistan, and an unflinching assessment of responsibility together with a day-by-day account of his own actions and observations as revenue minister and district magistrate in the border state of Bahawalpur during the months immediately following the division of the Punjab and the slaughter that followed. There can be no doubt that his power of swift decision, and his application of common sense amounting to brilliance, saved many lives; his account constitutes first-hand historical evidence of a high order. His *Gandhi and Modern India* is an admirable counterpoise to his *Warren Hastings*.

From 1965 to 1972 he was a fellow of All Souls, being the college's estates bursar in 1966–9, and from 1972 to 1982 he was at the India Office Library and Records, preparing for publication, with Nicholas Mansergh, the India Office documents on *The Transfer of Power 1942–7* (twelve volumes). He found time also to edit *Wavell: the Viceroy's Journal* (1973), a labour of love carried out with his usual clarity and distinction. When he died his last and most substantial book, *The British Conquest and Dominion of India* (1989), was still in proof. It was written, as always, with clarity, detachment, and mastery of complex material.

Moon's life was not all spent toiling at a desk. Before retiring from All Souls he bought a mixed farm near Aylesbury, which he later enlarged. He employed a manager, but took pleasure not only in the business of the farm but in the physical work of haymaking and harvest; he was a generous employer. He was a good horseman and enjoyed both hunting and racing. He sang in Oxford in the Bach Choir and had a particular admiration for the music of Handel.

Penderel Moon resembled in many ways an aristocrat of the Enlightenment. In appearance he was trim and slight; in personal habit, ascetic. In scholarship, as in farming, he combined the confident mastery of the professional with the detachment of the amateur of independent means. He was decisive in his opinions and often autocratic, a champion of the peasant but no egalitarian. In youth, he liked to surprise and even to shock, but he never took up a position merely for effect.

He married in 1966 Pauline Marion, daughter of the Revd William Everard Cecil Barns; the marriage was not a success and was soon dissolved; there were no children. Moon died 2 June 1987 at home at his farm in Wotton Underwood, Buckinghamshire.

[Private information; personal knowledge.]

PHILIP MASON

published 1996

MORRISON Herbert Stanley

(1888–1965)

Baron Morrison of Lambeth

Labour politician, was born in Brixton, London, 3 January 1888, the youngest in a family of four girls and three boys of Henry Morrison, police constable with a weakness for the bottle, and his wife, Priscilla Caroline Lyon, daughter of a carpet fitter in the East End of London. His mother had been in domestic service and, with six surviving children, the early years were hard but not marked by lack of the basic necessities. An eye infection shortly after birth deprived Morrison of the sight of his right eye, although this was a handicap which he generally overcame. He was educated at one of the Board schools set up under the 1870 Education Act, and, from the age of eleven, at St. Andrew's Church of England School, Lingham St., which he left at the age of fourteen to become an errand boy. After a spell as a shop assistant and as a switchboard operator (which gave him more time for reading), minor journalistic efforts helped to provide a living, and from 1912 to 1915 Morrison worked as circulation manager for the first official Labour paper, the *Daily Citizen*. From April 1915 he became part-time secretary of the London Labour Party and thereafter politics, either as an organizer or as a member of Parliament, was his sole occupation: and politics to Herbert Morrison meant the Labour movement. In his early years he took part in the local forums, heard such famous figures as George Bernard Shaw and Keir Hardie, and in 1906 he joined the Brixton branch of the Independent Labour Party. Following a common trend among left-wingers in London, he found this a rather pro-Liberal, north of England or Nonconformist type of organization, and himself preferred the more direct socialism of the Social Democratic Federation to which he transferred in 1907. To the London Left, free trade, anti-landlordism, and Home Rule for Ireland were all meaningless; Morrison was preoccupied—it was his lifelong preoccupation—with transport, health, education, and housing as provided by the local authorities for the citizens of the larger towns, and, above all, for London. Later he left the SDF and rejoined the ILP because he saw that it was more likely to win elections and achieve actual changes. As part of this interest he attended the Lambeth Metropolitan Borough Council—he was often the sole visitor—and unsuccessfully contested the Vauxhall ward for the ILP in 1912. In 1910 he had become secretary of the South-West London Federation of ILP branches and his work led steadily to the decision of the London Trades Council to call a conference and form the London Labour Party. After he became secretary to this new organization, in 1915, Morrison talked less and less about political theory, though he was opposed to the war of 1914–18 and to conscription. His concern was entirely with winning elections and carrying out pragmatic reforms, the common feature of which was to remedy social grievances in a manner which showed no prejudice against either governmental action or state ownership. If he resisted Popularism, he also rigorously opposed any Communist move 'to pour sand' into the Labour Party machine.

In many respects Morrison's greatest achievements in politics were in London between 1920 and 1940. He began by bringing his organization intact through the war of 1914–18, going on to win fifteen out of 124 seats in the 1919 London County Council elections. He realized that more was gained by steady work and preparation, by mastery of the immediate subject and its possibilities, than by all the street-corner oratory which so delighted the older generation of socialists. This work required the finding and training of candidates not only for the LCC but for the elections in twenty-eight boroughs. Once elected, these men had to be taught how to make speeches, conduct committees, and actually run the machinery of local government. In late 1919 the London Labour Party won a majority or became the largest party in sixteen boroughs. In 1919 Morrison became mayor of Hackney and in 1922 a member of the London County Council. He was soon the dominating figure.

Elected to Parliament for Hackney South in 1923 and 1929, Morrison was a strong supporter of Ramsay MacDonald and in the second Labour Government became minister of transport (1929). He proved to be a first-class minister, and was responsible for the 1930 Road Traffic Act and for the London Passenger Transport Bill of 1931. In the latter case, Morrison had been leading the Labour group on the LCC in opposition to a proposal to form a privately owned monopoly of London Transport. He became minister of transport just in time to prevent the Bill from passing and introduced his own measure, the creation of the London Passenger Transport Board. As a progenitor of the Board, Morrison was a firm believer in the autonomous public corporation as the best instrument for controlling a nationalized industry. He argued the case in his book *Socialization and Transport* (1933), which was in part a defence of his views against criticism from within the Labour Party. Other possibilities, such as workers' or joint control of an industry or management by a government department, had a strong traditional appeal to some socialists. By winning acceptance for his own view, Morrison in effect determined the form which was later given to the post-war nationalization Acts. He also insisted on fair compensation for stockholders and on the obligation to demonstrate the advantages of nationalization industry by industry. Because, as he thought, the case had not been made out for nationalization of the steel industry, he was opposed to that commitment in Labour's programme.

It was in the 1930s that Morrison achieved his greatest hold on the Labour Party. In part this was due simply to his personality and ability. A short, stocky figure with a quiff of hair combed back from his forehead, he was a first-rate debater and public speaker. He could put his party's view in the most reasonable, lucid, and engaging manner while never suggesting weakness and he was always ready to counter every attack. Also his achievements in London were a tonic to the Labour Party just when it most needed one. The annual conference found him in his element.

After Labour's exhilarating rise to power in the early 1920s, there had been the disappointing experiences of the two minority Governments, the defection of Ramsay MacDonald, and the débâcle of the 1931 general election. Morrison had begun in 1931 by wishing to remain in office with MacDonald, but after much hesitation he eventually stayed with the rest of the party when the 'national' Government was formed. In the face of these setbacks, the capture of the LCC in 1934 and the steady achievements thereafter were a most welcome sign that Labour could win and govern, achievements which in London were due to Herbert Morrison. Under him the LCC reformed public assistance, kept Poor Law officers out of the hospitals, built a new Waterloo Bridge despite government opposition, introduced the green belt, and pushed ahead with slum clearance and school building. Morrison was, in fact, a rather unusual type of Labour leader. He had not come up through the trade-union movement, nor was he one of the middle-class intellectuals who formed the other major group in the senior ranks. A working-class boy who was largely self-educated, he had risen by virtue of his organizational, tactical, and argumentative skills and he had no signs of a social inferiority complex. Indeed his bearing was a mixture of cockney brashness and the self-confidence which arose from knowledge, competence, and a solidly based political position. His clothes and his furniture were always bought at the Co-op. A further facet of Herbert Morrison's character which emerged strongly after his re-election in 1935 was his love of the House of Commons. As might have been expected, despite a shaky start, he took pleasure in mastering its rules of procedure. He was never overawed by the Palace of Westminster, but he valued its historical traditions and became an expert at using the House of Commons as part of the machinery of government.

His absence from the Commons from his defeat in 1931 until the general election of 1935, when he was re-elected for Hackney South with a majority of 5,000 was, however, to have a crucial effect on his subsequent career. Clement Attlee, hitherto junior to Morrison, who had been a Cabinet minister already, found himself deputy leader of the small group of Labour MPs in 1931 and when the leadership fell vacant in 1935 on George Lansbury's retirement, Attlee's claims were preferred to those of Morrison or Arthur Greenwood. When a 'national' Government was formed in 1940, Morrison became minister of supply and then, from October, home secretary and minister of home security. In large part this appointment arose from his close knowledge of London and Londoners because the chief task was to reassure the citizens that all possible measures were being taken to preserve them from air attack.

Herbert Morrison visited all the areas and units involved in Civil Defence, and, after some reluctance to remove fire-fighting from its local government base, he created the National Fire Service to secure better cooperation and more rapid action, and provided a proper Civil Defence uniform. This did much for morale, as did the Morrison indoor table shelter; and he went on to institute a Fire Guard with regular fire-watching duties. In all these activities Morrison typified the irrepressible London civilian who made a joke out of nights at the office or the factory, who rallied round after the raids, and would not let any German actions depress him.

In many ways, the climax of Morrison's career was the Labour landslide of 1945. He had prepared the ground for it in several respects. In the actual chain of events leading to the election, Morrison had played a considerable part. In 1940 he had insisted that the Labour Party divide the House at the end of the debate on the Norwegian fiasco and had thus given the impetus which led to the resignation of Neville Chamberlain. As one of the small group of Labour leaders who successfully occupied high office through the war, he had shown that such men could rule most effectively. And, when Churchill asked the Labour Party to continue with the Coalition until Japan was defeated, Morrison was instrumental in insisting that this was unsatisfactory and that the country wanted a general election.

It has often been said that Morrison constructed and managed the machine which channelled the enthusiasms of 1945 into decisive action at the ballot box. Of this there is less evidence. The Conservative Party had almost totally abandoned its organization while Transport House had kept in operation. But there was no expert electioneering on either side. As with the LCC campaigns, all that was done was to provide candidates, explain the legal position, and produce a manifesto and some centrally directed propaganda. But because Morrison had done this before in London and played a large part in the similar process at a national level in 1945, he, not unfairly, received a large measure of the credit for the victory.

Although he had many subsequent achievements and his highest offices and honours were bestowed after 1945, some aspects of his career raised doubts and Morrison himself had disappointments, which made this period perhaps less happy than the previous years had been. As the results of the election of 1945, when Morrison was elected for Lewisham East, became known, he suggested that Attlee should not accept the royal commission to form a Government until the parliamentary party had met to elect a leader. Ernest Bevin and Attlee himself resisted this argument; Sir Stafford Cripps and Harold Laski agreed with Morrison; Attlee ended the matter by going to the palace. Morrison in his *Autobiography* (1960) denied that, in supporting delay, he was seeking the post of prime minister for himself. Yet Laski, Ellen Wilkinson, and the others who were active on this occasion were quite clear that their candidate was Morrison and that he had given them his complete support. In fact, Morrison pressed his case in meetings of various Labour groups for several days after Attlee had been designated prime minister.

Again, in 1947, when Cripps was alarmed about the lack of leadership on economic affairs, Morrison became involved in the situation. But, in spite of these frictions, not uncommon in all Governments, few would deny Morrison the credit for many of the successes of the post-war Labour

Government. When he was minister of supply in 1940, Morrison had had some difficulty with economic problems, a field which he never mastered as thoroughly as he had general administration and the social services. This difficulty cropped up again between 1945 and 1947, when he was responsible, as lord president of the Council, for economic planning and co-ordination. In 1947 this task was given to Cripps at a new Ministry of Economic Affairs and Morrison was left to lead the House of Commons and to plan and carry through the legislative programme of the Government. In this task he excelled. His experience over the London Passenger Transport Act made him the authority on all the earlier nationalization measures, particularly of transport and electricity. Experienced members of the press lobby said it was a joy to watch him introduce these Bills, picking his way through the complexities and skirting the dangers like a cat walking across a mound of cans and broken bottles.

When it came to the question of steel, he was never adamant about public ownership and had wanted this item omitted from the 1945 election programme. Then, when the Cabinet took up the measure, Morrison was responsible for negotiations with (Sir) Ellis Hunter and (Sir) Andrew Duncan, the steel-masters' leaders. They produced a plan for increasing the powers of the Iron and Steel Board and allowing it to take over any firm which was not amenable to control. Aneurin Bevan, Bevin, and Cripps resisted this scheme throughout the summer of 1947 (when part of the time Morrison was seriously ill). In August the Parliamentary Labour Party discovered the situation, insisted on full nationalization, and the Bill was put in hand in October of that year. Although Morrison was much criticized for his 'hybrid measure', it was the most that could be achieved if the co-operation of the steel-masters was to be retained; and it would have given the Government a substantial measure of control.

In September 1947 Cripps openly admitted that he felt Bevin should take over from Attlee as prime minister, Hugh (later Lord) Dalton should become foreign secretary, and Attlee could remain as chancellor of the Exchequer. Cripps was almost equally critical of Morrison but still tried to win him over. Morrison said that he felt he should be prime minister and he went no further with the conspirators when it was clear that their objective was to elevate his chief enemy, Bevin. He left Cripps to put the proposal to Attlee who stopped the whole business by appointing Cripps to the Exchequer. Morrison's account of this in his *Autobiography* is not entirely frank. Eventually he agreed to be lord president of the Council, in which office he would have to co-ordinate Labour's policies. When Bevin fell ill in 1950, Morrison dithered over whether he wanted to become foreign secretary. The following year Attlee noted that: 'He seemed to want it badly and turned down every other suggestion I made to him, so in the end I appointed him. Rather bad luck for him, as it turned out.' This was because Morrison lacked all feeling for foreign affairs and was un-happy and uncomfortable in it so that his reputation suffered as a result. It is generally agreed that much of Morrison's touch, his sure-footedness in all matters of domestic policy and administration, deserted him when he moved to the Foreign Office in 1951. It has been suggested that for the first time his eyesight troubled him, when so much had to be read. More seriously, his judgement faltered. Even friendly critics pointed out that he knew Londoners perfectly, other English fairly well, the Scots and Welsh were strangers to him, and foreigners incomprehensible. This may not have been fair, but his tenure of the Foreign Office was neither successful nor fortunate. A Morrison Plan for Palestine was quickly disregarded but the chief problem confronting him was the decision of Mr Mossadeq's Government to take over the British-owned oil-wells at Abadan. Morrison was in favour of recovering them and admonishing the Persian Govern-ment by direct military action. It was left to Attlee to veto any such idea, pointing out that world and particularly Asian opinion would react vio-lently, that the Persians could not be denied the right to nationalize such assets, and that strong-arm action in defence of commercial interests could no longer be tolerated. Unable to act as he had wanted, Morrison's performance lacked clarity or decisiveness and his short spell at the Foreign Office did considerable harm to his political standing.

In opposition after 1951, Morrison played a prominent part but many felt that he was getting older and was not as effective as he had been in the 1940s. In 1955 Attlee retired and Morrison entered the leadership contest. In his *Autobiography* he says that his weakness was his 'inability to intrigue'. Yet there is small evidence of intrigue on the side of the victor, Hugh Gaitskell. There is little doubt that Attlee held on to the leadership until 1955 in order to prevent Morrison's succeeding. He resigned only when Morrison was sixty-seven and then after declaring that the Labour Party needed a leader who was born in the twentieth rather than in the nineteenth century. As deputy prime minister from 1945 to 1951 and as deputy leader of the party since then, as a man who had contested the leadership with Attlee as far back as 1935, Morrison had undeniable claims to the topmost position. There was also a definite campaign to prevent his succeeding, all of which may justify his meeting such efforts with all the resources open to a politician.

'In politics', it is said, 'there is no friendship at the top', and this appears to have been the case among some of the Labour leaders. Attlee was always on reasonable terms with Morrison but he complained that 'Herbert cannot distinguish between big things and little things' and this was probably one motive behind his desire to prevent Morrison from obtaining the leadership. It was while Attlee was ill in hospital in early 1951 and Morrison was presiding over the Cabinet that divisions arose and Aneurin Bevan and (Sir) Harold Wilson resigned. Attlee blamed Morrison for this and complained that the issue was not kept open for long enough—'he lost me two of my ministers'.

Herbert Morrison had not got on well with Bevan, but the most publicized disharmony was between Morrison and Ernest Bevin. For some reason, very possibly over trade-union representation on public bodies, the massive leader of the Transport and General Workers Union had decided as early as 1924 that Morrison was anti-union and to this he added a distaste for disloyalty of which he accused Morrison in 1945 when the attempt was made to replace Attlee. While Cripps's move to oust Attlee in 1947 apparently never riled Bevin, he continued to suspect Morrison. A major reason why Attlee had placed Bevin at the Foreign Office in 1945 was the feeling that his relations with Morrison were not easy enough to permit the close co-operation which would have been required had both men occupied posts on the home front.

After the Labour Party lost power in 1951, Morrison remained as a leading and very effective opposition spokesman. He had been elected a visiting fellow of Nuffield College, Oxford, in 1947 and was much aided there by (Sir) Norman Chester, especially when he turned to writing and in 1954 published *Government and Parliament, a Survey from the Inside*. The book was at once acclaimed as a notable account of British government and Morrison himself hoped it would become another Erskine May, the authoritative description which would be renewed every few years and continue long after he had died. While the book had considerable merits, especially in the lucid accounts of parliamentary procedure, the legislative programme, and the nationalized industries, it never attained the stature Morrison hoped for. One reason was that he lacked the academic turn of mind and, while the exposition was excellent, there was little analysis. Deeper criticisms are that the book is a first-rate description of how the system worked in theory, but that Morrison put in too few of the by-ways and circumventions of practice. A brilliant intuitive politician, he did not explain how he played by ear, but set out the actual score as it was on the official hymn sheet.

After his defeat for the party leadership, he rejected all attempts to persuade him to remain as deputy leader, although until the end of that Parliament he was still a frequent contributor to debates, as jaunty and pugnacious as ever. In the dissolution honours of 1959 he was made a life peer and the following year extended his activities by accepting the presidency of the British Board of Film Censors.

Morrison's *Autobiography* appeared in 1960. It provided little new information or insights into the period, but did give some interesting sidelights on the author and his relations with his colleagues. In it Morrison says of Attlee that 'he was one of the best mayors that Stepney ever had'. It would be true to say that Morrison himself was almost certainly the best leader whom the London Labour Party and the LCC have ever had, but it would not be enough. He was a great parliamentarian, effective in debate, a master of legislative and administrative detail, the father of an important account of British government and a man whose sincere desire to create better conditions for all was recognized by everyone engaged in British politics.

He died in Queen Mary Hospital at Sidcup 6 March 1965, and his ashes were scattered in London, on the river.

Morrison married in 1919 Margaret (died 1953), the daughter of Howard Kent, of Letchworth, a clerk at Euston station; they had one daughter. It was not a particularly happy marriage.

He married, secondly, in 1955, Edith, daughter of John Meadowcroft, of Rochdale. She wrote an enjoyable account of his second marriage (1977).

There are two portraits in chalk of Morrison, both in the National Portrait Gallery, one by Juliet Pannett (1961), the other by Sir David Low.

[Lord Morrison of Lambeth, *An Autobiography*, 1960; Bernard Donoughue and G. W. Jones, *Herbert Morrison, Portrait of a Politician*, 1973.]

JOHN P. MACKINTOSH

published 1981

MOSLEY Sir Oswald Ernald

(1896–1980)

Sixth Baronet

Politician and Fascist leader, was born at 47 Hill St., Mayfair, London, 16 November 1896, the grandson of Sir Oswald Mosley, fourth baronet, of Rolleston Hall, Burton-on-Trent, and the eldest of the three sons of Oswald Mosley (who succeeded to the baronetcy in 1915) and his wife, Katharine Maud, the second child of Captain Justinian Edwards-Heathcote, of Longton Hall, Stoke-on-Trent, and Betton Hall, Market

Drayton, Shropshire. The Mosleys were an old landed Staffordshire family, who had also, until 1846, been lords of the manor of Manchester.

When Mosley was five years old, his mother obtained a judicial separation from her husband, and took her three young children to live near her father's Shropshire house. Mosley's paternal grandfather, Sir Oswald, took a great interest in him, and encouraged him to spend a good deal of his time at Rolleston. His close relationship with his grandfather and his mother, who both adulated him, was to remain a strong influence in his life.

After three years at the private school West Down, Mosley went in 1909 to Winchester, where he developed considerable skill at boxing and fencing, achieving his first of many distinctions in the latter sport when, aged fifteen, he won the public schools championship at sabre and foil. He left Winchester at the end of 1912. In January 1914 he entered Sandhurst, but, after an incident the details of which still remain obscure, was rusticated in June of that year.

Recalled to Sandhurst at the outbreak of war, Mosley was commissioned into the 16th Lancers that October. He immediately applied to join the Royal Flying Corps, and was in the 6th Squadron near Poperinghe, as an observer, from December 1914 to April 1915. He returned to Shoreham-by-sea to take his pilot's licence; but in a foolish escapade he crashed his plane while performing a risky manoeuvre to impress his mother, and broke his ankle. He returned to the trenches with the 16th Lancers, but his injured ankle seriously worsened, and in March 1916 he was invalided out with a severe and permanent limp.

Part of the rest of the war was spent in the Ministry of Munitions and in the Foreign Office. In London, Mosley swiftly became a well-known figure in the salons of the great hostesses, and came into contact with many leading politicians. Encouraged by F. E. Smith (later Earl of Birkenhead) and Sir George Younger (later Viscount Younger of Leckie), Mosley became Conservative candidate for the Harrow Division of Middlesex, and won the seat in December 1918 by a very large majority. On 11 May 1920 he married Lady Cynthia Blanche, second daughter of the formidable Conservative politician Lord Curzon of Kedleston.

Mosley appeared to live, at this stage, an almost 'double life'. On the one hand, 'Tom' Mosley (as he was known to his intimates) and his wife led a brilliant social life. To Mosley's own considerable income Cynthia had brought the fortune bequeathed by her grandfather Levi Leiter, the Chicago millionaire. The gilded and handsome young couple became the smartest of the smart set. On the other hand, Mosley was showing a serious concern with politics. He saw himself as a representative of the 'younger generation', for whom the war had sown doubts about the traditional political creeds and line-ups. Under the influence of Lord Robert Cecil (later Viscount Cecil of Chelwood) he became an enthusiastic backer of the League of Nations. He strongly attacked military expenditure and foreign involvements, which were preventing spending on home needs. Far more devastating, however, was his opposition to the government's Irish policy, and in particular to the alleged reprisals operated by the Black and Tans. A series of critical speeches and questions, in late 1920, culminated in his crossing the House to sit on the opposition benches. He became the secretary of the newly formed Peace with Ireland Council. On this occasion his local party gave him a unanimous vote of confidence; but, by 1922, in view of his independent line on a variety of issues, it felt constrained to ask for an assurance of his party loyalty. This Mosley loftily declined to give, claiming complete freedom of action. A new Conservative candidate was adopted, and Mosley stood as an Independent in the election that followed the collapse of the coalition in 1922. He was returned with a large majority.

It has been suggested that Mosley's career consisted of a series of mistimed opportunities, of which the first was a revolt against the coalition only months before its end. It is clear, however, that Mosley would have broken with his party, or indeed with any party, at this stage, and that his confidence in his own views and abilities made him scorn the constraints of party discipline. The same pattern was to follow him through the rest of his career.

In the 1923 election Mosley held Harrow with a reduced majority. It was already obvious that, if his political career was to continue, he needed some party affiliation. He had developed contacts with the Liberals, but, given the situation in 1923–4, his eventual choice could hardly be in doubt. In March 1924, two months after Ramsay MacDonald formed the first Labour government, Mosley joined the Labour Party, becoming a member of the ILP.

In the 1924 election he stood against Neville Chamberlain at Birmingham Ladywood, and was narrowly defeated, returning to Parliament in December 1926, after winning the Smethwick by-election with a large majority. The intervening period had been put to good use; together with (Evelyn) John St. Loe Strachey he had developed a series of economic policies which challenged the conventional wisdom of the time, and owed much to J. M. (later Lord) Keynes; and by his active work on behalf of the miners' strike he had built up support on the Left.

He was already being regarded as a possible future leader of the Labour Party, despite the arrogance and self-confidence which repelled so many of his colleagues, and the apparent frivolity of his social life. In 1928 he succeeded to the baronetcy. In the 1929 election he was returned for

Smethwick, and his wife Cynthia became the Labour MP for Stoke-on-Trent. Mosley became chancellor of the Duchy of Lancaster in the new government.

J. H. Thomas, lord privy seal, had been given special responsibility for the unemployment problem, helped by Mosley, George Lansbury, and George Johnston. Friction was great between Mosley and Thomas, who stood, as did the chancellor of the Exchequer, Philip (later Viscount) Snowden, for orthodox solutions. Things came to a head with the Mosley memorandum of 1930 which made radical recommendations for economic recovery, involving state intervention and a public works programme. When it was rejected by the Cabinet, Mosley resigned on 20 May 1930.

He was already considering leaving the party. The experiences of Harrow, of Smethwick, and of innumerable miners' galas had convinced him that he had a popular appeal which could transcend the conventional party system. When his proposals were defeated at the party conference in October, he set about planning the New Party, which was launched on 1 March 1931. At first this party was conceived entirely in parliamentary terms. Mosley and four other MPs (including his wife) remained in Parliament under the new banner. Discussions about alliances took place. Mosley hoped for at least a dozen seats in the October elections; but the election results were disastrous, all twenty-four candidates being defeated.

In early 1932 Mosley visited Italy, and on his return set about creating a British Fascist movement. He was impatient with the parliamentary system which had rejected him, and, in the 1932 situation, when so many people were predicting the demise of democracy, saw the future as lying with a dictatorial system which, alone, could solve the problems of the modern economy. On 1 October the British Union of Fascists was launched.

The first two years of the new movement were successful and comparatively respectable. Mosley's outstanding oratory and charisma proved capable of swaying mass meetings. The main influence was Mussolini's Italy, which still mustered considerable respect in Britain; and, despite the rough tactics of some of the party's members at ground level, a great effort was made to convince the traditional Right of the movement's respectable credentials. Many Conservatives saw it as a kind of 'Tory ginger group'. But in 1934 the picture changed. The violence at the great Olympia meeting in June estranged a good number of supporters of this type, and during the year many people became aware of the violence, extremism, and anti-Semitism which underlay the surface, and shied away.

Mosley's response was to stress, as central policies of the movement, the very aspects which had caused this rejection. From late 1934, anti-Semitism became a major plank in the BUF's platform. Deprived of much of his middle-class support, Mosley turned to the streets. There he appears to have hoped to gain that popular acclaim which would be the basis for the new regime to be built on the ruins of democracy.

The calculation was mistaken. Membership fell rapidly. Within a year the movement had ceased to be of any political importance. Its activities got considerable press coverage, of course, but it never came near to possessing any political power, even in areas like the East End, where its anti-Semitic policies had their greatest effect. The movement now became much more influenced by Nazism, and in 1936 its name was changed to the 'British Union of Fascists and National Socialists'. Mosley's Keynesian policies of 1930 had been replaced by a heady and over-simplified mixture of corporatism, totalitarianism, patriotism, and racialism.

Mosley's personal life changed considerably in this period. Lady Cynthia Mosley died of peritonitis on 16 May 1933. In October 1936, in Berlin, Mosley privately married, in Hitler's presence, the Hon. Mrs Diana Guinness, third daughter of the second Baron Redesdale, and sister of Nancy Mitford, Jessica, and Unity.

From 1936 onwards the BUF mounted a peace campaign, denouncing the coming war as a conspiracy organized by the Jews. The campaign was of much less importance nationally than the widespread acceptance of Nazi Germany in far more respectable circles. It continued, however, into the first year of the war, and in May 1940 Mosley and his wife were arrested and detained under Regulation 18B. In November 1943 they were released, on humanitarian grounds, on account of Mosley's physical condition.

After the war Mosley concerned himself with justification of his pre-war attitudes, as in *My Answer* (1946) and *My Life* (1968), and also with the leadership, from 1948 to 1966, of the Union Movement, whose theme was European unity, based on racial criteria. After a short stay in Ireland, he lived mainly in France, in a house at Orsay, outside Paris; but he made forays into Britain. He stood for Parliament at North Kensington in 1959, in the aftermath of the Notting Hill race riots, and to his amazement lost his deposit. A similar result met him at Shoreditch in 1966. To his death he was convinced that in the event of a European crisis he still had a contribution to make. He died at his house at Orsay 3 December 1980.

Some have called Mosley one of the most intelligent politicians of this century. He was, however, singularly lacking in judgement. His were simple, uncomplicated enthusiasms. Even where the policies were subtle, and correct, as with the Strachey-inspired Keynesian theories of his Labour period, his commitment was simple, demanding, and obdurate; in the case of later 'conspiracy theories' this was even more so. In each case he had unbounded confidence in his own judgement and capabilities, and scorn for those around him. Behind all this lay almost a caricature of traditional public school values; patriotism, the belief in the 'manly' virtues, dislike of outsiders, and rejection of those whom he believed to be opposed to this pattern—whether Black and Tans terrorizing a civilian population, or Jewish capitalists undermining traditional English virtues. Personal ambition played a great part, too; but his decisions, at every point, achieved the opposite of what he desired. He continually gave the impression of a 'coming man', but his impatience defeated him.

By his first wife Cynthia he had two sons and a daughter, and by his second wife Diana two sons. His eldest son is Nicholas Mosley (born 1923), the author, who in 1966 became the third Baron Ravensdale in succession to his aunt, Irene Curzon, and who succeeded to the baronetcy on his father's death.

[Sir Oswald Mosley, *My Life*, 1968; Robert Skidelsky, *Oswald Mosley*, 1975; Maurice Cowling, *The Impact of Labour 1920–1924*, 1971; Kenneth Lunn and Richard Thurlow (eds.), *British Fascism*, 1980; Robert Benewick, *The Fascist Movement in Britain*, 1972; contemporary diaries and journals; numbers of *Action, Blackshirt*, and *Fascist Week*; Nicholas Mosley, *Rules of the Game: Sir Oswald and Lady Cynthia Mosley 1896–1933*, 1982, and *Beyond the Pale, Sir Oswald Mosley 1933–80*, 1983.]

RICHARD GRIFFITHS

published 1986

MOUNTBATTEN Louis Francis Albert Victor Nicholas

(1900–1979)

First Earl Mountbatten of Burma

Admiral of the fleet, was born at Frogmore House, Windsor, 25 June 1900 as Prince Louis of Battenberg, the younger son and youngest of the four children of Prince Louis Alexander of Battenberg (later Louis Mountbatten, Marquess of Milford Haven, admiral of the fleet), and his wife, Princess Victoria Alberta Elizabeth Marie Irene, daughter of Louis IV of Hesse-Darmstadt. Prince Louis Alexander, himself head of a cadet branch of the house of Hesse-Darmstadt, was brother-in-law to Queen Victoria's daughter, Princess Beatrice; his wife was Victoria's granddaughter. By both father and mother, therefore, Prince Louis was closely connected with the British royal family. One of his sisters married King Gustav VI of Sweden and the other Prince Andrew of Greece.

Prince Louis, 'Dickie' as he was known from childhood, was educated as befitted the son of a senior naval officer—a conventional upbringing varied by holidays with his German relations or with his aunt, the tsarina, in Russia. At Locker's Park School in Hertfordshire he was praised for his industry, enthusiasm, sense of humour, and modesty—the first two at least being characteristics conspicuous throughout his life. From there in May 1913 he entered the naval training college of Osborne as fifteenth out of eighty-three, a respectable if unglamorous position which he more or less maintained during his eighteen months there. Towards the end of his stay his father, now first sea lord, was hounded from office because of his German ancestry. This affected young Prince Louis deeply, though a contemporary recalls him remarking nonchalantly: 'It doesn't really matter very much. Of course I shall take his place.' Certainly his passionate ambition owed something to his desire to avenge his father's disgrace.

In November 1914 Prince Louis moved on to Dartmouth. Though he never shone athletically, nor impressed himself markedly on his contemporaries, his last years of education showed increasing confidence and ability, and at Keyham, the Royal Naval College at Devonport where he did his final course, he came first out of seventy-two. In July 1916 he was assigned as a midshipman to the *Lion*, the flagship of Admiral Sir David (later Earl) Beatty. His flag captain, (Sir) Roger Backhouse, described him as 'a very promising young officer' but his immediate superior felt he lacked the brilliance of his elder brother George—a judgement which Prince Louis himself frequently echoed. The *Lion* saw action in the eight months Prince Louis was aboard but suffered no damage, and by the time he transferred to the *Queen Elizabeth* in February 1917 the prospects of a major naval battle seemed remote. Prince Louis served briefly aboard the submarine K6—'the happiest month I've ever spent in the service'—and visited the western front, but his time on the *Queen Elizabeth* was uneventful and he was delighted to be posted in July 1918 as first lieutenant on one of the P-boats, small torpedo boats designed primarily for antisubmarine warfare. It was while he was on the *Queen Elizabeth* that his father, in common with other members of the royal family, abandoned his German title and was created Marquess of Milford Haven, with the family name of Mountbatten. His younger son was known henceforth as Lord Louis Mountbatten.

At the end of 1919 Mountbatten was one of a group of naval officers sent to widen their intellectual horizons at Cambridge. During his year at Christ's College (of which he became an honorary fellow in 1946) he acquired a taste for public affairs, regularly attending the Union and achieving the distinction, remarkable for someone in his position, of being elected to the committee. Through his close friend Peter Murphy, he also opened his mind to radical opinions—'We all thought him rather left-wing', said the then president of the Union, (Sir) Geoffrey Shakespeare.

While still at Cambridge, Mountbatten was invited by his cousin, the Prince of Wales, to attend him on the forthcoming tour of Australasia in the *Renown*. Mountbatten's roles were those of unofficial diarist, dogsbody, and, above all, companion to his sometimes moody and disobliging cousin. These he performed admirably—'you will never know', wrote the Prince to Lord Milford Haven, 'what very great friends we have become, what he has meant and been to me on this trip.' His reward was to be invited to join the next royal tour to India and Japan in the winter of 1921–2; a journey that doubly marked his life in that in India he learnt to play polo and became engaged to Edwina Cynthia Annette (died 1960), daughter of Wilfrid William Ashley (later Baron Mount Temple).

Edwina Ashley was descended from the third Viscount Palmerston and the Earls of Shaftesbury, while her maternal grandfather was the immensely rich Sir Ernest Cassel, friend and financial adviser to King Edward VII. At Cassel's death in 1921 his granddaughter inherited some £2.3 million, and eventually also a palace on Park Lane, Classiebawn Castle in Ireland, and the Broadlands estate at Romsey in Hampshire. The marriage of two powerful and fiercely competitive characters was never wholly harmonious and sometimes caused unhappiness to both partners. On the whole, however, it worked well and they established a formidable partnership at several stages of their lives. They had two daughters.

Early in 1923 Mountbatten joined the *Revenge*. For the next fifteen years his popular image was that of a playboy. Fast cars, speedboats, polo, were his delights; above all the last, about which he wrote the classic *Introduction to Polo* (1931) by 'Marco'. Yet nobody who knew his work could doubt his essential seriousness. 'This officer's heart and soul is in the Navy', reported the captain of the *Revenge*. 'No outside interests are ever allowed to interfere with his duties.' His professionalism was proved beyond doubt when he selected signals as his speciality and passed out top of the course in July 1925. As assistant fleet wireless officer (1927–8) and fleet wireless officer (1931–3) in the Mediterranean, and at the signals school at Portsmouth in between, he won a reputation for energy, efficiency, and inventiveness. He raised the standard of signalling in the Mediterranean Fleet to new heights and was known, respected, and almost always liked by everyone under his command.

In 1932 Mountbatten was promoted commander and in April 1934 took over the *Daring*, a new destroyer of 1,375 tons. After only a few months, however, he had to exchange her for an older and markedly inferior destroyer, the *Wishart*. Undiscomfited, he set to work to make his ship the most efficient in the Mediterranean Fleet. He succeeded and *Wishart* was Cock of the Fleet in the regatta of 1935. It was at this time that he perfected the 'Mountbatten station-keeping gear', an ingenious device which was adopted by the Admiralty for use in destroyers but which never really proved itself in wartime.

Enthusiastically recommended for promotion, Mountbatten returned to the Naval Air Division of the Admiralty. He was prominent in the campaign to recapture the Fleet Air Arm from the Royal Air Force, lobbying (Sir) Winston Churchill, Sir Samuel Hoare (later Viscount Templewood), and A. Duff Cooper (later Viscount Norwich) with a freedom unusual among junior officers. He vigorously applauded the latter's resignation over the Munich agreement and maintained a working relationship with Anthony Eden (later the Earl of Avon) and the fourth Marquess of Salisbury in their opposition to appeasement. More practically he was instrumental in drawing the Admiralty's attention to the merits of the Oerlikon gun, the adoption of which he urged vigorously for more than two years. It was during this period that he also succeeded in launching the Royal Naval Film Corporation, an organization designed to secure the latest films for British sailors at sea.

The abdication crisis caused him much distress but left him personally unscathed. Some time earlier he had hopefully prepared for the Prince of Wales a list of eligible Protestant princesses, but by the time of the accession he had little influence left. He had been King Edward VIII's personal naval aide-de-camp and in February 1937 King George VI appointed him to the same position, simultaneously appointing him to the GCVO.

Since the autumn of 1938 Mountbatten had been contributing ideas to the construction at Newcastle of a new destroyer, the *Kelly*. In June 1939 he took over as captain and *Kelly* was commissioned by the outbreak of war. On 20 September she was joined by her sister ship *Kingston*, and Mountbatten became captain (D) of the fifth destroyer flotilla.

Mountbatten was not markedly successful as a wartime destroyer captain. In surprisingly few months at sea he almost capsized in a high sea, collided with another destroyer, and was mined once, torpedoed twice, and finally sunk by enemy aircraft. In most of these incidents he could plead circumstances beyond his control, but the consensus of professional opinion is that he lacked 'sea-sense', the quality that ensures a ship is doing the right thing in the right place at the right time. Nevertheless he acted with immense panache and courage, and displayed such qualities of leadership that when *Kelly* was recommissioned after several months refitting, an embarrassingly large number of her former crew clamoured to rejoin. When he took his flotilla into Namsos in March 1940 to evacuate

(Sir) Adrian Carton de Wiart and several thousand Allied troops, he conducted the operation with cool determination. The return of *Kelly* to port in May, after ninety-one hours in tow under almost constant bombardment and with a fifty-foot hole in the port side, was an epic of fortitude and seamanship. It was feats like this that caught Churchill's imagination and thus altered the course of Mountbatten's career.

In the spring of 1941 the *Kelly* was dispatched to the Mediterranean. Placed in an impossible position, Admiral Sir A. B. Cunningham (later Viscount Cunningham of Hyndhope) in May decided to support the army in Crete even though there was no possibility of air cover. The *Kashmir* and the *Kelly* were attacked by dive-bombers on 23 May and soon sunk. More than half the crew of *Kelly* was lost and Mountbatten only escaped by swimming from under the ship as it turned turtle. The survivors were machine-gunned in the water but were picked up by the *Kipling*. The *Kelly* lived on in *In Which We Serve*, a skilful propaganda film by (Sir) Noël Coward, which was based in detail on the achievements of Lord Louis Mountbatten and his ship. Mountbatten was now appointed to command the aircraft-carrier *Illustrious*, which had been severely damaged and sent for repair to the United States. In October he flew to America to take over his ship and pay a round of visits. He established many useful contacts and made a considerable impression on the American leadership: '. . . he has been a great help to all of us, and I mean literally ALL', wrote Admiral Starke to Sir A. Dudley Pound. Before the *Illustrious* was ready, however, Mountbatten was called home by Churchill to take charge of Combined Operations. His predecessor, Sir Roger (later Lord) Keyes, had fallen foul of the chiefs of staff and Mountbatten was initially appointed only as 'chief adviser'. In April 1942, however, he became chief of Combined Operations with the acting rank of vice-admiral, lieutenant-general, and air marshal and with *de facto* membership of the chiefs of staff committee. This phenomenally rapid promotion earned him some unpopularity, but on the whole the chiefs of staff gave him full support.

'You are to give no thought for the defensive. Your whole attention is to be concentrated on the offensive', Churchill told him. Mountbatten's duties fell into two main parts: to organize raids against the European coast designed to raise morale, harass the Germans, and achieve limited military objectives; and to prepare for an eventual invasion. The first responsibility, more dramatic though less important, gave rise to a multitude of raids involving only a handful of men and a few more complex operations such as the costly but successful attack on the dry dock at St. Nazaire. Combined Operations were responsible for planning such forays, but their execution was handed over to the designated force commander, a system which led sometimes to confusion.

The ill results of divided responsibilities were particularly apparent in the Dieppe operation of August 1942. Dieppe taught the Allies valuable lessons for the eventual invasion and misled the Germans about their intentions, but the price paid in lives and material was exceedingly, probably disproportionately, high. For this Mountbatten, ultimately responsible for planning the operation, must accept some responsibility. Nevertheless the errors which both British and German analysts subsequently condemned—the adoption of frontal rather than flank assault, the selection of relatively inexperienced Canadian troops for the assault, the abandonment of any previous air bombardment, and the failure to provide the support of capital ships—were all taken against his advice or over his head. Certainly he was not guilty of the blunders which Lord Beaverbrook and some later commentators attributed to him.

When it came to preparation for invasion, Mountbatten's energy, enthusiasm, and receptivity to new ideas showed to great advantage. His principal contribution was to see clearly what is now obvious but was then not generally recognized, that successful landings on a fortified enemy coast called for an immense range of specialized equipment and skills. To secure an armada of landing craft of different shapes and sizes, and to train the crews to operate them, involved a diversion of resources, both British and American, which was vigorously opposed in many quarters. The genesis of such devices as Mulberry (the floating port) and Pluto (pipe line under the ocean) is often hard to establish, but the zeal with which Mountbatten and his staff supported their development was a major factor in their success. Mountbatten surrounded himself with a team of talented if sometimes maverick advisers—Professor J. D. Bernal, Geoffrey Pyke, Solly (later Lord) Zuckerman—and was ready to listen to anything they suggested. Sometimes this led him into wasteful extravagances—as in his championship of the iceberg/aircraft carrier Habbakuk—but there were more good ideas than bad. His contribution to D-Day was recognized in the tribute paid him by the Allied leaders shortly after the invasion: '. . . we realize that much of . . . the success of this venture has its origins in developments effected by you and your staff.'

His contribution to the higher strategy is less easy to establish. He himself always claimed responsibility for the selection of Normandy as the invasion site rather than the Pas de Calais. Certainly when Operation Sledgehammer, the plan for a limited re-entry into the Continent in 1942, was debated by the chiefs of staff, Mountbatten was alone in arguing for the Cherbourg peninsula. His consistent support of Normandy may have contributed to the change of heart when the venue of the invasion proper was decided. In general, however, Sir Alan Brooke (later Viscount Alanbrooke) and the other chiefs of staff resented Mountbatten's ventures outside the field of his immediate interests and he usually confined himself to matters directly concerned with Combined Operations.

His headquarters, COHQ, indeed the whole of his command, was sometimes criticized for its lavishness in personnel and encouragement of extravagant ideas. Mountbatten was never economical, and waste there undoubtedly was. Nevertheless he built up at great speed an organization of remarkable complexity and effectiveness. By April 1943 Combined Operations Command included 2,600 landing-craft and over 50,000 men. He almost killed himself in the process for in July 1942 he was told by his doctors that he would die unless he worked less intensely. A man with less imagination who played safe could never have done as much. It was Alan Brooke, initially unenthusiastic about his elevation, who concluded: 'His appointment as Chief of Combined Operations . . . was excellent, and he played a remarkable part as the driving force and main-spring of this organization. Without his energy and drive it would never have reached the high standard it achieved.'

Mountbatten arrived at the Quebec conference in August 1943 as chief of Combined Operations; he left as acting admiral and supreme commander designate, South East Asia. 'He is young, enthusiastic and triphibious', Churchill telegraphed C. R. (later Earl) Attlee, but though the Americans welcomed the appointment enthusiastically, he was only selected after half a dozen candidates had been eliminated for various reasons.

He took over a command where everything had gone wrong. The British and Indian army, ravaged by disease and soundly beaten by the Japanese, had been chased out of Burma. A feeble attempt at counterattack in the Arakan peninsula had ended in disaster. Morale was low, air support inadequate, communications within India slow and uncertain. There seemed little to oppose the Japanese if they decided to resume their assault. Yet before Mountbatten could concentrate on his official adversaries he had to resolve the anomalies within his own Command.

Most conspicuous of these was General Stilwell. As well as being deputy supreme commander, Stilwell was chief of staff to Chiang Kai-shek and his twin roles inevitably involved conflicts of interest and loyalty. A superb leader of troops in the field but cantankerous, anglophobe, and narrowminded, Stilwell would have been a difficult colleague in any circumstances. In South East Asia, where his preoccupation was to reopen the road through north Burma to China, he proved almost impossible to work with. But Mountbatten also found his relationship difficult with his own, British, commanders-in-chief, in particular the naval commander, Sir James Somerville. Partly this arose from differences of temperament; more important it demonstrated a fundamental difference of opinion about the supreme commander's role. Mountbatten, encouraged by Churchill and members of his own entourage, believed that he should operate on the MacArthur model, with his own planning staff, consulting his commanders-in-chief but ultimately instructing them on future operations. Somerville, General Sir G. J. Giffard, and Air Marshal Sir R. E. C. Peirse, on the other hand, envisaged him as a chairman of committee, operating like Eisenhower and working through the planning staffs of the commanders-in-chief. The chiefs of staff in London proved reluctant to rule categorically on the issue but Mountbatten eventually abandoned his central planning staff and the situation was further eased when Somerville was replaced by Admiral Sir Bruce Fraser (later Lord Fraser of North Cape).

Mountbatten defined the three principal problems facing him as being those of monsoon, malaria, and morale. His determination that Allied troops must fight through the monsoon, though of greater psychological than military significance, undoubtedly assisted the eventual victories of the Fourteenth Army. In 1943, for every casualty evacuated because of wounds, there were 120 sick, and Mountbatten, by his emphasis on hygiene and improved medical techniques, can claim much credit for the vast improvement over the next year. But it was in the transformation of the soldiers' morale that he made his greatest contribution. By publicity, propaganda, and the impact of his personality, he restored their pride in themselves and gave them confidence that they could defeat the Japanese.

Deciding what campaign they were to fight proved difficult. Mountbatten, with Churchill's enthusiastic backing, envisaged a bold amphibious strategy which would bypass the Burmese jungles and strike through the Andaman Islands to Rangoon or, more ambitious still, through northern Sumatra towards Singapore. The Americans, however, who would have provided the material resources for such adventures, nicknamed South East Asia Command (SEAC) 'Save England's Asiatic Colonies' and were suspicious of any operation which seemed designed to this end. They felt that the solitary justification for the Burma campaign was to restore land communications with China. The ambitious projects with which Mountbatten had left London withered as his few landing-craft were withdrawn. A mission he dispatched to London and Washington returned empty-handed. 'You might send out the waxwork which I hear Madame Tussauds has made', wrote Mountbatten bitterly to his friend (Sir) Charles Lambe, 'it could have my Admiral's uniform and sit at my desk . . . as well as I could.'

It was the Japanese who saved him from so ignoble a role. In spring 1944 they attacked in Arakan and across the Imphal plain into India. The Allied capacity to supply troops by air and their new-found determination to stand firm, even when cut off, turned potential disaster into almost total victory. Mountbatten himself played a major role, being personally responsible at a crucial moment for the switch of two divisions by air from Arakan to Imphal and the diversion of the necessary American aircraft from the supply routes to China. Imphal confirmed Mountbatten's faith in the commander of the Fourteenth Army, General W. J. (later Viscount) Slim and led to his final loss of confidence in the commander-in-chief, General Giffard, whom he now dismissed. The battle cost the Japanese 7,000 dead; much hard fighting lay ahead but the Fourteenth Army was on the march that would end at Rangoon.

Mountbatten still hoped to avoid the reconquest of Burma by land. In April 1944 he transferred his headquarters from Delhi to Kandy in Ceylon, reaffirming his faith in a maritime strategy. He himself believed the next move should be a powerful sea and air strike against Rangoon; Churchill still hankered after the more ambitious attack on northern Sumatra; the chiefs of staff felt the British effort should be switched to support the American offensive in the Pacific. In the end shortage of resources dictated the course of events. Mountbatten was able to launch a small seaborne invasion to support the Fourteenth Army's advance, but it was Slim's men who bore the brunt of the fighting and reached Rangoon just before the monsoon broke in April 1945.

Giffard had been replaced as supreme commander by Sir Oliver Leese. Mountbatten's original enthusiasm for Leese did not endure; the latter soon fell out with his supreme commander and proved unpopular with the other commanders-in-chief. A climax came in May 1945 when Leese informed Slim that he was to be relieved from command of the Fourteenth Army because he was tired out and anyway had no experience in maritime operations. Mountbatten's role in this curious transaction remains slightly obscure; Leese definitely went too far, but there may have been some ambiguity about his instructions. In the event Leese's action was disavowed in London and he himself was dismissed and Slim appointed in his place.

The next phase of the campaign—an invasion by sea of the Malay peninsula—should have been the apotheosis of Mountbatten's command. When he went to the Potsdam conference in July 1945, however, he was told of the existence of the atom bomb. He realized at once that this was likely to rob him of his victory and, sure enough, the Japanese surrender reduced Operation Zipper to an unopposed landing. This was perhaps just as well; faulty intelligence meant that one of the two landings was made on unsuitable beaches and was quickly bogged down. The invasion would have succeeded but the cost might have been high.

On 12 September 1945, Mountbatten received the formal surrender of the Japanese at Singapore. Not long afterwards he was created a viscount. The honour was deserved. His role had been crucial. 'We did it together', Slim said to him on his deathbed, and the two men, in many ways so different, had indeed complemented each other admirably and proved the joint architects of victory in South East Asia.

Mountbatten's work in SEAC did not end with the Japanese surrender; indeed in some ways it grew still more onerous. His Command was now extended to include South Vietnam and the Netherlands East Indies: 1½ million square miles containing 128 million inhabitants, ¾ million armed and potentially truculent Japanese, and 123,000 Allied prisoners, many in urgent need of medical attention. Mountbatten had to rescue the prisoners, disarm the Japanese, and restore the various territories to stability so that civil government could resume. This last function proved most difficult, since the Japanese had swept away the old colonial regimes and new nationalist movements had grown up to fill the vacuum. Mountbatten's instincts told him that such movements were inevitable and even desirable. Every effort, he felt, should be made to take account of their justified aspirations. His disposition to sympathize with the radical nationalists sometimes led him into naïvely optimistic assessment of their readiness to compromise with the former colonialist regimes—as proved to be the case with the communist Chinese in Malaya—but the course of subsequent history suggests that he often saw the situation more clearly than the so-called 'realists' who criticized him.

Even before the end of the war he had had a foretaste of the problems that lay ahead. Aung San, head of the pro-Japanese Burmese National Army, defected with all his troops. Mountbatten was anxious to accept his co-operation and cajoled the somewhat reluctant chiefs of staff into agreeing on military grounds. Inevitably, this gave Aung San a stronger position than the traditionalists thought desirable when the time came to form Burma's post-war government. Mountbatten felt that, though left wing and fiercely nationalistic, Aung San was honourable, basically reasonable, and ready to accept the concept of an independent Burma within the British Commonwealth; '. . . with proper treatment', judged Slim, 'Aung San would have proved a Burmese Smuts.' The governor, Sir Reginald Dorman-Smith, conceded Aung San was the most popular man in Burma but considered him a dangerous Marxist revolutionary. When Aung San was accused of war crimes committed during the Japanese occupation, Dorman-Smith wished to arrest and try him. This Mountbatten forestalled; but the hand-over to civil government in April 1946 and the murder of Aung San the following year meant that the supreme commander's view of his character was never properly tested.

In Malaya the problem was more immediately one of law and order. Confronted by the threat of a politically motivated general strike, the authorities proposed to arrest all the leaders. 'Naturally I ordered them to cancel these orders', wrote Mountbatten, 'as I could not imagine anything more disastrous than to make martyrs of these men.' Reluctantly he agreed that in certain circumstances Chinese trouble-makers might be deported, but rescinded that approval when it was proposed to deport certain detainees who had not had time to profit by his warnings. His critics maintained that sterner action in 1945–6 could have prevented, or at least mitigated the future troubles in Malaya, but Mountbatten was convinced that the prosperity of Malaya and Singapore depended on the co-operation of Malay and Chinese, and was determined to countenance nothing that might divide the two communities.

In Vietnam and Indonesia Mountbatten's problem was to balance nationalist aspirations against the demands of Britain's Allies for support in the recovery of their colonies. He was better disposed to the French than the Dutch, and though he complained when General (Sir) Douglas Gracey exceeded his instructions and suppressed the Viet Minh—'General Gracey has saved French Indo-China', Leclerc told him—the reproof was more formal than real. In Indonesia Mountbatten believed that Dutch intransigence was the principal factor preventing a peaceful settlement. Misled by Dutch intelligence, he had no suspicion of the force of nationalist sentiment until Lady Mountbatten returned from her brave foray to rescue Allied prisoners of war. His forces could not avoid conflict with the Indonesian nationalists but Mountbatten sought to limit their commitment, with the result that both Dutch and Indonesians believed the British were favouring the other side. He did, however, contrive to keep open the possibility of political settlement; only after the departure of the British forces did full-scale civil war become inevitable.

Mountbatten left South East Asia in mid-1946 with the reputation of a liberal committed to decolonization. Though he had no thought beyond his return to the navy, with the now substantive rank of rear-admiral, his reputation influenced the Labour government when they were looking for a successor to Viscount (later Earl) Wavell who could resuscitate the faltering negotiations for Indian independence. On 18 December 1946 he was invited to become India's last viceroy. That year he had been created first Viscount Mountbatten of Burma.

Mountbatten longed to go to sea again, but this was a challenge no man of ambition and public spirit could reject. His reluctance enabled him to extract favourable terms from the government, and though the plenipotentiary powers to which he was often to refer are not specifically set out in any document, he enjoyed far greater freedom of action than his immediate predecessors. His original insistence that he would go only on the invitation of the Indian leaders was soon abandoned but it was on his initiative that a terminal date of June 1948 was fixed, by which time the British would definitely have left India.

Mountbatten's directive was that he should strive to implement the recommendations of the Cabinet mission of 1946, led by Sir R. Stafford Cripps, which maintained the principle of a united India. By the time he arrived, however, this objective had been tacitly abandoned by every major politician of the sub-continent with the important exception of M. K. Gandhi. The viceroy dutifully tried to persuade all concerned of the benefits of unity but his efforts foundered on the intransigence of the Muslim leader Mahomed Ali Jinnah. His problem thereafter was to find some formula which would reconcile the desire of the Hindus for a central India from which a few peripheral and wholly Muslim areas would secede, with Jinnah's aspiration to secure a greater Pakistan including all the Punjab and as much as possible of Bengal. In this task he was supported by Wavell's staff from the Indian Civil Service, reinforced by General H. L. (later Lord) Ismay and Sir Eric Miéville. He himself contributed immense energy, charm and persuasiveness, negotiating skills, agility of mind, and endless optimism.

He quickly concluded that not only was time not on his side but that the urgency was desperate. The run-down of the British military and civil presence, coupled with swelling inter-communal hatred, were intensely dangerous. 'The situation is everywhere electric, and I get the feeling that the mine may go up at any moment', wrote Ismay to his wife on 25 March 1947, the day after Mountbatten was sworn in as viceroy. This conviction that every moment counted dictated Mountbatten's activities over the next five months. He threw himself into a hectic series of interviews with the various political leaders. With Jawaharlal Nehru he established an immediate and lasting rapport which was to assume great import-ance in the future. With V. J. Patel, in whom he identified a major power in Indian politics, his initial relationship was less easy, but they soon enjoyed mutual confidence. Gandhi fascinated and delighted him, but he shrewdly concluded that he was likely to be pushed to one side in the forthcoming negotiations. With Jinnah alone did he fail; the full blast of his charm did not thaw or even moderate the chill intractability of the Muslim leader.

Nevertheless negotiations advanced so rapidly that by 2 May Ismay was taking to London a plan which Mountbatten believed all the principal parties would accept. Only when the British Cabinet had already approved the plan did he realize that he had gravely underestimated Nehru's ob-jections to any proposal that left room for the 'Balkanization' of India.

With extraordinary speed a new draft was produced, which provided for India's membership of the Commonwealth, and put less emphasis on the right of the individual components of British India to reject India or Pakistan and opt for independence. After what Mountbatten described as 'the worst 24 hours of my life', the plan was accepted by all parties on 3 June. He was convinced that any relaxation of the feverish pace would risk destroying the fragile basis of understanding. Independence, he announced, was to be granted in only ten weeks, on 15 August 1947.

Before this date the institutions of British India had to be carved in two. Mountbatten initially hoped to retain a unified army but quickly realized this would be impossible and concentrated instead on ensuring rough justice in the division of the assets. To have given satisfaction to everyone would have been impossible, but at the time few people accused him of partiality. He tackled the problems, wrote Michael Edwardes in a book not generally sympathetic to the last viceroy, 'with a speed and brilliance which it is difficult to believe would have been exercised by any other man'.

The princely states posed a particularly complex problem, since with the end of British rule paramountcy lapsed and there was in theory nothing to stop the princes opting for self-rule. This would have made a geographical nonsense of India and, to a lesser extent, Pakistan; as well as creating a plethora of independent states, many incapable of sustaining such a role. Mountbatten at first attached little importance to the question, but once he was fully aware of it, used every trick to get the rulers to accept accession. Some indeed felt that he was using improper influence on loyal subjects of the Crown, but it is hard to see that any other course would in the long run have contributed to their prosperity. Indeed the two states which Mountbatten failed to shepherd into the fold of India or Pakistan—Hyderabad and Kashmir—were those which were subsequently to cause most trouble.

Most provinces, like the princely states, clearly belonged either to India or to Pakistan. In the Punjab and Bengal, however, partition was necessary. This posed horrifying problems, since millions of Hindus and Muslims would find themselves on the wrong side of whatever frontier was established. The Punjab was likely to prove most troublesome, because 14 per cent of its population consisted of Sikhs, who were warlike, fanatically anti-Muslim, and determined that their homelands should remain inviolate. Partition was not Mountbatten's direct responsibility, since Sir Cyril (later Viscount) Radcliffe was appointed to divide the two provinces. Popular opinion, however, found it hard to accept that he was not involved, and even today it is sometimes suggested he may have helped shape Radcliffe's final conclusions.

Mountbatten had hoped that independence day would see him installed as governor-general of both new dominions; able to act, in Churchill's phrase, as 'moderator' during their inevitable differences. Nehru was ready for such a transmogrification but Jinnah, after some months of apparent indecision, concluded that he himself must be Pakistan's first head of state. Mountbatten was uncertain whether the last viceroy of a united India should now reappear as governor-general of a part of it, but the Indian government pressed him to accept and in London both Attlee and George VI felt the appointment was desirable. With some misgivings, Mountbatten gave way. Independence day in both Pakistan and India was a triumph, tumultuous millions applauding his progress and demonstrating that, for the moment at least, he enjoyed a place in the pantheon with their national leaders. 'No other living man could have got the thing through', wrote Lord Killearn to Ismay; '. . . it has been a job supremely well done.'

The euphoria quickly faded. Though Bengal remained calm, thanks largely to Gandhi's personal intervention, the Punjab exploded. Vast movements of population across the new frontier exacerbated the already inflamed communal hatred, and massacres on an appalling scale developed. The largely British-officered Boundary Force was taxed far beyond its powers and Delhi itself was engulfed in the violence. Mountbatten was called back from holiday to help master the emergency, and brought desperately needed energy and organizational skills to the despondent government. 'I've never been through such a time in my life', he wrote on 28 September. 'The War, the Viceroyalty were jokes, for we have been dealing with life and death in our own city.' Gradually order was restored and by November 1947 Mountbatten felt the situation was stable enough to permit him to attend the wedding of Princess Elizabeth and his nephew Philip Mountbatten in London. He was created first Earl Mountbatten of Burma, with special remainder to his daughter Patricia.

Estimates vary widely, but the best-documented assessments agree that between 200,000 and 250,000 people lost their lives in the communal riots. Those who criticize Mountbatten's viceroyalty do so most often on the grounds that these massacres could have been averted, or at least mitigated, if partition had not been hurried through. Mountbatten's champions maintain that delay would only have made things worse and allowed the disorders to spread further. It is impossible to state conclusively what *might* have happened if independence had been postponed by a few months, or even years, but it is noteworthy that the closer people were to the problem, the more they support Mountbatten's policy. Almost every senior member of the British administration in India and of the Indian government has recorded his conviction that security was deteriorating so fast and the maintenance of non-communal forces of law and order proving so difficult, that a far greater catastrophe would have ensued if there had been further delay.

Mountbatten as governor-general was a servant of the Indian government and, as Ismay put it, 'it is only natural that they . . . should regard themselves as having proprietary rights over you'. Mountbatten accepted this role and fought doughtily for India's interests. He did not wholly abandon impartiality, however. When in January 1948 the Indian government withheld from Pakistan the 55 million crores of rupees owing after the division of assets, the governor-general argued that such conduct was dishonourable as well as unwise. He recruited Gandhi as his ally, and together they forced a change of policy on the reluctant Indian ministers. It was one of Gandhi's final contributions to Indian history. On 30 January he was assassinated by a Hindu extremist. Mountbatten mourned him sincerely. 'What a remarkable old boy he was', he wrote to a friend. 'I think history will link him with Buddha and Mahomet.'

His stand over the division of assets did the governor-general little good in Pakistan where he was believed to be an inveterate enemy and, by persuading Radcliffe to award Gurdaspur to India, to have secured that country access to Kashmir. When, in October 1947, Pathan tribesmen invaded the Vale of Kashmir, Mountbatten approved and helped organize military intervention by India. He insisted, however, that the state must first accede and that, as soon as possible, a plebiscite should establish the wishes of the Kashmiri people. When war between India and Pakistan seemed imminent he was instrumental in persuading Nehru that the matter should be referred to the United Nations.

The other problem that bedevilled Mountbatten was that of Hyderabad. He constituted himself, in effect, chief negotiator for the Indian government and almost brought off a deal that would have secured reasonably generous terms for the Nizam. Muslim extremists in Hyderabad, however, defeated his efforts, and the dispute grumbled on. Mountbatten protested when he found contingency plans existed for the invasion of Hyderabad and his presence was undoubtedly a main factor in inhibiting the Indian take-over that quickly followed his departure.

On 21 June 1948 the Mountbattens left India. In his final address, Nehru referred to the vast crowds that had attended their last appearances and 'wondered how it was that an Englishman and Englishwoman could become so popular in India during this brief period'. Even his harshest critics could not deny that Mountbatten had won the love and trust of the people and got the relationship between India and her former ruler off to a far better start than had seemed possible fifteen months before.

At last Mountbatten was free to return to sea. Reverting to his substantive rank of rear-admiral he took command of the first cruiser squadron in the Mediterranean. To assume this relatively lowly position after the splendours of supreme command and viceroyalty could not have been easy, but with goodwill all round it was achieved successfully. He was 'as great a subordinate as he is a leader', reported the commander-in-chief, Admiral Sir Arthur Power. He brought his squadron up to a high level of efficiency, though not concealing the fact that he felt obsolescent material and undermanning diminished its real effectiveness. After his previous jobs, this command was something of a holiday, and he revelled in the opportunities to play his beloved polo and take up skin-diving. In Malta he stuck to his inconspicuous role, but abroad he was fêted by the rulers of the countries his squadron visited. 'I suppose I oughtn't to get a kick out of being treated like a Viceroy', he confessed after one particularly successful visit, 'but I'd have been less than human if I hadn't been affected by the treatment I received at Trieste.' He was never less, nor more than human.

Mountbatten was promoted vice-admiral in 1949 and in June 1950 returned to the Admiralty as fourth sea lord. He was at first disappointed, since he had set his heart on being second sea lord, responsible for personnel, and found himself instead concerned with supplies and transport. In fact the post proved excellent for his career. He flung himself into the work with characteristic zeal, cleared up many anomalies and outdated practices, and acquired a range of information which was to stand him in good stead when he became first sea lord. On the whole he confined himself to the duties of his department, but when the Persians nationalized Anglo-Iranian Oil in 1951, he could not resist making his opinions known. He felt that it was futile to oppose strong nationalist movements of this kind and that Britain would do better to work with them. He converted the first lord to his point of view but conspicuously failed to impress the bellicose foreign secretary, Herbert Morrison (later Lord Morrison of Lambeth).

The next step was command of a major fleet and in June 1952 he was appointed to the Mediterranean, being promoted to admiral the following year. St. Vincent remarked that naval command in the Mediterranean 'required an officer of splendour', and this Mountbatten certainly provided. He was not a great operational commander like Andrew Cunningham, but he knew his ships and personnel, maintained the fleet at the highest level of peacetime efficiency, and was immensely popular with the men. When 'Cassandra' of the *Daily Mirror* arrived to report on Mountbatten's position, he kept aloof for four days, then came to the flagship with the news that the commander-in-chief was 'O.K. with the sailors'. But it was on the representational side that Mountbatten excelled. He loved showing the flag and, given half a chance, would act as honorary ambassador into the bargain. Sometimes he overdid it, and in September

1952 the first lord, at the instance of the prime minister, wrote to urge him 'to take the greatest care to keep out of political discussions'.

His diplomatic as well as administrative skills were taxed when in January 1953 he was appointed supreme Allied commander of a new NATO Mediterranean Command (SACMED). Under him were the Mediterranean fleets of Britain, France, Italy, Greece, and Turkey, but not the most powerful single unit in the area, the American Sixth Fleet. He was required to set up an integrated international naval / air headquarters in Malta and managed this formidable organizational task with great efficiency. The smoothing over of national susceptibilities and the reconciliation of his British with his NATO role proved taxing, but his worst difficulty lay with the other NATO headquarters in the Mediterranean, CINCSOUTH, at Naples under the American Admiral R. B. Carney. There were real problems of demarcation, but as had happened with Somerville in South East Asia, these were made far worse by a clash of personalities. When Carney was replaced in the autumn of 1953, the differences melted away and the two commands began to co-operate.

In October 1954, when he became first sea lord, Mountbatten achieved what he had always held to be his ultimate ambition. It did not come easily. A formidable body of senior naval opinion distrusted him and was at first opposed to his appointment, and it was not until the conviction hardened that the navy was losing the Whitehall battle against the other services that opinion rallied behind him. 'The Navy wants badly a man and a leader', wrote Andrew Cunningham, who had formerly been Mountbatten's opponent. 'You have the ability and the drive and it is you that the Navy wants.' Churchill, still unreconciled to Mountbatten's role in India, held out longer, but in the end he too gave way.

Since the war the navy had become the Cinderella of the fighting Services, and morale was low. Under Mountbatten's leadership, the Admiralty's voice in Whitehall became louder and more articulate. By setting up the 'Way Ahead' committee, he initiated an overdue rethinking of the shore establishments which were absorbing an undue proportion of the navy's resources. He scrapped plans for the construction of a heavy missile-carrying cruiser and instead concentrated on destroyers carrying the Sea Slug missile: 'Once we can obtain Government agreement to the fact that we are the mobile large scale rocket carriers of the future then everything else will fall into place.' The Reserve Fleet was cut severely and expenditure diverted from the already excellent communications system to relatively underdeveloped fields such as radar. Probably his most important single contribution, however, was to establish an excellent relationship with the notoriously prickly Admiral Rickover, which was to lead to Britain acquiring US technology for its nuclear submarines and, eventually, to the adoption of the Polaris missile as the core of its nuclear deterrent.

In July 1956 Nasser nationalized the Suez canal. Mountbatten was asked what military steps could be taken to restore the situation. He said that the Mediterranean Fleet with the Royal Marine commandos aboard could be at Port Said within three days and take the port and its hinterland. Eden rejected the proposal since he wished to reoccupy the whole canal zone, and it is unlikely anyway that the other chiefs of staff would have approved a plan that might have left lightly armed British forces exposed to tank attack and with inadequate air cover. As plans for full-scale invasion were prepared, Mountbatten became more and more uneasy about the contemplated action. To the chiefs of staff he consistently said that political implications should be considered and more thought given to the long-term future of the Middle East. His views were reflected in the chiefs' recommendations to the government, a point that caused considerable irritation to Anthony Eden, who insisted that politics should be left to the politicians. In August Mountbatten drafted a letter of resignation to the prime minister but, without too much difficulty, was dissuaded from sending it by the first lord, Viscount Cilcennin. He was, however, instrumental in substituting the invasion plan of General Sir Charles Keightley for that previously approved by the Cabinet, a move that saved the lives of many hundreds of civilians. On 2 November, when the invasion fleet had already sailed, Mountbatten made a written appeal to Eden to accept the United Nations resolution and 'turn back the assault convoy before it is too late'. His appeal was ignored. Mountbatten again offered his resignation to the first lord and again was told that it was his duty to stay on. He was promoted admiral of the fleet in October 1956.

With Harold Macmillan (later the Earl of Stockton) succeeding Eden as prime minister in January 1957, Duncan Sandys (later Lord Duncan-Sandys) was appointed minister of defence with a mandate to rationalize the armed services and impose sweeping economies. There were many embittered battles before Sandys's first defence white paper appeared in the summer of 1957. The thirteenth and final draft contained the ominous words: 'the role of the Navy in Global War is somewhat uncertain.' In the event, however, the navy suffered relatively lightly, losing only one-sixth of its personnel over the next five years, as opposed to the army's 45 per cent and the air force's 35 per cent. The role of the navy east of Suez was enshrined as an accepted dogma of defence policy.

In July 1959 Mountbatten took over as chief of defence staff (CDS). He was the second incumbent, Sir William Dickson having been appointed in 1958, with Mountbatten's support but against the fierce opposition of Field-Marshal Sir Gerald Templer. Dickson's role was little more than that of permanent chairman of the chiefs of staff committee but Sandys tried to increase the CDS's powers. He was defeated, and the defence white paper of 1958 made only modest changes to the existing system. Mountbatten made the principal objective of his time as CDS the integration of the three Services, not to the extent achieved by the Canadians of one homogenized fighting force, but abolishing the independent ministries and setting up a common list for all senior officers. During his first two years, however, he had to remain content with the creation of a director of defence plans to unify the work of the three planning departments and the acceptance of the principle of unified command in the Far and Middle East. Then, at the end of 1962, Macmillan agreed that another attempt should be made to impose unification on the reluctant Services. 'Pray take no notice of any obstructions', he told the minister of defence. 'You should approach this . . . with dashing, slashing methods. Anyone who raises any objection can go.'

At Mountbatten's suggestion Lord Ismay and Sir E. Ian Jacob were asked to report. While not accepting all Mountbatten's recommendations—which involved a sweeping increase in the powers of the CDS—their report went a long way towards realizing the concept of a unified Ministry of Defence. The reforms, which were finally promulgated in 1964, acknowledged the supreme authority of the secretary of state for defence and strengthened the central role of the CDS. To Mountbatten this was an important first step, but only a step. He believed that so long as separate departments survived, with differing interests and loyalties, it would be impossible to use limited resources to the best advantage. Admiralty, War Office, Air Ministry—not to mention Ministry of Aviation—should be abolished. Ministers should be responsible, not for the navy or the air force, but for communications or supplies. 'We cannot, in my opinion, afford to stand pat', he wrote to Harold Wilson (later Lord Wilson of Rievaulx) when the latter became prime minister in October 1964, 'and must move on to, or at least towards the ultimate aim of a functional, closely knit, smoothly working machine.' 'Functionalization' was the objective which he repeatedly pressed on the new minister of defence, Denis Healey. Healey was well disposed in principle, but felt that other reforms enjoyed higher priority. Though Mountbatten appealed to Wilson he got little satisfaction, and the machinery which he left behind him at his retirement was in his eyes only an unsatisfactory half-way house.

Even for this he paid a high price in popularity. His ideas were for the most part repugnant to the chiefs of staff, who suspected him of seeking personal aggrandizement and doubted the propriety of his methods. Relations tended to be worst with the chiefs of air staff. The latter believed that Mountbatten, though ostensibly above inter-Service rivalries, in fact remained devoted to the interests of the navy. It is hard entirely to slough off a lifetime's loyalties, but Mountbatten *tried* to be impartial. He did not always succeed. On the long-drawn-out battle over the merits of aircraft-carriers and island bases, he espoused the former. When he urged the first sea lord to work out some compromise which would accommodate both points of view, Sir Caspar John retorted that only a month before Mountbatten had advised him: 'Don't compromise—fight him to the death!' Similarly in the conflict between the TSR 2, sponsored by the air force, and the navy's Buccaneer, Mountbatten believed strongly that the former, though potentially the better plane, was too expensive to be practicable and would take too long to develop. He lobbied the minister of defence and urged his right-hand man, Solly Zuckerman, to argue the case against the TSR 2—'You know why I can't help you in Public. It is *not* moral cowardice but fear that my usefulness as Chairman would be seriously impaired.'

The question of the British nuclear deterrent also involved inter-Service rivalries. Mountbatten believed that an independent deterrent was essential, arguing to Harold Wilson that it would 'dispel in Russian minds the thought that they will escape scot-free if by any chance the Americans decide to hold back release of a strategic nuclear response to an attack'. He was instrumental in persuading the incoming Labour government not to adopt unilateral nuclear disarmament. In this he had the support of the three chiefs of staff. But there was controversy over what weapon best suited Britain's needs. From long before he became CDS, Mountbatten had privately preferred the submarine-launched Polaris missile to any of the airborne missiles favoured by the air force. Though not himself present at the meeting at Nassau between Macmillan and President John F. Kennedy at which Polaris was offered and accepted in exchange for the cancelled Skybolt missile, he had already urged this solution and had made plans accordingly.

Though he defended the nuclear deterrent, he was wholly opposed to the accumulation of unnecessary stockpiles or the development of new weapons designed to kill more effectively people who would be dead anyway if the existing armouries were employed. At NATO in July 1963 he pleaded that 'it was madness to hold further tests when all men of goodwill were about to try and bring about test-banning'. He conceded that tactical nuclear weapons added to the efficacy of the deterrent, but argued that their numbers should be limited and their use subject to stringent control. To use *any* nuclear weapon, however small or 'clean', would, he insisted, lead to general nuclear war. He opposed the 'mixed manned multilateral force' not just as being military nonsense, but because there were more than enough strategic nuclear weapons already.

What were needed, he told the NATO commanders in his valedictory address, were more 'highly mobile, well-equipped, self-supporting and balanced "Fire Brigade" forces, with first-class communications, able to converge quickly on the enemy force'.

Mountbatten's original tenure of office as CDS had been for three years. Macmillan pressed him to lengthen this by a further two years to July 1964. Mountbatten was initially reluctant but changed his mind after the death of his wife in 1960. Subsequently he agreed to a further extension to July 1965, in order to see through the first phase of defence reorganization. Wilson would have happily sanctioned yet another year but Healey established that there would be considerable resentment at such a move on the part of the other Service leaders and felt anyway that he would never be fully master of the Ministry of Defence while this potent relic from the past remained in office. Whether Mountbatten would have stayed on if pressed to do so is in any case doubtful; he was tired and stale, and had a multiplicity of interests to pursue outside.

His last few months as CDS were in fact spent partly abroad leading a mission on Commonwealth immigration. The main purpose of this exercise was to explain British policy and persuade Commonwealth governments to control illegal immigration at source. The mission was a success; indeed Mountbatten found that he was largely preaching to the converted, since only in Jamaica did the policy he was expounding meet with serious opposition. He presented the mission's report on 13 June 1965 and the following month took his formal farewell of the Ministry of Defence.

Retirement did not mean inactivity; indeed he was still officially enjoying his retirement leave when the prime minister invited him to go to Rhodesia as governor to forestall a declaration of independence by the white settler population. Mountbatten had little hesitation in refusing: 'Nothing could be worse for the cause you have at heart than to think that a tired out widower of 65 could recapture the youth, strength and enthusiasm of twenty years ago.' However, he accepted a later suggestion that he should fly briefly to Rhodesia in November 1965 to invest the governor, Sir Humphrey Gibbs, with a decoration on behalf of the Queen and generally to offer moral support. At the last minute the project was deferred and never revived.

The following year the home secretary asked him to undertake an enquiry into prison security, in view of a number of recent sensational escapes. Mountbatten agreed, provided it could be a one-man report prepared with the help of three assessors. The report was complete within two months and most of the recommendations were carried out. The two most important, however—the appointment of an inspector-general responsible to the home secretary to head the prison service and the building of a separate maximum security gaol for prisoners whose escape would be particularly damaging—were never implemented. For the latter proposal Mountbatten was much criticized by liberal reformers who felt the step a retrograde one; this Mountbatten contested, arguing that, isolated within a completely secure outer perimeter, the dangerous criminal could be allowed more freedom than would otherwise be the case.

Mountbatten was associated with 179 organizations, ranging alphabetically from the Admiralty Dramatic Society to the Zoological Society. In some of these his role was formal, in many more it was not. In time and effort the United World Colleges, a network of international schools modelled on the Gordonstoun of Kurt Hahn, received the largest share. Mountbatten worked indefatigably to whip up support and raise funds for the schools, lobbying the leaders of every country he visited. The electronics industry, also, engaged his attention and he was an active first chairman of the National Electronic Research Council. In 1965 he was installed as governor of the Isle of Wight and conscientiously visited the island seven or eight times a year, in 1974 becoming the first lord lieutenant when the island was raised to the status of a shire. A role which gave him still greater pleasure was that of colonel of the Life Guards, to which he was also appointed in 1965. He took his duties at Trooping the Colour very seriously and for weeks beforehand would ride around the Hampshire lanes near Broadlands in hacking jacket and Life Guards helmet.

His personal life was equally crowded. The years 1966 and 1967 were much occupied with the filming of the thirteen-part television series *The Life and Times of Lord Mountbatten*, every detail of which absorbed him and whose sale he promoted energetically all over the world. He devoted much time to running the family estates and putting his massive archive in order, involving himself enthusiastically in the opening of Broadlands to the public, which took place in 1978. He never lost his interest in naval affairs or in high strategy. One of his last major speeches was delivered at Strasburg in May 1979, when he pleaded eloquently for arms control: 'As a military man who has given half a century of active service I say in all sincerity that the nuclear arms race has no military purpose. Wars cannot be fought with nuclear weapons. Their existence only adds to our perils because of the illusions which they have generated.'

Some of his happiest hours were spent on tour with the royal family in their official yacht *Britannia*. He derived particular pleasure from his friendship with the Prince of Wales, who treated him as 'honorary grandfather' and attached great value to his counsel. When Princess Anne married, the certificate gave as her surname 'Mountbatten-Windsor'. This was the culmination of a long battle Mountbatten had waged to ensure that his family name, adopted by Prince Philip, should be preserved among his nephew's descendants. He took an intense interest in all the royal houses of Europe, and was a source of advice on every subject. Harold Wilson once called him 'the shop-steward of royalty' and Mountbatten rejoiced in the description.

Every summer he enjoyed a family holiday at his Irish home in county Sligo, Classiebawn Castle. Over the years the size of his police escort increased but the Irish authorities were insistent that the cancellation of his holiday would be a victory for the Irish Republican Army. On 27 August 1979 a family party went out in a fishing boat, to collect lobster-pots set the previous day. A bomb exploded when the boat was half a mile from Mullaghmoor harbour. Mountbatten was killed instantly, as was his grandson Nicholas and a local Irish boy. His daughter's mother-in-law, Doreen Lady Brabourne, died shortly afterwards. His funeral took place in Westminster Abbey and he was buried in Romsey Abbey. He had begun his preparations for the ceremony more than ten years before and was responsible for planning every detail, down to the lunch to be eaten by the mourners on the train from Waterloo to Romsey.

Mountbatten was a giant of a man, and his weaknesses were appropriately gigantic. His vanity was monstrous, his ambition unbridled. The truth, in his hands, was swiftly converted from what it was to what it should have been. But such frailties were far outweighed by his qualities. His energy was prodigious, as was his moral and physical courage. He was endlessly resilient in the face of disaster. No intellectual, he possessed a powerfully analytical intelligence; he could rapidly master a complex brief, spot the essential and argue it persuasively. His flexibility of mind was extraordinary, as was his tolerance—he accepted all comers for what they were, not measured against some scale of predetermined values. He had style and panache, commanding the loyal devotion of those who served him. To his opponents in Whitehall he was 'tricky Dickie', devious and unscrupulous. To his family and close friends he was a man of wisdom and generosity. He adored his two daughters, Patricia and Pamela, and his ten grandchildren. However pressing his preoccupations he would make time to comfort, encourage, or advise them. Almost always the advice was good.

Among Mountbatten's honours were MVO (1920), KCVO (1922), GCVO (1937), DSO (1941), CB (1943), KCB (1945), KG (1946), PC (1947), GCSI (1947), GCIE (1947), GCB (1955), OM (1965), and FRS (1966). He had an honorary DCL from Oxford (1946), and honorary LL Ds from Cambridge (1946), Leeds (1950), Edinburgh (1954), Southampton (1955), London (1960), and Sussex (1963). He was honorary D.Sc. of Delhi and Patna (1948).

Mountbatten was much painted. His head, by John Ulbricht, is held by the National Portrait Gallery, while portraits by Philip de László, Brenda Bury, Derek Hill, and Carlos Sancha are in the possession of the family. His state portrait by Edward Halliday hangs in the former viceroy's house, New Delhi, and by Da Cruz in the Victoria Memorial Building, Calcutta. A memorial statue by Franta Belsky was erected in 1983 on Foreign Office Green in London.

On Mountbatten's death the title passed to his elder daughter, Patricia Edwina Victoria Knatchbull (born 1924), who became Countess Mountbatten of Burma.

[Philip Ziegler, *Mountbatten*, 1985; family papers.]

PHILIP ZIEGLER

published 1986

NEHRU Jawaharlal

(1889–1964)

National leader and first prime minister of India, was born in Allahabad 14 November 1889, the eldest child of Pandit Motilal Nehru and his wife, Swarup Rani. Motilal was to become a leading advocate at the Allahabad high court, and he adopted a life-style which matched his professional eminence. He accepted the Anglo-Indian culture of the time and mixed easily with the British rulers of India. Swarup Rani, in contrast, remained uneducated and traditional in her beliefs. Although Jawaharlal had two younger sisters (one of whom was to become Mrs Vijayalakshmi Pandit), his parents were deeply possessive and ambitious for their son. Motilal wanted him to have the best English education money could buy and then to enter the Indian Civil Service and in 1905 took him to England to enter Harrow. After two unsatisfying years Jawaharlal decided to go on to Cambridge where he entered Trinity College. Although Motilal's support enabled him to live in great comfort and to travel widely, he was restless and drifting. He obtained a second class in part i of the natural sciences tripos (1910), which was rather better than he had expected. Meanwhile Motilal had changed his plans for his son and decided he should study law. In October 1910 Jawaharlal moved to London and the Inner Temple to read for the bar. Law too failed to win his interest but he passed the final examinations two years later, leaving in 1912 to return to India.

While Jawaharlal was in Britain Motilal had become active in the Indian National Congress: father and son began their long political dialogue. Jawaharlal was more sympathetic than his father with those Indians who challenged the moderate leadership of Congress. The extremist glorification of the Hindu past, however, had no attraction, and temperamentally he could never accept terrorist violence. His first meeting of Congress, in 1912, did not inspire him and for four years he led an aimless life, living at home and working for his father.

His marriage, on 8 February 1916, seemed only to increase his burdens. Motilal chose the bride. Kamala, daughter of Jawaharmal Kaul, a Delhi business man, was like Jawaharlal a Kashmiri Brahmin. Married at sixteen she was ten years younger than Jawaharlal. Kamala lacked Western education, had little in common with her husband, and in the Nehru household she was bitterly conscious of her inadequacies and felt helpless and jealous of her sisters-in-law. In November 1917 a daughter was born and named Indira, but Kamala's health was poor and by 1920 she was already suffering from tuberculosis.

Jawaharlal was drawn into active politics by Mrs Annie Besant's Home Rule League and showed a relish for agitation which suggested he was at last finding a cause. Then, in 1919, M. K. Gandhi launched his campaign against the Rowlatt Act. To Jawaharlal he seemed to offer brave and effective leadership in striking contrast with the spineless Congress politicians. Only Motilal's profound scepticism stopped Jawaharlal joining Gandhi's movement at once. Events during 1919, however, shook Motilal's faith in British intentions and the shooting of hundreds of Indian demonstrators at Amritsar on 13 April cast doubt on the proposed reforms.

In November 1919 Motilal was elected president of Congress. He urged acceptance of the constitutional reforms, but within twelve months Congress had turned away from electoral politics and embarked on a non-co-operation campaign under Gandhi's leadership. Jawaharlal joined with enthusiasm although he shared neither Gandhi's spiritual and moral preoccupations, nor his commitment to non-violence. In many ways they were worlds apart but the bond between them remained unbroken until Gandhi's death. Motilal, whose name and fortune had given Jawaharlal his start, was left with no option if he were to retain influence, both political and with his cherished son, but to join him in Gandhi's campaign. During these months Jawaharlal first travelled in the countryside and gained some inkling of the conditions in which the overwhelming mass of his fellow countrymen were living. The Westernized intellectual, who generally thought in English, forged links with men who barely if at all understood what he told them. In a way which he found inexplicable they extended to him their trust and confidence. Jawaharlal for the first time tasted the exhilaration of power.

On 6 December 1921 Motilal and Jawaharlal were both arrested and sentenced to six months in prison. After three months it was discovered that Jawaharlal had been improperly convicted and he was released. Following outbreaks of violence Gandhi had already called off the campaign and this had angered and bewildered Jawaharlal. His doubts disappeared when he attended Gandhi's trial and he returned to Allahabad to organize a boycott of foreign clothes. On 11 May 1922 he was back in prison, this time for eight months. Between December 1921 and June 1945 Jawaharlal was to spend almost nine years in prison. It served perhaps as an escape from the demands of mundane political activity, providing periods of study and reflection which led him later to describe prison as 'the best of universities'.

Meanwhile Congress had split, with Motilal a leader of the group wishing to return to electoral politics. Gandhi was strongly opposed. Jawaharlal was torn by the conflict of loyalty; temperament rather than conviction led him to look for some kind of compromise. He became secretary of the All-India Congress but the movement was in decline and disarray. Drawn into municipal politics, he won widespread respect as chairman of the Allahabad Municipal Board. The actor in him, however, aspired to a larger stage. But national politics were at a low ebb and Jawaharlal was depressed by the divisions in Congress. Kamala lost an infant son in 1924 and her health grew worse. Jawaharlal felt little regret when on 1 March 1926 he left India with his wife and daughter to seek medical treatment for Kamala in Europe. They settled in Geneva, Kamala's health showed little improvement, and European politics increasingly won Jawaharlal's attention.

During his stay in Europe Jawaharlal came in touch with socialist and anti-imperialist groups and laid the foundation of his knowledge of European and world affairs and his interest in both the Soviet Union, which he visited briefly, and China. He also became convinced that India's greatest obstacle in achieving national unity was religion, and that the country could advance socially and economically only through industrialization and socialist planning.

The Indian political scene was transformed by the appointment in 1927 of the statutory commission, chaired by Sir John (later Viscount) Simon, and the widespread hostility which this provoked. Early in December Jawaharlal sailed for home to play a leading role in a revived Congress culminating in his election as president, in succession to his father, at the end of 1929. He argued passionately for complete independence. Motilal in contrast accepted the goal of Dominion status. Congress was deeply split and faced a radical revolt. At the end of 1929 the conciliatory initiative of the viceroy, E. F. L. Wood, Lord Irwin (later the Earl of Halifax), trapped Jawaharlal in a personal crisis. Gandhi and Motilal at first responded favourably to Irwin's move. Against his judgement Jawaharlal felt unable to disagree. Gandhi saw personified in Jawaharlal the tensions which threatened to tear Congress apart and decided that not negotiations but another Gandhian campaign was the only way to preserve Congress unity. In March 1930 he set out on his 'salt satyagraha' and the next month civil disobedience began. It continued, with a number of breaks, into 1934 but faced increasingly determined and effective government action.

For much of the campaign Jawaharlal was in jail. From 1930 to the end of 1935 he was imprisoned four times and served a total of 1,460 days. Again he used the time to read, to think, and to write prolifically. *Glimpses of World History* (1934–5), written in the form of letters to his daughter, Indira, was followed by his *Autobiography* (1936). Although uneven, the book was written with passion and an engaging yet forthright style. Motilal was also in prison and his health began to deteriorate gravely. Jawaharlal was released at the beginning of 1931 in time to be with his father when he died on 6 February. The political scene did nothing to alleviate his grief. He could not support Gandhi's willingness to negotiate: the clash between nationalism and imperialism, he was convinced, could not be ended through compromise. So he ignored the Gandhi-Irwin Pact, involved himself in the peasant movement in the United Provinces, and was back in prison by the end of the year, irritated equally with Gandhi and with Congress, but unable to see any effective alternative course of action. In May 1935 Kamala's condition worsened and she sailed for Europe for further treatment. In September Jawaharlal's sentence was suspended on compassionate grounds and he flew to join her. She died 28 February 1936. Jawaharlal in his absence had been again elected Congress president and he left at once to return to India.

He arrived to find Congress deep in discussion on whether to accept the 1935 Government of India Act and seek elected office. Nehru was opposed to this but was in the minority and, in spite of his doubts, he campaigned vigorously, travelling over 50,000 miles in five months. To his surprise Congress won a remarkable victory in eight of the eleven provinces. Nehru saw it as a victory for secularism and socialism. He was mistaken: it heralded an intensification of communal feeling and marked a major step on the way to partition.

Congress government in the provinces had less interest for Nehru than the deepening world crisis. In 1937–9 he travelled widely outside India and was not surprised by the outbreak of war. His sympathies were with the Allies but his profound distrust of British intentions left him in anguished frustration. Deeply critical of Gandhi's individual civil disobedience campaign he nevertheless took part, was arrested on 31 October 1940, and, apart from nine months, he was in prison for the rest of the war. The viceroy, the Marquess of Linlithgow, had little sympathy with Congress while Britain was fighting for survival. Government viewed Nehru as the most dangerous leader in the country and was happy to see him behind bars. Japan's entry into the war led to the only attempt to break the political deadlock. Sir Stafford Cripps was sent out in March 1942 and Nehru attended the discussions with Maulana Azad, the leading Congress spokesman. Nehru hoped for a settlement which would enable Congress to co-operate in the war effort but the mission was a failure. Nehru, disillusioned and bitter, turned to Gandhi and his 'Quit India' movement as the only alternative to the break up of the national movement in a sea of communalism and disintegration. The Congress leaders were arrested and Nehru was in prison for almost three years. There he wrote his *The Discovery of India* (1946), which was part rambling cultural history, part autobiography, part exploration of the freedom movement and its links with the country's past.

When he was released on 15 June 1945 Nehru found M. A. Jinnah's movement for Pakistan a powerful force, and the general elections at the end of the year revealed the extent to which the political world had been polarized between Congress and the Muslim League. Nehru's gifts seemed ill-suited to the protracted negotiations that preceded independence. Deeply suspicious of British policy, even after the Labour Party came to office, unable to recognize the proponents of Pakistan as more than reactionary and self-seeking opportunists, increasingly shocked by the irrational and bloody outbursts of violence, Nehru found it difficult to give decisive leadership and his frustration led, on occasion, to intemperate outbursts. Yet events swept him into power. When Lord Wavell formed a provisional government in September 1946 Nehru became vice-president of the viceroy's council and held the external affairs portfolio. In spite of friction with Muslim League members of the Government Nehru, prime minister in all but name, began laying down policies for independent India.

Meanwhile a virtual war of succession was breaking out with savage rioting in many parts of the country. Nehru was appalled at this 'competition in murder and brutality'. The British Government on its part concluded that only a rapid transfer of power could avert a complete disintegration of civil order. Lord Mountbatten of Burma was appointed to carry this through and he recognized at once that such a transfer could take place only on the basis of partition. Nehru and Mountbatten had much in common and the sympathy and trust between them enabled

Nehru at a critical moment in the negotiations to persuade Mountbatten to revise his plans and avoid the danger of India being fragmented. At last Nehru resigned himself to the inevitability of partition and when, at midnight on 14 August 1947, the Constituent Assembly met to usher in Indian freedom, Nehru rose superbly to the occasion with a moving speech, eloquent and magnanimous. The rejoicing was brief, for free India under Nehru's leadership faced critical problems of great magnitude.

As prime minister Nehru dominated the first seventeen years of India's independence. It was in many ways a premiership of character rather than accomplishment, of continuity rather than change, yet what was achieved owed more to him than to any other leader. In building and preserving national unity, in strengthening parliamentary democracy, in seeking development through state planning, and in pursuing a foreign policy of non-alignment, he made a mark unmistakably his own.

Partition and the transfer of power brought massacre and panic; millions were uprooted, hundreds of thousands killed. Order was restored but communal feelings were dangerously inflamed. Gandhi returned to Delhi to try to stop the violence and was assassinated there in January 1948 by a Hindu extremist. Deeply shocked, Nehru told India 'the light has gone out.' For some months his passionate opposition to communalism appeared to be shared by his fellow countrymen, but this reaction was short-lived; within Congress itself Hindu communalists were strongly represented. Their strength was one element behind the election (against Nehru's wishes) of P. N. Tandon as Congress president in 1950. The election was also an attempt by Vallabhbhai Patel, long a rival to Nehru and now deputy prime minister, to limit Nehru's power and the influence of his office. The Patel-Tandon domination of Congress was short-lived. Patel died in December 1950, Nehru gathered support in Tandon's working committee and consolidated his power over the party by taking the presidency himself from 1951 to 1954. He accepted the necessity of working with the rightists both in Congress and in Cabinet but his victory established both his undisputed personal supremacy and also the dominance of Government over the Congress organization.

Independence made it necessary to integrate the former princely states whose relationship with the Crown was unceremoniously ended by the British. By 15 August 1947 almost all of them had acceded either to India or to Pakistan. Kashmir, with a predominantly Muslim population but a Hindu ruler, still had not. In October 1947, in an attempt to force the issue, Pathan tribesmen from Pakistan invaded Kashmir. The Maharaja opted for India, troops were sent in to support him, and a brief war between India and Pakistan followed. A Government under Sheikh Abdullah, an old friend of Nehru's, was installed and when the United Nations brought about a cease-fire in the fighting India agreed that a plebiscite should follow. It never did: Nehru's growing reluctance stemmed partly from a rift with the Sheikh who began to speak of an independent Kashmir and was eventually removed and imprisoned without trial, but perhaps more to his conviction that to hold a plebiscite would rekindle the communal violence of partition, place in peril the large Muslim population remaining in India, and strengthen those forces opposing Nehru's stand for a secular state. There is little doubt either that as a Kashmiri Brahmin long attracted by the mountainous beauty of his ancestral home Nehru's emotions were deeply involved in the fate of the state. The cease-fire line hardened into a *de facto* border and Kashmir remained divided. Although a pact between Nehru and Liaquat Ali Khan in April 1950 settled some of the outstanding issues between India and Pakistan, Kashmir remained a matter of bitter dispute.

Nehru used his enormous influence to nurture parliamentary democracy. Impatient as he could be with others, he was endlessly patient in establishing the traditions and conventions of the parliamentary system. The new constitution was inaugurated in January 1950 and India became a republic with a president as its constitutional head, but recognizing the British sovereign as head of the Commonwealth. The Indian union was established as a secular state with a federal structure but a strong centre. In these broad features, as in many of its details, Nehru's wishes were closely reflected. The achievements of the first years were consolidated in the first general election of 1951–2 when both communalist and Communist parties fared badly and Congress scored an overwhelming victory.

In one area Nehru achieved less than he hoped; that of social reform. The opposition to a reform and codification of personal and family law was too strong and it took all of Nehru's personal prestige to carry a number of separate acts providing, among other things, for divorce, monogamy, and equal rights of inheritance for women. The constitution itself formally abolished untouchability. The new constitutional and legal basis for individual rights and liberties had relatively little impact except among urban, Westernized classes, and many other reforms had a similar limited effect. Education was greatly expanded but with a striking imbalance between the urban and rural areas where a large majority of the population remained illiterate.

The other major area where change was sought was the economy. Nehru's belief in industrialization and in state planning, long a source of difference with Gandhi, went back many years. In 1950 the Planning Commission was created, with the prime minister as chairman, and this was followed by three Five Year Plans. The first (1951–6), which concentrated on agricultural production, appeared a great success. When it ended India was self-sufficient in food. But this achievement was not sustained; monsoon failures and the seemingly inexorable increase of population again created the need for imports. The second plan was more ambitious. After the Communist victory in China a sense of competition and national pride was involved in Indian development and Nehru was determined to show that democratic freedom need not be sacrificed to economic progress. The record was mixed. The plan cost nearly twice as much as the first, depended on substantial foreign aid, and eventually had to be cut back. The achievements, nevertheless, were striking: the steel, aluminium, and cement industries were greatly expanded, a number of new industries were started, and industrial production expanded 50 per cent in eight years (1951–9). But for all their success the plans did little to benefit the inhabitants of India's innumerable villages. Landlordism was abolished in the early years of independence, but agrarian conditions proved intractable. Nehru saw a powerful Congress as the key to national unity and he ruefully recognized that at the heart of this power in the states were deeply conservative small landholders hostile to any far-reaching changes. In 1952 the Community Development Programme was begun but change was slow; the economic disparity between rich and poor grew no smaller.

In foreign policy during the late 1940s and the 1950s Nehru's authority was almost unchallenged. He offered support and leadership to fellow Asian nationalists and welcomed the Communist rise to power in China. This concern with Asia brought him into conflict with the United States to whom Nehru's idea of non-alignment in the deepening East-West division seemed at best incomprehensible. One attraction of Commonwealth membership for Nehru was that, in a modest way, it offered a grouping other than the American or Soviet blocs, and enabled India to avoid complete reliance on the United States for foreign aid. In October 1950 the Chinese invaded Tibet and Nehru's enthusiasm for China waned, though he rebuffed Patel and others who urged a policy of confrontation. Thereafter Nehru was always apprehensive of China while still believing Sino-Indian friendship to be the only basis of stability in Asia. This seemed assured by the agreement between them of June 1954 and by the Bandung conference of Afro-Asian states the following year. At Bandung Nehru was unquestionably the elder statesman but it was Chou En-lai who took the centre of the stage. By this time Nehru's sustained advocacy of non-alignment had become more acceptable, or at least accepted, by the great powers. In 1955 Nehru visited the Soviet Union and Bulganin and Krushchev returned the visit later that year. When Nehru condemned the Anglo-French invasion of Suez he was in agreement with the United States, and his visit there in 1956 brought new understanding on both sides.

He was less forthright on the Soviet invasion of Hungary and this cost him support both at home and abroad.

If during the fifties Nehru's authority seemed undisputed there were times nevertheless when he bowed to pressure. One was in his response to the movement for redrawing the state boundaries along linguistic divisions. He saw the movement as a threat to national unity and the States Reorganization Act of 1956 was a tactical concession in an attempt to defuse separatism which was only partly successful. Cautious accommodation was also called for in the bitter disputes over the continued use of English as an official language.

In his last years, from 1959 until his death in 1964, Nehru faced increasing pressure internally and externally, and for the first time he experienced public criticism. Congress faced serious challenges from both conservatives and radicals and when in 1959 the Chinese reopened the whole boundary question and established direct control in Tibet right-wing opinion grew markedly. Nehru's room for manœuvre or negotiation narrowed. Heavy internal pressure forced him to approve the invasion of Portuguese Goa in December 1961 which sadly tarnished his reputation as a peace-maker and although the general election shortly afterwards renewed the Congress majority the pressure on Nehru did not diminish. Pressed by an army and by public opinion he agreed to a policy of asserting Indian presence in the border region with China. The discovery of a Chinese road across the desolate Aksai Chin plateau in north-east Kashmir provoked a strong anti-Chinese reaction in India. Nehru was shocked, felt he had been betrayed, and publicly expressed his bitterness. In October 1962 Chinese forces advanced into India but later withdrew to their earlier positions. Nehru believed the Chinese wished to destroy India's non-aligned status and the war certainly finished any idea of an Afro-Asian bloc headed by India and China.

Brief and local as it was, the war was a disaster for India's development plans, and during 1963 Nehru courageously sought to direct the surge of national feeling created by the war into saving as much as possible of the third Five Year Plan. He probably found greater satisfaction in the signing of the Nuclear Test Ban Treaty in August. The East-West antagonism which he had always opposed seemed at last to be diminishing.

On 8 January 1964 Nehru, then seventy-four years old, suffered a serious stroke. For five months he fought to regain his physical powers and was able to resume some of his official duties. The recovery was only partial and was brief, and he died in Delhi 27 May 1964. His only child Indira was prime minister of India from 1966 to 1977, and from 1980.

That Nehru was a good man is profoundly true and lay at the heart of his almost magical appeal. He was also an unusually complicated man, a leader harbouring powerful contradictory impulses: agitator and mediator, a politician often bored with politics and wanting power not for himself but for a cause, a Brahmin not without vanity who loathed caste, an aloof intellectual preferring his own company who had a unique relationship with the Indian masses. The young revolutionary came to face the dilemmas of power, and the impulsive intransigence of the pre-independence years gave way in great measure to a tough practicality. What persisted was the urge to persuade rather than coerce. His public speeches, often rambling and discursive, were in essence a remarkable course of public education, the fruit of a singularly well-furnished mind. Blessed with extraordinary gifts of intellect, of energy and physical resilience, and of a captivating presence, Nehru added to these qualities loyalty, courage, self-discipline, and a dedication to a free and democratic India in which dignity and well-being for the Indian people would be achieved and preserved.

There is a portrait by Edward I. Halliday (1954), and a bronze by Sir Jacob Epstein. A bronze statue of Nehru, holding a dove of peace (1966), is in Aurangabad, western India.

[Jawaharlal Nehru, *An Autobiography*, 1936; *Selected Works of Jawaharlal Nehru*, 1972; Michael Brecher, *Nehru: A Political Biography*, 1959; Sarvepalli Gopal, *Jawaharlal Nehru: A Biography*, vol. i, 1975, vol. ii, 1980; B. N. Pandey, *Nehru*, 1976.]

T. H. BEAGLEHOLE

published 1981

NKRUMAH K w a m e

(1909–1972)

First president of Ghana, was born in the village of Nkroful in the extreme south-west of the country. He believed that the most likely date of his birth was 18 September 1909. Being a male child born into the Akan tribe on a Saturday, he was called Kwame although baptized Francis Nwia Kofie, the priest recording the date of birth as 21 September, which is the date used officially. His mother, Nyaniban, a petty trader, whose only child he was, gave him a claim to two minor chieftaincies, those of Nsaeum and of Dadieo. His father was a goldsmith at Half Assini. At the age of six he went to the Roman Catholic school at Half Assini, where he later taught for a year before proceeding in 1926 to the Government Training College at

Accra, moving in 1928 to Achimota when the colleges merged. In 1930 he became a teacher at the RC junior school at Elmina, moving in 1931 to become head teacher at the RC junior school, Axim. In 1933 he became first indigenous teacher at the RC seminary at Amissano.

In August 1935 he left the Gold Coast for the USA where he enrolled at Lincoln University, taking a BA in economics and sociology in 1939 and a B.Theology in 1942. He took masters degrees in education and philosophy at the University of Pennsylvania. For a while he lectured at Lincoln which conferred its honorary LL D degree on him in 1951. There he began to write his pamphlet *Towards Colonial Freedom* with its Marxist interpretation of colonialism. In later years he described himself as a non-denominational Christian and scientific Marxist, finding no conflict. While in America he realized the importance of organization and determined to master the technique. This he was able to exercise in London (May 1945– November 1947) as joint secretary of the organizing committee for the fifth Pan-African Congress, which was held in Manchester in October 1945, and as secretary of the West African National Secretariat, which aimed at the unification of all colonies in West Africa.

In August 1947 the inaugural meeting was held at Saltpond in the Gold Coast of a nationalist movement, the United Gold Coast Convention (UGCC), which needed to reconcile its leadership by the local intelligentsia with the mass of people. Nkrumah was invited to become general secretary on the basis of his political activities in the USA and Britain. He accepted, determined to turn the UGCC into a popular movement. Within six months of his return in December 1947 some 500 branches were established. He was fortunate in the time of his return as a whole array of discontents had accumulated. The final annoyance came when the government declined to act over the dispute with traders about the high prices of imported goods, which led to an organized boycott in January– February 1948, and ended with disturbances on 28 February. The Watson commission of inquiry into the disturbances was impressed by the need to give Africans a greater share in the formation and execution of policy and made recommendations with that object. In his evidence to the commission, Nkrumah agreed that he had adopted communist views, though he denied ever being a party member. He was already a star speaker of the UGCC, having charisma and qualities of leadership, and was obviously a man with a mission. He established an anti-chief committee on youth organization (CYO) composed of thoroughgoing opponents of the existing social order, which, on 12 June 1949, formed the Convention People's Party (CPP) with the motto 'We prefer self-government with danger to servitude in tranquillity' and its policy 'Seek ye first the political kingdom and all things shall be added unto you.' The motto turned out to be as apt as the policy hope was naïve. Nkrumah resigned from the UGCC, leaving a party of chiefs, merchants, and professional men which, in the movement to universal suffrage, was doomed.

In January 1950 the CPP called a general strike in order to coerce the government on constitutional reform. A state of emergency was declared and seven CPP leaders who had openly instigated the strike were imprisoned for calling an illegal strike, Nkrumah and one other being also found guilty of sedition. All were released after the general election of February 1950 when Nkrumah received 22,780 votes out of a possible 23,122 in Accra Central. The CPP won 33 out of the 38 seats elected by direct franchise. So it continued: in the 1954 election on the basis of universal adult suffrage and the abolition of the three ex-officio ministers, the CPP won 72 of the 104 seats while at the 1956 general election which had to precede the grant of independence, the CPP won 71 seats. There was never a viable alternative government. Nkrumah's rise to power was swift: in 1951 he was leader of government business, in 1952 prime minister, in 1957 prime minister of Ghana, and in 1960 president of the republic, when he assumed the title Osagyefo (redeemer). He had found the political kingdom, albeit with the help of the Watson commission and the more flexible policy of the British government after the Suez crisis.

When he had achieved his first mission, the independence of Ghana, he turned immediately to his second, the unity of Africa, which became an *idée fixe* with him. In April 1958 he convened a conference of eight independent African states and toured them in May and June. Already there was disappointment in his party, especially among ex-servicemen, and also among the Ga people of Accra, who formed the Ga Shifimo Kpee (Ga Standfast Organization) against the influx of other tribal people into their area. As a tribal organization, it was unlawful. It operated conspiratorially, threatening violence, including indiscriminate murder by bomb-throwing in Accra. The police were reluctant to prosecute as they wished to conceal their sources of information. Nkrumah allowed those suspected to be detained under the Preventive Detention Act of 1958 which was intended to be used only in an emergency and was not expected to be used against members of opposition parties. By the end of 1960 318 detention orders had been made, although 255 of them were made in 1960 after the Act had been extended at the request of the police to detain the new kind of gangster that had emerged. Of the 788 persons released after the *coup* of January 1966, approximately half were political and the rest criminal detainees. None was executed for a political offence. On his side, it was argued that with two attempted assassinations and the bomb-throwing, Nkrumah was justified in detaining suspects. Nevertheless, he received general condemnation in the world's press, which in turn made him frustrated and withdrawn. Much of the political unrest was due to the complete dominance of the CPP and its increasing corruption.

Nkrumah tried to call a halt to the corruption and high living of ministers and party officials by making a broadcast at dawn, the hour when a chief made an important pronouncement, on 18 April 1961. After the subsequent investigations, six ministers, including some of Nkrumah's oldest colleagues, were asked to resign and six others had to surrender specified properties. Nkrumah made enemies but did little to suppress corruption because it arose largely as a by-product of his economic policy. At independence, Ghana had a viable economy, a good balance of payments and strong foreign exchange reserves. It was heavily dependent on the price and quantity of its exports of cocoa for its foreign exchange receipts and Nkrumah determined to reduce this dependence by diversifying the economy despite the obvious shortages of skilled manpower both within and outside the Civil Service. His haste was not balanced by the good luck which had helped him when he sought the political kingdom. The world price of cocoa declined catastrophically while the introduction of the cedi unattached to any international currency led to the large-scale smuggling of cocoa, foodstuffs, and manufactures across the border by those intent on holding hard currency.

By 1965 it was clear that Ghana would be unable to repay its international short-term debts of some £155 million. Apparently unaware of the disillusionment with him, Nkrumah went to North Vietnam to seek a peaceful solution to the conflict there. On 24 February 1966 he was deposed by the army in a coup which had been planned long before. It had been felt that he was leaning too far towards the East, that the deprivation of liberties had gone too far, and that the economy was crumbling. Nkrumah went into exile in Conakry, Guinea, where he was welcomed as co-president by President Sekou Touré. He died 27 April 1972, in Bucharest, Rumania, while being treated for cancer of the skin. The government of General I. K. Acheampong persuaded Sekou Touré to allow his body to be buried at Nkroful. His widow, formerly Fathia Halen Ritz, of Egypt, whom he married in 1957, their son, and two daughters were invited to reside in Ghana at the government's expense. It was felt by 1972 that the mania of denigration had gone too far. It was thought that, had he permitted a fair and open general election in 1964 and avoided many of the excesses, he might well have survived. As it was, his positive legacy was considerable: he was the chief protagonist of Pan-Africanism, playing a leading role in the formation of the Organization for African Unity (OAU); he introduced free elementary education for the first time in Africa and a free basic medical service; he built a network of roads and constructed the Tema harbour; he brought the massive Volta river hydro-electric project to completion, and did much besides. However, all was not well with Ghana politically, socially, and economically after 1960 and the Osagyefo had to pay the price of disillusion and failure.

Nkrumah was admitted to the Privy Council in 1959 and won the Lenin peace prize in 1962. He also received honorary doctorates.

[*The Autobiography of Kwame Nkrumah*, 1957; Geoffrey Bing, *Reap the Whirlwind*, 1968; D. J. Morgan, *The Official History of Colonial Development* (5 vols.), 1980; private information.]

D. J. MORGAN

published 1986

NOEL-BAKER Philip John

(1889–1982)

Baron Noel-Baker

Labour politician and winner of the Nobel peace prize, was born at Brondesbury Park, London, 1 November 1889, the sixth child in the family of three sons and four daughters of Joseph Allen Baker, Liberal MP and engineer, who came to England from Canada in 1876, and his wife, Elizabeth Balmer Moscrip, of Roxburghshire, New Brunswick, Canada. Joseph Baker had much to do with the development of London's tramway system. After the Quaker school, Bootham in Yorkshire, Philip went to Haverford College in Pennsylvania, USA. He entered King's College, Cambridge, in 1908 where he distinguished himself academically with a second in part i of the historical tripos (1910) and a first in part ii of the economics tripos (1912). He was university Whewell scholar in international relations in 1911 and was president both of the Cambridge Union (1912) and the University Athletic Club (1910–12), at that time a unique combination. He became vice-principal of Ruskin College, Oxford, in 1914.

During World War I, as a Quaker and conscientious objector, he served with the Friends' Ambulance Unit and received the Mons star and silver medal for valour (Italy, 1917) and the croce di guerra (1918). His first experience of public life came after the war, when he was a member of the British delegation to the Paris peace conference and then served with the secretariat of the League of Nations until 1922. He was an admirer of the League's creator, Viscount Cecil of Chelwood. He returned briefly to the academic world as Sir Ernest Cassel professor of international relations at the University of London from 1924 to 1929. He then became a Labour MP

567

for Coventry in 1929 and was made parliamentary private secretary to Arthur Henderson, the secretary of state for foreign affairs. He lost his seat in 1931 but Henderson chose him as his principal assistant when he presided over the disarmament conference of 1932–3. His academic and personal interest in disarmament was reflected in the efforts to end the private trade in arms which he described in a book *The Private Manufacture of Armaments* (1936).

In 1936 he was elected MP for Derby, a constituency (which became Derby South) which he held for thirty-four years. His ministerial career started with the wartime coalition government under (Sir) Winston Churchill in 1942 when he was appointed joint parliamentary secretary to the Ministry of War Transport. In 1945 he became minister of state to the Foreign Office under Clement (later Earl) Attlee and in the same year he was admitted to the Privy Council. He was then secretary of state for air in 1946–7 and for commonwealth relations from 1947 to 1950. His last government post was as minister for fuel and power in 1950–1. He was a very popular chairman of the Labour Party in 1946–7 and was chairman of the foreign affairs group of the Parliamentary Labour Party from 1964 until 1970.

After 1951 he was a member of the shadow cabinet for the next eight years in opposition. Slight and white-haired, sincere and eloquent, he dominated disarmament debates in the House of Commons with his total mastery of all the facts and figures. His work for disarmament was summarized in his major book, *The Arms Race—a Programme for World Disarmament* (1958), which with his other work was recognized by the award of the Nobel peace prize in 1959, the proceeds of which were used for the cause of disarmament. He received many subsequent honours, decorations, and honorary degrees and was made a life peer in 1977. He was a man of great charm and impressive intellect, who was widely liked, even by those who might have disagreed profoundly with some of his political views. It is likely that his uncompromising stand on disarmament prevented him from achieving the very high office to which his intelligence and political skills might otherwise have propelled him. The Labour governments of the time were reluctant to endorse the type of pacifism and multilateral disarmament which he saw as the only hope for the avoidance of future conflicts.

His life as sportsman and sports administrator spanned a century of transition in sport. Throughout his life he was closely associated with the Olympic Games, in which he ran twice (in 1912 and 1920, in the 1,500 metres race). In both races he self-sacrificingly arranged the way he ran in the final to make the victory of his team-mate more certain. Yet towards the end of his long life he saw many of his ideals in sport flouted; success in sport too often became the justification of political ideology. Perhaps in contrast to his international committees on disarmament, the results of which were disappointing, his International Council for Sport and Physical Recreation (of which he was the founder and president for sixteen years) seemed to bear more fruit. He had an immense belief in the importance of sport both for the individual and as a means of international understanding. At the age of ninety-one he made one of the last major speeches of his life at the Olympic Games in Baden-Baden, and received a standing ovation.

On 12 June 1915 at Worth, he married Irene (died 1956), the daughter of Francis Edward Noel, a British landowner, of Achmetaga in Greece. He first met his wife when they worked together in the Friends' Ambulance Unit in France. He added Noel to his name on marriage. There was one son of the marriage, Francis, who was for some years Labour MP for Swindon. Noel-Baker died at his Westminster home 8 October 1982.

[Personal knowledge.]

ROGER BANNISTER

published 1990

O'NEILL Terence Marne

(1914–1990)

Baron O'Neill of the Maine

Prime minister of Northern Ireland, was born 10 September 1914 at 29 Ennismore Gardens, Hyde Park, London, the third son and youngest of five children of Captain Arthur Edward Bruce O'Neill (2nd Life Guards), of Shane's Castle, Randalstown, county Antrim, MP for mid-Antrim and eldest son of the second Baron O'Neill, and his wife, Lady Annabel Hungerford Crewe-Milnes, eldest daughter of the Marquess of Crewe, statesman. Terence O'Neill's father became the first MP to die at the front (5 November 1914) and his mother married again in 1922. The young O'Neill was educated at West Downs School in Winchester, and at Eton. He spent much time in Abyssinia, where his stepfather was consul, and during the 1930s had several jobs, ending up at the Stock Exchange. After being commissioned at Sandhurst in May 1940, O'Neill joined the 2nd battalion of the Irish Guards, serving in Normandy and Holland. Both his brothers were killed in World War II.

In October 1946 O'Neill was returned unopposed as the Unionist member for Bannside in the Stormont parliament. He became parliamentary secretary to the minister of health in February 1948 and to the minister of home affairs in 1955. In 1956 he was sworn of the Privy Council (Northern Ireland) and became minister of home affairs and then of finance, forming a politically important relationship with a reform-minded private secretary, (Sir) Kenneth Bloomfield. Another important member of O'Neill's circle, *Belfast Telegraph* editor Jack Sayers, was 'never able to satisfy my mind about the Prime Minister's liberalism—it is far more intellectual than emotional and even then much of it emanates from Ken Bloomfield'. Nevertheless, the fact remains that when in 1963 O'Neill became prime minister of Northern Ireland—unlike his three Unionist predecessors—there was no trace of anti-Catholic bitterness on his record. Yet he was to disappoint some, at least, of his liberal friends.

The subsequent intensity of the sectarian conflict has obscured the fact that in his early years in office he was primarily concerned to win back Protestant support which the Unionist party had lost to the Northern Ireland Labour party in the period since 1958. 'Stealing Labour's thunder'—to use O'Neill's own term—rather than allaying Catholic resentments, was his main preoccupation.

O'Neill had a generous, even impulsive, streak and was capable of the occasional conciliatory grand gesture, such as his famous visit to a Catholic school. In the main, however, he espoused a rhetoric of planning and modernization by which nationalist grievances would be dissolved by shared participation in the benefits of economic growth. He saw little role for structural reform. His speeches in this early period resonate with a pious little-Ulsterism in which devolution emerges not just as an inevitable and reasonable historical compromise but as a responsive communal form of government superior to that of the class-based party system in the rest of the United Kingdom. That UK system was, however, economically sustaining the Stormont regime: a fact of which O'Neill was more aware than the Unionist electorate.

O'Neill's early lack of responsiveness to Catholic grievances was sharply criticized by liberal unionist groupings, such as the leadership of the Northern Ireland Labour party and the *Belfast Telegraph*, but in the short term O'Neillism was quite effective politically. The O'Neillite manifesto for the 1965 election crystallized the ideology of modernization—'Forward Ulster to Target 1970'. The result showed an average swing to the Unionist party of 7 per cent and was a major defeat for Labour.

Despite this electoral success, even then O'Neill was widely perceived to be a poor party manager. Normally secretive and aloof, at times he was capable of indiscreet and hurtful sarcasm at the expense of prickly senior colleagues. And, ironically, his 1965 triumph played a key role in marginalizing a party (Labour) which gave radicals from the Catholic community an outlet.

The emergence in 1968 of the civil rights movement, which included many such radicals, presented O'Neill with an excruciating dilemma: placating the reformers was likely to mean the consolidation of the internal unionist opposition. O'Neill chose the path of moderate, even modest, reform—'the five-point programme' of November 1968. For a brief moment, he seemed to have a real chance of gaining significant Catholic support whilst retaining that of a majority of Protestants. But the tactics of the radical wing of the civil rights movement, responding more to leftist politics than nationalist impulses, were to frustrate him.

The civil rights march led by the People's Democracy group in January 1969 was of decisive importance. This march was attacked at Burntollet bridge by Orange partisans and the subsequent deterioration in communal relations made O'Neill's position exceptionally difficult. Caught between the pressures generated by loyalist and nationalist militants, and having almost lost his seat in a snap election he called in February, he resigned in April 1969, though he retained substantial Protestant support even at the end. He accepted a life barony in 1970. In 1967 he had received an honorary LL.D. from Queen's University, Belfast.

O'Neill's legacy is ambiguous. Even the reputation of his path-breaking talks in 1965 with the taoiseach, Sean Lemass, suffered, amongst unionists at any rate, from later claims by Lemass's widow (bitterly repudiated by O'Neill) that they had been about 'Irish unity'. His famous statement on resignation continues to haunt his reputation: 'It is frightfully hard to explain to Protestants that if you give Roman Catholics a good job and a good house, they will live like Protestants ... they will refuse to have eighteen children on National Assistance ... in spite of the authoritative nature of their church.' He was a patrician figure out of touch with large sections of the population. O'Neill's political failure is made all the more tragic by the fact that he was essentially a man of decent tolerant instincts.

In 1944 O'Neill married (Katharine) Jean, daughter of William Ingham Whitaker, of Pylewell Park, Lymington. They had a daughter and a son. O'Neill died 12 June 1990 at his home in Lymington, Hampshire.

[*Ballymena Observer*, 13 November 1914; Terence O'Neill, *The Autobiography of Terence O'Neill*, 1972; Andrew Gailey (ed.), *John Sayers, a Liberal Editor*, 1993; Paul Bew and Henry Patterson, *The British State and the Ulster Crisis*, 1985.]

PAUL BEW

published 1996

ORMSBY GORE (William) David

(1918–1985)

Fifth Baron Harlech

Politician and ambassador, was born 20 May 1918 in London, the second son and third child in the family of three sons and three daughters of William George Arthur Ormsby Gore, fourth Baron Harlech, politician and banker, and his wife, Lady Beatrice Edith Mildred, daughter of James Edward Hubert Gascoyne-Cecil, the fourth Marquess of Salisbury. His elder brother died at the age of nineteen. He was educated at Eton and New College, Oxford (of which he became an honorary fellow in 1964). He obtained a third class in modern history in 1939 and joined the Berkshire Yeomanry in the same year, becoming a major (general staff) by the end of the war.

In 1950 he became Conservative MP for the Oswestry division of Shropshire and held the seat until 1961. After a few months as parliamentary under-secretary, he was appointed minister of state for foreign affairs at the beginning of the administration led by Harold Macmillan (later the Earl of Stockton) in January 1957. In this office much of his attention was devoted to disarmament negotiations, partly in Geneva and partly in New York during successive sessions of the United Nations General Assembly.

In November 1960 John F. Kennedy was elected president of the United States. Ormsby Gore, two years his junior, had been a close friend since Kennedy's pre-war years in London during his father's embassy. Macmillan, anxious to achieve the closest relations with the new president, who was a brother-in-law of his late nephew by marriage, the Marquess of Hartington, decided to send as British ambassador to Washington another nephew by marriage. Ormsby Gore resigned from the House of Commons and arrived in Washington in May 1961.

Until that point the new ambassador's career could be fairly described as remarkably nepotic. The success which he then made of his mission, however, sprang from qualities which could not be bestowed by family connection. Ormsby Gore was almost perfectly attuned to the new US administration. His friendship with the president strengthened rather than wilted under the strains of office and official intercourse. It was buttressed by the fact that he was also on close terms with Jacqueline Kennedy, as were the Kennedys with Lady Ormsby Gore (Sylvia, or Sissy, daughter of Hugh Lloyd Thomas, diplomat and courtier, whom he had married young in 1940, and by whom he had two sons and three daughters), whose shy but elegant charm made her an addition to the embassy and easily at home in the White House. President Kennedy much liked to have small dinner parties organized at short notice. The Ormsby Gores were probably more frequently invited on this basis than was anybody else, including even the president's brother and attorney-general. It was a wholly exceptional position for any ambassador to be in. It made him almost as much an unofficial adviser to the president as an envoy of the British government—although there was never any suggestion that British interests were not firmly represented in Washington during these years. His position was particularly influential during the Cuban missile crisis in October 1962.

Gore's special relationship may have caused some jealousy amongst other ambassadors but it in no way weakened his position in official Washington outside the White House. Other members of the administration—Robert McNamara, Robert Kennedy, McGeorge Bundy, Arthur Schlesinger—became his close and continuing friends, and after Kennedy's assassination he was even able to be a more than averagely effective ambassador for the first seventeen months of Lyndon Johnson's presidency. But the *raison d'être* of his embassy had gone. In February 1964 his father died and he became Lord Harlech. Later that year the Conservative government which had sent him as a political appointment to Washington was replaced by a Labour one. The new government was in no hurry to remove him. Nor should it have been. Apart from his effectiveness on the spot, his Kennedy years had shifted Harlech to the centre or even the left-centre of politics. After his return to England (in the spring of 1965) he was briefly (1966–7) deputy Conservative leader in the House of Lords, but he had lost any taste which he ever possessed for political partisanship and resigned after a year. This apart, all his subsequent semi-political activities were firmly centrist: the presidency of Shelter, the chairmanship of the European Movement (1969–75) and of the National Committee for Electoral Reform (from 1976). He was also twice concerned in a semi-official capacity with trying to find a multi-racial solution to the Rhodesian problem. In addition he was president of the British Board of Film Censors from 1965, the initiator and chairman of Harlech Television from 1967, and a director of a few other companies, although never centrally occupied with business. He was chairman of the Pilgrim Trust (1974–9) and of the British branch of the Pilgrims (a quite separate organization) in 1965–77. He was also the leading British figure in all Kennedy commemorative activities.

Sadly his own life then came to be almost as marked by tragedy and violent death as was that of the Kennedy family itself. In 1967 Sissy Harlech was killed in a car crash almost at the gates of their north Wales house. In 1974 his eldest son committed suicide. He surmounted these vicissitudes with fortitude and buoyancy, greatly assisted by his second marriage in 1969 to Pamela, the daughter of Ralph Frederick Colin, a New York lawyer and financier. They had one daughter. Pamela Harlech, a *Vogue* editor and talented compiler of books, brought vitality and verve to the marriage and had the gift of keeping her husband young. David Harlech at sixty-six looked no different from the way he had looked at fifty-six. He had no mountains left to climb, but he lived a life of style and grace, in which a large part was played by pleasure, tempered by high public spirit, good judgement, and unselfish instincts on all the main issues of the day. There seemed little reason why he should not continue for many years as an easy-going public figure of good sense and high repute. But tragedy struck again. On the evening of 25 January 1985, driving from London to Harlech, he was involved in a car crash (the third major one of his life) near to his constituency of the 1950s and the Shropshire homes of his earlier life. He died in hospital in Shrewsbury early the next morning. He was succeeded in the barony by his second son, Francis David (born 1954).

Ormsby Gore was admitted to the Privy Council in 1957 and appointed KCMG in 1961. He had honorary degrees from several American universities and from Manchester University (LLD, 1966).

[Personal knowledge.]

Roy Jenkins

published 1990

PERCY Henry Algernon George

(1871–1909)

Earl Percy

Politician and traveller, born at 25 (now 28) Grosvenor Square, London, on 21 Jan. 1871, was eldest son of Henry George Percy, Earl Percy, who became seventh duke of Northumberland in succession to his father in 1899. As Lord Warkworth he won at Eton the prize for English verse, and at Christ Church, Oxford, first class honours in classical moderations in 1891 and *literæ humaniores* in 1893, his class in the latter school being reputed one of the best of the year. He also obtained at Oxford in 1892 the Newdigate prize for English verse on the subject of St. Francis of Assisi, and his recitation of his poem in the Sheldonian Theatre was long remembered as one of the most impressive of these performances. In 1895 he contested

Berwick-on-Tweed as a conservative without success against Sir Edward Grey, but later in the year was chosen at a by-election for South Kensington, which he represented continuously till his death. Marked out from the first as a debater of ability, industry, and independence, he soon became conspicuous in a group of conservatives who sometimes adopted a critical attitude towards their leaders, and, in view of his future prospects, few felt surprise when, on Mr. Balfour becoming prime minister in July 1902, Earl Percy (as he had been styled since his father's succession to the dukedom in 1899) was appointed parliamentary under-secretary for India. Approving himself in this office by the immense pains which he took to master matters proper to his department, he passed to foreign affairs as under-secretary of state on the reconstruction of Mr. Balfour's cabinet in October 1903. Since his chief, Lord Lansdowne, was in the upper house, Lord Percy had occasion to appear prominently in the commons and to prove both his capacity and his independence, especially in dealing with Near Eastern matters, which had long engaged his interest, and had induced him once and again to visit Turkish soil.

Travel in the Near East divided his interests with politics. In 1895 he first visited the Ottoman dominions, when he returned with Lord Encombe from Persia though Baghdad and Damascus. He went back to Turkey in 1897 to make with Sir John Stirling Maxwell and Mr. Lionel Holland a journey through Asia Minor to Erzerum, Van, the Nestorian valleys, and the wilder parts of central Kurdistan. He returned by Mosul, Diarbekr, and Aleppo, and published his experiences in 'Notes of a Diary in Asiatic Turkey' (1898), a volume which showed strong but discriminating Turcophilism, sensitiveness to the scenic grandeur of the regions traversed, and growing interest in their history and archæology. True to the traditions of his family, he began to collect antiques, particularly cylinder seals; and subsequently extending his interest to Egypt, he applied himself to the study of hieroglyphics.

His most important tour in Turkey was undertaken in 1899. He then made his way with his cousin, Mr. Algernon Heber Percy, through Asia Minor and up the course of the southern source of the Euphrates to Bitlis and his Nestorian friends of Hakkiari. Thence he went on into the Alps of Jelu Dagh, traversing a little-known part of Kurdistan near the Turco-Persian border, and passed by Neri to Altin Keupri, whence he descended the Lesser Zab and Tigris on a raft to Baghdad. On his way out he had been received by Sultan Abdul Hamid. His second book, 'The Highlands of Asiatic Turkey' (1901), was inspired by his old sympathy for Turks, but also by a deepened sense of the evils of Hamidism, whose downfall he foresaw. Intolerant equally of Armenian and of Russian aspirations, he advocated agreement with Germany on Ottoman affairs.

He was in Macedonia in 1902, when appointed to office, and returned home through a wild part of North Albania, although not followed by the large Turkish escort which the solicitude of the Porte had prescribed for him. Thereafter parliamentary duties prevented him from making other than short recess tours, during one of which he took a motor-boat up the Nile, to practise for a projected cruise on the Euphrates, which he did not live to achieve. On Macedonian and indeed all Ottoman affairs his authority was acknowledged, although his views were not always welcome to the advocates of the *rayah* nationalists. An effective and thoughtful though not ambitious or frequent speaker, and a forceful but reserved personality, he had come to be regarded as a future leader in his party, when, to general sorrow, he died of pneumonia on 30 Dec. 1909, while passing through Paris on his way to Normandy. He was unmarried. He became a trustee of the National Portrait Gallery in 1901, and received in 1907 the degree of D.C.L. from the University of Durham.

[*The Times*, 31 Dec. 1909; private information.]

D. G. HOGARTH

published 1912

RADCLIFFE Cyril John

(1899–1977)

Viscount Radcliffe

Lawyer and public servant, was born in Llanychan, Denbighshire, 30 March 1899, the third of the four children (all sons) of Captain Alfred Ernest Radcliffe, of the Royal Lancashire Regiment, and his wife, Sybil Harriet, daughter of Robert Cunliffe, a London solicitor, who was president of the Law Society in 1890–1.

Radcliffe was at school at Haileybury. After service in the Labour Corps—because of his poor eyesight the only form of war service open to him—he entered New College, Oxford, as a scholar in 1919, and took first class honours in *literae humaniores* in 1921. He was a fellow of All Souls from 1922 to 1937. In 1923 he became Eldon law scholar and was called to the bar by the Inner Temple in 1924. He went into the chambers of Wilfrid (later Lord) Greene. He took silk in 1935, and by 1938, after Greene and Sir Gavin (later Viscount) Simonds were appointed to the bench, he had become the outstanding figure at the Chancery bar.

This meteoric legal career was interrupted by World War II. Radcliffe joined the Ministry of Information, and by 1941 had become its director-general. His gifts and skills complemented those of his minister, Brendan (later Viscount) Bracken, in an unlikely but effective partnership.

In May 1945 he resumed his practice at the bar; and in 1949 he was appointed a lord of appeal in ordinary, the first man (other than ex-law officers) for over sixty years to be appointed to the House of Lords direct from the bar.

In 1947 he was appointed chairman of the two boundary commissions set up with the passing of the Indian Independence Act of that year. The time he spent in India, and his eldest brother's death there while serving in the army, left him with a lifelong feeling for the country, and an intense admiration for the achievements, courage, and dedication of the early generations of British administrators there.

Over the next thirty years Radcliffe was the chairman of a series of public inquiries, including the royal commission on taxation of profits and income (1951–5); the constitutional commission for Cyprus (1956); committees on the working of the monetary system (1957–9) and on security procedures and practices in the public service (1961); the tribunal of inquiry into the Vassall case (1962); and committees of privy councillors on the *Daily Express* and D notices (1967) and on ministerial memoirs (1975–6). Though he continued to carry out judicial duties when he was not fully engaged on an inquiry, the law was no longer enough to satisfy his intellectual appetite; he enjoyed the succession of challenges provided by these public inquiries, whose reports reflected his own thoroughness, lucidity, and wisdom of judgement. The frequency with which his skill as a chairman was pressed into service led Sir A. P. Herbert to comment on 'Government by Radcliffery', but it is perhaps the fact that his achievements covered so diverse a range of activities that partly accounts for a sense that his outstanding gifts were never really put to full use.

He retired from judicial work in 1964. He became a trustee of the British Museum in 1957, and was chairman of the trustees from 1963 to 1968. He was chairman of the governors of the School of Oriental and African Studies from 1960 to 1975. He became the first chancellor of the University of Warwick in 1966. In his last ten years he withdrew increasingly into private life, partly in order to care for his wife but also because of his increasing disenchantment with the quality of public life.

Radcliffe was much in demand as a speaker and lecturer. He spoke, as he wrote, with exceptional lucidity and power, and with a sense of style well characterized as intellectual eloquence. He had an abiding interest in the arts, and assembled—but eventually disposed of—a small but distinguished collection of Impressionist paintings. For many years a trusted friend of Calouste Gulbenkian, he was disappointed not to be able to fulfil Gulbenkian's and indeed his own hope that he might become the first chairman of the Gulbenkian trustees.

Radcliffe was by common consent one of the outstanding intelligences of his generation. He had a capacious and powerful mind, disciplined by his academic and legal training, and nurtured by extensive reading, particularly in English history and literature. He cherished freedom and the liberal values, and order and the rule of law as the condition of freedom. He believed in the power of reason as a determinant of human conduct, and measured the foibles and follies of men with a detached and unsparing perceptiveness. He was a reserved and fastidious man. All this made him for some people unapproachable, and he had relatively few close friends; but their devotion was rewarded by the discovery of a keen sense of humour, a dry wit, and a warm and steadfast affection.

He was a man of middle height, with a large, square head: a high forehead, with crinkly brown—later silvery grey—hair brushed tight back from his forehead; a blunt mouth and a firm chin; and blue-grey eyes behind thick spectacles.

Radcliffe's principal publications were *The Problem of Power* (1951 Reith lectures, 1952, reissued with new preface, 1958), *The Law and its Compass* (1960 Rosenthal lectures, 1961), *Mountstuart Elphinstone* (Romanes lecture, 1962), *Government by Contempt: Whitehall's Way with Parliament and People* (1968), and *Not in Feather Beds* (a collection of speeches, lectures, and articles, 1968).

Radcliffe was appointed KBE in 1944 and GBE in 1948. As a law lord, he became a life peer and a privy councillor in 1949; and he was created viscount in 1962. He was elected FBA in 1968 and had many honorary degrees, including an Oxford DCL (1961).

Radcliffe married in 1939 Antonia Mary Roby (died 1982), the daughter of Godfrey Rathbone Benson, first Baron Charnwood, politician and man of letters. She was the former wife of John Tennant. There were no children of the marriage. Radcliffe died at his home in Hampton Lucy, Warwickshire, 1 April 1977. The viscountcy became extinct.

[*The Times*, 4 April 1977; Robert Stevens, 'Four interpretations' in *Law and Politics*, 1979; private information; personal knowledge.]

ROBERT ARMSTRONG

published 1986

(1874–1936)

Politician, was born in Bombay 28 March 1874, the son of Dorabji Shapurji Saklatvala, a Parsee merchant, of Bombay and later of Manchester, and Jerbai Tata, a sister of J. N. Tata, who, with his brother, founded the Tata Iron and Steel Works in India. Receiving his early education at St. Xavier's School and College in Bombay, Saklatvala studied law and was a member of Lincoln's Inn. For three years he prospected for coal, iron, and limestone in the Indian jungle, and considerably aided the production of the Tata firm. Welfare work in the plague hospitals and the slums of Bombay led to interest in Indian labour problems and association with the Indian Trade Union Congress. On accepting a position on behalf of the firm in London in 1905 (he did not resign his position of departmental manager until 1925), Saklatvala joined the National Liberal Club, but subsequently turned socialist, and in 1910 became active in the independent labour party, then affiliated to the labour party. He also joined the British socialist party and, for trade union association, the General Workers' Union and the National Union of Clerks. After the Russian revolution he assisted in the formation of a People's Russian Information Bureau and the communist party of Great Britain. In 1922 he first entered parliament as labour member for North Battersea, being the third member from India to be elected to the House of Commons, after Dabadhai Naoroji, a liberal, in 1892, and Sir M. M. Bhownagree, a conservative, in 1895. After the formation of the Third (Communist) International in 1919, Saklatvala sought to secure the adhesion of the independent labour party, and upon his failure concentrated upon communist activity. He was a founder member of the Workers' Welfare League of India, which aimed at the equalization of European and Asiatic labour standards. In 1923 he lost his seat, but regained it as a communist in 1924. Appointed in 1925 a member of an inter-parliamentary delegation to the United States of America, his visa was revoked by the United States secretary of state, Kellogg, on the ground that the United States did not admit revolutionaries.

Active in agitation during the General Strike in 1926, Saklatvala was imprisoned for two months on a charge arising out of a May Day speech in Hyde Park. In 1927 he visited India, but was refused permission to stay in Egypt *en route*. He was a strong critic of the Indian National Congress and of Gandhi's methods, in particular of the re-introduction of the spinning-wheel and the weaving of khaddar cloth. Upon his return to England his permit to re-enter India was cancelled at the request of the Indian government. At the general election of 1929 he again contested North Battersea, but was defeated. In 1934 he visited Russia, travelling widely through the territory bordering on India, and was greatly impressed by the developments in industry, agriculture, education, and general culture among its backward peoples.

Saklatvala married in 1907 Sehri, daughter of Henry Marsh, of Tansley, Derbyshire; their three sons and two daughters were initiated into the Parsee religion in 1927, a ceremony for which the father was censured by the communist party. He died in London 16 January 1936.

Although a cultivated man and personally popular among a wide circle of friends, Saklatvala figured as 'a stormy petrel' throughout the later years of his life in London. He viewed social conditions in Great Britain with abhorrence and was extreme in his utterances about the continuance of British rule in India.

[*The Times*, 17 January 1936; *Review of Reviews*, December 1922.]

J. S. MIDDLETON

published 1949

SASSOON Sir Philip Albert Gustave David

(1888–1939)

Third Baronet, of Kensington Gore

Politician and connoisseur, was born in Paris 4 December 1888, the only son of (Sir) Edward Albert Sassoon, second baronet, by his wife, Aline Caroline, daughter of Baron Gustave de Rothschild, of the French branch. He was grandson of Sir Albert Abdullah David Sassoon, first baronet, who had been born at Bagdad in 1818 and had accompanied his father, David Sassoon, when he moved to Bombay and there founded the great merchant house of David Sassoon & company. The Sassoons had been settled in Mesopotamia for many centuries, and local tradition claimed that they had been driven out of Spain in the fifteenth century.

Philip Sassoon was educated at Eton and Christ Church, Oxford. At nineteen years of age he chose British nationality, having, on account of his birth in France, the right to elect for one country or the other. In 1912 his father, who had been unionist member for Hythe since 1899, died, and he was returned to parliament in the same interest for the same constituency. He represented it without a break for twenty-seven years, until his death.

In 1933 he received the freedom of the borough. When war broke out in 1914 he held a commission in the Royal East Kent Yeomanry, and in December 1915 he was appointed private secretary to (Field Marshal) Sir Douglas (later Earl) Haig, commander-in-chief of the British armies. In this important position, which he held until after the armistice, his cosmopolitan social gifts were fully called into play, and he obtained a unique view of the war, and of the statesmen and generals who were conducting it. It was to Sassoon that Haig handed the piece of paper on which he had written the famous 'Backs to the Wall' order of the day, and the field-marshal subsequently gave it to him. He retained it until his death, when he bequeathed it to the British Museum.

In the years immediately following 1918 Sassoon busied himself with politics, with travelling, and with entertaining. He completed Port Lympne, near Hythe, the country residence which he had begun before the war, and on which he spent freely his great fortune. This house soon became famous for its meetings between the various statesmen and soldiers who were conducting the lengthy Peace Conference in Paris, and their host showed his own particular qualities of tact and considerateness. In 1924 Sassoon was appointed under-secretary of state for air, a post which he held until 1929, and again from 1931 until 1937. During the second period the secretary of state for air sat in the House of Lords, and in consequence Sassoon represented his ministry in the House of Commons. His annual speech on the introduction of the air estimates, invariably delivered without a single written note, was followed with attention by members of all parties, because of its careful reasoning and mass of skilfully presented detail. Sassoon's quick comprehension of the meaning of air power did much to rouse the public: while the personal interest which he took in the Royal Air Force and the enthusiasm with which he always sought to promote its welfare were of great service to the country. In 1929 appeared his only book, *The Third Route*, notable for its descriptive skill and for its power of humorous exaggeration, both of which distinguished equally his conversation. In 1937 he was appointed first commissioner of Works, a post which synthesized many of his energies, and wherein he was most happy. Although death cut short his tenure of this office, several memorials remain to his taste; notably his restoration of Sir James Thornhill's Painted Hall at Greenwich Hospital.

Honours, like great wealth, came to Sassoon early. He was sworn of the Privy Council in 1929, held numerous orders and decorations, British and foreign (including the G.B.E., 1922), and was for many years a trustee of the National Gallery (chairman of the board from December 1932 to 1936), the Tate Gallery, the Wallace Collection, and the British School at Rome. But, despite his successful career, his gifts were perhaps more those of an artist than of a politician. His kindnesses were, like his wit, creative, and in Port Lympne and Trent Park, New Barnet, he made works of art. The first preserved the qualities of his fire and brilliance as a young man, while the second reflected his more mature judgement. Besides being a judge of pictures, he was a connoisseur of furniture, china, and old silver—in fact of all beautiful or decorative objects. The exhibitions, such as 'Conversation Pieces' and 'The Age of Walnut', which were held, in aid of charity, each spring for many years in his London house were famous among art-lovers. These exhibitions were organized by Sassoon and by his cousin Mrs. David Gubbay, who acted as hostess for him at Trent and Port Lympne. No picture of life between the wars is complete without some account of one of these houses, filled always with politicians, painters, writers, professional golfers, and airmen. His great entertainments were imbued with his personality and with imagination, as if with a kind of magic, and he seemed to be surrounded by a constant activity in house and garden.

Sassoon died, after a month's illness, at his London house, 45 Park Lane, 3 June 1939. He was unmarried, and the baronetcy became extinct. His only sister married the fifth Marquess of Cholmondeley.

There are several portraits of Sassoon, notably a painting and a char-coal-drawing by J. S. Sargent, and a painting by Glyn Philpot, all three of which are in Lady Cholmondeley's possession.

[Sir P. Sassoon, *The Third Route*, 1929; private information; personal knowledge.]

OSBERT SITWELL

published 1949

SEELY John Edward Bernard

(1868–1947)

First Baron Mottistone

Politician and soldier, was born at Brookhill Hall, between Derby and Nottingham, 31 May 1868. His family were wealthy colliery owners in the Midlands, and his grandfather, for many years member of Parliament for Lincoln, was a noted Radical, who won notoriety by entertaining Garibaldi at his home in the Isle of Wight. Seely was the fourth son and seventh child of (Sir) Charles Seely, who became first baronet, by his wife, Emily, daughter of William Evans, of Crumpsall Grange, Lancashire. He was brought up in Nottinghamshire but spent most of his holidays in the Isle of Wight for which he retained a constant affection. From his Tudor manor there he was eventually to take his title. He was educated at Harrow (where he fagged for Stanley Baldwin) and at Trinity College, Cambridge. He graduated in 1890 and was called to the bar by the Inner Temple in 1897. While an undergraduate he had joined the Hampshire Yeomanry. When the South African war broke out he succeeded in arranging private but immediate transport to South Africa for his squadron, through the good offices of his uncle, Sir Francis Evans, chairman of the Union Castle Line. He served against the Boers for eighteen months and his remarkable courage, although occasionally bringing him into conflict with authority, won him distinction and several decorations: he was appointed to the D.S.O. in 1900.

During his absence in South Africa Seely was elected Conservative member for the Isle of Wight (1900). In Parliament his handsome appearance, friendliness, incisive speech, and ebullient unorthodoxy quickly singled him out as a coming man. With some of the younger Conservatives, in particular (Sir) Winston Churchill and Lord Hugh Cecil (later Lord Quickswood), 'Jack' Seely maintained a sustained attack on the Balfour Government's administration of the army. He left the Conservative Party in 1904 on the combined issues of protection and 'Chinese slavery', and resigning his seat was re-elected without opposition at a by-election. In 1906 he was narrowly elected as a Liberal for the Abercromby division of Liverpool. When Campbell-Bannerman formed his Government, Seely was 'left outside', but when Asquith became prime minister in 1908 he was appointed under-secretary to the Colonial Office and in 1909 was sworn of the Privy Council. Since his chief, Lord Crewe, was in the Lords, important work fell to the under-secretary, in particular the introduction of the measure which brought about the Union of South Africa. In 1911 Seely transferred to the War Office where in 1912 he succeeded Lord Haldane as secretary of state, an obvious choice having regard to his knowledge of army matters and his experience on the Committee of Imperial Defence. He worked in close accord with the chief of the imperial general staff, Sir John French (later the Earl of Ypres), whom he always held in affectionate admiration. French and Seely were responsible for the invitation to Foch to attend the British manœuvres in 1912 and active in preparing the army for the war with Germany which Seely believed to be inevitable. The mobility of the proposed Expeditionary Force and in particular the development of a Flying Corps were his especial interests.

Seely and his advisers had some immediate anxieties nearer home. During the later months of 1913 there was some discussion in the army—

and a great deal more outside—about the position of the armed forces should the Government be obliged to impose the policy of Home Rule for Ireland by force. In view of the speculation on this topic Seely wisely decided to confer in December with the general officers commanding in England, Scotland, and Ireland. At this conference, and after a discussion in which the secretary of state raised the whole question of the relations between the armed forces and the civil power, it was not disputed that officers who were domiciled in an area of disturbance—which in this case was Northern Ireland—should not be compelled to take part in any possible hostilities.

On 14 March 1914 a Cabinet committee of which Seely was a member decided to inform Sir Arthur Paget, commanding in Ireland, that there was reason to expect attempts to obtain arms and that certain depots in the north appeared to be insufficiently guarded. Paget replied that he was reluctant to move troops for fear of precipitating a crisis in the country. He was again summoned to London where by this time (Sir) Winston Churchill and Seely had persuaded themselves and the Cabinet that trouble was imminent; a view which the sudden departure of Sir Edward (later Lord) Carson for Belfast on the 19th did nothing to dispel. Certain movements of troops in Ireland were agreed. Paget was also instructed to talk to his officers in the sense of the discussions held in the previous December. The instructions, based on these discussions, which were given to him in writing in December, provided that Ulster-domiciled officers might 'disappear' but stated that other officers who from conscientious reasons were not prepared to carry out their duty as ordered were to say so at once and be dismissed the Service. No doubt Seely is to be blamed for agreeing to instructions which gave officers the opportunity of pronouncing judgement on orders which might be issued to them, but the position was embittered by political pressure from outside and Seely was naturally anxious to meet the wishes of Paget and his own leading military advisers. But the results of these instructions were serious for, although no precise record has been kept of what Paget said when he got back to Dublin, his observations gave rise to the impression that immediate action against Ulster was contemplated and resulted in his reporting to London without further explanation that Brigadier-General (later General Sir) Hubert Gough and fifty-seven of his officers in the 3rd Cavalry brigade stationed at the Curragh 'preferred dismissal if ordered north'. Gough was accordingly relieved of his command and ordered to report to the War Office with his three colonels.

On Monday morning, 23 March, Seely, in the presence of Paget, French, and the adjutant-general, Sir Spencer Ewart, reassured Gough about the Government's intentions, and agreed to provide written confirmation which Gough might show to his officers. Seely then went to a Cabinet meeting, which he had to leave before it concluded in order to attend the King to report on the situation. On his return, the Cabinet had broken up for luncheon and he failed to apprehend, from a few words with Asquith who was still in the room, that the document drafted for Gough by the adjutant-general and amended by the Cabinet was now inviolate. Seely, realizing that it did not entirely meet Gough's difficulties, accordingly added two paragraphs, one of which asserted that the Government had no intention of using the forces of the Crown 'to crush political opposition to the policy or principles of the Home Rule Bill'. In this he had the help of Lord Morley who was to answer for the Government in the Lords that afternoon. The revised memorandum, initialed by Seely himself, and by French and Ewart, was then handed to Gough. Later that day, on the prompting of (Sir) Henry Wilson who was in close touch with the Opposition, Gough sought additional clarification from French who, without informing Seely, gave Gough the further written assurance that his men would not be ordered to Ulster. Gough returned to his command, but the jubilation of his friends aroused strong feeling among the Liberal and Labour parties, many of whose members held that the Government had stooped to bargain with a troublesome group of officers. In the face of this it was out of the question for the Government to endorse the amended statement.

On 25 March in the House of Commons Seely took the entire blame, in an effort to avoid the resignations of the chief of the imperial general staff and the adjutant-general. Asquith, while repudiating the memorandum and making it clear that he thought the secretary of state had made an error of judgement, declined to accept Seely's resignation. During the next few days it became clear, however, that both French and Ewart felt that they must resign rather than dishonour their signatures. Strenuous efforts were made, between parliamentary storms, to retain French as chief of the imperial general staff. By 30 March, however, Asquith reluctantly concluded that the Government 'could not possibly survive any recognition, express or implied, of the Gough treaty, and it is equally clear that French will not remain except upon that footing. ... I see no way out of the imbroglio but for Seely to go also and I propose myself, for a time, to take his place.'

The Curragh incident thus cost Seely his portfolio, although he remained a member of the Committee of Imperial Defence. Asquith's subsequent decision not to 'purge' the army (because this would have disorganized the Expeditionary Force) was noted by both sides in Ireland to his great disadvantage. And the strains and stresses which the episode had revealed in the army were noted too in Germany.

The question whether Seely would have speedily returned to office after taking part in what, in his own words, 'looked like a private bargain with a few rebellious officers', was engulfed by the outbreak of war. To one of his active disposition it was perhaps not unfortunate that he was no longer a member of the administration. He left London on 11 August 1914, and remained in France with scarcely a break until 1918, for the majority of the time in command of the Canadian Cavalry brigade. He and his horse Warrior (about which he later wrote an engaging book) were conspicuous in many actions in which 'the luckiest man in the army' seemed to reflect by his remarkable gallantry the more romantic exploits of an earlier tradition. Seely was appointed C.B. in 1916, C.M.G. in 1918, and was five times mentioned in dispatches. In 1918 he was gassed and retired from active service with the rank of major-general. He became parliamentary under-secretary and deputy minister of munitions, moving as under-secretary to the Air Ministry in January 1919. In November he resigned on the prime minister's refusal to give the Air Ministry a separate secretary of state.

Seely was member for the Ilkeston division of Derbyshire from a by-election in 1910 (after an earlier defeat in the same year at Abercromby) until 1922 when, in common with many coalition Liberals, he was defeated. He was elected as a Liberal for the Isle of Wight in 1923 but was defeated in the following year. He devoted the rest of his life to the savings movement—he was chairman of the national committee (1926–43), and an active vice-chairman till his death—and to country pursuits. From 1918 he was lord lieutenant of Hampshire and the Isle of Wight. Ships and the sea were always his principal recreation and for much of his life he was coxswain of the Brooke lifeboat. He was created a baron in 1933.

Throughout his strenuous life Seely was conspicuous for a gay and brave bearing, not commonly found at Westminster, and this won him a wide company of friends who, apart from his own political party, included Balfour, George Wyndham, Birkenhead, MacDonald, Henderson, and Snowden. He was the author of two books of autobiography which, even in their titles, *Adventure* and *Fear, and be Slain*, faithfully revealed the tang of Seely's personality. Nor were his exciting experiences diminished in their telling.

Seely was twice married: first, in 1895 to Emily Florence (died 1913), daughter of the Hon. (Sir) Henry George Louis Crichton; secondly, in 1917 to the widow of his friend Captain George Crosfield Norris Nicholson, Evelyn Izmé, daughter of the tenth Baron and first Viscount Elibank. She survived him when he died in London 7 November 1947. There were three sons and four daughters of the first marriage and one son of the second.

The eldest son was killed at Arras in 1917 and the second son, Henry John Alexander (born 1899), succeeded as second baron.

A portrait by Sir William Orpen is in the Imperial War Museum; another by Sir Alfred Munnings of Seely mounted on Warrior is in the National Art Gallery at Ottawa.

[*The Times*, 8 November 1947; J. E. B. Seely, *Adventure*, 1930, *Fear, and be Slain*, 1931, and (Lord Mottistone), *My Horse Warrior*, 1934; Sir C. E. Callwell, *Sir Henry Wilson*, 2 vols., 1927; Sir F. B. Maurice, *Haldane*, 2 vols., 1937–9; private information.]

ROGER FULFORD

[Geoffrey Brooke, *Good Company*, 1954; A. P. Ryan, *Mutiny at the Curragh*, 1956.]

published 1959

SHINWELL Emanuel

(1884–1986)

Baron Shinwell

Politician, was born 18 October 1884 in Spitalfields, east London, the eldest in a family of thirteen children of Samuel Shinwell, a clothing manufacturer of Polish Jewish origin, and his Dutch wife, Rose Konigswinter. The family moved to Glasgow but Shinwell left school at the age of eleven to be apprenticed to the tailoring trade. He joined his first trade union, the Amalgamated Society of Clothing Operatives, at the age of seventeen and was elected to Glasgow Trades Council in 1906. He was to serve twice as its president. He became an early member of the Independent Labour party and was an active socialist crusader. In 1911 he was prominent on the Clyde during the national dock strike.

He continued his militant union activities during the war and was wrongly alleged to have been involved in the disturbances in George Square, Glasgow, between striking workers and the police on 'Red Friday' (31 January 1919). As a result, he spent over five months in Calton gaol, Edinburgh. He was now turning to thoughts of a political career. In the 1918 general election, he stood unsuccessfully as Labour candidate for Linlithgow (West Lothian); in 1922 he was elected to Parliament there.

He served as parliamentary secretary to the mines department in the first Labour government of Ramsay MacDonald in 1924. Defeated in the

1924 general election, he was re-elected in a by-election in 1928 and served in junior offices in the second Labour government, as financial secretary to the War Office in 1929–30 and again in the mines department in 1930–1. He had an immense admiration for MacDonald and tried in vain to persuade him not to head the 'national' government in August 1931. In the subsequent general election, Shinwell was defeated again.

He now decided to challenge MacDonald directly and in the 1935 general election handsomely defeated his old leader at Seaham Harbour. After a redistribution of seats, the constituency was later renamed Easington. Shinwell was always a pugnacious member of Parliament. In 1938 he caused a sensation by striking a Conservative, Commander Robert Bower (as it happened, a former naval boxing champion), when the latter made a hostile interjection in debate. During the war years Shinwell was a vigorous, though always patriotic, critic of (Sir) Winston Churchill's coalition government. He and the Tory sixth Earl Winterton were popularly christened 'Arsenic and Old Lace'. Shinwell was also prominent in Labour's policy-making committees, notably those dealing with coal and energy.

When Labour won the 1945 general election, Attlee appointed Shinwell to the cabinet as minister of fuel and power. Here he achieved the nationalization of coal in 1946 and also negotiated the so-called miners' charter with the National Union of Mineworkers. He caused much controversy by declaring that the middle class was 'not worth a tinker's cuss.' He served as chairman of the Labour party in 1947–8. However, his reputation slumped during the acute fuel crisis of January–March 1947, at a time of an exceptionally severe winter. He was accused of complacency and failing to plan to deal with basic problems of coal production. That October, much to his chagrin, Shinwell was demoted by Attlee to the War Office, outside the cabinet. Hugh Gaitskell took his place and thereby earned Shinwell's undying enmity, reinforced by Gaitskell's public school background. Shinwell was also attacked by younger men like James (later Baron) Callaghan for being less than ardent over nationalization. However, Shinwell proved to be a vigorous war minister, in tune with army sentiment, and Attlee reappointed him to the cabinet in March 1950 as minister of defence. Here Shinwell dealt energetically with the emergency in Malaya and war in Korea. In the summer of 1951 he urged the cabinet to send British troops to protect the oil refineries at Abadan, which the Persian government had nationalized, but he was successfully resisted by other ministers.

After Labour fell from office in 1951, Shinwell lost ground. He was defeated in elections for the party national executive in 1952 and left the shadow cabinet in 1955. Gaitskell was elected party leader that year;

Shinwell had backed his fellow veteran, Herbert Morrison (later Baron Morrison of Lambeth). However, despite being in his seventies, he continued to play a lively role in politics. He changed his stance on nuclear weapons and campaigned against the stationing of US Polaris submarines at Holy Loch. The election of Harold Wilson (later Baron Wilson of Rievaulx) as party leader after Gaitskell's death gave Shinwell new opportunities. Although now eighty, he was appointed by Wilson as chairman of the Parliamentary Labour party in October 1964, and worked hard to secure support for a government whose initial majority was only three. However, he came into conflict with ministers from 1966, especially with the equally aggressive foreign secretary, George Brown (later Baron George-Brown), since Shinwell was a vehement enemy of British entry into the European Common Market. He resigned as party chairman in 1967; in 1970 he became a life peer.

His career was still far from over. He became chairman of the all-party Lords' defence study group. He voted against his own Labour government in 1976 and in March 1982 resigned the party whip in protest against left-wing militancy, though he remained a Labour party member. He was now a legendary figure, and his hundredth birthday was celebrated in the House of Lords in 1984 (during a national miners' strike) with considerable enthusiasm.

With his stocky figure and Glaswegian accent, 'Manny' Shinwell was pugnacious in Parliament and on the platform. Appropriately, his enthusiasms included professional boxing. Though not religious, he was also much involved with the Jewish community. His performance in office was marred by the 1947 fuel crisis, while as a service minister he showed a jingoism some thought inappropriate. However, he had the gift of striking up friendships across the spectrum, including with the first Viscount Montgomery of Alamein and the editor of the *Sunday Express*, Sir John Junor. He was kindly towards the young. He was a major personality over sixty years, and a notable pioneer in Labour's long march to power in 1945. He wrote several autobiographical works, of which *Conflict Without Malice* (1955) is the most important. He was married (and widowed) three times. In 1903 he married Fay ('Fanny') Freeman (died 1954); they had two sons and a daughter. In 1956 he married Dinah (died 1971), daughter of Carol Ludwig Meyer, of Denmark. In 1972 he married Sarah, former wife of Alfred Hurst and daughter of Solomon Stungo. She died in 1977. Shinwell himself died 8 May 1986 at the age of 101, at his St John's Wood flat in London, and was cremated at Golders Green crematorium.

[Emanuel Shinwell, *Conflict Without Malice*, 1955, *I've Lived Through It All*, 1973, *Lead with the Left: my First Ninety-Six Years*, 1981, and *Shinwell Talking*, tape-recorded conversations edited by John Dexat, 1984; *The Times* and *Guardian*, 9

May 1986; Dalton papers, London School of Economics; Gaitskell papers, Nuffield College, Oxford; Labour party archives, Manchester; private information.]

KENNETH O. MORGAN

published 1996

SINCLAIR Sir John Alexander

(1897–1977)

Sailor, soldier, and intelligence director, was born 29 May 1897 in Fulham, the younger son and second of the four children of John Stewart Sinclair, later archdeacon of Cirencester (who was the grandson of Sir John Sinclair, first baronet), and his wife, Clara Sophia, daughter of John Dearman Birchall JP, of Bowden Hall, Gloucestershire. He was educated at Osborne and Dartmouth, finishing his education just in time to serve as a midshipman RN for the first two years of World War I. During that time he was almost continuously at sea, mainly in submarines, but scarcely ever free from seasickness. Soon after he had taken part in the landing of the Lancashire Fusiliers on the west beach at Gallipolli his health broke down completely and he had to be invalided out of the navy after only six years' service. During his long convalescence he was able to do some teaching at the Downs School, Winchester, where he had been a pupil formerly, until well enough to apply for a new career in the army. In 1918 he entered the Royal Military Academy, Woolwich, where he proved himself an outstanding cadet winning the sword of honour and other Academy prizes. Commissioned in the Royal Field Artillery in 1919, he served first with the Murmansk force in northern Russia and then in India. Returning to duty at Aldershot, he married in 1927 Esme Beatrice (died 1983), daughter of Thomas Kark Sopwith, of Maidstone, who was later archdeacon of Canterbury. There were two sons and two daughters.

After serving as adjutant in the Honourable Artillery Company (1929–31) he went on to the Staff College, Camberley (1932–3), and from 1938 to 1939 he was an instructor at the Senior Staff College at Minley. By the opening of World War II his reputation in the army was that of a studious and thoughtful soldier and a fine all-round sportsman. He began the war as an operational planner with the BEF. Although the British were always sceptical of one of its basic concepts, namely the impassability of the Ardennes to German armour, the British plans had to be fitted into the overall Gamelin plan. It was Alec Sinclair who drafted the operational order for the advance of the BEF to the river Kyle but having done so was himself almost immediately recalled to London to become GSO1 in Military Operations 4 close to the highest levels of command, and at a time when the planners had to take simultaneous account of the calls for re-inforcement and the possibility of evacuation. When this phase was over he had become brigadier and deputy director of operations. In 1941 he was appointed brigadier general staff South-Eastern Command and in 1942 deputy chief of the general staff Home Forces.

Promoted major-general he concentrated on training and planning for the Normandy invasion, though his hopes of himself joining the invasion forces were later dashed by the split up of Home Forces Command and the formation of the 21st Army Group of Sir B. L. Montgomery (later Viscount Montgomery of Alamein). Instead he was appointed director of military intelligence at the War Office in 1944 and thus found himself entering at the highest level a field that was new to him. Intelligence played a great part in the war and was at that time needed more than ever. He quickly showed that he had the qualities for the job; a capacity for detail, good judgement, and a ready acceptance of responsibility. 'Sinbad' Sinclair, as he was called by his colleagues, became a much-respected DMI and held the post until the end of the war.

Then, near the expected end of his military career, a new prospect opened for him. It was to become in 1951, after first serving as deputy director until 1950, the director of MI6, the civilian intelligence service responsible to the foreign secretary and the prime minister. The choice of a successful DMI, admired for his strong character and organizational skills, was particularly appropriate for the transitional period that lay ahead of the service. A large wartime organization had to be scaled down, new methods and standards of recruitment for permanent staff agreed, and old international alliances renegotiated for new peacetime tasks. He achieved these things in ways that lasted well, while at the same time directing current operations in his usual practical and responsible way. It was therefore unfair to his reputation that the only time he came to public notice was in connection with the intelligence operation of 19 April 1956 in which the diver Commander Lionel Crabb was lost when making an underwater inspection of a Russian ship awaiting in Portsmouth harbour the return of Khrushchev and Bulganin, who were on a goodwill visit to Britain. The intelligence urgencies of those times had led to a hastily planned operation for which he had to accept responsibility without having been able to supervise its details.

He retired in 1956 leaving behind him the reputation of a notable re-former and much-trusted chief. He was now free to enjoy twenty-one years of a happy and united family life at his home at East Ashling, Sussex, where he died 22 March 1977.

He was appointed OBE in 1940, CB in 1945, and KCMG in 1953. He was also a commander of the US Legion of Merit (1945).

[Personal knowledge.]

DICK WHITE

published 1986

SNOW Charles Percy

(1905–1980)

Baron Snow

Author and publicist, was born in Leicester 15 October 1905, the second of four sons of William Edward Snow and his wife, Ada Sophia Robinson. His father was a clerk in a shoe factory and a church organist, an FRCO. From a local elementary school Snow entered Alderman Newton's grammar school, Leicester, with a scholarship, and then studied science at the local university college (later Leicester University). He gained a first class degree in chemistry, followed by an M.Sc. (1928) in physics there, both London University external degrees, and proceeded, again by scholarship, to do postgraduate research at the Cavendish Laboratory in Cambridge. He became a fellow of Christ's College in 1930, the same year in which he gained a Ph.D. He was tutor of the college from 1935 to 1945 and was later a frequent visitor and honorary fellow. He had been a fairly good cricketer at school, and, at Cambridge, he enjoyed watching cricket at Fenner's with other bachelor dons such as G. H. Hardy to whom he dedicated *The Masters*; later, he became a member of the MCC.

Snow's research in infra-red spectroscopy failed, since it was built upon an intuition that careful experimental results did not confirm; in consequence he was not subsequently taken entirely seriously as a scientist. But he remained dedicated to science, with both a reasoned sympathy and a boyish enthusiasm for great scientists. His years at Cambridge coincided with a golden age of Cambridge physics, and he was starry-eyed about the achievements of the brilliant men whom he knew, and whom he thought (correctly) that the world in general and cultivated society in particular neither understood nor appreciated. It became his mission to explain their achievement. He read widely, increasingly in the body of European literature, and in the Cambridge English studies of Sir Arthur Quiller-Couch and Basil Willey: he adopted a posture of a cultured (and left-wing) serious interest in literature and the arts, which was deeply opposed as dilettantism by the growing body of professional scholars of English literature, especially the school represented by F. R. Leavis, university reader in English, with whom he later had a celebrated controversy. Snow published *Death under Sail* in 1932 and a second novel, *The Search*, in 1934, and in 1940 began what was to be a series, taking its title from the first book, *Strangers and Brothers*. It was this series that made his name.

Snow had three careers. He was a scientific administrator. He was a novelist and critic. He was a public man, much in demand to lecture, broadcast, and pontificate. Each career fed on the others. Though the *Strangers and Brothers* sequence was not directly autobiographical, each novel drew upon Snow's own experience, in *The Masters* (1951) of a Cambridge combination room, in *The Corridors of Power* (1964) of the relation between senior civil servants and politicians, in *The New Men* (1954) of the early attempts to develop a nuclear weapon. In form the novels harked back to the Victorian writers. Like Trollope, with well-described characters, scenes firmly set, and a strong plot, he deliberately avoided the lessons of Henry James and even more of James Joyce. The hero, Lewis Eliot, an academic lawyer, was an idealized version of the author himself made more sensitive, given to more suffering, and more respected.

In 1939 Snow joined a group organized by the Royal Society to deploy British scientific manpower; by 1942 he was director of technical personnel at the Ministry of Labour, under Ernest Bevin; and from 1945 until his retirement in 1960 he was a Civil Service commissioner in charge of recruiting scientists to government service. He was also a director of English Electric, a company designing and building nuclear power stations. He was appointed CBE in 1943, knighted in 1957, and became a life peer in 1964, joining (Sir) Harold Wilson's first government as parliamentary secretary of the newly created Ministry of Technology, which was intended to bring the benefit of technological revolution to a backward nation. Both the Ministry and Snow failed, and he left the government in 1966. As a back-bencher Snow became a popular member of the House of Lords, with his ungainly figure and heavy jowled features, frequently seen in its bar and dining-room, exchanging gossip with other heavyweights.

It was this full public life, and his own chequered emotional life till his marriage, that provided the scenes and personalities of his novels. He married, on 15 October 1950, the novelist Pamela Hansford Johnson (died 1981), by whom he had a much-loved son, Philip, who to Snow's joy became a scholar of Eton. She was the daughter of R. Kenneth Johnson and had been married previously to Gordon Stewart, by whom she had a son and a daughter. Snow's novels deal much with the unhappy private and inner lives of his characters, in dissonance with their active and often successful public lives; he was an acute observer both of public and private stress. The books are most gripping when dealing with Snow's own lived experience, they have narrative strength, and are useful documentary sources about life in the Civil Service, politics, and the universities. He rejoiced in the diverse social origins of the British élite. His own ascent from the working class to the peerage was a source of delight to him, and social mobility was a theme of his novels. They lack high art, the characterization is often shallow, and the prose pedestrian, showing little gift for wit, style, or literary craftsmanship. Yet, though he was dismissed like W. Somerset Maugham as a mere story-teller, his novels were widely read, discussed, and enjoyed, and seen as a genuine insight into these important parts of national life. He was a perceptive and generous critic, revealing especially in his weekly article for the *Financial Times* a wide and deep knowledge of European literature, especially of the French and Russian masters, as well as an encyclopaedic knowledge of science, history, and current affairs.

Some of Snow's novels were produced as plays, notably *The Affair* (Strand theatre, 1961–2), and *The Masters* (Savoy and Piccadilly theatres, 1963–4), both adapted by Ronald Millar.

Snow was a generous and affable host, a kind friend, and a supporter of young writers, notably his Leicester friend Harry Hoff (William Cooper), who emulated his career as a scientific administrator and novelist. Snow's generous and broad sympathies led him to see the strengths rather than the weaknesses of people, and similarly of countries like the United States and the Soviet Union, in both of which as well as in Britain, he was honoured with numerous academic awards. He sought to be a sympathetic interpreter of different styles of life, and thus to extend mutual understanding. This was the origin of his Rede lectures at Cambridge in 1959, *The Two Cultures and the Scientific Revolution*, in which his theme was that ignorance by humanists of modern science was as barbaric as ignorance of the arts by scientists. This doctrine endorsed a fashionable view and was part of a feeling, widespread at the time, that Britain's relatively poor economic performance was due to the lack of scientific and technological knowledge in the ruling group. F. R. Leavis attacked the thesis with passion, asserting that his own interpretation of culture, based upon that of T. S. Eliot, as a knowledge of what great artists said of life, was in direct conflict with Snow's more pedestrian view of culture as knowledge. This controversy to some degree proved Snow's point, since he held that the imaginative insights formerly the monopoly of artists and religious thinkers had now become the prerogative of those who (like Newton) voyaged through strange seas of thought alone.

It was this enthusiasm for science, its intellectual excitement and its potentiality for good which, like H. G. Wells, he communicated. It also led him into further controversy such as that aroused by *Science and Government* (1961) and its *Postscript* (1962), covering his Godkin lectures at Harvard in 1960, in which he denounced as highly dangerous the influence in scientific matters during the 1939–45 war exercised by F. A. Lindemann (Viscount Cherwell) over (Sir) Winston Churchill, using as his argument the disagreements between the 'Prof' and Sir Henry Tizard on the development of radar and the effectiveness of the strategic bombing of German towns. Snow's sympathies were clearly with Tizard.

His later years, again like Wells, showed disillusion with the government's attempts to sponsor the technological revolution, and disappointment at the senseless violence abroad and in the streets of London. He always showed in his writing an inner pessimism of despair and death, faced with stoic determination by the men in his novels who were professionally successful.

Snow died in London 1 July 1980.

[*The Times*, 2 July 1980; R. Greacen (ed.), *The World of Snow*, 1962; S. Weintraub (ed.), *C. P. Snow—a Spectrum: Science, Criticism, Fiction*, 1963; David Shusterman, *C. P. Snow*, 1975; William Cooper, *C. P. Snow*, 1959; personal knowledge.]

JOHN VAIZEY

published 1986

SNOWDEN Philip

(1864–1937)

Viscount Snowden

Statesman, was born in a two-roomed cottage in the hamlet of Ickornshaw, Cowling, near Keighley, in the West Riding of Yorkshire, 18 July 1864, the only son and the youngest of the three children of John Snowden, of Cowling, by his wife, Martha, daughter of Peter Nelson, also of Cowling. His father was a weaver in a mill, who had begun his working life on a handloom at home and still used it to make pieces for his family. Both parents had abilities above their station in life; and as showing the quality of the local Yorkshire stock it may be noted that the row of thirty to forty moorland cottages known as Middleton, which included Snowden's birthplace, included also those of two other labour members who sat with him at different times in parliament. The atmosphere was strongly radical and Wesleyan Methodist; and the boy imbibed early a familiarity with the Bible and an admiration for Gladstone, neither of which ever left him. Educated at a very elementary local school which the Act of 1870 turned into a board school, he escaped the weaving-mill by becoming a pupil-teacher; but, after three years this career was cut short by his parents' migration across the Lancashire border to Nelson, following the failure of the firm which employed them. The boy, then fifteen, became a clerk in an insurance office, where he remained for seven years. At twenty-two he passed a civil service examination, and was appointed a junior exciseman, serving subsequently at Liverpool, in the Orkneys, at Aberdeen, and at Plymouth.

It was not until 1891, when he was twenty-seven, that the event occurred which changed Snowden's life. Until then he had been physically active and powerful above the average; but a small cycling accident led to acute inflammation of the spinal cord and rendered him a chronic cripple. After two years he was invalided out of the civil service. During convalescence he studied socialism with a view to reading a paper on it at the local liberal club, and in the process he became a socialist. This was not very long after the birth of the independent labour party (at Bradford in January 1893); and in 1894 Snowden addressed a meeting for the party's Keighley branch. He scored a great hit, and for the following ten years (1895–1905) settled down to the career of an independent labour party propagandist. Before long his reputation became national, and in a particular kind of idealistic, semi-religious eloquence he had no superior. As a 'draw' at meetings where admission was charged for, he was second to Keir Hardie alone. About 1899 he settled at Keighley in order to serve on the town council and the school board, and to act as editor (for 8s. a week) of a local socialist paper. For the years 1903–1906 he was national chairman of the independent labour party. But it was a grinding struggle. His impaired physique had come near breaking-point, when in 1905 he married Ethel, daughter of Richard Annakin, of Harrogate, a lady who not only cared for him devotedly, but had sufficient means to enable him to work at less strain.

Meantime, in the 'khaki' general election of 1900, Snowden had made at Blackburn his first bid for parliament. With the tide running strongly for the conservatives he was defeated, but achieved great personal popularity and polled over 7,000 votes. He stood as an independent labour party candidate under the auspices of the labour representation committee, a body which he had helped to found at the famous Memorial Hall conference in London earlier in the year, and which in 1906 changed its name to the labour party. In 1902 he unsuccessfully fought a by-election at

Wakefield; but in 1906, with the tide in his favour, he was elected for Blackburn and remained one of its two members until 1918. No less than fifty-two other labour members were elected with him, of whom twenty-eight were, like him, returned under the labour representation committee to sit as an independent party.

Snowden in the House of Commons was at first handicapped by his physical infirmity, which precluded his jumping up to catch the Speaker's eye. But when once arrangements had been made to get round this, he proved himself a debater of the first rank. His style in the House differed from his platform style, in that the latter had been warming and idealistic and had helped materially to make British socialism a gospel of love, not hate; whereas in parliament he became much harder and terser, and developed along with remorseless logic a very formidable gift of sarcasm. Two subjects he especially made his own—the drink question and national finance. His authority on the latter became much enhanced in 1909, when Lloyd George in framing his famous budget appeared to have gone to Snowden for some of its ideas. When war came in 1914 Snowden happened to be out of the country; but on his return he worked hard to rally that minority in the labour movement which opposed the war. He succeeded in especially identifying with it the independent labour party, of which he once more became chairman for three years (1917–1920); and he was a constant champion of conscientious objectors. He paid for these unpopular courses by losing his seat at Blackburn in 1918.

For four years Snowden was out of parliament, but at the general election of 1922 he was returned for the Colne Valley division of his native county. When in January 1924 Ramsay MacDonald formed the first labour government, Snowden inevitably became chancellor of the Exchequer in it, and was sworn of the Privy Council. His budget was free trade and Gladstonian rather than specifically socialist. He abolished the protective 'McKenna duties', the corporation profits tax, and the inhabited house duty, besides lowering various taxes on commodities. He also lowered the taxes on popular entertainments, which he regarded as valuable rivals to the public-house. From November 1924 to June 1929 he and his party were out of office, although Snowden retained the Colne Valley seat. During this period occurred the General Strike of 1926. Snowden had no sympathy with it whatever, but in 1927 he made one of his most effective speeches against the government's trade union bill arising out of it. In the same year he quitted the independent labour party, which he regarded as having changed over from evolutionary to revolutionary socialism. When Mac-Donald formed his second Cabinet in 1929, Snowden almost automatically resumed his place at the Exchequer, such was his prestige in that field. His first task was to attend at The Hague an international conference upon the

Young Plan. Taking the view that it fleeced Great Britain for the benefit of her continental allies, he demanded and eventually obtained large changes in it. The preponderance of expert opinion has since been that his view was wrong and the changes unfortunate; but the John Bullish vigour with which he urged and carried them won the acclaim of his fellow countrymen, even in quarters hitherto hostile. His return was that of a conquering hero, and in due course he received the freedom of the City of London.

But the rest of Snowden's period as chancellor was darkened by the great depression, which began to reach Europe from the United States of America towards the end of 1929. In his 1930 budget he confronted an estimated deficit of £42,264,000. He met it chiefly by raising the income-tax from 4s. to 4s. 6d. in the £ and increasing the surtax to yield £12½ millions extra; while at the same time he spent £5 millions on regraduating the income-tax, so that about three-quarters of those paying it paid no more than before. Thus almost the whole of the new burdens were borne by incomes of over £1,000 a year. But the fall in trade and unemployment continued to grow; and in a debate on 11 February 1931 Snowden took parliament into his confidence, disclosing the extreme gravity of the country's situation and appealing to the parties for a common effort to overcome its difficulties. His appeal caused a great sensation, and was well received all over the House, except by the left wing of his own party. A three-party committee of seven was set up, with Sir George (later Lord) May as chairman, to review expenditure and explore possible economies. Three weeks later Snowden had to undergo a serious internal operation, which kept him away from the House for seven weeks. But it was completely successful, and he presented his budget on 27 April.

This time Snowden estimated a deficit of £37,366,000. But as the numbers of the unemployed had now grown to 2,600,000, he did not wish to impose new taxes, nor could he well propose economies pending the Report of the May Committee. He therefore raised the money by stopgap devices—mainly by taking £20 millions from the Exchange Account. The controversial side of the budget lay elsewhere. Snowden included in it certain land tax clauses, providing for a valuation with a view to an eventual tax on land values. Here he had trouble with the liberals, who if they voted with the conservatives could oust the government; but at last he got his clauses through. Meanwhile the economic crisis grew rapidly worse; foreigners with sterling balances tended to withdraw them, and the country's stock of gold fell. The run was stimulated by the publication on 1 August of the May Committee's Report, which estimated the probable deficit by the following April at £120 millions, and advised an immediate saving of £96 millions—over £80 millions out of social services. On 12

August the Economy Committee of the Cabinet met and the opposition leaders were summoned to London; and for the ensuing twelve days a many-sided negotiation went on, Snowden's version of which is given at length in his *Autobiography*. The upshot was the resignation of the labour ministry and the formation by MacDonald on 24 August of a new three-party 'national' ministry in which three other members of the old Cabinet—Snowden, J. H. Thomas, and Lord Sankey—retained their places. Snowden took part without enthusiasm, but from a strong sense of duty. He was assured that the ministry was not to be a coalition, but would deal with the immediate crisis only.

Snowden's own main contribution was a new budget, introduced by him on 10 September 1931. He estimated that the deficit on the current financial year would be £74,679,000, and the deficit on the following one would (on the same basis) reach £170 millions. A drastic scheme balanced both the figures—about half by cuts and half by new taxation. The speech in which he asked for and obtained these sacrifices was worthy of the occasion, and in it he perhaps touched his highest level. Incidentally the finance bill included clauses to facilitate the conversion of the £2,000 millions of 5 per cent war loan; and it was by using these that in 1932 Neville Chamberlain was able to convert the loan. But Snowden's troubles were not over, and on 21 September he had to suspend the gold standard, the speech in which he did so being again one of his best. There followed in October the general election. Snowden did not stand in it; after his severe illness in the spring he had decided not to; instead, he went to the House of Lords, being in November created Viscount Snowden, of Ickornshaw. But by two election letters and a broadcast address he made perhaps a larger contribution than anyone else to the government's victory at the polls.

In the reconstituted ministry Snowden became lord privy seal, and held that position until 28 September 1932. But a division soon developed in the Cabinet between protectionists and free traders, Snowden being particularly strong for free trade. An attempt was made to preserve unity by the famous 'agreement to differ', announced on 22 January 1932; but when in August the Ottawa Economic Conference was held and resulted in a scheme of preferential tariffs, the free traders felt their position to be impossible. The liberal party was split between Simonites and Samuelites, and the latter resigned with Snowden. It was the virtual end of his career in politics. He completed a valuable two-volume autobiography, which appeared in 1934, when he was seventy; and three years later he died at Tilford, Surrey, 15 May 1937. He had no children. He received the honorary degree of LL.D from the universities of Leeds (1927), Bristol (1929), and Manchester (1930).

Snowden's stature was curtailed by his infirmity, but he was very broad-shouldered, and gave an impression of his former strength. He was noticeably blond, with pale hair, a pale skin, and light-blue 'steely' eyes. Perhaps his most marked feature was his thin-lipped mouth, tightly pursed to utter his terse, hard phrases. Although a man of fundamental generosity and capable of great charm, he was not always over-easy to get on with; in the party it used to be said that he was not a good committee-man. In other respects he was very 'Yorkshire', with the uprightness, down-rightness, and impatience of sloth or crookedness which that conveys. He was a clear rather than a profound thinker, but his party owed much to him for the sure instinct with which he presented socialism in an English dress, rejecting the unassimilable elements of continental doctrine. No one in the movement could have been more completely working-class in origin; but he differed from most of his colleagues in not having graduated in the trade-union machine, and was never inclined, as some of them were, to put its claims above those of the democratic parliamentary state.

A bust of Snowden was made by the Hungarian sculptor Aloyse Ströbl, of which two castings exist: one is at the Treasury, the other at Leeds University library. A massive cairn of rough granite marks the spot on the wild moorland above Ickornshaw where in 1937 Snowden's ashes were scattered to the wind.

[Lord Snowden, *An Autobiography*, 2 vols., 1934; *The Times*, 17 May 1937; private information; personal knowledge.]

R. C. K. ENSOR

published 1949

SOAMES (Arthur) Christopher (John)

(1920–1987)

Baron Soames

Politician, was born 12 October 1920 in Penn, Buckinghamshire, the only son and youngest of three children of Captain Arthur Granville Soames, OBE, of the Coldstream Guards and Ashwell Manor, Penn, and his wife, Hope Mary Woodbyne, daughter of Charles Woodbyne Parish. He was educated at Eton and the Royal Military College at Sandhurst and commissioned in 1939 as a second lieutenant in the Coldstream Guards. He served in the Middle East, Italy, and France during the war, winning the croix de guerre (1942) while on attachment to the Free French brigade in the Western Desert, where his right leg was shattered by a mine explosion. In 1946 he was appointed assistant military attaché at the British embassy in Paris. In the following year he married Mary, youngest daughter of (Sir) Winston Leonard Spencer-Churchill, former prime minister.

In 1950 he entered Parliament as the Conservative member for Bedford. During Churchill's second premiership (1952–5), Soames acted as his parliamentary private secretary. He did much to keep the government going, masking the seriousness of his father-in-law's illness, when Churchill suffered a stroke in 1953. He went through the ranks of junior ministerial office before becoming secretary of state for war in 1958 (when he was sworn of the Privy Council), and serving in the cabinet in 1960–4 as minister of agriculture.

Having lost his seat in the 1966 election, he was an inspired choice by the government led by Harold Wilson (later Baron Wilson of Rievaulx) as British ambassador to France (1968–72). Soames took up his post at a difficult time, with President Charles de Gaulle continuing to obstruct British accession to the European Community. His term in Paris began inauspiciously with the leaking by the Foreign Office of the contents of a private conversation between him and de Gaulle (*l'affaire Soames*). A year later, de Gaulle was gone and Soames was able to establish a much warmer relationship with his successor, Georges Pompidou. This was the crucial period leading to the successful completion of negotiations for Britain's entry into the EC and Soames, himself a convinced European, played a major part in persuading the French government no longer to impede the negotiations. His excellent colloquial French, splendid hospitality, and ebullient personality endeared him to the Parisians.

Immediately following British entry into the EC, Soames became the first British vice-president of the European Commission and commissioner for external affairs, from 1973 to January 1977. He was a most effective commissioner. He played a major role in international trade negotiations and in establishing British influence in Brussels.

After a brief return to private life, Soames was invited to join Margaret (later Baroness) Thatcher's government in 1979 as lord president of the Council and leader of the House of Lords. Later that year he was given his most difficult task, being appointed governor of Southern Rhodesia to oversee the cease-fire and elections leading to the independence of Zimbabwe. When he set off from London the cease-fire had still not been agreed, much less brought into effect, and the prospects for the success of his mission were generally discounted by the press. Following the successful conclusion of the Lancaster House negotiations, a cease-fire was implemented under the supervision of the largely British Commonwealth monitoring force. Soames had the greatest difficulty with the Rhodesian military commanders on the one hand and sections of the Patriotic Front on the other throughout the period leading up to the elections, which were held in February 1980. He had to exercise responsibility with no more real power than he could win by bargaining with the contending parties. He set out to establish a personal relationship with the black political leaders, assuring Robert Mugabe that, if he won the elections, Soames would take the lead in helping the new government establish itself in a still uncertain, tense, and dangerous situation. When Mugabe did win he invited Soames to continue to serve as governor. In the ensuing period major steps were taken towards bringing together and forming into a single military command elements of the Rhodesian forces and those of the Patriotic Front, who themselves were split into two warring factions. Soames left Rhodesia having helped to bring an end to the war and to launch Zimbabwe as an independent nation, amidst near-universal plaudits.

On his return to Britain he had to deal with matters far less congenial to him, including a Civil Service strike. He found himself out of sympathy with the new economic strategy being pursued by Mrs Thatcher and her style of government. In 1981 he was dropped from the government. He remained thereafter very active in business, holding a number of important directorships until his death, including those of N. M. Rothschild's and the National Westminster Bank, and the chairmanship of ICL (UK).

Soames was a figure very much larger than life. His conversation could usually be heard in the next room. His convivial but forthright personality inspired strong loyalties among his friends and some resistance on the part of more sensitive souls. His hospitality and enjoyment of life were legendary. As ambassador in Paris, commissioner in Brussels, and governor of Rhodesia, he put up performances which could scarcely have been matched by anyone else. His success in all these capacities owed much to his wife, (Dame) Mary. They had three sons, one of whom, Nicholas, also became a Conservative MP and minister, and two daughters.

The academic distinctions Soames received included honorary doctorates from Oxford (1981) and St Andrews (1974). He was awarded the Robert Schuman prize in 1976. He was appointed CBE (1955) and GCMG and GCVO (1972), created a life baron in 1978, and appointed CH in 1980. He also was awarded, on his departure from Paris, the cross of grand officer of the Legion of Honour. He died from cancer 16 September 1987, at his home in Odiham, Hampshire.

[Private information; personal knowledge.]

ROBIN RENWICK

published 1996

(1889–1960)

Baron Somervell of Harrow

Politician and judge, was born at Harrow 24 August 1889, the second son of Robert Somervell, master and bursar (1888–1919) of Harrow School, and his wife, Octavia Paulina, daughter of the Rev. John Churchill. He went himself to Harrow, going up to Oxford in 1907 with a demyship at Magdalen. He obtained first class honours in chemistry (1911), a choice of subject surprising in light of his subsequent career, but typical of his exceptional mental energy and versatility. In 1912 he was elected a fellow of All Souls, an event which, like his first election to Parliament, he himself regarded as particularly memorable, since he was the first man who, having taken a degree in chemistry, was later elected to an All Souls fellowship. He joined the Inner Temple but his projected career was interrupted by the outbreak of war in which he served in India (1914–17) and Mesopotamia (1917–19), with the 1/9 Middlesex Regiment and as staff captain with the 53rd Infantry brigade; he was appointed O.B.E. in 1919.

Somervell had been called to the bar *in absentia* in 1916 and began practice in the chambers of W. A. (later Earl) Jowitt whose pupil he had been. Somervell's mental agility and temperament did not attract him to the ordinary run-of-the-mill common law practice; the art of cross-examination did not appeal to him, seeming indeed to his naturally kind heart apt to be unfair. His arguments were expressed briefly and lucidly, without any emotional or histrionic quality. He applied himself to the mentally exacting problems created by the commercial clauses of the Treaty of Versailles, gaining a considerable practice before the mixed arbitral tribunal established under the treaty.

He took silk in 1929 and soon began his political career. Politics had a special fascination for him since boyhood and his choice of profession was largely governed by his belief that the bar would provide a ready introduction to politics. At Oxford his friendship with Cyril, later Lord, Asquith of Bishopstone, had much inclined him to the Liberals, but the serious decline of that party, his disapproval of the performance of the Labour Party, and above all his admiration for Stanley Baldwin, whom he particularly respected for his freedom from class bitterness, self-esteem, or ambition, converted Somervell to the Conservative cause. He was defeated at Crewe in 1929 but was successful in 1931 and again, by a narrow majority, in 1935 when he characteristically refused a safer seat, preferring to remain where he had made and valued many local contacts.

To Somervell the House of Commons was both a goal and a home. In his view it was a truly democratic institution in which the ministers were in a real sense subject to the influence of the elected representatives of the nation. He was an assiduous attender, particularly in committees, and he genuinely enjoyed the discussions on public affairs. 'Having got a seat he sat in it.' His maiden speech was on the Statute of Westminster bill, when he found himself (as often, before 1940) in a measure of disagreement with (Sir) Winston Churchill.

In 1932 Somervell appeared as one of the leading counsel for the Bank of Portugal in the important case of *Waterlow & Sons* v. *Banco de Portugal* in the House of Lords. In the autumn of 1933 he succeeded Sir Boyd (later Lord) Merriman as solicitor-general and was knighted accordingly. Sir Thomas Inskip, later Viscount Caldecote, was attorney-general. As attorney-general himself from 1936 he had under him first his old friend Sir Terence O'Connor who had greatly influenced and helped him early in his political career; then Jowitt; and later Sir David Maxwell Fyfe, afterwards the Earl of Kilmuir. Somervell was sworn of the Privy Council in 1938.

The functions of a law officer *vis-à-vis* the heads of the various Ministries, a subject on which he addressed the Holdsworth Club in the university of Birmingham in 1946, gave exceptional scope to Somervell's qualities. His emphatic view was that, as a law officer, he should always be available to informal approach by the legal advisers of the various Ministries, a view which bore remarkable fruit during the war of 1939–45. Never afraid of quick decision, he was confident in his judgement which was undoubtedly sound and based on a robust common sense. He wished especially to avoid having to say 'if only you had told me of this before'. Nor was he a man ever to worry over hypothetical situations.

The exceptionally long period of his law officership included problems such as the budget leakage in 1936, the abdication of King Edward VIII, and the form of the Oath appropriate to the coronation of King George VI, a matter involving him in successful negotiations with the representatives of the Commonwealth countries. He also played an important part in debate on such measures as the incitement to disaffection bill and the government of India bill. He strongly supported the line taken by Neville Chamberlain at Munich. During the war his considerable energies were greatly called upon in connection with the very numerous statutory instruments which the exigencies of war demanded, with such legislation as the War Damage Act, and with the vexed problem of war crimes. In respect of all these exacting duties his lucidity, friendliness, and above all his quickness of mind gained him the respect of members of all parties. He applied himself to his duties, in back-bencher opinion, 'without publicity and with great ability and diligence'.

Somervell frequently began his day at the Law Courts at 8.30 a.m. and remained in the House until late risings, finding none the less time to prepare fully for his appearance in a complicated case next day. His remarkable energy was assisted by his capacity for decision without worry. But his intellectual capacities were not even exhausted by his pressing duties as a member of the bar, as a law officer, or later as a judge. He was an insatiable reader and found time to study diverse and complex subjects, upon which he would summarize his conclusions in papers prepared not for publication but for his own clarification, such as 'Christian Art 12th–15th Centuries', 'The Background to the New Testament', and 'Relativity'.

From 1940 to 1946 Somervell was recorder of Kingston upon Thames. His twelve years as a law officer ended with his appointment as home secretary in the caretaker Government of 1945. The defeat of the Conservative Party put an end to his political career but in 1946 he was appointed, on the recommendation of Jowitt, by now lord chancellor, a lord justice of appeal, a position which he held until 1954; for most of this time he presided over one of the divisions of the Court of Appeal. After the exertions of his ministerial work he felt judicial life to be relatively unexacting since he was able to reach clear conclusions rapidly and to deal speedily with the cases which came before his court. Frequently he would shorten the argument of counsel, not by putting questions critical of their arguments, but rather by summarizing them and then asking: 'That is your case, is it not?' or 'Do you see what I mean?' If Somervell's judgements were not always framed in careful literary style and were, in his own words, inclined to be slapdash, they were notable for lucidity and absence of prolixity. It was his strong view that our law suffered from too much verbal inflation, and of one of his colleagues he observed that 'he would never use one word when ten would do'. As in his political career, he earned the affection of his colleagues both in the court and at the bar.

In 1933 Somervell married Laelia Helen, daughter of Sir Archibald Buchan-Hepburn. They had no children. If 1933—the year of his marriage and his appointment as solicitor-general—had been a triumphant year for Somervell, 1945 was, by contrast, a bleak one. In that year the death of his wife after a long illness ended a perfect partnership and about the same time the defeat of the Conservative Party ended his career in politics which had been the principal focus of his mind and energies. Somervell tried to maintain as his home the Old Rectory at Ewelme in Oxfordshire which he had bought shortly after his marriage (and where he was buried) but in 1955 he felt compelled to abandon it. Thereafter he lived in chambers in the Inner Temple, paying frequent visits to All Souls. In 1953 he suffered a slight thrombosis. From this he recovered but in 1954 he assumed the less arduous work of a lord of appeal in ordinary, with a life peerage; he later became afflicted with a cancer which caused his judicial retirement in 1960 and his death in London 18 November of the same year. Meanwhile he had served in 1957 as treasurer of his Inn and in 1959 was made an honorary D.C.L. of Oxford; he had been elected an honorary fellow of Magdalen in 1946 and received an honorary LL.D. from St. Andrews in 1947. He had also been a governor of Harrow from 1944 to 1953 and for the last six years a most energetic and influential chairman of the governors.

Apart from reading Somervell derived great pleasure from music, especially the gramophone records of chamber music by the classical masters. He was for many years on the governing body of the Royal College of Music. He was also chairman of the reviewing committee on the export of works of art and from 1944–9 a trustee of the Tate Gallery. His pleasures throughout his life had never been the playing of games although at one time he was an enthusiastic if not greatly skilled horseman. For him the greatest enjoyment, whether alone or in company, lay in travel and the open countryside and its wild bird and animal life. He bore his last illness with extraordinary cheerfulness and courage, spending more and more of his time at All Souls, his love of which was demonstrated by his gift of the iron gate in the north-west corner of the Great Quadrangle which he did not live to see in place.

[Private information; personal knowledge.]

EVERSHED

published 1971

STRACHEY (Evelyn) John (St. Loe)

(1901–1963)

Politician and writer, was born at Newlands Corner, Merrow, near Guildford, 21 October 1901, the younger son and youngest of three children of John St. Loe Strachey, for many years editor of the *Spectator*. After the death of Lord Strachie in 1936 Strachey became heir presumptive to the baronetcy created for Sir Henry Strachey, secretary to Clive of India. His mother, Henrietta Mary Amy Simpson, was a granddaughter of the Victorian economist Nassau Senior. His sister married the architect (Sir) Clough Williams-Ellis.

Strachey was educated at Eton and Magdalen College, Oxford, which he left after two years, in 1922, without a degree; his parents feared the consequences of further studies on his health following peritonitis. His elder brother had died of pneumonia in his first year at Balliol. But John Strachey had already become known as an undergraduate journalist, as editor, with Robert (later Lord) Boothby, a lifelong friend, of the Conservative journal, the *Oxford Fortnightly Review*; he was also prominent in the Canning Club; wrote poems; and both acted in, and wrote plays for, undergraduate societies. On leaving Oxford he began to work on his father's *Spectator*, writing leading articles and reviews.

In 1923 Strachey joined the Labour Party, under the influence of Sidney and Beatrice Webb, and stood for Parliament unsuccessfully in 1924, for the Aston division of Birmingham, a nomination which he owed to the influence among Birmingham socialists of (Sir) Oswald Mosley, the ex-Conservative member who was candidate for Ladywood. Although Strachey remained a contributor to, and shareholder of, the *Spectator*, he now abandoned his expectation of becoming its editor when his father died, and became an active socialist writer and pamphleteer. With Mosley, he proposed new plans for the resolution of the nation's economic problems in *Revolution by Reason* (1925), and became editor of both the *Socialist Review* and the *Miner*. In 1929 he was returned for Aston and became parliamentary private secretary to Mosley, who had become chancellor of the Duchy of Lancaster in the new Labour Government. He supported Mosley in his campaigns on unemployment in 1930, and followed him into the New Party founded in 1931. For a time he was Mosley's closest collaborator, but broke away after six months, when it seemed that the New Party was turning against Russia, which Strachey had already twice visited.

On leaving Mosley, Strachey asserted himself as an independent member of Parliament, but lost his seat in the general election of 1931. The depression in Britain was by now at its worst, and Strachey found himself drawn towards the Communist Party. He wrote for the Communist cause a succession of influential books: notably *The Coming Struggle for Power* (1932) and *The Nature of Capitalist Crisis* (1935). Strachey was never a member of the Communist Party, although his second wife was, and he would have liked to have been; but the party leaders considered him not altogether dependable and, in any case, so long as he supported the cause, more useful outside than within. Strachey's was, in fact, the most powerful intellectual voice in the Communist movement in this country throughout most of the thirties, and, as such, influenced the Left Book Club, founded by (Sir) Victor Gollancz in 1936 with Strachey's help, which became more of a movement than a book club. Strachey wrote regularly in the club's monthly *Left News*, spoke at its many rallies throughout the country, and provided the club's choice for November 1936 (*The Theory and Practice of Socialism*) and for March 1938, when, in *What Are We to Do?*, he argued for a Popular Front. In the same year his pamphlet *Why You Should Be a Socialist* sold over 300,000 copies.

Although to Strachey socialism still meant Communism, he was by now beginning to move away from Communist orthodoxy. The Nazi-Soviet pact of 1939 in the end disillusioned him about Soviet motives. Other reasons for his break with Communism were: his admiration for J. M. (later Lord) Keynes and for Roosevelt, both of whom, the one in theory, the other in practice, seemed to suggest a middle way in politics; and his interest in and personal experience of psychoanalysis. His book, *A Programme for Progress* (the Book Club choice for January 1940), seemed too Keynesian and angered orthodox Communists even before Strachey finally decided to break with the party after the German invasion of Norway and Denmark in the spring. He did so in a letter published in the *New Statesman* (27 April 1940).

Left without a political base, Strachey joined the Royal Air Force and served some time as adjutant with a fighter squadron, then as public relations officer with a bomber group. He next moved to the Air Ministry, where he eventually joined the directorate of bomber operations and became widely known to the country for his air commentaries after the BBC 9 o'clock news. This fame helped him back into Parliament as a member for Dundee in 1945 and to the post of under-secretary of state for air in Attlee's administration where he dealt skilfully with demobilization and other Service problems. Marked out for promotion, he became minister of food in May 1946.

This appointment was the most critical in Strachey's life. In many ways he was well equipped: he had made himself an able economist; he liked, and understood the meaning of, power; he knew how to use civil servants to their best advantage; he had a gift for political simplification and explanation. All these qualities were necessary, since the Ministry of Food was a politically sensitive department at a time when shortages and rationing continued and, indeed, increased (notably with the introduction of bread rationing) despite the end of the war. Strachey established a temporary mastery over the House of Commons in 1946, but he was bitterly and often unfairly attacked by the Conservative press, particularly the Beaverbrook papers. By 1949 his reputation had been severely damaged by the failure of a plan to increase supplies of natural oil by growing ground-nuts on a large scale in Tanganyika. This scheme originated with the United Africa Company but was thought too large for private exploitation. The Cabinet asked the Ministry of Food to organize the scheme. After several years and over £30 millions had been invested, it was plain that ground-nuts could not be commercially or satisfactorily grown. The affair, exploited to the full by the press, hurt Strachey's political prospects, although he can be blamed only for an initial excess of zeal for the scheme, for failure to start with a 'pilot' plan, and for an excessive reliance on those whom he had named to carry out the scheme on the spot: in particular, his old friend (Sir) Leslie Plummer.

After the general election of 1950, Strachey, returned for West Dundee, became secretary of state for war, still without a seat in the Cabinet. The arrest of Dr Fuchs, the atomic spy, had led to doubts about security, and immediately upon Strachey's appointment the *Evening Standard* (2 March 1950) came out with headlines 'Fuchs and Strachey. A great new crisis. War minister has never disavowed Communism.' Strachey was advised not to sue on the grounds that the publicity would do more harm than good, although he wanted to and would certainly have been justified. Although less happy in his new post than at the Ministry of Food, and not in favour of the health service charges which brought the resignation of Aneurin Bevan, Strachey greatly admired Attlee's leadership, and remained in the Government until it was defeated in 1951. Thereafter, as shadow minister of war, he set himself to master the complexities of nuclear strategy.

In the years in opposition, Strachey attempted to steer a middle course between Gaitskellites and Bevanites in the Labour movement and accordingly incurred the obloquy of both. He voted for Hugh Gaitskell as successor to Attlee in 1955 and, in the late fifties, drew closer to the official leadership of the party. After Gaitskell died in 1963 Strachey worked for the succession of George Brown (later Lord George-Brown). Nevertheless, (Sir) Harold Wilson named him shadow Commonwealth secretary, and would have included him in his Cabinet in the following year had not Strachey died, in London, following a spinal operation, 15 July 1963.

During the fifties Strachey's main work, in his own view at least, was to attempt a new theoretical statement of his political position in a series of books: *Contemporary Capitalism* (1956), *The End of Empire* (1959), and *On the Prevention of War* (1962). In these the ex-Marxist of the thirties attempted to absorb Keynes, to analyse the real effect of empire on European economies, and to introduce the new theoretical American strategic thinking to a British audience. In 1962 he published a brilliant collection of essays, *The Strangled Cry*, mostly about the intellectual and psychological effect of Communism. In both personal and political life Strachey often seemed indecisive and perhaps evasive. He was, however, a man of great intellectual integrity, charm, and wit to his family and those who knew him well. He remained a man of culture while a politician. Physically, he was tall, somewhat ungainly, with a swarthy countenance relieved by friendly brown eyes. He remained an enthusiastic games player until late in life. As a writer, he was an extremely able expositor of complicated general ideas, whether those of Marx, Keynes, J. K. Galbraith or even Hermann Kahn.

He influenced the Labour movement towards Marxism in the thirties; away from it in the forties; and towards a realistic foreign and defence policy in the sixties.

Strachey was twice married: in 1929 to Esther (died 1962), only daughter of Patrick Francis Murphy, a wealthy department store owner of New York, who obtained a divorce in 1933; in that year Strachey married Celia, daughter of an Anglican clergyman, the Revd Arthur Hume Simpson; they had a son and a daughter.

The only known portrait is one by Celia Strachey which remained in her possession.

[Hugh Thomas, *John Strachey*, 1973; private information; personal knowledge.]

HUGH THOMAS

published 1981

TREVELYAN Humphrey

(1905–1985)

Baron Trevelyan

Diplomat, was born at Hindhead, Surrey, 27 November 1905, the younger son and fifth of six children of the Revd George Philip Trevelyan, rector of Carshalton, Surrey, and later vicar of St Stephen's, Bournemouth, and his wife, Monica Evelyn Juliet, daughter of the Revd Sidney Phillips, vicar of Kidderminster, and later honorary canon of Worcester. A second cousin of the historian George Macaulay Trevelyan and of Sir Charles P. Trevelyan, education minister in Ramsay MacDonald's two Labour administrations, he was educated at Lancing and Jesus College, Cambridge. He obtained a second class in part i (1926) and a first in part ii (1927) of the classical tripos. In 1929 he joined the Indian Civil Service.

From this early age Trevelyan showed that relentless determination to get to the core of the problems facing him, which was to mark his career in the public service and his work in the worlds of commerce and the arts after his retirement. Anxious to plumb the thought processes of Indian nationalism, when a junior district officer in the Madras governorate, he made a personal friend of the local Congress Party representative with whom he used to row at weekends. But such activities were frowned on as too eccentric by the local British community and, after enduring three years of criticism from that quarter, he secured a transfer to the Indian

Political Service in 1932 and the more congenial and rewarding work of liaison between New Delhi and the Indian states. There he remained for the next fifteen years, rising to the rank of political agent in the Indian states and joint secretary to the external affairs department of the government of India, for whom he went to Washington in 1944 to prepare the way for the first Indian embassy in the USA. Then, when independence came in 1947, he transferred to the Foreign Service.

From 1948 to 1950 Trevelyan served as counsellor of embassy in Baghdad and from 1951 to 1953 as economic adviser to the UK high commissioner in Germany. In 1953 he was appointed chargé d'affaires in Peking, Britain's first representative to the newly established communist government in China. For the first year the Chinese kept him very much at arm's length, but Trevelyan's tenacity, coupled with the new understanding with China that followed the 1954 Geneva conference, eventually enabled him to enjoy a reasonably businesslike relationship with Zhou Enlai.

In 1955 he became ambassador in Cairo until the breach of diplomatic relations fourteen months later following the Anglo-French attempt to seize the Suez canal by force. Although he never revealed his private abhorrence of his government's action, it was a tribute to the respect in which he was held by the Egyptians that both President Nasser and his foreign minister accepted that he was in no way privy to the conspiracy between Britain, France, and Israel.

After a brief interlude working with Dag Hammarskjöld as under-secretary general at the United Nations—a period he hated owing to Hammarskjöld's inability to delegate work—Trevelyan was sent in 1958 as ambassador to Iraq. Here the unpredictability of the new revolutionary leader, General Kassim, was to tax his patience and diplomatic skills to the utmost. Then in 1962, after a brief spell in the Foreign Office, he became ambassador in Moscow. This was at the end of the Cuban missile crisis and Trevelyan was to witness two years later how this foolish effort of brinkmanship helped to bring about the downfall of the Russian leader, Nikita Khrushchev.

On retirement from the Diplomatic Service in 1965 Trevelyan was offered the post of permanent under-secretary at the Foreign Office, but this he declined, not wishing to block the promotion of someone younger than himself. However he did agree, in 1967, to undertake, as high commissioner in Aden, the thankless but essential task of supervising Britain's withdrawal in the approach to independence.

Retirement from diplomacy did not permit Trevelyan to vegetate. In 1965 he had become president of the Council of Foreign Bondholders. The year 1969 saw him as a trustee of the British Museum and in the following year he became, in succession to Lord Eccles, chairman of the trustees and prime mover in staging at the Museum the exhibition of the Tutankhamun treasures. He was also a director of BP, GEC, and the British Bank of the Middle East. Furthermore, he wrote several memoirs of China, India, Russia, and the Middle East, among them *The India We Left* (1972) and *The Middle East in Revolution* (1970), which will always stand as models of brevity, lucidity, and illumination.

Trevelyan was without doubt the outstanding British diplomat of his time, an ambassador who enjoyed the trust of the governments to which he was accredited no less than his own. Whatever their differences, Jawaharlal Nehru, Zhou Enlai, Nasser, Kassim, and Khrushchev held him in the highest esteem as a man of total honour and formidable intellect. Although from a most distinguished clan, he outshone them in his achievements, which found their due reward in the Order of the Garter and a peerage, a distinction unique in modern times for one of his profession.

Possessed of a phenomenal physical and mental energy, he enthused and invigorated those who served with him, especially young people, putting them on their mettle and commanding authority without pomposity by the sheer pre-eminence of his razor-sharp mind. His recipe for a happy post was 'Not too civilized, too much work, bad climate, a spice of danger.' In his company there was never a dull or an idle moment, but rather always an opportunity to learn from his extraordinary knowledge of politics, art, culture, and music, whether of China, India, or the world of Islam. He was a keen pianist.

He was appointed OBE (1941), CIE (1947), CMG (1951), KCMG (1955), and GCMG (1965). He was made a life baron in 1968 and appointed KG in 1974. He was an honorary fellow of Jesus College and had honorary degrees from Cambridge (LLD, 1970), Durham (DCL, 1973), and Leeds (D.Litt., 1975).

In 1937 he married Violet Margaret ('Peggy'), daughter of General Sir William Henry Bartholomew, CMG, DSO, and later GCB, chief of the general staff in India. They had two daughters. Trevelyan died 8 February 1985 at home in Duchess of Bedford House, London W8.

[Humphrey Trevelyan, *Public and Private*, 1980; personal knowledge.]

ANTHONY NUTTING

published 1990

(1882–1972)

Civil servant, was born 23 August 1882, the sixth of the seven children and the youngest of the three sons of Harry Wilson, a furniture dealer, of Bournemouth, and his wife, Elizabeth Ann Smith. He was educated at Kurnella School, Bournemouth. He entered the Patent Office as a boy clerk in 1898, and passed into the second division of the Civil Service in 1900. In 1904 he enrolled as a 'night school' student at the London School of Economics, where he took a B.Sc. (Econ.) in 1908. He served in the labour department of the Board of Trade when the chief industrial commissioner was Sir George (later Lord) Askwith, and in 1915 he was made secretary of the committee on production and of the government arbitration committee under the Munitions of War Acts, of both of which Askwith was chairman. Wilson used later to say that it was on Askwith's techniques as an arbitrator and conciliator that he modelled his own.

The labour department of the Board of Trade became the nucleus of the Ministry of Labour which was created when David Lloyd George became prime minister in 1916. Wilson went to the new ministry, and by 1919 had become the principal assistant secretary in charge of the industrial relations and conciliation department. In this post he helped to implement the reports of the committee chaired by J. H. Whitley, as a result of which joint industrial councils were set up in a wide variety of industries and services which had hitherto had no formal negotiating machinery. In 1921, still under forty, he became the permanent secretary of the Ministry of Labour. With the extended powers of the new ministry he was able to play a more positive part in the settlement of industrial disputes at national level. He thus acquired considerable experience of industrial conciliation and an extensive knowledge of the personalities, organizations, and forces at work on both sides of industry; and he earned the respect and confidence not only of employers' and union leaders but also of his political masters. He was at the heart of the discussions and negotiations in which the government was involved at the time of the general strike in 1926.

When the Labour government took office in 1929, a team of officials was set up under the direction of the lord privy seal (J. H. Thomas) to deal with the problem of unemployment and to foster more active co-operation by the government in the reorganization and development of industry. Wilson was put at the head of this team, first as permanent secretary at the Ministry of Labour and then, from 1930, in a new appointment as chief industrial adviser to the government which enabled him to concentrate all his attention on the problems of industry and employment. He continued as chief industrial adviser under the national government of 1931. In July 1932 he accompanied the British delegation (which included Stanley Baldwin and Neville Chamberlain) to the imperial economic conference at Ottawa. He virtually took over the spadework of the British delegation, and was one of the main architects of the agreement, although his influence did not commend itself to those observers who would have favoured a larger commitment to imperial preference than the British government was prepared to make. This phase of his career culminated in his contribution to the reorganization of the cotton industry in 1935.

In 1935 Wilson was asked by the new prime minister (Stanley Baldwin) to join his staff as a personal adviser. Although conscious of the risk that this might arouse the jealousy and antagonism of his departmental colleagues, he accepted it as his duty to do so. Accordingly, while retaining his position and title as chief industrial adviser to the government, he was seconded to the Treasury for service with the prime minister: an unusual appointment which brought him to the prime minister's right hand, and to an office next door to the Cabinet Room in 10 Downing Street. He was involved as the prime minister's adviser over the whole range of business, including the crisis that led to the abdication of King Edward VIII.

Wilson expected this personal appointment to come to an end when Baldwin retired in 1937, but Neville Chamberlain asked him to 'stay around for a bit'; so he did, and made himself even more indispensable to the new prime minister than to his predecessor. In the deepening international crisis caused by the expanding ambitions of Hitler's Germany and Mussolini's Italy, Chamberlain was determined to prevent, if he could, or at least to defer for as long as possible, the outbreak of another European war. He disagreed with the policies and distrusted the attitudes of the Foreign Office, and reposed great confidence in Wilson as his principal adviser, on international as well as domestic affairs.

In this difficult and exposed position Wilson sought to work very closely with the permanent under-secretary of state at the Foreign Office, Sir Alexander Cadogan. But others in the Foreign Office, itself divided, distrusted him. They were suspicious of his inexperience of diplomacy, and resentful of his influence with the prime minister. They believed that he encouraged the prime minister in the view that other foreign policy objectives, and in particular co-ordination with French policy (and stiffening of French resolve where necessary), should be subordinated to the attempt to develop better understandings with Germany and with Italy; and they thought that he helped to foster in the prime minister's mind the illusion that the conduct of foreign relations resembled the handling of industrial disputes.

Wilson was the senior member of the small party of official advisers who accompanied Chamberlain on his visits to Berchtesgaden, Bad Godesberg, and Munich in September 1938, and Chamberlain sent him as an emissary to Hitler in Berlin between the visits to Bad Godesberg and Munich. Both before and after this time he had direct contact with various representatives of the German government, in the hope of discovering a basis for settling areas of dispute and reaching an Anglo-German agreement which would prevent war.

Early in 1939 Wilson was appointed to succeed Sir N. F. Warren Fisher as permanent secretary to the Treasury and official head of the Civil Service. He combined his new duties with his position with the prime minister until Chamberlain's resignation in May 1940. As permanent secretary to the Treasury he was concerned for the problems of war finance, but he concentrated mainly on directing the adaptation of the machinery of government to its wartime functions. He retired from the public service on reaching his sixtieth birthday in 1942.

Wilson's association in the public mind with 'the men of Munich' no doubt prevented him from being offered the further public appointments which might have been expected (particularly in wartime) to come the way of a retiring permanent secretary to the Treasury. From 1944 to 1951 he served as independent chairman of the National Joint Council for Local Authorities' Administrative, Professional, Technical, and Clerical Services. In 1956, when Nigel Nicolson (the Conservative member of Parliament for the Bournemouth constituency in which Wilson lived) publicly dissociated himself from the Eden government on the Suez affair, Wilson emerged briefly as one of Nicolson's strongest supporters in the disagreement which he had with his constituency association. Apart from that, his retirement from public affairs was complete.

Wilson had in the highest degree many of the attributes of a great public servant; intelligence, clarity of mind and expression, skill in conciliation, impartiality, and integrity. The attribute which made him especially valuable to ministers was his ability to see issues plain and clear, and then to present them plainly and clearly to his political chiefs. His experience as a negotiator led him to believe that, given a modicum of good will, there was no problem or dispute which could not be resolved by the use of an appropriate form of words; and his skill in devising such formulae was one of the qualities which most commended him to the ministers with whom he was associated, though it was sometimes felt that he was not always sufficiently mindful of the longer-term implications of the formulae which he produced. His qualities were valued equally by the ministers whom he served from both of the main political parties—J. H. Thomas, for instance, described him as 'a ruddy wonder'—and by the employers' and union leaders with whom he dealt. His industry and devotion to duty, to the exclusion of every other interest save that of family life, were tireless. He was at or near the centre of government for over twenty years. But his achievements in the rest of his career were eclipsed by the two pre-war years with Chamberlain. Close observers thought that in a difficult position he conducted himself with complete official propriety; but his association with the policy of appeasement attracted considerable obloquy, both at the time and subsequently, and it is arguable that to his misfortune and not primarily by his own fault he was thrust into a role at 10 Downing Street which ought never to have been allowed to take the form it did.

Wilson was not, as some said, the chief architect of the policy of appeasement: Chamberlain was nobody's puppet. But there can be no doubt of the loyalty and conviction with which he supported and helped the prime minister in carrying it out. It was not just a matter of professional loyalty to his minister, though that consideration would certainly have weighed with any civil servant with Wilson's sense of public duty. There was a high degree of intellectual and personal sympathy, even affinity, between the two men; and Wilson was convinced of the rightness of Chamberlain's policies. He believed that there was no need or cause for a war between Britain and Germany; that Germany's legitimate grievances and aspirations could be satisfied; that if they were satisfied Hitler would either not need or (for lack of support at home) not be able to go to war; and that a strong and non-communist Germany could be a bastion against what he saw as the supreme menace of Soviet communism. The aim of the policy of appeasement was thus, as he saw it, to avert war, not just to defer it. Even after the policy had failed to achieve that aim, however, Wilson continued to believe not only that it had been right in conception and intention but also that it had been advantageous and even necessary as a means of gaining time in which to demonstrate the inevitability of war beyond a peradventure, to rally the support of public opinion at home and in the Empire, and to bring the country's preparations to a point where, if war at last became inescapable, at least it could be faced with some hope of avoiding defeat.

Wilson was a slim figure of medium height, with a considerable presence: reserved, rather solitary, and of a grave mien and disposition; not given to laughter but with a ready smile. He was a very gentle and self-controlled man, virtually never moved to anger or even to raising his voice; and a man of great charm and unfailing courtesy, widely respected, and held in affection by many of his colleagues.

Wilson was appointed CBE in 1918, CB in 1920, KCB in 1924, and GCB in 1937. He was appointed GCMG in 1933, after the imperial economic conference in Ottawa. He was an honorary LL D at Aberdeen (1934) and Liverpool (1939); and became an honorary fellow of the London School of Economics in 1960.

Wilson married in 1908 Emily, daughter of John Sheather, a farmer of Beckley in Sussex; she died eighteen months after her husband, in October 1973. They had one son and two daughters. He died in Bournemouth, the town where he was born, 19 May 1972, nearly ninety years old.

[*The Times*, 26 May 1978, and other obituaries; biographies, diaries, and memoirs of contemporaries; personal recollections; private information.]

ROBERT ARMSTRONG

published 1986

WOLFF Sir Henry Drummond Charles

(1830–1908)

Politician and diplomatist, born in Malta 12 Oct. 1830, was only child of the rev. Joseph Wolff by his wife Lady Georgiana, daughter of Horatio Walpole, second earl of Orford. He was named Drummond after Henry Drummond, a founder, with his father, of the Irvingite church. After education at Rugby, under Tait, he spent some time abroad in the study of foreign languages. At the age of sixteen he entered the foreign office as a supernumerary clerk, and became a member of the permanent staff in 1849. In June 1852 he was attached to the British legation at Florence, and was left in charge during the autumn of 1852 in the absence of the minister, Sir Henry Bulwer (afterwards Lord Dalling). He returned to the foreign office in 1853, and in 1856 he was attached to Lord Westmoreland's special mission to congratulate Leopold I, King of the Belgians, on the twenty-fifth anniversary of his accession. When the conservatives took office in February 1858, Wolff became assistant private secretary to the foreign secretary, the earl of Malmesbury, and in October private secretary to the secretary for the colonies, Sir Edward Bulwer Lytton (afterwards Lord Lytton). Having been made C.M.G. and king of arms of the order in April 1859, he was secretary to Sir Henry Storks, high commissioner of the Ionian Islands, from June 1859 till the transfer of the islands to Greece in June 1864. Throughout this period Wolff took an active part in various commissions of inquiry set on foot to redress grievances and to promote the material welfare of the islanders. In 1860 he acted as delegate for the islands to the international statistical congress in London; in 1861 he was vice-president of a commission to arrange for Ionian exhibits in the London international exhibition of 1862, and helped in the establishment of an Ionian Institute for the promotion of trade and education. In Oct. 1862 he became K.C.M.G., and subsequently arranged the details of the transfer of the islands to Greece, which was effected in June 1864. On relinquishing his office he received a pension from the Greek government.

For the next few years he travelled much, and was mainly engaged in promoting various financial undertakings, a kind of work for which his wide popularity and his astuteness and fertility of resource gave him great advantages. In 1864 he assisted at Constantinople in arranging for the conversion of the internal debt of Turkey into a foreign loan. In 1866 he laid a project for a ferry across the English Channel before the emperor of the French. Subsequently he aided in the liquidation of a large undertaking entitled the International Land Credit Company, which had come to disaster. In 1870, during the war between France and Germany, he made three expeditions from Spa, where he was staying, into the theatre of the campaign. At the beginning of September, with two English companions, he visited the battlefield of Sedan a day or two after the surrender of the French army, meeting on his return journey the emperor of the French on his way to Germany. A fortnight later Wolff and Henry James (afterwards Lord James of Hereford) visited the battlefields of Gravelotte and Saarbrücken and the environs of Strasburg while invested by the German forces, and came under the fire of the French artillery. Early in Oct. 1870 he proceeded from Spa to Baden, and thence to Strasburg, which had then surrendered, and on to Nancy and Toul. He narrated his experiences in the 'Morning Post', and the narrative was privately printed in 1892 as 'Some Notes of the Past'.

Meanwhile he was actively interested in party politics. He was one of the select company of contributors to 'The Owl', a short-lived but popular satirical journal, which was started in 1864 by Algernon Borthwick (afterwards Lord Glenesk) but abandoned in 1870 in consequence of the pressure of other work. In 1865 he stood as a conservative for Dorchester, with 'the most disastrous results'. Afterwards he purchased from Lord Malmesbury a small building property at Boscombe, near Bournemouth, which he set to work to develop, and at the general election in 1874 he was elected conservative M.P. for Christchurch. He took at once an active part in the House of Commons. He spoke often on foreign policy, especially in connection with the Eastern question. He was prominent in defending the purchase by the British government of the Khedive's shares in the Suez Canal Company. In 1875 he was appointed a member of the copyright commission, and signed the Report presented in 1878, only dissenting on some points of detail. In 1876 he accompanied George Joachim (afterwards Lord) Goschen on a mission of inquiry into Egyptian finance to Egypt, in behalf of the Egyptian bondholders. During the Easter recess in 1878, when the revision of the treaty of San Stefano by a European congress was still in suspense. Wolff visited Paris, Vienna, and Berlin to ascertain the general feeling of European statesmen. In August 1878 he returned to employment under the foreign office, and was made G.C.M.G. Lord Salisbury selected him to be the British member of the international commission for the organisation of the province of Eastern Roumelia. After a preliminary discussion at Constantinople the commission established itself at Philippopolis in October. The Russian and British delegates were often at diplomatic odds, the former being openly hostile to the separation of the newly formed province from Bulgaria and seeking to give to it a fuller freedom from Turkish sovereignty than the treaty of Berlin sanctioned. Wolff appealed to the higher Russian authorities with considerable success. In April 1879 the organic statute was settled and signed. After assisting at the installation of the new governor-general, Aleko Pasha, Wolff returned to his parliamentary duties in England, and in September was created K.C.B. The Eastern Roumelian commission was further directed to draw up schemes for the administration of other European provinces of the Turkish empire, but before this task was approached, Gladstone's second administration began in England, and Wolff resigned (April 1880), being succeeded by Edmond (now Lord) Fitzmaurice.

At the general election in the spring of 1880 Wolff was elected for Portsmouth. At the opening of the new parliament he took a leading part in opposing the claim of Charles Bradlaugh to take the oath, receiving the active support of Lord Randolph Churchill and Mr. (afterwards Sir John) Gorst. In the result these three members formed the combination, subsequently joined by Mr. Arthur Balfour and known under the title of the Fourth Party, which, during the next five years, did much to enliven the proceedings of the House of Commons and to make uneasy the positions both of the prime minister, Mr. Gladstone, and of the leader of the opposition, Sir Stafford Northcote, afterwards earl of Iddesleigh. Wolff was an active and efficient colleague, taking his full share in parliamentary discussions and being especially useful in reconciling his companions' differences. He was personally responsible for the passing of a bill, which he had introduced in the previous parliament, enabling the inhabitants of seaside resorts to let their houses for short periods without losing their qualification to vote at elections. But his attention was mainly devoted to party warfare. On 19 April 1883, after the unveiling of the statue of Lord

Beaconsfield in Parliament Square, he first suggested to Lord Randolph Churchill the formation of a 'Primrose League', to be so named after what was reputed to be the deceased statesman's favourite flower. In the course of the following autumn the league was set on foot. The statutes of the new association were drawn up by Wolff and revised by a small committee. They prescribed a form of declaration by which members undertook 'to devote their best ability to the maintenance of religion, of the estates of the realm, and of the imperial ascendancy of the British empire', and they ministered to the weaker side of human nature by providing a regular gradation of rank with quaint titles and picturesque badges. The league, though at first somewhat scoffed at by the conservative leaders, was soon found to be a most efficient party instrument. In the dissension caused in the conservative party by Lord Randolph Churchill's advocacy of a frankly democratic policy, Wolff sided with his colleague, but he was too astute a politician to favour internal divisions, and was instrumental in procuring the reconciliation, which was effected in the summer of 1884. On Lord Salisbury's return to office in June 1885 Wolff was made a privy councillor, and in August was despatched on a special mission to Constantinople to discuss with the Turkish government the future of Egypt, which since 1882 had been in the military occupation of Great Britain. The British occupation, though accepted as a practical necessity, had not received formal recognition or sanction either from the Sultan or any of the powers. Wolff was instructed to arrange with the Porte the conditions on which the Sultan's authority should in future be exercised in Egypt and the methods for assuring the stability of the Khedive's government. After some months Wolff concluded with the Turkish government in Oct. 1885 a convention providing that the two governments should each send a special commissioner to Egypt who should in concert with the Khedive reorganise the Egyptian army, examine and reform all branches of the Egyptian administration, and consider the best means for tranquillising the Soudan by pacific methods. When these ends were accomplished, the two governments would consider terms for the withdrawal of the British troops from Egypt within a convenient period. Wolff went to Egypt as British commissioner under this convention. Moukhtar Pasha was the Turkish commissioner. At the end of twelve months Wolff returned to England in order to discuss the terms of a further arrangement with Turkey. In Jan. 1887 he proceeded to Constantinople, and there negotiated a second convention, signed on 22 May, which stipulated for the withdrawal of the British forces from Egypt at the end of three years, with the proviso that the evacuation should be postponed in the event of any external or internal danger at that time; that for two years after the evacuation Great Britain was to watch exclusively over the safety of the country; and that subsequently both the Sultan and the British government were each to have the right, if necessary, of sending a force to Egypt either for its defence or for the maintenance of order. In a separate note it was stated that the refusal of one of the Mediterranean great powers to accept the convention would be regarded by the British government as an external danger justifying the postponement of the evacuation. The governments of Austria, Germany, and Italy were favourably inclined to this arrangement, but the French government, which determinedly opposed it, intimated together with the Russian government that if it were ratified they would feel justified in occupying other portions of Turkish territory. The Sultan consequently refused to ratify it.

Wolff returned to England in July 1887. Lord Salisbury in a final despatch observed that the negotiations had defined formally the character of the English occupation and the conditions necessary to bring it to a close. The convention of Oct. 1885 remained in force as a recognition by the Porte of the occupation, and the continued presence of the Turkish commissioner in Egypt, though possibly not in all respects convenient, implied acquiescence in the situation.

Wolff's parliamentary career had been brought to a close by his defeat at Portsmouth in the general election of November 1885, while he was absent in Egypt. For the future his work was entirely in the diplomatic profession. In Dec. 1887 he was appointed British envoy in Persia, and proceeded to Teheran early in the following year. Here his versatile energy found ample occupation in watching the progress and development of Russian policy on the northern frontier, in devising plans for harmonious action by the two powers in lieu of the traditional rivalry between their legations, in promoting schemes for the development of British commercial enterprise, and in encouraging the Persian government in efforts for administrative and financial reform. Among the measures, which he was instrumental in promoting were the issue of a decree in May 1888 for the protection of property from arbitrary acts of the executive and the opening of the Karun river to steam navigation in October following. A concession obtained by Baron Reuter on the occasion of the Shah's visit to England in 1872, which was worded in such vague and comprehensive terms as to seem incapable of practical development, took, under Wolff's guidance, a business-like and beneficial shape in the establishment of the Imperial Bank of Persia. Some other schemes were less successful. A carefully considered project for the construction of a railway from Ahwaz on the Karun river in the direction of Ispahan failed to obtain sufficient financial support, and the concession of the tobacco régie to a group of English financiers, which seemed to promise considerable advantages to the Persian exchequer, excited such fanatical opposition that it was in the end abandoned some time after Wolff's departure from Persia. Wolff received the grand cross of the Bath in Jan. 1889, and was summoned home later in the year to attend the Shah on his visit to England. He accompanied the Persian sovereign during his tour in England and Scotland. On his way back to Teheran in Aug. 1889 Wolff passed through St. Petersburg, where he had an audience of the Emperor of Russia, and urged the importance of an agreement between the two countries on the policy to be pursued in Persia, obtaining an assurance that the new Russian minister at Teheran would be authorised to discuss any proposals, which he might be empowered to put forward for this object. He had intended in 1890 to visit India, but before his departure from Teheran he was struck down by a serious illness, during which his life was at one time despaired of. He recovered sufficiently to be brought to England, where he gradually regained strength, but his health was clearly unequal to a return to the arduous duties and trying climate of Teheran. In July 1891, somewhat against his will, he was transferred to Bucharest, and six months afterwards was appointed ambassador at Madrid. That post he held for eight years, till his retirement on pension in Oct. 1900. In June 1893 he effected a provisional commercial agreement with the Spanish government, pending the conclusion of a permanent treaty, and this arrangement was further confirmed by an exchange of notes in Dec. 1894. British relations with Spain gave no cause for anxiety, and Wolff's natural geniality and hospitable instincts secured him a general popularity, which was unimpaired by the war between Spain and the United States, when English public opinion pronounced itself somewhat clearly on the American side. After his retirement he lived for reasons of health quietly in England. He retained, however, his keen, restless interest in public affairs, his gift of amusing conversation, and his apparently inexhaustible fund of anecdote. Through life his good temper was imperturbable, and he delighted in mischievous humour, which was free from malice or vindictiveness. He professed in casual conversation a lower standard of conduct than he really acted upon, and despite his avowed cynicism he was by nature and instinct kind-hearted and always ready to assist distress. He became very infirm in the last few months of his life, and died at Brighton on 11 Oct. 1908.

He married at the British Consulate, Leghorn, on 22 Jan. 1853, Adeline, daughter of Walter Sholto Douglas, by whom he had two sons and a daughter. His widow was awarded a civil list pension of 100l. in 1909. His daughter, Adeline Georgiana Isabel, wife of Col. Howard Kingscote, was a prolific novelist, writing under the pseudonym of 'Lucas Cleeve'. Her chief works, which show an easy style and vivid imagination, include 'The Real Christian' (1901), 'Blue Lilies' (1902), 'Eileen' (1903), 'The Secret Church'

(1906), 'Her Father's Soul' (1907). She was a great traveller and an accomplished linguist. She predeceased her father on 13 Sept. 1908 at Château d'Œx, Switzerland. A cartoon portrait of Wolff by 'Spy' appeared in 'Vanity Fair' in 1881.

[Sir H. D. Wolff published in 1908 two volumes, entitled *Rambling Recollections*, which give a very entertaining though somewhat discursive account of his varied experiences. Other authorities are *The Times*, 12 Oct. 1908; *Foreign Office List*, 1909, p. 405; Winston Churchill's *Life of Lord Randolph Churchill*, 2 vols. 1906; Harold Gorst's *The Fourth Party*, art. on the Primrose League in *Encycl. Brit.* 11th ed.]

T. H. SANDERSON

published 1912

WOOD Edward Frederick Lindley

(1881–1959)

First Earl of Halifax

Statesman, was born at Powderham Castle, Devon, the home of his maternal grandfather, 16 April 1881. He was the fourth son and youngest of the six children of Charles Lindley Wood, later second Viscount Halifax, by his wife, Lady Agnes Elizabeth Courtenay, only daughter of the eleventh Earl of Devon. Born with an atrophied left arm which had no hand, he shrugged off his disability even as a child; the Christian belief which was the passion of his father's life and which permeated his own upbringing precluded self-pity. He quickly learned to shoot and ride to hounds, and as heir to great estates in Yorkshire, his three brothers having died young while he himself was between the ages of four and nine, was able to share without embarrassment the traditional pursuits of a countryman.

He was educated at Eton and Christ Church, Oxford, where in 1903 he took a first class in history followed by a fellowship at All Souls. He taught history, hunted twice a week, travelled round the world, and wrote a biography of John Keble (1909) reflecting the Anglo-Catholic faith he shared with his father. In 1909 his marriage to Lady Dorothy Evelyn Augusta Onslow, younger daughter of the fourth Earl of Onslow, brought lasting happiness and a family of three sons, and twin daughters only one of whom survived. The loyalty which at his wedding burdened him with a solid gold cup nearly two feet high as a tribute from the tenantry helped to ensure his election in January 1910 as Conservative member of Parliament for Ripon. He held the seat in December, and thereafter was returned unopposed until created a peer in 1925.

On the outbreak of war in 1914 Wood was serving as a yeomanry officer in the Yorkshire Dragoons. The failure of the allied armies to pierce the western front denied his regiment the mobile role of their hopes, confining them instead to a monotonous routine behind the lines. Wood was mentioned in dispatches in January 1917 and later that year returned to England at the invitation of Sir Auckland (later Lord) Geddes to serve for the rest of the war as an assistant secretary in the Ministry of National Service. In 1920, when not yet forty, he accepted the governor-generalship of South Africa but was obliged to withdraw when the Union expressed a preference for a man of cabinet rank or a member of the royal family. So he remained in the Commons where, although neither fluent nor brilliant, his thoughtful contributions to debate were heard with attention. His first ministerial office, as under-secretary for the colonies, began bleakly in April 1921. The secretary of state, (Sir) Winston Churchill, had wanted someone else and being much preoccupied with Middle Eastern problems made no time to receive him. The new under-secretary eventually forced his way into his chief's office, where a brisk exchange laid the foundations of co-operation. On a mission to the West Indies Wood studied the economics of sugar and demands for constitutional reform.

Wood felt an aloof distaste for the ways by which Lloyd George attempted to hold together his uneasy coalition. Characteristically, he had objected less to the activities of the 'Black and Tans' in Ireland than to the Government's evasiveness on the subject. He was also troubled by allegations that honours were being sold. He did not hesitate to vote for the downfall of Lloyd George in October 1922. In the new administration of Bonar Law he entered the Cabinet for the first time, as president of the Board of Education, and was sworn of the Privy Council. He found the work uncongenial, lacked interest in educational problems, and could not hope to inspire a department which was being financially starved; but he remained until the fall of Baldwin's government in January 1924. He was equally ineffective as minister of agriculture in Baldwin's second administration. However rooted his personal belief in the virtues of the land, he accepted an official policy that shrank from the expense of sustaining an enfeebled industry. He was released from frustration by his appointment in November 1925 as governor-general and viceroy of India, his name having been suggested to Baldwin by King George V.

For a man without overt ambition, Wood had risen swiftly to high office. Initially he owed it to family. His grandfather, the first Viscount Halifax, was one of the earliest secretaries of state for India and author of the dispatch recognizing British responsibility for Indian education. Yet in his own right the new viceroy was hardly less well equipped than his predecessors. Immensely tall, with a fine domed head and the face of an ascetic, he bore himself as majestically as Lord Curzon, and if intellectually he could not quite match that relentlessly energetic mind, he brought a calmer and more balanced temperament to the rule of 400 million people. Once only in five years, it was afterwards recalled, did he lose his temper— at the disappearance of a disreputable old hat to which he was much attached. Lord Irwin, as he was created in December 1925, landed at Bombay on Maundy Thursday, 1 April 1926. His aim, he told one of his staff in June, was 'to keep a contented India in the Commonwealth twenty-five years hence'. A few weeks later, on 17 July, speaking in Simla at the Chelmsford Club, one of the few open to both Europeans and Indians, he set the tone of his viceroyalty. In phrases of burning sincerity which accorded with the Indian mind he appealed in the name of religion for an end to communal strife between Hindu and Moslem: a theme to which he returned again and again. For as long as such hatreds persisted even the most sympathetic of viceroys would be reluctant to meet Indian demands for self-government.

The Act of 1919 which embodied the Montagu–Chelmsford reforms had provided for a statutory commission to report within ten years. Upon this Indian aspirations were fixed. Thus the announcement in November 1927 that the commission was to consist entirely of British members of Parliament affronted educated Indian opinion. Its chairman was Sir John (later Viscount) Simon, and its members included C. R. (later Earl) Attlee, who as prime minister in 1947 was to be responsible for granting independence to the subcontinent. Such names in 1927 were of no account among Indians and even those of temperate views determined to boycott an inquisition by foreigners into their country's fitness for self-government. Various attempts to associate Indians with the commission proved unsuccessful. Irwin afterwards admitted that he had been wrong in advising the secretary of state, Lord Birkenhead, not to include Indians. He had reasoned that a mixed body would fail to reach agreement; that the Moslems could be persuaded to co-operate with an all-British commission; and that the Hindus would follow suit, however reluctantly, rather than allow their traditional opponents to be heard unchallenged. For his part, Birkenhead feared that an alliance between British Labour and Indian members of a mixed commission might produce dangerously inconvenient majority conclusions. He must share responsibility for the gravest mistake of Irwin's viceroyalty.

As the Simon commission gathered its evidence in an atmosphere of glacial hostility, the viceroy searched for a formula of reconciliation. He acted as resolutely as any predecessor against increasing outbreaks of violence but came to recognize that only a generous gesture of friendship would break the sullen silence. The imaginative scheme which he evolved was in two parts—a Round Table conference embracing all parties in the British Parliament, all parties and interests in British India, and the Indian princes; and a formal declaration on dominion status. In this, as in subsequent policy, his hand was strengthened by a change of government at home. The second Labour Government of Ramsay MacDonald, which took office in June 1929, shared the viceroy's view that benevolent paternalism must give way to partnership no less in India than elsewhere throughout the Commonwealth. In the talks held in London during his leave that summer Irwin was to find in Wedgwood Benn (later Viscount Stansgate), the new secretary of state, a more accommodating ally than Birkenhead. It was therefore with confidence that in October the viceroy risked his reputation for statesmanship by publicly announcing a Round Table conference and the British Government's view that the natural issue of India's constitutional progress was dominion status.

The result was tragically disappointing. Among Indians, an initial restoration of faith in the motives of British rule rapidly gave way to mistrust and dismay at reports of the scornful fury which the viceroy's words had evoked in London. Birkenhead and Churchill were predictably vehement among Conservatives; Lord Reading condemned him with the authority of a popular ex-viceroy, his juridical mind outraged by the imprecision of the term dominion status; Simon was annoyed that Irwin had anticipated the commission's report. Hoping to save the situation by personal persuasion, the viceroy invited Indian political leaders, including M. K. Gandhi, to meet him in New Delhi. The conference was abortive. Disillusioned by unfriendly speeches at Westminster and unable to extract an early or exact date for the implementation of dominion status, Gandhi and his associates withdrew to plan a campaign of civil disobedience with complete independence as its ultimate goal.

Again India passed through the weary cycle of resentment, rebellion, repression, and reprieve. In the spring of 1930 Gandhi led a march to the sea to defy the salt laws which imposed a tax minute in its incidence but to the Indian imagination a symbol of oppression. Irwin, whose compassion concealed a steely regard for law and order, was reluctant to add martyrdom to the other spiritual qualities which elevated Gandhi above all other Indian leaders. But when defiance provoked violent and bloody riots, the viceroy did not hesitate to authorize his arrest and the use of full emergency powers against unlawful gatherings and a seditious press. So long as Gandhi remained in prison there could be peace of a sort but no progress. In January 1931, combining magnanimity with political shrewdness, Irwin ordered the release of the one man who could speak for India. They met eight times and after protracted discussion came to an understanding known as the Delhi Pact. Few proconsuls other than Irwin could have demonstrated a subtlety of mind to match that of Gandhi or driven so hard a bargain clothed in the language of friendship: there was to be an end to civil disobedience and the economic boycott of British goods; Congress was to be represented at future sessions of the Round Table conference to discuss India's future in an All-India Federation, Indian responsibility, and reservations or safeguards on such matters as defence, external relations, the position of minorities, and India's financial credit. Conservative opinion in England, which had begun to discern some good in a viceroy who refused to entertain criticisms of a much-tried police force or to commute death sentences for crimes of violence, reacted harshly both to the discussions and to their outcome. Irwin saw things differently. When asked whether Gandhi had not been tiresome he replied: 'Some people found Our Lord very tiresome.'

In a lifetime of public service, the viceroyalty must be accounted Irwin's most exacting task. But for all his vision, his sympathy and his administrative skill, he could not secure an immediate measure of constitutional progress or a calming of racial strife. Within a year of his sailing for England in April 1931 the second Round Table conference had ended inconclusively, civil disobedience was widespread, and Gandhi once more in prison. Irwin nevertheless imprinted on the Indian mind a remembrance of tact and patience and a courage which recognized neither political expediency nor physical fear. More than once his life was in danger, notably when his train was almost derailed by a terrorist bomb as he approached New Delhi to take up residence for the first time in the oriental Versailles created by Sir Edwin Lutyens and Sir Herbert Baker. His own preference in the capital was for the Anglican church of the Redemption, enriched by his private raising of funds and consecrated in the last days of his rule. Appointed G.C.S.I. and G.C.I.E. in 1926, he was made K.G. in 1931, becoming chancellor of the order in 1943.

In the autumn of 1931 Irwin was invited to become foreign secretary in Ramsay MacDonald's 'national' Government. He declined, preferring to savour the renewed enjoyment of Garrowby, his estate near York, and to prolong his reunion with his father whom he had hardly dared hope to see again. He was also aware that he had become something of an embarrassment to right-wing members of his own party. Such tensions, he felt, unfitted him for an office which should be as far removed as possible from parliamentary strife. In the summer of 1932, however, he was persuaded to return to the Board of Education. He liked in later years to recall how the proconsul fresh from the rule of a sub-continent was refused a new pair of curtains for his office. The appointment he found as drably uncongenial and as economically restricted as it had been earlier. He accepted it only when urged to place his knowledge of Indian affairs at the disposal of the Cabinet and assist Sir Samuel Hoare (later Viscount Templewood), the secretary of state, in the drafting and parliamentary progress of an immense government of India bill which did not reach the statute book until 1935. Two pleasures sustained him during this gruelling task. In 1932 he became master of the Middleton foxhounds and in 1933 he was nominated unopposed as chancellor of Oxford University in succession to Lord Grey of Fallodon. Early in 1934 his father died in his ninety-fifth year at the other family estate of Hickleton, in Yorkshire. It was a bereavement which, although scarcely unexpected, left the son conscious of an acute loneliness after the shared intimacies of half a century. Five months as secretary of state for war in 1935 revealed to him the paucity of our defences but did not impress him with an urgent need for rearmament. After the general election in November, Halifax, as he now was, became lord privy seal and leader of the House of Lords and on Baldwin's retirement in 1937 he was appointed lord president of the Council in Chamberlain's administration. During his tenure of both these offices without departmental responsibilities he applied himself increasingly to foreign affairs.

With Anthony Eden (later the Earl of Avon), who became foreign secretary in December 1935, Halifax at once established a harmonious relationship. Both were disturbed by the growing belligerency of Nazi Germany; neither, aware of British and French military weakness, was prepared in March 1936 to contemplate resistance to Hitler's occupation of the Rhineland. Exposed to scorn and easy abuse in later years, their caution at the time accurately reflected the attitude of many of their countrymen. What began increasingly to separate the two ministers was their contrasting approach to the efficacy of negotiation. Halifax believed that the Nazis were reasonable men whose ambitions could be modified by patient and persuasive discussion; Eden feared that without substantial rearmament such exchanges would be mistaken for weakness and serve only to encourage aggression. The doubts of the foreign secretary were justified by the visit which Halifax made to Germany in November 1937. Eden had reluctantly agreed that Halifax should meet Hitler in Berlin under guise of accepting an invitation, bizarrely addressed to him as master of the Middleton, to shoot foxes and to attend a hunting exhibition. By subsequently agreeing to journey to Berchtesgaden for his interview with Hitler, Halifax unwittingly cast himself in the role of eager supplicant; and by omitting to deliver an unambiguous warning against German designs on Austria and Czechoslovakia, as instructed by the foreign secretary, he deprived his mission of deterrent effect. 'He struck me as very sincere', Halifax recorded of his talk with the Führer. Other Nazi leaders he found likeable though slightly comic. The squire of Garrowby could well discern their social inadequacies; the Christian failed to detect their wickedness.

Eden resigned in February 1938: the essential issue was whether British foreign policy should emanate from the Foreign Office or from No. 10 Downing Street. In agreeing to succeed as foreign secretary Halifax implicitly accepted a more subordinate role than that of his predecessor, an understanding which weakened his tenure of the Foreign Office and delayed his conversion to robustness. He embarked on his duties assiduously but without enthusiasm. His knowledge of European history and thought was not profound and he never read *Mein Kampf*. He was nevertheless welcomed, even by Churchill, as a man whose desire for peace did not preclude a readiness to resist aggression. His attitude was soon put to the test. Three weeks after Halifax became foreign secretary, Hitler invaded Austria and incorporated it within the German Reich. Czechoslovakia now lay exposed to the same fate and German minorities on the Sudeten border were incited to demonstrate with increasing violence against the alleged oppression of the Czech Government. Three factors left Halifax little room for diplomatic manœuvre. The first was British military weakness, in spite of a slowly increasing preoccupation with rearmament. The second was a persistent and paralysing over-estimate of German military strength. The third was the geographical remoteness of Czechoslovakia. To guarantee the independence of Czechoslovakia in March 1938, either alone or in alliance with a debilitated France, was a risk Halifax dared not take. If his bluff had been called and Britain had been drawn into a declaration of war on Germany, it would have been without hope of protecting either Czechoslovakia from German tanks or London from German bombs. So in courteous tones which aroused only the contempt of the Nazi leaders he begged them to moderate their claims in the interests of world peace; simultaneously he urged the Czechs not to be so disobligingly slow in bowing to German demands. In July he dispatched Lord Runciman to Czechoslovakia as a mediator.

Responsibility for that chapter of appeasement in British foreign policy belongs more to Chamberlain than to Halifax. The foreign secretary did not attend, or resent not attending, any of the three meetings held successively at Berchtesgaden, Godesberg, and Munich in September 1938 at which the prime minister reached agreement with Hitler on the dismemberment of Czechoslovakia. Nor did he consider Chamberlain's dependence in foreign affairs on an adviser such as Sir Horace Wilson, who was not a member of the Foreign Office, a matter on which he should protest, much less resign. At two moments during the crisis Halifax did show to some advantage. Stiffened by Sir Alexander Cadogan, permanent under-secretary at the Foreign Office and his mentor in the realities of international affairs, he insisted on Chamberlain's rejection of the terms proposed by Hitler at Godesberg for the immediate occupation of the Sudeten territories. His gesture of defiance, however, was too belated to earn the Czechs more than a ten-day reprieve from Germany for their Sudeten territories and an empty guarantee of what was left of their country from Britain and France. Halifax also felt he must intrude on the welcome given to Chamberlain on his return from Munich. As they drove together through cheering crowds from Heston airport to Downing Street, he warned the prime minister that he should resist the temptation to consolidate his position by calling for an immediate general election and that he should strengthen his Cabinet by bringing in not only Churchill and Eden but also members of the Labour Party if they could be persuaded. In the event there was no general election; but neither was there an attempt to construct a truly national government dedicated to rearmament. Halifax was the one member of Chamberlain's administration who, by threatening resignation, might have ensured it. His quiescence did not spring only from loyalty to a leader and a friend. His lifelong resort to regular and unhurried worship brought him consolation at times of stress, a serenity transcending the cares of statecraft, and a detachment from the evil realities of life which was of no service to a foreign secretary. A humble acceptance of Divine Will protected him from self-reproach, even from self-examination, on the consequences of his actions; and a belief in immortality made the sufferings of those enslaved by the Nazis seem less tragic than they were.

Hitler's occupation in March 1939 of the truncated and wholly Slav remains of Czechoslovakia which had been denied him five months before roused British public opinion and caused Halifax's attitude to harden more than that of the prime minister. Although there were still echoes of appeasement in his speeches in the House of Lords, he recognized that to remain inactive in the face of Hitler's mounting threats towards Poland would be merely to postpone an unavoidable war against an enemy who drew strength from each successive plunder. An expanding programme of British rearmament, even if still inadequate, also engendered a growing spirit of confidence in the Foreign Office. So within a few days of the German march into Prague it was announced that Britain had guaranteed the independence of Poland. In April Italy invaded Albania and the British Government gave firm assurances of support to Greece and Romania. A measure of military conscription was introduced, although opposed by both the Labour and Liberal parties. In May Halifax sent a representative to Moscow for tripartite talks with Russia and France; clouded by mistrust, they were stifled in August by the conclusion of a Russo-German pact for the partition of Poland. Some held Halifax responsible for the belatedness and hesitancy of the British approach to Moscow. But whatever slender prospect there may have been at that stage of securing Russia as an ally against Germany was doomed by Russia's insistence that Britain should recognize her right of military intervention in the Baltic states and that Poland should agree to the entry of Soviet troops into her territory in the event of war with Germany. On 1 September German armies invaded Poland. There followed a day of confused exchanges with the French Government on the timing of an ultimatum before Britain was at war with Germany.

Halifax remained foreign secretary and directed his efforts to persuading the neutral nations to support the Allies or at least to withhold aid from Germany. In May 1940 a vote in the House of Commons reflected the disenchantment of all parties with Chamberlain's irresolute conduct of the war. Halifax escaped much of the odium, partly because he had been less personally identified than Chamberlain with Munich, partly because there was about him, as in India, an aura of disinterestedness and moral purpose which transcended the grievous consequences of British policy during his tenure of the Foreign Office. He was thus considered by many to be as suitable a successor as Churchill in the hours which immediately preceded Chamberlain's resignation as prime minister on 10 May. The prospect appalled him. He knew he did not possess those qualities of popular leadership and ruthlessness which the situation demanded; he realized how difficult if not impossible it would be for any prime minister to control the war effort from the remoteness of the House of Lords, with Churchill running defence. So it was with relief that he welcomed the choice of Churchill as leader of an all-party government. Among those who recorded initial disappointment on both public and private grounds was King George VI, whose friendship extended to granting Halifax the unusual privilege of walking through the garden of Buckingham Palace on his daily journey from Eaton Square to the Foreign Office. Halifax was invited by the new prime minister to remain at his old post and to continue as a member of the War Cabinet. After the German advance across the Low Countries and France and the escape of the British Expeditionary Force from Dunkirk, he flew with Churchill to Tours on 13 June for a fruitless meeting with Paul Reynaud, the French prime minister, five days before Marshal Pétain sued for peace.

In December Halifax's own fortunes took an unexpected turn when he was urged by Churchill to succeed Lord Lothian as British ambassador in Washington. In his sixtieth year he was justifiably reluctant to exchange an historic, influential, and by now familiar office of state for a 'high and perilous charge' among a people he barely knew. He was sensitive, too, to whispers that the prime minister would not be sorry to rid himself of a colleague whose long association with Chamberlain detracted from his usefulness at home. His sense of duty prevailed and in January 1941 he crossed the Atlantic in the newly commissioned battleship *King George V*. Although President Roosevelt paid Halifax the unusual compliment of greeting him personally in Chesapeake Bay, the welcome given to the ambassador elsewhere was discouraging. In spite of some sympathy for a nation under enemy fire, American public opinion was largely isolationist; and the initial difficulty of following so congenial an envoy as Lothian was aggravated by indiscretions from which Halifax's advisers failed to save him. He called on the chairman of the foreign affairs committee in the House of Representatives while lend-lease proposals for aid to Britain were being debated in Congress, thereby seeming to interfere in the decisions of the legislature; he accepted an invitation to hunt the fox, a sport suggestive of aristocratic leisure even more in the New World than in the Old; he made jokes about baseball. One humiliating incident, however, was turned neatly to advantage. Having been pelted with eggs in Detroit, he was widely, although incorrectly, reported as saying that the United States were fortunate to have eggs to throw, at a time when the ration in England was one a month. As the prospect of war with Japan loomed large, American critics of the supposedly belligerent and reactionary country he represented began to lose their influence. Halifax reinforced his growing popularity by extensive speaking tours, a burden made lighter both by the radiant sympathy of his wife and by the bonhomie of his cousin, friend, and stage-manager, Colonel Angus McDonnell. If most at his ease with landowners and mystics, Halifax soon learned to overcome his natural reserve among audiences which did not often include either. Nor, save in appearance, did he conform to the expected caricature of an English aristocrat. He reacted with good humour to intrusive curiosity and with deliberate charm to outspoken and sometimes ill-informed criticism of his country's alleged motives in India and elsewhere. Although he never quite achieved Lothian's ascendancy, no ambassador more adroitly or more successfully adapted himself to a role for which at heart he had little relish. A speech in Canada, however, on 24 January 1944, about the future of the Commonwealth, made a far less acceptable impression there.

The Japanese attack on Pearl Harbor in December 1941 welded Britain and the United States into alliance against Japan, Germany, and Italy. The emphasis of Halifax's task shifted accordingly from public relations to the strengthening of links between the two governments. To this end the

British missions, both civil and military, soon came to number 1,200 including no fewer than six fellows of All Souls. Halifax had already won the confidence of Cordell Hull, the secretary of state, with whom he transacted day-to-day diplomatic business. Even more fruitful was his intimacy with Harry Hopkins, the president's most trusted adviser, which won him unprecedented freedom of access to the White House. But however serviceable the easy relationship he established with Roosevelt, his personal influence in Washington was inevitably eclipsed by Churchill's periodic visits and his own exclusion from talks between president and prime minister. More than pre-war disagreements over India and the policy of appeasement, a fundamental difference in temperament separated them. One was accommodating, reflective, and cautious: the other resolute, impulsive, self-inspired. Thus the ambassador's wary affection and admiration for the prime minister as a war leader was qualified by doubts about the clarity of his judgement; and understandable irritation at being kept ignorant of decisions reached in private by Churchill and Roosevelt was sharpened by lesser grievances. He was exhausted by his guest's apocalyptic table-talk which flowed into the early hours of the morning and he complained of the cigars which left the embassy 'stinking like a third class smoking carriage'. Deep personal sorrow was added to restiveness when, towards the end of 1942, the second of his three sons was killed in battle and the third gravely wounded. A few months later he confided to Eden, his successor as foreign secretary, that he would like to be relieved of his appointment and come home. But he was persuaded to remain in Washington for another three years, thus bridging both Truman's elevation to the presidency on Roosevelt's death in April 1945 and the defeat of the Churchill government which brought Attlee to power three months later. In July 1944 he was created an earl.

On the abrupt cancellation by America of the lend-lease agreement at the end of the Japanese war, Halifax helped Lord Keynes in the protracted negotiations for a loan of 3.75 billion dollars from the United States Government. The sum was smaller and more hedged about with conditions than the British team had hoped for, but it was enough to tide a near-bankrupt nation over the immediate crisis. Halifax also took part in the conference at Dumbarton Oaks in 1944 which began to shape the charter of the United Nations and in the meetings at San Francisco, where he took a strong stand against the Russian interpretation of the Yalta formula on the unanimity rule in the proposed Security Council, whilst persuading Commonwealth delegates reluctantly to concur in the procedure recommended. His perceptive description of Molotov, the Soviet foreign minister, as 'smiling granite' did not, however, extend to an appreciation of Stalin's ambitions in Europe, much less to the formidable nature of the Communist society. When Churchill drew public attention to these dangers in a speech at Fulton, Missouri, in March 1946, Halifax tried to persuade him to qualify his words in his next speech. In this Halifax was unsuccessful, for Churchill felt it would be 'like going to see Hitler just before the war'. In May he returned to England and later that year was admitted to the Order of Merit.

The last years of his life were spent increasingly in familiar places and among old friends. In 1946 he rejoined the governing body of Eton, having originally been elected a fellow in 1936, and drew much refreshment from liturgical disputes with the provost, Lord Quickswood. As chancellor of Oxford, he gave a more than formal attention to the university's problems and took every opportunity of renewing his links with All Souls, 'a second home for more than fifty years'. Two more honours came to him in 1947 when he was appointed chancellor of Sheffield University and high steward of Westminster. He liked pageantry and found the wearing of ceremonial robes and insignia no burden either as chancellor of the Order of the Garter or as grand master from 1957 of the Order of St. Michael and St. George. As president of the Pilgrims he was able both to maintain his transatlantic friendships and to relive those evenings of sustained oratory which had never ceased to amaze him as ambassador. In 1947 he became chairman of the general advisory council of the B.B.C. He spoke from time to time in the House of Lords, enjoyed foreign travel, and wrote a gently evasive volume of memoirs, *Fulness of Days* (1957). But it was in taking up once more the threads of his family life in Yorkshire that he found true happiness and peace. He resumed the mastership of the Middleton hunt and immersed himself in farming, estate management, and local church affairs. A few weeks after celebrating his golden wedding he died at Garrowby 23 December 1959 and was buried at Kirby Underdale. He was succeeded by his eldest son, Charles Ingram Courtenay (born 1912). His youngest son, Richard Frederick, was minister of power (1959–63) and of pensions (1963–4), and his daughter, Anne, married the third Earl of Feversham.

Halifax's character was of baffling opaqueness. On some contemporary minds he left the imprint of statesmanship suffused by Christian faith; others suspected that his churchmanship concealed a strain of shrewd worldliness and expediency. Even the habitual ambiguity of his speeches might be variously interpreted either as a humble search for truth or as a form of verbal insurance against the unexpected. His rigid adherence to religious principles could make him seem heartless in his judgement of human frailty; thus he regarded divorce followed by remarriage, whatever the circumstances, as scarcely removed from bigamy. He loved family life and guarded his privacy well. But having been brought up by his father to think of racing as immoral and ballet as indecent, he observed with tolerant melancholy the addiction of his own sons to those pastimes. Among friends he was a lively talker with a smile of singular sweetness: his difficulty in pronouncing the letter 'r' added charm to a pleasant tenor voice. Those who saw him only on official occasions thought him aloof and consciously representative of an aristocracy whose continued and effortless lien on political power seemed anachronistic, even dangerous. Halifax sometimes doubted his fitness for a particular task yet believed in the ordered world into which he had been born and did not question his right to be called to high office. To his intimates he was a man of simple disposition; and the young, who are sensitive to pretentiousness, found him an enchanting companion.

There is a portrait of Halifax by Sir Oswald Birley at All Souls and another by Lawrence Gowing at Christ Church, Oxford. Lionel Edwards painted him with his father, then aged ninety-three, and his eldest son, at a meet of the Middleton hounds: the picture hangs at Garrowby.

[The Earl of Halifax, *Fulness of Days*, 1957; S. Gopal, *The Viceroyalty of Lord Irwin, 1926–31*, 1957; the Earl of Birkenhead, *Halifax*, 1965; private information; personal knowledge.]

KENNETH ROSE

published 1971

WOODCOCK George

(1904–1979)

General secretary of the Trades Union Congress, was born 20 October 1904, at Walton le Dale, Lancashire, the second of the four sons and of the five children of Peter Woodcock, cotton weaver (and later tackler), and his wife, Ann Baxendale. Woodcock went to Brownedge Roman Catholic Elementary School until he left for full-time employment as a cotton weaver when he was thirteen. At twelve, he had become a half-timer: one week he worked in the mill from 6 a.m. till 1 p.m. and attended school in the afternoon, the next week he went to school in the morning and worked in the mill till 5.30 p.m. At thirteen, he had two looms, and then three, and at fourteen he had four looms, as high as a weaver in those days could go.

His ambition was to become a professional footballer; his father and three uncles had played for Blackburn Rovers. Woodcock himself played for Brownedge in the Catholic League. He spent all his free time training, and later believed he had overdone it, for he suffered a long illness which ended his career as a weaver and a footballer.

He was a minor official of the Bamber Bridge and District Weavers' Union, and was active in the Independent Labour Party and the Labour Party. He was an election agent for Labour during the 1929 election, and at the same time worked for a TUC scholarship to Ruskin College, Oxford, which he won in 1929. In 1930 he won the Club and Institute Union scholarship, and in 1931 an extra-mural scholarship, being accepted by New College, Oxford. He took a first in philosophy, politics, and economics in 1933, and won the Jessie Theresa Rowden senior scholarship. He was later (1963) to be an honorary fellow of New College.

After two years (1934–6) in the Civil Service, Woodcock joined the TUC as head of the research and economic department. He remained in that post, working closely with Walter (later Lord) Citrine, the general secretary, until 1946; from the following year until 1960 he was assistant general secretary under Sir H. Vincent Tewson; and he was general secretary from 1960 until 1969. In 1969 he was appointed chairman of the Commission on Industrial Relations by Harold Wilson (later Lord Wilson of Rievaulx) but resigned two years later when Edward Heath tried to give the CIR legal functions under his Industrial Relations Act.

When he joined the TUC as its first young university-trained intellectual, the depression and unemployment were the dominant problems. Woodcock was captivated by the ideas of J. M. (later Lord) Keynes. He was proud of his part in the discussions which led to the 1944 white paper on employment policy, the charter of Britain's post-war economic consensus. There was one sentence he cherished, and he thought his career would have been worthwhile for it alone: 'The Government accept as one of their primary aims and responsibilities the maintenance of a high and stable level of employment after the war.' It was a sentence which was to dominate the thinking of all governments for thirty-five years, and to run like a silver thread through Woodcock's own life. For he foresaw—with an insight denied to most people in politics, Whitehall, industry, and the unions—that there was a price to be paid for full employment. From the era of Keynes, Ernest Bevin, and Sir R. Stafford Cripps to that of Harold Macmillan (later the Earl of Stockton) and Harold Wilson, Woodcock was wrestling with the unresolved problems of all western societies: how to combine free trade unionism with reasonable freedom from inflation.

For Woodcock realized that the commitment of governments to full employment had shifted the balance of power in industry, so that unions now were often more powerful than employers. He rejected the attempts by various politicians to reverse this process by legislation, arguing that this 'peremptory' method of reform, while it might appeal to ministers working within the time-span of a single Parliament, led inevitably into short cuts that would prove to be culs-de-sac. This, Woodcock believed, was true of legislation on both industrial relations and on incomes policy: they might have some temporary effect, but so long as free trade unions existed they would leave no permanent system. His own life was devoted to bringing about reform by voluntary methods. His obsession was with the relationship between trade unions and government. Woodcock maintained that since unions drew their new authority from full employment, rather than from better organization or greater militancy, it was in their interests to see that governments adopted—or continued to adopt—economic and financial policies which would maintain full employment. And only trade-union co-operation, particularly in wage fixing, could allow governments to persist with such policies.

Consequently Woodcock's later life, particularly during those nine years when he led the TUC, was devoted to the education of both politicians and his own colleagues who headed the major unions and served on the TUC general council, about the subtlety and fragility of this relationship. On the one hand, he would say to ministers that unions were by nature organizations which could only respond to governments, and that therefore governments must put them under pressure by challenging them to undertake difficult tasks. Simultaneously he would be arguing against those in the TUC who saw their role—particularly during Conservative governments—as being a protest movement. 'We have left Trafalgar Square', he would say, maintaining that the TUC's primary task was not protest, but to work with ministers and civil servants in the corridors of Whitehall, so that benign economic policies would add to their members' prosperity, and make it secure.

One of Woodcock's great achievements was to persuade the TUC in 1962 to take part in the National Economic Development Council, created by a Conservative chancellor of the Exchequer, J. S. B. Selwyn Lloyd (later Lord Selwyn-Lloyd). He hoped that it would ultimately develop into a major instrument of national planning, where the social partners—government, industry, and the unions—would commit themselves to policies of economic co-operation for the prosperity of all. When a Labour government was elected in 1964 Woodcock persuaded the TUC to accept a prices and incomes policy and individual unions to submit wage claims to the TUC before pursuing them. He agreed with the government's proposal to establish a royal commission on trade unions and employers' associations and was himself a member of it from 1965 to 1968.

In a paper Woodcock delivered to the British Association a few years before his death, he looked bleakly, and prophetically, at the alternatives: 'Neither the employers nor the trade unions could or would be willing to hand over their responsibilities or their powers to the State, and compulsion has been shown to be impracticable. The most likely alternative to co-operation is that governments will have to modify their commitment to maintain a high level of employment, and their consequential responsibilities for economic growth, stable prices and good industrial relations. If this country were to return to the industrial instability and the heavy unemployment of pre-war days, that would certainly not improve the ability of the trade unions collectively to secure greater social justice and fairness for their members.' Within three years of Woodcock's death, co-operation between government and unions had almost completely broken down, and there were three million unemployed in Britain.

Woodcock was also a member of the British Guiana constitutional commission in 1954, of the royal commission on the taxation of profits and incomes, 1952–5, and of the Radcliffe committee on the working of the monetary system, 1957–9. He was vice-chairman of the National Savings Committee (1952–75) and a member of the BBC advisory council.

George Woodcock delighted in conversation. He was a marvellous raconteur, particularly about his early life in Lancashire and at Oxford. An emotional man, he was an impassioned debater, by turns analytical and persuasive, his large and bushy eyebrows raised in protest at the irrationality of humankind. There was no more patient, and determined, exponent of the causes he believed in, but he retained a down-to-earth view that both politics and industrial relations were arts of the possible. This sometimes produced a Hamlet-like quality of philosophical introspection that those who knew how right his ideas were occasionally found irritating. Yet Woodcock throughout his career kept facing the unions with the fundamental question: 'What are we here for?' Although he knew his own answer, he could never persuade the trade-union leadership as a whole to think deeply enough about its response.

Woodcock had honorary degrees from Oxford (1964), Sussex (1963), Manchester (1968), Kent (1968), Aston in Birmingham (1967), Lancaster (1970), and London (1970). He became a freeman of the City of London in 1965. He was appointed CBE in 1953 and admitted to the Privy Council in 1967.

In 1933, while still a student, Woodcock married Laura Mary, also a devout Roman Catholic, daughter of Francis McKernan, an engine fitter, of Horwich in Lancashire. During his TUC years, they lived in Epsom, Surrey, where Mrs Woodcock was a magistrate and, successively, councillor, alderman, and mayor of the town. She was the first woman to be made a freeman of Epsom. They had a son and a daughter, both of whom went to Oxford. Woodcock died at Epsom District Hospital 30 October 1979.

[Personal knowledge.]

JOHN COLE

published 1986

WYNDHAM John Edward Reginald

(1920–1972)

First Baron Egremont and sixth Baron Leconfield

Civil servant and author, was born at Windsor 5 June 1920, the third child in the family of one daughter and three sons of Edward Scawen Wyndham and his wife, Gladys Mary, daughter of FitzRoy James Wilberforce Farquhar. His father, fifth son of the second Baron Leconfield, was a professional soldier in the Life Guards and commanded his regiment before leaving the army in 1923 to live at Edmonthorpe in Leicestershire where Wyndham spent his childhood. Wyndham was educated at Eton, where he edited the Eton College *Chronicle*, and went up to Trinity College, Cambridge, in 1939 to read history. The war interrupted his university career and he left after a year to try to join the armed forces but was turned down on grounds of defective eyesight. He then applied to go into the Civil Service and was accepted by the Ministry of Supply. Here, after working in the purchasing and requisitioning department, he was appointed private secretary to the parliamentary under-secretary, Harold Macmillan (later the Earl of Stockton). Thus began a remarkable working relationship, which was to last until Macmillan's retirement from active politics some twenty-four years later, and a personal friendship which endured to the end of Wyndham's life.

For the rest of the war Macmillan and Wyndham were together. In 1942 Wyndham went to the Colonial Office where Macmillan had been moved as parliamentary under-secretary of state in charge of the economic section; and in 1943 he left for north Africa to work under Macmillan whom Churchill made minister resident (with Cabinet rank) at Allied Force Headquarters in Algiers. From here his work took him to Italy in

1944 at the time of the Allied invasion and to Greece during the revolution. Wyndham was appointed MBE in 1945.

After the end of the war in Europe, he went back to London to the Air Ministry, under Harold Macmillan who had been made secretary of state for air in Churchill's caretaker government. In 1945, on the fall of the caretaker government, Wyndham was transferred for a year to Washington as private secretary to R. H. (later Lord) Brand, head of the British Treasury delegation and chairman of the British Supply Council in North America. Here he became involved in the negotiations for the celebrated American loan to Britain. On his return to England, Wyndham was offered a Treasury post in Egypt. But he left the Civil Service and made a journey with Macmillan (then in opposition) to Persia and India at the start of 1947. In this same year Wyndham joined the Conservative Research Department. Here he worked for five years alongside the brilliant band of young men—many of whom were later to make their mark in politics— assembled by the department's chairman, R. A. Butler (later Lord Butler of Saffron Walden). In 1952, however, he had to leave after the death of his uncle, the third Lord Leconfield, whose heir Wyndham was, to devote himself to the problems of his inheritance of the Wyndham family estates.

Family matters occupied the next few years. These included the negotiations with the Treasury over the large death duties and the principle, established for the first time, of the acceptance by the nation of works of art to help pay these. Wyndham moved to Petworth, and became a member of the West Sussex County Council and a magistrate. Then in 1955 Macmillan, by now foreign secretary, suggested that Wyndham might rejoin him as his private secretary. For a year the old relationship was renewed but in 1956 Wyndham had to return to Petworth again on his master becoming chancellor of the Exchequer; he was still negotiating with the Treasury over death duties and therefore could not work in that department. In this way Wyndham was absent from Whitehall throughout the Suez crisis and the succession of Macmillan to the prime ministership in January 1957. However in May 1957 the new prime minister wrote to ask if they might resume their old connection and later that year Wyndham joined the private office at 10 Downing Street. Here he remained until Macmillan's resignation in 1963, occupying a unique position of personal friend and professional adviser.

In 1963 Wyndham was created first Baron Egremont in recognition of his services during these years, and thus revived an extinct family title. He was introduced into the House of Lords on the same day as his father, who had recently succeeded as the fifth Baron Leconfield: the first time that father and son have taken their seats together.

Wyndham occupied the rest of his life with writing and the management of his estates. He contributed a column to the *Spectator*, and reviews and articles to other newspapers and periodicals; but the culmination of his literary work was his autobiography *Wyndham and Children First*, published in 1968, which enjoyed considerable commercial and critical success.

Wyndham had a remarkable, almost unique, effect upon the people he met during his short life. In the social world he was loved by a mass of friends, young and old, men and women. His wit, his charm, his originality and sometimes almost eccentricity, delighted all who knew him. In the political world it is difficult to find a parallel for the part he played. He brought to Whitehall all his humour, with its whimsical and often unexpected turns. Yet he was very discreet and very devoted to the interests of what he used to call his 'master'. Perhaps the only similar case was that of Montagu Corry (later Lord Rowton). Both served prime ministers with complete devotion; both were young, charming, and commanded not merely the affection but the respect of their chiefs. Both were recommended for peerages on their masters' resignation, the first by Lord Beaconsfield, the second by Harold Macmillan.

In 1947 Wyndham married Pamela, youngest daughter of Captain Valentine Maurice Wyndham-Quin, RN, younger son of the fifth Earl of Dunraven. They had two sons and one daughter. Egremont died at Petworth House, Sussex, 6 June 1972 and was succeeded by his elder son, (John) Max (Henry Scawen) Wyndham (born 1948). A drawing by Augustus John and a bust by Fiore de Henriques are in the possession of the family.

[Personal knowledge.]

HAROLD MACMILLAN

published 1986

YOUNGER Sir Kenneth Gilmour

(1908–1976)

Politician and reformer, was born 15 December 1908 at Colton, Dunfermline, Fife, the second child and younger son (there were also two daughters) of James Younger (later second Viscount Younger of Leckie), the son of the first Viscount, who was chairman of the Conservative Party. His mother was Maud, daughter of Sir John Gilmour, baronet, and sister of Sir John Gilmour, a Conservative secretary of state for Scotland. Such parentage did not prevent Younger from joining the Labour Party which he did as a young man after leaving New College, Oxford, which he had entered from Winchester. In 1930 he obtained a third class degree in philosophy, politics, and economics.

In 1932 Younger was called to the bar (Inner Temple) and practised up to 1939. During the war he served in the Intelligence Corps, finishing as a temporary major on the staff of Field Marshal Montgomery (later Viscount Montgomery of Alamein).

After the general election of 1945, at which he was returned as Labour member for Grimsby, he seemed set on a political career destined to take him to the highest office. Almost at once he was attached as parliamentary private secretary to the minister of state at the Foreign Office. Thus he put down the root of one of the interests he was to follow all his life, the promotion of international goodwill and the development of supranational institutions.

In December 1945 he was sent as a British alternate delegate to the UN and in 1946 was appointed chairman of the European committee of the United Nations Relief and Rehabilitation Administration. In 1947 he moved to the Home Office after a brief spell in the Ministry of Civil Aviation and there put down the root of his other interest, individual rights and penal reform.

In the Parliament of 1950–1 he was minister of state at the Foreign Office under Ernest Bevin. Owing to Bevin's ill health a great deal of the work fell to Younger in the difficult and shifting world of post-war international relations. These two, looking, as someone remarked, like an old polar bear attended by a lively cub, became a familiar and welcome sight in the House of Commons. Younger was an outstandingly efficient departmental minister who inspired trust and affection in those with whom he dealt, and some of the acclaim which has rightly been accorded to Bevin as foreign secretary should be shared by his minister of state. In 1951 he was made a privy councillor.

Though Younger joined the shadow cabinet after 1951 when Labour went into opposition his heart was not in the often negative and wearisome battles which an opposition must wage. He was essentially constructive. Nor could he pretend to an indignation he did not feel which is a faculty considered essential to the ambitious. He was in politics not for the glittering prizes but to achieve results in his chosen fields. When he felt this could be done better by service elsewhere he felt no great compulsion to stay in Parliament. So in 1959 he left the House of Commons and shortly afterwards became director of Chatham House—the Royal Institute of International Affairs.

Here he was able to return to one of his main interests—foreign policy. Younger realized sooner than most people that Britain was no longer an imperial power nor a superpower but that her role lay through the UN and world and regional co-operation. To such co-operation Younger believed Britain could bring particular talents through her long experience and through her position on the Atlantic seaboard of Europe and in the Commonwealth.

In the meantime he maintained his interest in legal and penal matters. From 1966 he was chairman of the advisory council on the penal system. In 1970 he was appointed chairman of the committee of inquiry into privacy. In 1972 he was a member of the committee on Northern Ireland chaired by Lord Diplock and for thirteen years from 1960 to 1973 chairman of the Howard League for Penal Reform. He served on many other bodies and was a governor of St. George's Hospital. In 1968 he was given an honorary doctorate by St. John's University, New York, and in 1972 appointed KBE.

He published and edited various Fabian and other essays connected with his public work. *A Study in International Affairs* (ed. Roger P. Morgan, 1972) was compiled in his honour.

His premature death deprived the country of an able and unselfish public servant and his friends of a delightful and incisive companion. His modesty, his innocent appearance, and his courtesy could mislead casual acquaintances. They would be brought up short by his precise and often radical opinions caustically expressed. He was no tolerator of slovenliness. Indeed at Chatham House he ruthlessly weeded out those whom he felt had nothing to contribute however venerable and respected they might be. His own contributions whether in formal meetings or private conversation were invariably to the point. He was in the tradition of practical reformers. He had no great interest in fashionable dogma but to the end developed his opinions from a firm belief in the possibility of improving the human lot by firm guidance of the institutions at our command. In 1934 he married Elizabeth Kirsteen, daughter of William Duncan Stewart JP, of Achara, Duror, Argyll, a wife who matched his abilities and his temperament. They had one son and two daughters. Younger died at his London home 19 May 1976.

[Personal knowledge.]

J. GRIMOND

published 1986